Personality

Personality

Third Edition

Jerry M. Burger

Santa Clara University

Brooks/Cole Publishing Company
Pacific Grove, California

Brooks/Cole Publishing Company
A Division of Wadsworth, Inc.

Printed in the United States of America

1 2 3 4 5 6 7 8 9 10———97 96 95 94 93

Library of Congress Cataloging in Publication Data

Burger, Jerry M.
    Personality: theory and research / Jerry M. Burger. — 3rd ed.
        p.   cm.
    Includes bibliographical references and index.
    ISBN 0-534-17220-2
    1. Personality   I. Title.
    BF698.B84   1993
    155.2 — dc20

Psychology Editor: Ken King
Editorial Assistant: Gay Meixel
Production Editor: Angela Mann
Managing Designer: Andrew Ogus
Print Buyer: Barbara Britton
Permissions Editor: Jeanne Bosschart
Designer: MaryEllen Podgorski
Copy Editor: Margaret Moore
Cover Design: MaryEllen Podgorski
Cover Painting: David Park, *Encounter*, n.d. Oil on masonite, 9.5 x 11.875. Gift of the Women's Board of the Oakland Museum Association.
Compositor: TypeLink, Inc.
Printer: R. R. Donnelley (Crawfordsville)

To Marlene

Contents in Brief

Contents

13 The Behaviorial/Social Learning Approach: Theory, Application, and Assessment   391

The Cognitive Approach: Relevant Research 504

Conclusions and Future Directions 529

Preface

Upon reaching his 40th birthday, Mick Jagger explained to a reporter, "I'm not getting older, I'm getting gooder." Upon completing the third edition of this book, I've come to see that the same description, corrected for grammar, can apply to textbooks as well as to rock stars. The changes in this edition are not as dramatic or widespread as the changes I made when writing the second edition. With a few exceptions, the differences between this edition and the last are more like refinements than overhauls. Throughout the book I've rewritten sentences and expanded points. As with the earlier revision, I've also updated the references extensively. In total, there are more than 220 new references in this edition, and more than 550 since the first edition. But those familiar with the earlier editions will also find a few big changes. Briefly, let me outline what's new and what's the same this time around.

What's New? I've expanded the five approaches to personality to six in this edition. I've added a theory and a research chapter on the biological approach to understanding personality. This addition reflects the field's growing recognition of biological influences in recent years. Some of the information in these chapters was covered elsewhere in the second edition. I have retained coverage of research on genetic influences, temperament, and Eysenck's personality theory. However, there are also a number of new topics in these chapters. The new material includes sections on evolutionary personality theory, cerebral asymmetry, mate selection, and the role of temperament in academic achievement.

I've also added topics and sections to some of the other chapters. I cover research on social anxiety in the trait research chapter, and added research on self-esteem to the humanistic research chapter. In the theory chapters readers will find new sections on the psychology of optimal experience, the revised frustration-aggression model, the hopelessness model of depression, and recent work on possible selves.

What's the Same? The philosophy that guided the organization and writing of the first two editions remains. I wrote this book to organize within one textbook the two approaches typically taken by instructors of an undergraduate personality course. On the one hand, many instructors focus on the great theories and theorists — Freud, Jung, Rogers, Skinner, and so on. Students in these classes gain insight into the structure of the mind and issues of human nature, as well as a background for understanding psychological disorders and psychotherapy. However, they are likely to be puzzled when they pick up a current journal of personality research only to find they recognize few, if any, of the topics. On the other hand, some instructors emphasize personality research. Students learn about current research on individual differences and personality processes. But they probably see little relationship between the abstract theories they may touch upon in class and the research topics that are the focus of the course.

But these two approaches to teaching the course do not represent separate disciplines that happen to share the word *personality* in their titles. Indeed, the structure of this book is designed to demonstrate that the classic theories stimulate research and that the research findings often shape the development and acceptance of the theories. Limiting a student's attention to either theory or research provides an unfortunately narrow view of the field.

Something else that remains from the earlier editions is my belief that students learn about research best by seeing *programs* of research, rather than a few isolated examples. There are 25 research programs covered in the six research chapters in this edition. In each case I have tried to illustrate how the questions being investigated are connected to a larger theory, how early researchers developed their initial hypotheses and investigations, and how experimental findings led to new questions, refined hypotheses, and ultimately a greater understanding of the topic. Through this process, students are exposed to some of the problems researchers encounter, the fact that experimental results often are equivocal, and a realistic picture of researchers who don't always agree on how to interpret findings.

Finally, I have retained and expanded many of the features of the previous edition in this third edition. Each of the theory chapters contains a section on application and a section on assessment. These sections demonstrate how the sometimes abstract theories relate to everyday concerns and issues and how each approach to understanding personality brings with it unique assumptions and problems when trying to measure personality variables. I've also expanded the number of personality tests students can take and score themselves. There are now 14 "Assessing Your Own Personality" boxes scattered throughout the book. I've discovered in my own teaching that, for example, discussions about locus of control research mean a lot more to students when they know how they scored on a locus of control test. This hands-on experience not only gives students a better idea of how personality assessment works, but often brings out a little bit of healthy skepticism about relying too heavily on such measures. I've retained the biographies of the prominent personality theorists in this edition. Feedback from students indicates that knowing something about the person behind the theory makes the theory come alive a little more. They also enjoy speculating about how the theorist's life affected the development of the theory.

Acknowledgments   Of course, it is important to acknowledge the contribution of all those who supported me in this endeavor. Thanks are extended to the people at Wadsworth, especially Ken King and his unwavering support and enthusiasm. I also would like to thank the many colleagues who reviewed various parts and versions of this manuscript. This list includes Elaine Donelson, Michigan State

University; Paul Karoly, Arizona State University; Elizabeth Lemerise, Western Kentucky University; Christopher T. Leone, University of North Florida; Lori J. Toedter, Moravian College; Robin R. Vallacher, Florida Atlantic University; Naomi Wagner, San Jose State University; and Elissa Wurf, Lehigh University. And, as always, I want to thank Marlene and Adam, whose understanding and support through all three editions has made this book possible.

What Is Personality?

On June 14, 1985, a group of armed terrorists hijacked TWA Flight 847 over Europe. The hijackers forced the crew to fly the plane to Beirut, Lebanon, where they presented their list of demands for the release of the hostages. During the first few hours of this ordeal, the terrorists took one American away from the others. Many passengers heard the man scream as he was beaten. Gunshots followed, then silence. At times the hijackers ran wildly up and down the aisles of the plane, randomly pointing their automatic weapons at hostages. A few passengers were released, but for 39 Americans the odyssey of terror was just beginning. They were removed from the plane and held by armed guards in unfamiliar and frightening locations. Some hostages were placed in dark and barren jail cells. They had no way of knowing how long their ordeal would last or if they would leave Beirut alive. It was not until June 30th, after 17 days of captivity, that the hostages were released unharmed.

How do you suppose you would have reacted if you had been in the hostages' place? The question may seem a simple one at first. Of course, anyone in this situation experiences great fear and anxiety, as each of the hostages expressed following their release. But as powerful as the situational forces were in determining the hostages' reactions, this type of event also creates an opportunity to observe some of the differences between people. For not all of the hostages from Flight 847 responded in the same way to their capture and abuse. One man reportedly offered the terrorists $2 million for his release. Another tried to convince his captors that he was "a promoter" of their cause and could be of great help to them in America. Two hostages secretly wrote their names on their stomachs so that they could be identified after they were killed. One group gathered every day for a prayer session. Another group worked on escape plans. The men in this latter group even watched their captors carefully whenever they shot their automatic weapons. They wanted to learn how to operate the guns in case they succeeded in capturing one. Five hostages kept hidden logs of their activities. One man chastised the hijackers for violating the rules of their religion. Some were resigned to their deaths, others carried on in hope.

Even after their release, the hostages displayed a wide variety of reactions to their captors. Some were openly sympathetic with the terrorists' cause, others were angry and bitter. One man described his captors as "vile, disgusting animals." But a few exchanged addresses with the terrorists and promised to write letters.

The behavior of the passengers from Flight 847 was in some ways typical of people who are suddenly thrown into a unique and traumatic situation. At first the demands of the situation cause nearly all people to react in a similar manner, in this case with fear and great stress. But soon each person's characteristic way of dealing with stressful situations emerges. Those characteristic differences between people — that is, their personalities — are the focus of this book.

The Person Versus the Situation

Is our behavior shaped by the situation we are in or by the type of person we are? In the hijack example, did the hostages act the way they did because of the events surrounding them, or were their behaviors more the result of the kind of person they were before getting on the plane? This is one of the enduring questions in psychology theory and research. The generally agreed-upon answer to the question today is that both the situation and the person contribute to behavior. Certainly we don't act the same way in all situations. Depending on where we are and what is happening, each of us can be outgoing, shy, aggressive, friendly, depressed, frightened, or excited. But it is equally apparent that not everyone at the same party, the same ball game, or the same shopping center behaves identically. The debate among psychologists has now shifted to the question of *how* the situation influences our behavior, as well as how our behavior reflects the individual.

We can divide the fields of study within psychology along the answer to this question. Many psychologists concern themselves with how people typically respond to environmental demands. These researchers recognize that not everyone in a situation reacts the same, but their objective is to identify patterns that generally describe what most people will do. Thus, a social psychologist might create several different situations in which subjects view a person in need of help. The purpose of this research is to identify the kinds of situations that increase or decrease helping behavior. However, personality psychologists turn this way of thinking completely around. We know there are typical response patterns to situations, but what we find more interesting is why Peter tends to help more than Paul, even when both are presented with the same request.

You may have heard the axiom "There are few differences between people, but what differences there are really matter." That tends to sum up the personality psychologists' view point. They want to know what makes you different from the person sitting next to you. Why do some people make friends easily while others are lonely? Why are some people prone to bouts of depression? Can we predict who will rise to the top of the business ladder and who will fall short? Why are some people introverted while others are so outgoing? We'll explore each of these questions in this book. Other topics we will cover include how your personality is related to hypnotic susceptibility, reactions to stress, how well you do in school, and even your chances of having a heart attack.

This is not to say the situation is unimportant or of no interest to personality psychologists. Indeed, as discussed in Chapter 7, many of the questions posed by

The outstanding characteristic of man is his individuality. There was never a person just like him, and there never will be again.
GORDON ALLPORT

personality researchers concern how a certain kind of person behaves in a particular situation. However, our emphasis is on what makes you different from the next person, that is, your personality. But before addressing that issue, we should start by defining what we mean by *personality*.

Defining Personality

Anyone who has been in college a while can probably anticipate the topic of the first lecture of the term. The philosophy professor asks "What is philosophy?" The first class meeting in a communication course centers on the question, What is communication? Those who teach geography, history, and calculus have similar lectures. And so, for traditional and practical reasons, we too begin with the basic question, What is personality?

Although a definition follows, bear in mind that psychologists do not agree on a single answer to this question. Indeed, personality theorists and researchers frequently question the nature of their field and how it differs from or relates to other areas of psychology, as well as other disciplines (Blass, 1984; Carlson, 1984). Nonetheless, the definition that guides the organization and topic selection of this book includes much of what we generally accept as personality theory and research today.

We define **personality** as *consistent behavior patterns originating within the individual.* At least four aspects of this simple definition need elaboration. First, personality is *consistent*. In other words, a person's behavior patterns display some stability. This consistency in behavior exists across time and across situations. We expect someone who is outgoing today to be outgoing tomorrow. We also are not surprised to find that someone who is competitive at work also is competitive in sports. We acknowledge this consistency in character when we say "He was not acting like himself" or "It was just like her to do that." Of course, this does not mean an extraverted person is boisterous and jolly all the time, on solemn occasions as well as at parties. Nor does it mean people cannot change. But if personality exists and behavior is not just a reflection of whatever situation we find ourselves in, then we must expect some consistency in the way people act.

Second, personality originates *within* the individual. This is not to say external sources do not influence personality. Certainly the way parents raise their children affects the kind of adult the child becomes. But behavior is not solely a function of the situation. The fear we experience while watching a frightening movie is the result of the film, but the different ways we each express or deal with that fear come from within.

Third, this definition focuses on the *individual's* behavior. Social psychologists know people are different and often respond in different ways to the same situation. However, these psychologists look at how the average person behaves in a given situation, ignoring individual differences. In contrast, personality psychologists acknowledge the importance of the situation but are more interested in understanding, for example, why some people respond to a challenge with increased effort while others react by giving up.

Finally, we will treat the term *behavior* rather broadly here. Although overt actions are of primary interest to personality psychologists, we cannot understand the actions without examining such things as thoughts, emotions, and attitudes. Thus, consistent patterns in the way we think about ourselves, our expectancies, and the way we classify events into cognitive categories are all part of personality.

Six Approaches to Personality

What are the sources of consistent behavior patterns? This is the basic question asked by personality theorists and researchers. One reason for the length of this book is that personality psychologists have answered this question in many different ways. To help make sense of the wide range of personality theories proposed over the past 90 years, we describe six general approaches to explaining personality. These are the psychoanalytic approach, the trait approach, the biological approach, the humanistic approach, the behavioral/social learning approach, and the cognitive approach. Each of the major theories of personality fits into one of these six general approaches.

But why so many theories of personality? I'll try to answer this question by way of analogy. Nearly everyone has heard the story about the five blind men who encounter an elephant. Each feels a different part of the animal and then tries to explain to the others what an elephant is like. The blind man feeling the leg describes the elephant as tall and round. Another feels the ear and claims an elephant is thin and flat, while yet another describes the long, slender elephant he feels when holding on to the trunk. The man feeling the tail and the one touching the elephant's side have a different image. The point to this story, of course, is that each man knows only a part of the whole animal. Thus, while each is partly correct, because he does not acknowledge that there is more to the elephant than he has felt, each provides an incomplete description of the animal.

In one sense, the six approaches to personality are analogous to the blind men. That is, each approach does seem to correctly identify and examine an important aspect of human personality. For example, psychologists who subscribe to the *psychoanalytic approach* argue that people's unconscious minds are largely responsible for important differences in their behavior styles. Other psychologists who favor the *trait approach* identify where along a continuum of various personality characteristics a person might lie. Psychologists advocating the *biological approach* point to inherited predispositions and physiological processes to explain individual differences in personality. In contrast, those promoting the *humanistic approach* identify personal responsibility and feelings of self-acceptance as the key causes of differences in personality. *Behavioral/social learning* theorists explain consistent behavior patterns as the result of habits learned from exposure to certain kinds of environments. Finally, those promoting the *cognitive approach* look at differences in the way people process information to explain differences in behavior.

It's tempting to suggest that by combining all six approaches we can obtain the larger, accurate picture of why people act in consistent behavioral patterns.

Unfortunately, the blind-men analogy is only partially applicable to the six approaches to personality. Although different approaches to a given issue in personality often vary only in emphasis, with each providing a legitimate, compatible explanation, in many instances the explanations of two or more approaches appear entirely incompatible. Thus, people who work in the field tend to align themselves with one or another of the six approaches as they decide which of the competing explanations they accept.

Returning to the blind men and the elephant, suppose someone were to ask how an elephant moves. The man feeling the trunk might argue that the elephant slithers along the ground like a snake. The man holding the elephant's ear might disagree, saying that the elephant must fly like a bird with its big, floppy wings. The man touching the leg would certainly have a different explanation. Although in some instances more than one of these explanations might be accurate (for example, a bird can both walk and fly), it should be obvious that at times not every theory can be right.

So, how do we know which approach is correct? One answer is through research. Indeed, on occasion research findings support one theory of personality over another. Unfortunately, the results of most studies can be explained within each of the approaches. It also is possible that one theory is correct in describing one part of human personality, whereas another theory is correct in describing other aspects.

Obviously, each of the six approaches we describe is of some value when explaining the existence of consistent behavior patterns. No doubt some theories will make more sense to you than others. But it is worth keeping in mind that each approach has been developed and promoted by a large number of respected psychologists. While not all of these men and women are correct about every issue, each approach has something of value to offer in our quest to understand what makes each of us who we are.

Two Examples: Aggression and Depression

To get a better idea of how the six approaches to understanding personality provide six different, yet legitimate, explanations for consistent patterns of behavior, let's look at two common examples. Because aggressive behavior and the suffering that comes from depression are widespread problems in our society, we should not be surprised to hear that psychologists from many different perspectives have attempted to account for these behaviors within their theories of personality. Indeed, some of the theories and research on these two topics have proven so useful that they are covered in detail later in the book.

Example 1: Aggression   We all have seen people who seem to be very aggressive — perhaps dangerously so. Aggressive adults often have a long history of violence and trouble with authorities. Adults with a pattern of arrests for assault typically possess a history of aggressive behavior that goes back to playground fights in childhood. Why are some people consistently more aggressive than others? Each of the six approaches to personality provides at least one answer. As you read about them, think about an aggressive person you have encountered. Which of the six explanations seems to do the best job of explaining this person's behavior?

Psychoanalytic theorists tend to explain behavior in terms of unconscious processes. The classic psychoanalytic explanation of aggression proposes that each of us possesses an unconscious death instinct—a desire to self-destruct. However, because a healthy personality does not self-destruct, these impulses may unconsciously be turned outward and expressed against others in the form of aggression. Later psychologists elaborated on another psychoanalytic concept, frustration, to explain aggression. These theorists argued that aggression results when we are blocked from reaching our goals. A person who experiences a great deal of frustration, perhaps someone who is constantly falling short of a desired goal, is a likely candidate for persistent aggressive behavior.

Personality theorists from the trait approach focus on individual differences in the stability of aggressive behavior. For example, many years ago a team of researchers measured aggressiveness in eight-year-old children by asking students in several classrooms such questions as "Who pushes or shoves children?" (Huesmann, Eron, & Yarmel, 1987). Twenty-two years later, the investigators again interviewed the subjects, who were now 30 years old. They discovered that the children who had been identified as aggressive in elementary school were the most likely to engage in aggressive behavior as adults. The children who pushed and shoved others often grew into adults who engaged in spouse abuse and violent criminal behavior.

Personality psychologists from the biological perspective also are interested in relatively stable patterns of aggressive behavior. They point to a genetic predisposition to act aggressively as one reason for this stability. Evidence now suggests that some people inherit more of a proclivity toward aggression than others do (Rushton, Fulker, Neale, Nias, & Eysenck, 1986). Although it is always difficult to tease out what is inherited from what is learned as the child grows up, some people may indeed be born with aggressive dispositions that, depending on their upbringing, result in their becoming aggressive adults. To understand the causes of aggressive behavior, psychologists from the biological perspective also compare aggressive and nonaggressive people on a number of physiological variables, such as testosterone level (DiLalla & Gottesman, 1991).

Psychologists with a humanistic approach to personality explain aggressive behavior in yet another way. Many of these theorists deny that some people are born to be aggressive. In fact, most have argued that people are basically good. They believe all people can become happy, nonaggressive adults if allowed to grow and develop in an enriching and encouraging environment. Problems develop when something interferes with this natural growth process. Aggressive children come from homes in which basic needs are frustrated. If the child develops a poor self-image, he or she may strike out at others in frustration. The solution is to provide a warm and accepting environment for the child to grow up in.

The behavioral/social learning approach contrasts in many ways with the humanistic view. According to this approach, people learn aggressive behavior in the same way they learn other consistent behaviors. Playground bullies find that aggressive behavior is rewarded: They get to bat first and have a choice of playground equipment because the other children fear them. The key to the behavioral interpretation is that rewarded behavior will be repeated. Thus, the playground bully probably will continue this aggressive behavior and try it out in other situations. If the aggression is continually met with rewards instead of punishment, the result will be an aggressive adult.

Children who watch other people get what they want with aggressive behavior also learn that aggression can be rewarding. Aggressive playmates can serve as powerful role models for children, who may learn that hurting others is sometimes useful. As we will see in Chapter 14, many people are concerned that the aggressive role models children watch routinely on television may be responsible for increasing the amount of aggressiveness in society.

Finally, cognitive psychologists approach the question of aggressive behavior from yet another perspective. Their main focus is on the way aggressive people process information. To better understand this, imagine you are walking alone through a park. Two teenage boys, walking about 30 feet behind you, suddenly quicken their pace and draw closer to you. What is your reaction? Perhaps the boys are in a hurry to get somewhere, perhaps they simply are more energetic and walk faster than you do. Maybe they are interested in catching up to you, to ask you for the time or for directions to the library. Or maybe they want to harm you. This situation, like many we encounter, contains a fair degree of ambiguity, and different people see it differently.

Cognitive personality psychologists argue that how you respond to this, or any, situation is a function of how you interpret it. Whether you see the circumstances as threatening, annoying, or benign will cause you to run away, prepare to fight, or move out of the way. The cognitive approach proposes that some people are more likely than others to interpret ambiguous situations as threatening. These people also are more likely to respond by acting aggressively.

The cognitive approach can help us understand why some adolescent boys act more aggressively than others (Dodge & Crick, 1990). Researchers have found that aggressive elementary schoolboys frequently interpret innocent actions by others as personally threatening (Dodge & Tomlin, 1987). For example, in one study investigators showed aggressive and nonaggressive boys a videotape in which one boy spills paint on another boy's art project, thus causing the first boy to win a painting contest (Dodge & Somberg, 1987). Although the videotape is deliberately unclear about whether the spill was malicious or accidental, the aggressive boys tended to interpret the action as intentional. Further, they were more likely than nonaggressive boys to say they would respond with anger. Other researchers have found that aggressive boys often fail to see their own behavior as aggressive but are quick to interpret other boys' actions against them as acts of aggression (Lochman, 1987). So it is not difficult to see why a 10-year-old boy who believes other people are constantly threatening and challenging him would exhibit consistently aggressive behavior. Unless he learns to interpret events in a less threatening way, the boy is likely to continue his aggressive behavior in adulthood.

Now, let's return to the original question: Why do some people show a consistent pattern of aggressive behavior? It should be clear by now that this question probably has no simple answer. Each of the six approaches to personality offers a different explanation. Which is correct? One possibility is that only one is correct and that future research will identify that theory. However, a second possibility is that each approach is partially correct. There may be six (or more) different causes of aggressive behavior. Still a third possibility is that the six explanations do not contradict one another but rather differ only in their focus. It is possible that hostility exhibited by aggressive boys is an expression of an aggressiveness trait that is relatively stable across many situations and over time (the trait approach). But it might also be the case that these boys tend to interpret ambiguous events as threatening (the cognitive explanation) because of past experiences in which they were assaulted (the behavioral/social learning explanation). These boys may also have been born with a tendency to respond to threats in an aggressive manner (the biological approach), but perhaps if they had been raised in a nonfrustrating environment (the psychoanalytic approach) or in a supportive home in which their basic needs were met (the humanistic approach), they would have overcome their aggressiveness. The point is that each explanation provides a starting point for understanding aggressive behavior. But how we explain aggressiveness, and what steps we take to deal with it, depends to a great extent on which of the six approaches we are coming from.

Example 2: Depression

Most of us know what it is like to be depressed. We have all had days when we feel a little "blue" or "melancholy." Like many college students, you may also have suffered through longer periods of intense sadness and a general lack of interest and motivation for anything. Although most of us fluctuate through changing moods and levels of interest and energy, some people seem more prone to depression than others. Because problems with depression are widespread today, many psychologists have offered explanations for its cause. Once again, each of the six approaches to personality has a different explanation for depression.

According to Sigmund Freud, the founder of the psychoanalytic approach, depression is anger turned inward. That is, people suffering from depression hold unconscious feelings of anger and hostility. For example, they may want to strike out at family members. But a healthy personality does not express such feelings overtly. In addition, psychoanalysts argue that each of us has internalized the standards and values of society, which typically discourage the expression of hostility. Therefore, these angry feelings are turned inward, and people "take it out" on themselves. As with most psychoanalytic explanations, this takes place at an unconscious level.

Trait theorists are concerned with identifying depression-prone people. Psychologists have long recognized that one of the best predictors of who will suffer from a serious bout of depression is whether the person has suffered from depression before. For example, one investigation found a very high correlation between measures of emotional temperament taken 12 months apart (Costa, McCrae, & Arenberg, 1980). That is, a person's general emotional level today is a very good indicator of that person's emotions, including depression, 1 year from now. More direct evidence for the stability of depression-proneness comes from

What causes depression? Depending on which approach to personality you adopt, you might explain depression in terms of anger turned inward, a stable trait, an inherited predisposition, low self-esteem, a lack of reinforcers, or negative thoughts.

an investigation that measured depression levels in a group of men when they were middle-aged and again 30 years later when they were elderly (Leon, Gillum, Gillum, & Gouze, 1979). The researchers also found an impressively high correlation between the men's depression levels at the two different times. One recent study found that depression levels in 18-year-olds could be predicted from looking at subjects' behavior from as early as 7 years old (Block, Gjerde & Block, 1991).

Biological personality psychologists use this evidence of depression-prone stability to argue that depression is more than a person's reaction to his or her particular circumstances. Evidence now exists that some people may inherit a genetic susceptibility to depression (Wender et al., 1986). In fact, some scientists have recently identified the gene they believe transmits this susceptibility. A person born with this vulnerability faces a much greater likelihood than the average individual of reacting to stressful life events with depression. Because of this inherited tendency, we can expect these people to experience repeated bouts of depression throughout their lives.

Humanistic personality theorists interpret depression in terms of self-esteem. That is, people who frequently suffer from depression are those who have failed to develop a good sense of their self-worth. A person's level of self-esteem is established while growing up and, like other personality concepts, is fairly stable across time and situations. The ability to accept oneself, even one's faults and weaknesses, is an important goal for humanistic therapists when dealing with clients suffering from depression.

The behavioral/social learning approach examines the type of environment surrounding the development of depression. Behaviorists argue that depression results from a lack of positive reinforcers in a person's life. That is, you may feel down and unmotivated because you see few activities in your life worth doing. A more extensive behavioral model of depression, covered in Chapter 14, proposes that depression develops from experiences with aversive situations over which people feel they have little control. This theory, called *learned helplessness*, maintains that exposure to uncontrollable events creates a perception of helplessness that is generalized to other situations. For example, people who find they cannot control whether they receive a promotion inappropriately believe they also cannot control other important aspects of their lives. The resulting pattern of helpless behavior resembles classic depression symptoms.

More recent investigations into the causes and development of learned helplessness have led some researchers to expand this model to include some cognitive features. These psychologists argue that besides experiencing an inability to control events, people must also interpret this lack of control a certain way. For example, people who attribute their inability to get a promotion to a temporary economic recession will not become as depressed as people who believe it is the result of personal inadequacies. Why then are some people more prone to depression than others? According to research, people maintain a fairly stable style of interpreting events. Someone who is frequently depressed probably has a tendency to interpret uncontrollable events in a depressing way.

A more elaborate cognitive explanation of depression, described in detail in Chapter 16, introduces the concept of a depressive schema. This model proposes that we use something like a depressive filter to interpret and process information. That is, depressed people are prepared to see the world in the most depressing terms possible. Because of this depressive schema, depressed people can easily recall depressing experiences. People and places they encounter are likely to remind them of some sad or unpleasant time. In short, people become depressed because they are prepared to generate depressing thoughts.

Which of these accounts of depression strikes you as the most accurate? If you have been depressed, was it because of your low self-esteem, because you experienced an uncontrollable situation, or because you tend to look at the world through depressing lenses? As we found when looking at aggression, more than one of these approaches may correctly explain depression. You may have found that one theory can explain an experience with depression you had last year, whereas another seems to better account for a more recent bout with depression.

In addition, the theories can at times complement each other. For example, the evolution of the learned helplessness model demonstrates how a behavioral/social learning theory of depression also can include cognitive mechanisms to help explain why some people are more likely than others to develop and maintain depressive episodes.

There is a final lesson to learn from these two examples: You need not align yourself with the same approach to personality when explaining different phenomena. For example, you may have found that the cognitive explanation for aggression made the most sense to you but that the humanistic approach provided the best account of depression. This demonstrates the main point of this section: Each of the six approaches to personality has something to offer the student interested in understanding consistent behavior patterns.

The Study of Personality: Theory, Application, Assessment, and Research

A thorough understanding of what we know of human personality requires more than the study of the various personality theories. It also requires that we review applications of some of the concepts promoted by the approach, methods for assessing personality within each approach, as well as research relevant to the issues introduced by the approach. Each of the four aspects of personality psychology—theory, application, assessment, and research—will be introduced briefly below and developed in detail as part of the coverage of each of the approaches.

Theory

Each approach to understanding personality begins with a theory. This theory usually comes from the writings of several important psychologists who have provided their own descriptions of consistent patterns of behavior. They explain the mechanisms that underlie human personality and how these are responsible for creating behaviors unique to a given individual. In most cases, theorists also attempt to explain how differences in personality develop. Many also describe methods, based on their theories, for changing personality. Most often, theorists present strategies for change as part of an approach to psychotherapy. Although each theory tends to emphasize a different aspect of personality, each theorist must wrestle with several issues when describing the nature of human personality. We'll introduce a few of these here. The way theorists from each of the six approaches generally deal with these issues appears in Figure 1.1.

There can scarcely be anything more familiar than human behavior. Nor can there be anything more important. Nonetheless, it is certainly not the thing we understand best.

B. F. SKINNER

Genetic Versus Environmental Influences Are people born with the seeds for their adult personalities already intact? Or are they born with no inherited personality orientation, with each healthy baby just as likely as any other to become a great humanitarian, a criminal, a leader, or a helpless psychotic? Naturally, there is

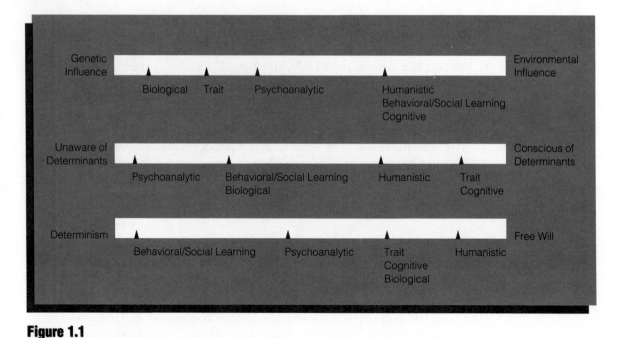

Figure 1.1

Position of the Six Approaches to Personality on Three Theory Issues

plenty of room for opinions in between these two views. But most personality theorists address this question: To what extent are our personalities the result of inherited predispositions, and to what extent are they shaped by the environment in which we grow up? There are sharp disagreements on this issue. Many biological and trait theorists argue that we too often fail to recognize the importance of inherited predispositions. To a lesser degree, psychoanalytic theorists also emphasize innate needs and behavior patterns, albeit unconscious. However, humanistic, behavioral/social learning, and cognitive theorists typically consider inherited influences on personality only briefly or not at all. To some extent the answer to this question is an empirical one. A growing amount of research implicates some inherited factors in the development of personality (see Chapter 10).

Conscious Versus Unconscious Determinants of Behavior   To what extent are people aware of the causes of their behavior? Sigmund Freud argued that much of what we do is under the control of unconscious forces, those that by definition we are not aware of. B. F. Skinner, an influential behavioral theorist, argued that people assume they understand the reasons for their actions, when in reality they do not. Behaviorists do not credit an unconscious mind with control of behavior but argue that we fail to recognize the extent to which environmental stimuli shape our behaviors. Psychologists advocating the biological approach argue that most people fail to recognize the extent to which biological factors influence their behavior, although we may occasionally be correct when, for example, we attribute our actions to something we "inherited from our parents." In contrast, trait and cognitive theorists rely heavily on self-report data in developing their theories and in their research. For example, they assume people can identify and report their level of social anxiety or how they organize information in their mind. However, each tends to hedge away from an extreme position on this issue. Like psychologists from the biological approach, trait theorists often talk about genetic causes of behavior, and cognitive psychotherapists acknowledge that people do not recognize the cognitive processes responsible for some of their problems. Humanistic theorists often take a middle-ground position on this issue. Although these theorists argue that no one knows us better than ourselves, they also acknowledge that many people do not understand why they act the way they do. Carl Rogers, a leading humanistic theorist, described an unconscious process he called *subception*. In subception, people perceive information but fail to bring that information into awareness if it threatens their self-image.

Free Will Versus Determinism   To what extent do we decide our own fate, and to what extent are our behaviors determined by forces outside of our control? This is an old issue in psychology that has spilled over from even older discussions in philosophy and theology. On the one extreme we find theorists from the behavioral/social learning approach called *radical behaviorists*. Perhaps most outspoken on this issue was B. F. Skinner, who argued that our behavior is not freely chosen but rather the direct result of the environmental stimuli to which we have been exposed. Thus, Skinner (1971) called freedom a myth. Psychoanalytic theorists typically take a less extreme position but nonetheless emphasize innate needs and unconscious mechanisms that leave much of human behavior outside of our control. On the other end of the spectrum are the humanistic theorists, who often identify personal choice and responsibility as the cornerstone of mental health. Humanistic psychotherapists frequently work to get their clients to recognize that they have more responsibility for the direction of their lives than society typically leads them to believe.

Although less clear on this issue, trait, biological and cognitive theorists probably fall somewhere between these others. Trait theorists and biological theorists often emphasize genetic predispositions that tend to limit development in certain areas. But none of these psychologists would argue that personality is completely dictated by these predispositions. Similarly, cognitive psychotherapists often encourage their clients to recognize how they cause many of their own problems and help them to develop strategies for avoiding future difficulties.

The ways personality theorists answer these and other questions shape their ideas on how personality develops and operates. As we will see in the next sections, how we conceive of personality then dictates the issues to which we apply the theory, the methods we use to measure personality assessment, and how we conduct research on relevant topics.

Application

Understanding the nature of human personality is an important goal for academic psychologists. However, psychology has a long history of applying the information it gains from its theories and research to questions and issues that directly affect people's lives. The most obvious example of this application in the field of personality is psychotherapy. Many of the major personality theorists also have been therapists who developed and refined their ideas about human personality in the course of dealing with clients and helping them to overcome their problems.

There are many different styles of psychotherapy. Which style psychotherapists choose is partly dictated by the assumptions they make about the nature of personality. The focus of therapy from a psychoanalytic perspective is, not surprisingly, on unconscious causes of the problem behavior. Humanistic therapists are more likely to work in a nondirective manner to provide the proper atmosphere for clients to explore their own feelings. Cognitive therapists try to change the way their clients process information, whereas behaviorists typically structure the environment so that desired behaviors increase in frequency while undesired behaviors decrease.

There are other ways in which psychologists apply personality to practical concerns. Information from personality research is used by psychologists working in educational settings to identify relevant characteristics in children, by industrial psychologists to design working environments to meet the needs of employees, and by counselors to help people decide which careers their aptitudes and abilities are best suited to. In short, because so many important questions and issues in our lives are concerned with individual differences, an understanding of how personality processes operate is often relevant when working with people.

Assessment

The usefulness of personality theories would be very limited if the concepts identified in these theories could not be measured. For example, if there were no way to determine who had high or low self-esteem, then psychologists could not examine how self-esteem develops or how people with high or low self-esteem differ. Without procedures to accurately assess this concept, psychologists could not help people with low self-esteem or further develop theories about self-esteem based on research findings.

Thus, psychologists from each of the six approaches have developed procedures for assessing the personality concepts of interest to them. You are probably familiar with some of these procedures. Perhaps the most common is the self-report inventory, in which test takers answer a series of questions about themselves. Results from these personality tests are usually given in terms of how the test taker's score compares with the scores of others who have taken the test.

However, personality psychologists measure individual differences in many other ways. The type of test used depends largely on the assumptions about personality made within the context of the particular theory. For example, a self-report inventory would not be useful for someone who approaches personality

Everyone else probably understands us better than we do ourselves.

CARL JUNG

It's difficult to make it through college without taking a personality test somewhere along the way. One reason self-report inventories are frequently used in personality research can be seen here—researchers can quickly collect information from a large number of people.

from the psychoanalytic perspective. This is because most of the important concepts in this theory lie in the unconscious mind, to which the person has no direct access. Asking people the extent to which they hold unconscious aggressive desires is not likely to prove very useful.

To avoid this problem, psychoanalytic psychologists have developed assessment procedures that do not rely on the test takers' ability to describe themselves. As described in Chapter 3, test takers typically provide responses to ambiguous stimuli, which a trained psychologist then interprets. Some psychologists refer to this as a *sign approach*. That is, the psychologist does not examine personality concepts directly but rather looks for signs of, for example, frustrated unconscious impulses.

Psychologists from the trait, biological, and humanistic approaches are more likely to use the self-report assessment procedures described above. Of course, this assumes test takers are able to provide accurate information about themselves. In contrast to psychoanalysts, theorists from these approaches generally are willing to make this assumption. Indeed, humanistic theorists argue that no one can know the client better than the client.

Behavioral/social learning theorists take yet another tactic in assessing personality concepts. These psychologists typically use what is called the *sample approach*. They are interested in overt behavior, not in structures and concepts that supposedly exist within our minds. To determine a person's consistent behavior patterns, these psychologists observe that person's behavior. For example, to determine how cooperative people are, behavioral psychologists might observe people working on a group task. A person who engages in a large number of cooperative behaviors (for example, helping others in the group, complimenting others on their work) would be identified as a cooperative person. These psychologists might also identify group members who tend to show leadership, aggressive, or nurturant behaviors during the task.

The goal of assessment for cognitive psychologists is to determine how people perceive the world and how they organize and process this information. Asking people to describe themselves or watching how they interact with others probably provides little information about cognitive structures and processes. Therefore, cognitive personality theorists typically ask test takers to work on some type of organizing task. For example, they might ask clients to indicate how two people are alike and how they are different from a third person. The categories test takers use to make these distinctions tell us something about how they typically classify the people they meet and how they generally process information.

In short, personality psychologists use a wide variety of assessment procedures. The method a psychologist chooses depends on his or her approach to personality. That approach determines which personality concepts are most important to measure and what procedures are most appropriate for getting at that information.

Research

Although the focus thus far has been on the differences among the six approaches to personality, one feature they all have in common is that each generates a great deal of relevant research. Sometimes this research tests the validity of principles and assumptions central to the theory. Other times researchers are only interested in examining a few of the concepts introduced by a personality theory.

Psychologists employ a large number of research methods in their efforts to uncover information about personality. A recent review traced the history of the various research methodologies employed by personality researchers (Craik, 1986). As shown in Figure 1.2, this study found that the popularity of different methods has fluctuated greatly over the history of personality research. For example, using biographies and doing field studies were popular early in this history, then fell off for a while, only to return in recent years. Projective tests and the use of observer judgments have always been popular. The persistent use of projective tests illustrates the continued popularity of the psychoanalytic approach throughout this time. Personality inventories have always been popular, but their use increased dramatically after World War II. The need to measure soldiers' aptitudes and other psychological variables during the war gave this method a boost it has enjoyed ever since. Similarly, laboratory methods have seen a large increase in popularity in recent years. Only naturalistic observation has largely disappeared from the personality researchers' arsenal.

We'll look at a number of relevant research programs in later chapters. However, to better appreciate this work we need to first look at how researchers go about designing their experiments and some of the pitfalls they need to avoid. These topics are addressed in the next chapter.

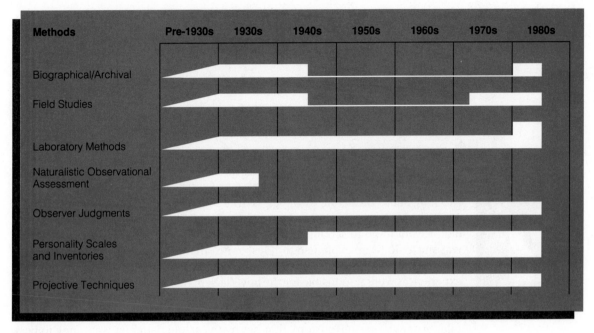

Figure 1.2

History of Personality Research Methods

Taken from Craik (1986), with permission.

Summary

1. Personality psychology is concerned with the differences between people. Although there is no agreed-upon definition, *personality* is defined here as consistent behavior patterns originating within the individual.

2. For convenience, the many theories of personality are divided into six general categories: the psychoanalytic, trait, biological, humanistic, behavioral/social learning, and cognitive approaches. Each approach provides a different focus for explaining individual differences in behavior. The six approaches can be thought of as complementary models for understanding human personality, although occasionally they present competing accounts of behavior.

3. A thorough understanding of human personality requires more than the study of theory. We'll also examine how each of the approaches is applied to practical concerns, how each deals with personality assessment, and some of the research relevant to the issues and topics addressed by the theories.

Personality Research Methods

2

Not long ago, "Desperate in Dallas" wrote to Ann Landers about her husband's 16-year-old cousin who was living with them. The boy didn't want to work, didn't want to go to school, and generally was a very messy house guest. What was she to do? Ann explained to "Desperate" that the boy's real problem was the rejection he had received from his parents earlier in his life. These early childhood experiences were responsible for the boy's lack of motivation. Within the next few weeks, Ann also explained to "Wondering in Boston" that a five-year-old boy became aggressive from watching too many violent programs on television. She told "Anonymous in Houston" that her five-year-old daughter was going to be a leader, and "Intrigued in Norfolk" that while some people are routinely incapacitated with minor aches and pains, others are capable of ignoring them.

In each of these examples, Ann Landers was explaining why a certain person engages in consistent behavior patterns, that is, the causes of that person's personality. Millions of people seem to think that she has something to say about behavior. But how does she know? Experience? Intelligence? A keen insight into human nature? Perhaps. In a way, Ann Landers represents one way we come to understand personality — through expert opinion. In a layman's sort of way, Ann Landers is similar to the great personality theorists who study the works of others, make their own observations, and then explain what they believe are the causes of consistent patterns of human behavior. For example, Sigmund Freud read widely about what his contemporaries were saying about human behavior. He worked and consulted with some of the great thinkers of the day who also were concerned about psychological phenomena. Freud also carefully observed his patients, who came to him with a variety of psychological problems. From the information gathered from all of these sources, Freud developed a new conception of human personality that he spent the rest of his career promoting.

Although more scholarly and rigorous than Ann Landers's one-paragraph diagnoses, Freud's theory often evokes a similar response: How does he know? Freud's writings are intriguing, and his arguments at times persuasive, but most personality psychologists want more than an expert's viewpoint before they accept a personality theory. They want empirical research. They want studies examining key predictions from the theory. They want some hard numbers providing strong evidence in support of the theory. This is not because an expert's views are of no value. Quite the contrary, the views and observations of personality theorists form the backbone of this book. But theories alone provide only part of the picture. Understanding the nature of human personality also requires an examination of what psychologists have learned from rigorous empirical investigations.

This chapter introduces some of the basic concepts of personality research. In addition, we will go over some of the ways to tell a good study from a weak one. Finally, because personality psychologists often rely on personality tests, we will review briefly some of the concepts associated with measuring individual differences in personality.

The Hypothesis-Testing Approach

Each of us on occasion speculates about the nature of personality. You may have wondered why you seem to be more self-conscious than others, why a friend seems to be depressed so often, or why you have so much trouble making friends when it seems to come so easily to others. In the latter case, you may have watched the way a popular student interacts with people she meets and compared this behavior with the way you typically act around strangers. If you are like most people, you may have even tried to change your behavior to be more like hers and then watched to see if this would have any effect on how others reacted to you.

In essence, the difference between this process and that used by personality psychologists lies only in the degree of sophistication. Like all of us, personality researchers speculate about the nature of personality. From observations, knowledge about previous theory and research, and careful speculation, these researchers generate hypotheses about why certain people behave in consistent, characteristic ways. Then, using rigorous experimental methods, they collect data to see if their explanations about human behavior are correct. Like pieces in a large jigsaw puzzle, each study makes another contribution to our understanding of personality. However, by the time you get to the end of this book it should be clear that this is one puzzle that will never be finished.

Theories and Hypotheses

Most personality research begins with a **theory**—a general statement about the relationship between constructs or events. Theories differ in the range of events or phenomena they explain. Some, such as the major personality theories discussed in this book, are very broad. For example, psychologists have used Freud's psychoanalytic theory to explain topics as diverse as what causes psychological disorders, why people turn to religion, and why certain jokes are funny. However, most personality researchers typically work with theories that are considerably more narrow in their application. For example, they might be concerned with the reasons some people are more motivated to achieve than others, or the relationship between a parent's behavior and a child's level of self-esteem. It might be useful to think of the larger theories, such as Freud's, as collections of more specific theories that share certain assumptions about the nature of human personality.

A good theory possesses at least two characteristics. First, a good theory is *parsimonious*. Scientists generally operate under what is known as the "law of parsimony" — that is, the simplest theory that can explain the phenomenon is the best one. As will be seen throughout this book, several theories can be generated to explain any one behavior. Some can be quite extensive and include many concepts and assumptions, whereas others explain the phenomenon in relatively simple terms. Which theory is better? Although it sometimes seems that scientists enjoy wrapping their work in fancy terms and esoteric concepts, the truth is that, if two theories can account for the phenomenon equally well, the simpler explanation is preferred.

Second, a good theory is *useful*. More specifically, unless a theory can generate testable hypotheses, it may be of little or no use to scientists. Ideas that cannot be tested are not necessarily incorrect. It's just that they do not lend themselves to scientific investigation. For example, throughout history people have explained psychological disorders in terms of invisible demons taking over a person's body. This may or may not be a correct statement about the causes of disorders. But unless this is somehow testable, the theory cannot be examined through scientific methods and is of little use to scientists.

However, theories themselves are never tested. Instead, investigators derive from the theory hypotheses that can then be tested in research. A **hypothesis** is a formal prediction about the relationship between two or more variables that is logically derived from the theory. Let's illustrate this with an example. As discussed in Chapter 12, many psychologists are interested in stable individual differences in loneliness. That is, they want to know why some people frequently suffer from feelings of loneliness, whereas others rarely, if ever, feel lonely. One theory proposes that consistently lonely people lack social skills that might enable them to develop and maintain satisfying relationships. Because this is a useful theory, many predictions can be logically derived from it (see Figure 2.1). For example, if the theory correctly describes the cause of loneliness, then we might expect consistently lonely people to make fewer attempts to initiate conversations than those who are not lonely. Another prediction might be that these lonely people have a poor perception of how they are being perceived by others. Yet another prediction might maintain that lonely people make more socially inappropriate statements than nonlonely people when they do engage in conversations.

Each of these predictions can be tested. For example, we might test the last prediction by recording conversations lonely and nonlonely people have with new acquaintances. Judges could evaluate the conversations in terms of number of appropriate responses, number of appropriate questions, and so on. If people who identify themselves as lonely make fewer appropriate responses during the conversation, the prediction is confirmed. We then say we have support for the theory. But notice that the theory itself is not tested directly. Theories are never

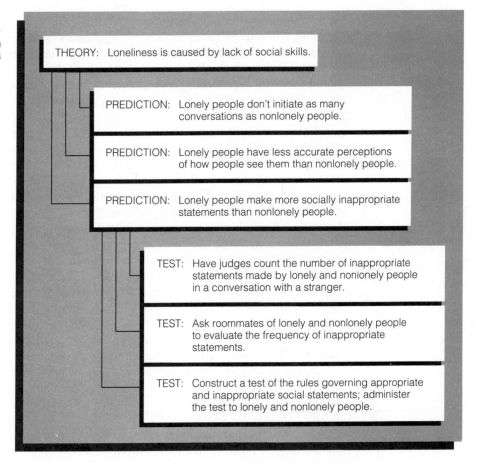

Figure 2.1

Example of the
Hypothesis-Testing
Approach

proved or disproved. Rather, a theory is more or less supported by the research and therefore is more or less useful to scientists trying to understand the phenomenon. The more often research confirms a prediction derived from a theory, the more faith we have that the theory is accurately describing the nature of things. However, if predictions are consistently not confirmed in empirical investigations, we are much less likely to accept the theory. Most likely, we would generate a new theory or modify the old one to better account for the research findings.

One aspect of hypothesis testing needs to be highlighted here. Most of the research reported in this book began with a theory from which predictions were derived and tested. However, not all research operates this way. Beginning researchers are sometimes tempted to start this process from the bottom, making specific predictions about how one variable affects another without any theoretical reason for why the variables might be related. For example, you might observe while jogging one day that you feel less pain and exhaustion on the days you think about something other than jogging. This might spawn the prediction that running while thinking about something distracting makes the running more bearable. You might even design an experiment in which some people run while concentrating on their running while others run while solving math problems in their heads. But even if your prediction were confirmed, what would this tell you? The information might be of some value to runners. But without a larger theory you would be unable to say much about human behavior outside of this situation.

But suppose you began your research with a theory concerning the relationship between focus of attention and the impact of stressors. One prediction that could be derived from this theory might be that distraction during physical exertion makes the effort less painful. This prediction then might be tested with the running study described above. The results from the study might then confirm the prediction and give support to the larger theory. In addition, predictions might be derived from this theory concerning the use of defense mechanisms to deal with anxiety, or how hypnosis helps people overcome pain, or why certain exercises help women reduce the discomfort of childbirth.

This is not to say that atheoretical research is meaningless. Many times psychologists working in applied areas are interested in understanding specific behaviors in specific situations. For example, market researchers may want to know if people are more likely to buy an orange box or a blue box of detergent. However, even in this case, market researchers who plan to continue work in this area with other products might find it more productive to begin with a theory about how colors are related to emotions.

Experimental Variables

Good research progresses from theory to prediction to experiment. The basic elements of an experiment are the experimental variables, which are divided into two types: independent variables and dependent variables. An **independent variable** determines how the groups in the experiment are divided. Often this is manipulated by the experimenter, such as when subjects are randomly assigned to different experimental conditions. An independent variable might be the amount of a drug each group receives, how much stress each group is exposed to, or the type of speech each group is presented with. For example, if level of stress is the independent variable, a researcher might tell Group A that they will receive intense electric shocks; Group B, mild electric shocks; and Group C, no shocks. Because each of the groups created by the independent variable receives a slightly different treatment, some researchers refer to the independent variable as the "treatment" variable.

By randomly placing subjects into different conditions, experimenters can create groups for comparison. However, many times an investigator wants to compare two or more groups that differ on some independent variable that the researcher cannot or chooses to not manipulate. For example, a researcher might want to compare first-born children with middle-born and last-born children. In this example, birth order is the independent variable, even though the investigator was not responsible for deciding which subjects would be in which groups.

A **dependent variable** is measured by the experimenter and used to compare the experimental groups. In a well-designed experiment, differences between groups on the dependent variable can be attributed to the different levels of the independent variable. For example, suppose an experimenter's hypothesis was that people reduce their anxiety about threatening events by obtaining as much information about the situation as possible. The researcher might want to use level of anxiety as the independent variable, perhaps by telling subjects they will soon receive either intense, moderate, or no electric shocks. The three groups might be compared on how many questions they ask the experimenter about the upcoming shock. In this case, the number of questions is the dependent variable. The results of such an experiment might come out like this:

	High Anxiety	Moderate Anxiety	No Anxiety
Average number of questions	5.44	3.12	1.88

If the experiment has been designed correctly, the investigator will attribute the difference in the dependent variable (the number of questions) to the different levels of the independent variable (anxiety). Because experimenters want to say that differences in the dependent variable are the result of the different treatment each of the groups received, some researchers refer to the dependent variable as the "outcome" variable.

However, most personality research is more complex than this example indicates. Researchers typically use more than one independent variable. In the information-seeking example, an experimenter might want to further divide subjects into groups some psychologists refer to as "repressors" and "sensitizers." As we'll explore in more detail in Chapter 6, people can be divided into those who tend to seek out information (sensitizers) and those who tend to avoid information (repressors) when faced with a threatening situation. In our example, the experimenter might change the hypothesis to predict that anxiety leads to a search for information, but only among sensitizers. Repressors might actually avoid information more when anxiety goes up. Thus, researchers might use two independent variables to divide subjects into groups. They could randomly assign subjects to either an anxiety (anticipate shocks) or a no-anxiety group, and within each of these groups identify those who are typically sensitizers and those who are typically repressors. If the dependent variable remained the number of questions asked of the experimenter, the results might turn out like those shown in Figure 2.2. This figure illustrates what is called an **interaction**. That is, how one independent variable affects the dependent variable depends on the level of the other independent variable. In this example, whether anxiety leads to an increase or a decrease in the number of questions asked depends on whether the subject is in the sensitizer or the repressor group.

Researchers also typically use more than one dependent variable in their experiments. In addition to the number of questions asked, researchers might want to measure how much time subjects spend examining the electric-shock

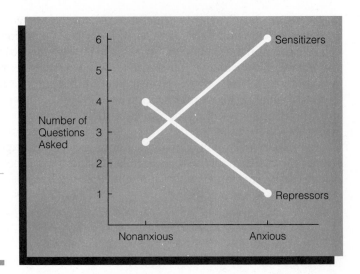

Figure 2.2

An Interaction
Between Two
Independent
Variables

machinery or how long they spend going over a written description of the procedures. The more often scores on these dependent measures fall in line with the predictions, the more support researchers can claim for the theory.

Types of Research

Like a carpenter or a physician, personality researchers must know how to use many different tools if they are to be effective in their job. There are many different ways to examine the causes of consistent behavior patterns. In this section we'll look at two of the more important ways of classifying personality research. In addition, we will examine a special type of research used frequently by personality psychologists: the case study method.

Manipulated Versus Nonmanipulated Independent Variables

Personality is so complex a thing that every legitimate method must be employed in its study.
GORDON ALLPORT

As described earlier, sometimes researchers randomly assign subjects to conditions, such as putting them into the high-anxiety or low-anxiety group, whereas other times they simply identify which group the subject already belongs to, such as sensitizers or repressors. The significance of this difference is illustrated in the following example. Suppose you are interested in the effect violent television programs have on the amount of aggression people display in real life. You recruit some subjects who watch a lot of violent TV shows and others who watch relatively few. The subjects are tested in several ways to determine which are more aggressive. Consistent with the experimental hypothesis, you find the subjects who watch a lot of violent television are more aggressive than those who watch relatively little violent TV. You might be tempted to conclude from this finding that watching violent television programs causes people to become more aggressive. However, based on this study alone, such a conclusion must be tempered. For example, it's possible these people watch violent TV shows precisely *because* they are aggressive. Perhaps they are more entertained by programs that include shootings, stabbings, and other violent acts. Thus, although the findings are consistent with the hypothesis, any statement about a cause-and-effect relationship must be qualified.

This example illustrates the fundamental difference between research using manipulated independent variables and research using nonmanipulated independent variables. An investigator who uses a **manipulated independent variable** begins with a large number of subjects and *randomly* assigns them to experimental groups. That is, each subject has an equally likely chance of being assigned to Experimental Condition A as to Experimental Condition B (or C, or D, and so on). We know all subjects are not exactly alike at the beginning of the experiment. Some are naturally more aggressive than others, some more depressed, some more intelligent. Each has different life experiences that might affect what he or she does in the experiment. However, by using a large number of subjects and randomly assigning them to experimental conditions, we assume that all of these differences will be evened out. Thus, although within any given experimental condition there are people with different aggressiveness levels, each condition should have the same *average* level of aggressiveness at the beginning of the experiment.

The experimenter then introduces the independent variable. For example, one group might be shown 30 minutes of violent television programming, while another group watches a baseball game, and still another group sits quietly and watches no television. Because we assume subjects in each experimental condition initially are nearly identical on the average, any differences between the groups after the presentation of the independent variable (in this case, the type of program) are attributed to the independent variable. That is, if we find the subjects who watched the violent TV shows are more aggressive than those who watched the nonviolent shows or those who watched no TV, then we have more confidence in concluding that watching the violent TV shows *caused* the subjects to act more aggressively.

This procedure contrasts with the use of nonmanipulated variables. A **nonmanipulated independent variable** exists without the experimenter's intervention. For example, we might divide subjects into male and female groups, or high self-esteem and low self-esteem groups. In neither case does the experimenter randomly assign a subject to be in one or the other condition. Returning to the earlier example, the experimenter who compared frequent and infrequent television viewers did not manipulate subjects into those two categories. Instead, the subjects had already determined which of the groups they belonged to without any action on the researcher's part.

The difficulty with this and other nonmanipulated independent variables is that the researcher cannot assume the people in the two groups are nearly identical on the average at the beginning of the experiment. For example, people who watch relatively little television might be more intelligent, might come from a higher socioeconomic level, or might be better educated than the more frequent viewers. We can be fairly certain that they have more time for activities besides television, such as reading or interacting with friends, than the frequent viewers. They also might differ in terms of self-esteem, experiences with aggression, diet, and, most notably, their level of aggression prior to participating in the experiment. Thus, any differences we find between the two groups could be caused by *any* of these differences, not necessarily by the amount of violent TV shows each group watches.

Because of this difficulty in determining cause-and-effect relationships with nonmanipulated independent variables, researchers generally prefer to manipulate variables. However, doing so is not always possible. Sometimes manipulating the variable is too expensive, too difficult, or unethical. This is a particular problem in personality research because many of the variables we want to study cannot be easily manipulated, if at all. Returning to our example, it would be next to impossible to tell some subjects, "You watch a lot of violent television during the next few years," and tell others, "You watch no violent television until I tell you it's OK." Instead, if we want to know about the long-term effects of exposure to violent TV, we have to accept our subjects as they are, understanding that many group differences exist at the outset of the study. Sometimes researchers try to control for some of these known differences, such as by comparing the education levels of the two groups. However, we can never be sure we have controlled for all the relevant variables.

But research employing nonmanipulated variables is not necessarily of little value. Many times, using such variables is the only way to reasonably examine a topic of interest. How else can we study the differences between introverts and extraverts without comparing two pre-existing groups? Much of what we know of personality comes from such studies, but researchers using nonmanipulated variables always must remain cautious when making statements about cause-and-effect relationships.

Laboratory Versus Field Research

Some personality research is conducted with volunteer subjects in a highly controlled and somewhat artificial laboratory. But sometimes researchers examine the behavior of people who don't realize a study is going on in a "real-world" setting. Some of the differences between these two types of research are illustrated in the following example.

As described in Chapter 4, one prediction derived from Sigmund Freud's theory of personality is that people who are tense and anxious find a humorous situation funnier than do people who are relatively anxiety-free. One way to test this prediction might be to find a group of people who are fairly anxious and another group that is generally relaxed. For example, you might go to an amusement park to find a group of people waiting in line for a frightening roller-coaster ride and another group waiting in line for a relatively safe and relaxing train ride.

The woman passing by never realizes that the papers were dropped on purpose and that whether or not she stops to help is being recorded by the hidden experimenter. An advantage of field research is that subjects act the way they naturally would when encountering such a situation.

You then could create a comical scene in front of each group. For example, you might have an actor trip and fall face-first into a cake he is carrying. Judges could be stationed around the scene to record how many people standing in line show visible signs of laughter.

Suppose you conducted this experiment and found that a higher percentage of the people in the roller-coaster line laughed than in the train line. What would you conclude? One possibility is that different anxiety levels were responsible for the different reactions. But there are other possibilities. For example, perhaps the kind of person who rides on roller coasters is generally more fun-loving and more likely to laugh than the train riders. It's possible the people in the train line have been standing there longer, or are at the end of their visit to the park and are looking for a relaxing ride. They might just be too tired to laugh.

But there are other problems with this study. How can we be sure the people lined up for the roller coaster are feeling anxious? After all, people who are afraid of such rides probably avoid them. How sure are you that the people are reacting to the scene you created and not something else? Perhaps something else has just happened in front of the train riders (for example, a child fell and hurt herself) that could have affected their moods.

In short, the difficulties in conducting this study illustrate the major limitation of field research: the loss of experimenter control over many relevant features of the investigation. A **field study** is conducted in a natural, as opposed to a laboratory, setting. Subjects act the way they ordinarily act and typically do not find out they are part of an experiment. However, this does not mean experimenters cannot introduce a little manipulation into the situation. A researcher might ask subjects to contribute to a charity, using a different type of appeal for people randomly assigned to different experimental conditions. Or, as in the humor example, the researcher might create a comical scene and observe how people react.

The major advantage of a field study is that researchers examine behavior taking place in a natural setting. We say the findings have greater *external validity* than those from laboratory investigations. That is, we are more confident they have some relationship to the way people behave. Because subjects are unaware of the experiment, they are likely to behave as they ordinarily do when responding to a request for money or seeing a person fall on a cake. The disadvantage, as seen in the humor example, is that the experimenter must forfeit control over many aspects of the situation that might have significant effects on the results.

In contrast, a large amount of experimenter control is the major advantage of **laboratory research**. Although the laboratory setting is artificial, in that the researcher creates an environment probably not found in the real world, it does allow us to examine the effects of only those variables of interest. Subjects are aware they are participating in a research project, and researchers can select subjects with the type of background and characteristics they prefer. Nearly all the crucial features of the situation are controlled by the researcher: what people see, what information they are exposed to, possible reactions, and so forth. Extraneous variables that might affect the results, such as age of subjects or amount of familiarity among subjects before the experiment begins, can be controlled as well.

Let's return to the anxiety-humor hypothesis. If you wanted to examine this hypothesis in a more controlled manner, you might begin by recruiting volunteer subjects and randomly assigning them to either a high-anxiety or a low-anxiety condition. For example, half of the subjects might be told they are to give a speech in front of a large group, and the other half not told this. You also might use a more direct measure of subjects' humor responses than possible in the field study. You could ask subjects to rate on a 10-point scale how funny they found the situation, rather than using judges to interpret their reactions.

But laboratory research has disadvantages, too. Experimenters often wonder if their laboratory findings are too artificial to tell them much about how people behave in a natural setting. Psychologists frequently discuss how the subjects' knowledge of being in an experiment affects how they act (Berkowitz & Donnerstein, 1982; Orne, 1962). For example, laboratory subjects may do what they think they are supposed to, rather than what they actually would do in a natural setting.

Thus, laboratory and field investigations each have advantages and disadvantages. Which procedure we choose depends on how concerned we are with controlling extraneous variables versus our desire to generalize the findings to real-world settings. The best program of research is one that tests hypotheses with both types of studies. A finding that turns up consistently in laboratory as well as field research allows researchers to control potentially important variables as well as demonstrate the real-world applicability of the phenomenon.

The Case Study Method

One method of research used more often by personality researchers than most other types of psychologists is the **case study method**: an in-depth evaluation of a single individual (or sometimes a few individuals) or a single group of people. Most typically, the subject is a psychotherapy patient suffering from a disorder of interest to the investigator. The researcher records in great detail the person's history, current behavior, and changes in behavior over the course of the investigation, which often lasts for years. Case study data are usually descriptive. That is, rather than reporting a lot of numbers and statistical analyses, the investigators usually describe their impressions of what the subject did and what it means. Researchers occasionally include quantitative assessments, such as recording how many times the person washes his or her hands in a 24-hour period. However, numbers from another group or another person with which to compare these data are rarely reported.

As we will see throughout this book, several prominent theorists have used the case study method when developing their ideas about personality. Sigmund Freud relied almost exclusively on his own in-depth analysis of patients when formulating ideas about personality. In fact, many of Freud's initial insights into the functions of the human mind came from his observations of one early patient, Anna O., whose story is told in Chapter 3. Gordon Allport, the first psychologist to promote the concept of traits, argued that we cannot capture the essence of a whole personality without an in-depth analysis of a single individual. Humanistic theorists, most notably Carl Rogers, developed their unique concept of human nature through the extensive evaluation of psychotherapy clients. Finally, the behaviorists, often regarded as the most scientifically rigorous of the personality researchers, have relied heavily on case studies to illustrate various aspects of their theories and the effectiveness of their therapies. For example, in Chapter 13 we will review John B. Watson's work with an orphaned infant named "Little Albert." This famous case study has been widely cited as evidence for the behaviorist explanation of abnormal behaviors.

Disadvantages of the Case Study Method   The widespread use of the case study method by prominent psychologists may surprise you at first, given some of the obvious weaknesses of this method. First is the problem of generalizing from any one case to other people. Just because one person behaves in a certain way doesn't mean all people behave that way. In fact, many of the case study subjects come to the attention of personality theorists when they seek out psychotherapy, no doubt because they feel different from others. One reason experimenters often randomly assign many people to conditions in their studies is to eliminate the bias that comes from examining just a few people who may or may not be representative of a larger population.

Second is the problem of determining cause-and-effect relationships with the case study method. For example, a patient with a fear of water may recall a traumatic experience of nearly drowning as a child. Although we can speculate that this earlier event is responsible for the fear, we cannot be certain that the fear wouldn't have developed without the experience. Because of this, researchers using case studies must be cautious when speculating about the causes of the behaviors they see.

Third, investigators' subjective judgments can often interfere with scientific objectivity in case study work. The expectancies researchers bring to a case study may cause them to see that which confirms the hypotheses and to overlook that which does not. As we will see in the next chapter, Freud in particular has been criticized for approaching his cases with his own biases. Some researchers, such as the behavior modification therapists described in Chapter 13, work on developing more reliable, less biased observation techniques. Nonetheless, the problem remains of deciding ahead of time which behaviors are worth recording and which should be ignored.

Advantages of the Case Study Method   With all of these weaknesses, why do so many personality researchers continue to use the case study method? One reason is that many of the concepts deemed important to these investigators are not easily examined with experimental methods. For example, Freud's concern with the deeper understanding of a person's unconscious mind is not easily examined in other ways. Some humanistic theorists argue that reducing an individual to a few numbers on a sheet of paper results in losing the "real" person altogether. The case study method also is valuable for generating hypotheses about the nature of human personality. Researchers then examine these hypotheses with more rigorous experimental procedures.

There are at least four situations in which the case study method is a particularly useful research tool. First, it is the most appropriate method when *examining a rare case.* Suppose you wanted to investigate the personalities of political assassins. You probably would be limited to exploring the background and perhaps the current behavior of only a handful of people who fall into this category. Similarly, therapists working with patients described as having multiple personalities often report their observations in a case study manner when recording information about what is probably a once-in-a-lifetime find.

The case study method also is appropriate when the researcher can argue that *the subject is essentially no different from all normal people* on the dimension being examined. For example, case studies of "split-brain" patients have uncovered important information about the functioning of the human brain. Subjects in these studies have had the corpus callosum (which connects the right and left halves of the cerebral hemisphere) severed as part of treatment for severe epilepsy. Because the physical functions of the brain are basically alike for all normally functioning people, studying the behavior of these few patients tells us much about the way our right and left brains would operate if not connected by the corpus callosum.

Still another appropriate use of the case study is *to illustrate a treatment.* Therapists often describe in detail the procedures they used to treat a particular patient and the apparent success or failure of the therapy. A prudent therapist will not argue that all people suffering from the disorder should be treated in this way, but rather will use the case study to suggest possible treatment programs other therapists might explore with their clients. A therapy procedure is most effectively demonstrated when the client's progress is compared at various stages of the treatment, such as comparing a no-treatment period with a treatment stage (Hayes, 1981).

Finally, an investigator might choose the case study method simply *to demonstrate possibilities*. For example, a researcher using one or two easily hypnotizable subjects might demonstrate impressive changes in behavior. Some deeply hypnotizable subjects have been reported to change skin temperature on one part of the body but not another, to form blisters on their hands, and to increase the size of their breasts. These studies are not intended to argue that all people are able to do these things but rather to illustrate some of the possibilities obtainable with hypnosis.

In summary, although the case study method has been used extensively by personality theorists and researchers, it has some serious drawbacks. Chief among these is the impossibility of determining the extent to which the subject is representative of the average person. Yet it would be unfair to say the case study does not have a place in personality research. When used properly and, more important, when the findings are interpreted properly, the case study method provides valuable insight into a large number of personality processes.

Statistical Analysis of Data

Suppose a waitress wanted to know, for obvious reasons, what kind of behavior elicits the largest tips from customers. Her hypothesis is that smiling and acting in a friendly manner will result in better tips than will acting in a more professional and efficient manner. She tests her hypothesis by alternating between the friendly and the professional approach each night for 14 nights. At the end of each evening, she counts her tips and records the data. Suppose these were her findings:

Friendly Approach	*Professional Approach*
$31.50	$36.90
42.75	31.75
39.60	38.00
32.00	32.25
41.10	33.60
29.45	39.30
30.20	30.60
$35.23 average	$34.63 average

Finally, let's suppose the waitress concludes from this study that the friendly approach indeed works best and that she changes to a friendly waitressing style from now on. The question is: Is this conclusion justified? We can see from her numbers that the friendly approach came up with a higher average tip than did the professional approach. But by now you probably have already wondered if an average of $35.23 is *reliably* different from an average of $34.63. Because of naturally occurring variation in the amount of tips made in an evening, we would not expect the averages to come out exactly the same, even if the waitress never changed her approach. One "condition" in this study would almost always come out at least a little higher than the other. So the question becomes: How much higher must one of the averages be before we can conclude that it is not just a chance fluctuation, but in fact represents a real difference between the two styles of waitressing? This is the question of **statistical significance**.

Statistical Significance

How can researchers tell if the different averages of their groups represent real effects or just chance fluctuations? Fortunately, statisticians have developed formulas that allow us to estimate the likelihood that the difference between our averages could have occurred by chance alone. There are many types of statistical tests, each appropriate for different types of data and different research designs. Some of the more common tests are an *analysis of variance*, a *chi-square test*, and a *correlation coefficient*.

Returning to the waitress example, if the two averages differed by an amount so small that it could have been caused by a chance fluctuation, then we say the difference has not reached a level of statistical significance. Conversely, if the difference is so large that in all likelihood it was not caused by chance but reflects a true difference between the two waitressing styles, we say the difference is statistically significant. In the latter case, we would conclude that one style of waitressing does seem to result in better tips than does the other style.

However, statistical tests do not really provide a yes or no answer to our question. All they tell us is the statistical probability that the difference between the groups was caused by chance. For example, suppose we apply a statistical test to the waitress's data and find that a difference this large might occur by chance one out of every four times. What could we conclude from this? That the different averages represent a real effect? It would be difficult to have much confidence in such a statement. We might have found a real difference, but there is a considerably high probability that the finding is just a fluke. So, when *can* we say we have a real difference? Traditionally, the significance level used by psychologists is .05. This means if the difference between the scores is so large that it would occur less than 5% of the time by chance, then the difference is probably genuine. However, as illustrated in Box 2.1, large differences can appear by chance, and a .05 probability level still allows for an incorrect conclusion of a real difference 1 out of 20 times.

Correlation Coefficients

The **correlation coefficient** is one of the statistics frequently used by personality researchers. This is the appropriate statistic when we want to understand

Predicting the Stock Market from the Super Bowl

Psychological researchers typically employ a significance level of .05 to determine whether a particular finding is one that occurs by chance or is likely to reflect real differences between groups of subjects. If a finding is unlikely to occur more than 1 in 20 times by chance, then we say it is statistically significant. But does this mean we can be confident the researcher has uncovered a genuine, reliable relationship whenever the finding reaches this level?

The answer is no. Remember, 1 out of 20 of these findings will occur by chance alone. To illustrate, Koppett (1978) reported a rather unusual relationship: He noted first whether a team from the original American Football League or National Football League won each Super Bowl (played in January), and then whether the stock market, as indicated by the New York Stock Exchange, went up or down that year. In his examination of the first 11 Super Bowls, this is what he found:

Year	Super Bowl Winner	Original League	Stock Market
1967	Green Bay	National	Up
1968	Green Bay	National	Up
1969	New York Jets	American	Down
1970	Kansas City	American	Down
1971	Baltimore	National	Up
1972	Dallas	National	Up
1973	Miami	American	Down
1974	Miami	American	Down
1975	Pittsburgh	National	Up
1976	Pittsburgh	National	Up
1977	Oakland	American	Down

Every time a National team won the Super Bowl, the stock market went up, and every time an American team won, the market went down.

Now, unless we are willing to believe that the outcome of the Super Bowl somehow affects the stock market, the obvious conclusion is that some relationships occur by chance alone. Psychologists are increasingly aware of the problem in reporting and accepting results that may be specious. To overcome the problem, researchers are encouraged to replicate their findings. In addition, researchers are beginning to use advanced statistical procedures called *meta-analyses* that help determine the overall strength of a research finding when all the studies testing a particular effect are examined (Cooper, 1990).

Nonetheless, 3 years later Koppett (1981) reexamined and updated his finding. He discovered the following:

Continued

the relationship between two measures. For example, we might be interested in the relationship between loneliness and depression. One way to investigate this relationship is to ask a large number of people to complete a loneliness scale as well as a depression inventory. If loneliness and depression are related, we would expect people who score high on loneliness to also score high on depression; similarly, those who score low on loneliness would score low on depression.

Figure 2.3 presents three possible outcomes from this research. Each point on the figure represents one subject's scores on both scales. The first outcome indicates that a subject's score on one scale is a fairly good predictor of that person's score on the other scale. In this case, if we know someone is high on loneliness, we know that person probably also is going to score high on depression. The second outcome indicates little or no relationship between the measures; knowing a subject's score on one scale gives us no information about what the other score will be. The third outcome, like the first, indicates that knowing a person's loneliness score *will* help us predict the depression score, but not in the way we might have anticipated. Here, a high score on one measure predicts a low score on the other.

After conducting the appropriate statistical test, we can reduce the data in each of the relationships shown in Figure 2.3 to a single number, the correlation coefficient. This number can range from 1.00 to -1.00. The closer the coefficient is to either of the extremes, 1.00 or -1.00 (and thus the farther away from 0), the stronger the relationship between the two measures. Returning to the figure, the first outcome indicates a fairly strong relationship between loneliness and depression. The correlation coefficient for this figure might be .60. Because a high score on one measure indicates a high score on the other measure, this is a *positive correlation*. For the second outcome, the correlation coefficient approaches .00,

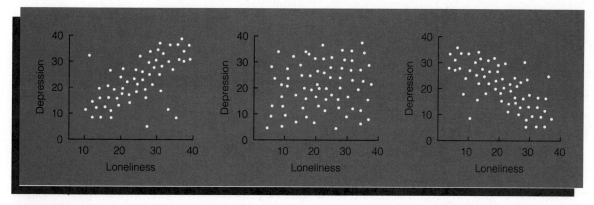

Figure 2.3

Three Possible Relations Between Loneliness and Depression

indicating no relationship between the measures. The third outcome might yield a correlation of -.60, also indicating a fairly strong relationship between the variables. We should note the third outcome is a *negative correlation*, but this does not mean it is less important than a positive correlation of the same magnitude. For example, if we had compared scores on a loneliness scale with scores on a sociability measure, we probably would have anticipated a high score on one would predict a low score on the other.

Problems to Look for When Examining Research

The man with creative ideas in philosophy or art can give wings to them at once; but in science . . . extensive painstaking experiment has to be done.

RAYMOND CATTELL

There is no such thing as a perfect experiment. I am confident any personality researcher would agree with that statement. When selecting experiments to cover in this book, I have tried to find those that logically flow from theory, with properly defined variables, appropriate comparison groups, and fairly clear results. In one respect, this is not difficult. Hundreds of good studies on personality and related areas are published each year. On the other hand, all studies have their weaknesses. For example, a well-designed laboratory experiment with clear interpretations might still be criticized for being artificial and thus unlikely to generalize outside of the particular research setting.

This is why prudent researchers temper the conclusions they draw from any one study, and instead work on programs of research that demonstrate and examine personality phenomena in several investigations using diverse methodologies. Although any given study may have weaknesses, we can be fairly confident about a hypothesis supported in several different investigations. However, some experiments clearly are weaker than others. In this section we will introduce some of the problems investigators face when designing their studies. Along the way we will cover some of the issues you, as a daily consumer of research reports in newspaper stories, radio and television reports, and advertisers' claims, should be aware of.

Experimental Confounds

There is an old story about a man who drinks scotch and water all night Monday and wakes up the next morning with a hangover. On Tuesday he switches to bourbon and water but wakes up the next morning in the same condition. Wednesday night he tries brandy and water all night long and once again wakes with a hangover. After pondering his condition, the man reaches the following conclusion: No matter how much he wants it, he'd better give up drinking water.

The story illustrates the problem of **experimental confounds**—that is, what happens when another variable is allowed to vary with the independent variable. In this case, the drinking of alcohol was confounded with the drinking of water. Each night the man drank alcohol he also drank water. As in this case, failure to recognize that more than one variable is being manipulated can cause us to draw unwarranted conclusions.

As described earlier, researchers who use manipulated variables assume that subjects randomly assigned to each of the conditions differ on the average *only* in their exposure to the different levels of the independent variable. That way we can attribute differences on the dependent variable to the effect of the independent variable. Unfortunately, it is not always easy to manipulate *only* the independent variable.

For example, as described in Chapter 14, the learned helplessness theory of depression proposes that depression begins when people discover they cannot control an important event in their lives. In experimental tests of this theory, researchers often give one group of subjects control over the termination of an aversive noise. Typically, by solving some problem subjects are able to end the noise within a few seconds after it starts on each of many trials. Another group is also presented with the noise, but can do nothing to turn it off. Researchers find that subjects who cannot control the noise act like people suffering from depression: They have a decrease in general motivation and perform more poorly on later tasks. Those who are allowed to control the noise do not show these behaviors. Although these findings are in line with the predictions, there is a problem here. That is, the two groups of subjects differ not only in the extent to which they are able to control the noise but also in the amount of noise they are exposed to. In other words, the amount of *control* and the amount of *noise* are *confounded* in this experiment. We have no way of knowing if the different levels of depression are the result of the differences in control or the differences in noise.

Today, learned helplessness researchers take care to see that subjects in this type of experiment receive identical amounts of noise. When the two groups of subjects are alike in every way except one, then we have more confidence

Much personality
research today is con-
ducted with under-
graduate college stu-
dents in laboratory
situations. Although
these situations give
investigators a great
deal of control, they
raise questions about
the generalizability
of the findings to
other settings and
populations.

concluding that differences on the dependent variables (depression level) are the
result of differences on the independent variable (the amount of control).

Nonrandom Samples

Not long ago, a popular men's magazine reported the results of a survey on
American sexual behavior. Casually glancing at some of the tables and graphs, the
reader soon discovered that more than a third of the men and women surveyed
had engaged in sex in a public place, nearly 60% reported having two sexual
encounters with two different partners within a 24-hour period, and more than a
third said they had participated in sex with more than one partner (*Playboy*,
1983). A casual reader might begin to feel ignored by the sexual revolution.
However, a careful reader would have noticed the description of people who were
included in the sample.

    As it turns out, this particular survey was one in which readers of this "adult-
oriented" men's magazine cut out and mailed in their responses on a survey form
printed in an earlier issue. Thus, even assuming all the respondents were honest
in their answers (which itself is questionable), it is difficult to say these people are
representative of the American public. More likely, the readers of this magazine
hold more liberal attitudes about sex, are more interested in sexual behavior, and
are more willing to experiment with different forms of sexual expression than is

the average person. Thus, although the findings may be interesting, they tell us very little about the sexual behavior of Americans.

The problem with this survey is its use of a **nonrandom sample**. Ideally, subjects in a study are representative of the particular group of people the researcher is interested in. If we want to draw conclusions about all adults, then theoretically every adult should have an equal chance of participating in the experiment. If the investigator wants to know about people with low self-esteem, then every person who fits this description should have an equally likely probability of being selected to be in the study. Obviously, in almost all cases this is impossible. But researchers should make certain that their subjects are at least representative of the larger group. If subjects are different from the larger group in some significant way—they might be older, less educated, or more liberal—then investigators must be especially cautious in generalizing the research results to other types of people.

Many of the studies reported in this book suffer from nonrandom samples, because academic researchers often rely on student volunteers in their studies. Typically, college students are more intelligent, more affluent, better educated, and younger than the average American. Therefore, it is difficult to know how representative they are of adults in general (Carlson, 1984; Sears, 1986). Nonrandom sampling does not make the findings useless, but it does mean we need to be cautious when drawing conclusions for people who do not belong to this group.

Comparison Groups

A few years ago, a certain beer company broadcast commercials consisting of live "taste tests" during football games. The commercials ran throughout the season, culminating in a large, live test during the Super Bowl broadcast. One hundred "loyal" drinkers of another brand of beer were asked to indicate which of two unlabeled glasses of beer tasted better. Not surprisingly, a large percentage of these drinkers chose the sponsor's beer over their usual brand. The brewer concluded, of course, that its beer tasted better.

The problem with this demonstration is that there is no appropriate comparison group against which the findings can be matched. What would have happened if 100 of the *sponsor's* "loyal" drinkers had been given the choice? It is possible just as many of these people would have selected the *rival's* product. If that were the finding, we would more reasonably conclude that a large number of beer drinkers are simply unable to tell which beer they prefer, or are drinking the wrong beer. In other words, without an appropriate comparison group, drawing any conclusions about the test is difficult.

A **comparison group**, sometimes called a control group, is composed of subjects who differ from the experimental group in a specific way. Usually subjects in the comparison group do not receive a particular treatment that the experimental group receives. By comparing the results of the comparison group and the treatment group, we can determine if the treatment has had an effect.

To illustrate this point, suppose we were interested in the relationship between emotion and aggression. We might randomly assign people to two conditions. The subjects in Group A are made depressed, while the subjects in Group B are made happy. Then we give each person the opportunity to act aggressively, and we rate the behavior on a 10-point scale. Finally, suppose that we find the following average aggression scores for the two groups (with 10 being the most aggressive):

	Depressed	Happy
Aggression score	7.53	2.91

Assuming we manipulated mood and measured aggression appropriately, what would you conclude? That being depressed causes people to act aggressively? Maybe. But these data might also be interpreted to mean that being happy reduces aggression. What's needed is a comparison group that receives *neither* treatment. Depending on how aggressive we found *that* group to be, we could arrive at any of three conclusions. Consider these three possibilities:

	Depressed	Comparison	Happy
Possible outcome 1	7.53	7.50	2.91
Possible outcome 2	7.53	5.20	2.91
Possible outcome 3	7.53	2.93	2.91

Perhaps happiness reduces aggression (outcome 1), perhaps depression increases aggression (outcome 3), and perhaps both conditions affect aggression levels (outcome 2). Without the comparison group, we don't know which conclusion to draw.

You can find abundant examples of this problem when watching news commentators interpret election results. For example, I once observed a well-known correspondent comment on several candidates who had spent large amounts of money on their election bids but had lost. He concluded from this situation that spending money has no impact on voter preference. Although that may be true, the lack of an appropriate comparison group should caution us against drawing this conclusion. What is needed here (but which, of course, is impossible) is a condition in which the same candidates in the same situation run for office *without* spending large amounts of money. For example, it is possible that a candidate who spends heavily and obtains 48% of the vote might have received only 20% without the heavy spending. Similarly, winning an election when spending money does not mean the election would have been lost otherwise. Like the therapist who declares the treatment a success because the client gets better, unless there is an appropriate comparison group, this type of conclusion needs to be tempered.

Prediction Versus Hindsight

Which person would you find more impressive: the one who can explain *after* a basketball game why the winning team was victorious, or the one who accurately predicts *before* the game which team will win and why? Most of us probably would be more impressed with the second person. After all, anyone can come up with legitimate explanations after the facts are in. People who really understand the game should be able to anticipate what will happen when two teams meet.

In a similar manner, if a scientist has a legitimate theory, we can expect him or her to make reasonably accurate predictions of what will happen in an experiment before the data are in. Remember, the purpose of research is to provide or not provide support for a hypothesis. Researchers generate a theory, make a hypothesis, and collect data that either support or do not support the hypothesis. Suppose a researcher were interested in the relationship between self-esteem and helping behavior but had no clear prediction of what this relationship might be. If the study finds that high self-esteem people help more than lows, the researcher might conclude that this is because people who feel good about themselves maintain that evaluation by doing good things. Do the data in this case support the hypothesis? From a scientific standpoint, the answer is that they do not. This is because the hypothesis was generated *after* the results of the study were seen. With that sequence, there is no way the hypothesis *wouldn't* be supported by the data. If the study had found that low self-esteem people help more, the same researcher might have concluded that this is because these people are attempting to improve their self-image by doing good things. With no possibility that the hypothesis might not be supported, the hypothesis has not really been tested.

This is not to say researchers should ignore findings they haven't predicted. On the contrary, such findings are often the basis for future hypotheses and further research. But explaining everything after the results are in explains nothing. You can hear examples of this problem at the close of the stock market each day. If the president of the United States gives a speech and the stock market goes down, analysts tell us it was because of the speech. However, if the stock market had gone up, no doubt the analysts would attribute the rise to the speech as well.

Replication

When investigators conduct a well-designed experiment and uncover statistically significant results, they usually report the findings in a journal or perhaps at a professional conference. Too often, such findings are then cited as something researchers have uncovered and are generally treated as "fact." But psychologists are becoming increasingly aware of the difficulty of relying on one research finding for their facts.

There are many reasons a researcher might find a statistically significant effect. There could be something peculiar about the people in the sample. There might be something special about the time the research was conducted — perhaps an unusual mood in the country, or on campus, caused by an important event. Or the finding could have occurred by chance. You will recall researchers typically rely on a .05 significance level. This means 1 out of every 20 times an effect is found at this level, it is the result of chance and does not represent a real difference between the conditions.

The way to deal with this problem is **replication**. The more often an effect is found in experiments, the more confidence we can have that it reflects a genuine relationship. Replications often use subject populations different from those used in the original research. This helps to determine whether the effect applies to a larger number of people or is limited to the kind of subject used in the original sample. For example, researchers often discover that an effect found with male subjects is not found with female subjects.

Yet determining the strength of an effect by how often it is replicated is not always easy. One difficulty has been termed the "File Drawer" problem (Rosenthal, 1979). That is, investigators tend to publish and report research only when they find a significant effect. When an attempt at replication fails, the researcher may decide something has gone wrong — perhaps the wrong materials were used, perhaps something was not done the way the original researcher did it, and so on. And so the research is stored away in a file drawer and never reported. The result is that a well-known research finding may, in fact, be difficult to replicate. But because the failures at replication are stored away in file drawers, we might not realize the problem exists.

Personality Assessment

Sometimes Americans seem obsessed with measuring personality. Popular magazines often promote short tests, or "quizzes," to measure how good a roommate you are, what type of romantic partner you need, or the type of vacation spot that matches your personality. Although the magazines rarely claim their tests are based on any scientific investigations, the popularity of these tests suggests that readers find them at least interesting, if not believable. There is something about calculating a test score that gives credibility to an untested 10-item quiz.

On a more sophisticated level, personality psychologists also have been accused of sometimes putting too much faith in the numbers generated by their personality tests (see Chapter 7). Personality assessment is a central part of much personality research. If we are going to study need for achievement, self-esteem, anxiety, and so on, we need to measure these concepts as accurately as possible. Similarly, psychologists working in such areas as education, personnel, and counseling rely on personality tests to determine if a child should be placed in a special class, if an employee should be promoted to a new position, or if a client needs admission to a psychiatric hospital.

In each case, it is the responsibility of the people using the test to see that it accurately measures the concept they are interested in. Unfortunately, not all personality tests are as good as psychologists would prefer, and there are limits to the appropriate use of the scores the tests generate. But how can we tell a good test from a bad one, or how can we determine if the test score measures what it is we want to measure? Before using any standardized test, we need to examine its *reliability* and its *validity*.

Reliability

Suppose you took a personality test today and it indicated that, compared to others your age, you were high on the trait independence. That is, more than most people you enjoy being on your own and making your own decisions.

Taking a Personality Test

Personality researchers frequently use standardized personality tests to measure individual differences among people. Several examples of these tests appear throughout this book. The first one is presented below. You can determine your score and how you compare with others who have taken this test by indicating the extent to which each of the following statements is characteristic of you. Use the following scale to indicate your responses:

> 0 = Extremely uncharacteristic of me
> 1 = Somewhat uncharacteristic of me
> 2 = Neither characteristic nor uncharacteristic of me
> 3 = Somewhat characteristic of me
> 4 = Extremely characteristic of me

_____ 1. I'm concerned about my style of doing things.
_____ 2. I'm concerned about the way I present myself.
_____ 3. I'm self-conscious about the way I look.
_____ 4. I usually worry about making a good impression.
_____ 5. One of the last things I do before I leave my house is look in the mirror.
_____ 6. I'm concerned about what other people think of me.
_____ 7. I'm usually aware of my appearance.

The test you have just taken is the Public Self-Consciousness Scale (Fenigstein, Scheier, & Buss, 1975). The scale was designed to measure the extent to which you typically are concerned about and pay attention to what others think of you. To determine your score, add the values you assigned to each of the seven test items. You can compare your score with the norms Fenigstein and his colleagues found in a large sample of undergraduate students. The males in the sample had an average score of 18.9, and the females 19.3. The standard deviation for both groups was 4.0, indicating that about two thirds of the people in the sample had scores that fell within four points of these averages.

How reliable is this test? Fenigstein and his colleagues asked a group of students to respond to the scale items 2 weeks after they had taken the identical test. When they compared the scores from the first and second administrations, the researchers found a test-retest correlation of .84. This means that the extent to which the test subjects scored high or low on the test did not change much over the 2-week period. In other words, the test has good reliability.

But a test must also have good validity before it is useful. Several investigations since the publication of the Public Self-Consciousness Scale indicate that it does seem to be measuring how concerned people are with the impression they make on others. For example, those who score high on this scale are more concerned with fashion and are more likely to conform to social pressure than are those scoring low. More information about the scale is presented in Chapter 7.

However, suppose next week you take the test again and this time your score indicates you are relatively low on independence. Which of these scores reflects your true level of independence? Unfortunately, you have no way of knowing from this test if you are an independent or a dependent person. The test suffers from poor reliability.

A test has good **reliability** when it measures *consistently*. One indication of this is how consistently the test measures over time. In the independence test example, there is little consistency and therefore low reliability. Many factors can contribute to poor consistency over time. Often the questions or the scoring procedures are too vague. For example, a test of creativity might use judges to make subjective assessments of how creative a subject's drawing is. Unfortunately, today's drawing could strike a judge as highly creative, but tomorrow the judge might see the same drawing as ordinary and boring. In this case, the test's low reliability would render it useless for determining how creative a given person is.

A good test maker provides information about the test's reliability over time. The most common way to report this information is with a **test-retest reliability** coefficient. To determine this coefficient, researchers first administer the test to a large number of people. Some time later, usually after a few weeks, the same people take the test again. The scores from the first administration are correlated with those from the second by way of a simple correlation procedure. The higher the correlation coefficient, the better the reliability.

Unfortunately, a reliability coefficient does not provide a simple answer to the question of whether or not the test is reliable. Determining a test's reliability is not a yes-or-no question. On the one hand, a test-retest coefficient of .90 is probably reliable enough to meet most people's needs (although not if extremely high reliability is required). On the other hand, a reliability coefficient of .20 is no doubt too low for most purposes. But what about something in between? Is a test with a reliability coefficient of .50 or .60 acceptable? The answer depends on the experimenter's needs and the availability of alternative, more reliable tests. Sometimes the nature of the concept being measured contributes to low reliability. For example, tests given to young children often have lower than desirable levels of reliability. The test might be used anyway because typical fluctuations in a child's mood, attention, or effort during testing create inconsistencies in answers and therefore limit the reliability of any test.

Another aspect of reliability is **internal consistency**, the extent to which the items on a test measure the same thing. Let's say 10 items on a 20-item test of extraversion accurately measure the extent to which the test taker is an extraverted person. Because half of the items measure extraversion, the overall score probably is somewhat indicative of the person's true level on this dimension. But because half of the items measure something besides extraversion, the usefulness of the score is limited. This test suffers from poor internal consistency.

Statistical tests can be used to determine how well the responses on each test item correlate with the responses on other items. A statistic called an *internal consistency coefficient* can be calculated. A high coefficient indicates most of the items are measuring the same concept; a low coefficient suggests items are measuring more than one concept. A careful test maker calculates the test's

Box 2.2

The Barnum Effect

Personality tests provide researchers, therapists, and psychotherapy clients with information about the individual's personality. Test scores are often presented to clients, and the personality features they reveal are then described by the therapist. Clients may discover, for example, that they are higher than average in aggressiveness or low in feelings of self-worth. These findings may then become the focus of further therapy. The widespread use of personality tests by therapists from nearly all perspectives attests to the usefulness that has been attributed to them.

However, along with this perceived usefulness comes a danger. Both the therapist and the client could fall victim to the "Barnum Effect," accepting as true "individual" test feedback that applies to virtually everyone. To demonstrate this phenomenon, Ulrich, Stachnik, and Stainton (1963) administered two short personality tests to undergraduate students. One week later, the students were given a written description of their personalities, the description supposedly based on the test results. In reality, all students were given the same description, part of which read as follows:

You have a strong need for other people to like you and for them to admire you. You have a tendency to be critical of yourself. You have a great deal of unused capacity which you have not turned to your advantage. While you have some personality weaknesses, you are generally able to compensate for them.

Subjects were then asked to give their reactions to the test, including a rating, ranging from "excellent" to "very poor," on how well the description applied to them.

When they believed the test interpretations were made by a competent psychologist, 53 of 57 students rated the interpretation as either good or excellent.

Continued

internal consistency and includes in the final version only those items that "hang together" to measure the same concept.

Validity

Reliability alone does not determine a test's usefulness. You will notice that reliability data tell us only that a test is measuring something consistently. But they tell us nothing about *what* the test is measuring. That is why we also must examine data concerning the test's validity.

Validity refers to the extent to which a test measures what it is designed to measure. As with reliability, the question is not whether a test does or does not

Even when the interpretations were supposedly made by an inexperienced student, 75% of the students rated the interpretation the same way. Some of these subjects' written responses were particularly interesting:

On the nose! Very good. I wish you had said more, but what you did mention was all true without a doubt.

I believe this interpretation applies to me individually, as there are too many facets which fit me too well to be a generalization.

The interpretation is surprisingly accurate and specific in description.

It appears to me that the results of this test are unbelievably close to the truth. For a short test of this type, I was expecting large generalizations for results, but this was not the case.

There are some important implications from these types of findings. First, psychologists could easily get a false sense of accuracy about their interpretations when the client so readily agrees with the assessment (Forer, 1949). Second, both the psychologist and the client could place more weight on the results of a personality test than it merits (Iennarella & Kaplan, 1988). Third, clients could react to these Barnum assessments with changes in their behavior. For example, subjects who were given Barnum assessments indicating that they were open-minded later presented more open-minded evaluations of campus issues than did those not given this assessment (Petty & Brock, 1979).

In short, although assessments from personality tests may be quite valuable in better understanding an individual's personality, they should be approached with some caution. Instead of accepting personality tests as a means of penetrating the self, we might better view these instruments as but one method of evaluation that probably should be taken with at least a small amount of healthy skepticism.

have validity. Rather, the question is how well the validity of the test has been demonstrated. As with the reliability question, this requires test users to make subjective judgments of how well the test seems to be measuring what they want to measure.

Validity is relatively easy to determine for some kinds of tests. For example, if the purpose of a test is to predict how well students will do on an upcoming exam, researchers simply compare the test scores with the exam scores to determine what is called the *predictive validity* of the test. However, the validity of most concepts of interest to personality researchers is not determined this easily. These psychologists are usually interested in measuring hypothetical constructs, such as intelligence, masculinity, or social anxiety. **Hypothetical constructs** are useful inventions by researchers to describe concepts that have no physical reality. That is, no one can be shown an "intelligence." We can see behaviors and test performances that suggest a high intellectual functioning, but intelligence remains a theoretical entity researchers find useful.

The problem hypothetical constructs present for personality researchers is in determining if a test measures something that, in reality, is but a useful abstract invention. How can you know if your test is measuring self-esteem? People who agree with the test item "I am not as competent as most people in sporting events" might have low self-esteem. Then again, they might just have poor athletic ability, or they might be depressed. The task facing personality researchers is establishing the test's **construct validity**, that is, demonstrating that the test scores accurately reflect the test takers' level on the hypothetical construct dimension. Fortunately, a researcher can do several things to determine the construct validity of a test. Unfortunately, deciding whether or not the test has enough validity for its use comes down to a subjective judgment made by the test user. Some of the ways construct validity can be established are described below.

Face Validity   Perhaps the most obvious way of deciding if a test measures what it says it measures is to look at the test items. A test that asks subjects "Do you feel nervous interacting with others?" or "Are you uncomfortable meeting new people?" probably would be accepted by most of us at first glance to be measuring something like social anxiety. The test would have good **face validity**. That is, on the face of it, the test appears to be measuring social anxiety.

Although most tests probably have high face validity, not all do. Some hypothetical constructs don't lend themselves to these kinds of obvious questions. For example, how would you design a test to measure creativity? Asking people "Are you creative?" probably won't help much. Instead, you might ask subjects to write an ending to a story or to name as many uses as they can think of for an ordinary object like a milk bottle. These tests might be good measures of creativity, but the face validity would be less certain than with a more straightforward measurement procedure.

Congruent Validity   Suppose you are interested in using a new intelligence test that reportedly takes less time to administer and is more economical than the more commonly used tests. You'd probably want to see how scores from this new test compare with scores on an established intelligence test. But suppose you gave both tests to a group of subjects and found a correlation between the test scores of only .20. Because scores on the two tests are not very related, a subject could come out with a high score on one intelligence test and a low score on the other, leaving you to wonder which is the true measure of intelligence. This is not to say that the old scale is measuring intelligence and the new scale is not, but rather that they cannot both be measuring the same construct.

The **congruent validity** of a test, sometimes called convergent validity, is the extent to which scores from the test correlate with other measures of the same construct. If two tests are measuring the same construct, then the scores from the two tests should be highly correlated. However, you need not limit this to correlations with other personality tests. For example, if I were trying to deter-

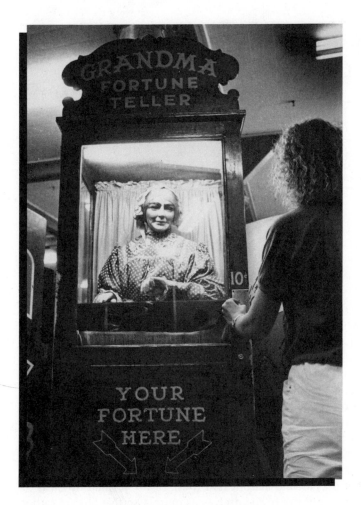

For 10 cents this fortune-teller may reveal that "good things will happen to you, but some misfortune will come your way as well." By making general statements that could apply to almost anyone, mechanical as well as human fortune-tellers are capitalizing on the Barnum Effect when they convince customers that the future is foreseeable.

mine the construct validity of a new measure for anxiety, I might compare test scores with anxiety levels as rated by a team of professional psychologists.

Discriminant Validity In contrast to congruent validity, **discriminant validity** refers to the extent to which a test score does *not* correlate with the scores of theoretically unrelated measures. Let's return to the problem of designing a creativity test. It is important to show that such a test is measuring only creativity and not simply something that resembles creativity, such as intelligence. To establish the discriminant validity of the test you would need to give both the creativity test and a standard intelligence test to a group of subjects. If scores from the two tests are highly correlated, someone might argue that your creativity test does not measure creativity at all, but simply intelligence. Notice that even a low correlation does not tell you what the test *is* measuring, but rather what it is *not* measuring. Nonetheless, this is an important step in establishing the construct

validity of the test.

Behavioral Validation

Reprinted by permission of NEA, Inc.

Behavioral Validation **Behavioral validation**, predicting behavior from test scores, is an extremely important step in establishing construct validity. Suppose you divided subjects into a high group and a low group based on their scores on an assertiveness test and then watched how they acted when they received poor service or when someone cut in front of them in line. We would expect the high-assertiveness subjects to complain about the service or ask the intruder to move to the end of the line, whereas the low-assertiveness subjects tolerate these inconveniences. But what if the two groups of subjects show no differences in their assertive behavior? In this case, the validity of the test might be in doubt.

In this example, it is possible that subjects responded to test items by describing how they thought they would act but that these responses had no basis in reality. Some people might think of themselves as quite assertive but act rather meek when a real need for assertion arises. Therefore, it is possible for a test to have face validity, congruent validity, and discriminant validity, and still have questionable construct validity. If test scores cannot predict behavior, then we must question the usefulness of the test. However, we should note that a failure to predict behavior from a test score can be caused by many other factors, such as measuring the wrong behavior or measuring the behavior incorrectly. This issue is discussed in Chapter 7.

In summary, a good personality test is one with established reliability and validity. Before using any test in research or practice, psychologists should examine the available data concerning the test's reliability and validity to determine if they are satisfactory for the intended use. If a test shows signs of poor consistency and little validity, then what the test is *really* measuring is questionable. Using such a test could result in findings that may or may not have anything to do with the topic the psychologist wants to examine.

Summary

1. Most personality psychologists examine theories about personality processes through scientific research. Most of this research is based on the hypothesis-testing approach, in which hypotheses are derived logically from theories. These hypotheses are then tested in experiments, and the theory either is or is not supported. A good theory is parsimonious and capable of generating many testable hypotheses.

2. One important distinction in personality research concerns whether independent variables are manipulated by the researcher. When researchers examine nonmanipulated variables they have less confidence in making statements about cause and effect. Another important distinction is whether the investigation is conducted in a laboratory or in the field. Laboratory research gives researchers more control over relevant variables, but at the expense of external validity. Many personality researchers use the case study method. Although case studies have some limitations, such as questionable generalizability to other populations, they also possess some unique advantages over other methods.

3. Researchers often compare scores from two or more groups. They use statistical tests to determine if the difference between the groups is the result of chance fluctuations or if it represents a genuine effect. Traditionally, researchers use a correlation coefficient when analyzing their data. A correlation coefficient tells us the direction and size of a relationship between two measures.

4. Researchers face many potential problems when designing their experiments. These include experimental confounds, the use of nonrandom samples, and lack of appropriate comparison groups. Predicted results are better than those explained in hindsight, because the latter approach does not allow for hypothesis testing. Researchers are becoming increasingly aware of the need to replicate their findings, but obtaining reliable information about how often an effect is not replicated is a problem.

5. Personality researchers often use personality tests in their work. To determine the usefulness of a test, researchers should examine evidence for the test's reliability and validity. Reliability can be gauged through test-retest correlations and internal consistency coefficients. Validity is determined through face validity, congruent validity, discriminant validity, and behavioral validation. Researchers must use subjective judgments in deciding if tests are reliable and valid enough for their needs.

Key Terms

theory A general statement about the relationship between constructs or events.

hypothesis A formal prediction about the relationship between two or more variables that is logically derived from a theory.

independent variable The experimental variable used to divide subjects into groups.

dependent variable The experimental variable measured by the experimenter and used to compare groups.

interaction An experimental outcome in which the effect of one independent variable on the dependent variable depends on the level of another independent variable.

manipulated independent variable An independent variable for which subjects have been randomly assigned to an experimental condition.

nonmanipulated independent variable An independent variable for which condition assignment is determined by a characteristic of the subject.

field study An investigation conducted in a natural setting instead of a laboratory, with subjects who are unaware they are participating in an experiment.

laboratory research Highly controlled research conducted in an artificial setting created by the researcher.

case study method An in-depth examination of one subject or one group.

statistical significance The likelihood that a research finding represents a genuine effect rather than a chance fluctuation of measurement.

correlation coefficient A statistic that indicates the strength and direction of a relationship between two variables.

experimental confound A variable that is inadvertently manipulated or allowed to vary along with the independent variable.

nonrandom sample A research sample for which not all members of the target population have had an equally likely chance of being selected.

comparison group An experimental condition, usually a no-treatment group, that differs from other conditions in a specific way and helps to rule out alternative hypotheses.

replication An investigation that finds results similar to those found in an earlier investigation.

reliability The extent to which a test measures consistently.

test-retest reliability A measure of a test's reliability, as indicated by the correlation between scores on the same test given to the same people at different times.

internal consistency The extent to which test items are interrelated and thus appear to measure the same construct.

validity The extent to which a test measures what it is designed to measure.

hypothetical construct Imagined entity created by scientists to aid in explanation and investigation.

construct validity The extent to which a test measures the hypothetical construct it is designed to measure.

face validity A method for establishing a test's validity, in which test items appear to measure what the test was designed to measure.

congruent validity A method for establishing a test's validity by correlating the test scores with other measures of the same construct.

discriminant validity A method for establishing a test's validity by demonstrating that its scores do not correlate with the scores of theoretically unrelated measures.

behavioral validation A method for establishing a test's validity by predicting behavior from test scores.

Suggested Readings

Barber, T. X. (1976). *Pitfalls in human research: Ten pivotal points.* New York: Pergamon. Theodore Barber underscores an often overlooked source of error in psychology research — the researcher. He outlines 10 ways human error can interfere with good scientific research.

Kazdin, A. E. (Ed.) (1986). Special issue: Psychotherapy research. *Journal of Consulting and Clinical Psychology, 54*(1). The articles in this special issue discuss how researchers deal with some of the unique problems associated with psychotherapy research, such as small sample sizes and special populations.

West, S. G. (Ed.) (1986). Special issue: Methodological developments in personality research. *Journal of Personality, 54*(1). Several prominent personality researchers discuss the history of personality research methods and recommendations for future directions. Specific chapters are devoted to methodological issues that surface throughout this book, including person-situation interactions, factor analysis, and genetics research.

The Psychoanalytic Approach
Freudian Theory, Application, and Assessment

3

Although people have speculated about the nature of personality for years, the first acknowledged personality theorist did not emerge until the late 1800s. Then, an Austrian neurologist began proposing such outrageous notions as sexual desires in young children, unconscious causes for baffling physical disorders, and the treatment of sick minds through a time-consuming, expensive procedure in which patients lie on a couch while the doctor listens to them talk about seemingly irrelevant topics. That neurologist, Sigmund Freud, continued to develop, promote, and defend his ideas despite intense criticism. By the time of his death in 1939, Freud had written numerous volumes, was recognized as the leader of an important intellectual movement, and had changed the thinking of psychologists, writers, parents, and lay people for years to come.

Freud's influence on psychology and 20th-century thought is so widespread that most of us underestimate the effect his theory has had on our thinking. For example, if you are like most adults in this culture, you freely accept the idea that what you do is sometimes influenced by an unconscious part of your mind. We often say things like ''I must have done that unconsciously.'' We have no trouble believing a movie character who acts like a violent maniac at times but later can't remember what he has done. Although Freud was not the first to talk about the unconscious, no one before or since has placed so much emphasis on unconscious processes in explaining human behavior.

Do you believe that dreams reveal inner fears and desires? If so, you again are espousing an idea that Freud popularized. Although people have been interpreting dreams for thousands of years, Freud was the first to incorporate dream interpretation into a larger psychological theory. Dream interpretation has become so closely connected with psychology that many people are disappointed (or maybe relieved) after their first contact with psychotherapy when their therapist doesn't ask about their dreams. When you share your dreams with friends and try to guess their hidden meanings, you are informally following a therapeutic procedure outlined by Freud nearly 100 years ago.

Freudian references have permeated our language, our literature, even our motion pictures. When Woody Allen's character exclaims in *Annie Hall* that he is one of the few men who suffers from penis envy, many members of the audience probably did not recognize the reference to classic Freudian theory. Thus, an understanding of Freudian psychology is part of a good liberal arts education.

You'll appreciate references to ego, Freudian slips, libido, the unconscious, repression, denial, and the like much more when you understand the theory whence they came.

Freud Discovers the Unconscious

How did a Viennese neurologist come to change the way we think of humankind? There is little in Freud's early history to indicate that greatness awaited him. Although Freud was a respected member of the medical community, his interests began to drift. In 1885 he went to Paris to study with another neurologist, Jean-Martin Charcot. Charcot was experimenting with early versions of hypnosis and its use in curing what then were believed to be unusual physiological problems. Shortly thereafter, Freud returned to Vienna and began work with a prominent physician, Joseph Breuer. Like Charcot, Breuer was using hypnosis to treat hysterical patients. Hysteria is a disorder that consists of a variety of physical symptoms. Patients often display blindness, deafness, an inability to walk or to use an arm. Most physicians of that day treated hysteria as if it were a physically based illness. However, Breuer and Freud developed another interpretation.

Discussions about one of Breuer's patients, a woman with the pseudonym Anna O., probably set the direction for the rest of Freud's career. According to Breuer, Anna O. experienced a number of hysterical symptoms, including paralysis of her left arm, hallucinations, and speaking only in English despite her German native tongue. Under hypnosis, Anna O. would talk about her daydreams and hallucinations and about past traumatic events. During her final hypnosis session, she discussed her experiences with her dying father and some associated hallucinations about a black snake. After this session, the paralysis in her arm was gone and she could once again speak German.

In 1895 Freud and Breuer published *Studies in Hysteria*, in which they presented the case of Anna O. and the use of hypnosis in treating hysteria. Freud continued to use hypnosis to treat his hysterical patients but soon grew disillusioned with its limitations and began looking for alternative methods. Slowly he recognized the importance of allowing patients to say whatever came into their mind. He discovered that, even without hypnosis, under the right circumstances patients would describe previously hidden material that seemed related to the causes and cure of their hysterical symptoms. The development of this technique, called *free association*, was a significant step in the development of Freud's theory.

One startling discovery Freud made with these early patients was that memories uncovered during free association often concerned traumatic sexual experiences, many of which supposedly had occurred in early childhood. He gradually concluded that these early sexual experiences were responsible for the hysterical symptoms expressed by his adult patients. At this point, Freud was well along the way in his transition from neurologist to psychologist. He continued to work with hysterical patients and wrote about his observations and the development of his theories, convinced that he was on the threshold of important psychological discoveries.

ever, while working in the laboratory of one of his instructors, Ernst Brücke, Freud became discouraged at his chances for advancement. In addition, he had fallen in love with Martha Bernays, and wanted to earn enough money to marry her and give her a comfortable life style. So, upon completing his degree, he left the lab and went into private practice.

It was during his subsequent four-year engagement to Bernays (they were finally married in 1886) that Freud won a research grant to travel to Paris to observe Jean-Martin Charcot's work with hypnosis. It was also during this time that he began to develop his ideas about the power of the unconscious mind. By this time Freud had begun pondering many of the insights that would later make up his theory. His work with Joseph Breuer, observations of his own patients, and a great deal of introspection finally blossomed into his 1900 book *The Interpretation of Dreams*. Although it took several years to sell the 600 original printings of the book, it signaled the beginning of the professional recognition that Freud had sought back in medical school.

Sigmund Freud was born in 1856 in Freiberg, Moravia (now part of Czechoslovakia). In 1860 his family moved to Vienna, where Freud spent virtually the rest of his life. Freud's ambition to amount to something important surfaced early. He typically excelled in school, and while in medical school at the University of Vienna was determined to make an important discovery and thereby make a name for himself. How-

Continued

Yet Freud's writings sold poorly at first. In fact, his work met with great opposition in the academic and medical communities. Freud's open discussion of infantile sexuality and omnipresent sexual motives did not sit well with the puritanical standards of Victorian Europe. His approach to treatment was so radical that many respected physicians considered it absurd. Nonetheless, Freud continued his work and his writing and soon developed a small following of scholars who traveled to Vienna to study with him. These scholars formed the

Vienna Psychoanalytic Society, with Freud as its great figurehead and leader.

Sigmund Freud, continued

Something about Sigmund Freud has attracted the attention of numerous biographers. The most complete of these is the three-volume biography by Ernest Jones (1953–1957). Despite his much sought-after fame, in many ways Freud was a private person. Consequently, most biographers have glued together the facts we have about Freud's life with a large amount of speculation. Perhaps the most interesting part of this speculation concerns the extent to which Freud's description of human personality reflects his own personality and life experiences. Not surprisingly, Freud's relationship with his parents is of particular interest. Although his father had several children from an earlier marriage, Sigmund was his mother's first child and apparently the apple of her eye. His mother was only 21 when he was born and almost as close in age to her son as she was to her husband. Biographers agree that an especially close relationship was formed. Freud's mother sometimes referred to him as her "Golden Sigi." In contrast, Freud's relationship with his father appears to have been cold, if not occasionally hostile. Freud arrived late to his father's funeral, something he later identified as an unconsciously motivated behavior.

Freud reported struggling with guilt feelings over his relationship with his father many years after his father's death.

It is not difficult to see how Freud's description of the Oedipus complex—sexual attraction for the mother and competitive hostility toward the father—may have been a kind of projection of his own feelings toward his parents. Freud hints at this insight at many places in his writings. Indeed, he often relied on his own introspection to test the accuracy of his clinical intuition. He is reported to have reserved a half hour each night for this self-analysis.

Freud's marriage was a long and relatively happy one, producing six children. The youngest child, Anna, held a special place in her father's heart. She followed in her father's professional footsteps, eventually taking over a leadership role in the psychoanalytic movement and becoming a respected psychoanalytic theorist in her own right. Freud created a situation filled with interesting Oedipal possibilities when he conducted Anna's psychoanalysis himself. Freud and his family fled from their home and Nazi persecution when Germany invaded Austria in 1938. They escaped to London where Freud died of cancer the next year.

Later, many members of this society would come to disagree with Freud and leave the ranks to develop their own personality theories and form their own professional organizations. But as we will see, the flavor of their theories remained unmistakably Freudian.

Gradually Freud's theory gained acceptance within the growing field of psychology. In 1909 Freud was invited to the United States to present a series of lectures on psychoanalysis at Clark University. For Freud, the occasion marked the beginning of international recognition of his work. He continued to develop his theory and write about psychoanalysis until his death 30 years later. Many consider Freud the most influential psychologist in the relatively short history of the field, as well as one of the most important scholars of the century.

The Freudian Theory of Personality

The Topographic Model

The key starting point in understanding the Freudian approach is the division of the human personality into three parts. Freud originally divided personality into the *conscious*, the *preconscious*, and the *unconscious*. This division is known as the **topographic model**. The **conscious** contains those thoughts you are currently aware of. This material changes constantly as new thoughts enter your mind and others pass out of awareness. When you say something is "on your mind," you probably mean the conscious part of your mind. However, the conscious can deal with only a tiny percent of all the bits of information stored in your mind. There are also an uncountable number of thoughts you *could* bring into consciousness fairly easily if you wanted to. For example, what did you have for breakfast? Who was your third-grade teacher? What did you do last Saturday night? This large body of retrievable information comprises the **preconscious**.

Although many people consider the material in the conscious and preconscious parts to be fairly exhaustive of the thoughts in our minds, Freud described these as merely the tip of the iceberg. The vast majority of our thoughts, and the most important from a psychoanalytic viewpoint, are found in the **unconscious**. This is the material you have no immediate access to. According to Freud, you cannot bring unconscious material into consciousness except under certain extreme situations, as we will discuss later. Nonetheless, this unconscious material is responsible for much of your everyday behavior. Understanding the influence of the unconscious on our behavior, particularly what might be termed "abnormal" behavior, is perhaps the essence of appreciating the psychoanalytic perspective.

The Structural Model

Freud soon discovered that the topographic model was limited in its ability to describe the structure of human personality. He therefore introduced the **structural model**, which further divides personality into the *id*, the *ego*, and the *superego*. Just as we often say, "One part of me wants to do one thing, and another part of me wants to do something else," so did Freud conceive of the personality as made up of parts often not at peace with one another.

Freud maintained that at birth there is but one personality structure, the **id**. This is the selfish part of you, concerned only with satisfying your personal desires. Actions taken by the id are based on the **pleasure principle**. That is, the id is concerned only with what brings immediate personal satisfaction, regardless

Figure 3.1

Relationship of the
Id, Ego, and Su-
perego to the
Three Levels of
Awareness

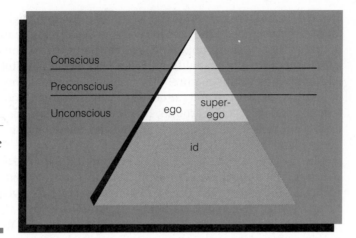

of any physical or social limitations. When babies see something they want, they reach for it. It doesn't matter whether the object belongs to someone else or may be harmful. And this *reflexive action* doesn't disappear when we become adults. Rather, Freud maintained that our id impulses are ever present and are held in check by other parts of a healthy adult personality.

Obviously, our pleasure impulses would be frustrated most of the time if the id relied solely on reflexive action to get what it wants. Therefore, Freud proposed that the id also uses **wish fulfillment** to satisfy its needs. That is, if the desired object is not available, the id will imagine what it wants. If a baby is hungry and doesn't see food nearby, the id imagines the food and thereby at least temporarily satisfies the need. Another example of wish fulfillment in Freudian theory is the images in our dreams.

If you react skeptically to the idea of id impulses and wish fulfillment operating within your own mental system, this may be because Freud described the id as buried entirely in the unconscious. As shown in Figure 3.1, id impulses remain out of our awareness. Indeed, because many of these impulses center on themes of sexuality and aggression, it is probably good that we are not aware of this unconscious material.

As children interact with their environment during the first two years of life, the second part of the personality structure gradually develops. The actions of the **ego** are based on the **reality principle**. That is, the primary job of the ego is to satisfy id impulses, but in a manner that takes into consideration the realities of the situation. Because id impulses tend to be socially unacceptable, they are threatening to us. The ego's job is to keep these impulses in the unconscious. Thus, if you deny that you have the kinds of thoughts Freud says are in your id, it is because your ego is working effectively to keep those thoughts out of your awareness. Unlike the id, your ego moves freely between the conscious, pre-conscious, and unconscious parts of your mind.

However, the ego's function is not simply to frustrate the aims of the id. Rather, Freud maintained that human behavior is motivated by instincts and

In its relation to the id, [the ego] is like a man on horseback, who has to hold in check the superior strength of the horse, [but] is obliged to guide it where it wants to go.

SIGMUND FREUD

57

directed toward tension reduction. Very young children might be allowed to grab food off their parents' plates and may be watched carefully enough so that they do not touch hot or sharp objects that might harm them. Thus, early in life, and perhaps occasionally in adulthood, reflexive actions can result in the reduction of tension. But as infants mature, they need to understand the physical and social limits on what they can and cannot do. If you are hungry, your id impulse may be to grab whatever food is around. But your ego understands that this action can lead to problems. The ego devises strategies for obtaining food in a way that doesn't land you in a lot of trouble.

By the time a child is about five years old, the third part of the personality structure, the **superego**, is formed. The superego represents society's — and in particular, the parents' — values and standards. The superego places more restrictions on what we can and cannot do. If you see a $5 bill sitting on a table at a friend's house, your id impulse might be to take the money. Your ego, aware of the problems this might cause, attempts to figure out how to get the $5 without being caught. But even if there is a way to get the money without being caught, your superego will not allow the action: Stealing money is wrong, even if you don't get caught. The primary weapon the superego brings to the situation is guilt. If you take the money anyway, you'll probably feel bad about it later and may lose a few nights sleep before returning the $5 to your friend. Some people have roughly translated the concept of the superego into what we call "conscience."

But the superego does not merely punish us for moral violations. It also provides the ideals the ego uses to determine if a behavior is virtuous and therefore worthy of praise. Because of poor child-rearing practices, some children fail to fully develop their superegos. As adults, such people have little inward restraint from stealing or aggressing against others. In other people, the superego can become too powerful, or "supermoral," and burden the ego with impossible standards of perfection. Here the person could suffer from relentless *moral anxiety* — an ever-present feeling of shame and guilt — for failing to reach standards no human can meet.

The three parts of the personality are in a constant state of struggle with one another. In the healthy individual, a strong ego does not allow the id or the superego too much control over the personality. The goal is to find ways to satisfy the demands of both the id and the superego. But that, of course, isn't easy. The id says, "I want it." The ego might reply, "I'll see if I can get it for you." But the superego says, "You'd better not." According to Freud, our unconscious mind is a continuous battlefield for these various parts of the personality. The ego needs to mediate between the two more extreme delegations while also serving reality.

Instincts and Tension Reduction

The three parts of the mind provide the structure, the three parts of the personality provide the characters. But what sets Freud's system in motion? Freud maintained that human behavior is motivated by strong internal forces he called *Triebe*, roughly translated as drives, or instincts. According to Freud there are two major categories of instincts: the life or sexual instinct, generally referred to as **libido**,

LECTURE TONIGHT — FREUDIAN PSYCHOLOGY

I FIND THAT THE ID, THE EGO, AND THE SUPEREGO ARE MUCH EASIER TO UNDERSTAND IF YOU THINK OF THEM AS LARRY, MOE AND CURLY.

© 1988 by NEA, Inc. THAVES 8-24

and the death or aggressive instinct, known as **Thanatos**. Although Freud originally maintained the two forces were in opposition, he later suggested that the two often combine, thus intertwining what we do with both erotic and aggressive motives.

Freud attributed most human behavior to the life or sexual instinct. However, he used this description in a very broad sense. Sexually motivated behaviors include not only those with obvious erotic content but also nearly any action aimed at receiving pleasure. Late in his career Freud added the death instinct— the desire we all have to die and return to the earth. However, this unconscious motive is rarely expressed in the form of obvious self-destruction. Most often, the death instinct is turned outward and expressed as aggression against others. The wish to die remains unconscious.

Freud was greatly influenced by much of the scientific thought of his day. Among the ideas he adapted from other sciences was the notion of a limited amount of energy. Energy within a physical system does not disappear but exists in finite amounts. Similarly, Freud argued that we each have a finite amount of psychic energy which more or less powers the psychological functions. This means that energy spent on one part of psychological functioning is not available for other uses. Thus, if the ego has to expend large amounts of energy to control the id, it has little energy left to carry out the rest of its functions efficiently. One goal of Freudian psychotherapy is to help troubled patients release unconscious impulses being held in check, thereby freeing up the energy available for daily functioning.

In the Freudian model, the eventual goal of human behavior is to reach a tensionless state. However, psychological tension is created whenever an instinct is activated. This state is roughly comparable to feelings of excitation, nervousness, and arousal. Thus, hunger activates our need to find and consume food. We experience the unpleasantness associated with tension until we engage in the correct behavior (eating) and the tension dissipates.

Defense Mechanisms

Fortunately, the unconscious thoughts and impulses Freud wrote about are kept out of our awareness. Not only could acting on these impulses result in all kinds of social and legal problems, but we might also have difficulty accepting some of the more distasteful thoughts we supposedly hold deep inside. Classic psychoanalytic cases involve such unconscious themes as hatred for one's parent(s), aggression toward one's spouse, incestuous thoughts, memories of traumatic childhood experiences, and similar notions perhaps best kept in the unconscious.

In keeping this material out of consciousness, the ego is attempting to reduce or avoid anxiety. **Anxiety** is an unpleasant emotional experience similar but not identical to feelings of nervousness, worry, agitation, or panic. Awareness of certain unacceptable material creates anxiety. The feeling that unacceptable unconscious thoughts are about to express themselves into consciousness also can create vague feelings of anxiety. Freud called this *neurotic anxiety*.

How does the ego deal with anxiety-provoking material? The ego has many techniques at its disposal to deal with unwanted thoughts and desires. These are known collectively as **defense mechanisms**. Some of the principal defense mechanisms are reviewed below.

Repression Freud called repression "the cornerstone on which the whole structure of psychoanalysis rests" (1914/1963, p. 116). It is clearly the most important of the defense mechanisms. **Repression** is an active effort by the ego to push threatening material out of consciousness or to keep such material from ever reaching consciousness. For example, one night a boy sees his father physically assault his mother. When later asked about the experience, the boy insists he has never seen anything at all like that. He may not be lying. Instead, he may have found the scene too horrifying to accept and therefore simply repressed it out of consciousness. According to Freud, each of us uses repression, for we all have material in our unconscious mind we would rather not bring into awareness. As efficient as this seems, it is not without a cost. Because repression is a constant, active process, it requires the ego to constantly expend energy. Repressing a large number of powerful thoughts and impulses leaves our ego with little remaining energy with which to function. Without a strong ego, the battle for a stable personality can be lost.

Sublimation According to Freud, sublimation is the only truly successful defense mechanism. Unlike repression, the more we use sublimation, the more productive we become. **Sublimation** is the channeling of threatening unconscious impulses into socially acceptable actions. For example, your aggressive id impulses can get you into trouble if you direct them at the people you might want to. But sublimating these impulses into, say, boxing or football, is acceptable, because in our society aggressive athletes are considered heroes and rewarded for their actions. Sublimation is productive because the id is allowed to express its aggression, the ego doesn't have to tie up energy holding back the impulses, and the athlete is loved and admired for aggressive play. We can speculate that daring

According to Freud,
participation in
aggressive sports
allows the expression
of unconscious aggres-
sive impulses in
a socially acceptable
manner. Football
players might be
engaging in subli-
mation with each
tackle.

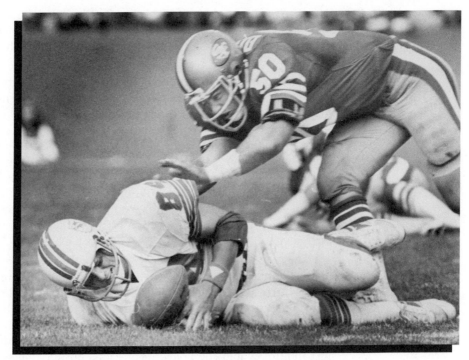

race car drivers or police squad members who volunteer to dismantle live bombs may be sublimating suicidal tendencies or a fascination with death.

Displacement   Like sublimation, **displacement** involves channeling our impulses to a nonthreatening object. For example, a woman whose boss yells at her might want to strike back at the employer, but a functioning ego will keep that impulse in check. Instead, she might express her aggression by yelling at her husband or children. Although doing so could create other problems, it's probably less threatening than losing her job. Freud noted that many of our apparently irrational fears, or phobias, are merely symbolic displacements. For example, Freud speculated that a fear of horses expressed by the son of one of his clients was really a displaced fear of the father.

Denial   When we use **denial**, we simply refuse to accept that certain facts exist. This is more than saying we do not remember, as in repression. Rather, we insist that something is not true, despite all evidence to the contrary. For example, a widower who loved his wife deeply may act as if she were still alive long after her death. He may set a place for her at the table or tell friends that she is just away visiting a relative. To the widower, this charade is more acceptable than admitting consciously that his wife has died. Obviously, denial is an extreme form of defense. The more we use it, the less in touch with reality we are and the more difficulty we will have in functioning. Nonetheless, in some cases the ego will resort to denial rather than allow certain thoughts to reach consciousness.

Reaction Formation   One of the most interesting defense mechanisms described by Freud is **reaction formation**. Here the person attempts to hide from a threatening idea or urge by acting in a manner opposite to his or her unconscious desires. For example, a young woman who constantly tells people how much she loves her mother could be masking strong unconscious hatred for the mother. People who militantly get involved with antihomosexuality or antipornography crusades could, according to the Freudian view, unconsciously hold a strong interest in homosexuality or pornography. It is as if the possibility of the thought — for instance, hating one's mother — is so unacceptable that the ego must prove how incorrect the notion is. How could a woman who professes so much love for her mother really hate her deep inside?

Intellectualization   One way for the ego to handle threatening material is through **intellectualization**, which means removing the emotional content from the idea. By examining the idea in a strictly intellectual, unemotional manner, we can bring some thoughts into consciousness or allow them to remain in consciousness without anxiety. For example, a woman might imagine her husband, for whom she holds unconscious hostility, being involved in a gruesome automobile accident, under the guise of unemotionally pondering the importance of wearing seat belts.

Projection   Sometimes we attribute an unconscious impulse to other people instead of to ourselves, which is called **projection**. By projecting the impulse onto another person, we free ourselves from the perception that we are the one who actually holds this thought. For example, we may deny that we have any unusual sexual desires while maintaining that other people do. The man who declares that the world is full of distrustful and cheating people may unconsciously know that he is distrustful and a cheater.

Through the use of these and other defense mechanisms, the healthy ego successfully keeps anxiety-provoking material out of awareness. All of us use defense mechanisms, for failure to keep threatening thoughts from our consciousness would create tremendous anxiety. Nevertheless, the use of too many defense mechanisms, with the exception of sublimation, can result in tying up much of the ego's energy and sometimes in losing touch with reality.

Psychosexual Stages of Development

One of the most controversial contributions Freud made to psychology is his theory of personality development. Freud believed that the essence of the adult personality is formed during the first five or six years of life. Although adults sometimes blossom into seemingly different kinds of people than they were in childhood, Freud maintained that the roots of this adult personality were well formed during the early years. In addition, Freud often interpreted psychological phenomena within a sexual framework. Consequently, his explanation of early personality development largely centered on sexual themes. According to Freud, each of us progresses through a series of developmental stages during childhood. Because the chief identifying character of each stage concerns primary erogenous zones and sexual desires, and because each has an influence on the adult personality, they have been labeled the **psychosexual stages of development**.

The importance of the stages lies in the concept of **fixation**. Remember that Freud believed the personality operates on psychic energy called libido. In Freud's view, as children progress through each of the psychosexual stages, they inevitably leave behind a small amount of libido that has been tied up in resolving relevant crises during that stage. In most people this still leaves an adequate amount of psychic energy to operate the adult personality. Unfortunately, sometimes a child encounters a particularly traumatic experience or an excessive amount of gratification at one of the stages. This results in the tying up, or fixating, of a large amount of libido. Consequently, the ego has less energy available for normal adult functioning. In addition, the adult expresses characteristics reminiscent of the earlier stage at which the energy is fixated. Some examples, presented below, will help explain the process.

The first stage each child goes through is the **oral stage**. During this period, which spans approximately the first 18 months of life, the mouth, lips, and tongue are the primary erogenous zones. You only need to watch a six-month-old baby for a few minutes to realize that everything must go into the mouth. Traumatic experiences during this time, such as traumatic weaning or feeding problems, may result in the fixation of psychic energy and the development of oral personality characteristics. People who develop oral personalities are said to be dependent on others as adults, although fixation that occurs after the child has teeth may result in excessive aggression as an adult. These oral-personality characteristics express the infantile need for oral satisfaction. Adults you know who smoke or drink excessively, or who are constantly putting their hand or some other object to their mouth, probably would be diagnosed as having oral personalities within the Freudian system.

When children reach the age of about 18 months, they enter the **anal stage** of development. According to Freud, the anal region becomes the most important erogenous zone during this period. Not coincidentally, it is during this stage that most children are toilet trained. Traumatic toilet training may result in fixation and an anal personality. People with an anal personality may be orderly, stubborn, or generous, depending on how their toilet training progressed.

The most important psychosexual stage, the **phallic stage**, occurs when the child is approximately three to six years old. During this period, the penis or clitoris becomes the most important erogenous zone. It is during the later part of this stage that the child goes through the famous **Oedipus complex**, named for the Greek mythological character who unknowingly married his mother. Freud argued that children at this age develop a sexual attraction for their opposite-sex parent. Thus, young boys have strong incestuous desires toward their mothers, while young girls have these feelings toward their fathers.

According to Freud, adult oral personalities develop when traumatic childhood experiences cause the fixation of an excessive amount of psychic energy at the oral stage of development. Smoking, drinking, and excessive eating are characteristic of an oral personality.

Youngsters are not without their share of fear about this situation. Boys develop **castration anxiety**, the fear that their father will discover their thoughts and cut off the son's penis. If the boy has seen his sister's genitals, he is said to conclude that this fate has already befallen her. Girls, upon seeing male genitals, are said to develop **penis envy**, the desire to have a penis, coupled with feelings of inferiority and jealousy because of its absence. How do children resolve this situation? Freud's explanation very neatly ties up several psychological questions. Children eventually repress their desire for their opposite-sex parent (whom they realize they probably can never have as long as the other parent is around). Then, as a type of reaction formation, children identify with the parent of the same sex.

The resolution of the Oedipus complex serves a number of important functions. By identifying with the same-sex parent, boys begin to take on masculine characteristics, and girls, feminine characteristics. Identification with the parents also fits nicely with the development of the superego. This is the age at which the child adopts the values and standards of the parents, in the form of the superego. However, as we will explore a bit more in the next chapter, the Oedipal

After resolution of the Oedipus complex, children pass into the latency stage. For several years boys will prefer to play with other boys, and girls with other girls. All of this ends with puberty.

desires are repressed, not eliminated. Thus, Freud maintained, they can still influence our behavior in a number of unsuspected ways.

After resolution of the Oedipus complex, the child passes into the **latency stage**, the time before puberty. Sexual desires abate during these years, only to return strongly when the child reaches puberty and the genital stage, the final stage of sexual development. During the latency stage, boys and girls seem uninterested in each other. A look at any playground will verify that boys play with other boys and girls play with other girls. Once the child reaches puberty and the **genital stage**, the erogenous urges return and are focused in the adult genital regions. If the libido has progressed to this stage without leaving large amounts fixated at earlier stages, then normal heterosexual functioning is possible.

Getting at Unconscious Material

If we accept that the largest and most important part of our mind is unconscious and thereby out of our awareness, we may be tempted to challenge the usefulness of Freud's theory. That is, even if our behavior is determined by unconscious conflicts, of what value is it to talk of such things if they remain unavailable to us?

The Freudian response to this question is that there are many ways for a trained psychoanalyst to learn about what is going on in a person's unconscious mind. Freud believed that strong id impulses must be expressed. Because the true nature of these impulses must be repressed by a strong ego, they are often expressed in a disguised or somewhat altered form. However, if we know what to look for, we can see the "true" meaning behind much of this expression. This is probably why many people respond to psychologists as if somehow, like a mind reader, they know exactly what other people are thinking. Although that's certainly not the case, Freud did believe that there are many ways in which our actions betray our true, albeit unconscious, thoughts and desires. Following are seven different techniques that Freudian psychologists use to get at unconscious material.

Innocent dreams . . . are wolves in sheep's clothing. They turn out to be quite the reverse when we take the trouble to analyze them.
SIGMUND FREUD

Dreams   Freud called our dreams the "royal road to the unconscious." In 1900 he published *The Interpretation of Dreams*, presenting for the first time a psychological theory of what our dreams really mean. According to Freud, dreams provide the id impulses with a stage for expression. They are a type of wish fulfillment. That is, they represent what we would really like to have. Many people immediately reject the notion of dreams as wish fulfillment, on the basis of dreams they've had that they certainly wouldn't want to come true. Others ask how the scrambled nonsense that makes up many of our dreams could somehow represent hidden desires. But Freud cautioned that we should distinguish between the **manifest content** of a dream (what the dreamer sees and remembers) and the **latent content** (what is really being said). Overt expression of many of our unconscious thoughts and desires would be difficult for us to face upon waking; that's why they were repressed in the first place. Therefore, Freud maintained, these ideas are expressed in disguised form in our dreams. This is why we often laugh about silly and absurd dreams. They may seem like nonsense to us, but to a Freudian therapist they may be filled with valuable clues about our unconscious thinking.

The key to Freudian interpretation of dreams is understanding that many of our unconscious thoughts and desires are represented *symbolically* in the dream. For example, dreams involving penises, sexual intercourse, and vaginas might be disturbing to us, whereas we probably wouldn't feel threatened by a dream about a fountain, an airplane, or a cave. Thus, unconsciously we take the threatening content and translate it into symbols before it appears in our dreams. In this manner, the impulses are expressed and the conscious mind is not threatened. "The dreamer does know what his dream means," Freud wrote. "Only he does not know that he knows it and for that reason thinks he does not know it" (1916/1961, p. 101).

Freud believed that the trained psychoanalyst could recognize many of the obvious and widely used symbols that appear in our dreams. Thus, the therapist recognizes that a house represents the human body, one's parents are disguised as a king and a queen, children are represented as small animals, birth is associated with water, a train journey is a symbol for dying, and clothes and uniforms represent nakedness.

But the vast majority of Freudian dream symbols are sexual. In Victorian Europe, the time when Freud was developing his theory, people were particularly inhibited about sex. Thus, the expression of sexual matters needed to be well disguised in dreams. According to Freud, male genitals are represented in dreams by "things that resemble it in shape." Freud (1916/1961) lists several such common symbols, including sticks, umbrellas, trees, knives, rifles, pencils, and hammers. Female genitals are symbolically represented by bottles, boxes, rooms, doors, and ships. Sexual intercourse is hidden in such activities as dancing, riding, and climbing. In fact, reading Freud's long list of sexual symbols, it's hard to think of many dreams that can't be interpreted sexually. Although Freud's emphasis of sex has been criticized by some of his followers, the idea that our dreams contain at least some symbolic representations of untold sexual desires remains widely accepted among psychologists and lay people.

Projective Tests   Children and young lovers often play a game of describing what they see in the formation of clouds in the sky. One person might see a group of people, another a mountain scene, and still another the face of a famous person. Of course, no one is incorrect, for there are no real pictures in the clouds. But where are these images coming from? The answer, from a Freudian perspective, is that these responses are coming from the people's own minds and reflect what they see but ordinarily might not describe. Their descriptions of what they find in vague objects like clouds represent another way of getting at unconscious material.

Projective tests present subjects with ambiguous stimuli and ask them to respond with a story, the identification of objects, or perhaps a drawing. As with the cloud formations, there are no right or wrong answers. Rather, responses are individual and indicate what is going on deep inside the mind, which the person may not be aware of. We'll review some of the different projective tests used by psychologists later in this chapter.

Free Association   Take a few minutes to clear your mind of thoughts. Then allow whatever comes into your mind to enter. Say whatever you feel like saying, even if it is not what you expect and even if you are a little surprised or embarrassed by what comes out. If you are successful in allowing these free-flowing ideas into your awareness, you have experienced what some call the fundamental rule of psychoanalysis: free association. During psychoanalysis, the patient is encouraged to use **free association** to temporarily bypass the censoring mechanism the ego employs. Ordinarily we block out distasteful, seemingly trivial, or silly thoughts so as to protect ourselves from this material or to keep from sounding foolish. However, according to Freud, such intrusions contain valuable psychological material. Because these thoughts are normally excluded from consciousness, they provide keen insight into that part of the mind not seen in our everyday censored conversations.

But free associations are not easy to tap. Our egos have activated considerable energy to repress certain thoughts and are not likely to let this material just ease into consciousness. Sometimes patients simply slip into long silences and report that nothing comes to mind or cunningly verbalize all kinds of unimportant ideas in an effort to avoid the crucial but threatening material. One technique designed to help overcome such problems is the word association test, in which the subject is asked to respond to the therapist's words with whatever word pops into his or her mind first. The therapist quickly runs through a list of seemingly unrelated words, the responses to which seem obvious: *black–white, mother–father, Sunday–school*, and so on. If the therapist moves quickly enough, and if the patient truly expresses the very first word that comes to mind, both patient and therapist could be surprised by the responses. For example, a patient might respond to *mother* with *fear* or to *love* with *shame*. Where did those responses come from? Why were those associations made? In Freudian terms, the association exists in the unconscious and was able to slip into consciousness momentarily during the test. If the patient has no trouble making associations to most words but suddenly "blocks" on one item (for example, *mother*), it may suggest some associations about the word that almost, but not quite, came into consciousness. A trained therapist probably would return to this material later in the test.

Freudian Slips   We all occasionally make what are called slips of the tongue. A husband might refer to his wife by her maiden name or say that her mind is really her "breast" feature. These slips can be embarrassing and funny, but to Freud they were insightful. The husband who refers to his wife by her maiden name may unconsciously wish he'd never married this woman. Although the statement sounds innocent — an accidental slip — it may be loaded with underlying feelings. We call these misstatements **Freudian slips**.

An excellent example of a Freudian slip was shown in the motion picture *Ordinary People*. A young man filled with guilt over his brother's death talks to his therapist about a recent attempt to kill himself by slashing his wrists. When attempting to say that his mother will never get over the incident, he blurts out, "If you think *I* could ever forgive me" instead of "If you think *she* could ever forgive me." He pauses and realizes that the truth, buried so deep for so long, has just slipped out. Recovery has taken its first step.

Hypnosis   Freud's early experiences with hypnosis first unlocked his curiosity about the unconscious. Freud believed that the ego was somehow put into a suspended state during a deep hypnotic trance. A successful hynotist could thus bypass the ego's censoring process and get directly to unconscious material. Early experiences with hypnosis told Freud there was more to the human mind than what we can bring into awareness. When people asked him for proof of the unconscious, he often pointed to hypnosis. "Anyone who has witnessed such an experiment," he wrote, "will receive an unforgettable impression and a conviction that can never be shaken" (1938/1964, p. 285).

Because Freud saw hypnosis as a pipeline to the unconscious, it is easy to see how hypnosis would be a valuable tool indeed for a psychotherapist seeking to uncover unconscious material. Yet Freud was quick to acknowledge some of the drawbacks of hypnosis. Chief among them is that not all patients are equally susceptible to hypnotic suggestion. In addition, as will be seen in Chapter 4, not all psychologists agree with Freud's description of hypnosis as a pathway to the unconscious. The question of exactly what hypnosis is remains a matter of great controversy.

"Accidents"   Suppose you have just had a fight with your friend and you "accidentally" knock off a shelf an irreplaceable statue belonging to your friend. The statue shatters beyond repair. You apologize, saying that you did not mean to do it. But is this really an accident? In Freud's view, many actions that appear to be caused accidentally are in fact motivated behaviors stemming from unconscious impulses. Freud might argue that you were unconsciously expressing an aggressive desire to hurt your friend when you broke the statue. Patients who claim they "accidentally" forgot their regular meeting with a therapist are seen as displaying what Freud termed *resistance*. Consciously, such patients believe they simply did not remember the appointment. Unconsciously, there has been a deliberate effort to thwart a therapist who may be close to uncovering threatening material buried deep in the unconscious. Similarly, reckless drivers can be viewed as setting themselves up for an "accident" in order to satisfy an unconscious desire to harm themselves—a desire too threatening to be allowed into awareness. These examples are "accidents" only in the sense that we do not *consciously* intend them—but not in the sense that they are unintended.

Symbolic Behavior   Just as our dreams are interpreted by Freudian psychologists as symbolic representations of our unconscious desires, so too can many of our daily behaviors be taken as symbolic gestures of these unconscious thoughts. Behaviors acted out symbolically pose no threat to the ego, because they are not perceived for what they are. But these actions do allow the expression of unconscious desires. An excellent example is found in the case of a patient who held a great deal of hostility toward his mother, although not at a conscious level. To the therapist, this unconscious hostility was the root of the patient's problems and was expressed through an interesting doormat the patient purchased for his home. On the doormat was a design of several daisies—innocent enough. But the design's significance lay in the fact that the patient's mother had a favorite flower, the daisy. She had daisies on her dishes and pictures of daisies all around the house. In short, the daisies symbolized the mother. The good son enjoyed rubbing his feet and stomping on the daisies—symbolically acting out his hostility toward his mother—every time he entered the house.

When we apply Freud's symbols of dream interpretation to everyday behaviors, we can readily see symbolic action everywhere. What can we say about the woman who joins the rifle team? The man who explores caves? The person who flies an airplane for a hobby? The person who constantly borrows pencils without returning them? It is interesting to note that Freud was a habitual cigar smoker who, despite painful operations for cancer of the jaw, apparently continued to smoke until his death. We can only wonder if Freud ever recognized that the cigar was an obvious phallic symbol that he would not abandon even when faced with death.

Application: Psychoanalysis

Freud was not only the father of psychoanalytic theory, he also was the first person to outline and advocate a system of psychotherapy to treat psychological disorders. During his early years with Breuer, Freud saw that many disorders were psychological rather than physical in origin. Through his experimentation with hypnosis, he came to see that the causes of these disorders were buried in a part of the mind and not easily accessible to awareness. Slowly Freud developed various methods to get at this material, beginning with hypnosis and gradually changing to free association. As he gained insights into the causes of his patients' disorders and the structure and functioning of human personality, Freud developed a system of therapy to treat, and eventually eliminate, the disorder.

This system of psychotherapy is called **psychoanalysis**. Its goal is to bring crucial unconscious material into consciousness, where it can be examined and dealt with by the ego in a rational manner. Once the unconscious material surfaces into consciousness, it must be dealt with in such a manner that it does not manifest itself in some new disorder. Instead, the therapist and the patient work together to help the ego once again exercise appropriate control over the id impulses and the oppressive superego. In some ways, the therapist and the patient are like explorers searching through the patient's mind for crucial unconscious material. But the therapist is also like a detective who must evaluate cryptic messages about the underlying cause of the disorder as the patient unconsciously, but cunningly, works to mislead and frustrate the therapist's search.

Typically, psychoanalysis patients lie on a couch while the therapist sits behind them, out of sight. The patient is encouraged to speak freely, without any distractions from the room or the therapist that might inhibit free association. Unfortunately, the process of digging through layers of conscious and unconscious material, as well as avoiding the obstacles and misdirection thrown in the way by the threatened ego, is a lengthy one. Patients usually require several hour-long therapy sessions a week for a period of perhaps several years. Consequently, psychoanalysis is expensive and therefore usually limited to those who can afford it.

The bulk of time spent in psychoanalysis is devoted to getting at the crucial unconscious material causing the disorder. Because the ego has devoted so much energy and is so strongly motivated to repress this material, this part of therapy can be difficult. Freud used a variety of methods to get at unconscious material, including free association, dream interpretation, and hypnosis. Unlike later systems of psychotherapy, in psychoanalysis the therapist actively interprets for patients the significance of their statements, behaviors, and dreams. But Freud cautioned that therapists should not reveal the true meaning too soon. Beginning therapists are often tempted to interpret the unconscious meaning behind an act or a statement to a patient as soon as they understand it themselves. However, this could be threatening for the patient's ego, causing him or her to construct new and less permeable defenses for the unconscious material.

Freud maintained that the therapist's job is to interpret dream symbols for patients until they understand the true meaning of their dreams. We find an excellent example of this in one of Freud's famous case studies, the case of Dora. Dora was an 18-year-old patient from an affluent family. She complained of headaches and other physical problems. One area of trauma for Dora concerned a married couple, Mr. and Mrs. K. Mrs. K. was having an affair with Dora's father, and to make things more complicated, Mr. K. had made sexual advances toward Dora, which she reacted to with disgust and anger. One day during therapy, Dora related the following dream:

> A house was on fire. My father was standing beside my bed and woke me up. I dressed quickly. Mother wanted to stop and save her jewel-case; but Father said: "I refuse to let myself and my two children be burnt for the sake of your jewel-case." We hurried downstairs, and as soon as I was outside I woke up. (1901/1953, p. 64)

To the untrained listener, this dream seems innocent and meaningless enough, similar to dreams we all have experienced and given little thought to. But for Freud, it was filled with clues about the causes of Dora's problems. With a little questioning Freud learned that shortly before the dream had occurred, Mr. K. had given Dora an expensive jewel case as a present. With this information, Freud had all the pieces he needed to understand the dream. He explained to Dora:

> Perhaps you do not know that "jewel-case" is a favourite expression for the female genitals. . . . The meaning of the dream is now becoming even clearer. You said to yourself: "This man is persecuting me; he wants to force his way into my room. My 'jewel-case' is in danger, and if anything happens it will be Father's fault." For that reason in the dream you chose a situation which expresses the opposite—a danger from which your father is *saving* you. Mr. K. is to be put in the place of your father just as he was in the matter of standing beside your bed. He gave you a jewel-case; so you are to give him your jewel-case. . . . So you are ready to give Mr. K. what his wife withholds from him. That is the thought which has had to be repressed with so much energy, and which has made it necessary for every one of its elements to be turned into its opposite. The dream confirms once more what I had already told you before you dreamt it—that you are summoning up your old love for your father in order to protect yourself against your love for Mr. K. (p. 69)

Freud interpreted several important psychoanalytic concepts for Dora. He identified her use of symbols and repression of her true desires. He explained how she used reaction formation—dreaming the opposite of what she really wanted—and how her repressed desires for her father affected her behavior. Not surprisingly, Dora had difficulty accepting this interpretation at first. According to Freud, part of the therapist's job is to help patients obtain a reasonable understanding of psychoanalytic theory and some of the concepts that affect their behavior.

Ironically, one of the first signs that therapy is progressing is the development of **resistance**. For example, patients might declare that therapy isn't helping them and they want to discontinue it. Or they might lapse into long silences, return to material already discussed, miss appointments, or insist that certain topics aren't worth exploring. These attempts at resistance may indicate that the therapist and patient are getting close to the crucial material. The threatened ego is desperately attempting to defend against the approaching demise of its defenses as crucial unconscious material is almost ready to burst into consciousness.

Another necessary step in psychoanalysis is the development of **transference**. Here the emotions associated with other people in past situations are displaced onto the therapist. For example, a patient might talk to and treat the therapist as if the therapist were a deceased parent. Unconscious emotions and speeches buried deep and long are unleashed, feelings that often lie at the heart of the patient's disorder. Freud warned that handling transference was a delicate and crucial part of the therapy process. In particular, therapists must avoid **countertransference**, in which they react to the patient as if the therapist were the object of transference. Returning to the example, the therapist must avoid taking on the role of the deceased parent.

The bulk of time spent in psychoanalysis is devoted to bringing the unconscious conflict to the surface. At this point the therapist works with the emotionally vulnerable patient to resolve the conflict at a conscious level and integrate it into the new personality. Successful treatment releases the psychic energy the ego has expended in repressing the conflict. Once freed, the patient can live a happy, normal life.

Assessment: Projective Tests

Psychoanalysts are faced with a unique problem when developing ways to measure the personality constructs of interest to them. By definition, the most important concepts are those the test taker is unable to report directly. If a patient can readily identify psychological conflicts, they are obviously not buried deeply enough in the unconscious to be of much value to a Freudian therapist. The solution is to bypass direct reporting altogether. As with other methods psychoanalysts use to get at unconscious material, the purpose of projective tests is to generate responses from test takers that can then be interpreted by a trained therapist.

As mentioned earlier in this chapter, projective tests present test takers with ambiguous stimuli, such as inkblots or vague pictures. Subjects respond by describing what they see, telling stories about the pictures, or somehow providing a reaction to the material. The test stimuli are designed to provide no clear clues about a correct or an incorrect response. Therefore, subject responses tend to be highly idiosyncratic. One person may see a bat and an elephant, while another identifies a classroom and a woman in mourning. As the name implies, psychoanalysts consider these responses projections from the unconscious. The ambiguous material provides an opportunity for the expression of pent-up impulses. However, as with other expressions of these impulses, the significance of the responses is not apparent to the test taker.

This psychologist is administering one of the most widely used personality tests: the Rorschach inkblot test. The subject tells him what she sees on the card, but whether these responses provide a valid assessment of her personality remains a controversy.

Types of Projective Tests

More than 50 years ago, Hermann Rorschach designed the most famous projective test, the **Rorschach inkblot test**. This test consists of 10 cards, each containing nothing more than a blot of ink, sometimes in more than one color. Test takers are instructed to describe what they see in the inkblot. They are free to use any part of the inkblot and usually are allowed to give several responses to each card. Although some of the cards may be quite suggestive, they are, of course, nothing more than inkblots.

Inkblot test responses can be analyzed with any of several scoring systems developed over the years. However, most psychologists probably rely on their personal insights and intuition in interpreting responses. Unusual answers and recurring themes are of particular interest, especially if they are consistent with information revealed during therapy sessions. For example, most therapists probably would find significance in the responses of a patient who sees nothing but dead people, graves, and tombstones in each card. Similarly, patients who see people committing suicide, bizarre sexual acts, or violent behavior probably provide their therapists with topics to explore in the next therapy session.

Another widely used projective test is the **Thematic Apperception Test (TAT)**. This test, designed by Henry Murray, consists of a series of cards containing ambiguous pictures. Test takers are asked to tell a story about the scene — who the people are, what is going on, what has led up to the scene, and what the

Box 3.1

Projection from an Assassin

On May 15, 1972, presidential candidate George Wallace was shot and permanently disabled by a 21-year-old attempted assassin. Surprisingly, the young man, Arthur Bremer, had little interest in politics. In fact, records later uncovered about his travels suggested that Bremer had made earlier attempts to shoot then-President Richard Nixon. A search into Bremer's past revealed a quiet but deeply troubled person who apparently believed that the assassination would make some kind of sense out of what he saw as his confused and unproductive life.

The ensuing investigation into Bremer's background produced the following composition. Bremer had written it a few years earlier, while he was a senior in high school. Entitled "Guitar," the composition describes a boy named Paul who takes weekly guitar lessons from an instructor named George. Bremer received an A on the composition. His teacher commented: "An excellent creation of the troubled young man of today's and yesterday's world." In retrospect, it is easy to see how the story of Paul was a projection of the writer's self-image and inner troubles. Much like a story produced from a TAT card or a Rorschach inkblot, these excerpts from "Guitar" can be seen as highly revealing of inward feelings:

In all the families on television, the mother was a pretty high school graduate and never thought of not feeding her kids meals. The mothers of television always smiled at their kids and kissed their foreheads. My mother was not like that. My mother did not kiss me. She would not say "hello" to me after I came into the house from school.

Continued

outcome is going to be. Although most of the cards contain images of people, their facial expressions, as well as the nature of the relationship between the people and what they are doing, are intentionally vague. Thus, test takers may see love, grief, guilt, anger, anguish, indifference, or hate in the people's faces. The characters may be fighting, plotting, loving, or unaware of each other. They may be in for a happy, sad, horrifying, pathetic, or disappointing end to their situation. Such differences in stories are viewed as significant clues to the subject's inner personality, a part of the person we might not otherwise see. Although therapists often rely on their intuition when interpreting test responses, many use the relatively objective scoring procedures developed by the test developers. As will be seen in Chapter 8, this test has been widely used in personality research.

Yet another projective test used by many therapists is the **Human Figure Drawing test**. The ambiguous stimulus here consists of a blank piece of paper and the instructions to draw a picture for the psychologist. In many cases, test

I used to hate those television mothers. Now I hate Mom. I dreamed about Donna Reed, my television mother, cooking dinner for me and kissing my forehead. I remember how he would come home after work. He would be tired and have a hungry gut. He would complain that Mom was not feeding my younger brother or him or me. Mom would shout. Dad would swear, and my younger brother would cry. Mom and Dad threw things at each other. I could hear them even though I was in the bedroom and my pillow was over my ears. I tried to think about pretty Donna Reed while Dad shouted and swore.

It was Wednesday again and I went to twentieth and Greenfield. George wanted to talk with my parents about getting rid of the plain guitar I rented from the music school. He wanted Dad to buy a $215 electric guitar and amplifier. There were always a lot of expensive guitars on display at the music school. Dad and I went to twentieth and Greenfield on Saturday, and I knew I was not going to get the guitar. Dad always said, "Live within your means," whenever he did not want to spend money. I stood beside Dad in the music school. I did not argue, because I knew I was not going to get the dumb guitar. George and Dad talked a long time.

When they talked, I just looked at my shoe laces. I dreamed my shoe laces were big snakes and they were crawling up my legs, and it was dark, and I was lost in Africa, and Dad was too busy to save me. Mom was talking to that nice man next door, and they were smiling at each other and too busy for me. Donna Reed was pulling at the snakes to save me, but I did not care. I pushed Donna Reed away from me. I wanted to die. I wanted to be cremated and have the ashes thrown in George's face. I did not like Dad either.

Next day I threw a brick and broke the big display window at the music school. I ran fast and nobody knew who did it.

takers are simply instructed to "draw a person," but sometimes psychologists ask them to draw a family or a tree. The Human Figure Drawing test has many uses, including a measure of intelligence in children (Harris, 1963). However, most often it is used as an indicator of psychological problems (Koppitz, 1968). Psychoanalysts view the person drawn by the test taker as a symbolic representation of the self.

The notion that children's drawings provide a peephole into their inner thoughts and feelings has a strong intuitive appeal. For many years, schoolteachers have taken note of children who never seem to draw smiles on the faces of the characters they sketch. Similarly, children who frequently draw monsters or ghoulish creatures could be reflecting a deeper problem. Scoring systems are available for assessing these potential problems, but a glance at the drawings presented in Figure 3.2 suggests that the children who drew these pictures may need psychological counseling.

Figure 3.2

Human Figure Drawings by Emotionally Disturbed Children

From Koppitz (1968); reprinted by permission of Grune & Stratton, Inc., and the author.

Evaluation of Projective Tests

Like most things related to Freudian theory, a great deal of controversy surrounds the use of projective tests. Critics point to the unacceptably low indices of reliability and validity typically found in research with these tests, particularly the Rorschach inkblot test (Aiken, 1979; Peterson, 1978). For example, there is little evidence of stability over time on the inkblot test. A test taker's score today might be very different from that person's score a month from now. Similarly, internal consistency indicators are low, which means that the interpretation given to one card's responses doesn't correlate very well with the interpretation given on other cards. Another problem surfaces in studies looking at "inter-judge reliabilities," which generally find disappointingly low agreement rates between two or more people scoring the same test responses. Thus, there is some question about the Rorschach test's ability to generate reliable results. As such, many critics challenge whether the inkblot procedure should be treated as a test at all, but rather should be thought of as a highly structured interview.

In addition, thousands of validity studies have been conducted with the Rorschach inkblot test, relating the test to everything from creativity to intelligence to sexual orientation. However, after reviewing these investigations, one reviewer concluded that there is a "general lack of predictive validity for the Rorschach [which] raises serious questions about its continued use in clinical practice" (Peterson, 1978, p. 1045). In short, without adequate reliability and validity data, skeptics challenge the usefulness of projective tests, the Rorschach test in particular, in measuring personality.

Nonetheless, the Rorschach inkblot test and many other projective tests continue to be among the most widely used psychological instruments. One reason for this is that many therapists believe projective tests should not be subjected to the strict psychometric standards applied to other psychological tests. For example, they argue that internal consistency cannot be adequately tested, because each item on the test is likely to arouse different unconscious conflicts. Stability over time also is difficult to establish because of subjects' tremendous mood fluctuations between test sessions. However, this brings into question the use of projective tests to assess personality, which generally is defined as a relatively stable entity.

The difficulty in establishing good validity data for projective tests can be attributed to at least two features of these tests. First, test results are usually presented in general, interpretive terms, rather than as predictions of specific kinds of behaviors. Conclusions such as "He is struggling with his sexuality" or "She has some ambivalence about her relationship with her parents" are not easy to test in a support—no support fashion in an empirical investigation. A second, related problem is that few good criteria exist for testing many of the conclusions drawn from projective tests. That is, if a therapist concludes from a Rorschach test that the patient has a certain type of unconscious conflict, what objective criterion does the researcher use to establish the validity of this claim? Indeed, if therapists had easy access to unconscious material, they wouldn't need to use projective tests in the first place.

Many psychologists will no doubt continue to use projective tests regardless of what research says about the instruments. This is because even though the tests may not provide an adequate measure of a patient's personality, they can be quite useful in providing insights about patients' problems and directions for further exploration that might not be obtained in other ways. For example, therapists working with children sometimes allow a child to play with a family of dolls. If children act out a drama in which the mother and father dolls are cruel to the child doll, they may be expressing something about how they perceive their home in a way that isn't easily expressed through other means.

However, many psychologists warn against overinterpreting responses to projective tests. The child in the previous example could merely be acting out a scene from a recent television program. Because the validity of the test remains open to challenge, psychologists are usually advised not to rely too heavily on the tests in making diagnoses. Instead, projective tests should be viewed as providing but one source of information about a patient. This should be taken into consideration along with information collected through interviews, observation, case histories, and other types of tests. Unfortunately, like other psychological tools, projective tests have a potential for misuse as well as for insight.

Strengths and Criticisms of Freud's Theory

None of the approaches to personality covered in this book can spark an argument as quickly as Freudian theory. Every clinical psychologist and personality researcher has an opinion on the value and accuracy of Freud's theory. Although there are few who accept all of Freud's observations and postulates unquestioningly, adherents of the Freudian view typically defend strongly the assumptions about the nature of human functioning that underlie the approach. Critics tend to be equally passionate in their evaluations. Let's look at some of the issues in that debate.

Strengths

Even if all of Freud's ideas were to be rejected by modern personality theorists, he would still deserve an important place in the history of psychology. Freud's was the first comprehensive theory of human behavior and personality. One tribute to Freud's influence is the need most subsequent personality theorists have found to point out where their theories differ from or correct weaknesses in Freud's works. Many of these psychologists built their theories on the foundation laid by Freud, borrowing key psychoanalytic concepts and assumptions. As we will see in Chapter 5, many of those who studied Freud or were trained in the Freudian tradition went on to develop and promote their own versions of psychoanalytic theory. Most psychology historians credit psychoanalytic theory with setting the direction for personality theory for many decades to follow. Thus, the shape of more recent approaches to personality, even though far removed from psycho-

Freud's greatest achievement probably consisted in taking neurotic patients seriously.

CARL JUNG

analytic theory, probably has been influenced in many ways by the field of personality as pictured by Freud.

Freud can also be credited with developing the first system of psychotherapy. Today, treating psychological disorders through discussions with a therapist is an accepted way of dealing with life's problems. Although psychotherapy might have evolved without Freud, it certainly would not have evolved the way it did. The use of such techniques as free association, hypnosis, and dream interpretation have become standard tools for many therapists. Indeed, some patients are disappointed to find their therapist has no couch and does not plan to hypnotize them or interpret their dreams. Nonetheless, surveys reveal that a large number of young as well as experienced psychotherapists identify themselves as "psychoanalytic" in perspective (Smith, 1982; Spett, 1983).

Finally, Freud can be credited with popularizing and promoting important psychological principles and concepts. For example, the concept of anxiety has played a key role in the work of many psychotherapists, personality theorists, and researchers from numerous areas of psychology. As will be seen in Chapters 4 and 6, many of the topics researched by psychologists today have their roots in one or more of Freud's concepts, even though they no longer carry much of the Freudian flavor. The point is that by placing these concepts onto the menu of psychological topics many years ago, Freud was able to influence the subject matter of personality research today.

Criticisms

Although Freud's ideas were so revolutionary they were rejected initially by the medical and academic communities of the day, some writers have argued that these ideas may not have been so original or ground-breaking. For example, one investigator discovered that between 1870 and 1880 at least seven books that included the word *unconscious* in the title were published in Europe (Whyte, 1978). Because the educated elite in Europe was relatively small at the time, another researcher concluded that "at the time Freud started his clinical practice every educated person must have [been] familiar with the idea of the unconscious" (Jahoda, 1977, p. 132). Other historians point out that Freud probably had access to the works of people already writing about different levels of consciousness, free association, and infantile sexuality (Jahoda, 1977; Jones, 1953–1957). In addition, many "Freudian" ideas appear in literature that predates Freud's work. For example, the Russian novelist Fyodor Dostoyevski, who died in 1881, described in his works such things as unconsciously motivated behaviors, erotic symbolism in dreams, intrapsychic conflict, and even hints of an Oedipus complex.

Thus, a case can be made that Freud's "revolutionary" ideas were not so new and foreign to European thinking at the time. We can offer three points in Freud's defense. First, Freud often cited earlier works on topics similar to the ones he was introducing. This is especially true in his early writings. Second, Freud was the first person to organize many loosely related ideas into one theory of human behavior. Without a unified theory detailing the relationship among the unconscious, dream interpretation, and infantile sexuality, it is doubtful whether any of these vague notions would have been developed much further by the scientists who were familiar with them. Third, Freud initiated a lifelong program of investigating the various concepts in his theory. The work Freud and his followers did with their patients provided the data on which psychoanalytic theory was developed. While many of Freud's major contributions may have had predecessors in earlier writings, there is a large difference between introducing an idea and organizing, integrating, and developing many ideas into a comprehensive model of human behavior.

A second criticism often made of Freudian theory is that many of the hypotheses generated from the theory are not testable. Recall that one criterion for a valuable scientific theory is whether it can generate hypotheses that can be either supported or not supported. But critics point to the difficulty of determining a situation or research finding that would fail to support Freud's theory. For example, if a Freudian therapist concludes that a patient has a strong unconscious hatred for her sister, what sort of evidence could be used to show that the conclusion is incorrect? What if the patient says she cannot remember any negative feelings toward her sister? The patient is obviously repressing them. What if the patient describes how much she loves her sister? Obviously, a reaction formation. And if the patient says she has harbored some negative feelings toward her sister? Then the therapist has been successful in bringing the material into consciousness. If the hypothesis cannot be unsupported, then neither can it be truly supported. This makes the theory considerably less useful to scientists.

In Freud's defense, we can hardly accuse him of being unconcerned with finding evidence to support his theory. Indeed, he referred to many parts of his theory as "discoveries," the products of detailed examinations of patients' statements during various stages of psychoanalysis. Although some aspects of Freudian theory may be difficult to test, part of the difficulty may be researchers' failure to develop adequate experimental methods. However, as shown in the next chapter, some clever methods for examining various Freudian concepts have been devised in recent years, and others no doubt will be developed in the future.

Freud relied heavily on case study data as evidence for the various aspects of his theory. However, this is the basis of another criticism, in that these data were most certainly biased. First, Freud's patients hardly represented typical adults. Not only did they come from relatively wealthy and well-educated European families, but they also were suffering from psychological disorders at the time. It is a large leap to say that the minds of these patients function the same as the mind of the average psychologically healthy adult. Second, all information we have about these patients was filtered through Freud. Thus, it is possible that Freud recognized and recorded only those statements and behaviors that supported his theory and ignored or failed to notice those that did not. Third, it is possible that (consciously or unconsciously) Freud caused his patients to say the things he wanted to hear. Psychotherapy patients can at times be highly vulnerable to accepting whatever a person in a position of authority tells them and may be highly motivated to please that person. For example, it is interesting to note that when interpreting Dora's dream, Freud wrote that the dream only confirmed what he already knew. Of course, this criticism is not limited to Freud but applies to all case studies based on private interactions between therapists and their patients. Unless the therapist invites others to listen in on the sessions and form their own impressions, the data will almost always be subject to the interpretation and influence of the therapist.

A final group of criticisms concern disagreements with the points of emphasis and tone of Freud's theory. Many of Freud's early followers eventually broke away from the group and developed their own theories because they felt Freud ignored or deemphasized important influences on personality. For example, some were concerned about Freud's failure to recognize how experiences beyond the first five years of life could affect personality. Others disagreed with Freud's emphasis on instinctual influences on personality at the expense of important social and cultural influences. Still others took issue with Freud's tendency to concentrate on the negative parts of personality — on psychological disorders — rather than on the daily functioning and positive aspects of personality. Because of these and other limitations of Freud's theory, many neo-Freudians developed theories that corrected these points within a framework that was basically Freudian. Some of their contributions are reviewed in Chapter 5.

Summary

1. The first comprehensive theory of personality was developed by Sigmund Freud about 100 years ago. After working with hypnosis to help patients suffering from hysteria, Freud came to understand the power of unconscious influences on our behavior. According to his theory, the human personality can be divided into conscious, preconscious, and unconscious parts. In addition, the human personality can be divided into the id, the ego, and the superego.

2. According to Freud, psychological activity is powered by psychic energy, called libido. Intrapsychic conflict creates tension, and the goal of human behavior is to return to a tensionless state.

3. Within Freud's theory, a healthy personality is one in which the ego is able to control id impulses and superego demands. To this end, the ego often uses defense mechanisms. These include repression, in which traumatic information is pushed out of awareness. Other defense mechanisms include sublimation, displacement, reaction formation, denial, intellectualization, and repression. With the exception of sublimation, the ego uses these defense mechanisms at a cost.

4. Among the most controversial aspects of Freud's theory is his explanation of the psychosexual stages of development. Freud maintained that young children pass through stages of development characterized by the primary erogenous zone for each stage. Children pass through oral, anal, and phallic stages on their way to healthy sexual expression in the genital stage. Excessive trauma during these early years may cause psychic energy to become fixated, and the adult personality will reflect the characteristics of the fixated stage of development. An important step in the development of adult personality takes place with the resolution of the Oedipus complex at the end of the phallic stage.

5. Psychoanalysts have developed several methods for getting at unconscious material. Freud called dreams the "royal road to the unconscious." He interpreted the symbols in his patients' dreams to understand their id impulses. In addition, Freudian psychologists use projective tests, free association, and hypnosis to get at this material. Clues about unconscious feelings also may be expressed in Freudian slips, "accidents," and symbolic behavior.

6. Freud also developed the first system of psychotherapy, called psychoanalysis. Most of the time in this lengthy therapy procedure is spent bringing the unconscious sources of the patients' problems into awareness. A Freudian therapist actively interprets the true (unconscious) meanings of the patients' words, dreams, and actions for them. One of the first signs that psychoanalysis is progressing is resistance, in which a patient stops cooperating with the therapeutic process in order to halt the therapist's threatening efforts to bring out key hidden material.

7. Many Freudian psychologists rely on projective tests to measure the concepts of interest to them. Typically, test takers are asked to respond to ambiguous stimuli, such as inkblots. Because there are no real answers, responses are assumed to reflect unconscious associations. The use of projective tests is controversial. Critics point to unacceptably low indicators of reliability and validity. However, if used correctly, these tests may provide insights into patients' personalities and sources of psychological problems.

8. Among the strengths of the Freudian approach is the tremendous influence Freud had on personality theorists for many years to follow. In addition, Freud developed the first system of psychotherapy and introduced many concepts into the domain of scientific inquiry. Critics point out that many of Freud's ideas were not new and that many aspects of his theory are not testable. Others criticize his use of biased data in developing his theory. Many of those who studied with Freud also disliked his emphasis on instinctual over social causes of psychological disorders and the generally negative picture he painted of human nature.

Key Terms

topographic model Freud's original model of personality structure, in which personality is divided into three different levels of awareness.

conscious In Freud's topographic model, the part of personality that contains the thoughts which we are currently aware of.

preconscious In Freud's topographic model, the part of personality that contains thoughts that can be brought into awareness with little difficulty.

unconscious In Freud's topographic model, the part of personality that contains material that cannot easily be brought into awareness.

structural model Freud's model of personality that divides personality into the id, the ego, and the superego.

id In Freud's structural model, the part of personality concerned with immediate gratification of needs.

pleasure principle The principle on which the id operates, in which pleasure is the sole reason for behavior.

wish fulfillment The satisfaction of id impulses through imagining the desired object.

ego In Freud's structural model, the part of personality that considers external reality while mediating between the demands of the id and the superego.

reality principle The principle on which the ego operates, in which the external consequences of an action are considered.

superego In Freud's structural model, the part of personality that represents society's values.

libido The limited amount of psychic energy that powers mental activity.

Thanatos The self-destructive (death) instinct, often turned outward in the form of aggression.

anxiety An aversive emotional state experienced as feelings of nervousness, worry, agitation, and panic.

defense mechanisms Devices the ego uses to keep threatening material out of awareness and thereby reduce or avoid anxiety.

repression A defense mechanism in which the ego pushes threatening material out of awareness and into the unconscious.

sublimation A defense mechanism in which threatening unconscious impulses are channeled into socially acceptable behaviors.

displacement A defense mechanism in which a response is directed at a nonthreatening target instead of the unconsciously preferred one.

denial A defense mechanism in which a person denies the existence of a fact.

reaction formation A defense mechanism in which people act in a manner opposite their unconscious desires.

intellectualization A defense mechanism in which the emotional content of threatening material is removed before bringing it into awareness.

projection A defense mechanism in which one's own unconscious thoughts and impulses are seen in other people.

psychosexual stages of development The innate sequence of development made up of stages characterized by primary erogenous zones and sexual desires.

fixation The tying up of psychic energy at one psychosexual stage, which results in adult behaviors characteristic of that stage.

oral stage The psychosexual stage of development in which the mouth, lips, and tongue are the primary erogenous zone.

anal stage The psychosexual stage of development in which the anal region is the primary erogenous zone.

phallic stage The psychosexual stage of development in which the genital region is the primary erogenous zone and in which the Oedipus complex develops.

Oedipus complex A child's sexual attraction at about age 5 for their opposite-sex parent and the consequent conflicts.

castration anxiety The fear a boy experiences during the phallic stage of development that his father will cut off his genitals.

penis envy A girl's desire to have a penis and to be like a male.

latency stage The psychosexual stage of development that follows resolution of the Oedipus complex and in which sexual desires are weak.

genital stage The final psychosexual stage in which the ability to engage in adult sexual behavior is developed.

manifest content Dream material as perceived in symbolic form.

latent content The real meaning of dreams as expressed in symbols.

projective tests Tests designed to assess unconscious material by asking subjects to respond to ambiguous stimuli.

free association A procedure used in psychoanalysis in which patients say whatever comes into their mind.

Freudian slip A seemingly innocent misstatement that reveals unconscious associations.

psychoanalysis The system of psychotherapy developed by Freud that focuses on uncovering the unconscious material responsible for the patient's disorder.

resistance A stage in psychoanalysis in which the patient acts to prevent the therapy from progressing further.

transference A stage in psychoanalysis in which the patient transfers unconscious feelings about another individual to the therapist.

countertransference In psychoanalysis, the therapist's transferring of unconscious feelings about another individual to the patient.

Rorschach inkblot test A projective test in which subjects are asked to describe what they see in a series of inkblots.

Thematic Apperception Test (TAT) A projective test in which subjects are asked to tell stories about a series of ambiguous pictures.

Human Figure Drawing test A projective test in which subjects are asked simply to draw a person.

Suggested Readings

Freud, S. (1923/1962). *The ego and the id.* New York: Norton. It's difficult to develop a full appreciation for Freud's theory and the manner with which he argued his case without reading some of his writings. This book, in which Freud introduced many of the central concepts in his structural model of personality, often appeals to the curious student.

Freud, S. (1930/1961). *Civilization and its discontents.* New York: Norton. If you are going to read but one of Freud's books, this might be the best choice. Freud applied his model of personality to the question of how society can function given the hedonistic nature of human beings. Students from a wide range of interests often find this book the most thought-provoking of Freud's works.

Gay, P. (1988). *Freud: A life for our time.* New York: Norton. One of the most widely acclaimed biographies of Sigmund Freud. Biographer Peter Gay presents an extensive and comprehensive account of Freud's life that provides the reader with an appreciation of the man and his theory.

The Freudian Approach
Relevant Research

4

When I describe Freud's theory to undergraduates, I typically find two different reactions. On the one hand, some students are impressed with Freud's insight into human behavior. Psychoanalytic theory helps them understand some of their own feelings and behaviors and the conflicts they wrestle with. "It really applies to me," a student told me recently. "Now I see why I do some of the things I do. Now I understand how symbolic some of my behaviors are."

On the other hand, many students eye Freudian theory with skepticism and even ridicule. Sexual feelings in children, unconscious meanings in dreams, Oedipal desires for one's opposite-sex parent, and the like strike these students as little more than a Freudian fantasy taken too seriously. While it probably is the case that we embrace those personality theories that fit our own perceptions of human behavior, a scientific approach to personality requires more than faith in one theory over another. What we need is evidence that Freud was correct i[n] his characterization of human nature and psychological processes. We ne[ed] research.

Critics of the psychoanalytic approach often charge that Freud was un[con]cerned with validating his theory. But Freud's writings are filled with "a pa[ssion]ate desire to discover ways in which the validity of psychoanalytic finding[s] be established," wrote one historian. "The search for validation perva[des] entire work" (Jahoda, 1977, p. 113). However, Freud sought validation [in] case study reports rather than empirical experiments. He used staten[ents] patients made during therapy to support his descriptions of personali[ty. For]tunately, as described in Chapter 2, case studies have several weakn[esses] make reliance on these data alone questionable. Although Freud's pat[ients' statements consistent with his theory, we must wonder about Fre[ud's] seeing and recording what he expected and the generalizability of th[ese] to all people.

Another criticism of Freud's work is that many parts of h[is theory] untestable. As described in the previous chapter, some aspects of [it] do not easily translate into experiments. Although some of the dif[ficulties encoun]tered by researchers may be overcome with clever innovations ar[d anal]ogy, it is probably correct to say that at least part of Freud's theo[ry does not lend] itself to being examined through experimental methods. Fortu[nately, re]searchers have succeeded in deriving testable hypotheses from

Dre[ams con]cern[ed] we d[o] sleep [ ] by tri[ ]

SIGMU[ND]

This has resulted in a considerable amount of empirical work on some of the issues introduced by Freud. We'll look at four relevant topics in this chapter.

First, we'll examine some of the ways researchers have used dream interpretation to explore unconscious conflicts. Next, we'll look at how researchers have struggled to find ways to examine Oedipal impulses in the laboratory. This is followed by research on one specific aspect of Freud's theory. Freud described in detail the unconscious motives underlying humor. Several predictions have been derived and tested from this work. Finally, we'll look at the phenomenon that first piqued Freud's curiosity about the unconscious — hypnosis.

Dream Interpretation

You are sleeping. Slowly the clouds inside your restful mind form the images of your dreams. These images are vague at first, but soon you recognize a classroom and classmates familiar to you. It's your second-grade room, everything the way you remember it, except that you are an adult now, sitting in your old desk. Suddenly you notice another important difference between yourself and your classmates — you're the only one not wearing any clothes. You try to conceal this fact with your arms as best you can, but your teacher and some of the students notice. You bolt from the room, past a group of dancers, until you find yourself on a battlefield. Tanks, bazookas, and rifles are aimed at you from every side. Your only escape is to fly, which you do by leaping into the air Superman-style. You soar to a nearby cave, where you hide from the battle outside.

Then you wake up, heart pounding. Because you make an effort to think about the dream, the detailed images remain vivid in your memory all morning. If you are like most people in this society, you probably wonder just what this dream means. Your curiosity reflects one of Freud's legacies to 20th-century Western culture. The notion that dreams contain hidden psychological meaning was promoted and popularized by Freud. If you took this dream to a Freudian therapist, you likely would be told it is loaded with classic symbolism, which in the Freudian tradition means sexual symbolism. For example, you'd probably be told dancing and flying represent sexual intercourse, guns and tanks are penises, and caves are wombs.

Freud interpreted his patients' dreams as a means of understanding their unconscious conflicts and desires. Many therapists since have used dream interpretation as one of their therapeutic tools. But how accurate is dream interpretation? One problem patients sometimes encounter is that different therapists develop entirely different interpretations of the same dream. Other psychologists deny that dreams have any significance at all, or they challenge the ability of therapists to understand the significance of dreams. Who is correct? An examination of the research on dream interpretation obviously would be helpful. We can divide this research into studies about *what* people dream and those focusing on *why* people dream. However, like other aspects of Freudian psychology, this research still leaves much room for interpretation by believers and skeptics.

*...ms are never con-
...d with trivialities;
... not allow our
...o be disturbed
...les.*

...ND FREUD

The Meaning of Dream Content

According to Freud, the content of our dreams contains much information about what's in our unconscious. Occasionally a dream contains images or evokes emotions that we feel must mean something. But for the most part our dreams are absurd, vague, or just silly images that seemingly have no relation to anything. Of course, Freud might say the reason for this is that the important unconscious material has been disguised through symbolism. Later psychoanalytic theorists have argued that dreams represent unconscious preoccupations (Hall, 1953). That is, our unresolved conflicts surface during our sleeping hours. Identifying what people dream about provides a clue about the sources of their unconscious conflicts.

One example of how dream researchers look for these clues is found in research comparing how often male and female characters occur in dreams. Several investigations have found that while about half of the characters in women's dreams are male and half are female, men are more likely to dream about male characters (Hall, 1984; Hall & Domhoff, 1963). As shown in Table 4.1, this difference is found at all ages and in nearly every culture. Hall (1984) estimated from the combined findings of all these studies that males make up about 50% of the characters in women's dreams, but about 65% of the characters in men's dreams.

Why are nearly two thirds of the characters in men's dreams other males? Hall (1984) explains this finding in terms of differences between the male Oedipus complex and the female counterpart, the Elektra complex. According to Freudian theory, males never completely overcome their conflicts with their fathers. Because of displacement, men also experience greater conflict with men generally than do women. They therefore are preoccupied with this conflict at an unconscious level, and this preoccupation surfaces in the form of male characters in their dreams.

Another example of how unconscious preoccupation shows up during our sleep is seen in recurrent dreams. Most of us have experienced a dream that we believe we have had before. For some people the same dream occurs every night for several nights in a row. Sometimes a dream appears off and on for months or even years. From a psychoanalytic perspective, the dream reappears night after night because the conflict expressed in the dream is important yet remains unresolved. This helps to explain why recurrent dreamers also are more likely to suffer from anxiety and generally poor adjustment during the waking hours than are people not experiencing recurrent dreams (Brown & Donderi, 1986). The unconscious conflict surfaces in the dream at night but is expressed in the form of anxiety during the day.

But what of the most provocative aspect of Freud's dream interpretation theory, that seemingly innocent objects and actions are symbolic representations of sexuality and sexual activity? This is a difficult hypothesis to test directly, but some support is found in research on *who* is most likely to dream of, for example, snakes and flying. According to some psychoanalytic researchers, people currently experiencing high levels of anxiety are most likely to engage in the

Table 4.1

Percentage of Male and Female Dream Characters

Age of Subjects	Country/ Culture	Males	Females
		Percent Male Characters	Percent Male Characters
2–4	United States	59	49
7–12	United States	67	54
10–13	United States	69	52
	Guatemala	72	43
	Peru	68	50
14–17	United States	66	56
	Guatemala	68	46
	Peru	59	57
	Zulu	81	49
	Cuna	59	55
College	United States*	60	48
	Australia	55	48
	Mexico	59	61
	Peru*	34	39
	Zulu	82	54
	India	71	46
	Nigeria	81	50
Adult	United States	66	52
	Ifaluk	80	53
	Tinguian	61	66
	Alor	68	58
	Skolt	73	48
	Hopi	63	51

Source: Taken from Hall (1984), with permission.
*Figures combined from more than one sample.

"symbolic expression of sexual arousal" (Wallach, 1960). This is said to follow because their anxiety prevents them from expressing their sexual desires in more direct ways, thus forcing the expression of these feelings through symbols. To test this hypothesis, researchers asked subjects in one study to keep diaries of their dreams and their daily level of anxiety for 10 days (Robbins, Tanck, & Houshi, 1985). Consistent with the psychoanalytic position, the higher subjects' anxiety levels, the more often classic Freudian sexual symbols (pencils, boxes, flying) appeared in their dreams.

In summary, although testing some of Freud's views on dream interpretation directly has proven difficult, several investigations have found the content of subjects' dreams often are consistent with Freud's predictions. Of course, many of these findings are open to alternative explanations. For example, men may dream about males more than women because they come into contact with more men during the day (Urbina & Grey, 1975). Similarly, recurrent dreams might be caused by issues with which the dreamer is well aware, rather than indicating unconscious conflicts. At any rate, examining the content of dreams has proven a useful research methodology and has produced some intriguing, albeit sometimes difficult to explain, findings.

The Function of Dreams

A more challenging question than what people dream is why people dream. Freud maintained that unconscious impulses cannot be suppressed forever. Therefore, one of the major functions of dreams is to allow the symbolic expression of these impulses. Dreams provide a safe and healthy outlet for expressing unconscious conflicts. But researchers had to wait for technology to catch up with theory before they could investigate this aspect of Freud's work.

In the 1950s, researchers discovered that mammals experience two distinctly different kinds of sleep (Aserinsky & Kleitman, 1953). Each night we alternate between periods of REM and non-REM sleep. The name REM comes from "rapid eye movement," because this period usually is accompanied by rapidly moving eyes underneath closed lids. REM sleep is sometimes called *paradoxical sleep*, because while our muscles are especially relaxed during this time, our brain activity, as measured by an instrument called an *electroencephalograph*, is similar to the waking state. Most adults spend one-and-a-half to two hours a night in REM sleep, spread over several periods.

The significance of this discovery for personality researchers is that REM sleep is filled with dreams, whereas non-REM sleep has almost no dreams. Thus, the discovery of REM sleep created new opportunities for dream researchers. For example, suddenly researchers could look at the effects of depriving people of REM sleep, they could correlate psychological variables with the length and amount of REM sleep, and they could wake people during REM sleep to capture dreams that might be lost by morning (cf. Arkin, Antrobus, & Ellman, 1978; Cohen, 1979).

What did REM sleep research find about the relationship between dreaming and mental health? Early researchers maintained that REM sleep, and therefore dreaming, was necessary for maintaining one's mental health and that depriving someone of REM sleep might create serious psychological disturbances. However, subsequent researchers have challenged this conclusion (Hoyt & Singer, 1978; Vogel, 1975). But dreaming does seem to have some positive psychological effects. For example, REM sleep appears to prepare us for dealing with anxiety-arousing or ego-threatening material. People deprived of REM sleep have more difficulty with potentially stressful tasks (McGrath & Cohen, 1978).

The psychological value of REM sleep was demonstrated in one experiment in which subjects were shown a film about autopsy procedures (Greenberg,

Pillard & Pearlman, 1978). The film showed a physician performing an autopsy in gruesome detail and was selected for the study because it invariably created high levels of anxiety in viewers. Some subjects saw the film before and after being deprived of REM sleep. These subjects had a more difficult time coping with their anxiety, as indicated by physiological measures, than did subjects not deprived of REM sleep. The subjects allowed to dream between showings of the film somehow were better able to work through their anxiety. These subjects were significantly less disturbed by the film the second time they saw it.

Other research suggests that dreams may also allow us to work through unresolved problems while we sleep. Subjects in one study were told they had performed poorly on an IQ test just before going to sleep (Cohen & Cox, 1975). The subjects who reported dreaming about the experiment during the night were in a better mood the next day than were those who did not. This suggests that by dreaming about the problem subjects were able to somehow resolve or deal with it better. Consistent with Freud's observations, the dreams appeared to have a positive function.

Although some of these findings suggest Freud was correct when he argued that dreaming was necessary for healthy psychological functioning, other research findings challenge Freud's position. For example, why do newborn babies experience as much as eight hours of REM sleep per day? What unconscious conflicts are they working out? For that matter, REM sleep has been found in nearly all mammals and possibly even in human fetuses (Crick & Mitchison, 1983). At best, we can say that REM sleep serves functions other than dreaming and the unconscious release of tension.

Nonetheless, feelings that at least some of our dreams contain important psychological messages, and that dreaming serves some important psychological function, are difficult to abandon. Psychologists and lay people probably will always be enchanted with, frightened by, and curious about the crazy stories that play in our mind while we sleep.

The Oedipus Complex

Perhaps no aspect of Freudian theory brings a stronger reaction from supporters and detractors than the Oedipus complex. Psychoanalysts consider the Oedipus complex and the consequences of its resolution a cornerstone of Freud's theory. Critics often ridicule the notion that 5-year-old boys have sexual thoughts about their mothers. Freud's only evidence for the existence of an Oedipus complex came from therapy sessions with his patients or interviews with the parents of young patients. Freud said all males go through this period but fail to recall it because they repress Oedipal desires upon resolving the issue.

Early researchers occasionally sought support for Freud's theory through empirical research. For example, a significant correlation was found between the physical characteristics men prefer in their wives and the way they describe their mothers (McElroy, 1950). This finding could be interpreted as evidence for unresolved Oedipal wishes; the men were seeking in their wives a symbolic relationship with their mothers. Unfortunately, most of these findings suffered from viable alternative explanations. For example, mothers might model characteristics that men become accustomed to and appreciate in women. Little wonder then they seek out a wife with similar characteristics. The problem these researchers faced was that they were dealing with variables they could not manipulate (Chapter 2). To rule out alternative explanations, investigators ideally need to randomly assign people to conditions and manipulate the independent variable.

Unfortunately, this presents something of a problem for psychoanalytic researchers. How can you manipulate what's in a person's unconscious mind? Of course, we can introduce Oedipal thoughts to one group by having them read a passage about a five-year-old's lust for his mother. But then the information would be in the conscious as well as (perhaps) the unconscious mind. What psychoanalytic researchers need to demonstrate is that *unconscious* Oedipal thoughts affect men's actions. But how?

Subliminal Psychodynamic Activation

Lloyd Silverman and his colleagues came up with an answer to this problem (Silverman, 1976; Silverman & Fishel, 1981; Silverman & Weinberger, 1985; Weinberger & Silverman, 1987). They introduced a procedure called **subliminal psychodynamic activation**. Subjects in these experiments look into an apparatus called a **tachistoscope**. They stare at a dark or blank screen while the experimenter flashes an image on the screen for a fraction (4 one thousandths) of a second. Silverman demonstrated that people cannot tell what image they have seen when it is presented this quickly. That is, the information is not retained in consciousness. However, he argued that the image *has* been exposed long enough to register in the *unconscious*. If Silverman was correct, then the subliminal psychodynamic activation procedure allows researchers to place images and information in the unconscious minds of some subjects but not others. If subjects are randomly assigned to different image conditions, and if they then behave in different ways consistent with Freud's predictions, we can produce evidence in support of psychoanalytic theory.

To date, researchers have conducted approximately 100 studies with this procedure (Weinberger & Silverman, 1987). Silverman and his colleagues have claimed a great deal of success in supporting Freudian theory. For example, Freud postulated that depression results from aggressive impulses turned inward. When depressed people were presented with tachistoscopic aggressive images, they became more depressed (Silverman, 1976). Similarly, psychoanalytic theory suggests that stutterers unconsciously relate speaking with defecation. When stutterers were presented with tachistoscopic images of a dog defecating, their stuttering increased (Silverman, Klinger, Lustbader, Farrell, & Martin, 1972). Can evidence for the Oedipus complex be found with this procedure as well?

Research on the Oedipus Complex

According to psychoanalytic theory, unresolved Oedipal wishes are expressed in a number of everyday activities. For example, sexual contact with a female is

The experimenter controls the frequency and duration of the image exposure with this tachistoscope. The subject stares into the dark screen, awaiting the rapid presentation of the image. Some researchers claims this procedure allows them to implant messages into the unconscious part of the subject's mind.

interpreted as symbolic sexual contact with one's mother. Competition in sports or business is seen as a manifestation of unconscious desires to compete with and defeat one's father for the love of one's mother. If the theory is correct, then we should be able to increase these activities by introducing relevant thoughts into a person's unconscious mind through the subliminal psychodynamic activation method.

Silverman and his colleagues tested this hypothesis by examining competition among males in a simple dart-throwing game (Silverman, Ross, Adler, & Lustig, 1978). According to Freud, men try to defeat other men in such games because of unresolved Oedipal desires to symbolically defeat their fathers. Male college students were randomly assigned to groups and presented with different sets of tachistoscopic images. One group saw images of two men looking unhappily at each other, with the caption "Beating Dad Is Wrong." These images were designed to increase Oedipal conflict. A second group saw images of two men smiling, with the caption "Beating Dad Is OK." These images were supposed to decrease Oedipal conflict. A comparison group saw only images of people walking, with the caption "People Are Walking." Their Oedipal conflicts should not have been affected by the presentations.

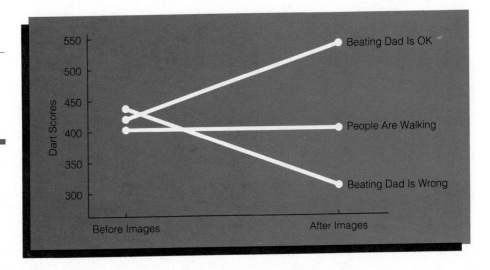

Figure 4.1

Dart-Throwing Scores Before and After Subliminal Messages

The men were told they were competing with one another for cash prizes. Silverman compared how well they did in the dart-throwing competition before and after they were exposed to the images. Results from one of these experiments are shown in Figure 4.1. Subjects presented with the conflict-increasing message ("Beating Dad Is Wrong") performed more poorly, whereas those given the conflict-reducing message ("Beating Dad Is OK") did better. The researchers explain this finding in terms of Freudian theory. When unconscious Oedipal conflict was increased or decreased, the men's competitiveness with another male, symbolic of competition with their fathers, changed accordingly.

Might there be something else about these subliminal messages that could account for these findings? Silverman and his colleagues have examined various possibilities (Silverman & Fishel, 1981). For example, they changed the messages to "Beating Mom Is Wrong" and "Beating Mom Is OK." These messages are similar to the ones used in the first study, but without the competition-with-father information. As predicted, these non-Oedipal messages had no impact on the dart game. When Oedipal conflicts were reduced through the tachistoscopic message "Winning Mom Is OK," dart throwing also improved. Taken together, these studies seem to provide that elusive support for Freud's description of the Oedipus complex.

Problems with Replication

Research with subliminal psychodynamic activation has attracted a great deal of attention from personality researchers. Because discussions of the Oedipus complex often lead to strong attacks and defenses, we should not be surprised to find Silverman's research evokes similarly strong reactions. Many critics simply have a hard time accepting the findings. Silverman (1982a, 1982b) suggested that because these psychologists have already rejected Freudian theory, they try to reject

Box 4.1

Creating Freudian Slips in the Laboratory

Freud maintained that slips of the tongue often reveal unconscious thoughts. According to Freud, the man who introduces himself to an attractive woman with "Excuse me, but we haven't been properly seduced," is telling more about his real intentions than he probably wants to. But while most of us can recall embarrassing examples of Freudian slips that seem to confirm Freud's position, researchers are faced with a problem that makes much research on Freudian topics difficult: How can we examine Freudian slips experimentally? By their nature, Freudian slips occur when we least expect them. Laboratory subjects could talk a long time without ever uttering a usable slip of the tongue.

Fortunately, researchers have come up with a few clever ways to get around this problem. For example, male subjects in one experiment were asked to complete some innocent-looking sentences (Motley & Camden, 1985). Half the subjects did this in the presence of an attractive and scantily-clad female experimenter, half with a male experimenter. Which group would Freud expect to make more slips of the tongue? When completing sentences such as "With the telescope, the details of the distant landscape were easy to . . ." the men in the female-experimenter group were more likely to say "make out" than were the other subjects. More blatantly, for the sentence "The lid won't stay on regardless of how much I . . ." these men were more likely to answer "screw it." In another study, men were asked to read quickly-presented word pairs (Motley, Camden, & Baars, 1979). Again, some responded in the presence of the sexually arousing female experimenter, others with a male experimenter. As expected, in front of the female, subjects were more likely to read *bine-foddy* as "fine body" and *lood-gegs* as "good legs."

While these findings tend to support Freudian theory, researchers are quick to point out that alternative interpretations are possible. For example, linguists can explain these slips in terms of cognitive connections and activation of linguistic pathways. Essentially, they argue that the sexual connotation in these situations activates our memory of similar kinds of information. This creates a kind of cognitive pathway between the beginning of the sentence and the double-entendre word, thus making selection of the sexually related word more likely. Thus, while evidence for Freudian slips exists, the debate over Freud's explanation continues.

the entire lot of experiments based on whatever methodological weakness they can find in one or two studies. While there may be some truth to this reasoning, other researchers have uncovered serious questions about the subliminal psychodynamic activation procedure (Allen & Condon, 1982; Balay & Shevrin, 1988; Condon & Allen, 1980; Fisher, Glenwick, & Blumenthal, 1986; Haspel & Harris, 1982; Heilbrun, 1980, 1982; Oliver & Burkham, 1982).

The most serious problem has been the difficulty with replication. Recall from Chapter 2 that psychologists are increasingly concerned about replicating their findings. An experiment might yield seemingly significant results for any number of unknown reasons. There might be something peculiar about the laboratory, the subjects, or the procedure that is not obvious to the investigators. Experimenters might have inadvertently tipped off subjects as to what they were supposed to do. Then again, some differences occur by chance alone. Therefore, before researchers accept a finding as factual, they often want to know that it can be found consistently in different laboratories. The need for replication is especially strong when dealing with a topic and findings as controversial as those in the Oedipus complex experiments.

Unfortunately, several investigators have not been able to replicate Silverman et al.'s (1978) results. For example, Heilbrun (1980) made three carefully designed efforts to conduct the dart-throwing study in a manner identical to the original investigation, yet could not find significant differences between conditions. A similar failure to replicate this effect was reported by Haspel and Harris (1982). Still, the subliminal psychodynamic activation procedure has been used successfully by other researchers (Dauber, 1984; Frauman, Lynn, Hardaway, & Molteni, 1984; Geisler, 1986).

So what are we to conclude from all of this? At least two features of research with Freudian theory are evident. First, because of the skepticism that surrounds much of this theory, researchers looking for empirical support should be ready to supply solid, replicable findings and be prepared for challenges from critics. Second, many of the key aspects of Freud's theory remain difficult to investigate empirically. Silverman and his colleagues are to be commended for their ambitious and clever efforts to explore unconscious influences on behavior through the subliminal psychodynamic activation process. Yet difficulties in replicating some of the original findings suggest that the evidence for Freudian theory obtained from this method is far from convincing. Perhaps technological advances will allow future investigators to develop better, less controversial methods for testing psychoanalytic theory.

Humor

On January 28, 1986, the space shuttle *Challenger* exploded 73 seconds after liftoff. Debris from the flaming craft scattered into the Atlantic Ocean. All seven crew members died. Millions watched television replays of the accident in shock and disbelief. Many cried openly. A nation went into mourning.

Why bring up this tragic incident as an introduction to a section on humor? Because within two days after the disaster, I probably had heard more than a half-dozen *Challenger* jokes. Many people I encountered were eager to be the first to tell me the latest one. A radio disc jockey was suspended from his job when he shared a series of *Challenger* jokes on the air.

What is it that brings out this tasteless humor? Every highly publicized tragedy seems to be followed by a series of related jokes. This type of humor has taken many forms over the years, but never seems to disappear or go out of style. In recent years cruel, tasteless humor has shown up as "dead baby" jokes, "Helen Keller" jokes, and "Mommy Mommy" jokes. In Freud's day they took the form of "marriage broker" jokes, which always began with a young man visiting a broker to arrange a marriage with an appropriate young woman. For example,

> The bridegroom was most disagreeably surprised when the bride was introduced to him, and drew the broker on the one side and whispered his remonstrances: "She's ugly and old, she squints and has bad teeth and bleary eyes. . . ."
> "You needn't lower your voice," interrupted the broker, "she's deaf as well." (Freud, 1905/1960, p. 64)

The typical response to this humor is laughter or a smile, followed by a half-serious complaint about the joke being "gross" or in poor taste. Yet these jokes remain popular and continue to proliferate in different forms. Why?

Freud's Theory of Humor

In his 1905 book *Jokes and Their Relation to the Unconscious*, Freud presented an extensive analysis of humor. Although he recognized "innocent" jokes, such as puns and clever insights, Freud was more concerned with "tendentious" jokes — jokes that provide insight into the unconscious of the joke teller as well as the one who laughs. Naturally, Freud saw two kinds of tendentious jokes, those dealing with hostility and those dealing with sex. Hostile jokes include those with overt aggressive intentions, such as insulting jokes and satire. But Freud also identified jokes with disguised hostility, such as those about marriage or ethnic groups. On the other hand, you probably have no trouble recognizing jokes about sex (even if you don't always get them).

Why do so many people enjoy this type of humor? According to Freud, these jokes allow the expression of impulses ordinarily held in check. Although we may have unconscious urges to attack certain people or groups of people, our egos and superegos generally are effective in preventing outward acts of violence. However, we can express these same aggressive desires in a socially appropriate manner through an insulting joke. "By making our enemy small, inferior, despicable or comic," explained Freud, "we achieve in a roundabout way the enjoyment of overcoming him" (1905/1960, p. 103).

A person who laughs at [an obscene joke] . . . is laughing as though he were the spectator of an act of sexual aggression.
SIGMUND FREUD

Similarly, we can discuss taboo sexual topics through the socially appropriate outlet of sexual humor. Open discussions of sex are inappropriate in many social settings. Yet jokes on sex are often not only tolerated but encouraged and rewarded as well. I have seen some normally conservative and proper people who would never bring up the topic of sex in public deal with all kinds of normally taboo topics simply by repeating a joke "someone told me."

Freud noticed that the laughter following a hostile or sexual joke rarely is justified by the humor content of the joke. Most sexually oriented jokes actually contain very little humor. So why do we laugh? Freud explained this in terms of tension reduction. The description of aggression or sexual behavior at the beginning of the joke creates tension. The punch line allows a release of that tension. We get pleasure from many jokes not because they are clever or witty but because of the reduction of tension and anxiety. Freud might have interpreted the jokes following the *Challenger* tragedy in terms of the tension generated by the sudden awareness of death and unpredictable disaster. "Strictly speaking, we do not know what we are laughing at," Freud explained. "The technique of such jokes is often quite wretched, but they have immense success in provoking laughter" (1905/1960, p. 102).

Research on Freud's Theory of Humor

Look at the picture on page 98. Think of a caption that is as humorous or funny as possible. When high school students were asked to write funny captions to such pictures, they gave responses filled with aggressive and sexual themes (Nevo & Nevo, 1983). However, the students made almost no references to sex or aggression when asked what they might say if actually in that situation. According to the researchers, the students "used Freud's techniques as if they had read his writings." For example, one picture without any obvious sexual content depicted only that a man was late for an appointment. Yet students still came up with captions such as "I was in bed with Brigitte Bardot," "I met a couple of girls," and "I was late because I was with your wife."

Was Freud correct when he wrote that people find aggressive and sexual humor funny? Several investigations support this observation (Deckers & Carr, 1986; Kuhlman, 1985; McCauley, Woods, Coolidge, & Kulick, 1983; Pinderhughes & Zigler, 1985). In most cases, subjects rate cartoons containing aggression or sex as funnier than cartoons without these themes. For example, subjects in one experiment rated "Far Side" and "Herman" cartoons funnier when one of the characters experienced pain than when there was no pain or violence (Deckers & Carr, 1986).

At least three additional predictions can be derived from Freud's theory of humor. If Freud is correct, then we should especially enjoy hearing hostile jokes when the victim of the joke is someone we dislike. In addition, if aggressive humor releases tension as Freud said, then exposure to aggressive humor should lower the likelihood that someone will act aggressively. Finally, Freud's theory makes the fairly straightforward prediction that anxious people find situations funnier than those who are less anxious. Researchers have tested all three of these predictions. Let's see how Freud's theory has held up.

Preference for Hostile Humor   If hostile humor allows us to satisfy aggressive impulses, then we should find that humor particularly funny when it is aimed at a person or group we don't like. Researchers have found some support for this

Write a funny caption for this picture.

prediction (Wicker, Barron, & Willis, 1980; Zillmann, Bryant, & Cantor, 1974). For example, how people reacted to political cartoons aimed at Richard Nixon and George McGovern during the week before the 1972 presidential election depended on who they planned to vote for. People found cartoons lightly assaulting the other candidate funnier than those assaulting their candidate.

An extension of this prediction can be made for *when* people find hostile humor funny. Freud argued that hostile humor provides us with a cathartic release of tension by allowing the expression of hostility in a socially acceptable and pleasurable way. If Freud is correct, then people in a hostile mood should have more unexpressed hostility and therefore should experience greater pleasure when the pent-up tension is released. This hypothesis was tested in a study in which experimenters intentionally angered some subjects with insulting remarks about their grammar, handwriting, and general intelligence (Dworkin & Efran, 1967). Subjects then listened to comedy recordings that expressed either hostile or nonhostile feelings. Consistent with the Freudian view, angry subjects found the hostile humor funnier than nonangry subjects. Apparently the hostility aroused by the experimenter created increased tension that was released when listening to the hostile comedian.

Reducing Aggression with Hostile Humor   We've often heard that humor can turn away anger. Suppose you were confronted with an angry person and wanted to defuse the situation with a joke. What kind would you tell — one with obvious hostile content or an innocent, nonhostile joke? Common sense says to try the nonhostile joke, but Freudian theory says just the opposite. Remember, Freud said hostile humor provides a cathartic release of tension. Therefore, the way to reduce the angry person's need to act aggressively is to reduce that tension. Hostile humor should do the trick better than nonhostile humor.

Unfortunately, research support for this prediction is mixed. Several studies have found a decrease in hostility after exposing subjects to hostile humor. For example, the experimenter in one study insulted subjects and then had them rate either hostile or nonhostile jokes (Leak, 1974). Subjects who read hostile jokes said they liked the experimenter more often than did the ones who read nonhostile jokes. Presumably the hostile humor defused their angry feelings. Similarly, angry subjects in another study were given the opportunity to administer electric shocks to a woman after reading some *Playboy* cartoons (Baron, 1978b). Subjects who read cartoons in which women were exploited gave less intense and shorter shocks than did subjects who read nonexploitive cartoons. Again, the hostile cartoons appeared to have defused some of their aggression. Finally, angry black Americans who listened to a black comedian make fun of white segregationists in one study felt less aggressive than did those who listened to a nonhostile comedian (Singer, 1968).

All of these findings suggest Freud may have been correct about hostile humor reducing the likelihood of aggression. In some cases, exposing people to hostile humor seems to provide an outlet for tension reduction that lowers the need to aggress. Unfortunately, the relationship between humor and aggression is more complex than this. For example, angry women exposed to a hostile comedy routine in one study became *more* hostile toward an experimenter who had insulted them (Berkowitz, 1970). In another study, angry subjects allowed to shock an unseen victim gave more electric shocks after reading hostile cartoons than did those who read nonhostile cartoons (Baron, 1978a). Thus, sometimes hostile humor reduces aggressiveness, yet other times it increases.

What can we conclude about this prediction from Freudian theory? Quite possibly hostile humor defuses aggressive tendencies in some situations. But hostile humor has the potential to do more than reduce tension. For example, as we will discuss in Chapter 14, people often imitate modeled aggression. The aggression described or shown in hostile jokes and cartoons might be imitated by an angry reader. In addition, hostile humor may be arousing in some cases. Once again, arousal has been identified as a contributing factor in aggression (Zillmann, 1979). In short, although Freud may be correct about the tension-reducing capabilities of hostile humor, we need to know more about how such humor affects the overall tendency to act aggressively.

Level of Tension and Funniness Observe a group of listeners the next time a good storyteller tells an obscene joke. Skilled joke tellers elaborate on the details. They allow the tension level to build gradually as they set up the punch line. Listeners smile or blush slightly as the joke progresses. According to Freud, this long buildup creates greater tension and thus a louder and longer laugh when the punch line finally allows a tension release.

Freud said the more tension people experience before a punch line, the funnier they'll find the joke. This prediction was tested in an experiment in which subjects were asked to work with a laboratory rat (Shurcliff, 1968). Subjects in the low-tension condition were asked to hold the rat for five seconds. They were told, "These rats are bred to be docile and easy to handle, and I don't think you will have any trouble." In the moderate-tension condition, subjects were asked to take a small sample of the rat's blood. They were told the task was easier than it looked. Finally, subjects in the high-tension group were given a bottle and syringe and asked to take two cubic centimeters of blood from the rat. The experimenter stressed the difficulties involved and warned the rat might bite.

The punch line occurred when subjects reached into the cage and discovered a toy rat. Consistent with Freud's theory, subjects in the high-tension group thought the situation was funnier than did subjects in the other conditions. The pleasure they derived from the release of tension apparently led to their enjoyment of the joke.

Interpreting the Research Findings   Although inconsistencies exist, researchers have uncovered some evidence in support of Freud's theory of humor. People often find jokes and cartoons funnier when they contain sexual and aggressive themes. People also appear to enjoy hostile humor more when it is aimed at someone they dislike and when they feel hostile. Hostile humor may reduce tension, although this does not necessarily reduce hostility, and jokes are funnier when the listener's tension level is built up before the punch line.

Does all of this mean that Freud was correct in his description of the nature of humor? Perhaps. One problem researchers face when interpreting these studies is that alternative explanations are often possible (Kuhlman, 1985; Nevo & Nevo, 1983). For example, many findings can be explained in terms of incongruity (McGhee, 1979). According to this analysis, humor results from an incongruity between what one expects in a situation and what happens. Thus, the reason people find sexual and aggressive humor funny may be because sex and aggression are inconsistent with expected standards of behavior in most settings. For example, imagine a scene in which two sophisticated women bump into each other at a department store. Imagine further that they either get into a physical fight or say something with sexual connotations. We may find this situation funny for the reasons outlined by Freud. But it might also bring a laugh because we do not expect women to act this way when shopping. At any rate, Freud's theory has clearly met one criterion for a good theory: It has generated a number of hypotheses and a significant amount of research.

Hypnosis

A psychologist is giving a classroom demonstration of hypnosis. Several student volunteers sit in the front of the room. They are told to relax and that they are becoming drowsy. The hypnotist tells them they are in a state of deep hypnosis and that they will do whatever he says. Soon the students close their eyes and sit peacefully yet attentively in their chairs. The hypnotist begins the demonstration by asking them to extend their left arm and to imagine a weight is pulling it down. Suddenly the arms of several students begin to move downward, just as if a weight were pulling on their arms. A few arms drop immediately; others drop slowly over several repetitions of the instructions. Still other students remain unaffected, with arms extended straight out. Later the hypnotist tells the students a fly is buzzing around their head. Some react swiftly, perhaps swatting at the imaginary fly, others react slowly or only slightly, and others continue to sit calmly. Before taking them out of hypnosis, the psychologist tells the students they won't remember what has happened until they are told to. When later asked about what they recall, some remember nothing, others a few details, and others practically everything that happened.

This description of a hypnotic induction and susceptibility test is typical of those used in hypnosis research. Although considerable disagreement remains over the nature of hypnosis, most researchers agree that hypnosis includes an induction procedure in which subjects are told they are going to be hypnotized, followed by suggestions to perform certain tasks to demonstrate the degree of hypnosis. These tasks range from the simple ones used in hypnosis research, such as dropping your arm, to the entertaining performances of stage hypnosis subjects, such as yelling like Tarzan or trotting up and down the aisles warning that the British are coming.

Although modern hypnosis has existed in some form for more than 200 years, it remains an intriguing and often misunderstood phenomenon shrouded in mysticism and curiosity. Yet hypnosis also carries a number of potentially useful applications. For example, many people have dental work performed under hypnosis, without the need of painkillers. Police investigators sometimes use hypnosis to help witnesses remember crime details. And many psychoanalytically oriented therapists believe hypnosis can uncover unconscious material crucial to overcoming patients' problems. Despite these many uses, psychologists still quarrel about just what they are dealing with. We'll explore some of the different opinions on this matter next, then examine individual differences in hypnotic susceptibility.

What Is Hypnosis?

There are many theories about the nature of hypnosis. For convenience, we'll group these into two camps. One group describes hypnosis similar to the way Freud did. They believe hypnosis taps an aspect of the human mind that is otherwise difficult to reach. These theorists say that hypnotic subjects fall into a "trance" or that they experience an "altered state of consciousness" like sleeping. On the other side we find theorists who reject the notion that hypnotized people operate under an altered state of awareness. They skeptically maintain there is nothing mysterious about hypnotic phenomena—that all the "amazing" things people do under hypnosis can be explained in terms of basic psychological processes applicable to hypnotized and nonhypnotized people.

Psychoanalytically Influenced Theories   Freud believed hypnosis allowed him to interact with a highly hypnotizable patient's unconscious mind. Somehow the barrier to the unconscious was weakened during hypnosis, allowing easier access to crucial unconscious material. Many psychoanalytic therapists still use hypnosis

From being in love to hypnosis is evidently only a short step. There is the same humble subjection, the same compliance, the same absence of criticism toward the hypnotist as toward the love object.
SIGMUND FREUD

Like the volunteers in this classroom demonstration, most people respond to simple suggestions during hypnosis. However, why these subjects go along with the hypnotist's suggestions remains a matter of controversy.

this way. For example, Milton Erickson (1967) developed several techniques to confuse and distract the conscious so that contact with the unconscious could be made. Other psychoanalytic theorists have expanded the Freudian explanation. For example, one team of psychologists proposed that the ego forms a new subsystem during hypnosis (Gill & Brenman, 1967). According to this theory, the ego creates a kind of pocket in which the formerly unconscious material that surfaces during hypnosis is stored. The ego monitors this pocket of information during hypnosis but keeps it out of conscious awareness once hypnosis is terminated.

A more recent elaboration of the psychoanalytic position has been proposed by Ernest Hilgard (1973, 1977). According to this **neodissociation theory**, deeply hypnotized subjects experience a division of their conscious. Part of their conscious enters a type of altered state, but part remains aware of what is going on during the hypnotic session. Hilgard says this second part acts as a ''hidden observer'' monitoring the situation. The hypnotized part of the conscious is not aware of the observer part.

Hilgard used *pain analgesia* experiments to illustrate how the hidden observer works. He placed highly hypnotizable subjects into a hypnotic state and told them they would not experience pain. Their arms were then lowered into ice water for several seconds. Like any of us, these people reported severe pain almost immediately after their arms touched the water when not hypnotized. However, when hypnotized, they appeared to withstand the icy water with little evidence of suffering.

But this ability to withstand pain under hypnosis has been demonstrated before. The new twist Hilgard added was then asking subjects to report their experiences through "automatic writing" or "automatic talking." He found subjects could keep one arm in the cold water while writing with the other arm that the experience is quite painful. Hilgard interpreted this as a demonstration of the division of consciousness that occurs under hypnosis. The hypnotized part denies the pain, but the hidden observer is aware of what is going on.

Nontrance Theories of Hypnosis Psychoanalytic theories of hypnosis describe hypnotized people as being in a type of trance. Subjects are said to experience a state of consciousness different from being awake. But many other theorists challenge this assumption. They point out there is nothing a person can do under hypnosis that cannot be done without hypnosis. For example, subjects who are relaxed, but not hypnotized, and asked to imagine a weight pulling their arms down will experience increased heaviness in their arms.

How do these skeptical psychologists explain some of the unusual things people do when hypnotized? Most use concepts such as expectancy, motivation, and concentration to explain hypnotic phenomena (Barber, 1970; Barber, Spanos, & Chaves, 1974; Sarbin, 1988; Sarbin & Coe, 1972; Spanos, 1986). For example, I sometimes ask a student in my class to stand up and spin like a top. In every case the student complies. When I ask them why they are doing this, they say it is because I asked them to. No one has ever said it was because they were hypnotized. Yet most people who see hypnotized subjects stand and spin like tops at the hypnotist's request say the people act that way because they are hypnotized. What is the difference between these two situations? Does the hypnotist use certain magical words that suddenly transform the subjects into a trance? Nontrance theorists argue that hypnotized and nonhypnotized people stand up and spin for the same reason: They think they are supposed to.

Nontrance theorists also are critical of "hidden observer" demonstrations (Spanos & Hewitt, 1980; Stava & Jaffa, 1988). They argue that the highly susceptible subjects in these experiments are told what the hidden observer is supposed to do and therefore experience what they believe they are supposed to experience. When researchers told subjects in one study that their hidden observer would experience *less* pain, the "hidden observers" indeed reported less, not more, pain (Spanos & Hewitt, 1980). In another experiment, some subjects were given instructions to experience less pain when *not* hypnotized (Spanos & Katsanis, 1989). These subjects reported as much pain reduction as did hypnotized subjects given these same instructions.

Nontrance theorists also argue that the psychoanalytic position is circular. If we ask why hypnotic subjects run around making chicken noises, we are told it is because they are hypnotized. But if we ask how we can tell that subjects are hypnotized, we are shown how they run around making chicken noises. The concept becomes inarguable and therefore useless in explaining the phenomenon.

Psychologists from both camps continue to debate the nature of hypnosis. Psychoanalytic theorists demonstrate unusual behavior under hypnosis, such as pain analgesia, deafness, and age regression. Nontrance theorists counter with demonstrations of the same phenomena without hypnosis or challenge the accuracy of the description. For example, people who claim to go back to an earlier age typically do a poor job of recreating what they really were like at that time (Nash, 1987). Let's look now at one example of this research that has attracted a lot of attention from both sides of the controversy.

Posthypnotic Amnesia   Hypnotic subjects often are told they will not remember what has happened during hypnosis until the hypnotist tells them to. Indeed, many of these subjects recall little or nothing of the experience until given permission. **Posthypnotic amnesia** has not escaped the attention of novelists and scriptwriters, whose characters sometimes engage in all manner of heinous acts while seemingly under the control of an evil hypnotist. While there is no evidence that hypnosis can be used this way, some subjects do claim to forget what they did when hypnotized. Why?

Psychoanalytically oriented theorists explain that the experience either has been repressed out of consciousness (Erickson, 1939) or has been recorded in a part of the mind not accessible to consciousness. For example, Gill and Brenman (1967) say the experience is recalled only by the pocket of the conscious mind created by the ego during the hypnosis. Information in this pocket remains inaccessible until the ego allows it to enter awareness. However, nontrance theorists argue that hypnotic subjects expect to not recall what happens to them and therefore make no effort to remember (Coe, 1978; Sarbin & Coe, 1979; Spanos, Radtke, & Dubreuil, 1982). They argue that under the right circumstances subjects can be convinced to make the effort to recall. For example, how long would posthypnotic amnesia continue if subjects were offered $1,000 each to describe what happened while they were hypnotized?

A team of researchers found a less expensive way to test this possibility (Howard & Coe, 1980; Schuyler & Coe, 1981). Some highly hypnotizable subjects were hooked up to a physiograph machine and told the experimenter was measuring physical changes during hypnosis. However, others were told the machine allowed the experimenter to tell when they were lying. The experimenter explained that the machine ''is very sensitive and functions in the same manner as a lie detector. It can tell if you are withholding information.'' In truth, the machine had no such capabilities, but the subjects believed that it did. Although they were told under hypnosis they would remember nothing, when it came time to report what they could remember about the hypnotic experience, subjects in the ''lie detector'' condition remembered significantly more than subjects in the other condition. Apparently, they believed they would be caught for saying they could not remember when they really could.

Other methods to encourage subjects to breach posthypnotic amnesia also demonstrate that the ''forgotten'' information is more accessible than psychoanalytic theorists acknowledge. Three such methods were used in one experiment (Coe & Sluis, 1989). Some subjects were told that a lie detector indicated they definitely were lying when they said they could not remember anything else about the hypnosis experience. Other subjects were shown a videotape of their hypnotic experience, while still others were simply encouraged to be honest. All three of these procedures led subjects to report information they previously had said they couldn't remember. In short, demonstrations of posthypnotic amnesia do not provide the strong evidence for an altered state of consciousness that some psychologists have claimed.

To conclude, the nature of hypnosis remains a mystery. Psychoanalytic theorists continue their attempts to demonstrate an altered state of consciousness different from the waking state. Nontrance theorists continue to challenge these demonstrations. We should point out that the nontrance theorists do not challenge the usefulness of hypnosis or the honesty of the subjects. Few subjects believe they are intentionally deceiving the hypnotist. Just as you act the way you believe a student is supposed to act when in school, hypnotic subjects behave the way they believe hypnotic subjects are supposed to when under hypnosis.

Hypnotic Susceptibility

Not everyone responds the same to a hypnotist's suggestions. Some hypnotic subjects sing like Frank Sinatra, stick their arms in ice water, or report seeing objects that aren't really there. Others begrudgingly close their eyes but fail to react to any of the hypnotist's requests. Most people fall somewhere in between. One of the first things students ask me after a hypnosis demonstration is why some people are so susceptible while others are not. What makes a good hypnotist? What kind of person makes the best subject?

Despite stage hypnotists' claims to be the best at their trade, research shows hypnotic susceptibility is largely a subject variable. The difference between hypnotists for the most part lies in showmanship. Highly susceptible subjects respond to anyone they perceive to be a legitimate hypnotist. In fact, to standardize procedures, many researchers put hypnotic induction procedures on tape. Research assistants play the tape for subjects with no apparent loss in responsiveness. Beginning hypnotists are sometimes disappointed when their subject fails to respond to suggestions, wondering what they did wrong. Had they given intelligence tests, they probably would not blame themselves for a subject who did poorly. But so many performers have promoted the idea of "good" and "bad" hypnotists that it is a difficult concept to shake.

There are a few techniques hypnotists can use to increase the responsiveness of their subjects, especially those subjects who are a bit skeptical at the beginning of the experience (Lynn et al., 1991). People are more susceptible to hypnotic suggestions when the situation is defined as hypnosis and when their cooperation is secured and trust established before beginning. But most hypnotists use these techniques routinely and still find large differences in hypnotic susceptibility. More evidence that hypnosis is a subject variable comes from the finding that hypnotic susceptibility is a fairly stable individual difference. People who are highly responsive to one hypnotist's suggestions probably will also be responsive to another hypnotist. Moreover, how responsive you are to hypnotic suggestions today is an excellent predictor of how susceptible you will be years from now. One team of researchers found an impressive correlation of .71 between hypnotic susceptibility scores taken 25 years apart (Piccione, Hilgard & Zimbardo, 1989).

Box 4.2

Stage Hypnosis

Few audience members are disappointed with a good stage hypnosis show. For some reason it is very entertaining to see a volunteer from the audience sing like Elvis Presley or run up and down the aisles looking for Lady Godiva. Stage hypnotists often bill themselves as the world's best, and people who see the performance are usually convinced of the billing.

However, susceptibility to hypnotic suggestion is more a function of the subject than the hypnotist. The difference between a good hypnotist and a bad one is only a matter of showmanship. Performers take advantage of situational variables and use techniques that virtually guarantee a successful show.

Meeker and Barber (1971) outlined techniques stage hypnotists use to ensure an entertaining performance. These range from techniques based on well-researched social-psychological principles to trickery to outright deception. Some of these techniques are described below.

Selecting Responsive Subjects
Motivation to become hypnotized is one of the most important determinants of how responsive a subject will be. Stage hypnotists often line 10 to 15 chairs across the back of the stage and announce that only the first people to fill the seats will be allowed to participate in the show. A mad scramble for the seats ensues, with the most highly motivated members of the audience quickly and efficiently selected. After a quick induction procedure, the hypnotist may give the group a few quick tests of susceptibility. Those who fail to respond to these early suggestions (perhaps because of stage fright or a "see if you can hypnotize me" attitude) are asked in a polite whisper to leave the stage. The hypnotist is left with a group of extremely responsive volunteers within a few minutes.

Continued

The question then becomes: What kind of person makes the best hypnotic subject?

Early research in this area looked for personality trait measures that correlated with hypnotic susceptibility. Researchers speculated that the best subjects might score high on measures of sensation seeking, imagination, or intelligence and low on measures of dogmatism, independence, extraversion, and so on. Unfortunately, very few correlations were found, and replications were seldom reported (Barber, 1964; Dana & Cooper, 1964; Hilgard, 1965; Kihlstrom, 1985). Short of hypnotizing the subject, no measure was found that reliably predicted susceptibility to hypnosis. Even Freud could not tell beforehand which patients

The Social Psychology of Performance
Several social-psychological factors influence subjects' willingness to cooperate with the performer and put on a good show. For example, subjects have been given the perfect excuse for acting silly—they're hypnotized. The ham in each of us is bound to come out in this situation. Audience reactions encourage wild behavior. The laughter becomes reinforcing, and volunteers may compete to see who can put on the best show.

Tricks to Increase the Appearance of Responsiveness
Although a very entertaining show is possible without them, some hypnotists have tricks to make the audience believe subjects are more responsive than they really are. A hypnotist may whisper instructions that the audience can't hear. Subjects may be told to respond for the sake of the show. Another technique is to fail to challenge subjects. A hypnotist may tell subjects that their arms have become rigid but never ask subjects to try to bend their arms, just in case they can do it.

Deception to Improve the Show
Although it isn't necessary, hypnotists have been known to use stooges—audience plants who work with the hypnotist. Even with genuine volunteers, several deceptive procedures can make hypnosis seem more amazing. Hypnotized subjects may be suspended between two chairs like a human plank. Subjects appear to be so deeply hypnotized that they defy basic structural limits. The audience doesn't realize that most people can perform this task easily when awake. It looks much harder than it is. Other hypnotists demonstrate their ability to eliminate pain through hypnosis by running a flame from a candle, match, or cigarette lighter over the subject's skin. This is impressive until you try it on yourself. As long as you move the flame quickly and don't get too close, or have the flame pointing upward, away from the skin, it's easy to perform this "incredible" task without the aid of hypnosis.

would be highly susceptible. He asserted only that "neurotics can only be hypnotized with great difficulty and the insane are completely resistant" (1905/1960, pp. 294–295).

However, later research identified a few personality variables other than neurosis and insanity that predict hypnotic susceptibility. These studies succeeded where earlier efforts had failed because investigators measured traits that more directly related to the hypnotic experience. For example, a person's ability to become immersed in a role is related to hypnotic susceptibility (Sarbin & Coe, 1972). This may be why drama students are more responsive to hypnotic suggestions than are nondrama students (Coe & Sarbin, 1966).

The most successful efforts to predict hypnotic susceptibility from personality traits come from work on a trait called **absorption** (Tellegen & Atkinson, 1974). People who score high on measures of absorption have the ability to become highly involved in sensory and imaginative experiences. They are open to new experiences and are prone to fantasies and daydreams (Roche & McConkey, 1990). Numerous studies have found that people who score high on measures of absorption are more susceptible to hypnotic suggestions than those who score low (Glisky, Tararyn, Tobias, Kihlstrom, & McConkey, 1991; Nadon, Hoyt, Register, & Kihlstrom, 1991). Thus, if you are the kind of person who gets involved in a good book or a movie and blocks out all experiences around you, you probably also are a responsive hypnotic subject.

Beyond this, three important variables affect hypnotic susceptibility: attitude, motivation, and expectancy. People with a positive attitude toward hypnosis are more susceptible than are those who view hypnosis with suspicion and mistrust (Cronin, Spanos, & Barber, 1971; Diamond, Gregory, Lenney, Steadman, & Talone, 1974). In addition, subjects' motivation to experience hypnosis affects susceptibility (Hilgard, 1970). The more people want to experience hypnosis, the more responsive they will be. Finally, what subjects expect to happen during the hypnotic experience affects their susceptibility. Subjects told in one study that responding to suggestions was difficult were not as susceptible as those told it was easy (Barber & Calverley, 1964). Similarly, subjects who first watched a highly responsive model react to a hypnotist's suggestions were more susceptible than those who watched a nonresponsive model (Klinger, 1970).

In a recent demonstration of the power of expectancies, investigators went so far as to trick subjects into changing their expectations about how susceptible to hypnosis they would be (Wickless & Kirsch, 1989). Some subjects in this study took a battery of personality tests. Two days later, after the tests were supposedly scored by expert psychologists, all subjects were given the same bogus feedback: The tests indicated that they would be highly susceptible to a hypnotist's suggestions. Other subjects were placed in a dimly lit room and asked to imagine that some lights across the room would, for example, turn red or begin flickering. What these subjects did not know is that the experimenter controlled the lights so that they really did begin to turn red or flicker when subjects tried to have these experiences. The experimenter explained that the subject's ability to imagine these things so vividly indicated that he or she would be an excellent hypnotic subject. Finally, to really change expectations, some subjects went through *both* of these procedures.

The subjects then were hypnotized and tested for their level of susceptibility. As shown in Figure 4.2, the subjects who had their expectancy levels raised were significantly more responsive to the hypnotist's suggestions than those who did not go through these experiences. In short, the findings demonstrate again that people tend to act under hypnosis the way they think they are supposed to act. This is why audience volunteers who expect to see people acting bizarre in a hypnosis show tend to act bizarre when they are hypnotized.

Studies demonstrating the researcher's ability to increase hypnotic susceptibility by changing expectations raise another point. Although hypnotic susceptibility is a fairly stable personality variable, is it possible to train people to be more

Figure 4.2

Hypnotic Suscep-
tibility as a
Function of
Expectations

Adapted from Wickless
and Kirsch (1989).

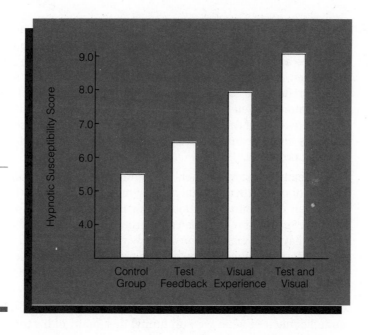

responsive to hypnotic suggestions? Personality traits and skills, such as the ability to become absorbed in a situation, probably are not changed easily. However, a subject's attitudes, expectancies, and motivations may be. Several recent investigations report success in training initially poor hypnotic subjects to increase their level of susceptibility (Gfeller, Lynn, & Pribble, 1987; Gorassini & Spanos, 1986; Spanos, Robertson, Menary, Brett, & Smith, 1987). In each of these investigations, subjects who initially were not very responsive to hypnotic suggestions participated in skill-training procedures. This training included the development of positive attitudes toward hypnosis and changing the subject's expectancy about hypnosis from one of passively receiving suggestions to actively taking part in responding. One investigation found that subjects who had gone through this training still showed signs of elevated responsiveness when hypno-tized a year later (Gorassini, Sowerby, Creighton, & Fry, 1991). In short, if you are a fairly unresponsive hypnotic subject, there may be something you can do to improve your susceptibility. However, how responsive you become probably is limited by your ability to become absorbed in the situation.

Summary

1. A common thread runs through the four topics covered in this chapter. In each case, evidence supporting the Freudian position has been produced by researchers, yet questions about how to interpret these findings remain. While it seems fair to conclude that some empirical support has been obtained for Freud's theory, in no case is this support clear and unequivocal.

2. Researchers examining the content of dreams find that men tend to dream about male characters twice as often as they dream about female characters. Some researchers interpret this finding as evidence of men's preoccupation with other men, a holdover from unresolved Oedipal impulses. Recurrent dreams are said to reflect the same preoccupation. The discovery of REM sleep allowed investigators to better examine the function of dreams. Although it is not clear that deprivation of REM sleep is related to psychological disorders, some research indicates that dreaming may help the sleeper work through and deal with ongoing problems.

3. For many years, researchers have sought methods to manipulate unconscious information and thereby study such Freudian notions as the Oedipus complex. Silverman's subliminal psychodynamic activation procedure may provide such a method. Subjects in Silverman's experiments exposed to tachistoscopic messages often behave in a manner consistent with Freudian theory. In a series of studies, men performed better or worse when receiving messages designed to increase or decrease Oedipal conflict. However, many researchers have been unable to replicate some of these findings.

4. Freud outlined a theory of humor, arguing that sexual and aggressive themes underlie much of what we find funny. In support of his theory, researchers find that people think hostile humor is funnier when it is aimed at someone they dislike and when they are in a hostile mood. In addition, some research indicates that hostile humor reduces the likelihood of aggression, as Freud predicted. However, other studies find the opposite. Finally, the more tension people experience before receiving a punch line, the funnier they find a joke. Although many research findings are consistent with Freud's theory, many also are open to alternative interpretations.

5. Many researchers and therapists explain hypnosis in a manner similar to Freud's description. However, other psychologists challenge the notion of altered states of consciousness and a trance. Although hypnotic subjects often act as if they are acting out of their unconscious, skeptical researchers explain these phenomena in terms of expectancies, motivations, and relaxation. Hypnotic susceptibility is largely a subject variable. People who generally are able to become absorbed in a situation tend to be responsive hypnotic subjects. In addition, attitudes, expectancies, and motivations play a role. There is some evidence that people can increase their susceptibility with training, but how much this helps probably is limited.

Key Terms

subliminal psychodynamic activation A research procedure that attempts to place images into the unconscious through very rapid tachistoscopic exposure.

tachistoscope An instrument capable of presenting very rapid visual images.

neodissociation theory Ernest Hilgard's theory, which maintains that consciousness is divided into aware and unaware parts during hypnosis.

posthypnotic amnesia Hypnotic subjects' inability to recall what occurred during hypnosis after the hypnotist tells them they will not remember.

absorption The ability to become highly involved in sensory and imaginative experiences.

Selected Readings

Balay, J., & Shevrin, H. (1988). The subliminal psychodynamic activation method: A critical review. *American Psychologist, 43,* 161–174. The authors review 23 years of subliminal psychodynamic activation research. Their analysis is highly critical, detailing methodological flaws in much of this research. The authors discuss what this research has taught us about psychoanalytic theory and the procedures used to examine unconscious conflicts.

Barber, T. X. (1969). *Hypnosis: A scientific approach.* New York: Van Nostrand Reinhold. Very clear and persuasive presentation of the skeptics' case against a trance interpretation of hypnosis. Since the publication of this book, Barber's work has been a thorn in the side of those arguing that hypnosis is an altered state of consciousness.

Brody, N. (Ed.) (1987). Special issue: The unconscious. *Personality and Social Psychology Bulletin, 13*(3). A collection of empirical and review articles outlining current efforts by personality researchers to examine unconscious processes. Articles include explorations of unconscious influences on memory, perception, hypnosis, and anxiety.

Hilgard, E. R. (1977). *Divided consciousness: Multiple controls in human thought and action.* New York: Wiley. Ernest Hilgard presents his neodissociation theory of hypnosis in this book. The "hidden observer" experiments are described, and implications for psychology beyond hypnosis are discussed.

The Psychoanalytic Approach
Neo-Freudian Theory, Application, and Assessment

5

Historians, scholars, teachers, and textbook writers have used a number of images and metaphors to describe Sigmund Freud's work and influence. Some picture Freud defiantly marching against the stream of contemporary thought and values. Others describe him as a pioneer blazing new trails into the previously unknown territory of the unconscious mind. I've also seen Freud compared with a diligent detective piecing together clues about the true nature of the human mind or a shrewd lawyer cutting away the ego's defenses one by one. But the metaphor I like best compares Freud with a tree. Like a giant oak standing in the middle of a grove, Freud's theory is the oldest and most formidable of the many psychoanalytic approaches to understanding personality. Just as the oak drops acorns that sprout into their own trees, so did Freud's Psychoanalytic Society generate several scholars who went on to develop their own theories of personality. However, like the surrounding saplings that resemble the great oak, the ancestry of these later personality theories is clearly Freudian.

The collection of scholars who gathered to study with Freud in Vienna included some of the leading thinkers of the day. Not surprisingly, many of these psychologists eventually developed their own ideas about the nature of personality. Unfortunately, Freud and some of his followers often viewed these contributions as more than elaborations or professional disagreements. Sometimes the failure to adhere strictly to psychoanalytic theory as espoused by Freud was seen as blasphemy. Freud apparently viewed almost any deviation from or disagreement with his works as something akin to treason. Gradually, many followers left the Psychoanalytic Society, sometimes forming their own associations and new schools of psychology.

Although none of the theorists described in this chapter ever developed as much fame or influence as Freud, each made a substantial contribution to the psychoanalytic approach to personality theory. Although at the time their differences with Freud may have seemed great, with the perspective of time we can see that their contributions more accurately were elaborations of Freud's theory, rather than radically new approaches to personality. Hence, these theorists have come to be known as the neo-Freudians. For the most part, the neo-Freudian theorists retained the concept of the unconscious as a key determinant of behavior. Most also agreed with Freud about the impact of early childhood experiences on personality development, although many felt that later experiences also influenced adult personality. Most of these theorists also readily accepted such Freudian concepts as defense mechanisms and dream interpretation. In short, the neo-Freudian theories should be viewed as different perspectives within the general psychoanalytic approach to personality.

One feature that remains from the tradition of loyalty and divisions found in that early group of theorists is the tendency to treat the theory's developer more like a prophet than a theorist. For example, we hear people identify themselves as a Jungian or an Adlerian psychologist. Although space doesn't allow more than a brief examination of a few of the major theorists' contributions, students often find one or two of the neo-Freudians has a certain grasp on the nature of human personality that is particularly insightful and thought-provoking for them. In that spirit, I hope the following brief presentation will serve as a starting point for future reading and thought.

Limits and Liabilities of Freudian Theory

If you were to plow through the many volumes written by Freud in his lifetime, you most certainly would find parts of his theory difficult to accept or in need of some elaboration. Although there were many aspects of Freud's theory that later students of psychoanalysis disagreed with, three of the theory's limits and liabilities played a key role in the development of the neo-Freudians' approaches.

First, many of these theorists rejected the idea that the adult personality is formed almost in its entirety by the time a child is five or six years old. While acknowledging that early childhood experiences have a significant impact, many neo-Freudians argued that later experiences, particularly in adolescence and early adulthood, are also important in shaping personality. Are you basically the same person you were five or ten years ago? Many of us would reply that we most definitely are not. Yet according to Freud, the roots of our personalities today lie in our childhood, not in our later experiences.

Second, many neo-Freudians challenged Freud's emphasis on instinctual influences on personality. They argued that he failed to recognize many of the important social and cultural forces that shape who we are. For example, Freud attributed many of the differences he saw between the personalities of men and women to inherent biological differences between the sexes. However, later theorists, most notably Karen Horney, argued that the culture we grow up in plays a large role in creating these differences. Of course, Freud did not ignore social influences altogether. But he failed to give them enough attention to satisfy many of his followers.

Deference for Freud's gigantic achievement should show itself in building on the foundations he has laid.

KAREN HORNEY

Third, some psychologists disliked the general negative tone of Freudian theory. They argued that Freud concentrated on the negative parts of personality. At times he painted a pessimistic and in some ways degrading picture of human nature—people largely controlled by instincts and unconscious forces. Later theorists, both psychoanalytic and otherwise, presented a more positive view of humankind and the human personality. For example, many addressed the posi-

tive features of the ego and emphasized the role of conscious rather than unconscious determinants of behavior. Many spoke of growth experiences and the
satisfaction people obtain from reaching their potential. These alternative views
can be uplifting to those who find Freudian theory just a little depressing.

Alfred Adler

Alfred Adler was the first member of the psychoanalytic group to break with
Freud. The year was 1911, and it was clear to both men that their differences were
fundamental. Unfortunately, the professional dispute became personal as well.
Freud saw Adler's disagreements more as defections than points of discussion.
When Adler left the Vienna group, several members left with him. Friendships
were severed, and accusations were tossed about. Adler went on to develop his
own society, establish his own journal, and even select a name for his new
psychology. He called his approach *individual psychology*. Some of Adler's more
important contributions to our understanding of personality are outlined below.

Striving for Superiority

Adler maintained that all of us begin life with a sense of inferiority. This is to be
expected from a weak and helpless child, surrounded by and dependent for
survival on larger and stronger adults. However, Adler argued that this perception
marked the beginning of a lifelong struggle to overcome these feelings of inferiority. He called this struggle a **striving for superiority**. Whereas Freud based
his motivational constructs on sexual and aggressive themes, Adler maintained
that the striving for superiority was *the* motivating force in life. All other motives
could be subsumed within this single construct. It is difficult to overstate the
importance Adler placed on this concept. "I began to see clearly in every psychological phenomenon the striving for superiority," he wrote. "It lies at the root of
all solutions of life's problems and is manifested in the way in which we meet
these problems. All our functions follow its direction" (in Ansbacher & Ansbacher, 1956, p. 103).

Thus, for Adler, virtually everything we do is designed to establish a sense of
superiority over life's obstacles and thereby overcome our feelings of inferiority.
Why do we strive to obtain good grades, to excel at athletics, to reach a position of
power? Because achieving these things moves us a step further away from our
feelings of inferiority. Moreover, the more inferior we see ourselves, the stronger
our striving for superiority. For example, Franklin Delano Roosevelt was disabled
by polio. Nonetheless, perhaps *because* of this disability, he aspired to become one
of the most influential figures of the 20th century. However, in some cases
excessive feelings of inferiority can have the opposite effect. Some people develop
an **inferiority complex**, a belief that they are so vastly inferior to everyone else
that they experience feelings of helplessness rather than an upward drive to
establish superiority.

But Adler did not equate achievement with mental health. Instead, he argued that well-adjusted people express their striving for superiority through concern for the *social interest*. For example, successful businesspeople achieve a sense of superiority and personal satisfaction through their accomplishments, but only if they reach these goals with consideration for the welfare of others. Success means providing consumers with a good product at a fair price that will make everyone's life a little happier. In contrast, poorly adjusted people express their striving for superiority through selfishness and a concern for personal glory at the expense of others. For example, politicians who seek public office for personal gain and power are poorly adjusted. Those who seek office to help right some of society's wrongs exhibit well-adjusted superiority striving.

Parental Influence on Personality Development

Like Freud, Adler believed that the first few years of life are extremely important in the formation of the adult personality. However, Adler also placed great emphasis on the role of the parents in this process. Two types of parental behavior almost certain to lead to personality problems for the child later in life are *pampering* and *neglect*.

Parents who give their children too much attention and overprotection run the risk of pampering. This pampering robs the child of independence, may cause even stronger feelings of inferiority, and can create the basis for adult personality problems. For example, some parents are afraid to punish or otherwise stifle "bratty" behavior. They may try to protect the child from scary rides, aggressive playmates, and many other ugly truths about life. As a result, the child grows up with an incomplete ability to deal with many of life's problems. You may know some of these formerly pampered children who, as adults, have difficulty living on their own, making their own decisions, and dealing with the daily hassles and frustrations that make up all of our lives. Allowing children to struggle with problems and make some of their own decisions, even if this means making mistakes, is good for them in the long run. Otherwise, their adult lives will be characterized by "extreme discouragement, continuous hesitation, oversensitivity, impatience, support," Adler wrote. "These are always evidence that a patient has not yet abandoned his early-acquired pampered style of life" (in Ansbacher & Ansbacher, 1956, p. 242).

To avoid producing a pampered child, parents should allow children to be independent, to make a few of their own choices and, inevitably, their own mistakes. However, it is also possible to do this too much. Children not given enough attention are, in Adler's words, *neglected*. They likely will grow up cold and suspicious of others. These neglected children become adults incapable of developing strong interpersonal relationships, and they may simply be unable to love.

We all know people who seem unable to return affection. They are uncomfortable with intimacy and may be ill at ease with closeness or touching. We also know people who are extremely dependent on others, who expect to receive but have never learned to give of themselves. To an Adlerian psychologist, this

To be human means to feel inferior. At the beginning of every psychological life there is a deep inferiority feeling.

ALFRED ADLER

Alfred Adler
1870–1937

Alfred Adler's career serves as an excellent example of one man's lifelong striving to overcome feelings of inferiority. Adler was born in Vienna in 1870, the third of six children (one older brother and one older sister). Adler spent much of his childhood in his older brother's shadow. A series of childhood illnesses, particularly rickets, left Adler physically unable to keep up with his brother and other playmates in athletic and outdoor games. He almost died of pneumonia at age four and twice was almost killed when run over by carts in the streets. Because of his physical inferiority, Adler received special treatment from his mother. However, this ended with the birth of his brother. "During my first two years my mother pampered me,"

he recalled. "But when my younger brother was born she transferred her attention to him, and I felt dethroned" (in Orgler, 1963, p. 2).

Adler also experienced feelings of inferiority in the classroom. He achieved only mediocre grades and did so poorly at mathematics one year he had to repeat the course. His teacher advised his father to take the boy out of school and find him an apprenticeship as a shoemaker. But this episode only seemed to motivate Adler. He studied furiously and soon became the best mathematics student in the class. He went on to receive his medical degree from the University of Vienna in 1895.

Adler never studied under Freud, nor did he ever undergo psychoanalysis, as required for becoming a practicing psychoanalyst (Orgler, 1963). The two theorists' association began in 1902 when Freud invited Adler to attend his discussion group after Adler had defended Freud's theory of dream interpretation against attacks in the local newspaper. Adler eventually was named the first president of the group in 1910.

However, growing disagreements with Freud led to Adler's resignation in 1911. Several members joined Adler in forming what was originally called the Society for Free Psychoanalytic Research—a name intended to express their objection to Freud's required adherence to his theory. Adler later changed the name of the association to Individual Psychology, established a journal, and received wide acceptance of his alternate interpretation of strict Freudian theory. As in his other battles to overcome early feelings of inferiority, so did Adler succeed in climbing out of Freud's shadow.

extreme coldness or excessive self-centeredness indicates a lifelong pattern that began with either excessive neglect or excessive pampering by the parents. These people may be helped through psychotherapy, but not until they have offended and alienated many people who otherwise might have been their friends or lovers.

Birth Order

Adler was the first psychologist to emphasize the role of **birth order** in shaping personality. That is, by virtue of the order of their birth, first-born children in a family are different in personality from middle-born children, who are different from last-born children. According to Adler, first-born children initially are subjected to excessive attention from their parents and thus to *pampering*. First-time parents rarely seem to have enough film and seldom miss an opportunity to tell friends and relatives about the new arrival. However, this pampering is short-lived. With the arrival of the second child, the first-born is "dethroned." Now attention must be shared with, if not relinquished to, the newest member of the family. The first-born's perception of inferiority is likely to be strong. Adler suggested that among first-borns we often find "problem children, neurotics, criminals, drunkards, and perverts."

Adler's assessment of middle children — Adler himself was a middle child — was more positive. These children are never afforded the luxury of being pampered, for even when they are the youngest there is always another sibling or two around demanding much of the parents' time. Adler argued that middle children develop a strong superiority striving, always in an effort to catch and surpass the older siblings. This tendency to challenge and overcome others in every sort of competition continues throughout the second-born's lifetime. "Even when he is grown up and outside the family circle," Adler explained, "he often still makes use of a pacemaker by comparing himself with someone whom he thinks more advantageously placed and tries to go beyond him" (in Ansbacher & Ansbacher, 1956, p. 379).

Although Adler believed that first-borns made up the greatest proportion of problem children, he felt that last-borns were a close second. These children are pampered throughout their childhood by all members of the family. Although older children often remark at how their little brother or sister "gets away with murder," which would not have happened "when I was that age," Adler argued that this treatment carries a definite price. A spoiled child is a very dependent child — a child without much personal initiative. Last-born children also are vulnerable to strong inferiority feelings, for everyone in their immediate environment is older and stronger.

Before applying Adler's descriptions to the members of your own family, you should note that research on birth-order effects has not always found support for Adler's predictions (Falbo, 1981; Zajonc, Markus, & Markus, 1979). Although birth order does appear to play a role in personality development, research indicates that the relationship may be a complex one dependent on many other variables.

According to Adler, younger brothers and sisters always see themselves as less capable than their older siblings. This is the beginning of a lifelong struggle to excel and thereby overcome these feelings of inferiority.

As this brief taste of his theory makes clear, Adler's interpretation of the causes of human personality contrasts sharply with Freud's on several important points. For example, Freud described the motives behind the successful businessperson in terms of sublimation. These people are simply expressing unacceptable unconscious motives in socially acceptable ways. Freud might say that defeating business rivals, particularly businessmen, satisfies an unconscious desire to compete with and defeat one's father, a motive left over from the Oedipus complex. However, Adler explained this same achievement behavior as an expression of superiority striving, perhaps influenced by the treatment the businesspeople received from their parents. He might also have guessed that these high achievers are second-born children.

Carl Jung

Perhaps the most bitter of all the "defections" from the Freudian camp was Carl Jung's break with the psychoanalytic circle. In Freud's eyes, Jung was the heir apparent to the leadership of the movement. Jung served as the first president of the International Psychoanalytic Association. However, in 1914, after long and intense disagreement with some of the basic aspects of Freud's theory, Jung resigned from the association. In the years that followed, he continued his work as a psychotherapist, traveled extensively around the world to observe other cultures, and eventually established his own school of psychology, named *analytic psychology.*

Carl Gustav Jung
1875–1961

While biographers debate the extent to which Freud's personality theory reflected his own unconscious, Carl Jung candidly described how his ideas about personality came from his own introspection and experiences. Jung was born in 1875 in Kesswil, a small town in Switzerland. He was a highly introspective child who kept to himself largely because he felt no one would understand the inner experiences and thoughts with which he was preoccupied. Jung spent many childhood hours pondering the meaning of dreams and supernatural visions he experienced. When he was 10 he carved a 2-inch human figure out of wood. He kept the figure hidden, spoke to it when alone, and sometimes wrote to it in secret codes.

Jung's desire to understand human personality led him to the young field of psychiatry. He earned his medical degree from the University of Basel in 1900, then went to Zurich to study with Eugen Bleuler, a leading authority on schizophrenia, and later went to Paris to work with Pierre Janet, who was pioneering work on consciousness and hypnosis. Naturally, Jung's curiosity about the human mind soon brought him into contact with Freud's work. After reading Freud's *The Interpretation of Dreams*, Jung began a correspondence with Freud. When they finally met in 1907, the two men are said to have engaged in a conversation that lasted 13 hours. Jung soon became a close colleague of Freud's, even accompanying him on his 1909 trip to lecture at Clark University. It was during this trip that Jung came to appreciate how intolerant Freud was of their disagreements about the nature of personality. Jung formally parted with the Vienna group in 1913.

Jung spent the next seven years in virtual isolation, exploring the depths of his own unconscious. He immersed himself in his fantasies, dreams, and visions in an effort to discover the true nature of personality. Scholars disagree on whether this was a period of voluntary introspection or a lengthy psychotic episode. Jung's autobiography, published just before his death, provides evidence for both interpretations. "An incessant stream of fantasies had been released, and I did my best not to lose my head but to find some way to understand these strange things," he wrote. "From the beginning there was no doubt in my mind that I must find the meaning of what I was experiencing in these fan-

Continued

tasies. When I endured these assaults of the unconscious I had an unswerving conviction that I was obeying a higher will" (1961, pp. 176–177).

Jung reports being visited during these years by various figures and images. He came to see these figures as the archetypal characters that make up the collective unconscious. Jung was convinced of their existence outside of his own mind. For example, he described in detail conversations with a figure he called Philemon. "I held conversations with him, and he said things which I had not consciously thought," Jung wrote. "For I observed clearly that it

was he who spoke, not I. . . . I went walking up and down the garden with him, and to me he was what the Indians call a guru" (1961, p. 183).

Jung emerged from these years of introspection with a new theory of personality. He devoted the rest of his career to a private practice, travel, reading, and studying. His observations during these experiences, combined with his continued introspection, resulted in numerous volumes and lectures about human personality that continue to mystify and excite readers from around the world.

Many students who have a difficult time appreciating Freudian theory have an even more difficult time understanding what Jung was saying about humankind. Part of the problem lies in Jung's frequent incorporation of ancient mythology and Eastern religious views into his writings and theories. These are often unfamiliar and sometimes mysterious to students. But I find that once the initial difficulty with terms and unusual concepts passes, many students find Jung's work among the most intriguing and thought-provoking of the personality theories.

The Collective Unconscious

If you were like most newborn children, you had no difficulty recognizing and developing a strong attachment to your mother. When you were a little older, you probably expressed at least some fear of the dark. When you became a little older yet, you probably had no difficulty accepting the idea that there was a God, or at least some superhuman existence that created and controlled nature. According to Jung, all people have these experiences. If we were to examine history, talk with people from other societies, and thumb through the legends and myths of the past, we would find these same themes and experiences throughout the various cultures of humankind, past and present. Why is this?

Jung's answer was that we all have a part of our mind that Freud neglected to talk about. He called this part the **collective unconscious**, as distinguished from the *personal unconscious*. Like the unconscious Freud talked about, the collective unconscious consists of unconscious thoughts and images. However, these thoughts were never repressed out of consciousness. Instead, each of us was born with this unconscious material, and it is basically the same for all people.

According to Jung, just as we inherit physical characteristics from our ancestors, so do we inherit unconscious psychic characteristics.

The collective unconscious is made up of **primordial images**. Jung described these images as potentialities for responding to the world in a certain way. Thus, newborns react so quickly to their mother because the collective unconscious holds an image of a mother for each of us. Similarly, we react to the dark or to God because of unconscious images inherited from our ancestors. Jung referred to these images collectively as **archetypes**. Among the many archetypes Jung described were the mother, the father, the wise old man, the sun, the moon, the hero, God, and death. The list was almost inexhaustible. Jung maintained there are "as many archetypes as there are typical situations in life."

Before examining some of the Jungian archetypes, we need to appreciate what Jung was proposing. Jung was aware of how mystical this theory sounds to many people when first encountering it. I have seen many students scoff at the idea that each of us is born with a collection of unconscious material that directs our actions and that, like all unconscious material, we have no direct access to. However, the notion of a collective unconscious is "no more daring than to assume there are instincts," Jung argued. "If the assertion is made that our imagination, perception, and thinking are likewise influenced by inborn and universally present formal elements, it seems to me that a normal functioning intelligence can discover in this idea just as much or just as little mysticism as in the theory of instincts" (1936/1959, p. 44).

Some Important Archetypes

Although the number of archetypes may be limitless, a few are particularly important in Jung's writings. Among the more interesting are the anima and the animus, the shadow, and the self.

The **anima** is the feminine side of the male; the **animus** is the masculine side of the female. No matter how much a masculine man might wish to deny it, deep inside is a feminine counterpart. Deep inside every feminine woman is a masculine self. A principal function of this archetype is to guide the selection of a romantic partner and the subsequent relationship. Jung described the process of looking for a mate as the projection of our anima or animus onto potential partners. Jung explained that "a man, in his love choice, is strongly tempted to win the woman who best corresponds to his own unconscious femininity—a woman, in short, who can unhesitatingly receive the projection of his soul" (1928/1953, p. 70). Less poetically, Jung is saying that each of us holds an unconscious image of the man or woman we are looking for. The more someone matches our projected standards, the more we want to develop a relationship with that person. Whereas people in love might prefer to "count the ways," Jung believed the real reason for the attraction lies in the hidden part of our minds inherited from our ancestors through the centuries.

Although the name may be a bit melodramatic, the **shadow** contains the unconscious part of ourselves that is essentially negative, or, to continue the

What attracts this man and woman to one another? According to Jung, these two have projected their anima and animus onto the partner and apparently have found a good fit.

metaphor, the dark side of our personalities. The shadow is located partly in the personal unconscious, as part of repressed negative feelings, and partly in the collective unconscious, as an inherited evil side of humankind. Jung observed that evil was personified in myths and stories in all cultures. In Judeo-Christian writings this archetype is symbolized in the Devil.

Good versus evil is perhaps the most common theme in all literature in all cultures, because the collective unconscious of all people readily grasps the concept. Indeed, Jung described it as central to human functioning. Well-adjusted people are able to incorporate their good and evil parts into a wholeness of self. Jung recommended that we get in touch with and accept the repressed material of the shadow. Otherwise, we will continue to project these evil thoughts onto people of our same sex. Thus, Jung argued that the objectionable characteristics we see in other people may simply be projections of our own objectionable selves. The more we project, the less we're in touch with reality and the more suspicious and hostile we are in our relationships.

The *self* is the organizing and unifying archetype. Working with the ego, the self allows us to feel a sense of unity and oneness, of becoming what we are supposed to become, or, in Jung's term, *self-realization*. When we complain about feeling "torn apart" or "coming to pieces," it means that the self archetype is not working well.

Evidence for the Collective Unconscious

Part of the difficulty people often have in understanding or appreciating Jungian psychology is that this elaborate theory is, at best, hard to support with scientific evidence. However, Jung did not create his theory out of sheer fantasy. Rather, through a lifelong process of studying modern and ancient cultures, and through his career as a psychotherapist, Jung arrived at what was for him indisputable proof that the collective unconscious, as well as the other constructs in his theory, were genuine and important parts of our personalities.

However, Jung's "evidence" does not consist of hard data from rigorous laboratory experiments. Instead, Jung examined mythology, cultural symbols, dreams, psychosis, and even alchemy. The logic behind this approach is that if a collective unconscious exists that is basically the same for each of us, then the primordial images should be found in some form in all cultures and across time. For example, primordial images are often expressed in dreams. But they also serve as symbols in art, folklore, and mythology. People suffering from psychosis may also express these archetype-based images.

Therefore, Jung provides as evidence for the collective unconscious the recurrence of certain images and symbols from all of these sources. For example, why does a symbol like a vulture appear in the dreams of people today in the same basic way it appeared in the religious writings and ancient mythologies of cultures unknown to the dreamer? Jung described an early discovery of such a "coincidence" when he talked with a mental patient suffering from a type of schizophrenia:

> One day I came across him there, blinking through the window up at the sun, and moving his head from side to side in a curious manner. He took me by the arm and said he wanted to show me something. He said I must look at the sun with eyes half shut, and then I could see the sun's phallus. If I moved my head from side to side the sun-phallus would move too, and that was the origin of the wind. (Jung 1936/1959, p. 51)

A few years later, while reading Greek mythology, Jung came across a description of a tubelike element hanging from the sun. According to the myth, the tube was responsible for the wind. How could such an image appear in both the hallucinations of the patient and the stories of the ancient Greeks? Jung explained that the image existed in the collective unconscious of the Greek storytellers as well as psychotic patients and therefore in the collective unconscious in us all.

Jung was probably the most prolific writer among the neo-Freudians. Like Freud, he eventually managed to touch on most aspects of human behavior. Later in this chapter we will review his description of personality types and his views on religion. While most of the neo-Freudians wrote of personality in less mysterious and more tangible terms than Freud did, Jung's thinking took him in the opposite direction. Perhaps the unique flavor of his theory is what has kept his writings so popular for so many years.

Erik Erikson

In the summer of 1927, a young artist wandering about Europe took a job in a school established for the children of Sigmund Freud's patients and friends. This artist, Erik Homburger, who had never received a university degree, became friendly with the psychoanalysts and was later trained by them. After changing his name from Homburger to Erikson, he began to practice psychotherapy and eventually to espouse his own views on the nature of human personality. Although Erikson retained several Freudian ideas in his theory, his own contributions to the psychoanalytic approach were numerous. We will discuss two of these contributions here.

Erikson's Concept of the Ego

Whereas Freud saw the ego as the mediator between id impulses and superego demands, Erikson believed that the ego performed many important constructive functions. To Erikson, the ego is a relatively powerful, independent part of personality that works toward such goals as establishing one's identity and satisfying a need for mastery over the environment. Appropriately, Erikson's approach to personality has been called *ego psychology*.

According to Erikson, the principal function of the ego is to establish and maintain a sense of *identity*. He described identity as a complex inner state that includes a sense of our individuality and uniqueness, as well as a sense of wholeness and continuity with the past and the future. The often overused and misused term **identity crisis** comes from Erikson's work. He used this term to refer to the confusion and despair we feel when we lack a strong sense of identity. Many of us have gone through periods in our lives when we weren't certain of ourselves, our values, or our direction in life. Perhaps you have experienced a time when you felt uncertain about yourself, when you were no longer sure that what you were doing held any value for you. These experiences with identity crises are typical in adolescence but are by no means limited to young people. Many middle-aged people have gone through similar trying periods.

Although identity crises can occur at any time, Erikson believed that they are more likely to occur when certain social conditions shake the basic foundation of people's lives. For example, rapid social change, the threat of war, and drastic rearranging of political and social power all can lead to a loss of stability, a threat to personal values, and feelings of uncertainty. Some people have argued that the

Erik Homburger Erikson

1902–

In reflecting back over the early years of his life, Erik Erikson observed that "it seems all too obvious . . . that such an early life would predispose a person to a severe identity crisis" (1975, p. 31). Indeed, Erikson's struggle with his identity led him to behavior he would later identify as somewhere between neurotic and psychotic. Yet these struggles also provided him with a keen insight into the problems associated with identity, particularly among adolescents and young adults.

Erik was born in Frankfurt, Germany, in 1902, the son of a Danish father and a Jewish mother. His father abandoned the family before Erik was born. Three years later his mother married a Jewish physician, Theodor Homburger, and for many years told her son that Dr. Homburger was his real father. Erikson's identity was further confused by his physical features. Although living in a Jewish family, he retained most of the physical features of his Scandinavian father — blond hair, blue eyes, and he was tall. "Before long, I was referred to as 'goy' in my stepfather's temple," he wrote, "while to my schoolmates I was a 'Jew' " (1975, p. 27). World War I broke out during Erik's early adolescence. By then he was aware of his real father and felt torn between loyalty to Germany and his growing identity as a Dane.

Erik's need to find his own identity erupted upon graduation from public school. His father pushed medical school, but Erik felt the need to resist this expectation. He decided instead that he was an artist and spent the next few years wandering about Europe. His travels eventually brought him to Vienna and into contact with Anna Freud, Sigmund's daughter and a noted psychoanalyst herself. Except for a Montessori teaching credential, his psychoanalytic training with Anna Freud was the only formal education he received after leaving home. Somewhere during these years Erik changed his name to Erik Homburger Erikson, obviously reflecting his changing sense of identity.

Erikson fled the rise of the Nazis in 1933 and settled in Boston. He has held positions with numerous universities since, including Harvard, Yale, the University of California at Berkeley, and the University of Pennsylvania. His first book, *Childhood and Society*, was not published until 1950, when Erikson was nearly 50 years old. During the past four decades, like the mature adults he writes about, Erikson has continued his personal and professional development.

rapid changes in today's society may leave us particularly vulnerable to identity crises. But, as Erikson reflected, "Times of change . . . what other times are there, in our memory?" (1968, p. 104).

Personality Development Throughout the Life Cycle

Freud believed the personality was largely formed during the first few years of life. When we think back over our lives, most of us can see that much of what we are indeed had roots in those early years. Yet I find people frequently point to important changes in their personalities in more recent years. Young adults often describe dramatic changes in personality over a very short period of time. Erikson (1950/1963) maintained that personality development continues throughout a person's lifetime. He outlined eight different stages that he believed we all progress through, each crucial in the development of personality (Figure 5.1).

According to Erikson, each of these eight stages is present in some form at birth. However, each becomes important during a specific period in our lives, marked by a turning point, or *crisis*, in personality development. How we resolve each of these crises determines the direction our personality development will take and influences how we resolve later crises. Each stage is characterized by two alternative ways to resolve the crisis. One of these is adaptive, but the other can lead to adjustment problems. As you read about these stages, you may want to recall how you resolved the crises for the stages you have already passed through. If you're like most students, you'll find more than a grain of truth in Erikson's scheme.

Basic Trust Versus Mistrust   During the first year or so of life, newborns are almost totally at the mercy of those around them. Whether infants are given loving care and have their needs met or whether their cries go unnoticed is the first turning point in the development of personality. The child whose needs are met develops a sense of *basic trust*, what Erikson calls "the most fundamental prerequisite of mental vitality." The sense of basic trust is "a pervasive attitude toward oneself and the world . . . an essential trustfulness of others as well as a fundamental sense of one's own trustworthiness" (Erikson, 1968, p. 96). For the child who receives adequate love and attention, the world is a good place, people are loving and approachable. Unfortunately, some infants never receive the loving care they need. As a result, they develop a sense of *basic mistrust*. These children begin a lifelong pattern of estrangement and withdrawal from others, trusting neither themselves nor other people.

Autonomy Versus Shame and Doubt   By the second year of life, children are actively developing a sense of who they are relative to the rest of the world. They want to see what they can do — is the world something they can control or something that controls them? This age is filled with a series of tests to determine the extent and limits of the child's own power. Children allowed to develop a sense of *autonomy* will feel independent, be self-expressive, and develop self-confidence. However, just as Adler warned against pampering children, Erikson observed that overly protective parents hinder the development of a sense of autonomy in children this

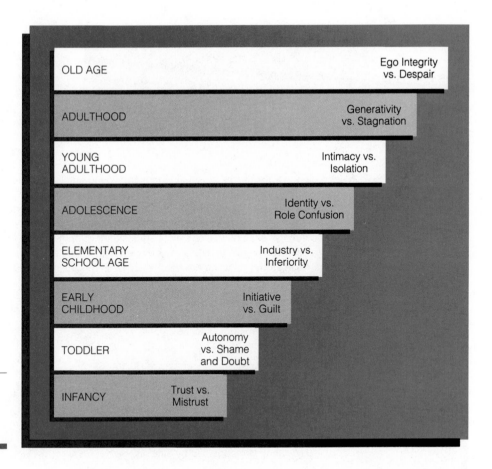

Figure 5.1

Erikson's Eight
Stages of
Development

OLD AGE	Ego Integrity vs. Despair
ADULTHOOD	Generativity vs. Stagnation
YOUNG ADULTHOOD	Intimacy vs. Isolation
ADOLESCENCE	Identity vs. Role Confusion
ELEMENTARY SCHOOL AGE	Industry vs. Inferiority
EARLY CHILDHOOD	Initiative vs. Guilt
TODDLER	Autonomy vs. Shame and Doubt
INFANCY	Trust vs. Mistrust

age. If not allowed to explore and gain a sense of personal mastery and influence, children develop feelings of *shame and doubt*. These are the children who hide their faces when addressed by adults.

The feeling of self-control that most children develop at this stage is the beginning of the perception of free will. Children who develop strong feelings of autonomy will enjoy exercising control over their own destiny later in life. Their self-confidence allows them to challenge and conquer tough obstacles. In contrast, children who develop feelings of shame and doubt may forever be followers, dependent and unsure people who lack the belief in their own abilities required for survival in highly competitive fields.

Initiative Versus Guilt   The next few years of life (roughly equivalent to Freud's phallic stage) are crucial in the development of the child's sense of *initiative*. The successful resolution of this crisis leads to a sense of ambition and purpose. Initiative directs the sense of autonomy that children bring from the previous stage. With the development of initiative comes the pleasure of undertaking a task

A Sense of Personal Identity

According to Erik Erikson, most teenagers and young adults struggle to form a sense of personal identity. As with the other stages of development, how well you resolve this crisis sets the pattern for future personality development and adjustment. Ochse and Plug (1986) developed a scale to measure the extent to which adults have successfully passed through each of Erikson's eight stages of development. The items for the identity formation versus role confusion stage are presented below. You can take this part of the test yourself by indicating *how often* each of these statements applies to you, using the following four-point scale:

    1 = Never applies to me
    2 = Only occasionally or seldom applies to me
    3 = Fairly often applies to me
    4 = Very often applies to me

_____ 1. I wonder what sort of person I really am.
_____ 2. People seem to change their opinion of me.
_____ 3. I feel certain about what I should do with my life.
_____ 4. I feel uncertain as to whether something is morally right or wrong.
_____ 5. Most people seem to agree about what sort of person I am.
_____ 6. I feel my way of life suits me.
_____ 7. My worth is recognized by others.

Continued

"for the sake of being active and on the move." Failure to develop a sense of initiative can lead to feelings of *guilt* and resignation rather than initiative.

The conscience, too, is developed during this stage, as are the beginnings of sexual self-images, important for future identity. By the time children leave this stage of development they are no longer babies or toddlers, but young boys and girls. If a strong sense of initiative has been developed, then the person has a "sense of purpose . . . a steadily growing conviction, undaunted by guilt, that 'I am what I can imagine I will be'" (Erikson, 1968, p. 122). This conviction will direct the child in later years, perhaps providing the motivation to make it through college or the confidence to "market" himself or herself within the business community.

Industry Versus Inferiority   We all can look back on our elementary school days and recall with fondness or pain our achievements and the discovery of personal limits. Most children enter this age thinking there is little they can't do. But soon

A Sense of Personal Identity, continued

_____ 8. I feel freer to be my real self when I am away from those who know me very well.

_____ 9. I feel that what I am doing in life is not really worthwhile.

_____10. I feel I fit in well in the community in which I live.

_____11. I feel proud to be the sort of person I am.

_____12. People seem to see me very differently from the way I see myself.

_____13. I feel left out.

_____14. People seem to disapprove of me.

_____15. I change my ideas about what I want from life.

_____16. I am unsure as to how people feel about me.

_____17. My feelings about myself change.

_____18. I feel I am putting on an act or doing something for effect.

_____19. I feel proud to be a member of the society in which I live.

To obtain your score, first reverse the values you assigned to items 1, 2, 4, 8, 9, 12, 13, 14, 15, 16, 17, and 18. That is, for these items, change an answer of 1 to 4, 2 to 3, 3 to 2, and 4 to 1. The values for the remaining items stay the same. Then add the values for all 19 items.

Ochse and Plug (1986) found average scores for this scale between 56 and 58 when they administered it to South African citizens between the ages of 15 and 60. The standard deviation for this score was between seven and eight, indicating that the majority of people obtain scores that fall within seven or eight points of these average scores. Scores considerably higher than this indicate a particularly well-developed sense of identity, whereas significantly lower scores suggest the test taker is still progressing through the identity development stage.

they begin to compete with other children. Inevitably, they compare their achievements with those of others their age, both in the classroom and on the playground. If children experience success, feelings of competence grow that set them well on their way to becoming active and achieving members of society. But experiences with failure can lead to feelings of inadequacy and to a poor prognosis for productivity and happiness. It is during this time, before the turmoil of puberty and the teenage years, that we develop either a sense of *industry* and a belief in our strengths and abilities or a sense of *inferiority* and a lack of appreciation for our talents and skills.

Identity Versus Role Confusion At last—or perhaps too soon—we reach the teenage years, a time of rapid changes and relatively short preparation for adulthood. The teenage years may be the most difficult time of life. The turmoil of transcending from playground concerns and simple solutions to a sudden bout with life's important questions can be disturbing, even cruel. Erikson was well aware of the significance of these years. Young men and women begin to ask the all-important question, "Who am I?" If the question is answered successfully, they develop a sense of *identity*. They make decisions about personal values and religious questions. They understand who they are and can accept and appreciate themselves. But unfortunately, many people fail to develop this strong sense of identity and instead develop *role confusion*.

In this search for identity, adolescents may join cliques, commit to causes, or drop out of school and drift from one job and situation to another. An acquaintance of mine, apparently struggling with role confusion, bounced from devout Christianity to alcohol and drugs, to Eastern religions, to social causes, and to conservative politics — all during his high school years — in an effort to "find" himself. Ten years later, at our high school class reunion, I found that he had spent the decade drifting to different parts of the country, different jobs, several colleges, and was currently thinking of becoming a rock star. His failure to develop a strong sense of identity had clearly impeded his later personality development.

Intimacy Versus Isolation The teen years dissolve swiftly into young adulthood, when the development of intimate relationships attains primary importance. Young men and women begin to seek out a special relationship within which to develop *intimacy* and grow emotionally. This need to develop a "true and mutual psychological intimacy" with another person includes friendships as well as romantic encounters. Although the development of intimacy within these special relationships typically results in marriage or a romantic commitment to one person, this need not always be the case. One can share intimacy without marriage and, unfortunately, marriage without intimacy.

People who fail to develop intimacy during this stage face emotional *isolation*. They may pass through many superficial relationships without finding the satisfaction of closeness and emotion promised by genuine relationships. Indeed, they may avoid relationships calling for emotional commitment or increased intimacy. The "swinging singles" life style has its advantages and may be pleasant for a while, but failure to move beyond this can seriously retard emotional growth and personal satisfaction.

Generativity Versus Stagnation As men and women approach the middle years of life, they develop a concern for guiding the next generation. Parents find their lives enriched by the influence they can have on their children. Childless adults may find this enrichment as well, through their interactions with young people. For example, we often find these people volunteering to help with youth groups or taking an active role in the rearing of nieces and nephews. A sense of personal satisfaction comes from such work.

Adults who fail to develop a concern for the development of young people suffer from a sense of *stagnation* — a feeling that this is where it all ends, a sense of boredom and personal impoverishment. We've all seen parents whose lives are filled with continued meaning and interests through raising their children. Unfortunately, we've also seen parents who obtain little pleasure from this process. As a result, they become bored and generally dissatisfied with their lives. Failure to see

Erikson described old age as a time for either feelings of integrity and satisfaction with life or feelings of despair and contempt for others.

the potential for personal growth in the development of their children is tragic for parent and child alike.

Ego Integrity Versus Despair   Inevitably, most of us keep our appointment with old age. But, according to Erikson, we still have one more crisis to resolve. Reflections on past years and experiences, as well as the inevitability of our approaching death, cause us to develop either a sense of integrity or feelings of despair. Men and women who look back on their lives with satisfaction will pass through this final developmental stage with a sense of *integrity*. "It is the acceptance of one's one and only life cycle . . . as something that had to be and that, by necessity, permitted of no substitution," Erikson wrote. "And an acceptance of the fact that one's life is one's own responsibility" (1968, p. 139).

People who fail to develop this sense of integrity fall into *despair*. They realize that time is now all too short, that the options and opportunities available to younger people are no longer there. A life has passed, and those who wish they could do it all differently will express their despair through disgust and contempt for others. Although few things in life are sadder than an older person filled with despair, few things are more satisfying than an elderly person filled with a sense of integrity.

Karen Horney

Unlike many of the neo-Freudians, Karen Horney (pronounced Horn-eye) was not a student of Freud's. Instead, Horney studied Freud's work indirectly and later taught psychoanalysis at the Berlin Psychoanalytic Institute and the New York Psychoanalytic Institute. But, like many of the others, she soon began to question some of the basic tenets of Freudian theory. In particular, Horney found she could not accept some of Freud's views concerning women — views she believed to be misleading, perhaps insulting. Horney rejected Freud's description of inherent differences between the personalities of men and women, and instead recognized the impact cultural and social forces had on these differences. Eventually, she became so convinced of the importance of these factors that she and the members of the New York Psychoanalytic Institute agreed that she should leave the institute. She resigned in 1941 and founded her own American Institute for Psychoanalysis.

Horney emphasized the role of cultural and social influences on personality development throughout her work. She argued that all neurosis is culture-dependent, in that the norms for behavior are defined by the particular culture (Horney, 1937). For example, among Native Americans being extremely passive or extremely aggressive is considered either abnormal *or* highly desirable, depending on the particular tribe. Horney pointed out that working hard even after all of one's needs have been ensured is a highly admired behavior in America. But in ancient Greece the same behavior was considered "positively indecent." This analysis contrasts with the Freudian view, which describes neurotic behavior in terms of innate intrapsychic conflicts that are not dependent on the particular social setting. This emphasis on social influences is illustrated in two of Horney's contributions to the psychoanalytic approach: her views on neurosis and on feminine psychology.

Neurosis

We all know people who fit Horney's description of neurotic. Let me give three examples of people I have met. One is a woman who at first appears friendly and warm. She's always doing things with people, always quick to pass along a compliment. But people soon find that her attention turns into demands. She can't stand to be alone, can't accept the idea that her friends or romantic partners would be interested in doing anything without her. Although her relationships never work out for long, she inevitably "falls in love" almost as soon as she meets the next man. The second example is a man who was disliked by almost everyone he went to college with. Few people escaped his sarcastic, sometimes biting, comments. He seemed to hold everyone he encountered with contempt. I never heard him say a nice thing about anyone. Today he is a successful, if not cutthroat, businessman. The third example is a woman who works in a small office tabulating figures. She rarely socializes with the other people who work for the same company, so now most of them have stopped asking her to join them. She has few friends and spends most of her evenings by herself.

Karen Horney
1885–1952

Karen Danielsen was born in Hamburg, Germany, in 1885, the daughter of a sea captain and his young, second wife. From her earliest years on, she faced the injustices and rejection that came from being a rebellious woman in a man's world. Her father was a strict authoritarian who used Bible verse to promote his views on the superiority of men. Karen's older brother, Berndt, was awarded opportunities, including college and an eventual law degree, that her father believed unnecessary for a female. Karen responded to this by vowing in elementary school to always be first in her class, and at age 12 decided she would one day go to medical school.

Karen's mother persuaded her father to allow Karen to go to college, where she met and married Oskar Horney in 1909. In 1915 she received her medical degree from the University of Berlin, one of the very few female students in one of the few schools to accept women. She underwent psychoanalysis as part of her psychoanalytic training but found it insufficient for dealing with her lifelong bouts with depression. At one point, her husband was reported to have rescued her from a suicide attempt (Rubins, 1978). Despite her depression, her doubts about psychoanalysis, and a number of personal problems—including the premature death of her brother, a strained marriage, and eventual divorce—her career prospered. She worked at the Berlin Psychoanalytic Institute and later emigrated to America where she joined the New York Psychoanalytic Institute in 1934.

However, it was not in Horney's character to check her growing dissatisfaction with several important aspects of Freud's theory. This open questioning created great strain with the other members of the institute, who in 1941 voted to disqualify her as an instructor. According to most reports of this event, Horney received the vote in a dramatically silent room. She responded by leaving the meeting in a dignified and proud manner, without uttering a word. Horney went on to establish her own highly successful American Institute for Psychoanalysis. By the time of her death in 1952, it was clear she had made great progress in her battle against the male-dominated and paternalistic psychoanalytic school of thought.

According to Horney, what these three people have in common is that each is extremely unhappy, desperately fighting off inner feelings of inadequacy and insecurity. Although they eventually drive everyone away with their chosen external behavior, on the inside they are scared and pitiful people trapped in a self-defeating interpersonal style. These styles are in fact a type of defense mechanism to ward off their feelings of anxiety.

What is it in the backgrounds of these people that has led them to what they are today? Freud conceived of neurosis in terms of fixated energy and unconscious battles between various aspects of the personality. But Horney said this behavior starts with disturbed interpersonal relationships during childhood. In particular, she believed children often grow up in a home that creates intense feelings of anxiety. Some children develop a sense "of being isolated and helpless in a potentially hostile world" (1945/1966, p. 41). The ways a parent can generate these feelings are almost endless:

> . . . direct or indirect domination, indifference, erratic behavior, lack of respect for the child's individual needs, lack of real guidance, disparaging attitudes, too much admiration or the absence of it, lack of reliable warmth, having to take sides in parental disagreements, too much or too little responsibility, overprotection, isolation from other children, injustice, discrimination, unkept promises, hostile atmosphere, and . . . [a] sense of lurking hypocrisy in the environment. (1945/1966, p. 41)

In short, parenting is not an easy job. Whereas having and raising children is one of the most important functions within our society, there is practically no training for the job and few restrictions exist on who can raise children and how they should be raised. And so we end up with too many children who lack a sense of personal worth, who are afraid and unsure of how to deal with their parents, who fear unjust punishment from their parents for reasons they can't understand, who feel insecure and inadequate, and who desperately want but fail to receive the warmth and support they need. These children are confused, afraid, and anxious.

How do the children deal with this anxiety? According to Horney, children growing up in one of these neurotically infested homes soon develop strategies for coping with their environment. On the positive side, these strategies usually are successful in alleviating some of the anxiety in the short run. Unfortunately, as the child continues to rely on these strategies they develop into "neurotic trends"—styles of interacting with others that become ingrained in the personality.

Horney maintained that neurotics adopt one of three general interaction styles in their efforts to avoid further anxiety-provoking experiences. She called these styles moving toward people, moving against people, and moving away from people. As you read about each of these styles, you'll no doubt see behaviors that you sometimes engage in yourself. That is healthy. Horney explained that nonneurotic people can be flexible in their use of the three styles. In contrast, neurotic people are characterized by their inflexible reliance on only one of these styles for all of their social interactions.

Moving Toward People   Some children learn to deal with their anxiety by emphasizing their helplessness. They become extremely dependent on others, compulsively seeking affection and acceptance. The reduced responsibility and sympathy they receive from others provides temporary relief from their feelings of insecurity and anxiety. Unfortunately, this may soon become their style of interacting — a style that carries over into adulthood. A person who relies on this style "needs to be liked, wanted, desired, loved; to feel accepted, welcomed, approved of, appreciated; to be needed, to be of importance to others, especially to one particular person; to be helped, protected, taken care of, guided" (Horney, 1945/1966, p. 51).

Although these people claim a need for love, they are incapable of genuine love or of deep, rewarding relationships. They often believe that if only they can find love, everything else will be all right. They may indiscriminately attach themselves to whomever is available, for any relationship is better than loneliness or feeling helpless and unwanted. If you've ever been involved with someone who meets this description, you undoubtedly can appreciate the futility of pursuing the relationship. Such people do not love, they cling. They do not give, they only take. They do not share affection, they demand it. Inevitably, the relationship is doomed. "The relationship from which he expects heaven on earth only plunges him into deeper misery," Horney explained. "He is all too likely to carry his conflicts into the relationship and thereby destroy it" (1945/1966, p. 62).

Moving Against People   One way to handle anxiety is to cling to others, another is to fight. Some children find that aggressiveness and hostility are the best means of dealing with a poor home environment. They compensate for feelings of inadequacy and insecurity by pushing around and hurting other children. They are rewarded with a fleeting sense of power and respect from other children, but no real friendships. When these children become adults, this neurotic style takes on more sophisticated forms, but it remains an expression of hostility. These neurotic adults retain their ever-present need to exploit others, to take advantage of weaknesses, to be in control, to be powerful.

Horney explained that this neurotic style is characterized by *externalization*, similar to Freud's concept of projection. That is, these adults believe that all people are basically hostile and out to get what they can. They respond to this perception by doing unto others before they can do unto them. Love and other positive emotions are considered silly and sentimental. They enter into relationships only when there is something to be gained. Consequently, relationships with neurotics who adopt this style are necessarily shallow, unfulfilling, and ultimately painful.

Moving Away from People   Some children adopt a third strategy to deal with their anxiety. Instead of interacting with others in a dependent or hostile manner, the child may choose to simply tune out the outside world and eventually the inside world as well. Who needs them? This style is characterized by a striving for self-sufficiency and independence. The desire for privacy is strong. These neurotics seek out jobs requiring little interaction with others. In general, they avoid affection, love, sympathy, and friendship. Because emotional attachment might lead to the kind of pain they remember from childhood, they develop a numbness to any emotional experience. The safest way to avoid anxiety is simply to avoid involvement. This is certainly the wrong kind of person to fall in love with — affection cannot be returned, it is not even felt. Thus, for both participants, the relationship will be shallow and unrewarding.

The Ineffectiveness of Neurotic Strategies In one respect, the three neurotic strategies are successful, in that they allow the person to avoid anxiety, at least for a while. However, eventually these interpersonal styles are bound to be more frustrating and problematic than helpful. If applied compulsively to all situations, none of these three styles can result in a satisfying interpersonal relationship. Without help, these neurotics are doomed to a life of emptiness, the price they pay for their escape from anxiety. Those of us who must interact with them understand the frustration and misery from the other side. Our interactions are rarely pleasant, and long-term relationships are usually disastrous. Yet the neurotic remains trapped in this style. "The compliant type looks at his fellow man with the silent question, 'Will he like me?' " Horney explained. "The aggressive type wants to know, . . . 'Can he be useful to me?' and the detached person's first concern is, 'Will he interfere with me . . . or will he leave me alone?' " (1945/1966, pp. 80-81).

Feminine Psychology

As a psychoanalyst in the 1930s, Horney found herself a woman in a man's world. Many of her initial doubts about Freud's theory began when she found she couldn't agree with some of Freud's disparaging views of women (see Box 5.1). To begin with, Freud maintained that the essence of female development could be found in the concept of penis envy, the desire of every young girl to be a boy. Horney (1967) countered this male-flattering position with the concept of *womb envy*, which maintains that men are jealous of women's ability to bear and nurse children. Horney did not suggest that men are therefore dissatisfied with themselves, but rather that each sex has attributes that the other admires. However, she did suggest that men compensate for their inability to have children through achievement in other domains.

Horney also pointed out that Freud's observations and writings took place at a time when many people considered women as inferior to men in many ways. If a woman living in that era complained that she wished she were a man, it was probably because of the restrictions and burdens placed on her by the culture, not because of inherent inferiorities. In a society where both men and women are free to become whatever they desire, there is little reason to think that girls want to be boys, or vice versa. Once again, Horney was emphasizing the importance of cultural versus innate influences on personality. She saw any apparent differences between the personalities of men and women as largely determined by the social environment they grow up in. In this respect, Horney was well ahead of her time. Her death in 1952 did not allow her to see how feminists would later use her ideas to promote the cause of sexual equality.

Box 5.1

The Freudian View of Women

Karen Horney was one of the earliest critics of Freud's portrayal of women. While writers still debate the extent to which Freud believed that women were inferior to men, it is clear that he often described females in terms that at least implied their inferiority. At various places in his work he suggested that women develop weaker superegos, that neurosis in women is more difficult to cure, and that women unconsciously desire to become men (Freud's notion of penis envy).

Rejection of some of these views came initially from female psychoanalysts, such as Horney and Clara Thompson. Thompson argued that Freud saw women only as a counterpart to men. Thus, instead of accepting childbearing as an important function, Freud described it as compensation for the woman's lack of a penis. Thompson, like Horney, also said that Freud confused the role women were relegated to during his era with a woman's true potential.

Later critics have pointed out some of the long-term influence that Freudian views about women may have had. Because Freudian thinking has influenced generations of psychotherapists and permeated 20th-century thought, these derogatory images of women could be damaging to women generally. Therapists convinced that female patients are naturally inclined toward submissiveness and are of weaker moral character may attempt to get these patients to accept their lot instead of pursuing "masculine" interests. According to Thompson, women growing up in an environment in which they were assumed to be inferior by women as well as men may continue to unconsciously accept that inferiority, even after they have consciously freed themselves from the view. Defenders of Freud point out, however, that he may merely have been a spokesperson for the male-dominant attitudes of his day, rather than an active shaper of those attitudes.

Harry Stack Sullivan

Unlike the other neo-Freudian theorists covered here, Harry Stack Sullivan was born and trained in America. After a rather poor education—Sullivan flunked out of college and obtained a medical degree from a soon-defunct medical school—he went to work as a psychoanalyst. From his experience with psychoanalysis, particularly in treating schizophrenic patients, Sullivan developed his own theory of personality. In many ways, the link with Freudian theory is apparent. Sullivan retained concepts like anxiety and the unconscious. However, he also placed more emphasis on the interpersonal causes and consequences of these Freudian mechanisms than did most psychoanalytic writers. This emphasis places Sullivan's approach somewhere between that of Freudian psychoanalysis and the more recent social learning theorists (see Chapter 13).

According to Sullivan, personality does not even exist in the absence of interpersonal relations, whether real or imagined. A personality "can never be isolated from the complex of interpersonal relations in which the person lives and has his being" (Sullivan, 1953, p. 10). Instead, we can understand people only by observing how they respond to various types of interpersonal situations. Under Sullivan's system, the concept of "self" develops from and has meaning only within our relations with other people. Two of Sullivan's contributions that illustrate his blend of Freudian theory with a more social orientation are presented here. These are his concept of personifications and his description of the stages of personality development.

Personifications

Like Freud, Sullivan placed heavy emphasis on the role of anxiety in his theory. However, Sullivan maintained that feelings of anxiety come from interpersonal experiences. Mothers who experience tension when interacting with their babies communicate their feelings of anxiety to the child. At first the baby has no way to deal with these feelings. However, over the course of a lifetime people learn which behaviors are associated with anxiety and which reduce or eliminate anxiety. One particularly useful mechanism for reducing anxiety is *selective inattention*. According to Sullivan, one effective way to reduce the impact of anxiety-provoking information is to ignore or reject it. If a recent fight with your spouse threatens your sense of security, think of something less threatening. However, like the defense mechanisms described by Freud, the short-term gain in reduced anxiety comes at a price. By paying less and less attention to relevant information, people develop false impressions of reality.

In particular, people develop a false sense of who they are. This process is important in shaping what Sullivan called **personifications** — mental images we have of other people and of ourselves. The most noteworthy of the personifications are those related to the self. According to Sullivan, we all form images of ourselves, and these images fall into three basic categories. The *good-me* personification consists of those aspects of ourselves that we feel good about, that have been rewarded in the past. Most important, these are the behaviors associated with feelings of security, or put another way, without anxiety. In contrast, the *bad-me* personification reflects those parts of our experiences that we would rather not think about, that have not been rewarded. These behaviors are associated with anxiety. We can easily think of examples of these first two personifications. Sometimes we feel content and pleased with our actions. Other times we wince in shame and embarrassment when we think about past words and actions. The feelings you get when thinking about such an embarrassing experience are probably what Sullivan meant by interpersonal anxiety.

Harry Stack Sullivan
1892–1949

Perhaps more than with any other theorist, Harry Stack Sullivan's descriptions of personality development seem distinctly autobiographical. Sullivan's emphasis on the importance of good interpersonal relations, particularly during the adolescent years, may reflect some of his own difficulties and traumas. For example, when Sullivan proposed that a mother's anxiety is transferred to her child, he probably was aware of his troubled relationship with his own mother, who appeared to have suffered from depression. Sullivan's childhood was a lonely and isolated one. He was an only child (two older brothers had died in infancy) and the only Irish Catholic in a Protestant neighborhood.

Sullivan's emphasis on the importance of adolescent relationships probably reflects his turbulent teenage years. When

Sullivan was 8 he developed a strong friendship with a 13-year-old, Clarence Bellinger. Biographers disagree on whether this was a homosexual relationship (Chapman, 1976; Perry, 1984) but acknowledge that it was generally perceived to be. Although Bellinger also became a psychiatrist, their relationship was terminated after Sullivan's adolescent years.

Sullivan's academic background was hardly the stuff great scholars are made of. He was suspended his first year at Cornell University in 1909, after failing all his classes. A few years later, without an undergraduate degree, he entered the Chicago College of Medicine and Surgery, a school of questionable academic quality. Sullivan's diploma was held up a few years until he could make his final tuition payment, and the school folded shortly thereafter. Nonetheless, following World War I, he developed a reputation for his successful treatment of schizophrenic patients in private hospitals in Baltimore and Washington, D.C. In 1927, Sullivan unofficially adopted one of these patients, 15-year-old James, who lived with Sullivan the rest of his life. Sullivan never married. He died from a brain hemorrhage in 1949, at age 56.

The good-me and bad-me personifications exist largely at the conscious level. But Sullivan identified a third self personification, the *not-me*. This represents those aspects of ourselves that are so threatening that we *dissociate* them from the self system and maintain them in our unconscious. According to Sullivan, people are aware of and experience their not-me personification only when sleeping or when schizophrenic. This process of dissociation is similar to Freud's concept of repression. Like repression, dissociation requires a constant effort to keep parts of the self in the unconscious.

Developmental Epochs

Like Freud, Sullivan identified the importance of early childhood experiences in the development of adult personality. He was particularly interested in the relationship between a child and its mother. However, like Erikson, Sullivan argued that personality development continues well beyond the first few years of life. Sullivan believed there were seven distinct stages of personality development — what he called **developmental epochs**. (See Table 5.1.) He called these infancy, childhood, the juvenile era, preadolescence, early adolescence, late adolescence, and adulthood. Unlike Freud, who described developmental stages in terms of an innate biological clock, Sullivan maintained that the stages are largely socially determined. Children go through a particular stage in a particular way partly because of biological changes associated with the stage, but partly because of the typical situation they find themselves in at that age. Children growing up in significantly different cultures probably go through quite different developmental stages.

A key feature of Sullivan's developmental scheme is the significance ascribed to the adolescent years, comprising three of the seven stages. Although the ability to develop adequate, nonanxious relationships begins with the baby's interactions with its mother, Sullivan argued that what happens during the preadolescent and teenage years is crucial for the development of satisfying interpersonal relations. The failure to form satisfying interpersonal relationships often lies at the core of many adult psychological disorders. This contrasts sharply with Freud, who traced disorders back to intrapsychic conflicts from early childhood. Let's look more closely at the three adolescent stages.

The *preadolescent epoch*, the fourth stage of personality development in Sullivan's theory, begins around eight or nine years of age. This stage is characterized by a new need — the need to develop an intimate relationship with a peer. "It is a specific new type of interest in a *particular* member of the same sex who becomes a chum or a close friend," Sullivan explained. "Something very . . . like full-blown, psychiatrically defined *love*" (1953, p. 245). Consistent with Sullivan's theorizing, most of us have seen children this age who become inseparable buddies. Sometimes children this age form larger same-sex gangs. But Sullivan argued that these gangs are still comprised of sets of two. The development of this special friendship serves a couple of psychological functions. It is where the child first develops a sensitivity to other people's needs. In addition, the acceptance and friendship the child experiences validate the preadolescent's sense of worth. Thus, developing this preadolescent relationship is an important step in interpersonal

Table 5.1

Sullivan's Developmental Epochs

Epoch	Appearance Signaled by
Infancy (0–1 year)	Birth
Childhood (1–5)	The acquisition of early speech
Juvenile era (6–8)	The need for playmates
Preadolescence (9–12)	The need for an intimate relationship with a same-sex "chum"
Early adolescence (13–17)	Puberty and a sex drive; the need for an intimate relationship with a member of the opposite sex
Late adolescence (18–early 20s)	Interest in developing a long-term sexual relationship; interest in occupational and financial matters
Adulthood	Establishment of career, adult friendships, and long-term sexual relationship

development. Children who fail to experience such a relationship may experience loneliness — painful feelings that can last through adult life — and they may have difficulty with relationships later in life.

With the onslaught of puberty, the preadolescent period gives way to the *early adolescent* epoch. Along with the physical changes ushered in with puberty come strong feelings of sexual attraction, what Sullivan called *lust*. "After lust gets underway, it is extremely powerful," Sullivan wrote. "In fact, one . . . may well think that lust is the most powerful dynamism in interpersonal relations" (1953, p. 266). The intimacy with a member of the same sex that was achieved in the preadolescent years is replaced with a need for intimacy with a member of the opposite sex.

However, Sullivan observed that in Western society satisfying these new-found needs often leads to "collisions" with other needs. The adolescent must distinguish and balance three needs: the need for personal security (freedom from anxiety), the need for intimacy, and the need for "lustful satisfaction." For many adolescents, feelings of self-worth take a beating during these years. Too often, self-worth becomes synonymous with sexual attraction and performance. Thus, teenagers who feel they are not sexually attractive or who lag behind their peers in sexual activity may experience low self-esteem. In the decades since Sullivan made these observations, there is little evidence that this link between self-worth and sexuality has loosened. Ads for any number of products communicate to us daily that the most desirable people are those who are the sexiest. Further conflicts come from parents, who often don't know how to deal with their children's sexual activity. Sullivan noted that too often parents resort to ridicule or some other type of interference that further shatters the sensitive adolescent self-image.

Many teenagers (and adults) also struggle to resolve their need for intimacy with their sexual desires. This is particularly difficult in a society that sends mixed messages about how to express sexual desires. The double message seems to be, "Sex is dirty, filthy, and disgusting—so save it for someone you love." Sullivan speculates that this conflict is in part responsible for the old "double standard" of sexual behavior for adolescent boys, which separates the girls to have sex with from the girls to have relationships with.

At the end of the teenage years we reach the *late adolescent epoch*. Here the concern is with developing satisfying sexual activity, presumably within a long-term relationship. In addition, this stage marks the transition into the concerns adults must deal with: occupation, financial matters, and the like. Sullivan was quick to point out that how well people pass through this stage depends to a great extent on opportunity. People lucky enough to go to college or who have other professional opportunities have a better chance of moving smoothly into adulthood.

It is also during the late adolescent stage that people often pay the bill for earlier anxiety-reducing tactics. By using selective inattention, some people have developed extremely distorted personifications of themselves. Consequently, their ability to develop satisfying relationships and progress professionally is severely hampered. "Many late adolescents show such superficially incomprehensible falsifications in the person's view of himself," Sullivan observed, "that he is not apt to learn very much . . . unless somebody goes to a great deal of trouble to put him through educative experience" (1953, p. 301). Of course, because this experience is likely to produce anxiety, Sullivan expected most people to resist such help.

Erich Fromm

If you are like most people, you have occasionally felt that life was becoming too overwhelming, that you just wanted someone stronger and wiser to suddenly appear and take care of you and all your problems. Maybe you've thought about how nice it would be to become a child again, to be free from the worries and responsibilities of adulthood. Erich Fromm, a German-born psychologist and relative latecomer to the psychoanalytic field, centered his theory of personality around these feelings of anxiety and the need to escape. His interest in this phenomenon was triggered in part by his observations of the Nazi party's rise to power in Germany in the 1930s. What would cause people to identify with and carry out the desires of the Nazi leaders? Fromm explained this phenomenon within the context of his theory of personality in his famous book *Escape from Freedom* (1941/1965), published at the beginning of World War II.

Erich Fromm
1900–1980

Erich Fromm was born in 1900 in Frankfurt, Germany. As a Jewish child growing up in an anti-Semitic environment, he soon developed an appreciation for the role of sociopolitical forces in shaping human behavior. This awareness was reinforced when he was 14 and World War I broke out in Europe. As an adolescent, Fromm was overwhelmed by the irrationality and destructiveness of the war that surrounded him. These experiences left him with a lifelong curiosity about the nature of human beings. "When the war ended in 1918," he later wrote, "I was a deeply troubled young man who was obsessed by the question of how war was possible, by the wish to understand the irrationality of human mass behavior, by a passionate desire for peace and international understanding" (Fromm, 1962, p. 9).

Fromm sought and found answers to his questions from two sources. Freud helped him understand individual personalities, and Karl Marx explained the sociopolitical influences. Fromm studied Freud and Marx extensively while in school. He received his Ph.D. from the University of Heidelberg in 1922 and studied psychoanalysis at the Berlin Psychoanalytic Institute. Fromm's thinking was also shaped through his firsthand observations of the rise of the Nazis in Germany until 1934, when he emigrated to the United States and watched the developments in Europe from abroad. His interests in psychoanalysis and social issues merged in his 1941 book *Escape from Freedom*, in which he explained the Nazi movement with what some have called a "sociopsychoanalytic" interpretation.

Fromm's career reflected that same curious blend of psychoanalysis and socialism found in his writings. He taught at a number of universities, including Columbia, Bennington College, Yale, Michigan State, New York University, and the National University of Mexico in Mexico City. At the same time, he maintained an active interest in political philosophy and was often involved in many social and political issues.

According to Fromm, the rise of modern democracy has freed humankind in the sense that we no longer are forced into a certain niche in a larger feudal system. We are free to be and do whatever we please. Yet it is this very freedom that creates the greatest problem for us. Once we emerge on our own, we are faced with enormous personal responsibilities, we are isolated, we are alone. Freedom can be frightening. Fromm described it as an "unbearable state of powerlessness and aloneness." As we become aware of our individuality, we become aware of all that we cannot control and come painfully face-to-face with our insignificance. According to Fromm, we respond to this perception of insignificance in one of two ways: We either escape from freedom or we progress toward "positive freedom."

Mechanisms of Escape

Fromm identified three main strategies people use to overcome the feelings of powerlessness and anxiety that accompany freedom. First is **authoritarianism**, the tendency to "fuse one's self with somebody or something outside of oneself in order to acquire the strength which the individual self is lacking" (1941/1965, p. 163). Fromm described the people who used this method of escape as *authoritarian characters*. They reflect an ironic combination of striving for submission as well as striving for domination, or in Fromm's terms, *masochism* and *sadism*. On the one hand, these authoritarian characters try to overcome their feelings of inferiority and helplessness by tying themselves to more powerful people or concepts. On the other hand, they also are motivated to dominate others. This latter sadistic tendency can take the form of exploiting others, causing them physical and mental pain and making them dependent on the authoritarian person. It is just this two-sided authoritarianism that Fromm observed in the members of the Nazi party, obedient to authorities while sadistic to their victims.

According to Fromm, the tendency to submit to higher forces and the need to express power over subordinates are both elaborate defenses against feelings of powerlessness. Because they are mere defenses, they are inadequate and neurotic. Aligning oneself with powerful people and exploiting and controlling others may succeed in generating a sense of personal strength, but authoritarian characters are unable to develop their personalities in a positive direction.

Fromm used this escape from freedom concept to interpret psychological phenomena in a manner slightly different from that of other psychoanalytic theorists. For example, whereas Adler maintained that striving for power and superiority was a positive force, Fromm saw such striving as neurotically motivated and harmful. Instead of striving for superiority, Fromm said people seeking power were striving to escape individuality and freedom. Similarly, Freud described the child's identification with the same-sex parent as a means of resolving the Oedipus complex. However, Fromm suggested that young children identify with the stronger parent because they find it more and more difficult to be independent.

A second mechanism of escape is **destructiveness**. Here the person attempts to overcome life's threatening situations by destroying them. Fromm was

Fromm's most important book, *Escape from Freedom*, was written in part to explain the rise of totalitarianism in Nazi Germany. According to Fromm, citizens joined the Nazi party as an escape from their perception of personal freedom.

struck by the tremendous amount of destruction he found throughout the world. Although destructiveness is unconsciously motivated, people who engage in it as a response to life's anxieties usually rationalize away these antisocial actions. Fromm cited love, duty, and patriotism as common rationalizations for destructive acts. Thus, people who say they are fighting for love of country or out of a sense of duty may in reality be unconsciously striving to overcome feelings of powerlessness and isolation.

Fromm argued that the majority of people in today's society use **automaton conformity**, yet another mechanism of escape. To avoid the anxiety associated with freedom, most of us seek out our own little niche from which we historically have escaped. We find a secure job and life style where we can become a cog in a larger machine. By acting as everyone else acts, we can temporarily escape our own individuality and thereby escape from the threatening aspects of personal freedom. "The individual ceases to be himself; he adopts entirely the kind of personality offered to him by cultural patterns; and he therefore becomes exactly as all others are and as they expect him to be," Fromm wrote. "The person who gives up his individual self and becomes an automaton, identical with millions of other automatons around him, need not feel alone and anxious any more" (1941/1965, pp. 208-209).

Poets, novelists, artists, wanderers, and philosophers often comment on the lack of individuality in modern society. We dress alike, talk alike, tend to follow the same fads, like the same music, adopt the same values, and buy the same products as almost everyone else in our culture. Are your values, career goals, likes, and dislikes really yours, or have you merely adopted the standards and rules set for you by society? Even "nonconformists" often adopt the nonconformist styles of others. Fromm argued that the thoughts, feelings, and actions most of us believe to originate from within are usually just reflections of the external world and the restrictive roles we have adopted. As long as we continue in that role, we avoid facing the threatening prospect of becoming our genuine selves. But we also miss out on the experience that Fromm called *positive freedom*.

Positive Freedom

Those who do not escape from freedom through one of the mechanisms described above may succeed in continuing the process of *individuation*. Individuation begins when children become aware of themselves as separate and unique beings. It develops into a growing understanding and appreciation of ourselves for what we are. "There is nothing of which we are more ashamed than of not being ourselves," Fromm wrote. "And there is nothing that gives us greater pride and happiness than to think, to feel, and to say what is ours" (1941/1965, p. 288). Fromm called this process of appreciating and acting like our real selves **positive freedom**.

The key to developing positive freedom is *spontaneity*—allowing ourselves the emotional and intellectual expression that otherwise might be hidden in some type of escape strategy. We express these inner feelings when we stop to appreciate the beauty of a sunset or allow ourselves to fall in love. Love is the "foremost component" of spontaneity. In his popular book *The Art of Loving* (1956/1974), Fromm explained that, because love is an art, it requires the effort and knowledge that other types of art demand. We do not merely "fall" in love or experience the pleasant sensation of love. Love is an active process in which we continue to develop our sense of individuality. The end product of spontaneity and individuation is happiness.

Application: Psychoanalytic Theory and Religion

The psychoanalytic theorists did more than describe personality and develop treatments for psychological disorders. In many ways, these writers offered an important new perspective on humankind and the enduring philosophical issues about the human condition. Inevitably, their questions overlapped with the ones traditionally addressed by theologians: Are people inherently good or bad? Why should we sacrifice personal pleasure for the common good? Are religious experiences genuine, or do they reflect an underlying disorder?

Why do people feel deeply about their religious beliefs? This is one of the questions addressed by Freud and many of the neo-Freudian theorists. Freud declared religion a delusion, while Jung pondered over the nature of religious experiences throughout his career.

In a style that typified his career, Freud directly challenged conventional thinking about many religious issues. In two of his books in particular, *The Future of an Illusion* and *Civilization and Its Discontents*, he assaulted widely held religious beliefs. Although Freud understood that organized religion could provide some solace for uneducated people, he lamented its widespread acceptance by intelligent people. "The whole thing is so patently infantile, so foreign to reality," Freud wrote, "that to anyone with a friendly attitude to humanity it is painful to think that the great majority of mortals will never be able to rise above this view of life" (1930/1961, p. 21).

Why, then, do so many people believe? According to Freud, religious behavior represents a form of neurosis stemming from the baby's feelings of helplessness and longing for a powerful protector, presumably the father. These feelings are "permanently sustained by fear of the superior power of Fate." Thus, Freud calls religion a type of collective wish fulfillment. To protect ourselves from a threatening and unpredictable world, we project our imagined savior from this predicament outward in the form of a God. To Freud, God is but an unconscious father figure generated in an infantile way to provide us with feelings of security.

Not surprisingly, Freud's views on religion have generated considerable reaction from theologians and religious scholars. Some have embraced his position, many have argued against it. Discussion of the psychoanalytic interpretation of religion was expanded in the writings of several neo-Freudians. The neo-Freudian theorist who stimulated the most discussion about the intersection between psychology and religion was Carl Jung.

Jung, whose father was a minister in the Swiss Reformed Church, addressed religious issues in numerous places in his writings. It is apparent from these references that Jung struggled with religious issues throughout much of his life, often wavering between favorable and unfavorable impressions of modern religion. He once referred to "the religious myth," yet at another point he described religious experience as "a great treasure" providing "a source of life, meaning, and beauty" (Bechtle, 1984).

Jung often insisted that the question of God's existence was outside the realm of science and hence nothing he could provide answers about. His interest was with humankind's eternal need to find religion. Why does religion surface in all cultures? Why is some entity similar to the Judeo-Christian God found in each of these cultures? Jung's answer was that each of us inherits a God archetype in our collective unconscious. This primordial image causes God-like images to surface in the dreams, folklore, artwork, and experiences of people everywhere. We can easily conceive of a God, find evidence for His existence, and experience deep religious feelings because we were born with a kind of unconscious predisposition for Him.

Scholars continue to debate if Jung meant by this that God exists only in our collective unconscious and therefore that the traditional description of God as an external entity is a myth (Bianchi, 1988). Although at times Jung does appear to argue that God exists only in the human mind, other references suggest he was not ready to make such a bold statement. In contrast, Erich Fromm (1966) was more direct in expressing a similar view of God as the projection of an internal image. God, he said, was "a historically conditioned expression of an inner experience" (p. 18).

Jung maintained that organized religions often took advantage of powerful archetypal symbols in promoting themselves to followers. Indeed, he described Christ as a symbol, with the four points on the cross representing the good versus bad and the spiritual versus material aspects of our being. As with other archetypes, symbolic representations with religious connotations appear in a number of places. In addition to religious art and scripture, Jung said religious symbols are often found in our dreams and in the hallucinations of psychotic patients.

Toward the end of his career, Jung seemed to take a more favorable approach to organized religion. He acknowledged that religion often provided followers with a sense of purpose and feelings of security. According to Jung, many patients seek out psychotherapy when their religion fails to provide reassurance and solace. Thus, modern psychotherapy has taken on the role once reserved for the clergy. Of particular importance for many of Jung's patients was the need to resolve the good and evil sides of their personalities. Therapists try to help these patients through a variety of therapy techniques. However, Jung argued that modern religions have developed their own practices to achieve the same end. For example, churches use confession, absolution, and forgiveness to symbolically help followers reconcile the evil side of their selves with the good.

Erich Fromm also was fascinated by the seemingly universal human need for religion. He explained this need within his theory of escape from freedom. People turn to the powerful authority of the church to escape the sense of powerlessness

The religions of mankind must be classed among the mass-delusions. No one, needless to say, who shares a delusion ever recognizes it as such.
SIGMUND FREUD

and loneliness that accompanies their awareness of individuality. "People return to religion . . . not as an act of faith but in order to escape an intolerable doubt," Fromm wrote. "They make this decision not out of devotion but in search of security" (1950, p. 4). The notion that we are individuals, responsible for ourselves and for finding our own meaning in life, is frightening to many people. Religion provides an escape from these fears.

Thus, according to Fromm, the same anxieties and insecurities that cause some people to align themselves with powerful political and social forces lead other people to religion. Submission to an authoritarian leader gives many people a sense of strength and security. Similarly, by surrendering their sense of who they are to a God people obtain the satisfaction of feeling protected by an awe-inspiring power.

However, Fromm also drew a distinction between *authoritarian religions* and *humanistic religions*. The former emphasize that we are under the control of a powerful God, while in the latter God is seen as a symbol of our own power. In a humanistic religion "man must develop his power of reason in order to understand himself, his relationship to his fellow men and his position in the universe," Fromm wrote. "Man's aim is to achieve the greatest strength, not the greatest powerlessness" (1950, p. 36). Authoritarian religions deny people their personal identity. Humanistic religions provide an opportunity for personal growth. Thus, while condemning some religions, Fromm recognized the potential for continuing the process of individuation and finding happiness in others.

Today the writings of Freud, Jung, Fromm, and some of the other psychoanalytic theorists are studied and debated by theology students around the world. Some scholars have even looked into these theorists' backgrounds to understand what there might have been in their childhoods to generate such a rejection of modern religion (cf. Meissner, 1984). But while most theologians probably reject these psychoanalytic interpretations of religious behavior, few are able to ignore them.

Assessment: Measuring Types

Because most neo-Freudian theorists did not fall far from the Freudian tree, they share many assumptions about personality assessment with Freudian psychologists. For example, most agree that crucial information needed to understand psychological disorders is often buried in the unconscious. Therefore, neo-Freudian psychologists rely heavily on the projective techniques, reviewed in Chapter 3, to measure personality. Neo-Freudian psychotherapists commonly use the Rorschach inkblot test and similar measures to tap into otherwise inaccessible regions of the mind.

However, unlike most Freudians, many neo-Freudians do not limit their assessment of personality to projective measures. One example of this is the identification of psychological types, as described by Carl Jung. Although Jung maintained that the roots and structure of different personality types are based in the unconscious, later Jungian psychologists found they could identify these types through clients' self-reports of their overt behaviors and feelings. As we will see, the use of Jung's types theory and the inventory designed to measure personality types has become quite popular in such areas as psychological counseling, career counseling, and education.

Jung's Theory of Psychological Types

Like many early psychologists, Carl Jung was struck by individual differences in personality. As he struggled to make sense of the many different personalities he encountered in his practice and travels, Jung eventually arrived at an important distinction. "There is a whole class of men who at . . . a given situation at first draw back a little as if with an unvoiced 'no,' and only after that are able to react," he wrote. "And there is another class who, in the same situation, come forward with an immediate reaction, apparently confident that their behavior is obviously right" (1933, p. 85). You probably can think of examples of these two types. We all know people who are apprehensive about entering a social gathering. They are likely to wait for someone to approach them rather than initiating a conversation themselves. We also know people who can enter the same gathering and begin interacting with no hesitation.

This distinction reflects what Jung identified as the two basic *attitudes*. The former case he called *introversion*, in which the dominant tendency is to channel psychic energy inward. Introverts tend to focus their attention to their inner worlds; they are introspective and withdrawn socially. For other people the dominant tendency is to focus psychic energy outward. This *extraversion* is characterized by an outgoing, active style and an interest in people and the external world.

But Jung soon recognized there were more than two types of people in the world. So he began to look at the relationship between a person's consciousness and experience, or how we perceive and make sense of the world. "I had always been impressed by the fact that there are a surprising number of individuals who never use their minds if they can avoid it," he wrote, " . . . [and] others who seemed to live . . . as if the state they had arrived at today were final, with no possibility of change . . . they seemed devoid of all imagination" (1964, p. 48).

From such observations, Jung identified what he called the four basic *functions*: sensation, intuition, thinking, and feeling. Sensation and intuition are the *irrational functions*, in that they are concerned with how we perceive information. Thinking and feeling are the *rational functions*, concerned with reason and judgment. "*Sensation* tells you that something exists; *thinking* tells you what it is; *feeling* tells you whether it is agreeable or not; and *intuition* tells you whence it comes and where it is going" (Jung, 1964, p. 49).

Of course, each of us uses all four functions, but Jung argued that one of these becomes our dominant mode of experience. If sensing is your dominant mode, you tend to focus on the immediate experience. You probably have developed excellent powers of observation and a keen memory for detail. However, if intuition is dominant, you are more likely to perceive experience in terms of possibilities and relationships with other concepts. You rely on insight and hunches, are often imaginative and abstract. On the other hand, people with a

Table 5.2

Jung's Eight Psychological Types

| Function | Attitude | |
	Extraversion	Introversion
Thinking	Focus is on learning about the external world. Practical, objective thinker. Interested in facts. Sometimes appears cold and impersonal. Makes a good scientist. Interested in using logic and applying rules.	Interested in understanding own ideas. Reflective, interested in philosophical issues and the meaning of one's own life. May be stubborn, distant, or arrogant. More interested in understanding himself or herself than in examining other people.
Feeling	Likely to be moody, capricious. Easily conforms to the group norm. Likes to follow fads and fashions. Can be highly emotional at times. Can change emotions quickly in a new situation.	Has deep emotional experiences, but keeps them to himself or herself. May appear silent and perhaps self-assuredly cold, but actually hiding strong emotions just under the surface. Often a nonconformist.
Sensing	Interested in experiencing the external world. Often sensual and can become obsessed with pleasure seeking. May live life for the pleasure of the moment.	More interested in own thoughts and inner sensations than external objects. May only be able to express himself or herself only through an outlet such as art or music, and these expressions typically are not understood by many.
Intuitive	Constantly seeking new challenges and interests in the external world. Gets bored easily with jobs and relationships. Enjoys novel situations. Tends to be unstable and flighty.	Likes to explore new and different ideas but has difficulty developing insights or communicating them to other people. May consider self a prophet or dreamer whose ideas will be carried out by others. Often fails to understand reality or social norms, thus totally impractical in planning.

dominant thinking function analyze perceived information in a logical, objective manner. These people actively and critically dissect all arguments and logic thrown their way. Finally, if your dominant function is feeling, you interpret information in terms of values and subjective impressions. You are more concerned with the human element than the technical one when making decisions.

The two attitudes and four functions create eight different personality types. Although Jung acknowledged that not all people within a category will be alike, he nonetheless maintained that the two-by-four framework represented distinctions inherent in the structure of the human psyche. Prototypic descriptions of the eight kinds of people in this system are presented in Table 5.2.

Measuring Psychological Types: The Myers-Briggs Type Indicator

By far the most popular method for measuring Jung's psychological types is the **Myers-Briggs Type Indicator** (Myers & McCaulley, 1985). Approximately two million people take this personality test each year. The full version of the measure asks test takers to describe themselves on 166 items. In keeping with Jungian theory, the measure is designed to identify which type category the test taker belongs to. This contrasts with the trait approach described in Chapter 7, in which the goal is to place a person's score along a continuum of possible strengths.

The Myers-Briggs Type Indicator divides people into categories along four dimensions. Jung's eight personality types are created by dividing people into Extraversion-Introversion, Sensing-Intuitive, and Thinking-Feeling categories. In addition, the test makers have included a Judgment-Perception division. People with a *judging* attitude tend to ignore new information as soon as they have enough facts to make up their minds. People with a *perceptive* attitude are open to new information. They are curious and inquisitive. By dividing people along each of these four lines, test makers can identify 16 different personality types. Thus, someone who is extraverted, intuitive, feeling, and perceptive is very different from someone who is extraverted, intuitive, thinking, and judging.

The Myers-Briggs test has been most widely used among counselors in nonclinical settings, such as career counseling, pastoral counseling, education, and business organizations (DeVito, 1985). For example, many counselors find scores on the Myers-Briggs are particularly useful in helping clients select careers. An extravert probably will not be happy in a job requiring long hours of isolated work, whereas an introvert might not do well in a job requiring a great deal of socializing and group activity. A list of the kinds of jobs best suited for the different personality types is shown in Table 5.3.

Psychological type scores are also of value to educators. What type of person does best in school? At first glance, Jung's theory would seem to provide some straightforward answers to this question. The Myers-Briggs test constructors argue that introversion helps academic performance, because advanced learning requires people to deal with concepts and ideas, something introverts are suited for (Myers & McCaulley, 1985). In addition, they argue that the ability to work with abstraction and theory, the specialty of intuitive types, will be a plus. Some evidence supports these predictions (Myers & McCaulley, 1985).

However, few of us are good at all types of learning. If psychological types are related to academic achievement, the proper question might be what *kind* of learning is a particular *type* of person best at? For example, extraverts seem to do better than introverts in learning groups (Haber, 1980; Kilmann & Taylor, 1974). Intuitive people do best when allowed to study what they want at their own pace (Carlson & Levy, 1973). One study found judging people are better than perceivers at implementing what they learn in study skills training, presumably because they are disposed to use what they learn (Robyak & Patton, 1977). Thus, the key to effective use of the Myers-Briggs test for educational counseling might be to match the personality type with the type of learning.

Table 5.3

Optimal Career Settings for Personality Types

Type	Career Setting
Extraverts	Work requiring group interactions, meeting with people, and social gatherings. Lots of travel, speeches, variety.
Introverts	Quiet, solitary desk work. Few interruptions. Jobs requiring concentration and thinking.
Thinking	Work including a lot of problem solving, especially when logic is required. Work with numbers, problems with clear solutions.
Feeling	Service jobs, especially those that benefit underprivileged groups. Work provides personal satisfaction.
Sensing	Work requiring attention to details. Short-term, tangible, and immediate goals and relevance.
Intuitive	Nonrepetitive tasks with new challenges. Abstract problems requiring insight and contemplation.
Judging	Highly organized and structured work. Tasks that can be completed before new ones are begun.
Perceptive	Work requiring an ability to adapt to new circumstances. Tasks calling for new, open-minded approaches to problems.

Strengths and Criticisms of Neo-Freudian Theories

Strengths

The primary strength of the neo-Freudian theories as a whole is their elaboration of several important influences on behavior that Freud had ignored or deemphasized. For example, most of these theorists identified the role played by social factors in the formation and change of personality. Many, most notably Erikson and Sullivan, described the ways personality develops beyond the first few years of life. And many theorists presented a much more optimistic and flattering picture of humankind than Freud had. Most described the ego more in terms of positive functions than as an arbitrator between the demanding id and superego.

The neo-Freudians also introduced many new concepts into the psychological literature. For example, birth order, archetypes, authoritarian personality, and personifications can be traced directly to some of the neo-Freudian theorists. As with Freudian theory, many of these ideas have made their way into our everyday language. Many people speak of identity crises, introversion, and inferiority complexes without recognizing the references to Erikson, Jung, and Adler.

Another gauge of the usefulness of a personality theory is the extent to which it influences later theorists and the development of new systems of psychotherapy. In this respect the neo-Freudian contributions can claim some success. The optimistic tone about humans that characterized many neo-Freudians' views helped to pave the way for the humanistic personality theories that developed a few decades later. Similarly, the emphasis on social aspects of personality development undoubtedly was a considerable step in the evolution of later social learning approaches to personality. And the techniques and approaches developed by each of the neo-Freudians almost certainly influenced later specific approaches to psychotherapy. For example, Albert Ellis (1973), who has developed and popularized a modern approach to psychotherapy called *rational emotive therapy* (see Chapter 15), notes that his system "owes a great debt to Alfred Adler" and argues that the psychotherapy method might not have evolved the way it did without Adler's ground-breaking work. Similarly, Sullivan's emphasis on the social environment surrounding schizophrenia laid the foundation for modern family-oriented approaches to psychotherapy.

In short, the neo-Freudian theorists did much to make parts of the psychoanalytic approach palatable to later psychologists and nonpsychologists. In fact, these theorists provided a bridge between Freud's concepts and many later personality theories. However, no individual neo-Freudian theorist, or even the theories taken as a whole, has ever reached the level of acclaim that Freud did. Part of this can be explained through some general weaknesses in the theories, as outlined below.

Criticisms

Many of the same weaknesses critics point to in Freud's theory are also present in some of the neo-Freudian works. For example, many who challenge Freudian theory because of the questionable data on which Freud based his conclusions have even greater reservations about some of the neo-Freudian theories. In particular, many of Jung's conclusions about the nature of the collective unconscious are based on data from myths, legends, dreams, occult phenomena, and artwork. Fromm's work has been criticized for being more descriptive than scientific, and his interpretation of history, which he uses to support his theory, has been challenged. Although many neo-Freudians incorporated anthropological and historical data as well as research from other areas of psychology (most notably, child development) into their works, these theorists still based their conclusions largely on data from patients undergoing psychotherapy. As such, they are subject to scientific criticism on the basis of biased data, with the resulting implications for their applicability to normal, functioning adults.

A second problem with the neo-Freudians as a group is that they often oversimplified or ignored important concepts. None dealt with so many topics in so much depth as Freud. Consequently, the neo-Freudians sometimes failed to effectively address concepts central to psychoanalytic theory, which has led some people to criticize neo-Freudian works as incomplete or limited accounts of personality and human behavior. For example, Erikson has been criticized for what some consider to be a superficial treatment of the role of anxiety in the development of psychological disorders. Sullivan has been attacked for not giving enough attention to hereditary factors. Similarly, Fromm has been criticized for placing too much emphasis on the role of social forces. Indeed, some of the strongest criticisms of Fromm's work center on his recommendation for sweeping social reforms he claimed would improve the lot of humankind. And Adler has been accused of oversimplifying in his attempt to explain many complex behaviors in terms of just one concept, the striving for superiority.

In defense of the neo-Freudian theorists, we can say that while they may have overstated their case at times, they were probably trying to distinguish their approaches from earlier ones. For example, Adler took pride in being able to reduce several Freudian notions to a single concept. In addition, because none of these theorists was as prolific as Freud, it's perhaps unreasonable to expect any of them to have treated as many concepts in as much depth as Freud.

Summary

1. Many psychologists who studied with Freud eventually broke away from the Vienna group to develop their own theories of personality and establish their own schools of psychology. Collectively, these theorists are known as the neo-Freudians, because they retained many basic Freudian concepts and assumptions. Among the limits they saw in Freud's theory were his failure to recognize personality change after the first few years of life, his emphasis on instinctual over social influences, and the generally negative picture he painted of human nature.

2. Alfred Adler introduced the concept of striving for superiority to account for most human motivations. He argued that we are motivated to overcome feelings of helplessness that begin in infancy. Adler also identified parental pampering and neglect as two sources of later personality problems. He argued that middle-born children were the most achieving and were less likely to experience psychological disorders than were first-borns or last-borns.

3. Carl Jung proposed the existence of a collective unconscious that housed primordial images he called archetypes. The collective unconscious contains material each of us inherited from past generations and is basically the same for all people. Among the most important of the archetypes are the anima and the animus, the shadow and the self. Jung pointed to the recurrent surfacing of archetypic symbols in folklore, art, dreams, and psychotic patients as evidence for their existence.

4. Erik Erikson emphasized the positive function of the ego in his theory. One of the ego's most important functions is to develop and maintain a sense of identity. Erikson outlined eight stages of personality development that we pass through during our lifetimes. At each stage we are faced with a crisis and one of two means to resolve the crisis. These choices then set the direction for personality development later in life.

5. Karen Horney rejected Freud's emphasis on instinctual causes of personality development. She argued that the differences Freud saw between the personalities of men and women were more likely the result of social factors than inherited predispositions. Horney maintained that neurotic behavior is the result of interpersonal styles developed in childhood to overcome anxiety. In time, these styles become inflexible and result in an inability to establish satisfying relationships. She identified three neurotic styles, which she called moving toward people, moving against people, and moving away from people.

6. Among Harry Stack Sullivan's contributions to psychoanalytic theory is the notion of personifications. These are mental images we have of others and ourselves. Of particular importance are the images we have of ourselves, which Sullivan identified as the good-me, the bad-me, and the not-me. Sullivan also outlined stages of personality development that extend well past the first few years of life. In particular, he emphasized the importance of the adolescent years, characterized by a need for intimacy and a need to satisfy sexual desires.

7. Erich Fromm argued that many people are motivated to escape from their perception of personal freedom and individuality. Some escape through authoritarianism, identifying with a powerful figure while also assaulting those with less power. Other mechanisms of escape include destructiveness and automaton conformity. In the latter case, people accept the norms handed to them by society and erase their feelings of uniqueness and individuality. Fromm argued that the key to happiness and personal adjustment is the development of feelings of individuation. The key to this positive freedom is spontaneity, and the most important component of spontaneity is love.

8. One important application of psychoanalytic theory is to religion. Freud was highly critical of organized religion, calling it wish fulfillment and a type of neurosis. Jung explained humankind's persistent need for religion in terms of a God archetype. Whether Jung meant that the notion of an external God was an illusion is uncertain. He saw modern psychotherapy taking the place of organized religion when patients became disenchanted with the answers provided by their religion. Fromm argued that the universal need for religion stems from the need to escape from freedom.

9. Among the personality assessment instruments to come out of the neo-Freudian theories is the Myers-Briggs Type Indicator. This test measures psychological types, as outlined by Jung. Test scores divide people into types along four dimensions: extraversion-introversion, sensing-intuitive, thinking-feeling, and judgment-perception. The 16 resulting types can be used by job counselors and education counselors to match people with the most appropriate career and education opportunities.

10. Among the strengths of the neo-Freudian theories as a group are the contributions they made to Freudian theory. In addition to correcting some of the limitations they found in Freud's work, many of the theorists introduced important concepts to the field of psychology. Many later approaches to personality were no doubt influenced by one or more of these theorists. Criticisms of the neo-Freudians include the use of biased and questionable data to support the theories. In addition, critics have charged that some of the theories are oversimplified and incomplete in places.

Key Terms

striving for superiority The primary motivational force in Adler's theory, which is the person's effort to overcome feelings of inferiority.

inferiority complex Feelings of being vastly inferior and helpless compared to others.

birth order Where people are placed among siblings according to the order of their birth.

collective unconscious The part of the unconscious mind containing thoughts, images, and psychic characteristics common to all members of a culture.

primordial images The images that make up the collective unconscious.

archetypes Primordial images that predispose us to comprehend the world in a particular manner.

anima/animus The archetype that is the feminine side of the male (anima) or the masculine side of the female (animus).

shadow The archetype that contains the evil side of humanity.

identity crisis A period in one's development characterized by a strong concern for developing a sense of self.

personification A mental image of oneself or of another person.

developmental epochs The seven stages of personality development in Sullivan's theory.

authoritarianism A mechanism to escape the perception of freedom, characterized by striving for submission and domination.

destructiveness A mechanism to escape the perception of freedom, characterized by destructive acts.

automaton conformity A mechanism to escape the perception of freedom characterized by conforming to societal standards.

positive freedom A healthy response to the perception of freedom, characterized by spontaneity and individuality.

Myers-Briggs Type Indicator Popular personality test used to assess Jung's psychological types.

Suggested Readings

Erikson, E. H. (1963). *Childhood and society* (2nd ed). New York: Norton. In this revised edition of his classic work, Erikson provides his most complete description of the eight stages of development. He also applies his approach to personality to such varied topics as Sioux Indian customs and Adolph Hitler's childhood.

Fromm, E. (1941/1965). *Escape from freedom*. New York: Avon. This is Fromm's most important and most influential work. Fromm outlines his theory of personality in this very readable and thought-provoking book, including explanations of the mechanisms of escape from freedom and the rise of Nazi Germany.

Horney, K. (1945/1966). *Our inner conflicts: A constructive theory of neurosis*. New York: Norton. Karen Horney is probably the best writer among the neo-Freudians, and this book is probably the most lucid yet comprehensive of her writings. Horney explains the causes and consequences of neurosis, including her descriptions of the three basic neurotic styles.

Jung, C. G. (Ed.). (1964). *Man and his symbols*. New York: Dell. If, like many students, you are intrigued by Jungian psychology, this might be a good starting point for finding out more about this theory. Jung wrote the first chapter in this book shortly before his death, with the intention of communicating his ideas to a nonacademic audience.

Neo-Freudian Theories
Relevant Research

6

The half-century or more that has passed since many of the neo-Freudian theorists broke away from the Freudian pack allows us to see how much more these theorists had in common with Freud than they probably realized themselves at the time. Just as their theories are better thought of as elaborations of Freud's basic psychoanalytic approach, so is the research covered in this chapter relevant for both Freudian and neo-Freudian approaches to personality. In truth, some of the topics covered here might also have been included in the chapter on research relevant for Freudian theory. I decided to place the three research topics for this chapter here because each seems to relate to psychoanalytic theory the way neo-Freudian psychology relates to Freud's works. That is, in each area researchers have taken concepts introduced by Freud and adapted these in ways Freud probably would object to. In many cases, the researchers acknowledge the birthplace of these concepts by retaining many of the terms introduced by Freud. We can only imagine what Sigmund would say if he could see how some of his concepts have been altered from their original psychoanalytic form.

The first example of this adaptation of psychoanalytic concepts is the research on anxiety and coping strategies. Anxiety plays a central role in Freud's theory, as well as many of the neo-Freudian theories. Although most neo-Freudian theorists continued to emphasize the importance of unconscious sources of anxiety, more recent research has centered on the conscious efforts we make to reduce or eliminate anxiety. We'll look at some of the ways people cope with stressful events and individual differences in coping styles.

As was typical of the theorists who followed Freud, several researchers interested in the causes of aggression reinterpreted some of Freud's concepts to explain the relationship between frustration and aggression. They retained many Freudian terms in their theorizing, such as sublimation, displacement, and catharsis. Their work has spawned a large amount of research on the causes of aggression, some of which we will examine here.

Finally, recent research on the concepts of individuation and deindividuation is relevant for psychologists interested in the issues of identity and individuation described by many neo-Freudian writers. We'll look at why people sometimes act in uncharacteristic ways, while other times they prefer to accentuate their individuality.

Anxiety and Coping Strategies

Imagine you are watching a scary movie. A young woman walks unsuspectingly through an innocent-looking garden at night. A psychopathic killer creeps up in the moonlight. From somewhere horns start blaring. You squirm in your seat. You want to close your eyes and make it go away, but you also want to see. What do you do? If you are like most people, you may use some strategy for dealing with these feelings of anxiety. You may tell yourself that "it's only a movie" or that "these things don't really happen." If you are convincing, you may succeed in reducing your anxiety until the killer is chased back into the woods.

Anxiety and strategies for alleviating anxiety have played an important role in the works of many psychoanalytic theorists. What is anxiety? Although there are many definitions (cf. Monat & Lazarus, 1985), most researchers probably would agree that anxiety is an unpleasant emotional experience. When you experience anxiety, you have feelings of worry, panic, fear, and dread. It is probably the emotional experience you would have if you were suddenly arrested or if you discovered that a diary containing some of your deepest secrets had been passed around among friends.

Although he changed his thinking about anxiety several times during his career, Freud identified three types of anxiety in his last major writing in this area. First, there is *reality anxiety*, or objective anxiety, which is a response to a perceived threat in the real world. We experience this type of anxiety when we suddenly confront a dangerous wild animal or narrowly escape an automobile accident. In cases of reality anxiety, we are aware of the dangerous situation responsible for our emotional reaction.

Because of his emphasis on unconscious aspects of human behavior, it is perhaps not surprising that Freud devoted more attention to two other types of anxiety: neurotic anxiety and moral anxiety. In neither of these cases are we consciously aware of what we are feeling anxious about. *Neurotic anxiety* is experienced when unacceptable id impulses are dangerously close to breaking into consciousness. It is this type of anxiety that leads the ego to utilize defense mechanisms. *Moral anxiety* is brought about by the superego in response to id impulses that violate the superego's strict moral code. Generally this is experienced as guilt.

Many neo-Freudian theorists adopted Freud's concept of anxiety in their writings. For example, Sullivan (1953) considered anxiety a cornerstone for his theory. The neurotic coping styles described by Horney also are said to develop in an effort to reduce and avoid anxiety. These theorists accepted the Freudian notion that some experiences with anxiety stem from unconscious conflicts, although they emphasized the interpersonal and cultural role in this process more than did Freud. For example, Sullivan said anxiety could be overcome by developing solid relationships with others — what he called *interpersonal security*. Horney agreed that unconscious impulses often triggered anxiety, but largely because they came into conflict with cultural standards. "The frequency with which anxiety is generated by sexual impulses is largely dependent on the existing cultural attitude toward sexuality," she wrote. "I do not see that sexuality as such is a specific source of anxiety" (1937, p. 66).

Gradually, neo-Freudian psychologists began using the term *defense mechanism* to refer to the strategies people employ to cope with the various sources of threat in their environments (Snyder, 1988). Adler, Anna Freud, and others promoted this new way of looking at defense mechanisms in place of Sigmund Freud's description of unconscious processes protecting the ego from instinctual forces (Snyder, 1988). Most of the research on anxiety and coping today is concerned with conscious efforts to reduce anxiety with known sources.

Anxiety is a part of our daily experiences, from potentially dangerous situations to nagging everyday annoyances. Some people seem to fall apart under the strain, whereas others hold up fairly well. Although we occasionally cannot understand why we feel so anxious and sometimes make incorrect assessments of what is causing our problems, most of the time we think we know what is making us anxious and usually do something about it.

A great deal of research has been conducted on the strategies people use to deal with their anxiety. You will recall that Horney identified anxiety-coping strategies as the source of neurotic interpersonal styles. According to Horney, children faced with excessive anxiety develop styles of interacting with others that temporarily reduce their anxiety but which create long-term adjustment problems. More recently, researchers have investigated coping strategies for everyday sources of anxiety. These strategies appear to be part of a well-adjusted person's repertoire for dealing with some of the difficulties life throws our way.

Reactions to Stressful Stimuli

What do you do when faced with a potentially stressful situation, such as waiting for your dentist to start drilling or getting ready to go to a job interview? If you are like most people you don't just accept the potential pain or fear as part of life. Researchers find that people actively employ strategies to reduce their anxiety (Lazarus, 1968, 1974). For example, subjects in one study were shown a rather grisly film on industrial safety (Koriat, Melkman, Averill, & Lazarus, 1972). The film depicted several serious accidents, including a scene in which a saw drove a board through the abdomen of a workman, who died writhing and bleeding on the floor.

How did subjects react to the film? Some of the strategies subjects reported using are listed in Table 6.1. Interestingly, the two most common strategies resemble some of the unconscious defense mechanisms described by Freud. That is, many subjects used a form of denial to deal with their anxiety: They convinced themselves the accident was not real. Others used a form of intellectualization: They tried to view the film in an emotionally detached manner. Another interesting aspect of these results is the wide variety of techniques subjects used to overcome anxiety. One quarter told themselves the gruesome scenes were actually humorous. Nearly half used strategies that were classified as "something else"—idiosyncratic responses used by very few subjects. This last finding suggests that each of us learns our own particular methods for dealing with anxiety. People who have seen a large number of frightening films probably have learned some rather unusual, but very effective, methods for reducing their anxiety.

Table 6.1

Detachment Strategies Used During Anxiety-Provoking Film

Strategy	Percentage of Subjects Using	Percentage of Subjects Using as First Choice
1. I constantly tried to remind myself that it was a film rather than a real occurrence.	56.4	21.3
2. I watched the film concentrating on the technical aspects involved in its production.	52.6	22.3
3. I concentrated on the details involved in the cause of the accidents and possible ways of their prevention.	14.1	2.6
4. I told myself that the workers were actually responsible for what happened.	14.1	5.1
5. I tried to adopt a humorous attitude toward what happened.	25.6	5.1
6. I told myself that such accidents are inevitable.	2.6	0
7. Something else.	43.6	21.8

Source: Adapted from Koriat, Melkman, Averill, & Lazarus, (1972).

The effectiveness of these learned strategies was illustrated in some studies that looked at anxiety levels in new and experienced sky divers (Epstein & Fenz, 1965; Fenz & Epstein, 1967). Most of us would agree that parachuting from an airplane many thousands of feet above the ground is an anxiety-provoking experience. In one study, sky divers with more than 100 jumps behind them were compared with those with fewer than 10. The parachutists wore equipment that allowed the researchers to monitor their physiological signs of anxiety throughout the process, from before arriving at the airport to after the landing. As shown in Figure 6.1, both groups began their jumping experience with the same increase in arousal. The inexperienced jumpers' arousal levels continued to rise up to the jump. However, after the experienced sky divers boarded the plane, their arousal appeared to level off. Apparently they had learned over their many jumps how to keep their arousal levels from getting too high.

Types of Coping Strategies

It should be evident from the research presented thus far that people respond to anxiety-provoking situations with active efforts to reduce the anxiety. Through different learning histories, each of us develops a wide variety of techniques for

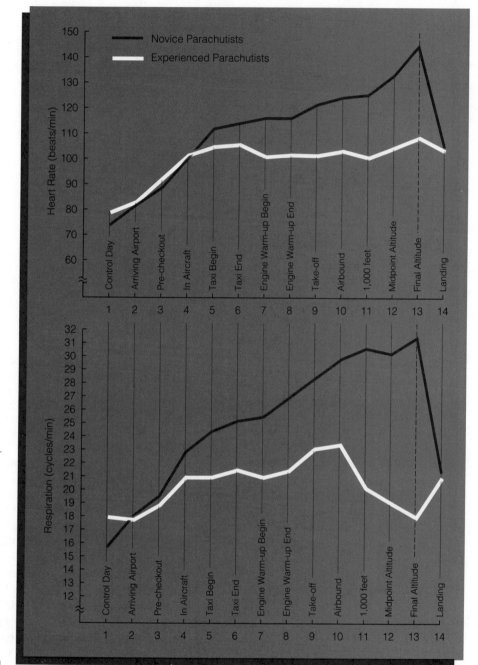

Figure 6.1

Physiological Responses to Approaching Jump by Inexperienced and Experienced Parachutists

Adapted from Fenz and Epstein (1967); reprinted by permission of Elsevier Science Publishing Co., Inc. Copyright 1967 by The American Psychosomatic Society, Inc.

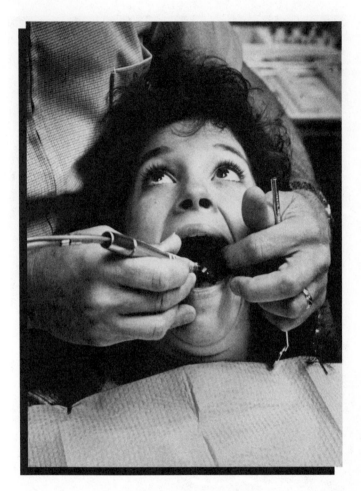

How do you handle the anxiety in this situation? You might try to think of something besides what the dentist is doing, or think about the value of good dental hygiene. What you probably won't do is concentrate on the potential pain.

dealing with threatening situations. Recently, investigators have asked whether it is possible to categorize all of these types of responses into a few general categories, or *coping strategies.*

What kinds of coping strategies do you use when faced with a problem? Experimenters asked one group of subjects to pick the most important problem they had faced during the previous year (Holahan & Moos, 1987). Subjects then were given a list of possible coping strategies generated from earlier research (Billings & Moos, 1981) and asked which ones they had used. The list is shown in Table 6.2.

Consistent with past work in this area, the subjects used a wide variety of coping strategies to deal with their problems. In addition, the researchers were able to group the various coping responses into three major categories. First, there were the *active-cognitive strategies*, in which a person actively thinks about the situation in an effort to make things better. For example, if your biggest problem

Table 6.2

List of Coping Strategies

Active-Cognitive Strategies

Prayed for guidance and/or strength

Prepared for the worst

Tried to see the positive side of the situation

Considered several alternatives for handling the problem

Drew on my past experiences

Took things a day at a time

Tried to step back from the situation and be more objective

Went over the situation in my mind to try to understand it

Told myself things that helped me feel better

Made a promise to myself that things would be different next time

Accepted it; nothing could be done

Active-Behavioral Strategies

Tried to find out more about the situation

Talked with spouse or other relative about the problem

Talked with friend about the problem

Talked with professional person (e.g., doctor, lawyer, clergy)

Got busy with other things to keep my mind off the problem

Made a plan of action and followed it

Tried not to act too hastily or follow my first hunch

Got away from things for a while

Knew what had to be done and tried harder to make things work

Let my feelings out somehow

Sought help from persons or groups with similar experiences

Bargained or compromised to get something positive from the situation

Tried to reduce tension by exercising more

Continued

Table 6.2

List of Coping Strategies *continued*

Avoidance Strategies
Took it out on other people when I felt angry or depressed
Kept my feelings to myself
Avoided being with people in general
Refused to believe that it happened
Tried to reduce tension by drinking more
Tried to reduce tension by eating more
Tried to reduce tension by smoking more
Tried to reduce tension by taking more tranquilizing drugs

Source: Taken from Holahan and Moos (1987), with permission.

was breaking up with a boyfriend or girlfriend this past year, you may have coped with this by convincing yourself that you were better off in the long run because of the experience, or by focusing on why things went wrong and how this can help you to be happier in your next relationship.

The second group of coping strategies were *active-behavioral strategies*. Here the person takes some action to improve the situation. For example, if your problem last year was doing poorly in school, you may have responded by getting some tutoring, learning more effective study habits, or taking some remedial classes to better prepare for future courses.

Finally, the researchers identified a group of coping responses they called *avoidance strategies*. These are efforts to deal with the anxiety by keeping the anxiety-provoking situation out of awareness. For example, if you discovered this past year that a loved one was suffering from a serious health problem, you may have responded by not thinking about the person or even by trying to convince yourself that the problem was not as serious as people were telling you.

Other investigators have divided coping strategies into those dealing with the problem and those dealing with the emotional reaction to the problem (Lazarus & Folkman, 1984). **Problem-focused strategies** are directed at taking care of the problem and thereby overcoming the anxiety. These include the various steps of "defining the problem, generating alternative solutions, weighing the alternatives in terms of their costs and benefits, choosing among them, and acting" (Lazarus & Folkman, 1984, p. 152). **Emotion-focused strategies** are designed to reduce the emotional distress. These include "avoidance, minimization, distancing, selective attention, positive comparisons, and wresting positive value from negative events" (p. 150).

In one investigation, men and women between ages 45 and 64 were asked how they had coped with a series of real-life events they had experienced during the past 7 months (Folkman & Lazarus, 1980). Subjects indicated their coping strategies on a checklist of possible responses. This list contained some emotion-focused strategies ("I tried to look on the bright side of things") and some problem-focused strategies ("I made a plan of action and followed it"). More than 1,300 examples of stressful experiences were examined. The researchers found that subjects used an emotion-focused strategy, a problem-focused strategy, or both, in more than 98% of the cases.

Which are the most effective coping strategies for reducing anxiety? First, there is evidence that the use of *some* coping mechanism is typically more effective in reducing anxiety than is using no mechanism. For example, ex-smokers in one study used some type of coping strategy to deal with the anxiety associated with kicking the habit. They were more than four times as likely to succeed at quitting smoking than were those who failed to use any coping techniques (Shiffman, 1985). The use of coping strategies also was found effective for reducing depression among couples experiencing stress in their marriages (Mitchell, Cronkite, & Moos, 1983). One survey asked adults about the types of coping responses they typically used and how effective they perceived each of 27 coping mechanisms to be (McCrae & Costa, 1986a). The researchers found that the more people relied on strategies generally agreed to be effective, the higher they scored in measures of happiness and general life satisfaction.

Thus, people tend to use coping mechanisms when faced with anxiety, and there is evidence that the use of these strategies is at least somewhat effective. But are all coping strategies equally effective? Should we encourage people to use one kind of strategy over another? The answer is that the effectiveness of any coping strategy depends on a number of variables.

One of these variables is time. Although more than one strategy for coping with a problem can be effective, one team of researchers pointed out that some coping strategies appear to work against one another (Suls & Fletcher, 1985). That is, avoidance strategies focus attention away from the anxiety-provoking situation or the person's reaction to the situation. On the other hand, active strategies, whether problem focused or emotion focused, call for us to focus our attention on the situation and thereby be better able to take action. But how can both kinds of strategies, working in seemingly opposite directions, be effective? How can paying attention to *and* not paying attention to the problem help to reduce anxiety?

To answer this question, the researchers reviewed 43 studies reporting on the effectiveness of one or both of these strategies (Suls & Fletcher, 1985). They found, indeed, that both avoiding the anxiety-provoking situation and paying attention to it were associated with more efficient coping than was not using any coping mechanism at all. The researchers found the key to unraveling this puzzle when they looked at the effectiveness of the strategies over time. Avoidance strategies generally were more effective in the short-run, but over time attention strategies appeared to be more successful.

If you look at some of your own experiences with anxiety, you may be able to see why this is so. Some problems do go away after a day or two. By simply not thinking about those problems, we might be able to weather the storm with an avoidance strategy. Paying attention to the problem at this time might only create more anxiety. However, many times problems do not go away. Ignoring financial problems will not make them disappear, although we might feel better for a few days if we avoid thinking about them. For long-term relief from anxiety, we may be forced to attend to the problem and do something about it.

Another variable that may be important in deciding which coping strategy to use is the availability of means to deal with the problem (Folkman, 1984). That is, engaging in a problem-focused strategy might be effective in some cases, but there are problems for which we possess no tools to repair the situation. Two psychologists recently demonstrated this point in a dramatic way (Strentz & Auerbach, 1988). In conjunction with the FBI and some domestic airline companies, the researchers staged a four-day hostage abduction. Pilots, copilots, and flight attendants, who had volunteered to participate in the exercise, were allowed to experience what it would be like to be taken hostage by terrorists. Great effort was taken to make the situation as realistic as possible:

> A group of five terrorists (Special Agents of the FBI) took quick and complete control of the subjects with sufficient force and noise to assure complete cooperation. Automatic weapons (blanks) were fired; blank firing adapters were not used, adding to the realism for hostages who might be familiar with these weapons. Terrorists' faces were covered with a ski mask or kaffiyeh (a Middle Eastern headpiece). Flash bangs (tactical hand grenades) were exploded (creating noise and a bright light, but no fragmentation). The van's driver and his assistant were both wearing concealed blood bags. During the shooting they broke the bags by hand and allowed the blood to soak into their clothing as they turned to face the hostages and fell to the floor. . . . Hostages were commanded to place their hands on the tops of their heads and make no other moves until so ordered. They were told that a violation of this order would result in their death. While some terrorists provided cover, two terrorists removed the hostages, one at a time, from the van and placed them on the ground spread-eagle face down. They were immediately searched, handcuffed with their hands behind them, and their heads were covered with pillow cases. (Strentz & Auerbach, 1988, pp. 654–655).

Measures taken throughout the study showed that, as expected, the subjects experienced high levels of anxiety. How did they cope with this anxiety? Before the kidnapping, some of the subjects were instructed in the use of emotion-focused coping strategies. They were told to try not thinking about the situation, or even to engage in fantasy thinking. Other subjects were instructed to use problem-focused strategies. These included ways to communicate to one another, how to gather information about their circumstances, and how to maintain a composed appearance.

Which coping strategy was most effective? Remember, there was little or nothing the hostages could do about the situation they found themselves in. But they might have been able to deal with their emotional reaction to that situation. Consequently, subjects instructed to use the emotion-focused strategies experienced lower levels of anxiety than did the subjects who used the problem-focused strategies. Like a lot of the problems we face, the solutions to the kidnapping were out of their hands. When there are few actions we can realistically take to solve a problem, we're probably better off not paying attention to the circumstances (Folkman, 1984).

However, this does not mean that emotion-focused strategies are always better. One study found that problem-focused strategies were more effective than emotion-focused strategies in helping people avoid depression (Vitaliano, De-Wolfe, Maiuro, Russo, & Katon, 1990). However, the problem-focused strategies were more effective *only* when the problems the subjects faced were ones they could do something about. When the solution to the problem was out of the person's control, there was no benefit in trying to attack the problem directly.

Other research suggests that if a means to resolve the problem is available, then taking quick action to eliminate it might prove the more prudent course of action. For example, a student who frets over not understanding the material in a math class could do himself or herself a favor by seeking help right away instead of waiting for a sudden insight. In a more dramatic example, one team of researchers looked at how soldiers suffering from combat stress coped with the long-term emotional reactions to their combat experiences (Solomon, Avitzur, & Mikulincer, 1989). The investigators examined the coping strategies and social functioning of Israeli soldiers who had suffered excessive combat stress during the 1982 Lebanon War. They found that the soldiers who used problem-solving strategies were more successful in their social functioning than the soldiers who relied on emotion-focused strategies. Moreover, the soldiers who increased their use of emotion-focused strategies during the years that followed the combat experience showed the poorest ability to cope. Apparently these soldiers would have benefited more from trying to deal with their problems directly, rather than trying to simply change the way they felt.

In short, different types of coping strategies seem to work in different situations. The key for dealing with anxiety might be to know when to employ which type of strategy. Fortunately, most of us have a number of coping strategies in our repertoires. If one approach for dealing with an anxiety-provoking situation doesn't work, perhaps another approach will.

Individual Differences in Coping Strategies: Repression-Sensitization

I once was involved in a situation at a local Red Cross office concerning the showing of a potentially anxiety-provoking film to expectant parents. The topic of the film was Sudden Infant Death Syndrome (SIDS), an illness that mysteriously kills thousands of infants annually. One group of parents did not want to expose themselves to anything that suggested their child could die in infancy. The other group argued that they wanted to know as much as possible about any such situation to prepare themselves in case the unfortunate event should happen to them.

The differences in opinion clearly reflected a different strategy for dealing with anxiety. The two groups of parents might have been divided along a personality dimension researchers call **repression-sensitization**. At one end of this dimension are people who typically respond to threatening situations by avoiding them. These *repressors* try to not think about the situation and thereby succeed in avoiding the anxiety as much or as long as possible. We see this strategy at work when people advise us that "worrying about it will do no good" and "try to think of something else to take your mind off it." If you have ever put off seeing a doctor or talking to a professor because you expected the encounter to be stressful, you have used the repression strategy.

On the other end of the dimension are the *sensitizers*. These people typically deal with a stressful situation by finding out as much as possible, as soon as possible, and thereby put themselves in a position to take the most effective action. You may have employed this strategy if you tried to get as much information as possible about a scheduled medical procedure or spent a great deal of time thinking about an upcoming job interview.

Although each of us has used both strategies at different times, researchers also find relatively stable tendencies to use one of these strategies more than the other (Byrne, 1961, 1964; Byrne, Barry, & Nelson, 1963; Weinberger, Schwartz, & Davidson, 1979). That is, some people tend to use the repression strategy when faced with a stressful situation, whereas others are more likely to turn to a sensitization strategy. Moreover, like other individual differences, we tend to resort to our preferred strategy regardless of the type of stressful event we encounter (Chabot, 1973).

Repression-Sensitization and Coping with Anxiety   Which person typically deals more effectively with anxiety — the sensitizer who faces problems head on or the repressor who ignores problems until forced to do something? Answering this question is not easy, in part because sometimes attending to a problem may be the best strategy for overcoming the source of the anxiety whereas other times this may result in nothing but a lot of wasted worrying. But researchers also face the problem of relying on subjects' self-reports of how anxious they are. For example, sensitizers typically admit to experiencing more anxiety in their lives than do repressors (Cook, 1985; Pagano, 1973; Weinberger, Schwartz, & Davidson, 1979). But perhaps this only reflects the repressors' failure to acknowledge their anxiety.

One way around this problem is to measure anxiety levels some other way. This was done in an experiment in which subjects anticipated receiving either fairly painful electric shocks or a mild vibrating sensation (Scarpetti, 1973). In addition to asking repressors and sensitizers to report their feelings on a questionnaire, the researchers assessed anxiety through skin conductance measures. Consistent with earlier findings, sensitizers *reported* feeling more anxious in the shock condition than did the repressors. But the skin conductance data, shown in Figure 6.2, tell a different story. In truth, the repressors experienced a significant *increase* in arousal in the shock condition, whereas the sensitizers effectively reduced their arousal. Thus, when we ask if repressors or sensitizers are more anxious, we need to specify which level we are referring to. Repressors may seem calm in the face of imminent danger, when sensitizers express their fears. But in reality the repressors may be the most anxious while the sensitizers keep calm.

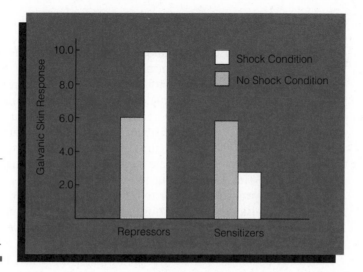

Figure 6.2

Mean Galvanic
Skin Responses
During Shock/
Vibration Trials

Data from Scarpetti (1973).

Repression-Sensitization and Health   A number of researchers have argued that repressors and sensitizers also have a different approach to health care (Chabot, 1973). If you think about the earlier descriptions of repression and sensitization, you can see why this might be the case. Sensitizers should be examining themselves constantly for information about the state of their health, whereas repressors should avoid such information. Consequently, sensitizers probably rush to a doctor at the first sign of a health problem, whereas repressors pretend the problem doesn't exist or that it will go away. Consistent with this reasoning, researchers find that hospital patients are more likely to be sensitizers than repressors (Tempone & Lamb, 1967). Similarly, sensitizer college students are more likely than repressors to visit the campus health center (Byrne, Steinberg, & Schwartz, 1968) or seek help from the campus counseling center (Thelen, 1969).

Researchers also find differences among repressors and sensitizers faced with health problems they cannot ignore. One group of investigators looked at the coping styles of chemotherapy patients, all of whom were suffering from Hodgkin's lymphoma or breast cancer (Ward, Leventhal, & Love, 1988). Although the repressors were no different from the sensitizers in terms of the stage of the disease or the amount of time they had been on chemotherapy, the repressors reported that they experienced fewer and less severe side effects from their treatment than did the other patients.

Although these findings suggest that sensitizers are overly concerned about health problems and repressors not concerned enough, another interpretation is possible. The sensitizers' style of constant worry may make them less healthy. Thus, sensitizers may really need more health care than do repressors. It is also possible that a history of poor health causes people to adopt a sensitization style. In other words, perhaps the poor health brought about the sensitization, not the other way around.

A couple of experiments point out the difficulty in drawing strong conclusions on this issue. In one study, male prisoners' visits to the prison medical officer were divided into those that genuinely required medical attention and those that did not (Gayton, Bassett, Tavormina, & Ozmon, 1978). Sensitizer prisoners requested more unnecessary visits than did repressors, but they also requested more *justified* visits. Thus, not only did these sensitizers think they needed more medical attention, they probably really did. In another study, researchers examined old test scores of patients in a veterans hospital (Dattore, Shontz, & Coyne, 1980). They found that cancer victims' scores, taken before the cancer developed, were significantly higher on a scale measuring repression than were the scores of other patients. This evidence suggests that the repressors may have failed to attend to early warning signs or to adhere to health practices that might have reduced their risk of cancer. Thus, although sensitizers may go to a doctor unnecessarily at times, perhaps this concern ultimately succeeds in keeping them healthier than those who ignore their health.

In conclusion, people do not sit by passively when faced with anxiety-provoking situations. Each of us develops various cognitive strategies for reducing our discomfort. Researchers have placed these various strategies into general categories, such as emotion-focused or problem-focused strategies. Which of these strategies is most effective may depend on the availability of some means to solve the problem and on how long the problem lasts. Finally, researchers find stable individual differences in our tendencies to use either a repressor or a sensitizer approach to stressful situations.

Frustration and Aggression

Suppose you are at the library late one night trying to read an article from a professional journal for one of your classes. You wade through the big words and jargon on the first few pages, hoping to make more sense of the writing as it progresses. You come to what appears to be the main point of the article, so you read each word slowly, carefully. Still you don't get it. So you read the last few paragraphs again. But again it doesn't make any sense. One more try, but no luck. You're running out of time and patience. What do you feel like doing?

Most people in this kind of situation experience high levels of frustration. They might respond by pounding their fists on the table or swearing at the author. If you're not in a public place, you might feel like throwing the journal across the room. You may have even yelled at your roommate or a friend when in a similar situation. What this example illustrates is the connection between frustration and aggression.

Few events in our lives command as much attention as those with an element of aggression. From playground fights to muggings to war, attempts by one human to inflict pain on another have been among the most widely researched human behaviors. Naturally, the psychoanalytic approach to personality has much to say about this topic. In fact, the first effort to explain the association between frustration and aggression appears to come from some of Freud's early writings. He proposed that frustration of the libido causes aggression. When our pleasure-seeking impulse is blocked, we experience a "primordial reaction" of aggressing against the obstacle. Naturally, our egos keep us from assaulting anyone and everyone who spoils our fun. Therefore, Freud argued that we often *displace* our aggression. Because we can't attack the police officer who won't let us drive as fast as we want, we displace the aggressive impulse by yelling at employees, friends, or family members.

Freud later changed his views on the causes of aggression. After witnessing the mass destruction of human life in World War I, he introduced the concept of a death instinct, *Thanatos*. Freud claimed we all have an instinctual desire to destroy ourselves. Because a fully functioning ego does not allow self-destruction, the instinct is turned outward toward others. However, it was Freud's original position that later inspired researchers interested in the causes of aggression. Although many of these researchers identified themselves more closely with behaviorism (Chapter 13), the psychoanalytic flavor of their theorizing is unmistakable. We cover the research here because it provides an excellent example of the neo-Freudian style: The researchers accepted many of Freud's basic notions but reinterpreted them in more social and less psychic terms. Although Freud spoke of frustrated libidinal impulses, the research we will cover here deals with frustrations of which we are generally aware.

Men are not gentle creatures who want to be loved. They are, on the contrary, creatures among whose instinctual endowments [is] a powerful share of aggressiveness.
SIGMUND FREUD

The Frustration-Aggression Hypothesis

In 1939 a team of psychologists translated Freud's early work on aggression into the **frustration-aggression hypothesis** (Dollard, Doob, Miller, Mowrer, & Sears, 1939). The hypothesis states that "aggression is always a consequence of frustration . . . that the occurrence of aggressive behavior always presupposes the existence of frustration and, contrariwise, that the existence of frustration always leads to some form of aggression" (p. 1). One attractive feature of this model is its simplicity. Notice the psychologists argue there is but one cause of aggression (frustration) and one response to frustration (aggression). A student frustrated in efforts to get on the honor roll, a baseball player frustrated in attempts to break out of a batting slump, a rat frustrated in its effort to find a piece of cheese, all should respond with aggression. And anyone who acts aggressively should have experienced some frustration.

The researchers adopted another psychoanalytic notion to explain when aggression will stop. They proposed that aggression ceases when we experience a **catharsis**, loosely conceived of as a release of tension. Freud discussed catharsis in terms of a release of psychic energy. However, aggression researchers concerned with catharsis describe tension in terms of arousal, energy levels, and muscle tension. The frustrated student who kicks her books across the room and the slumping batter who pounds his bat against the dugout wall should feel their tensions subside. Until the frustration builds tension levels up again, we should expect no further outbreaks from the student and the batter.

At first glance, the frustration-aggression hypothesis makes some sense. You may have felt the urge to throw a difficult-to-understand book across the room. We've all seen how a little shoving in a long line can lead to angry words, if not an

Although hitting the machine probably won't get you a drink or your money back, you might feel better. In this case, the frustration of not getting the drink leads to the aggression which may lead to a cathartic release of tension.

occasional fist. But given all of the frustrating experiences in our lives, why don't we spend most of our time acting aggressively? To account for this, some of the original theorists modified their positions, again borrowing from psychoanalytic theories (Doob & Sears, 1939; Miller, 1941; Sears, 1941). They proposed that frustration sometimes leads to an *indirect* expression of aggression. Indirect aggression can be expressed in many ways. One is through displacing the aggression to a new target, such as taking frustrating working conditions out on your spouse. Another is to attack in an indirect manner. For example, we might not hit our bosses, but we can make their jobs a little harder or spread malicious gossip about them. Finally, we can use sublimation (another concept adapted from psychoanalytic theory). For example, a frustrated person might run a few miles or play a hard game of basketball to work out tension. Thus, frustration always leads to aggression, but not always in the most obvious forms.

Testing the Frustration-Aggression Hypothesis

Because of its simplicity, the frustration-aggression hypothesis can be examined through three basic questions. First, can something other than frustration cause aggression? Second, does frustration always lead to aggression? And third, does aggression lead to catharsis and a reduction of aggression?

The answer to the first question is the easiest. Today most researchers accept that there are many causes of aggression other than frustration. For example, people sometimes act aggressively to obtain money or power, or out of a sense of duty or patriotism. Arousing music or a good orator also can spawn aggressive behavior. However, answering the other two questions has required a considerable amount of research.

Does Frustration Always Lead to Aggression?   Several investigations have found that frustrated subjects act more aggressively than do nonfrustrated subjects (Berkowitz, 1989). For example, experimenters in one study intentionally provoked unsuspecting people standing in lines in stores, banks, and ticket windows (Harris, 1974). Because previous studies have shown greater frustration the closer people are to their goal, experimenters cut in front of either the third person in line (close to the goal) or the twelfth person in line. The experimenters glanced back to notice the subject's response and, after 20 seconds, apologized and left.

The subjects' responses were coded for verbal and nonverbal aggression. For example, subjects saying ''Watch it'' or ''This is my place'' were given one point. Those making ''threatening, abusive, or extended comments'' were given two points. Nonverbal responses included ''unfriendly, threatening, or obscene gestures'' and pushing and shoving. As shown in Table 6.3, the frustrated subjects toward the front of the line expressed more aggression than did the less frustrated subjects toward the end.

Table 6.3

Mean Aggression Points for Subjects Toward the Front
and Toward the Back of the Line

	Verbal Aggression	Nonverbal Aggression	Total Aggression
Front of line	.619	.625	1.244
Back of line	.256	.263	.519

Source: Adapted from M. B. Harris (1974); reprinted by permission of Academic Press, Inc.

Figure 6.3

Aggression Level of Hockey Players as a Function of Team's League Standing

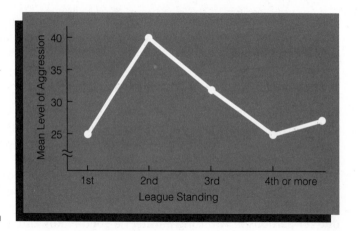

Adapted from Russell and Drewry (1976); reprinted by permission of Plenum Publishing Corporation.

Another team of researchers demonstrated the frustration-aggression effect when they examined the frequency of aggressive acts by professional Canadian hockey players (Russell & Drewry, 1976). The number of penalties assessed for violent play, challenges to the game officials, and so forth, were recorded for each game over two seasons. As shown in Figure 6.3, the hockey players' violence was related to their team's rank in the league standings. First-place teams and teams toward the bottom of the standings showed relatively little aggression. However, once again the players closest to their goal (the second-place team) were the most violent. Presumably the little frustrations of the game were more aggravating for these players than for those who were first or those so far from first they had little to lose.

These and other studies demonstrate that frustration is one cause of aggression. But does it always lead to aggression? This is a difficult question to answer for many reasons. Certainly very minor frustrations don't translate into aggression. There must be a minimal amount of frustration before the tendency to aggress surfaces. However, reformulations of the original frustration-aggression hypothesis maintain that aggression sometimes is disguised, such as when expressed through displacement.

Whether people displace their aggressive tendencies was tested in an experiment in which subjects were first asked to work on some anagram problems (Konecni & Doob, 1972). Some subjects found the task frustrating, especially because another "subject" (a confederate of the experimenter) annoyed and harassed them throughout this time. Other subjects were not harassed or frustrated on the task. Subjects then were given the opportunity to "grade" another subject on a creativity task. The means of grading was electric shock. They were told to give this other person painful (but not harmful) shocks for uncreative responses. Although no actual shocks were delivered, the number of shocks subjects thought they were giving was used as a measure of aggression.

How was displacement tested in this study? Some subjects were fortunate enough to find that the person who had earlier annoyed them (or not, depending on condition) was the one hooked up to the shock apparatus. For other subjects

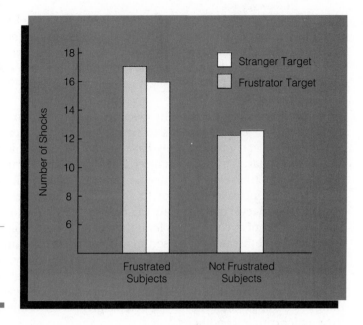

Figure 6.4

Mean Number of Shocks Delivered

Data from Konecni and Doob (1972).

the person receiving the shock was a stranger. The results from this part of the experiment are shown in Figure 6.4. Not surprisingly, subjects given the chance to shock the person who had frustrated them gave more shocks than did the nonfrustrated subjects. However, frustrated subjects given the opportunity to shock a *stranger* also delivered more shocks than did the nonfrustrated subjects. In this condition, the aggression was displaced onto an innocent bystander. The findings illustrate that although frustration often leads to aggression, this may take many forms. Frustration-based aggression at the office might be displaced onto drivers on the way home or to the delivery boy who accidentally throws the newspaper on the roof.

Thus, frustration sometimes leads to direct acts of aggression against the person frustrating us and sometimes causes us to displace our aggression to a convenient target. But does this mean that significant frustrations *always* lead to some kind of aggression? The answer is no. Researchers have identified a number of situations in which frustrated people do not appear to act aggressively (Berkowitz, 1989). Most obviously, the fear of punishment will often prevent us from responding to frustration with aggression. Moreover, most of us have learned that nonaggressive solutions to our problems will be more rewarding in the long run. Consequently, it is very unlikely that you will lash out physically at the person at the next library table whose loud chattering frustrates your desire to study.

Does Aggression Lead to Catharsis and Reduced Aggression?   No doubt when you have been angry, someone has told you to "let off a little steam." Some therapists advise clients to strike plastic dolls or use foam-rubber bats to work off their tensions and thereby create an atmosphere free from potential violence. This popular line of thinking captures one prediction from the frustration-aggression hypothesis: Our need to aggress is reduced after we experience a cathartic release of tension. Thus, perhaps the best way to deal with frustration is to express our feelings against some harmless target. Unfortunately, while this advice is entirely consistent with the frustration-aggression hypothesis, it is not supported by empirical research.

We can first ask if there is any evidence for a reduction of tension following aggression. The answer appears to be yes, but only under certain conditions. Subjects in several investigations have shown a sudden drop in physiological arousal after attacking another subject, usually through electric shock (Hokanson & Burgess, 1962; Hokanson & Edelman, 1966). Angered subjects' blood pressure levels tend to increase just prior to shocking someone else, then return to a normal arousal level more quickly than for subjects not allowed to shock. However, a number of circumstances limit this effect. For example, aggression against a powerful and threatening person may actually increase arousal (Hokanson & Shetler, 1961). Other studies find that people who feel guilty about hurting others may also show an increase rather than a decrease in arousal after pressing the shock button (Schill, 1972). Nonetheless, researchers generally agree that something resembling a cathartic release of tension does occur following aggression, at least under certain conditions.

Does this mean that aggression leads to a decrease in the need to aggress? Apparently not. Experiments with a wide variety of subject populations and procedures find that aggression actually produces an *increase* in the tendency to aggress. For example, subjects in one study were asked to participate in three successive tasks (Geen, Stonner, & Shope, 1975). First, they were asked to give their opinions on some controversial issues. Another subject (again, a confederate) graded the quality of their opinions by giving either few or many electric shocks. Thus, half the subjects were made angry and half were not. Next, the tables were turned. It was the confederate's turn to get shocked for making mistakes on a maze task. Sometimes the subjects were the ones to do the shocking, sometimes they watched the experimenter do the shocking, and sometimes the confederate received no shocks. Consistent with the frustration-aggression hypothesis, when angry subjects were allowed to retaliate against the confederate, they experienced a significant drop in blood pressure — a cathartic reaction. At this point the frustration-aggression hypothesis predicts that these subjects would be less inclined to act aggressively than the angry subjects who were not given an opportunity to attack the confederate.

To test this prediction, the third part of the experiment gave all subjects an opportunity to shock the confederate, this time as a means of grading his performance on a decoding task. Subjects set the shock level from 1 (mild shock) to 10 (extreme shock) whenever the confederate made a mistake. Who gave the most severe shocks — the subjects who had experienced catharsis or those who had not? As shown in Table 6.4, the frustration-aggression hypothesis was not supported. The subjects who had experienced the release in tension after retaliating against the confederate actually showed the *highest* level of aggression when given another opportunity.

Table 6.4

Mean Shock Level Set by Subject during Third Phase of Experiment

Treatment of Confederate on Second-Phase Task	Treatment of Subject by Confederate in Phase I	
	Attacked	Not Attacked
Subject shocked confederate	6.65	3.92
Experimenter shocked confederate	4.13	3.62
Confederate received no shocks	5.20	3.20

Source: From Geen, Stonner, and Shope (1975); reprinted by permission of Russell G. Geen.

Several studies have produced similar effects. Although the opportunity to aggress may provide a cathartic release of tension, it also seems to produce an increase, rather than the predicted decrease, in aggression. Why should this be the case? Geen and Quanty (1977) provide some answers. First, acting aggressively may lead to a *disinhibition* to aggress in the future. Most of us have strong inhibitions about physically hurting other people. However, once we violate that rule it may be easier to attack in the future. Such is the case of soldiers who find that using a weapon against another human being becomes easier and easier the more they do it.

Another reason for the aggression-breeds-aggression findings may be the presence of *cues for aggression*. As described in Chapter 14, some studies indicate that seeing something we associate with violence (for example, a gun) increases our tendency to act aggressively. By observing our own aggressive actions, we may witness additional aggressive cues that may spur us to more aggression. Finally, because the cathartic release of tension that comes with aggression feels good, acting aggressively may be reinforcing. As discussed in Chapter 13, behaviors that lead to pleasant consequences are likely to be repeated. Thus, rather than creating a reduction in aggression, catharsis may actually create a tendency to increase aggression.

A Revised Frustration-Aggression Hypothesis

In many ways the original frustration-aggression hypothesis has weathered more than half a century of research and analysis rather well. Few other theories in psychology have generated as much research or survived to such a ripe age. However, as described above, only some of the predictions derived from the original hypothesis have been supported in empirical research. Consequently, on the 50th anniversary of the model, psychologist Leonard Berkowitz proposed a reformulation of the original frustration-aggression hypothesis.

Berkowitz (1989) argues that frustrations cause us to act aggressively because they are aversive. Things that frustrate us are unpleasant, and it is the unpleasantness that we are responding to when we react to frustrating circumstances with aggression. According to this analysis, *any* unpleasant event increases the likelihood that we will act aggressively. The kinds of frustrations researchers examine often lead to aggression because blocking a person's ability to reach a desired goal is especially unpleasant. Berkowitz argues that researchers should not be asking if a particular event is frustrating, but rather how unpleasant it is.

This reformulation has several advantages over the original frustration-aggression hypothesis. First, the new model explains why all frustrations do not lead to aggression. Frustration leads to aggression only to the extent that it is perceived as unpleasant. Second, the revised hypothesis helps us understand why certain thoughts increase or decrease the likelihood of acting aggressively. Researchers find that people act more or less aggressively toward someone who frustrates them depending on whether they believe the person's actions were deliberate and hostile or done accidentally. For example, you may be very frustrated if you do poorly on a test because your roommate went home for the weekend with your textbooks in the back of his or her car. However, you will have a very different reaction to this frustration if you believe your roommate was unaware of the books than if you determine that he or she deliberately hid the books because of jealousy over your good grades. Although the original formulators of the frustration-aggression hypothesis gave little consideration to these kinds of cognitions, Berkowitz's revised hypothesis can account for these findings rather easily. Thoughts that create negative feelings make the whole experience more unpleasant and increase the chances of aggression. Thoughts that decrease negative feelings are less likely to lead to aggression.

The revised frustration-aggression hypothesis also allows us to make some interesting predictions. According to the reformulation, any unpleasant event can increase the likelihood of aggression. Consistent with this notion, researchers have found that such irritations as cigarette smoke, loud noise, and high temperatures increase the amount of punishment subjects give to innocent bystanders (Berkowitz, 1989). When frustrated people experience some of these unpleasant conditions, the chances that they will respond aggressively increase. We can expand the revised hypothesis even further to propose that unpleasant states as depression, not normally associated with hostility, might increase the chances that someone will respond aggressively to frustration. Finally, we can predict from the new hypothesis that giving something pleasant to a frustrated person will decrease the likelihood of aggression even if the source of frustration remains (Baron, 1984). Thus, if you win a large amount of money in a lottery we might predict that the hostility you had been experiencing as a result of a frustrating calculus class is likely to disappear.

In conclusion, although the frustration-aggression hypothesis has stimulated research for more than five decades, it has received only partial support from these investigations. While it is probably true that frustration can be responsible for aggression, there are occasions when frustration does not produce aggression and when aggression is caused by sources other than frustration. While there is evidence for a cathartic release of tension following aggression in some circumstances, that expression of aggression probably leads to more, not less, future aggression. Berkowitz's revised frustration-aggression hypothesis takes care of many of the shortcomings of the original model, but how well research supports some of the new predictions from this reformulation remains to be seen.

Individuation and Deindividuation

A researcher named Robert Watson (1973) once examined historical and anthropological reports of warfare in 23 different cultures. He compared the behavior of cultures that changed their physical appearance during battle (for example, masks, makeup) with those that did not. He found that 80% of the cultures that changed their appearance also reportedly engaged in torture and mutilation of their enemies. Only 12.5% of those who did not change their appearance did this. The findings suggest that something about not looking like themselves helped the warriors from these cultures act in a more savage, less human way.

Ugly and difficult-to-explain acts against others are not limited to distant cultures. In this country, quiet, respectable people sometimes get arrested when demonstrations turn into riots. Otherwise law-abiding citizens often participated in lynchings in the Old South. Middle-class citizens frequently yell "jump" to potential suicide victims or gather around grisly automobile accidents. You may have acted so out of character at a party or concert that you later had difficulty trusting your memory.

Why do people sometimes fail to act like themselves? One answer to this question stems from research on individuation and deindividuation. **Individuation** is a state in which we feel differentiated from others; we see ourselves as unique and different from the norm. **Deindividuation** is the opposite. It is a state in which people become less aware of themselves and their personal standards of behavior—a state where we find behavior described as "out of character."

The extent to which people develop and identify their uniqueness and individuality is a theme that runs through much of the writing of the neo-Freudian theorists. Erickson and Sullivan outlined the developmental sequence through which people develop a sense of identity. Horney also maintained that a psychologically healthy individual develops and expresses a sense of uniqueness and independence. Fromm based much of his theorizing about the need to escape from freedom on the notion of individuation. Fromm argued that as we mature we come to see ourselves as a separate entity, autonomous from the rest of the world. Although he agreed that developing a sense of identity and self has its positive side, Fromm was concerned about the fear most of us have in exercising our sense of uniqueness and individuality. "The child becomes more free to develop and express its own individual self unhampered by those ties which were limiting it," he wrote. "But the child also becomes more free *from* a world which gave it security and reassurance" (1941/1965, p. 46).

These neo-Freudian theorists generally were concerned with a relatively stable sense of identity and individuation. However, more recent researchers use the terms *individuation* and *deindividuation* to refer to temporary states in which people either maintain a strong sense of self despite pressure to focus on the norm or act in a manner that goes entirely against the way they normally behave. This research not only relates back to some of the concerns of the psychoanalytic theorists but also has implications generally for the study of personality. Let's begin with the latter phenomenon. Why don't people always act like themselves?

Deindividuation

According to deindividuation theory, certain situational variables reduce our awareness of ourselves and thereby create a state of deindividuation (Zimbardo, 1970). Some of these variables are listed in Table 6.5. Anything that focuses our attention away from who we are and what we believe in seems to work. Whenever you feel you're an anonymous member of a large group and not accountable for your actions, you probably are experiencing some level of deindividuation. Dances, concerts, cocktail lounges, and other situations are often arranged to encourage this effect. For example, cocktail lounges often feature low lights, arousing music, and consciousness-altering drinks, which creates a situation very different from the ones we encounter in our daily activities. Consequently, people often say and do things they later regret. People walking out of a cocktail lounge into a bright parking lot sometimes feel like Dorothy when she opened the door to her house and stepped into Oz. It's like passing into another world.

What kinds of things do people do when in a deindividuated state? Zimbardo (1970) describes two kinds of behavior. First, there are the negative, antisocial behaviors we have already alluded to. These behaviors are described as "selfish, greedy, power-seeking, hostile, lustful, and destructive" (p. 251). However, deindividuation can lead to normally unexpressed, positive behaviors as well. These include "intense feelings of happiness and sorrow, and open love for others." Research demonstrates that both positive and negative behaviors are possible when people lose a sense of themselves.

Deindividuation and Antisocial Behavior   According to deindividuation theory, a decreasing awareness of one's self increases the likelihood of antisocial behavior. Several laboratory studies have found support for this prediction. For example, subjects allowed to remain anonymous and dressed in bulky lab coats and hoods gave what they thought were longer electric shocks to another student than did subjects who wore large name tags and their own clothes throughout the experiment (Zimbardo, 1970). Other procedures that increase anonymity, decrease responsibility, heighten arousal, and so on, also increase aggression in laboratory studies. Deindividuated subjects are more likely than others to give electric shocks (Johnson & Downing, 1979; Prentice-Dunn & Rogers, 1980; Rogers & Prentice-Dunn, 1981), to make loud noises to disrupt other people (Mann, Newton, &

Table 6.5

Situational Variables Affecting Deindividuation

1. *Anonymity.* In certain situations other people don't know who we are. Being in the dark, being among strangers, concealing our appearance behind a mask—all of these create a feeling of anonymity.

2. *Lessened responsibility.* Some situations create the perception of lessened personal responsibility. When there are many people to share the blame for an act or when someone else can clearly be blamed, we may feel as if we can get away with anything.

3. *Groups.* Crowds of people engaging in unrestrained behavior, for instance, at rock concerts or political rallies, can cause us to get caught up with the behavior of the group and to become less aware of ourselves.

4. *Arousal.* Arousal can result from exercise, an exciting speech, music, sexually arousing stimuli, and the like.

5. *Novel situations.* In some situations we are not sure how to behave. We haven't had the opportunity to learn the norms for behavior, nor are we aware of the situational cues that provide this information.

6. *Altered states of consciousness.* Alcohol and drugs can create a state of consciousness in which self-awareness and concern with evaluation are diminished.

Innes, 1982), and even to throw objects at a courageous (if not stupid) research assistant (Diener, 1976).

But deindividuation research also lends itself to studies outside the laboratory. For example, once a year millions of children participate in an activity that theoretically creates as deindividuating a situation as ever created in a laboratory: Halloween trick-or-treating. Consider the variables: anonymity provided by a costume, a mask, and darkness; the novelty of a once-a-year event; the presence of many other children acting in a similar manner; and the arousal caused by the holiday hype and running from door to door. The situation is ripe for unrestrained behavior.

One team of researchers sought to capitalize on this naturally occurring deindividuation one Halloween night (Diener, Fraser, Beaman, & Kelem, 1976). In each of 27 homes an experimenter unknown to the neighborhood children greeted visitors at the door and pointed to a table with a bowl of candy bars and a bowl filled with pennies and nickels. The experimenter told the children to take just one piece of candy and left the room. Naturally, a concealed observer watched and recorded the children's behavior. The investigators examined three variables. First, the experimenter asked half the children their names and where they lived, while the other half remained anonymous. Second, the observer noted if the child was in a group or alone. Third, the experimenter sometimes assigned responsibility for missing candy or money to the smallest child in the group under various conditions. Sometimes the child was asked for his or her name, sometimes left anonymous. The combination of variables created the seven conditions shown in Table 6.6.

Table 6.6

Percentages of Trick-or-Treaters Taking Extra Candy and/or Money

Condition	% Transgressors
Nonanonymous	
Alone	7.5
Group	20.8
Anonymous	
Alone	21.4
Group	57.2
Assigned Responsibility	
None anonymous	10.5
Only leader identified	27.3
All anonymous	80.0

Source: Adapted from Diener, Fraser, Beaman, & Kelem, (1976); reprinted by permission of E. Diener.

The experimenters wanted to know how many children would take extra candy or some money when the experimenter left the room. As the table shows, the more deindividuation variables present, the more likely the children were to take something extra. Only 7.5% of the children who appeared at the door alone and who were asked to identify themselves took extra candy or money. When children came to the door in a group, remained anonymous, and saw that responsibility was given to another child (the most deindividuated condition), eight out of ten children were guilty of stealing.

Evidence for more serious antisocial consequences of deindividuation comes from studies examining newspaper accounts of ugly crowd behavior. One of these studies looked at incidents of "crowd-baiting," in which crowds encourage potential suicide victims perched on tall buildings to jump (Mann, 1981). Consistent with deindividuation theory, more crowd-baiting took place when the gathered crowd was large, when the episode took place after dark, and when the episode lasted several hours (thus resulting in more frustration and arousal). Another study looked at accounts of atrocities committed by lynch mobs (Mullen, 1986). The researcher found that mobs were more likely to engage in atrocious acts (shooting, burning, or dismembering the victim) when the number of people in the mob was large. In other words, instead of increasing the chances that someone in the group will object to the heinous behavior, a large crowd appears to increase the likelihood that people will participate in such actions. Like the masked warriors who torture and dismember their enemies and the trick-or-treating children who steal candy, the members of these groups seem to act in uncharacteristically antisocial ways when deindividuating variables take over.

Deindividuation and Positive Behaviors Acting out of character doesn't always mean acting in an antisocial manner. For example, we usually don't express open affection and positive emotional feelings in public. Although you may have the urge to hug that attractive person who sits next to you in class or to tell a coworker how much you enjoy working with her, you probably won't act on those desires. The picture we get is of people restraining their feelings as we all walk quietly and properly past each other with rarely more than an occasional passing word.

But what would happen if these people found themselves in a deindividuated situation? One team of researchers conducted a study to find out (Gergen, Gergen, & Barton, 1973). College students signed up for what they believed was an investigation of "environmental psychology." An experimenter explained that they and some other subjects would be placed in a totally dark chamber. "There are no rules . . . as to what you should do together," they were told. "At the end of the time period you will each be escorted from the room alone, and will subsequently depart from the experimental site alone. There will be no opportunity to meet the other participants." Subjects were then ushered into a dark 10-by-12-foot room with seven other people, some male and some female.

What would you do in this situation? The anonymity, novelty, and group nature of the situation make it ripe for deindividuated behavior. The researchers used infrared cameras, concealed tape recorders, and postsession questionnaires to examine subjects' reactions. They found subjects quickly replaced verbal interactions with physical ones. Subjects moved about, touched, hugged, and "moved within approximately 30 minutes to a stage of intimacy often not attained in years of normal acquaintanceship" (p. 130).

These subjects were compared with another group placed in the same situation, but with one exception: The lights were left on. The differences were dramatic. As shown in Table 6.7, while dark-chamber subjects moved about touching one another, subjects in the light chamber kept to themselves. The anonymity and other deindividuating characteristics of the dark chamber apparently led to the intimate contact.

Avoiding Deindividuation If deindividuation is partly responsible for riots, mob violence, lynchings, lootings, and the like, how might we use what we know about deindividuation to prevent or overcome this antisocial behavior? The answer is dramatically illustrated in Harper Lee's (1960) novel, *To Kill a Mockingbird*. At one point in the story, Atticus Finch stands between a black man unjustly accused of raping a white woman and an angry, drunken mob intent upon lynching the man. Atticus's five-year-old daughter arrives on the scene, spots a familiar face in the crowd, and addresses the man by name. "Hey, Mr. Cunningham. How's your entailment gettin' along?" she asks. She also asks about his son. Mr. Cunningham is suddenly taken out of the mob and made aware of himself. He answers the girl, turns away from the scene, and tells the other men to clear out. The girl has unknowingly shattered Mr. Cunningham's state of deindividuation and thereby prevented the lynching.

The lesson from this example is that increasing self-awareness reduces deindividuation and therefore should reduce the possibility of destructive behavior. In a less dramatic fashion, college students in one study were given the opportunity

Table 6.7

Frequency of Behaviors Under Dark and Light Conditions

Behavior	Dark	Light
Touched accidentally	100%	5%
Touched purposefully	90%	0%
Hugged another	50%	0%
Sexually aroused	80%	30%
Moved to middle of room	90%	15%

Source: Adapted from Gergen, Gergen, and Barton (1973); reprinted by permission of *Psychology Today* © 1973 APA.

to cheat on a test (Diener & Wallbom, 1976). Some students were made self-aware by taking the test in front of a mirror and by listening to themselves on a tape recorder. Only 7% of these students cheated. However, when these self-awareness features were missing from the testing session, 71% cheated. Similarly, when researchers placed a large mirror behind the candy table in a replication of the trick-or-treat study, the children identified by the experimenter were less likely to steal (Beaman, Klentz, Diener, & Svanum, 1979). However, the mirror did not affect the children allowed to remain anonymous. The researchers speculated that the mirror may have reminded the masked and costumed children of their anonymity.

Interpreting Deindividuation Findings Why do deindividuation variables lead to uncharacteristic behaviors? One Freudian-sounding interpretation says deindividuation leads to "a lowered threshold of normally restrained behavior" (Zimbardo, 1970). That is, deindividuation allows for the release of impulses normally held in check. Sometimes these are good, such as the release of feelings of affection, but other times the darker side of our personalities is allowed to come forth.

An alternative way of looking at deindividuation concerns whether our behavior is under the control of internal or external standards (Diener, 1979, 1980; Prentice-Dunn & Rogers, 1980, 1983). Ordinarily we rely on internal standards to determine our actions. However, sometimes our attention is focused away from ourself and toward external sources. Under deindividuation conditions, we fail to think about how the action fits with our values. We may even fail to think about the consequences of our actions. Consequently, behavior falls under the control of the mob or group. If everyone else is acting in an antisocial manner, we are more likely to go along with the crowd than when in more self-aware circumstances (Lindskold & Propst, 1981).

This interpretation helps to explain why deindividuation sometimes leads to aggression and sometimes leads to affection. When our attention is focused outward and our behavior is more under the control of external cues than internal values, we are likely to go along with external demands. Depending on what the situational cues suggest, deindividuation can result in either helping or hurting those around us. This helping-or-hurting response to deindividuation has been demonstrated in laboratory research (Johnson & Downing, 1979; Spivey & Prentice-Dunn, 1990). For example, compared to individuated subjects, deindividuated subjects in one experiment either administered more electric shocks or gave away more money, depending upon what they had seen a model do before them (Spivey & Prentice-Dunn, 1990). Consequently, unlike the more Freudian explanation, the focus-of-attention interpretation also does not assume that we all possess antisocial impulses we ordinarily are able to restrain. However, in either case, researchers agree that certain situations we have come to call "deindividuating" create the potential for uncharacteristically destructive or surprisingly intimate behavior.

Individuation

When deindividuated, people lose their sense of identity and instead become an anonymous part of the crowd. But what about the opposite state? Are there not situations in which people refuse to go along with the crowd and instead stand fast to their own ideas and standards? Researchers have identified such situations, which they describe as a state of individuation (Maslach, 1974; Maslach, Santee, & Wade, 1987; Maslach, Stapp, & Santee, 1985). We see examples of individuation when people dress differently from the norm or take positions on social issues different from their peers and colleagues.

In general, people prefer to individuate themselves when they believe there is something to be gained from such an action. For example, sometimes standing out from the crowd means attention and admiration from others. Identifying yourself as different from the rest can be daring and exciting. In fact, if it doesn't mean social rejection, most of us probably prefer to feel special rather than one of the masses. Studies find that people who want to separate themselves from a group often try some attention-getting behavior, such as sitting on the floor when everyone else remains in chairs (Maslach, 1974). Sometimes they disclose personal information that sets them apart from the others, such as telling about secret desires or beliefs that surely few people hold. Another way to individuate yourself is to make a lot of references to your actions, state your name frequently, and in general act in a more unconventional way than do the people around you. In short, you can individuate yourself by acting the opposite of people who prefer to remain *de*individuated.

Although our desire to individuate fluctuates from situation to situation, we also can identify a relatively stable degree to which people are willing to engage in behaviors that publicly differentiate them from everyone else (Maslach, Stapp, & Santee, 1985). We all know people who seem to go out of their way to stand out in a crowd. They're the ones always wearing unusual clothes or sporting a strange hair style. However, we also know people who never seem to stand out from the

Individuation

To what extent are you willing to individuate yourself from others? To obtain a better idea of this, you can respond to the following items. Indicate the extent to which you would be willing to do each of the following, using this five-point scale:

1 = Not at all willing to do this
2 = Somewhat unwilling to do this
3 = Neither willing nor unwilling to do this
4 = Somewhat willing to do this
5 = Very much willing to do this

_____ 1. Give a lecture to a large audience.
_____ 2. Raise your hand to ask a question in a meeting or lecture.
_____ 3. Volunteer to head a committee for a group of people you do not know very well.
_____ 4. Tell a person that you like him/her.
_____ 5. Publicly challenge a speaker whose position clashes with your own.
_____ 6. Accept a nomination to be a leader of a group.
_____ 7. Present a personal opinion, on a controversial issue, to a group of strangers.
_____ 8. When asked to introduce yourself, say something more personal about yourself than just your name and occupation.
_____ 9. Give an informal talk in front of a small group of classmates or colleagues.
_____10. Speak up about your ideas even though you are uncertain of whether you are correct.
_____11. Perform on a stage before a large audience.
_____12. Give your opinion on a controversial issue, even though no one has asked for it.

To find your score, simply add together your 12 answers. Maslach, Stapp, & Santee (1985) found a mean score of 37.7 and a standard deviation of 8.8 when they administered this scale to university undergraduates. People who score on the high end of this dimension are more willing than average to make themselves stand out in a crowd. Consistent with the individuation concept, research shows high scorers are less likely to conform to group pressure than are those scoring low on the scale (Maslach, Santee, & Wade, 1987; Santee & Maslach, 1982).

group, who go to great lengths to avoid drawing excess attention to themselves. A scale designed to measure this individual difference is found on page 188.

In conclusion, people tend to act more or less like themselves depending on the conditions they find themselves in. When situational variables draw attention away from oneself, deindividuation may set in, with antisocial or positive consequences. When people believe acting differently from others means rewards, they may take actions to individuate themselves. However, some people are more likely than others to do this.

Summary

1. People do not passively accept their discomfort when faced with an anxiety-provoking situation. Instead, each of us has learned to take steps to reduce that anxiety. Researchers have categorized these actions into general coping strategies. One of these divides coping responses into emotion-focused and problem-focused strategies. Which of these strategies will be more effective in reducing the anxiety depends on the availability of means to solve the problem and the length of the anxiety-provoking event. Other researchers examine people's relatively stable tendencies to use either a repressing or a sensitizing response to anxiety. Research finds that while sensitizers are more aware of their anxiety, repressors may actually be the ones with the strongest response to stressful situations. Sensitizers are more likely than repressors to seek out medical help, but the reasons for this remain unclear.

2. The frustration-aggression hypothesis maintains that frustration always causes aggression and that aggression has but one cause, frustration. Subsequent research finds that while frustration sometimes leads to aggression, it does not always do so, and there probably are causes of aggression other than frustration. The frustration-aggression hypothesis also maintains that aggression leads to a cathartic release of tension and a reduction in the tendency to aggress. However, while researchers find evidence for catharsis following aggression, this tends to increase the likelihood of further aggression. Recently, a revised frustration-aggression hypothesis proposed that frustration leads to aggression because it is aversive and therefore, like other aversive experiences, increases the likelihood of aggression.

3. When situational variables draw people's attention away from themselves and their internal standards of behavior, they are said to be in a state of deindividuation. In this state, people are more likely to act in uncharacteristic ways, including antisocial behavior, such as aggression, as well as positive behaviors, such as expressing affection. Deindividuation can be avoided by increasing feelings of self-awareness. At other times people prefer to stand out from a crowd, or individuate. People are most likely to individuate when they perceive rewards for separating themselves from others. Researchers also find individual differences in the tendency to engage in individuating behavior.

Key Terms

emotion-focused strategies Coping strategies designed to reduce emotional distress.

problem-focused strategies Coping strategies directed at taking care of the problem causing the anxiety.

repression-sensitization A personality dimension for a person's typical response to threat, with information-avoidance behaviors at one end and information-seeking behaviors at the other.

frustration-aggression hypothesis A theory that maintains that frustration always causes aggression and that all aggression is caused by frustration.

catharsis A release of tension or anxiety.

individuation A state in which people feel unique and differentiated from others.

deindividuation A state in which people are relatively unaware of themselves and their personal standards of behavior.

Suggested Readings

Berkowitz, L. (1989). The frustration-aggression hypothesis: An examination and reformulation. *Psychological Bulletin, 106,* 59–73. This is a concise but excellent summary of a half-century of research on the frustration-aggression hypothesis. Berkowitz also outlines his reformulation of the original model.

Lazarus, R. S., & Folkman, S. (1984). *Stress, appraisal and coping.* New York: Springer. This highly influential book has helped to define stress and coping strategies for researchers working in this area.

Zimbardo, P. G. (1970). The human choice: Individuation, reason, and order versus deindividuation, impulse, and chaos. In W. J. Arnold & D. Levine (Eds.), *Nebraska Symposium on Motivation, 1969* (pp. 237–307). Lincoln: University of Nebraska Press. Although not the first statement on deindividuation, this chapter probably was instrumental in stimulating a considerable amount of research on the topic in the years that followed. Zimbardo also describes deindividuation in terms that sound very psychoanalytic at times.

The Trait Approach
Theory, Application, and Assessment

Suppose for the moment that you have joined a national pen-pal club. The club assigns you a pen pal from a region of the country far away from where you live. The first letter you receive from your new writing partner is short and to the point. Your pen pal asks simply: *What kind of person are you?* Describing your physical features is relatively easy, and giving facts about your hometown, number of siblings, and so on takes almost no time at all. But how do you describe your personality to someone you have never met?

If you are like most people, you probably tackle this problem in one of two ways. You might start by describing what type of person you are — a quiet type, an independent type, an outgoing type. The other approach is to describe your characteristics — you are studious, shy, and friendly. In either case you are describing yourself in terms of relatively stable features, either by classifying yourself as a *type* of person or by identifying the extent to which you hold certain *traits*. This is what the trait approach to personality is all about. Trait researchers identify types or traits that describe a large number of people and that can be used to predict behavior.

Efforts to describe personality have been around as long as people have used language. Gordon Allport (1961) counted more than 4,000 adjectives in the English language that can be used for this purpose. An early challenge for personality psychologists was combining all of these characteristics into a usable structure. The first attempt to identify and describe these characteristics was to develop *typology* systems — a way to discover how many types of people there are and identify each person's type. For example, the ancient Greeks divided people into four types: sanguine (happy), melancholic (unhappy), choleric (temperamental), and phlegmatic (apathetic). William Sheldon (1942) argued for three basic personality types, each identified on the basis of general physique: endomorphic (obese), mesomorphic (muscular), and ectomorphic (fragile). The three types were said to differ not only in terms of physical appearance but in personality as well.

However, few researchers use a strict type approach today, because the approach makes several assumptions that are not easily justified. For example, the type approach assumes that each of us fits into one personality category and that all people within a category are basically alike. Further, the approach assumes the behavior of people in one category is distinctly different from the behavior of people in other categories. You can't be a little of category A and a little of B. You must be either A or B. These assumptions obviously are difficult to meet. Even Sheldon described people in terms of how much they resembled one of the three body types. Although typologies are still popular with lay audiences (zodiac signs, for instance), today the trait approach has replaced the type approach.

The Trait Approach

Personality as Trait Dimensions

Almost any personality characteristic you can think of—test anxiety, self-esteem, achievement motivation—can be illustrated with the trait continuum shown in Figure 7.1. That is, we can expect a wide range of behaviors along this continuum. Some people are very high in self-esteem, whereas others suffer from feelings of worthlessness. We also can take any given person and place him or her somewhere along the continuum. We are all more or less aggressive, more or less friendly, and so on. Finally, if we were to measure a large group of people and place their scores at appropriate points along the continuum, we probably would find that the scores are *normally distributed*. This means that relatively few people score extremely high or extremely low and that most of us bunch up somewhere toward the middle of the distribution.

A **trait** is a dimension of personality used to categorize people according to the degree to which they manifest a particular characteristic. The trait approach to personality is built upon two important assumptions. First, trait psychologists assume that personality characteristics are relatively stable over time. It would make little sense to describe people as high in self-esteem if they feel good about themselves one day but bad the next. Of course, it also defies common sense to assume that people always maintain an identical level of self-esteem regardless of circumstances. But while the trait approach acknowledges that we all have our ups and downs, over a long period of time a relatively stable level of self-esteem can be identified and used to predict behavior.

The second assumption is that the characteristics show stability across situations. For example, aggressive people should exhibit higher-than-average amounts of aggression during family disagreements as well as when playing football. Again, we all act more aggressive in certain situations than in others. But the trait approach assumes that over many different situations a relatively stable *average* degree of aggressiveness can be determined. As discussed later, these assumptions of trait stability across time and situations have not gone unchallenged.

Special Features of the Trait Approach

The trait approach to personality differs from the other approaches presented in this book in several important ways. The trait approach generally is less con-

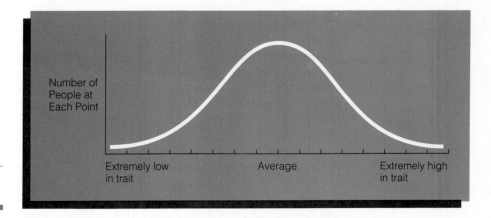

Figure 7.1

Trait Continuum

cerned with understanding one person than in understanding how people at certain points on the trait distribution behave. Trait researchers usually aren't interested in predicting one person's behavior in a given situation. Instead, they try to describe how people who score on a certain segment of the trait continuum might generally be expected to behave. Thus, a typical study might compare people who score relatively high on a social anxiety scale with those who score relatively low. Researchers might find that on the average people high in social anxiety talk less in a group situation than do those low on this trait. However, they probably would not attempt to predict any one person's behavior. Surely a few high-anxiety people in the study would talk a lot, whereas a few low-anxiety subjects would say very little. The goal of this kind of study is to identify differences between the *typical* behavior of someone who falls into one of the two groups. This contrasts with the psychoanalytic approach, in which therapists try to understand the behavior of one particular person.

Another distinguishing feature of the trait approach is that, compared to theorists from other approaches, trait theorists often place less emphasis on identifying the mechanisms underlying behavior. Rather than explaining *why* people behave the way they do, many trait researchers focus on describing personality and predicting behavior. This is an important step in understanding the causes of behavior, but when psychologists try to explain behavior with traits alone, they often fall victim to the problem of circular reasoning. For example, if asked to explain why Bob hit Scott, we might say "because Bob is aggressive." If we are then asked how we know Bob is aggressive, we might answer "because he hit Scott." We could substitute any word for "aggressive" in this example, and the logic would be just as compelling.

However, it would be incorrect to conclude that trait researchers are only interested in describing traits. Identifying traits and predicting behavior is often just the first step in the explanatory process. As the examples in the next chapter illustrate, trait researchers often examine the processes behind the behaviors characteristic of people high or low on a particular trait. For example, trait researchers have looked at the parenting styles that lead to a high need for

Achievement, and psychologists interested in social anxiety have examined the underlying concerns of shy people that cause them to avoid social encounters.

One of the major advantages of studying personality through the trait approach is that we can easily make comparisons across people. A trait description places people on a personality continuum relative to others. When we say someone is feminine, we are saying that the person is more feminine than most people. A researcher who concludes "People high in self-consciousness have difficulty making friends" is really saying that these people have a more difficult time making friends than do people who score at the lower end of this continuum.

Finally, the trait approach has relatively little to say about personality change. Information collected by trait researchers is useful to therapists making diagnoses and charting progress during therapy. In addition, many of the characteristics examined by trait researchers, such as self-esteem and social anxiety, are relevant to a client's personal adjustment. But research findings on personality traits typically provide only a direction for how to change people who may be too high or too low on a personality dimension. Trait psychologists are more likely to be academic researchers than practicing therapists. Thus, no major schools of psychotherapy have evolved from the trait approach to personality.

Important Trait Theorists

As you read this book, you may notice references to traits and trait measures scattered throughout the chapters dealing with other approaches to personality. This is testimony for how widely accepted the trait concept has become in personality psychology. Personality psychologists from nearly every approach, as well as psychologists from many other fields of psychology, use traits and trait measures in their work. The expansion of the trait approach from virtually nothing 70 years ago to its prominent influence today can be attributed in part to the pioneering work of the psychologists whose theories will be reviewed in depth here. These theorists went beyond proposing and examining a few trait dimensions. They also described the nature of traits, the structure of personality, and the relationship between traits and other aspects of psychology.

Gordon Allport

The first recognized work on traits by a psychologist did not appear until 1921, when Gordon Allport, along with his brother Floyd, published *Personality Traits: Their Classification and Measurement*. Gordon Allport also taught what is believed to be the first college course on personality in the United States, in 1924. Although psychologists and lay people today frequently speak of traits, much of Allport's work in the early years of his career was indeed ground-breaking. When only one year out of his bachelor's degree program, the unconventional Allport somehow managed to arrange a meeting with Sigmund Freud. Allport wanted to talk psychology, but Freud spent much of the time inquiring about Allport's unconscious motives. As far as Allport was concerned, there were obvious, conscious reasons for his behavior. But Freud's limited orientation wouldn't allow him to see the obvious. "Psychologists would do well," Allport concluded from the visit, "to give full recognition to manifest motives before probing the unconscious" (1968, p. 384).

Describing Traits   Unlike Freud, whom he accused of blindly adhering to psychoanalytic theory, Allport acknowledged the limitations of the trait concept from the beginning. Certainly behavior is influenced by a variety of environmental factors, he noted, and it is virtually impossible to use traits to predict specifically what one person will do. Yet, "in a person's stream of activity there is, besides a variable portion, likewise a constant portion," he argued. "And it is this constant portion we seek to designate with the concept of trait" (1961, p. 333). Allport also believed that our traits have physical components in our nervous systems. He maintained that scientists would one day develop technology advanced enough to identify personality traits by examining the structure of our nervous systems.

But Allport soon discovered one similarity he shared with Freud. His personality theory also ran into a wall of scientific resistance. Many psychologists of the day rejected his notion of traits. Allport asked why these same psychologists readily accepted such concepts as habits, drives, needs, and unconscious complexes, but not traits. Traits were similar to habits, but not as narrow. For example, brushing your teeth every morning is a habit, but brushing your teeth, washing your hands, keeping your clothes clean, and so on, are part of "a wider system of habits . . . a trait of *personal cleanliness*" (1961, p. 345). Allport argued that traits also were similar to, but not quite the same as, the accepted concept *attitudes*. Attitudes have specific referents and are either favorable or unfavorable. We express attitudes with phrases such as "I like that candidate" or "I do not care for that philosophy." However, behind these expressions of attitudes lie more generalized traits, such as authoritarianism or kindliness. Of course, again like Freud, Allport's determination (a trait on which he was high) eventually won the day. Today it is hard to imagine the field of personality without personality traits.

Dispositions are never wholly consistent. What a bore it would be if they were — and what chaos if they were not at all consistent.

GORDON ALLPORT

Nomothetic Versus Idiographic Approaches to Personality   So far we have described traits and trait research along the lines of what Allport called the **nomothetic approach** to personality measurement and description. That is, we have been looking at research on what Allport called *common traits*, "those aspects of personality in respect to which most people within a given culture can be profitably compared" (1961, p. 430). Researchers working on common traits compare all of their subjects on measures of assertiveness, anxiety, intelligence, and so on, because they believe nearly all people can be described along these dimensions. This type of research provides important information about the relationship between traits and behavior. In fact, Allport referred to nomothetic research as "indispensable" for an understanding of human personality.

But Allport also championed another way of researching personality traits that he believed was too often ignored. Rather than forcing all people into categories selected beforehand by the researcher, the **idiographic approach** is concerned with identifying the unique combination of traits that best accounts for

Gordon W. Allport
1897–1967

Gordon Allport was born in Montezuma, Indiana, in 1897 to a family of three older brothers, including seven-year-old Floyd. Young Gordon did not fit in well with the children he grew up with. "I was quick with words, poor at games," he wrote. "When I was ten a schoolmate said of me, 'Aw, that guy swallowed a dictionary'" (1967, p. 4). Allport was persuaded by

his brother Floyd to attend Harvard. This was the beginning of an academic and professional shadow in which the younger Allport was to spend many of his early adult years. Not only did Gordon follow his brother to both undergraduate and graduate degrees at Harvard, but he also chose Floyd's field of study, psychology. Floyd was the teaching assistant for Gordon's first psychology class. Later, Gordon took a course in experimental psychology from his brother, served as a subject in some of his research, and helped him with the editing of the *Journal of Abnormal and Social Psychology*.

Although the brothers both studied psychology, Gordon soon developed a very different view of the field. Floyd was a social psychologist and went on to achieve substantial recognition in this field. However, Gordon came to believe that human behavior could best be understood in ways different from the ones promoted by his colleagues. Indeed, in graduate school the budding personality psychologist identified himself as quite different from the other psychology

Continued

the personality of a single individual. To illustrate Allport's point, take a few minutes to make a list of the five or ten traits that you believe are the most important in describing your behavior. Have a friend do the same and then compare the two lists. You most likely will discover that the two of you have compiled two very different lists of traits. You might have used *independent* or *genuine* to describe yourself. Yet it may not have occurred to your friend to think of himself or herself in terms of independence or genuineness. Similarly, the traits your friend came up with might never have crossed your mind when making out your self-description.

students. "Unlike most of my student colleagues," Allport wrote, "I had no giftedness in natural science, mathematics, mechanics (laboratory manipulations), nor in biological or medical specialties" (1967, p. 8). After confessing these feelings to one of his professors, he was told, "But you know, there are many branches of psychology."

"I think this casual remark saved me," Allport later reflected. "In effect he was encouraging me to find my own way in the . . . pastures of psychology" (1967, p. 8). This he did, despite much early resistance to his notion of personality traits. Perhaps the earliest of these confrontations came in graduate school when Allport was given 3 minutes to present his research ideas at a seminar at Clark University in front of the famous psychologist Edward Titchner. His presentation about personality traits was followed by total silence. Later, Titchner asked Allport's advisor: "Why did you let him work on that problem?"

But Allport was not discouraged. He went on to a distinguished career, most of it at Harvard. His 1937 book, *Personality: A Psychological Interpretation*, outlined his theory of personality traits and was well received by many psychologists. Two years later Allport was elected president of the American Psychological Association. In 1964 he received the prestigious Distinguished Scientific Contribution Award from that same organization.

Allport's decision to wander off into different pastures of psychology was appropriate for the man who championed the idea of individual differences. This decision also took him out of his brother's shadow, perhaps best symbolized when Gordon later became the editor of the *Journal of Abnormal and Social Psychology* himself. He identified his confrontation with Titchner as a turning point in his career. "Never since that time have I been troubled by rebukes or professional slights directed at my maverick interests," he said. "Later, of course, the field of personality became not only acceptable, but highly fashionable" (1967, p. 9).

Allport referred to these five to ten traits that best describe an individual's personality as **central traits**. Of course, there also are **secondary traits** that play a smaller role in the makeup of our personalities. But if we want to understand one particular person, Allport's recommended strategy is to first determine what the important traits are for this individual and then determine where he or she falls on each of these dimensions. Although the number of central traits varies from person to person, Allport proposed that occasionally a single trait will dominate a personality. These rare individuals can be described with a **cardinal trait**. Allport pointed to historical figures whose behavior was so dominated by a single trait that the behavior became synonymous with the individual. Thus, we speak of people who are Machiavellian, Homeric, or Don Juans.

The advantage of using the idiographic approach is that the person, not the researcher, determines what traits to examine. With the nomothetic approach, the investigator measures traits that are central for some of the subjects, but only secondary for others. For example, a test score indicating a person's level of sociability is of great value when sociability is a central trait, but of limited value when it is not. Allport illustrated the idiographic approach in his study of an elderly woman who used the pseudonym Jenny Masterson. In his book *Letters from Jenny*, Allport (1965) examined more than 300 letters written by Jenny over a 12-year period. Allport identified eight of the woman's central traits with this method. Although time-consuming, this idiographic research contributed to a much more enlightening portrait of Jenny than could have been attained by obtaining test scores from her on a few preselected dimensions.

Functional Autonomy and the Proprium   Allport disagreed with Freud on another important aspect of personality theory: the relationship between childhood and adult personalities. According to Freud, the roots of adult personality are planted during childhood. Although they may appear different, the motives that underlie your adult personality are a reflection of the motives that guided your behavior as a child. However, Allport argued that although childhood behaviors may *resemble* adult behaviors, they don't necessarily represent the same underlying motives.

For example, many children who read frequently because their parents insist on it become avid readers as adults. But this does not mean the adults read for the same reasons they did in childhood. The behavior that was once a means to an end (pleasing the parents) has become **functionally autonomous**. That is, reading is now enjoyable for its own sake. Similarly, new employees who need their paychecks to survive might work very hard to make sure they are not fired. But many of these people continue to work hard even after attaining job security and comfortable salaries. The behavior that was once motivated by a need for money continues without that motivation. Allport agreed that we can often trace a certain adult behavior back to earlier times. But he argued that there is no reason to assume the adult behavior and the earlier behavior stem from the same motive.

Allport was particularly interested in the process by which children develop a sense of self. We all talk about a "self" and recognize our individuality and identity as something separate from others. But how does this notion develop? According to Allport, at birth children have no concept of themselves as distinct from their environment. Gradually they come to sense that their bodies are somehow different from other objects in the world. Babies soon discover that, unlike other parts of the environment, they can control the movement of their bodies and sense when a part of their body has been touched. From here the child develops a sense of self-identity and self-esteem, until finally the full sense of a self has evolved. Allport agreed with the neo-Freudians, who argued that the development of personality continues long after the first few years of life. Like Erikson and Sullivan, he believed identity development continues throughout adolescence.

Personality, like every other living thing, changes as it grows.
GORDON ALLPORT

However, as an academic research psychologist, Allport had mixed feelings about this notion of the self. He was well aware of the difficulty in defining and measuring something as conceptually fuzzy as a "self." He referred to the self as "an awesome enigma" for personality psychologists but argued it was too important to be ignored for the sake of convenience. To avoid confusion with similar concepts used by other psychologists, Allport developed the term **proprium** to describe all aspects of the self united under a single concept. Once again, the history of personality research has validated Allport's intuition. As you will see, today the self plays a central role in many humanistic psychologists' theories (Chapter 11) and more recently in the theorizing and research by cognitive psychologists (Chapters 15 and 16). By introducing and promoting concepts like traits, central traits, and the self, Allport assured himself a prominent place in the history of personality psychology.

Raymond Cattell

Like Allport, Raymond Cattell is an academic researcher who considers traits the basic elements of personality. Also like Allport, Cattell draws a distinction between traits common to most people in a culture and those relatively unique to the individual. However, Cattell has conducted his research with a slightly different goal in mind: to discover and identify the basic elements of human personality.

Unlike other personality theorists, Cattell did not begin with insightful notions about the makeup of human nature and then set out to measure those features. Rather, he borrowed the approach taken by other sciences. Cattell's first college degree was in chemistry. Just as chemists did not begin by guessing what chemical elements must exist, Cattell argued, so psychologists should not begin with a preconceived list of personality traits. Instead of trying to verify our intuition about what personality must be, he proposed using empirical methods.

The central goal directing much of Cattell's work is discovering just how many different personality traits there are. Psychologists have identified, measured, and researched hundreds of personality traits. But certainly many of these traits are related. Being sociable is not entirely different from being extraverted, although we can identify some fine distinctions. By grouping together those traits that are related and separating those that are independent, Cattell reasoned that we should be able to identify the basic structure of personality.

In his quest to discover this structure, Cattell employed a sophisticated statistical technique called **factor analysis**. Although a complete understanding of the procedure is beyond the scope of this book, an example can illustrate how factor analysis can be used to determine the number of basic personality traits.

Suppose you had tests to measure the following 10 traits: aspiration, cooperativeness, determination, endurance, friendliness, kindliness, openness, persistence, productivity, and tenderness. You could give these tests to a group of subjects and obtain 10 scores per person. You might then use correlation coefficients (Chapter 2) to examine how scores on one test compare with scores on the other nine tests. For example, you might find that friendliness and tenderness scores are highly correlated: If a person scores high on one test you can predict

Raymond B. Cattell
1905–

Raymond Bernard Cattell was born in Staffordshire, England, in 1905, the same year Alfred Binet developed the first standardized intelligence test. Cattell's happy childhood was interrupted when England entered World War I, when he found himself treating wounded and maimed soldiers in a makeshift wartime hospital. He later realized how these experiences planted a concern for humanity that would not fully blossom until the end of his undergraduate study at London University. A few months before graduating from the university with honors, Cattell decided to abandon his plans for a career in the physical sciences. "Soon my laboratory bench began to seem small and the world's problems vast," he wrote. "Gradually I concluded that to get beyond human irrationalities one had to study the workings of the mind itself" (1974, p. 64).

His decision to study psychology, which "was then regarded, not without grounds, as a subject for cranks," led

Continued

with some confidence that the person will also score high on the other test. Looking at the pattern of correlation coefficients, you might discover that the tests tend to cluster into two groups. That is, five of the tests are highly correlated with each other, but not with the other five tests. This second group of five tests are similarly correlated among themselves, but not with the tests in the first group. The two groups might look something like this:

Group A	Group B
aspiration	cooperativeness
determination	friendliness
endurance	kindliness
persistance	openness
productivity	tenderness

him to graduate work at London University. There Cattell — and psychology — stumbled into a fortunate association. Cattell was hired as a research assistant for the famous psychologist and mathematician Charles Spearman, who was studying the relationship between measures of intelligence. Spearman found evidence for a single general concept of intelligence, as compared to models arguing for many unrelated aptitudes. In the course of this research, Spearman developed the statistical procedure known as factor analysis.

Cattell soon recognized how factor analysis could also be used to understand the structure of personality. Although psychoanalysis was the dominant school of thinking among personality psychologists in England at the time, Cattell set about to change that.

"The real unraveling of drive structure and the concepts of 'ego,' 'superego,' conflict, anxiety, and other dimensions of human temperament," he concluded, "required measurement, experiment, and multivariate analysis" (1974, p. 65).

Although always an Englishman at heart, Cattell was tempted to America by an offer to work with the learning theorist E. L. Thorndike at Columbia. From there he worked at Clark, Harvard, and Duke, before joining the faculty at the University of Illinois in 1944, where he spent most of his career. Cattell has always been a hard worker, sometimes even going into his office on Christmas day. The result has been hundreds of research articles and dozens of books. His decision to study personality clearly was psychology's gain and physical science's loss.

Although you originally measured 10 traits, a reasonable conclusion would be that you actually measured two larger personality dimensions, one having to do with achievement and the other with interpersonal warmth. This is a simple illustration of Cattell's basic approach. By analyzing data from various sources with factor analyses, he has attempted to determine how many of these basic elements there are. He believes these **source traits** are the ones that ultimately constitute the human personality.

Unfortunately, the use of factor analysis is not as neat and clear-cut as this example suggests. If it were, we would have been able to figure out how many source traits there are a long time ago. One of the more serious limitations is that the procedure is limited by the type of data chosen for analysis. For example, what would happen if you took a few tests out of the previous example and inserted a few new ones, such as independence, absent-mindedness, and honesty? Most likely, this would change the number of categories (called *factors*) and the traits associated with (or, in factor analytic terms, "loaded on") them.

In response to this problem, Cattell divided his data into three types. Although this by no means ensures that his data include all potential personality traits, it does allow for a comparison of the factors obtained across the three types of data. Cattell examined life record data (*L-data*), questionnaire data (*Q-data*), and objective test data (*T-data*).

L-data are personality assessments from actual behavior throughout a person's lifetime. These data might include report cards, ratings by friends or employers, military conduct reports, and so on, and can also include observations a researcher makes without the person's knowledge. The main point is that because subjects do not provide the information directly, there is little room for deception or exaggeration.

Q-data are obtained from personality questionnaires. These are perhaps the easiest data to collect, and thus most factor analytic studies use this kind of data. Of course, people's ability and willingness to report about themselves affects the accuracy of this information.

T-data are in many ways the most desirable. Typically, investigators collect these data by observing subjects in settings that resemble real-life situations. For example, we might observe how people prepare themselves for an upcoming challenge or how they interact in a social setting. Cattell argues that this information is relatively uncontaminated by deception because the subject does not know the purpose of the test.

Although many similarities are found, the three types of data do not always produce identical personality factors. However, enough consistency has been found to lend credence to Cattell's claim of getting at the underlying structure of personality. Because they are easier to collect, data from personality questionnaires have received the most attention and stimulated the most research. Cattell has developed a widely used personality test to measure the 16 source traits that frequently emerge in his factor analyses. The traits measured on the Sixteen Personality Factor Inventory (16 PF, for short) are listed in Table 7.1.

As we will see later in this chapter, Cattell's strategy for identifying the basic structure of personality traits has stimulated a great deal of research in recent years. By introducing the question of personality structure and pioneering early research on this issue, Cattell has done much to shape the trait approach to understanding personality.

Henry Murray

Although most trait theorists reject much of psychoanalytic theory, Henry Murray responded to his early exposure to the psychoanalytic theorists in a different way. Early in his career Murray had the opportunity to interact extensively with Carl Jung. Jung's strong influence can be seen in the emphasis Murray gave to the unconscious in his writings. Among Murray's principal contributions to the field of personality is the Thematic Apperception Test (described in Chapter 3). Like many psychoanalytic tests, the TAT is a projective measure designed to get at material not readily accessible to conscious thought.

Table 7.1

Cattell's 16 PF Source Traits

Factor	Low Score Description	High Score Description
A	reserved, detached, critical, aloof, stiff	outgoing, warmhearted, easygoing, participating
B	less intelligent, concrete-thinking	more intelligent, abstract-thinking, bright
C	affected by feelings, emotionally less stable, easily upset, changeable	emotionally stable, mature, faces reality, calm
E	humble, mild, easily led, docile, accommodating	assertive, aggressive, stubborn, competitive
F	sober, taciturn, serious	happy-go-lucky, enthusiastic
G	expedient, disregards rules	conscientious, persistent, moralistic, stoic
H	shy, timid, threat-sensitive	venturesome, uninhibited, socially bold
I	tough-minded, self-reliant, realistic	tender-minded, sensitive, clinging, overprotected
L	trusting, accepting of conditions	suspicious, hard to fool
M	practical, "down-to-earth" concerns	imaginative, bohemian, absentminded
N	forthright, unpretentious, genuine but socially clumsy	astute, polished, socially aware
O	self-assured, placid, secure, complacent, serene	apprehensive, self-reproaching, insecure, worrying, troubled
Q_1	conservative, respecting traditional values	experimenting, liberal, free-thinking
Q_2	group-dependent, a "joiner" and sound follower	self-sufficient, resourceful, prefers own decisions
Q_3	undisciplined self-conflict, lax, follows own urges, careless of social rules	controlled, exacting, willpower, socially precise, compulsive
Q_4	relaxed, tranquil, unfrustrated, composed	tense, frustrated, driven, overwrought

Source: Reprinted by permission of the Institute of Personality and Ability Testing.

Murray called his approach *personology* and identified the basic elements of personality as needs. He was not very concerned with *viscerogenic needs*, such as the need for food and water. Rather, his work centered on understanding **psychogenic needs**, which are similar to the traits described by other theorists. A psychogenic need is a "potentiality or readiness to respond in a certain way under certain given conditions (1938, p. 124)." In keeping with his psychoanalytic background, he postulated that these needs are largely unconscious. Murray eventually arrived at a list of 27 psychogenic needs (see Table 7.2).

Henry A. Murray
1893–1988

Henry Murray was born to a wealthy family in 1893, in a house on the site of what today is Rockefeller Center in New York City. Murray's background and early training gave little clue that he would someday not only settle on personality psychology as a career, but come to be recognized as one of its most influential theorists. According to his own analysis, "[my] record consisted of nothing but items which correlated negatively, to a highly significant degree, with the records of the vast majority of professional psychologists" (1967, p. 286). He attended one psychology lecture as an undergraduate, found it a boring topic, and walked out. Instead, he earned his bachelor's degree in history in 1915, followed by a medical degree from Columbia in 1919. After working a few years in embryology, Murray went to Cambridge University in England, where he earned a doctorate in biochemistry in 1927.

But during the latter years of his academic training, Murray was exposed to and enthusiastically embraced the writings of Carl Jung. He was particularly impressed with Jung's description of psychological types. While studying in England, he arranged to meet with Jung in Vienna in 1925. These conversations convinced Murray to turn his attention to psychology. After working at the Harvard Psychological Clinic and receiving formal psychoanalytic training, Murray accepted a position at Harvard, where he taught until his retirement in 1962. Like most turns in his career, Murray was struck by the improbability of becoming a lecturer in psychology, given that he had a very weak background in psychology and suffered from a stuttering problem.

Nonetheless, Murray's academic career was long and successful. But this commitment to psychology did not end his professional diversity. He took a brief break from academia in 1943 when he was recruited by the Office of Strategic Services, a forerunner of the Central Intelligence Agency, to apply his understanding of personality to the selection of undercover agents. Murray also became something of a literary scholar, although he confessed once that "in school, [I] had received [my] consistently worst marks in English." He had a particular passion for the writings of Herman Melville and became an authority on Melville's life. Murray died in 1988 at the age of 95.

Table 7.2

Murray's Psychogenic Needs

Need	Description
Abasement	To surrender. To comply and accept punishment. To apologize, confess, atone. Self-depreciation. Masochism.
Achievement	To overcome obstacles, to exercise power, to strive to do something difficult as well and as quickly as possible.
Affiliation	To form friendships and associations. To greet, join, and live with others. To cooperate and converse sociably with others. To love. To join groups.
Aggression	To assault or injure another. To murder. To belittle, harm, blame, accuse, or maliciously ridicule a person. To punish severely. Sadism.
Autonomy	To resist influence or coercion. To defy an authority or seek freedom in a new place. To strive for independence.
Blamavoidance	To avoid blame, ostracism, or punishment by inhibiting asocial or unconventional impulses. To be well behaved and obey the law.
Counteraction	Proudly to refuse admission of defeat by restriving and retaliating. To select the hardest tasks. To defend one's honor in action.
Defendance	To defend oneself against blame or belittlement. To justify one's actions. To offer extenuations, explanations, and excuses. To resist "probing."
Deference	To admire and willingly follow a superior allied other. To cooperate with a leader. To serve gladly.
Dominance	To influence or control others. To persuade, prohibit, dictate. To lead and direct. To restrain. To organize the behavior of a group.
Exhibition	To attract attention to one's person. To excite, amuse, stir, shock, thrill others. Self-dramatization.
Harmavoidance	To avoid pain, physical injury, illness, and death. To escape from a dangerous situation. To take precautionary measures.
Infavoidance	To avoid failure, shame, humiliation, ridicule. To refrain from attempting to do something that is beyond one's powers. To conceal a disfigurement.
Nurturance	To nourish, aid, or protect a helpless other. To express sympathy. To "mother" a child.
Order	To arrange, organize, put away objects. To be tidy and clean. To be scrupulously precise.
Play	To relax, amuse oneself, seek diversion and entertainment. To "have fun," to play games. To laugh, joke, and be merry. To avoid serious tension.
Rejection	To snub, ignore, or exclude another. To remain aloof and indifferent. To be discriminating.
Sentience	To seek and enjoy sensuous impressions.
Sex	To form and further an erotic relationship. To have sexual intercourse.
Succorance	To seek aid, protection, or sympathy. To cry for help. To plead for mercy. To adhere to an affectionate, nurturant parent. To be dependent.
Understanding	To analyze experience, to abstract, to discriminate among concepts, to define relations, to synthesize ideas.

Source: From *Explorations in Personality,* edited by Henry A. Murray. Copyright 1938 by Oxford University Press, Inc.; renewed 1966 by Henry A. Murray. Reprinted by permission of the publisher.

Psychogenic Needs of U.S. Presidents

Americans often vote for their presidents based on what they perceive to be the candidates' personalities. But does personality have anything to do with a president's ability to lead? Psychologist David Winter (1987) provides some answers to this question. He examined the first inaugural address of each U.S. president to give such an address, from Washington to Reagan. The speeches were coded for evidence of three of Murray's psychogenic needs—Achievement, Affiliation, and Power. Here are Winter's findings:

President	Date	Ach	Aff	Pow
Washington, George	1789	39	54	41
Adams, John	1797	39	49	42
Jefferson, Thomas	1801	49	51	51
Madison, James	1809	55	51	57
Monroe, James	1817	57	46	51
Adams, John Quincy	1825	48	51	37
Jackson, Andrew	1829	43	47	45
Van Buren, Martin	1837	42	48	40
Harrison, William Henry	1841	32	41	40
Polk, James	1845	33	41	50
Taylor, Zachary	1849	53	53	41
Pierce, Franklin	1853	49	44	50
Buchanan, James	1857	46	47	42
Lincoln, Abraham	1861	36	45	53
Grant, Ulysses	1869	56	47	36
Hayes, Rutherford	1877	51	48	48

Continued

According to Murray, each of us can be described in terms of a personal hierarchy of needs. For example, if you have a strong need for a lot of close friends, then you would be said to have a high need for Affiliation. The importance of this need is not so much how it compares with the affiliation needs of other people, but rather how strong it is compared to some of your other needs. Suppose you have a big test tomorrow, but your friends are having a party tonight. If your Achievement need is higher on your personal need hierarchy than your need for Affiliation or Play, you'll probably stay with your books. If your

Box 7.1, continued

		Ach	Aff	Pow
Garfield, James	1881	46	35	49
Cleveland, Grover	1885	53	46	63
Harrison, Benjamin	1889	37	45	45
McKinley, William	1897	47	41	46
Roosevelt, Theodore	1905	62	38	38
Taft, William Howard	1909	44	38	58
Wilson, Woodrow	1913	66	49	53
Harding, Warren	1921	48	57	42
Coolidge, Calvin	1925	44	46	45
Hoover, Herbert	1929	68	45	48
Roosevelt, Franklin	1933	53	44	61
Truman, Harry	1949	56	65	78
Eisenhower, Dwight	1953	43	57	49
Kennedy, John	1961	50	85	77
Johnson, Lyndon	1965	55	59	49
Nixon, Richard	1969	66	76	53
Carter, Jimmy	1977	75	59	59
Reagan, Ronald	1981	60	51	63

Note: Ach = achievement. Aff = affiliation. Pow = power.

As we can see in this table, Jimmy Carter displayed the highest level of need for Achievement. John Kennedy ranked highest in Affiliation need, and Harry Truman's speech reflected the greatest need for Power.

Winter also found these personality differences were related to the president's behavior once in office. For example, the higher the president's need for Power, the more likely the country would go to war during his presidency. However, a high need for Power also was related to incidents in which the president avoided war in a crisis situation. Both of these actions are related to the president's style, as reflected in his personality. "The power motive is a leader characteristic associated with dramatic, crisis-oriented, perhaps confrontational foreign policy," Winter wrote, "which may end peacefully but which can easily end in war" (1987, p. 201).

Achievement need, although high, is not quite as strong as these other needs, your grade probably will suffer.

Murray recognized that a simple need hierarchy would be insufficient for predicting behavior. He therefore introduced the concept of **press**, the environmental forces that interact with needs to determine behavior. For example, your need for Order won't affect your behavior without an appropriate press, such as a messy room. If you have a strong need for Order, you probably begin cleaning up your room when it is only slightly disheveled. If you have a relatively weak need for Order, you might wait until the room is too messy to move around in — and even then, the cleaning might be motivated more by a need to please your roommates than to see things arranged neatly.

Murray drew a distinction between the real environment, the *alpha press*, and the perceived environment, the *beta press*. If people at a party are friendly and approachable, my Affiliation need might interact with that alpha press to create social behavior. However, if I misperceive these same people as cold and unfriendly, the beta press won't interact with my Affiliation need, and I won't act sociable. Understanding the beta press therefore is more important for predicting behavior than knowing what the situation is really like.

In addition to the TAT, Murray's principal legacy to the field of personality is the research his personology theory has stimulated. Several of Murray's psychogenic needs have been subjected to intense research, often by his students who went on to become important personality researchers in their own right. Among the more extensively researched are the need for Power, the need for Affiliation, and as presented in the next chapter, the need for Achievement.

Recent Factor Analytic Research:
The Big Five

From the early days of research on personality traits, investigators have been interested in the relationship between personality traits. That is, although we can identify thousands of traitlike adjectives to describe people, Cattell and others have demonstrated that certain traits tend to go together and that we can group the thousands of individual traits into a much smaller number of personality dimensions. Identifying and describing the basic dimensions of personality has been an ongoing issue in personality research for decades (John, 1990). And although there may never be complete agreement on this issue, recently researchers have noticed a surprisingly consistent finding in factor analytic studies of personality. Several different teams of investigators using many different kinds of personality data have repeatedly found evidence for five dimensions of personality (Costa & McCrae, 1988; Goldberg, 1990; McCrae & Costa, 1986b, 1987; McCrae, Costa, & Busch, 1986; Noller, Law, & Comrey, 1987; Peabody & Goldberg, 1989). Although there is still some confusion about the fifth factor (and the possibility of small sixth and seventh factors), the researchers have consistently uncovered factors that look like the ones listed in Table 7.3.

The Big Five

The five factors shown in Table 7.3 have shown up in so many studies using a variety of methods that researchers have begun to refer to them as the "**Big Five**." Suppose you spent hours completing a large number of personality tests. Research suggests that we can describe the bulk of information obtained from these

Table 7.3

The Big Five Personality Factors

Factor	Characteristics
Extraversion	Sociable versus retiring Fun-loving versus sober Affectionate versus reserved
Agreeableness	Softhearted versus ruthless Trusting versus suspicious Helpful versus uncooperative
Conscientiousness	Well organized versus disorganized Careful versus careless Self-disciplined versus weak willed
Neuroticism	Worried versus calm Insecure versus secure Self-pitying versus self-satisfied
Openness	Imaginative versus down-to-earth Preference for variety versus preference for routine Independent versus conforming

Source: Adapted from McCrae and Costa (1986b).

tests along five basic dimensions. First, your test answers tell us about your level of *Extraversion*, or your general level of activity and sociability. Next, we can combine information from the various tests to get an idea of your level of *Agreeableness*, or how trusting and helpful a person you are. Similarly, this information can tell us about how controlled and self-disciplined you are (*Conscientiousness*), how insecure and nervous you tend to be (*Neuroticism*), and how imaginative and open to new experiences you are (*Openness*). Alert students have recognized that the beginning letters of these five dimension labels cover the OCEAN of human personality.

Many researchers have been impressed with the pervasiveness of the Big Five regardless of how personality is measured. The five factors tend to show up not only when researchers factor-analyze subject responses on self-report trait inventories but also when researchers examine the traits and terms people use to describe their friends and acquaintances (Botwin & Buss, 1989; Goldberg, 1990) and when teachers describe their students (Digman & Inouye, 1986). The five factors also emerge in studies with elementary school children and appear to be fairly stable over time (Digman, 1989). In short, evidence from many different sources indicates strongly that the traits which make up our personalities can be organized along five basic personality dimensions.

Criticism and Limitations of the Big Five Model

Although research on the five-factor model has produced impressively consistent findings and an unusually high level of agreement among personality researchers, the model is not without its criticisms. First, there is considerable debate about what the five factors mean (Digman, 1989; Digman & Inouye, 1986). For example, these factors may simply represent the five dimensions that are built into our language. That is, although personality may in reality have a very different structure, our ability to describe personality traits is limited to the adjectives available in our language, which may fall into five primary categories. It may also be the case that our cognitive ability to organize information about ourselves and others is limited to using just these five dimensions. Thus, although people may describe personality as if all traits can be subsumed under five factors, this may not accurately capture the complexities and subtleties of human personality.

In response to this concern, many researchers have begun looking for the existence of the five factors in languages other than English (Church & Katigbak, 1989; John, 1990; Paunonen, Jackson, Trzebinski & Forsterling, 1992). The initial results of these studies have been promising, indicating that the five-factor model does not merely reflect the structure of the English language but may describe a universal pattern of describing personality.

Second, there remains some disagreement about the structure of the five-factor model of personality. For example, some factor analytic studies find patterns that do not fit well within the five-factor structure (Waller & Ben-Porath, 1987). Sometimes researchers find more than five factors, sometimes fewer. This has led some researchers to refer to "The Big Five, plus or minus two" (Briggs, 1989). Other investigators point out that the five factors do not always look the same when comparing one study to another. Indeed, researchers disagree on what to call some of the factors. This has prompted some critics to ask "which Big Five?" In response to this criticism, proponents have argued that the similarities between the factors uncovered using different methods and different populations are really quite remarkable (John, 1990).

Third, the five-factor model has been criticized for being atheoretical (Briggs, 1989). That is, researchers did not anticipate ahead of time how many factors they would generate from their factor analytic studies or what those factors might be. As described in Chapter 2, this lack of prediction ahead of time leaves the results of the research open to any number of explanations. Some personality theorists have speculated that there may be evolutionary reasons for the development of five major dimensions of personality, others have guessed that the five factors might relate to some kind of neurological structure. But because these hypotheses were generated after the results of the research were seen, we have no evidence to tell us *why* these particular factors tend to emerge in our research.

Nonetheless, if personality researchers continue to find evidence for the five-dimension model of personality, would this mean that trait theorists would be better off examining only five main traits instead of the hundreds they now investigate? The answer is no. In almost all cases, examining a specific trait probably will be more useful for predicting behavior than measuring only the more global personality dimension (Briggs & Cheek, 1986; Wolfe & Kasmer, 1988). For example, being sociable and being adventurous may be part of the larger personality concept Extraversion. However, if we want to understand how people act in social situations, it probably is more useful to examine their sociability scores than to measure only the more general dimension of extraversion. This is exactly what researchers found when looking at cooperative and competitive behavior (Wolfe & Kasmer, 1988). Although extraversion scores predicted who would act cooperatively and who would act competitively, researchers obtained even better predictions when they looked at scores from two of the traits that made up extraversion: sociability and impulsivity. One team of researchers found they could account for nearly twice as much of the variance in subjects' behavior when they looked at 16 specific traits than when the scores were combined into six general factors (Mershon & Gorsuch, 1988).

Another example makes the point even clearer. Scales designed to measure the Big Five personality dimensions usually combine subscales measuring anxiety with subscales measuring depression as part of the more global dimension Neuroticism (Briggs, 1989). Although it makes sense that both anxiety and depression contribute to this larger dimension, surely psychotherapists and researchers will almost always want to know which of these emotional difficulties their clients and subjects are suffering from.

In summary, although questions and issues remain, personality psychologists appear to have a reasonably clear answer to one of the central questions posed by the early trait theorists: How are the traits that make up the human personality organized? Our data to date tell us that these traits probably are organized around five basic personality dimensions.

The Situation Versus Trait Controversy

The trait concept has come a long way since Allport's early battles to gain acceptance among the psychologists of his day. The use of trait measures has been embraced by psychologists from nearly every perspective working in a wide variety of settings. Since World War II, many psychologists in mental health settings have relied on trait measurements as a primary basis for diagnosing psychological disorders. Patients admitted to mental health facilities often spend several hours taking tests that yield scores on a variety of traitlike measures. Educators became enchanted with achievement and aptitude measures that could be used to classify children and to identify problem cases. Anyone who has gone through the American education system in recent years can recall hours of such tests, often beginning in the first grade. And for several decades now academic personality researchers have been busy developing trait measures and correlating them to a number of behaviors. In short, personality trait measurement has become a widely used psychological tool.

Criticisms of the Trait Approach

Unfortunately, along with the widespread use of personality trait measurement came the possibility of abuse. Walter Mischel (1968), among others, criticized the way many psychologists were using and interpreting test scores. "It was not uncommon to take responses to inkblots, and such specific signs as the use of the white spaces or the color of the blots, . . . to predict such distal outcomes as potential incarceration, or probable parole violation, or psychiatric prognosis," he wrote. "On the basis of very little behavior sampling, all sorts of behaviors were predicted, and key decisions were made about people's fate" (1983, pp. 579–580).

Although some critics have accused Mischel of denying the existence of personality traits, Mischel argues that this was never his point (Mischel, 1973, 1979, 1983, 1990). Mischel maintains his complaint is with the overinterpretation of personality test scores. He argues that trait measures, as well as other types of test scores, do not predict behavior as well as many psychologists claim. Because of this, heavy reliance on these scores when predicting someone's future behavior cannot be justified. In addition, Mischel argues there is little evidence for consistency of behavior across situations. Let's look at each of these criticisms in depth.

Trait Measures Do Not Predict Behavior Well At the heart of this argument is the issue of whether your personality or the situation determines your behavior. Do you act the way you do because of the situation you are in or the kind of person you are? Advocates on one extreme argue that the situation determines behavior almost exclusively. Although proponents of **situationism** don't assert that everyone acts the same in a given situation, they often refer to individual differences merely as "error variance." Advocates on the other extreme claim that stable individual differences are the primary determinants of how we act.

Early in this debate, some psychologists sought an answer to the question by measuring how well personality scores and how well situations were able to predict people's behavior. Typically this research found that both the person and the situation were related to behavior and that knowing about *both* personality and situation was better than having information about only one (Endler & Hunt, 1966, 1968).

Unfortunately, there is a major weakness in this approach. The results of any such investigation are limited by the type of situation and the kind of personality variable examined. For example, we can think of situations in which nearly all people react the same. It would be absurd to try to predict whether high- or low-self-esteem people will run outside when a building catches on fire. Although the situation would account for nearly all of the variance in this case, it would be incorrect to conclude that differences in self-esteem are therefore not related to behavior. They simply aren't related to this behavior in this situation. However, if we look at other behaviors in other situations, such as how people react to

Can personality psychologists predict behavior? Yes, of course we can — sometimes.

WALTER MISCHEL

criticism, we probably will find large differences between high- and low-self-esteem subjects.

Today most psychologists agree that both the person and the situation determine behavior (Endler & Magnusson, 1976; Magnusson, 1990). Knowing that a person is high in aggressiveness or that a particular situation is frustrating does not help us predict behavior as well as knowing both of these facts. Thus, while people high in aggressiveness may be more prone to act aggressively than those scoring low on this dimension, and frustrating situations are more likely to produce aggression than are nonfrustrating situations, we would expect the highest amount of aggression when an aggressive person is placed in a frustrating situation. This way of looking at the relationship between traits, situations, and behaviors is called the **person-by-situation** approach.

Nonetheless, arguments remain over the validity of using personality trait scores to predict behavior. Mischel (1968) pointed out that personality trait scores rarely correlate with measures of behavior above the .30 or .40 correlation coefficient level. This "personality coefficient," as it is derogatorily called, statistically accounts for only about 10% of the variance in behavior. While these numbers confirm that personality is related to behavior, there remains a considerable amount of behavior that single trait scores do not explain.

There Is Little Evidence for Cross-Situational Consistency In one of the earliest studies on personality traits, a research team spent several years looking at honesty in more than 8,000 elementary school children (Hartshorne & May, 1928). They measured honesty in 23 different ways (lying, cheating, stealing, and so on) and found an average intercorrelation among these measures of only .23. Because personality traits are assumed to show some consistency across situations, this finding has been widely cited as a challenge to the trait approach. Knowing that a child is honest in one situation, such as telling the truth to a parent, may tell us little about whether the child will cheat on the playground or steal something from another child's desk.

Mischel also challenges the evidence for cross-situational consistency (1984; Mischel & Peake, 1982, 1983). Although people *appear* to show fairly strong consistency in behavior across situations, Mischel refers to this as "more apparent than real." For many reasons we tend to see behavior consistency that, on close examination, is not really there (Nisbett & Ross, 1980). For example, people often see what they expect to see. If I expect Karen to be unfriendly, I tend to notice when she insults someone but ignore the times when she pays a compliment. In addition, we typically see people in only one type of situation or role and fail to realize fully the extent to which the situation, not the person, is responsible for the behavior. For example, students sometimes are surprised to find that their stuffy, conservative professor is a fun-loving, adventurous person outside the classroom. Sometimes the way we treat people causes them to act more consistently than they otherwise might. If I assume Ron is going to be hostile, I probably will approach him in such a confrontive way that he will react with hostility. For all of these reasons we may see people acting more consistently across situations than they really are.

In Defense of Personality Traits

Naturally, attacks on something as central to personality theory as the use of traits have not gone unchallenged. Responses to Mischel's criticisms center around the question of how behaviors and traits are measured and the importance of the percentage of variance these traits explain.

Aggregating Data Seymour Epstein (1979, 1980, 1983, 1986) is one of those researchers who responded to Mischel's attacks. He argues that, on the surface, the situationists' view is absurd. If there were no consistency in behavior over time and across situations, how would we know who to marry or who to hire? Without predictable behavior patterns, we might as well marry someone at random, for our spouse's behavior would change unpredictably from day to day depending on the situation.

Epstein argues that researchers often fail to produce strong links between personality traits and behavior because they don't measure behavior correctly. The typical investigation uses a personality trait score to predict *one* measure of behavior, such as the number of minutes spent on an activity or the likelihood of volunteering for a charity drive, as indicated on a seven-point scale. This approach violates a basic concept in psychological testing. A behavior score based on one item or one measure is so low in reliability that it is almost impossible to find a correlation with any other score higher than the .30 to .40 "personality coefficient."

To understand this principle, think about why a final examination would never consist of just one true-false question. A student who knows the material well might miss one particular item for any number of reasons. But over the course of, say, 50 items, the student who knows the material well is likely to get a higher score than the student who does not. In psychometric terms, the 50-item test has a greater internal consistency (Chapter 2) and is thus a better indicator of the student's knowledge.

Epstein argues that the same problem is found in most trait studies. Most behaviors are measured on essentially one-item tests. A personality trait may be a good predictor of behavior, but we would never know it because we haven't measured behavior reliably. It's the same reason a best-of-seven World Series is played instead of a one-game world championship.

As an alternative to one-item measurement, Epstein proposes that researchers **aggregate data**. If you want to measure how much time students spend studying, you'll obtain a much better score by observing their behavior each night over the course of a few weeks than by observing just one night. Epstein (1979) demonstrated this point when he examined the relationship between scores on an extraversion-introversion scale and the number of social contacts initiated by college students, as recorded in daily diaries. Although we would predict that extraverts initiate more social contacts than do introverts, the correlation between any *one day's* total of social contacts and extraversion scores was relatively insignificant. However, the correlation between the scale score and the student's *two-week* total of initiated social contacts was an impressive .52.

Identifying Relevant Traits   Another reason personality trait measures usually fail to break the .30 to .40 barrier is that researchers may be looking at the wrong traits. Researchers often overlook which personality traits are important and which are not. Recall Allport's distinction between central and secondary traits: Traits are more likely to predict behavior if they are central traits. For example, suppose you were interested in the trait "independence." You might give an independence scale to a large number of subjects, then correlate the scores with how independently people acted in some subsequent situation. But in doing this, you probably would group together those people for whom independence is an important (central) trait and those for whom it is a relatively unimportant (secondary) trait. You would undoubtedly do better in predicting independent behavior by limiting your sample to subjects who consider independence an important personality dimension. By including subjects for whom the trait is only secondary, you dilute the correlation between the trait score and the behavior.

To illustrate this problem, researchers identified people who were either fairly consistent or relatively inconsistent in two kinds of behavior, "friendliness" and "conscientiousness" (Bem & Allen, 1974). The goal was to predict six measures of friendly behavior (for example, how friendly the subject was while waiting for the experiment to begin) and six measures of conscientiousness (for example, how well the student kept up with class readings). As Table 7.4 shows, correlation coefficients obtained for high-consistency subjects and low-consistency subjects showed a noticeably different pattern. Correlations between measures of friendliness averaged .57 for the consistent subjects, but only .27 for the inconsistent ones. Similarly, correlations for the conscientiousness data averaged .45 for the high-consistency subjects and .09 for the low-consistency subjects.

More recent studies have produced similar findings. For example, researchers identified "traited" and "untraited" subjects on the extent to which they generally felt in control of the events in their lives (called *locus of control*; see Chapter 14). When the investigators correlated trait scores with how many practice trials subjects took for a laboratory task, they found a nonsignificant .09 correlation. However, when they looked at just the subjects for whom the trait was fairly consistent, they found a correlation of .50 (Baumeister & Tice, 1988).

These findings demonstrate that personality trait measures can be strong predictors of behavior, but only if the trait is relevant or, in Allport's terms, a central trait for the individual. Other researchers point out that some personality variables may be more stable than others generally. For example, researchers find that how loud or timid people are tends to be relatively consistent across different social situations (Funder & Colvin, 1991). Other researchers have produced correlations significantly higher than the .30 to .40 range by using two or more traits in combination to predict behavior (Ahadi & Diener, 1989). In short, if researchers take care to select appropriate traits they can indeed use trait scores to predict behavior.

Table 7.4

Mean Correlations between Trait Measures in Low- and High-Consistency Subjects

	High-Consistency Subjects	Low-Consistency Subjects
Friendliness Measures		
Self-report	.57	.39
Mother's report	.59	.30
Father's report	.60	.16
Peer's report	.54	.37
Group discussion	.52	.37
Spontaneous friendliness	.59	.01
All friendliness variables	.57	.27
Conscientiousness Measures		
Self-report	.41	.11
Mother's report	.56	.10
Father's report	.49	.22
Peer's report	.49	.16
Returning evaluations	.40	.06
Course readings	.32	−.12
All conscientiousness variables	.45	.09

Source: Adapted from Bem and Allen (1974); reprinted by approval of Daryl J. Bem.

The Importance of 10% of the Variance   A final argument on the side of personality traits concerns the significance of .30 to .40 correlation coefficients. Mischel and others have criticized trait theory on the basis of the weak relationship between trait measures and behavior. But how high does a correlation have to be before it is considered important? Funder and Ozer (1983) provide some insightful data on this point. They looked at several social-psychological (situation-focused) investigations often cited for their "important" findings. The researchers converted the data from these studies into correlation coefficients and found that they ranged from .36 to .42. In other words, the "important" effects of these situational variables were, statistically speaking, no more important than the effects deemed weak by critics of personality trait theory. The point is that something which accounts for 10% of the variance of human behavior is fairly important given the complexity of behavior (see Box 7.2). Although the abuses of trait scores Mischel cites cannot be justified by this argument, it would be wrong to conclude that a finding is unimportant just because the correlation coefficient is only .30.

Box 7.2

How Important Is "Significant"?

One of the issues raised during the situation versus trait controversy concerns the importance of accounting for a small but statistically significant amount of variance. Nobody denies that correlations in the .30 to .40 range often are *statistically* significant. That is, the findings probably reflect a real relationship and not just chance fluctuation (Chapter 2). But, critics argue, a research finding can be statistically significant yet still account for so little variance as to be relatively meaningless. The question then becomes: How large does a statistically significant research finding have to be before it is considered important?

One psychologist recently provided some information that may be useful in answering this question. Robert Rosenthal (1990) examined some recently acclaimed research in the field of medicine. For example, one large study made headlines when researchers found that aspirin significantly reduces the risk of heart attacks. In fact, the investigators ended the experiment earlier than planned because the results were clear and to continue to give one group of patients placebo pills instead of aspirin would have been unethical. Obviously, the researchers considered this to be an important finding. Yet when Rosenthal examined the data he found the researchers were dealing with a correlation of around .03 that accounted for less than 1% of the variance! Rosenthal cites other important medical findings, including research on the causes of alcohol abuse and the effectiveness of AZT in treating AIDS symptoms. In each case the correlations are noticeably lower than those typically found in personality trait research.

One point these observations make is that *importance* is a subjective judgment. When dealing with medical treatments, being able to reliably save a relatively small number of lives is important. Rosenthal's data also remind us that many of the behaviors we are interested in are determined by a large number of causes. No one will ever discover a single cause for why people suffer from schizophrenia or why consumers buy one product over another. The purpose of most studies on these topics is to try to account for *some* of the variance in these behaviors. Similarly, we should not expect that a single personality score will account for all or even most of the variance in a given behavior. When we think about all the complex influences on our behavior, we probably should be impressed that personality psychologists can explain even 10% (and sometimes more).

Current Status of the Trait Debate

Although the fervor has declined in recent years, the importance and use of personality trait measures remains a topic of debate (cf. Kenrick & Funder, 1988; Mischel, 1990). Mischel is to be credited for alerting psychologists to the abuses of trait scores. Another positive outcome of the debate is the attention that has been drawn to the issues of data aggregation and the identification of subject-relevant traits, although just how much these procedures will be used in future research remains to be seen.

Psychologists will no doubt continue to develop measures for personality traits and use traits in their research for some time to come. But the continuing controversy over traits should keep researchers aware of the problems with this type of investigation. Some of the abuses Mischel objected to also are declining as many psychologists now examine information from a number of relevant sources before making diagnoses or recommending a certain type of education program. Finally, the discussion over traits should spark a continued search for more sophisticated and better methods of measuring individual differences.

Application: Educational Testing

On a given Saturday morning in the fall of each year, we can find tens of thousands of high school students hunched over desks in classrooms throughout the continent laboring over pages of test questions. How well the students answer these questions will determine where and whether they go to college, whether they receive financial assistance for their education, and perhaps how much they and their parents will expect from them once they reach a college classroom. For most of these students, taking a college entrance examination is not a novel experience. From the earliest elementary school grades, students become accustomed to taking tests designed to measure their aptitudes and academic achievements.

Some of the earliest examples of traitlike measures come from people working in education. For example, at the direction of the Minister of Public Instruction in Paris, a scholar, Alfred Binet, collaborated with a psychiatrist, Theodore Simon, to develop the first measure of intelligence in 1905. Lewis Terman of Stanford University revised and expanded Binet's scale in 1916 (renamed the *Stanford-Binet* test). Within a few decades, measuring intelligence became a standard practice in education.

Following World War II, educational psychologists developed numerous tests to measure specific aptitudes and skills. Separate intelligence tests were developed for preschool, school-aged, and adult subjects. School psychologists used these tests to identify children requiring special education programs. School administrators examined test scores to see how much their students were learning. Colleges and universities came to rely on standardized tests for selecting students into undergraduate, graduate, and professional schools.

Decisions based on scores from these tests can dramatically affect test takers' lives. For example, an incorrect decision about a child's learning disability can change the entire direction of the child's education. Trained psychologists know better than to base such decisions on test results alone. Yet, tests would not be used so widely if they did not have some influence in many of these decisions. Because improper use of aptitude and achievement tests can lead to severe injustices, we should not be surprised that many of the tests and test users have come under criticism in recent years. Let's look at two examples of this situation more closely.

College Admission Tests

Each year more than a million college-bound students take a lengthy college admission test. Most colleges and universities require scores from either the Scholastic Aptitude Test (SAT) or the American College Testing Program test (ACT). Like most trait measures, these tests provide an overall scholastic aptitude score that places each student somewhere on a normal distribution of scores ranging from outstanding to very poor. Although committees usually give more weight to grades and other evidence of academic performance when making admission decisions, admission test scores often play an important role. In one survey, only 2% of the schools contacted identified these test scores as "the most important" factor for deciding admission. However, another 43% said test scores were "a very important" factor (Hargadon, 1981).

Critics of admission tests challenge the validity of test scores for predicting academic performance (Nairn, 1980). Like critics of personality traits, they point to low correlations between test scores and college grade-point averages. However, as with most trait measures, studies find correlations between .30 and .40 for the relationship between test scores and measures of academic performance (Linn, 1982). In other words, admission tests predict about 10% of the variance in college performance. Further, when combined with other information, such as grades, prediction of college performance becomes even better than when looking at test scores or grades alone (Linn, 1982).

The parallels with the personality trait debate should be obvious. Just as psychotherapists should never rely solely on a test score to make a diagnosis, university committees should not make admission decisions on the basis of test scores alone. Nonetheless, when used correctly, admission test scores provide valuable information about academic potential. Given all of the many reasons why students do well or poorly in college, we should perhaps be impressed with .30 to .40 correlations. No test will ever be able to predict with much precision what a student's GPA will be, and no test user should ever expect as much from one test score.

Intelligence Tests

Among the most widely used and controversial of the tests used by educational psychologists are those designed to measure intelligence. One of the ironies of this widespread use is that there is very little agreement among experts in the field as to what intelligence is and just what these tests are measuring. Nonetheless, there is general agreement among test users that the scores derived from these tests measure something very much like a trait. That is, it is widely held that people can be placed on a continuum of intelligence, ranging from extremely low to extremely high. Very few people are found on the extremes of this dimension, and most people fall somewhere near the middle. Most intelligence scale results are reported as *IQ* (*Intelligence Quotient*) scores, with an average score of 100. All but a few percent of the people who take the test fall within the 130 to 70 range. Although most educators acknowledge that this IQ score is comprised of many different aptitudes and skills, they nonetheless often look first to the overall intelligence score when evaluating a student's aptitude and potential.

Many tests exist for measuring intelligence, but two have remained the most popular for many years now (Lubin, Larsen, Matarazzo, & Seever, 1985). One is the *Stanford-Binet* test, originated by Binet and revised by Terman. The other is the set of tests developed by David Wechsler. These are the *Wechsler Adult Intelligence Scale* (WAIS-R, latest revision), the *Wechsler Intelligence Scale for Children* (WISC-R), and the *Wechsler Preschool and Primary Scale of Intelligence* (WPPSI). The Wechsler scales are administered by a trained psychologist in a one-on-one setting and typically take an hour to an hour and a half per test. Testers obtain subscale scores for six "verbal" measures and six "performance" measures from the adult test. Verbal measures include tests of vocabulary, arithmetic problems, and general information. Performance tests look at how well test takers can use test materials to form geometric figures and their ability to solve various kinds of puzzles.

Like most trait measures, intelligence scores tend to be fairly stable over time. Although correlations between IQ scores taken at an early age and those taken as adults are rather low, two IQ scores taken from the same adult several years apart tend to correlate quite well, often around .80. When compared to correlations found with other trait measures, intelligence scores are quite stable. Even Walter Mischel (1968), while generally critical of trait stability findings, acknowledges that measures of intelligence are among the most stable of any individual differences.

Although intelligence scores are fairly stable over time, this should not be taken to mean that intelligence level is fixed by nature and unamenable to environmental influence. While psychologists generally agree that intelligence is largely influenced by inheritance (Bouchard & McGue, 1981), there is great disagreement about how set one's IQ level is at birth. The importance of this debate surfaces when we look at racial differences in IQ scores. It is a fact that black children in America tend to score an average of 10 to 15 points lower on most intelligence tests than do white children. Some psychologists have interpreted this to mean that blacks may be genetically less intelligent than whites (Jensen, 1969).

However, critics are quick to point out that black children often grow up in an environment that is less intellectually stimulating than that of the average white family (Scarr-Salapatek, 1971). Because intelligence does appear partially determined by the environment, we should only be surprised if we find no differences between blacks and whites. *That* would be the finding to support a fixed, inherited intelligence level. Indeed, researchers have found that black children adopted by white families of reasonable socioeconomic means develop IQ scores no different from those of adopted white children (Scarr & Weinberg, 1976).

Beyond this, critics have raised the issue of culture-bound intelligence tests. They argue that the questions asked on most intelligence tests reflect what white, middle-class Americans consider important. For example, one subtest on the Wechsler tests asks about general knowledge. The assumption behind these questions is that while all children are exposed to this information, the more intelligent ones will attend to and retain it. But clearly a child growing up in a black culture is exposed to different information than one growing up in white, middle-class culture. Because of this problem, many psychologists have been working to develop "culture-free" intelligence tests, and recent versions of the adult and children's Wechsler tests have been revised to account for some of this problem.

In summary, many of the aptitude tests used in educational settings are concerned with relatively stable individual differences. The scores they produce can be thought of as trait measures and can be placed on a normal distribution. Many of the controversies surrounding the use of personality trait scores also surface with the use of these aptitude measures. Like personality trait researchers, educational psychologists have become increasingly concerned about test validity and appropriate interpretation of test scores.

Assessment: Self-Report Inventories

It is unlikely you have reached college age without taking a number of self-report inventories. You may have received interest and abilities tests from a counselor, achievement and aptitude tests from a teacher, or personality and diagnostic inventories from a therapist. You may have even given yourself a few of those magazine quizzes for your own entertainment and curiosity. For a number of reasons, self-report inventories are more widely used than any other form of personality assessment. Typically these are pencil-and-paper tests that ask subjects to respond to questions about themselves. Relatively simple scoring procedures allow the tester to generate a score or set of scores that can be compared with others along a trait continuum. Hundreds of self-report inventories have appeared over the past 50 years, some carefully constructed with attention to reliability and validity, others not.

Self-report inventories are popular among professional psychologists for several reasons. They can be given in groups and can be administered quickly and easily by someone with relatively little training. Contrast this with the Rorschach inkblot test, which must be administered and interpreted by a trained psychologist one subject at a time. In addition, scoring a self-report inventory is relatively easy and objective. Researchers typically count matched items or total the response values. Finally, self-report measures usually have greater face validity than do other instruments. That is, we can be reasonably sure from looking at the items on a self-esteem test that they actually measure self-esteem. Although face validity alone does not establish the value of a test (Chapter 2), psychologists are less likely to disagree about what the test is measuring when the intent of the items is so obvious.

Some Frequently Used Self-Report Inventories

Self-report inventories come in all forms and sizes. Some have fewer than 10 items, others more than 500. Some provide detailed computer analyses on a number of subscales and comparison groups, others a single score for a specific trait dimension. To provide a flavor of some of the ways psychologists use self-report inventories, examples of two general types of tests will be presented here. First, we will examine some multidimensional inventories. These tests typically are used in applied settings, to aid in mental health diagnoses or in employment and promotion decisions. Scores are derived for a number of dimensions, and psychologists typically look at the overall personality profile as painted by the pattern of subscale scores, instead of any one specific dimension. Next, we will look at some popular single-trait inventories. These tests typically are developed and used by personality researchers interested in studying a particular personality trait. These inventories usually contain about 15 to 40 test items. Most provide only one score, but occasionally two or three subscale scores can be calculated.

Multidimensional Inventories   *The Minnesota Multiphasic Personality Inventory.*   A recent survey found mental health professionals use the MMPI more than any other self-report inventory (Lubin et al., 1985). This popularity has increased steadily since the test's development in the 1940s (Lubin, Larsen, & Matarazzo, 1984). Today clinical psychologists, guidance counselors, personnel psychologists, and school counselors give the MMPI regularly to their patients and clients.

The MMPI contains more than five hundred true-false items. These items generate several scale scores that are combined to form an overall profile of the test taker. The original scales were designed to measure psychological disorders. Thus, psychologists obtain scores for such dimensions as depression, hysteria, paranoia, and schizophrenia. However, most psychologists look at the overall pattern of scores, rather than one specific scale, in making their assessments. Of particular interest are scores that are significantly higher or lower than those obtained by most test takers. A sample profile is shown in Figure 7.2.

Many additional MMPI scales have been developed since the original scales were presented. Researchers interested in a particular disorder or concept usually determine those items that separate a normal population from the group they are interested in. For example, to develop a creativity scale, you would identify those test items that highly creative people tend to answer differently from people who are not very creative. MMPI answer sheets can be mailed to companies for

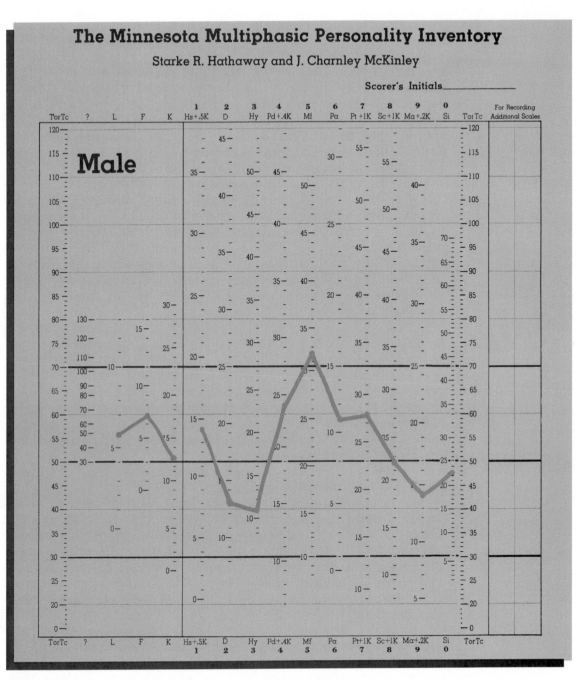

Figure 7.2

Sample MMPI Profile

The scales identified by numbers 1 through 0 are Hypochondriasis, Depression, Hysteria, Psychopathic Deviancy, Masculinity-Femininity, Paranoia, Psychasthenia (anxiety), Schizophrenia, Mania, and Social Introversion. Reprinted by permission of the University of Minnesota Press.

computerized scoring, although the basic scoring procedure is not particularly time-consuming.

The California Psychological Inventory   The MMPI scales are useful to psychologists working with psychiatric patients but are of less value to counselors working with more normal populations. For this reason, Gough (1956/1987) designed the California Psychological Inventory (CPI). Although about half the items are taken from the MMPI, the 18 scales that make up the CPI are quite different from those on the MMPI. Testers obtain scores for such traits as responsibility, tolerance, self-acceptance, flexibility, and self-control.

While the MMPI was designed to assess psychopathology and to help psychologists with diagnoses, the CPI provides valuable information with more everyday problems. For example, a woman who has difficulty in interpersonal relationships may score low on the CPI scales of sociability, flexibility, and tolerance, but high on the dominance scale. This profile would help her counselor understand why the woman has difficulties in relationships and provide some direction for helping her with this problem. Similarly, CPI profiles can be of value when helping clients select occupations or when working through conflicts within families.

The Edwards Personal Preference Schedule   The EPPS is of particular interest to personality researchers, as well as mental health professionals. The EPPS measures 15 of Henry Murray's psychogenic needs (Edwards, 1959). Thus, the test yields scores on the test taker's need for Affiliation, need for Achievement, need for Order, and so on. Consistent with Murray's theory, the test is constructed so that the strength of each need is compared with the strength of other needs. The profile of scores resembles the hierarchy of needs Murray talked about. That is, we not only can compare the strength of the need with others who have taken the test, but we also can see how strong each of the test takers' needs are compared to the other 14 needs measured with this test.

Personality researchers use the profile generated from the test to make predictions based on Murray's theory. For example, the relative strength of a subject's need for Order and need for Affiliation should help us predict what a person will do when faced with a messy room *and* a friend's invitation to go out. The test also is used by counselors, particularly when matching a client's need with the demands of a certain job or professional school. For example, a man with a high affiliation need and a low achievement need might not be well suited for graduate school.

Single-Trait Inventories   In addition to the large profile inventories, there are many personality trait scales that measure only one trait or sometimes only a few related traits. These tests usually are developed by academic researchers interested in better understanding a specific personality trait. Typically the scales are used to identify people who fall on the upper and lower ends of the trait continuum. Researchers then examine the backgrounds, attitudes, and behaviors of these two groups of people. Of course, these research findings often have implications for dealing with psychotherapy patients, such as those concerned with self-esteem or interpersonal style. Although perhaps hundreds of these types of trait measures are currently being used by researchers, space permits the introduction of only a few here.

The Authoritarian Personality Scale   Shortly after the fall of Hitler's Nazi Germany and the end of World War II, a group of psychologists began an extensive research program designed to better understand the causes of anti-Semitism (Adorno, Frenkel-Brunswick, Levinson, & Sanford, 1950). Their work led to the notion of a personality that is prone to prejudice and attracted to fascism. These researchers identified nine characteristics that make up this personality and used the term *authoritarian personality* to describe someone who portrays most of these characteristics. Their research was based heavily on the psychoanalytic model, particularly the works of Erich Fromm. Thus, the investigators placed great emphasis on child-rearing patterns in the development of this personality pattern and used such concepts as projection to explain authoritarian behavior.

The authoritarian characteristics Adorno et al. (1950) identified include a rigid adherence to traditional middle-class values, a preoccupation with power and toughness themes, a general hostility and cynicism toward people, and a submissive attitude toward authoritarian figures. These researchers developed the *F-Scale* (F for Fascist) to measure authoritarianism. Most of the research with this scale has produced results consistent with the description of the authoritarian personality. For example, people who score high on the F-Scale are more likely to be prejudiced (Klein, 1963) and more likely to project their own feelings and attitudes onto others (Granberg, 1972) than are those who score low. One interesting application of this research has been to understand how jurists go about deciding if a defendant is guilty or not guilty (Berg & Vidmar, 1975; Bray & Noble, 1978; Ryckman, Burns, & Robbins, 1986). Researchers find that because high authoritarians are relatively closed-minded and concerned with upholding traditional values, they are more likely to convict the person on trial and often recommend a harsh punishment.

The Self-Monitoring Scale   The Self-Monitoring Scale (Snyder, 1974; Snyder & Gangestad, 1986) was designed to measure the extent to which people observe, regulate, and control the public display of themselves. High self-monitors are very concerned about the image other people have of them and go to great lengths to create the impression they find most desirable. Low self-monitors are less likely to share this concern and are not as likely to alter their public appearance depending on who they are interacting with.

Researchers find high and low self-monitors differ on a large number of behaviors (Snyder, 1987). For example, high self-monitors are better at expressing their emotions through facial movements, at deceiving others, and at reading others' facial expressions than are low self-monitors. High self-monitors tend to approach friendships in an activity-based orientation. That is, they select friends based on what the person can do. High self-monitors are likely to have one friend for concerts, another for sports, and so on. Low self-monitors are more likely to approach friendship in an affect-based orientation. That is, they select friends because of a more global attraction and are as likely to call the same person to play tennis as to go shopping. Because they are more concerned with images, high self-monitors are more likely to select their dates on the basis of physical attractiveness, whereas low self-monitors are more likely to date someone with a pleasant personal style.

Sex Guilt and Sex Anxiety Scales   If you have ever made the mistake of introducing a sexual topic into a conversation with people you do not know well, you are aware that people differ on how comfortable they are with sexual behavior and sexually related issues. Some people are very interested in the topic and feel free to discuss it; others are quite uncomfortable and inhibited. Some of these differences can be measured on the Sex Guilt Scale (Mosher, 1966, 1968). People scoring high in sex guilt generally feel as if they should be punished for violating societal standards of sexual conduct. They tend to feel guilty about engaging in, or sometimes even just thinking about, sexual behavior outside of narrow socially acceptable standards. Researchers speculate that high sex guilt develops in families in which a generally negative view of sexuality is fostered.

Not surprisingly, differences in sex guilt have been related to differences in many sexually related behaviors (Mosher, 1979). For example, people high in sex guilt are reluctant to use effective contraception. Researchers find high sex-guilt people are not so guilt-ridden that they refrain from premarital intercourse but that they feel guilty enough to be inhibited about using contraception (Gerrard, 1982, 1987).

Other researchers have focused their attention on a related concept, *sex anxiety*. Sex anxiety scales measure the extent to which people generally feel anxious when dealing with sexual issues (Janda & O'Grady, 1980). As with sex guilt, people high in sex anxiety are less likely to engage in sexual activities and are uncomfortable dealing with sexually related matters.

The Desirability of Control Scale   Although each of us typically wants control over the events in our lives, people differ on the strength of this motivation. Whereas some people want to control every situation and every encounter, others are quite content to let someone else take control. Burger and Cooper (1979) developed the Desirability of Control Scale to measure these individual differences. People who score high on this scale prefer to make their own decisions, take on leadership roles in a group situation, and take precautions to avoid situations where they might lose control (for example, checking everything on a car before a long trip). Those scoring at the low end of the scale are more comfortable letting others make decisions for them and probably are not overly concerned with influencing people or taking responsibility for group projects.

Researchers find that individual differences in desire for control are related to a large number of behaviors (Burger, 1992). As compared to lows, people high in desire for control do better in achievement situations and are less likely to conform to social pressures. This follows from their high need to demonstrate mastery over challenging tasks and from their motivation to make their own decisions instead of going along with the crowd. However, people who have a high need for control also may be more prone to depression, more susceptible to feeling crowded when a lot of people are around, and more likely to be fooled into believing they have control over a chance outcome in a gambling situation. It seems that a high desire for control can be an asset when genuine control over a situation is obtainable, but it can lead to frustration and depression when encountering events over which control is not possible.

The Self-Consciousness Scale   Although each of us feels self-conscious on occasion, some people have this experience more often than others. Fenigstein, Scheier, and Buss (1975) developed the Self-Consciousness Scale to measure the extent to which people are disposed to focus attention inward on themselves. Two related constructs are measured with this scale. First, the test assesses *private self-consciousness*, the extent to which test takers are aware of their own moods, attitudes, and bodily states. Next, the scale provides a measure of *public self-consciousness*. This score indicates the extent to which people are aware of and concerned with outward appearances. Someone scoring high on this part of the scale often experiences what you might have felt the last time you stood in front of a group of people and were concerned about what they were thinking of you. The items on the public self-consciousness subscale were presented in Chapter 2.

As with other well-researched trait measures, individual differences in both of these self-consciousness subscales have been linked to relevant behaviors (Fenigstein, 1987; Scheier & Carver, 1981). Because they are more in tune with their attitudes and feelings, people high in private self-consciousness are more likely to base their behaviors on internal standards and beliefs instead of going along with the crowd. These high scorers also are more consistent in expressing their attitudes and are more aware of their emotional reactions to events. People high in public self-consciousness are more concerned with fashion and their physical appearance than are those low on this trait. They also are more aware of what others think of them and conform to social pressure to avoid negative evaluations. As you might suspect, people who score high in public self-consciousness also tend to score high on self-monitoring.

Sensation-Seeking Scale   We all know people who are more than willing to try sky diving, hang gliding, or some other thrill-seeking adventure despite the dictates of common sense. Zuckerman and his colleagues (Zuckerman, 1971; Zuckerman, Kolin, Price, & Zoob, 1964) developed the Sensation-Seeking Scale to assess the extent to which people seek out situations that provide "varied, novel and complex sensations and experiences." People who score high on this scale have a strong need for thrills and adventure-seeking. They are attracted to activities that involve an element of danger or risk. High sensation-seekers often seek out new and novel experiences. They find routine and repetitive experiences boring.

More than two decades of work on this trait has uncovered some interesting differences between high and low sensation-seekers (Zuckerman, 1979, 1983). For example, people scoring on the high end of the scale are more likely to have tried drugs and alcohol. They are more likely to have engaged in premarital sexual behavior and are generally more sexually responsive than are low sensation-seekers. Not surprisingly, high sensation-seekers also are more likely to volunteer for such experiences as hypnosis, encounter groups, meditation, and even sensory deprivation (although they find the latter more uncomfortable than do lows). Highs are more likely to try risky sports, such as scuba diving and parachute jumping, and are more likely to take risks with these, such as staying under water a little longer than recommended when scuba diving. Researchers find that high and low sensation-seekers also differ on several physiological measures, such as brain activity and hormone level. This evidence has led some researchers to suggest that individual differences in sensation-seeking may have a biological basis (Zuckerman, 1983).

Problems with Self-Report Inventories

Despite their widespread use, self-report inventories have problems that need to be considered when constructing a scale or interpreting test scores. Researchers who use self-report inventories still must depend on the subjects' ability and willingness to provide accurate information about themselves. Sometimes these inaccuracies can be identified and test scores discarded, but more often the misinformation probably goes undetected.

Faking   Sometimes test takers intentionally give misleading information on self-report inventories. For example, they may "fake good" on scales used to make employment decisions. Why would people admit something negative about themselves if an employer is using that information to decide who to hire? Most people are motivated to describe themselves as hard-working and well adjusted. On the other hand, there are situations in which people are motivated to "fake bad." That is, sometimes test takers want to make themselves look worse than they really are. For example, someone who wants to escape to a "safe" hospital environment might try to come across as having psychological problems.

What can a tester do in these cases? First, important decisions probably should not be made on test data alone. An employer would be foolish to promote a man who scored high on a leadership measure if that person has never shown leadership qualities in five years of employment. Test makers sometimes build safeguards into tests to reduce faking. If possible, the purpose of a test can be made less obvious, and filler items can be added to throw the test taker off track. However, these efforts probably are at most partially successful. Another option is to test for faking directly. The MMPI contains scales designed to detect faking. The test makers compared responses of subjects instructed to fake good or fake bad with the responses of other populations. For example, they found certain items that distinguished between fakers and genuine schizophrenics. People trying to look schizophrenic tend to check these items, thinking they indicate schizophrenia, but real schizophrenics do not. When testers detect fakers they can either throw out the results or adjust the scores on other scales to account for the faking tendency.

Carelessness and Sabotage   Although the person administering a test usually approaches the testing very seriously, this cannot always be said for the test taker. Subjects in experiments and newly admitted patients can get bored with long tests and not bother to read the test items carefully. Sometimes they don't want to admit to poor reading skills or their failure to fully understand the instructions. As a result, some or all of their responses will be made at random or after only very briefly skimming the question.

Even worse, subjects sometimes report frivolous or intentionally incorrect information to sabotage the research project or diagnosis. I once found a test answer booklet that appeared normal at first, but at second glance discovered that the test taker had spent the hour-long research session filling in answer spaces to form obscene words. A similar lack of cooperation is not uncommon among those who resent medical personnel or law enforcement officials.

The best defense against this problem may be to explain instructions thoroughly, stress the importance of the test, and maintain some kind of surveillance throughout the testing session. Beyond this, tests can be constructed to detect carelessness. For example, the Edwards Personal Preference Schedule presents several test items more than once. The tester examines the repeated items to determine if the subject is answering consistently. A person who responds A one time and B the next when answering two identical items might not be reading the item or might be sabotaging the test.

Response Tendencies   Before reading this section, you may want to take the test presented on pages 230–231. The test is designed to measure a response tendency called **social desirability** — the extent to which people present themselves in a favorable light. This is not the same as faking, in which people answer test items in a manner they know is inaccurate. People high in social desirability unintentionally present themselves in a way that is slightly more favorable than the truth. A look at the items on the Marlowe-Crowne Social Desirability Scale illustrates the point. For example, few of us thoroughly investigate the qualifications of *all* candidates before voting. Yet someone who looks at the qualifications of *many* candidates might exaggerate the truth and answer "true" on this item. What can be done about this? By measuring social desirability tendencies directly, a tester can adjust the interpretation of other scores accordingly. However, some researchers have questioned whether this adjustment actually improves the validity of the scores (McCrae & Costa, 1983).

Social desirability scores are useful when testing the discriminant validity of a new personality scale (Chapter 2). For example, suppose you developed a self-report inventory for friendliness. Most of your items would be fairly straightforward, such as "Do you make a good friend?" High scores on this test might reflect an underlying trait of friendliness, but they also might reflect the test takers' desire to present themselves as nice people. For this reason, test makers often compare scores on their new inventory with scores on a social desirability measure. If the two are highly correlated, they have no way of knowing which of the two traits their test is measuring. However, if scores on your friendliness inventory did not correlate highly with social desirability scores, you could have more confidence that people who score high on the scale are genuinely friendly and not just those who want to be seen that way.

But presenting oneself in a favorable light is not the only response tendency that testers have to worry about. Some people are more likely than others to agree with test questions. If you ask these people, "Do you think the governor is doing a

Response Tendencies

To better understand the concept of response tendency, take the following test.

Instructions: Listed below are a number of statements concerning personal attitudes and traits. Read each item and decide whether the statement is true or false as it pertains to you personally.

_____ 1. Before voting I thoroughly investigate the qualifications of all the candidates.

_____ 2. I never hesitate to go out of my way to help someone in trouble.

_____ 3. It is sometimes hard for me to go on with my work if I am not encouraged.

_____ 4. I have never intensely disliked anyone.

_____ 5. On occasion I have had doubts about my ability to succeed in life.

_____ 6. I sometimes feel resentful when I don't get my way.

_____ 7. I am always careful about my manner of dress.

_____ 8. My table manners at home are as good as when I eat out in a restaurant.

_____ 9. If I could get into a movie without paying and be sure I was not seen I would probably do it.

_____ 10. On a few occasions, I have given up doing something because I thought too little of my ability.

_____ 11. I like to gossip at times.

_____ 12. There have been times when I felt like rebelling against people in authority even though I knew they were right.

_____ 13. No matter who I'm talking to, I'm always a good listener.

_____ 14. I can remember "playing sick" to get out of something.

_____ 15. There have been occasions when I took advantage of someone.

_____ 16. I'm always willing to admit it when I made a mistake.

_____ 17. I always try to practice what I preach.

Continued

good job?" they probably will say yes. If you ask them a little later, "Do you disapprove of the way the governor is handling things?" they probably will say yes again. This *acquiescence* (or agreement) *response* can translate into a problem on some self-report scales. For example, if the score for the trait is simply the number of "true" answers on a scale, then someone with a strong acquiescence tendency would score high on the scale, regardless of the content of the items. Just how seriously acquiescence response tendencies distort test scores is still a matter of debate (Nunnally, 1978). However, to be safe, many test makers word half the items in the opposite direction. That is, sometimes "true" is indicative of

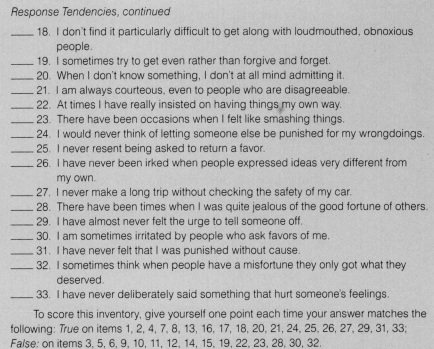

Response Tendencies, continued

_____ 18. I don't find it particularly difficult to get along with loudmouthed, obnoxious people.

_____ 19. I sometimes try to get even rather than forgive and forget.

_____ 20. When I don't know something, I don't at all mind admitting it.

_____ 21. I am always courteous, even to people who are disagreeable.

_____ 22. At times I have really insisted on having things my own way.

_____ 23. There have been occasions when I felt like smashing things.

_____ 24. I would never think of letting someone else be punished for my wrongdoings.

_____ 25. I never resent being asked to return a favor.

_____ 26. I have never been irked when people expressed ideas very different from my own.

_____ 27. I never make a long trip without checking the safety of my car.

_____ 28. There have been times when I was quite jealous of the good fortune of others.

_____ 29. I have almost never felt the urge to tell someone off.

_____ 30. I am sometimes irritated by people who ask favors of me.

_____ 31. I have never felt that I was punished without cause.

_____ 32. I sometimes think when people have a misfortune they only got what they deserved.

_____ 33. I have never deliberately said something that hurt someone's feelings.

To score this inventory, give yourself one point each time your answer matches the following: *True* on items 1, 2, 4, 7, 8, 13, 16, 17, 18, 20, 21, 24, 25, 26, 27, 29, 31, 33; *False:* on items 3, 5, 6, 9, 10, 11, 12, 14, 15, 19, 22, 23, 28, 30, 32.

You have just taken the Marlowe-Crowne Social Desirability Scale, designed to measure the social desirability response tendency. Crowne and Marlowe (1960) report a mean score on this scale of 13.72 for undergraduate college students, with a standard deviation of 5.78. As explained in the text, people who score high on this measure tend to present themselves in a favorable light that probably does not reflect reality. Another frequently used measure of social desirability is the Edwards Social Desirability Scale (Edwards, 1957).

the trait and sometimes "false" is. In this case, any tendency to agree or disagree with statements should be balanced out.

In summary, self-report inventories have many advantages over other assessment methods. However, testers cannot always assume that test takers' responses are accurate indicators of their traits. Careful test construction and administration can prevent or limit some of these problems, but the extent to which self-report inventories reflect what the test takers want or are able to say about themselves probably will always remain unknown.

Strengths and Criticisms
of the Trait Approach

In many ways the trait approach to personality is different from the other approaches examined in this book. Trait theorists tend to be academic researchers instead of therapists. Their focus is on describing and predicting behavior, rather than behavior change or development. In addition, they rarely try to understand the behavior of just one person. These differences give the trait approach some unique advantages, but they are the source of criticisms as well.

Strengths

The empirical nature of the work by Allport, Murray, and other early trait psychologists sets them apart from the founders of other personality theories. Rather than relying on intuition and subjective judgment like Freud and many of the neo-Freudians, these trait theorists used objective measures to examine their constructs. Some of these theorists, such as Cattell, specifically allowed the data to determine the theory, which was then subject to further empirical validation. This approach reduces some of the biases and subjectivity that plague data used in other approaches.

Another strength of the trait approach is its many practical applications. Mental health workers routinely use trait measures when evaluating clients. As we have seen, educational psychologists have embraced traitlike measures in their work. In addition, psychologists working in industrial and organizational settings often use personality trait measures in hiring and promotion decisions. Job counselors frequently rely on trait scores to match clients with careers. Although this widespread use of trait measures invites abuse if the scores are used incorrectly, the popularity of these measures attests to the value many psychologists place on them.

Like any important theoretical perspective, the trait approach has generated a large amount of research. Personality journals are filled with investigations about a variety of personality traits. Many new personality scales are developed and published each year. As we will see in the next chapter, much of this research stems directly from the work of some of the theorists covered in this chapter. Predicting behavior from personality trait measures has become a standard feature in research by clinical, social, industrial-organizational, educational, and developmental psychologists.

Criticisms

Criticisms of the trait approach often are based not so much on what the approach says but rather on what it leaves out. Trait psychologists describe people in terms of traits, but they usually do not explain how these traits develop or what can be done to help people who suffer from extreme scores. For example, what do we do for people who have extreme scores on measures of test anxiety, self-consciousness, and assertiveness? Knowing about these scores can help teachers and employers match people with the tasks and jobs best suited to them, but no schools of psychotherapy have come out of the trait approach. The failure of the trait approach to do more than identify potential problems limits its usefulness.

Another criticism concerns the lack of an agreed-upon framework. Although all trait theorists use empirical methods and are concerned with the identification of traits, there is no single theory or underlying structure that ties all of the theories together. We can see the confusion this creates by asking how many basic traits there are. Allport talked about a large number of traits. Murray reduced personality to 27 psychogenic needs. Cattell found somewhere between 16 and 20 basic elements of personality. And more recent investigations suggest that the number is really five. Without an agreed-upon framework, it is difficult to gain a cohesive overview of the approach or to see how research on one aspect of personality traits fits with research in other areas.

Summary

1. The trait approach assumes we can identify individual differences in behaviors that are relatively stable across situations and over time. Trait theorists usually are not concerned with any one person's behavior but rather in describing behavior typical of people at certain points along a trait continuum.

2. Gordon Allport was the first acknowledged trait theorist. Among his contributions were the notion of central and secondary traits, nomothetic versus idiographic research, functional autonomy, and the proprium.

3. Raymond Cattell's work concerns identifying the basic structure of personality. He used a statistical procedure called factor analysis to determine how many basic traits make up the human personality. Cattell also identified the importance of examining different kinds of data in this type of research.

4. Henry Murray identified psychogenic needs as the basic elements of personality. According to Murray, a need will affect behavior depending on where it lies on a person's need hierarchy and the kind of situation the person is in, known as the press.

5. Recent research provides fairly consistent evidence that human personality is structured along five basic dimensions. Although questions remain, the evidence to date tends to support the five-factor model. However, researchers probably can do a better job of predicting behavior by examining specific traits than measuring a more global dimension.

6. An enduring controversy in personality concerns the relative importance of traits compared to situational determinants of behavior. Critics charge that traits do not predict behavior well and that there is little evidence for cross-situational consistency. Trait advocates answer that if traits and behaviors are measured correctly, a significant relationship can be found. In addition, they maintain that the amount of variance in behavior explained by traits is considerable and important.

7. Educational psychologists often use trait measures in their work, particularly when measuring academic aptitude and intelligence. Because the decisions these psychologists make with test scores often have important influences on test takers' lives, much controversy surrounds the use of these tests. In particular, college admission tests and intelligence tests have come under fire. Many psychologists acknowledge the limits to appropriate test usage and are working to improve the validity of these tests.

8. Trait researchers rely heavily on self-report inventories in their work. Some of the most commonly used multiple-trait inventories include the Minnesota Multiphasic Personality Inventory, the California Psychological Inventory, and the Edwards Personal Preference Schedule. Popular single-trait scales include the Self-Monitoring Scale, the Self-Consciousness Scale, and the Sensation-Seeking Scale. Test users need to be aware of problems inherent in self-report inventories. These include faking, carelessness and sabotage, and response tendencies.

9. Like other approaches to personality, the trait approach has strengths and criticisms. The strengths include a strong empirical base, a host of practical applications, and the large amount of research generated. Criticisms include the limited usefulness of the approach for dealing with problem behaviors and the lack of an agreed-upon framework.

Key Terms

trait A dimension of personality used to categorize people according to the degree to which they manifest a particular characteristic.

nomothetic approach A method of understanding personality that compares many people along the same personality dimensions.

idiographic approach A method of studying personality through in-depth analysis of one individual and the dimensions relevant to that person's personality.

central traits The five to ten traits that best describe a person's personality.

secondary traits Traits besides the central traits that describe a person's personality.

cardinal trait A single trait that dominates a person's personality.

functional autonomy The maintenance of a behavior pattern for reasons other than those that originally caused the behavior.

proprium In Allport's theory, the aspect of personality containing all the features of the self.

factor analysis A statistical procedure used to determine the number of dimensions in a data set.

source traits The basic dimensions of personality in Cattell's theory.

psychogenic need In Murray's theory, a relatively stable predisposition toward a type of action.

press An environmental feature that interacts with psychogenic needs to determine behavior.

Big Five The five basic dimensions of personality found in many factor analytic studies.

situationism An approach to understanding behavior that maintains behavior is largely or exclusively determined by the situation rather than by personality characteristics.

person-by-situation approach An approach to understanding behavior that maintains behavior is a function of the person as well as the situation.

aggregate data Combining scores from more than one measure of the same concept to obtain a more reliable assessment of a variable.

social desirability The extent to which test takers tend to respond to items in a manner that presents them in a positive light.

Suggested Readings

Allport, G. W. (1961). *Pattern and growth in personality.* New York: Holt, Rinehart & Winston. This book, written toward the end of Allport's career, provides the best and most complete description of his theory of personality. Allport's intention to write to undergraduates with little or no background in psychology comes across in this well-written and comprehensive account of trait theory.

John, O. P. (1990). The "Big Five" factor taxonomy: Dimensions of personality in the natural language and in questionnaires. In L. A. Pervin (Ed.), *Handbook of personality: Theory and research* (pp. 66–100). New York: Guilford. A summary of the research and issues surrounding the five-factor model of personality traits. This chapter also includes an excellent history of the research leading up to recent Big Five studies.

Kenrick, D. T., & Funder, D. C. (1988). Profiting from controversy: Lessons from the person-situation debate. *American Psychologist, 43,* 23–34. A review of what personality psychology has learned 20 years after Mischel first challenged trait theory. The authors conclude that the usefulness of traits was reestablished during these years and that the defense of traits which developed from the controversy was good for the field of personality.

The Trait Approach
Relevant Research

8

In preparing this chapter, I paused to conduct a brief, partially scientific survey. I examined the last three issues of the *Journal of Personality*, the *Journal of Research in Personality*, and the personality section of the *Journal of Personality and Social Psychology*. These journals are prominent outlets in which personality psychologists publish their most recent research. Of the 66 relevant articles in these journals, I counted 50 that included at least one trait measure. That is, in 75.8% of these studies, researchers measured individual differences and used these scores to compare people who fell on different parts of the trait continuum.

This finding supports an assertion I have made for a while—that the trait approach has become so entrenched in personality research today, for many psychologists personality research has become synonymous with the measurement and examination of traits. Of course, many of the studies I examined dealt with topics relevant to the other approaches to personality. For example, one study dealt with individual differences in absorption and hypnotic susceptibility. However, the use of trait measures has become so widespread that it appears to have become part of the research arsenal of experimenters from all perspectives. In addition, if you were to conduct a similar survey of research journals in developmental psychology, social psychology, clinical psychology, industrial-organizational psychology, and other fields, I suspect you would also run across a liberal use of trait measures.

This prolific use of the trait concept presents a problem for the author of a personality textbook—how to review relevant research on traits within one chapter. The strategy I have adopted is to select three topics from the many available. I selected these examples of trait research because they illustrate three issues currently under investigation by a large number of trait researchers and because each illustrates in a slightly different way how research in this area evolves and develops. This research also illustrates problems often encountered by trait researchers in their quest to better understand individual differences on a specific dimension.

Sometimes research on a specific personality trait is stimulated by a larger personality theory. For example, one of the psychogenic needs postulated by Henry Murray—the need for Achievement—has been studied by psychologists for more than four decades. We'll examine some of what researchers have discovered about this trait and how psychologists develop new ways to investigate a well-researched concept.

We also will look at a personality concept that came to the attention of trait researchers via the medical community. The Type A behavior pattern was originally used by medical professionals to identify candidates for heart disease. This concept soon piqued the interest of personality psychologists, who subsequently found that Type A relates to a large number of behaviors. Thus, research on Type A behavior has taken a different course than is typical for trait concepts. Although investigators usually attempt to understand a trait first and then apply it to human concerns, Type A research began as an applied concept and later came under the scrutiny of academic investigators. The abundance of studies about Type A behavior illustrates that either approach can be fruitful.

Finally, we'll look at how personality trait research can help us better understand a common interpersonal problem, namely social anxiety or shyness. This research was initiated in the mid-1970s when psychologists realized that we knew very little about the causes or remedies of this sometimes painful experience (Zimbardo, 1977). As we will see, today numerous investigations have provided psychology with a much better idea of who suffers from social anxiety and why.

The Need for Achievement

Look at the picture on page 238. What is happening? Who do you think this person might be? Think of a story that might be told about him. How is the story resolved? There are no right or wrong answers to these questions. One person might see a man deep in thought, weighing all the possible solutions to an important problem to accomplish something of value. Another person might say the man is bored with his job, daydreaming about where he would rather be, and contemplating an excuse to leave the office early to spend the afternoon with his friends or family.

Each of these scenarios represents a kind of response that might be found when using the Thematic Apperception Test, designed by Henry Murray and described in Chapter 3. Like other projective tests, the TAT presents subjects with ambiguous stimuli — in this case, pictures to tell a story about. Because the pictures are intentionally vague, different types of stories are assumed to reflect the subjects' individual differences in motives. David McClelland, along with his colleagues, has used the TAT over the past few decades to study one of Murray's psychogenic needs in depth. In this section we will examine some of their work on the need for Achievement (McClelland, 1961, 1985; McClelland, Atkinson, Clark, & Lowell, 1953; Stewart, 1982).

The **need for Achievement**, as described by Murray, is the desire "to accomplish something difficult; to master, manipulate or organize . . . to overcome obstacles and attain a high standard; to excel one's self" (1938, p. 164). To assess this need, McClelland and his colleagues gave subjects several TAT pictures to tell stories about. They scored the stories with an objective coding scheme and obtained a need for Achievement score for each subject. Let's return to your story about the man in the picture. If you saw a man working hard to reach an

Who is this person?
What is he doing?
How will things turn
out? Whether you see
a man thinking about
a difficult business
problem or dreaming
about going fishing
may indicate your
own level of need for
Achievement.

important goal, this might be interpreted as reflecting your own high need for Achievement. If you gave these kinds of responses consistently to the TAT pictures McClelland uses, you no doubt would end up with a high need for Achievement score. On the other hand, if your stories stressed affiliation and personal enjoyment at the expense of achievement, your score would be quite low.

Like other trait measures, need for Achievement scores are assumed to reflect relatively stable individual differences that can be compared with the scores of other people along a continuum. Although the use of the TAT to measure this trait has been a subject of controversy (Atkinson, 1982; McClelland, 1980; Reuman, Alwin, & Veroff, 1984), it has provided some consistent and theoretically sound findings in a large number of investigations. One reason for the continued popularity of the need for Achievement concept is that it fits well with the American concern for economic growth and success in business (Spence, 1985) and theoretically can be used to identify the business and finance leaders of tomorrow.

High Need for Achievement Characteristics

What is a high need for Achievement person like? We should note that McClelland was not interested in all types of achievement, but rather with *entrepreneurial* behavior. Thus, his concern was with understanding and predicting behavior in the business world rather than, for example, the arts or science.

What kind of need for Achievement would you guess a businessperson has who takes chances to get ahead, whose goal is to succeed against high odds? You may be surprised to find that such behavior is *not* indicative of a high need for Achievement. One of the prominent features of high-need achievers is that they are only moderate risk takers. They want to succeed, but they also are highly motivated to avoid failure. They take small risks, such as a fairly secure business venture with a moderate chance of failure. But they rarely take large risks, such as placing all of their money on a highly speculative investment with potentially large payoffs. Their desire to achieve is too high to take such a large chance on failure.

Another characteristic related to a high need for Achievement is an energetic approach to work. But high-need achievers don't simply work harder at everything. They usually get pumped up only for tasks with the potential for some personal achievement. Routine and boring jobs hold no more interest for them than for anyone else. But if a job requires some creative and original input — thereby providing a sense of personal accomplishment — a high-need achiever probably will work harder and persist longer than most of us. Maybe this is why researchers sometimes find a positive correlation between need for Achievement and academic performance (Spence & Helmreich, 1983), but sometimes do not (McClelland, 1980).

High need for Achievement people also prefer jobs that give them personal responsibility for outcomes. They want credit for success but are also willing to accept blame for failure. In fact, the opportunity to receive concrete feedback about their performance is important to high-need achievers. This helps to explain why high need for Achievement people typically choose careers in the business world. Some professionals receive little immediate and clear feedback about how they are doing. For example, a social worker may never see any clear evidence of helping clients who pass through a community mental health clinic. In contrast, sales, productivity, and profit figures provide members of the business world with constant barometers of their performances. This need for immediate feedback is complemented by the high need for Achievement person's need to anticipate future possibilities and make long-range plans. These people succeed in business in part because they look ahead, anticipate many courses of action and possible pitfalls, and thereby increase their chances of obtaining the goal of personal achievement.

Raising High Need for Achievement Children

Why do some people become highly successful entrepreneurs, whereas others show little interest in making their millions in the business community? Is there something business-oriented parents do to create a high need for Achievement in their children? Although research provides no simple answers to these questions, McClelland believes some parenting practices do help to produce a high need for Achievement in children. In essence, parents can promote the development of this need by providing support and encouragement long enough to allow the child to develop a sense of personal competence, but not so long that the child is

Achievement Motivation

Although McClelland and his colleagues rely on the TAT to measure need for Achievement, other researchers have developed methods requiring less time to administer and less expertise to interpret. One of these measures, developed by Robert Helmreich and Janet Spence, divides the need for Achievement into three factors. The *work* factor represents "the desire to work hard and to do a good job," the *mastery* factor reflects "a preference for difficult, challenging tasks and for meeting internally prescribed standards of performance excellence," and the *competitiveness* factor describes "the enjoyment of interpersonal competition and the desire to win" (Spence & Helmreich, 1983, p. 41). You can take their Work and Family Orientation Questionnaire to measure your own level of each of these need achievement factors. Rate yourself on each item, using the following scale:

1 = Strongly agree
2 = Somewhat agree
3 = Neither agree nor disagree
4 = Somewhat disagree
5 = Strongly disagree

Work

_____ 1. It is important for me to do my work as well as I can even if it isn't popular with my coworkers.
_____ 2. I find satisfaction in working as well as I can.
_____ 3. There is satisfaction in a job well done.
_____ 4. I find satisfaction in exceeding my previous performance even if I don't outperform others.
_____ 5. I like to work hard.
_____ 6. Part of my enjoyment in doing things is improving my past performance.

Mastery

_____ 1. I would rather do something at which I feel confident and relaxed than something which is challenging and difficult.*

Continued

robbed of independence and initiative. "What is desirable . . . is a stress on meeting certain achievement standards somewhere between the ages of six and eight," McClelland explained. "Neither too early for the boy's abilities nor too late for him to internalize those standards as his own" (1961, p. 345).

The prescription for raising a high need for Achievement child thus seems to be finding that fine line between too much parental involvement and not enough. Parents should encourage achievement in young children, reward them, and

Achievement Motivation, continued

_____ 2. When a group I belong to plans an activity, I would rather direct it myself than just help out and have someone else organize it.

_____ 3. I would rather learn easy, fun games than difficult thought games.*

_____ 4. If I am not good at something, I would rather keep struggling to master it than move on to something I may be good at.

_____ 5. Once I undertake a task, I persist.

_____ 6. I prefer to work in situations that require a high level of skill.

_____ 7. I more often attempt tasks that I am not sure I can do than tasks that I believe I can do.

_____ 8. I like to be busy all the time.

*Reverse point value when scoring this item (for example, 5 = 1).

Competitiveness

_____ 1. I enjoy working in situations involving competition with others.

_____ 2. It is important to me to perform better than others on a task.

_____ 3. I feel that winning is important in both work and games.

_____ 4. It annoys me when other people perform better than I do.

_____ 5. I try harder when I'm in competition with other people.

Your score on each of the three subscales is the total of the point values for the items on that scale. To better understand the meaning of your scores, you can compare them with some means Spence and Helmreich obtained for four different types of populations:

	Work		Mastery		Competitiveness	
	Males	Females	Males	Females	Males	Females
College students	19.8	20.3	19.3	18.0	13.6	12.2
Varsity athletes	21.2	21.9	20.4	20.9	15.7	14.3
Businesspersons	21.1	20.7	22.3	22.1	14.6	13.8
Academic psychologists	21.1	21.9	21.5	22.4	11.7	11.1

From Spence & Helmreich (1983); reprinted by permission of W. H. Freeman and Company, Publishers.

show enthusiasm for their accomplishments. But too much parental involvement can stifle children's sense of independence and undermine their perception of mastery and accomplishment.

Beyond this, our understanding of how to develop a high need for Achievement child is limited. This is shown in an interesting longitudinal study conducted by McClelland and Pilon (1983). The researchers interviewed parents of five-year-olds in 1951 concerning various child-rearing practices. Twenty-six to 27

When to let go and when to hold on? The mother might decide to let the boy fall a few times, but in the process allow him to develop a sense of mastery and independence. However, she might also want to protect him just a little longer so that he can retain his sense of security and confidence. McClelland argues that such decisions have an impact on the child's need for Achievement.

years later, they located the children and tested them for need for Achievement. What child-rearing behaviors were related to high need for Achievement? The best predictors were a rigid feeding schedule and intense toilet training during the early years. Although we might conclude from this that a general parental style emphasizing orderliness and control was responsible for developing a high need for Achievement, McClelland disagrees. He speculates, like Freud, that specific experiences in early childhood, such as rigorous toilet training, may be related to adult personalities.

Predicting Achievement Behavior in Individuals and Cultures

How do these high need for Achievement characteristics translate into actual behavior in the business world? One obvious prediction is that college students scoring high on measures of need for Achievement will become the business leaders of the future. To test this, McClelland (1965) compared male students with high and low achievement needs on their choice of jobs in the business world 14 years later. Consistent with the theory, 83% of the subjects in entrepreneurial positions had been earlier classified as having a high need for Achievement. In contrast, 79% of the nonentrepreneurs had been in the low need for Achievement group. Not surprisingly, then, people with a high need for Achievement are more likely to be economically upwardly mobile, whereas people low in this need more often slide down the economic prosperity ladder (Littig & Yeracaris, 1965).

A careful reader may have noticed that nearly all of McClelland's work was conducted with males. There are reasons for this. When this work was begun in the 1950s, relatively few women entered the business world and even fewer had opportunities to advance into high managerial positions. Because McClelland was concerned with entrepreneurs, it was reasonable to limit study to males. Obviously, things have changed quite a bit since then. As career aspirations and opportunities for women have changed over the past few decades, we have seen a comparable increase in need for Achievement among female college students (Veroff, Depner, Kulka, & Douvan, 1980). Are these scores also related to achievement in the business world? A study by Jenkins (1987) suggests that they are. She measured need for Achievement among female seniors in 1967. Fourteen years later these women were contacted again. Consistent with the findings for males, the earlier need for Achievement scores predicted job choice and job characteristics for the women who entered the work force.

In short, research indicates that people with a high need for Achievement are likely to be successful in the business world. However, some recent research suggests that this may not always be the case. Although high-need achievers are motivated to reach personal goals of accomplishment, this strong need also might interfere with effective performance in some positions. For example, success in upper management and executive positions often depends on the person's ability to delegate authority and motivate others. Someone who is too concerned about his or her own accomplishments might have a difficult time relinquishing control over details and effectively relying on subordinates. This may explain why McClelland and Boyatzis (1982) found that need for Achievement was related to success for low-level managers but not for those higher up the corporate ladder. Another example of this phenomenon comes from an intriguing study that examined need for Achievement and effectiveness among American presidents (Spangler & House, 1991). Presidents whose inaugural speeches indicated a high need for Achievement (see Box 7.2) usually are rated by historians as relatively ineffective leaders.

Although there may be exceptions, research clearly indicates that differences in need for Achievement are related to individual achievement behavior. But McClelland has taken his work one step further. He began to wonder if it were possible to identify whole cultures in which need for Achievement is a prominent feature. Why have some countries developed out of World War II into economic superpowers, whereas others have floundered in economic despair? One possibility is that the citizens in some societies are raised in an atmosphere that fosters a generally high need for Achievement. According to McClelland's theory, these are the societies most likely to develop and prosper economically. If this is the case, then we should be able to predict the economic rise and fall of nations from need for Achievement scores.

But how can such an intriguing hypothesis be tested? McClelland (1961) developed some fairly clever methods to measure the general level of achievement that cultures emphasize. In one series of studies, he decided that children's books were a good indication of a culture's level of achievement motivation. For example, if the books were full of achievement themes — building a boat, starting a successful business, overcoming obstacles to achieve something of merit — then we might conclude that the culture emphasizes achievement and the children are being socialized in this manner. Next, a measure of economic development was needed. In this particular set of studies, McClelland decided on growth in the use of electrical energy. Nations prospering economically typically grow dramatically in the amount of electricity they use, because of the transition from manual labor to automation. These two measures were calculated for a large number of nations, and the correlation coefficients shown in Table 8.1 were computed. The number of achievement themes in children's stories significantly predicted subsequent levels of electricity usage.

However, as also shown in the table, an attempt to update the effect complicates the interpretation of these findings (Beit-Hallahmi, 1980). When researchers correlated McClelland's story data with more recent changes in growth of electricity usage they found that the impressive correlations in the original data dwindled to a nonsignificant .11 level. Why might this be the case? One possibility is that the world has changed. Although there may have been a time earlier in this century when personality variables, such as the need for Achievement, had a strong influence on a nation's economic development, world economy today is too complex for such an influence. It is also quite possible that growth in electricity use is no longer the correct measure of economic growth. Indeed, energy conservation is emphasized in developed countries these days. Nonetheless, given the difficulties built into this type of research, McClelland's original findings are quite impressive and thought-provoking.

But there is yet another step in this research program. If increased need for Achievement within a nation's business community is related to economic growth, then it may be possible to improve economic conditions by changing need for Achievement levels among business leaders. To this end, McClelland has developed and conducted short training programs in various cultures (McClelland, 1978; McClelland & Winter, 1969). For the most part, these programs have been a success. For example, a 2-year follow-up in small communities in India found businessmen in McClelland's program started more new businesses, invested more money, and hired more people than did those who hadn't participated.

Resultant Achievement Motivation

Clearly, the need for Achievement is a good predictor of many achievement-related behaviors. But, as with any complex behavior, this is only part of the story. Imagine a man who has a strong desire to achieve, yet who also has a tremendous fear of what will happen if he were to fail. He is offered an opportunity to move up

Table 8.1

Correlations Between Need for Achievement Themes in Children's Literature and Economic Development

Year of Stories	Years of Electric Growth	Correlation
1925	1925–1950	.46
1950	1952–1958	.43
1950	1950–1967	.39
1950	1952–1976	.11

Source: From Beit-Hallahmi (1980); reprinted by permission of Sage Publications, Inc., and the author.

in his company to a powerful managerial position. If he does well, the company and he will prosper. If he does poorly, the company will suffer and he may find himself out of a job. There is a good chance the man in this example would turn down the promotion, despite his high need for Achievement. Although a person's need for Achievement is related to achievement behavior, other personality variables play a role as well.

John Atkinson, who worked with McClelland on the original need for Achievement studies, has examined some of these additional variables. In his original formulation, Atkinson (1957) concluded that the *tendency to achieve* could be predicted from the *motive to approach success*, similar to McClelland's need for Achievement, and the *tendency to avoid failure*. Atkinson described this latter concept as "a disposition to avoid failure and/or a capacity for experiencing shame and humiliation as a consequence of failure" (1957, p. 360). In other words, an achievement situation, such as a final exam, is a highly traumatic event for many people. Their concern for what will happen if they fail pulls them in the opposite direction from their achievement need. Mathematically, the tendency to approach success (T_S) and the tendency to avoid failure (T_{AF}) determine the tendency to achieve (T_A) in the following manner:

$$T_A = T_S - T_{AF}$$

This level of one's tendency to achieve is referred to as **resultant achievement motivation**.

Subsequent researchers have added additional variables to this formula. For example, Atkinson (1974) proposed that the extent to which a person seeks extrinsic rewards (for example, money) is a relatively stable individual difference that also can affect the tendency to achieve. Another relevant variable, the *motive to avoid success* (or, more commonly, the **fear of success**), was introduced later and received considerable attention inside and outside academic psychology. Horner (1972) asked male and female students to write stories about hypothetical events, such as a woman named Anne who found herself at the top of her medical school class. An examination of the stories suggested that a large percentage of the women harbored a fear of succeeding in a traditionally male field. For example, 65% of the women wrote stories indicating something bad would happen because of Anne's success in medical school, such as men not liking her. Only 10% of the men wrote fear-of-success stories about a man at the top of his medical school class.

The social and political implications of this finding were not ignored. If the stories were a reflection of how the women felt about themselves, then the majority of college women suffered from a fear of competing with men that might counter whatever achievement needs pushed them into the business world. However, subsequent research has failed to replicate this sex difference (cf. Tresemer, 1976). Many women do show signs of a fear of success, but so do many men (Hoffman, 1974). Perhaps we can conclude that both men and women may desire promotions, power, and the fruits of success, but they also may fear the increased competition, corporate politics, higher expectancies, and greater worries that come with success. Understanding how these fears interact with need for Achievement should help us predict who will succeed and who will falter in the competitive business world.

An Attributional Approach to Achievement Motivation

Imagine for a moment that you have just received an F on a midterm exam (remember, this is only hypothetical). How would you react? Because passing the class is important to you, you no doubt will spend part of the next few days trying to figure out why you did so poorly. You might conclude there was something peculiar about the test — the professor selected bizarre points to test on or wrote ambiguous questions. Another possibility is that personal problems kept you from studying as much as you would have liked. Then again, you might decide that you really don't have what it takes to be a college student, no matter how hard you study.

How you respond to the poor midterm grade and how well you do on the next test depend in part on which of these explanations you adopt. For example, if the problem is not enough study time, you can set aside extra time for the final exam. But if the problem is a lack of ability, then there is little reason to try next time. This example illustrates yet another important influence on achievement behavior: the attributions people make for their successes and failures.

Bernard Weiner (a student of Atkinson's) and his colleagues have examined extensively the relationship between attributions and achievement (Weiner, 1979, 1985, 1990). According to their model, we often ask ourselves in an achievement situation why we have done as well or as poorly as we have. The answer to this question then determines how we feel about the performance and what we will do in similar situations in the future.

There are many ways to analyze the kinds of attributions people give for their performances, but Weiner has focused on three dimensions. First, there is the *stability* dimension. We can explain our performance with stable causes, such as intelligence, or with unstable causes, such as luck. In addition, an attribution may be either internal to us, such as the amount of effort put forth, or external, such as a difficult test. Weiner labels this dimension *locus*. Finally, there is the dimension of *control*—whether we can control or not control the cause of the success or failure.

By examining attributions along these three dimensions, researchers have had some success in predicting how people respond to successes and failures. For example, performing well on a test, being promoted in an organization, or winning a tennis match should enhance your self-esteem, but only if you believe the reason for success is internal. If you win a tennis game because your opponent is a lousy tennis player or had the sun in her eyes (external attributions), then you probably won't feel very good about the victory. How a person responds to future events often depends on the perceived stability of the cause of the performance. If you lose the tennis match because your opponent is a better player (stable), then you probably will not expect to win next time you two play. However, if you attribute the loss to some unstable bad luck, then you might be eager for another match. This analysis helps to explain why most people continue to participate in sports, even though not everyone can be a winner. Research indicates that most of us attribute our losses to unstable sources, thus keeping alive hope of winning the next time (Grove, Hanrahan, & McInman, 1991).

The attributional model also suggests a relatively easy way to improve achievement motivation: Change people's attributions. Wilson and Linville (1982, 1985) did just that with a group of college freshmen. Subjects in this study were students who, like many freshmen, didn't do very well their first and second semesters in college. The researchers explained to some of these students that the causes of low grades during one's freshman year usually are only temporary. In other words, they replaced stable attributions (for example, "I am not a good student") with unstable ones. As a result, the students with the new attributions not only got better grades during the next semester but also did better when they later took the Graduate Record Exam. The implications for education, sports (see Box 8.1), the business world, and other achievement domains are obvious.

In summary, research on need for Achievement has expanded considerably since the original work on this trait appeared in the early 1950s. Murray's theory stimulated McClelland's work. McClelland identified and described the behavior of high need for Achievement people. He then expanded his work to the questions of how parents influence a child's achievement motivation and how societies rise and fall economically as a result of different types of socialization. Later researchers found that these same behaviors and accomplishments also were characteristic of high need for Achievement females. Atkinson and others added to the original formula for predicting achievement behavior, and Weiner demonstrated the role of attributions in this process. All of this suggests that Murray's original need for Achievement concept was indeed a fertile one.

Attribution Training on the Basketball Court

Improvement at any sport requires a great deal of hard work and, above all, practice. Most athletes recognize that you need to hit a lot of baseballs, take a lot of chip shots, and spend time rehearsing your gymnastic routine over and over if you hope to get better at your sport.

But most coaches and trainers also recognize that whether an athlete improves or declines in performance is also a function of his or her motivation level. Research on at-

Continued

Type A–Type B Behavior Patterns

In the 1950s some physicians became frustrated over their inability to identify which of their patients were likely to suffer from cardiovascular problems. Although they knew high blood pressure, smoking, obesity, and inactivity all contributed to the risk of heart disease, combinations of these factors still were unable to predict new cases with much accuracy (Jenkins, 1971, 1976). But some physicians noticed that their heart attack patients seemed to act differently than their other patients (Friedman & Rosenman, 1974). Heart attack victims were

tributions and achievement suggests that how an athlete explains victories and defeats may have a lot to do with how well he or she does in the next game or contest. In particular, we could speculate from this research that athletes who attribute their poor performance to a lack of ability will develop a lower level of motivation than athletes who attribute the same poor performance to a lack of effort. The high jumper who says "I just can't jump any higher" and the tennis player who believes "That's the best I'll ever be able to serve" probably will not be as motivated as the jumper or server who says "I didn't win this time, but if I try just a little harder, I might be able to do it next time."

The effects of attributions on athletic motivation and performance were tested in a study with high school basketball players (Miserandino & Hoffman, 1990). Half the players on the varsity boys team received feedback suggesting their performance on a shooting drill was the result of their effort. Half the players did not receive this feedback. The feedback was given during practice three times a week for a period of 4 weeks.

The players were tested before and after the 4-week period on a 25-shot drill. The boys who had not received the effort attribution feedback showed no improvement during this time. However, the boys who had been trained to attribute their performance to effort improved their shooting from a 48% success rate to 58.4%. As most basketball fans will recognize, this much improvement can often be the difference between winning and losing a game.

more active, more energetic, and more driving than those without heart problems. In short, they seemed to have different personalities.

This personality dimension was identified as the *coronary-prone behavior pattern*, because it seemed to consist of a variety of behaviors that were part of a consistent overall pattern. Today this dimension is more commonly referred to as **Type A–Type B**, or just Type A. Strictly speaking, the name is an inappropriate one, because it is not a true typology. Instead of identifying two types of people, A and B, we can better understand the concept in terms of a trait continuum, with extreme Type A people at one end and extreme Type B people at the other.

Who would you rather ride with—a Type A or a Type B driver? If you think about the components that make up the Type A personality, the answer should be clear. Type A people hate to waste time and usually want to be in control. Consequently, when you see someone speed up to make it through a yellow light or change lanes to pick up a car length or two, you're probably watching a Type A driver. It's the same person who peeks out the corner of his or her eye at the other street's traffic light, just to be ready to take off when the light changes green (Wright, 1988). And when stuck in heavy traffic, the Type A driver is the one inching up to the next car's bumper and perhaps honking a horn in a futile attempt to get things moving.

One team of investigators compared the driving records of Type A and Type B bus drivers (Evans, Palsane, & Carrere, 1987). As expected, the Type A drivers had more accidents and had received more official reprimands for their poor driving than the Type B drivers. These researchers also looked at the behavior of bus drivers traveling through the heavy and poorly regulated traffic in India. The Type A drivers were more likely to pass other vehicles, apply their brakes, and honk their horns than were the Type B drivers. So, before lending your car to a friend, you might want to find out if that person is Type A or Type B.

What kind of people are likely candidates for heart attacks? Typical A people are strongly motivated to overcome obstacles and driven to achieve and to meet goals. They are attracted to competition, enjoy power and recognition, and are easily aroused to anger and action. They dislike wasting time and do things in a vigorous and efficient manner. They often find more easygoing people a source of frustration. On the other hand, Type B people are relaxed and unhurried. They may work hard on occasion, but rarely in the driven, compulsive manner of Type A people. These people are less likely than Type A's to seek competition or to be aroused to anger or action. Naturally, not all people classified as Type A or Type B fit these profiles exactly, and there are times when Type A people behave in a Type B manner and vice versa. But, as with other traits, researchers can identify the extent to which each of us behaves, on the average, like a Type A or a Type B person.

Early research found the Type A construct was a good predictor of heart disease (Cooper, Detre, & Weiss, 1981). For example, Type A males in one 8½-year study had more than twice the incidence of heart disease than did Type B males (Rosenman et al., 1975). In another study, Type A was a better predictor of heart attacks than cholesterol level or cigarette smoking (Jenkins, Zyzanski, & Rosenman, 1976).

Which person is a Type A and which a Type B? Wasting precious time in a waiting room can be quite stressful for a Type A person, but may be a little concern to a Type B.

Type A as a Personality Variable

What these medical researchers were examining, of course, is a personality variable. Naturally, a trait as intriguing as Type A soon caught the attention of personality researchers. Consequently, in the 1970s psychologists began conducting research to identify the behavioral differences between Type A and Type B people.

Some of the most useful findings from this early work identified three major components of the Type A trait (Glass, 1977). First, Type A people have a higher *competitive achievement striving*. For example, Type A's work harder than Type B's at achievement tasks regardless of outside pressure, such as deadlines. Second, Type A people show a sense of *time urgency*. They feel time is important and shouldn't be wasted. Type B's procrastinate whereas Type A's jump right in. No surprise, therefore, that Type A students volunteer for experiments earlier in the term than do Type B's and show up earlier to participate (Gastorf, 1980; Strube, 1982). Finally, Type A's are more likely than Type B's to deal with a frustrating situation with *aggressiveness and hostility* when provoked. In one experiment, Type A subjects gave more electric shocks to another "subject" in what was supposedly a learning experiment than did Type B subjects, but only when the other person had irritated them (Glass, 1977).

During the past two decades, psychologists have conducted hundreds of experiments on Type A behavior. This research has compared Type A and Type B people on a wide variety of behaviors, including driving habits, study habits, reactions to failure, and reactions to persuasive messages. Several scales have been developed to measure this personality difference, including measures of Type A in children (Steinkamp, 1990). Although medical researchers continue to explore the relationship between Type A and health, most of the research conducted on this concept today is being done by personality psychologists fascinated by the many applications of this individual difference variable.

Type A as a Motive for Control

Much of the research on Type A has been focused on identifying the psychological processes underlying the differences in behavior. One particularly interesting hypothesis to come out of this work attributes differences in Type A and Type B behavior to differences in a motivation for control. For example, after identifying the three components of the Type A behavior pattern, Glass (1977) concluded that they could be reduced to one underlying concept. He argued that all three behaviors represent a desire to exert control over the environment, in his words, "a strategy for coping with uncontrollable aversive events" (1977, p. 7). Type A people react to challenging achievement situations because the challenge is a threat to their sense of personal control. The irretrievable loss of time represents a similar threat. An aggressive response to a frustrating or threatening event may be the quickest and most efficient means of regaining control over the situation.

We should note that the differences between Type A and Type B behavior can be explained in terms other than a need for control (Matthews, 1982). For example, one prominent interpretation suggests that Type A people are best characterized by a strong need for self-appraisal (Freedman & Phillips, 1989; Strube, 1987; Strube, Boland, Manfredo, & Al-Falaij, 1987). That is, Type A behavior may reflect a desire to obtain an accurate impression of one's abilities. Nonetheless, it is useful to examine the research findings on Type A behavior within the framework of the control motivation hypothesis. If a general control motive is the underlying difference between Type A and Type B people, then we can make several predictions about how these people should react to situations where control is a relevant issue. As will be seen, much of this research has been done, and the control hypothesis has held up quite well.

If Type A people differ from Type B's in their need for control, then they should react differently when faced with the possibility of losing control. This hypothesis was tested in one study in which the blood pressure of Type A and Type B people was measured while they worked on easy, moderately difficult, and extremely difficult tasks (Holmes, McGilley, & Houston, 1984). Subjects were asked to repeat lists of two, five, or seven numbers in backward order. As shown in Figure 8.1, arousal levels generally went up as subjects worked on more difficult tasks. However, the most difficult task, and therefore the one that posed the greatest threat to subjects' perception of control, aroused Type A subjects more than Type B's. Similar results have been found when examining heart rate (Ortega & Pipal, 1984) and pulse rate (Pittner, Houston, & Spiridigliozzi, 1983).

Figure 8.1

Systolic Blood Pressure While Working on Task

Adapted from Holmes, McGilley, and Houston (1984); reprinted by permission of David Holmes.

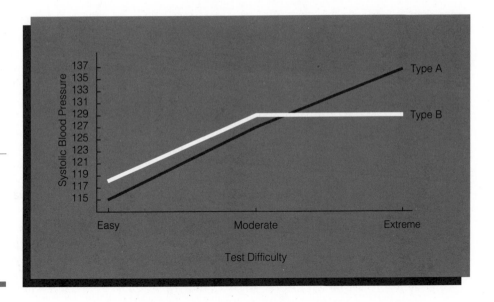

Type A people respond to control-threatening situations with greater arousal generally than do Type B's. Part of this may be an intentional effort to mobilize themselves for the upcoming challenge, but some of this arousal may also be out of the Type A person's control. This increase in physiological response may also provide a clue about why Type A people are more likely to suffer from cardio-vascular disease.

How do Type A people deal with this arousal? They might simply acknowl-edge they are having difficulty. But this would be tantamount to admitting to a loss of control. Therefore, one way Type A people deal with signs of physiological stress is to deny them. For example, Type A's and Type B's in one study were asked to exert themselves on a treadmill test (Carver, Coleman, & Glass, 1976). The Type A's pushed themselves more on the test than did the Type B's, but reported feeling less fatigue. In other studies, Type A's have been found to deny they are having trouble when threatened with shock or loud noise (Pittner & Houston, 1980; Weidner & Matthews, 1978). Similarly, Type A women are less likely to express physical complaints associated with menstruation than are Type B women (Mat-thews & Carra, 1982). Thus, Type A people respond more strongly to control-threatening situations than do Type B people, but they are less likely to attend to these physiological responses.

Type A people usually work harder than Type B's on achievement tasks, but not always. Consistent with the control motive hypothesis, Type A's work hard on challenging tasks but let their motivation wane when given an easy task that does not measure their ability to exercise control (Fazio, Cooper, Dayson, & Johnson, 1981). They also set higher goals for themselves than do Type B's (Ward & Eisler, 1987). But what really seems to fire Type A's is competition. What greater threat to a Type A's sense of control than to be told there will be only one winner? Their blood pressure and heart rates go up when simply being told they are competing against another person (Van Egeren, 1979). Type A's even seem to be *attracted* to competition, perhaps for the thrill of the challenge. In one study, Type A subjects expressed greater confidence in their ability to do well at a game when told they were competing against another subject (Gotay, 1981). Telling Type A people that others were able to solve a problem they could not is a particularly effective way to motivate them (Schwartz, Burish, O'Rourke, & Holmes, 1986).

In sum, researchers have identified characteristic ways Type A and Type B people respond to a wide variety of situations. In addition, each of these findings is consistent with the notion that Type A's differ from Type B's in terms of their motivation for control. The results of several additional studies point to the same conclusion. For example, Type A's are more likely to want something after being told they can't have it (Rhodewalt & Comer, 1982; Rhodewalt & Davison, 1983). They are more likely to dominate others when in a group discussion (Yarnold, Mueser, & Grimm, 1985), and they are less likely to give control of a task to others, even if someone else might be able to do a better job (Strube, Berry, & Moergen, 1985). In short, research evidence tends to support the hypothesis that Type A's have a stronger need to exercise control than do Type B's.

Type A and Achievement

Because Type A's are stimulated by challenges and competition, and generally driven and hard-working, it might seem obvious that they will be higher achievers than Type B's. However, we can also make the opposite case. Friedman and Rosenman (1974) point out that the Type A style may lead to more quantity than quality. Because they have a sense of time urgency, Type A's may not spend the time necessary to consider alternative approaches or develop creative answers to difficult problems. Type B college students perform better than Type A's when a delay between problem presentation and responding is required (Glass, Snyder, & Hollis, 1974). Thus, it is unclear whether Type A behavior is an asset or a liability in achievement situations.

A starting point in answering this question is to examine academic performance among Type A and Type B college students. One investigation found that Type A students received more academic honors and participated in more extracurricular activities than did Type B students (Glass, 1977). Further, this research revealed that Type A students participated in more sports, received more athletic awards, and participated in more social activities in high school than did Type B students. This superiority of Type A students might be explained by the way they look at grades. Type A students see grades as more important than do Type B's. They also take more credit hours of classes and expect to do better (Ovcharchyn, Johnson, & Petzel, 1981). Thus, Type A students appear to rise to the challenge of getting good grades and, more often than not, meet that challenge.

But does this higher achievement by Type A's carry over into actual work settings? Some research suggests that it does. One survey of managers from 12 large companies found the majority of the managers were classified as Type A (Howard, Cunningham, & Rechnitzer, 1977). Further, Type A managers had higher salaries than did their Type B counterparts. Type A also is a significant predictor of how rapidly professionals rise in their fields (Mettlin, 1976). One study found Type A research psychologists published more articles and were more widely cited (a measure of work quality) than were Type B researchers (Matthews, Helmreich, Beane, & Lucker, 1980). Subsequent analysis of the results of this last study suggested that this higher achievement reflects the Type A person's attraction to work and motivation to perform well (Helmreich, Spence, & Pred, 1988). Finally, Type A workers have higher aspirations than do Type B's (Mettlin, 1976) and put in longer hours (Howard, Cunningham, & Rechnitzer, 1977).

All of these studies point to the same conclusion: Type A people put in more effort and achieve more in work environments than do Type B people. Therefore, it should not be surprising to hear that Type A measures correlate with measures of achievement motivation (Matthews et al., 1980; Matthews & Saal, 1978). But before concluding that Type A is the personality to be, consider a few additional points. Although achieving more, Type A's are not as happy with their jobs as are Type B's (Howard, Cunningham, & Rechnitzer, 1977). It also may be the case that Type B's still do better at tasks that require some thinking and careful consideration of ideas. Finally, some research suggests that the hard-working, driving Type A style may be hazardous to your health. We return to that issue next.

Type A Behavior and Health Revisited

As described earlier, most of the initial research on Type A behavior uncovered a significant relationship between measures of Type A–Type B and the likelihood of developing coronary disease. Unfortunately, subsequent research has not always found this link (cf. Dembroski & Costa, 1987; Fischman, 1987; Matthews & Haynes, 1986). Several major investigations report low or nonexistent relationships between Type A behavior and coronary problems (see Table 8.2). How can we interpret these findings? It seems unlikely that Type A behavior once caused heart disease but that all of a sudden, around 1980, it no longer did. It also does not seem likely that all of the earlier studies somehow incorrectly identified a relationship that does not exist. Although it is always a possibility that through some type of sampling error or other methodological flaw the earlier investigations produced a significant effect that was not really there, the robustness of this finding across several different investigations, as well as nonscientific observation of the behavioral styles of heart attack patients, makes many researchers believe that some relationship between Type A behavior and health problems exists.

Many explanations have been offered for why measures of Type A do not always predict cardiovascular problems. Two seem particularly promising. The first concerns the way the Type A construct is measured. The second explanation examines the individual components that make up the Type A behavior pattern.

Measuring Type A: A Question of Validity   Recall from Chapter 2 that researchers using individual difference measures must be concerned with the question of validity. That is, does the test measure what it is supposed to measure? There are many ways to measure Type A behavior, but do all of these measure the same construct? The original medical researchers decided Type A behavior could best

Table 8.2

Relationship of Type A–Type B and Coronary Heart Disease (CHD) in Nine Major Studies

Study	Subjects/Length	Type A Measure	Type A–CHD Link
Western Collaborative Group Study	3,200 CHD-free middle-aged men/ 8 years	Structured interview	Yes
Framingham Heart Study	1,600 CHD-free middle-aged men & women/8 years	Framingham Type A Scale (self-report)	Yes, in women and white-color men
French-Belgian Cooperative Heart Study	3,200 CHD-free men/ 5 years	Bortner Rating Scale (self-report)	Yes
Belgian Heart Disease Prevention Trial	1,900 CHD-free middle-aged men/ 5 years	Jenkins Activity Survey	Yes
Recurrent Coronary Prevention Project	800 male CHD patients/ 5 years	Structured interview	Yes
Multiple Risk-Factor Intervention Trial	(1) 12,700 high-risk, CHD-free men	Jenkins Activity Survey	No
	(2) 3,100 of these/ 7 years	Structured interview	No
Multicenter Post-Infarction Program	500 CHD patients/ 3 years	Jenkins Activity Survey	No
Aspirin Myocardial Infarction Study	2,300 CHD patients/ 3 years	Jenkins Activity Survey	No
Honolulu Heart Program	2,100 CHD-free men/ 8 years	Jenkins Activity Survey	No

Source: Taken from Fischman (1987). Reprinted with permission from *Psychology Today* magazine. Copyright © 1987 (P. T. Partners, L.P.).

be assessed by observing subjects in a structured interview. These investigators observed such things as how quickly subjects spoke and whether or not they used exaggerated hand and face gestures.

Perhaps because the use of the structured interview technique is so difficult and time-consuming, many researchers soon developed self-report measures of Type A for their research. The most popular of these is the Jenkins Activity Survey (Glass, 1977). Items on this test ask subjects to respond to such questions as "How often does your job stir you to action?" and "Ordinarily, how rapidly do you eat?" Some advocates of the structured interview procedure quickly rejected the self-report method of assessment (Rosenman, 1986). They argued that Type A's theoretically lack the insight into their own behavior necessary to accurately answer the items on the test.

Unfortunately, whatever the Jenkins Activity Survey is measuring may not be the same as what is being measured by other assessment procedures. As shown in Table 8.2, most of the failures to uncover a significant relationship between Type A behavior and heart disease have occurred when investigators were using the Jenkins Activity Survey. Thus, it may be that whatever factor is responsible for the link between Type A behavior and cardiovascular problems is not being measured to the same degree with the different instruments.

Subsequent research findings have supported the suspicion that Type A as measured in a structured interview may be quite different from Type A as measured with the Jenkins Activity Survey. Subjects in one of these experiments attempted to trace a complicated pattern they could see only by looking in a mirror (Contrada, 1989). This task may sound easy at first, but subjects soon discover that it is quite difficult. As expected, Type A subjects, as determined through a structured interview procedure, showed an increase in their heart rates as they worked on the challenging task. However, subjects' Type A scores derived from the Jenkins Activity Survey were not related to the changes in heart rate.

A recent study adds yet another interesting twist to the question of how to measure Type A (Suls & Wan, 1989). A review of more than 37 studies found that Type A people experience significantly more emotional distress than Type B people. However, this finding appears only in studies that used self-report inventories to determine Type A. Studies that used the structured interview method found no such relationship.

In short, the Type A research provides a clear example of the importance of determining the validity of a personality measure. Two tests that claim to measure the same personality construct may not in fact measure the exact same variable. Although this observation helps to explain some of the difficulty researchers have had replicating earlier studies on cardiovascular problems, a close examination of Table 8.2 suggests that this may be only part of the problem.

Identifying the "Toxic Component" A second explanation for the discrepant findings between early Type A research and more recent investigations concerns breaking the Type A behavior pattern down into its components. As you may recall, Type A is actually a collection of several behaviors that tend to go together. In essence, when we measure Type A we are measuring many different behavior tendencies. It is possible that only one or two of these behavior tendencies is really responsible for health problems. Perhaps because other behaviors are measured along with these few health-related behaviors, we can expect to find only weak and sometimes nonsignificant associations between Type A behavior and cardiovascular disease.

This line of reasoning has led some researchers to look for the "toxic component" of Type A behavior. If we can discover which of the many behaviors that make up the Type A pattern is responsible for health problems, we can do a better job of predicting those problems and designing programs for their prevention. For example, one promising line of research suggests that the time-urgency component of Type A behavior may play a strong, independent role in heart disease (Wright, 1988).

However, most of the evidence to date points to what researchers have identified as the **Potential for Hostility** (Dembroski & Costa, 1987; Musante, MacDougall, Dembroski, & Costa, 1989). People who score high on measures of Potential for Hostility experience "combinations of anger, irritability, resentment, and related negative effects" in response to the type of common, daily frustrations and inconveniences we all experience. They react to these minor annoyances with "expressions of antagonism, disagreeableness, rudeness, surliness, critical-ness, and uncooperativeness" (Dembroski & Costa, 1987). For example, people high in Potential for Hostility might become upset when stuck in a slow-moving line at the post office or when they misplace something and can't find it right away. Most of us have learned to take these minor inconveniences in stride, but some people become highly irritated.

Several investigations have found that scores on a measure of Potential for Hostility (as assessed through the structured interview method) significantly predict coronary artery disease (Dembroski & Costa, 1987). More important, in each of these investigations a global measure of Type A failed to predict any health problems. The reason for this latter finding may be that while Potential for Hostility is part of the overall Type A score, its connection with health problems may get "washed out" when other unrelated behaviors are used to determine the overall Type A score. What this also means is that not all Type A behaviors may be bad for your health. The workaholic who pushes himself or herself with ever greater challenges and who prefers to work through lunch might not be headed for an early heart attack afterall. If this person does not let minor setbacks and little frustrations upset him or her, it may be possible to be productive *and* healthy.

In summary, after more than 30 years of research, what can we say about the Type A behavior pattern? Clearly, Type A is a useful personality variable, related to many important behaviors. The observations made by those physicians many years ago have held up fairly well, with modification. Perhaps the safest conclu-sion at this point is that Type A is not necessarily a source of cardiovascular problems. Whereas some Type A behaviors may be bad for your health, hard work alone probably is not.

Social Anxiety

I took a few moments at a recent psychology conference to take note of the different ways my colleagues went about meeting and greeting other profes-sionals. I positioned myself in the corner of a large room and watched as people entered what was designated as a "social hour." The event was scheduled so that people in the field could meet one another and perhaps exchange a few ideas about each others' work. Some people seemed quite at home in this setting. One woman in particular amazed me with her ability to introduce herself to someone she obviously had never met and immediately begin what appeared to be a lively

Social Anxiety

Indicate the extent to which each of the following statements describes you. Indicate your answers with a five-point scale, with 1 = Not at all characteristic and 5 = Extremely characteristic.

_____ 1. I often feel nervous even in casual get-togethers.
_____ 2. I usually feel uncomfortable when I am in a group of people I don't know.
_____ 3. I am usually at ease when speaking to a member of the opposite sex.
_____ 4. I get nervous when I must talk to a teacher or boss.
_____ 5. Parties often make me feel anxious and uncomfortable.
_____ 6. I am probably less shy in social interactions than most people.
_____ 7. I sometimes feel tense talking to people of my own sex if I don't know them very well.
_____ 8. I would be nervous if I were being interviewed for a job.
_____ 9. I wish I had more confidence in social situations.
_____10. I seldom feel anxious in social situations.
_____11. In general, I am a shy person.
_____12. I often feel nervous when talking to an attractive member of the opposite sex.
_____13. I often feel nervous when calling someone I don't know very well on the telephone.
_____14. I get nervous when I speak to someone in a position of authority.
_____15. I usually feel relaxed around other people, even people who are quite different from me.

You have just completed the Interaction Anxiousness Scale developed by Leary (1983a). The scale was designed to measure social anxiety surrounding what Schlenker and Leary (1982) call *contingent interactions*. This is the anxiety we sometimes experience in unrehearsed social encounters, such as when meeting new people or when on a date, as compared with the kind of anxiety people experience when delivering a prepared speech before a group. Interaction anxiousness includes what we commonly refer to as shyness and dating anxiety.

People who score high on the scale tend to experience social anxiety more often and more intensely than those who score low. To obtain your score, first reverse the values for your answers to items 3, 6, 10, and 15 (that is, 1 = 5, 2 = 4, and so on). Then add all 15 answer values together. Researchers find a mean score on the scale of about 39 for undergraduate students, with a standard deviation of about 10 (Leary, 1986).

Although social interaction comes easily to many people, others feel consistently left out. Researchers find that social anxiety is a serious problem for a large number of people.

and pleasant conversation. But other people approached the social hour in a very different manner. One man stopped about two feet inside the door and examined the proceedings for a few minutes. Then he slowly worked his way around the exterior of the room, looking for someone to talk to. When people did talk to him he appeared to smile nervously. The man seemed to look at the floor more than the person he was speaking to, and his conversations never seemed to last more than about 30 seconds. After about 10 minutes he left.

It would not be difficult to speculate that these two visitors to the social hour probably fall on opposite ends of the personality trait we call social anxiety. The man was clearly very anxious in this situation and behaved in a manner most people would identify as shy. I would guess that the woman has never suffered from shyness. Although most people probably would consider the woman's behavior normal and appropriate for a social gathering, researchers are discovering that the shy man's experience may be more common than most of us realize. In fact, shyness appears to be one of today's most widespread social problems. Researchers consistently find that about 40% of the people they survey identify themselves as shy (Zimbardo, 1977, 1986). Approximately another 40–50% say they have been shy before or are shy in certain situations. This leaves only a very small percentage of people who do not know the pain of social anxiety or shyness.

Social anxiety is anxiety related specifically to social interactions or anticipated social interactions. People suffering from social anxiety experience many of the usual anxiety symptoms—increased physiological arousal, inability to concentrate, feelings of nervousness. But socially anxious people recognize that the source of their discomfort is the social encounter they are now or soon will be engaged in. Although everyone has on occasion been at least a little nervous about an upcoming interview or date, as with other trait variables we can identify a relatively stable tendency for people to experience social anxiety. That is, each of us can be placed along a continuum for how much social anxiety we typically experience.

Social anxiety is the same as or related to many other constructs investigated by psychologists and communication researchers. The names for these concepts include shyness, dating anxiety, communication anxiety, reticence, and stage fright. Although some psychologists draw a distinction between social anxiety and some of these related concepts (Buss, 1980; Leary, 1983b), most researchers today appear to use the terms *social anxiety* and *shyness* synonymously. Concepts like dating anxiety and stage fright are often regarded as specific examples of the larger concept of social anxiety. Moreover, scales designed to measure social anxiety, shyness, and related constructs are highly correlated with one another (Anderson & Harvey, 1988). Consequently, we will use the terms *social anxiety* and *shyness* interchangeably here.

However, it also is important to recognize that social anxiety is *not* the same as introversion. Whereas introverts often choose to be by themselves instead of in social settings, the vast majority of socially anxious people do not like their shyness. Nearly two thirds of the socially anxious people in one study identified their shyness as "a real problem," and one quarter of the shy subjects said they would be willing to seek professional help to overcome their social anxiety (Pilkonis, 1977a).

Characteristics of Socially Anxious People

People who suffer from social anxiety have a difficult time in many social situations. Socially anxious people report feeling awkward and nervous when they have to talk to others (Cheek & Buss, 1981). They are very concerned about what others will think of them, and become very self-conscious when they meet new people or have to talk in front of a large audience. Quite often socially anxious people think about what they are doing wrong, how stupid they must sound, and how foolish they must look (Ickes, Robertson, Tooke, & Teng, 1986). Shy people often stumble over their words, say the wrong thing, and show outward signs of nervousness, such as perspiration and shakiness. These feelings of awkwardness are not merely in the minds of socially anxious people. The people they are talking to also identify shy people as more tense, inhibited, and unfriendly than nonshy people (Cheek & Buss, 1981). Shy people are more likely than most people to feel ashamed or embarrassed about what they say or do in social situations. This is probably why shy people also are more likely than nonshys to blush (Leary & Meadows, 1991).

At times socially anxious people become so concerned about how they are coming across that it interferes with their ability to carry on a conversation. Shy people sometimes report that they are so self-conscious and nervous that they cannot think of anything to say. They may allow the conversation to fall into silence, which can be extremely uncomfortable for someone already suffering from social anxiety (Pilkonis, 1977b). Their high level of anxiety also makes shy people more susceptible to what is known as the "next in line" effect (Bond & Omar, 1990). That is, socially anxious people are so concerned about speaking in front of others that they suffer high levels of anxiety right before and after it is their turn to talk. As a result, socially anxious people have a difficult time remembering what the person who spoke before them and the one who spoke after them said. Their anxiety keeps them from attending to and remembering the other speeches.

As noted earlier, shy people are not introverts. Rather, they would like to have a larger network of friends than they do. In particular, shy people often say that they would like more people they could turn to when they need help (Zimbardo, 1977). Unfortunately, their shyness often keeps them from developing more friends or asking the friends they have for help when they are in need. One study found that shy students were less likely to talk to a counselor about career advice than were nonshy students (Phillips & Bruch, 1988). Researchers in another study deliberately asked subjects to work on a task that could not be completed without asking for help from another subject (DePaulo, Dull, Greenberg, & Swaim, 1989). Nonetheless, the socially anxious subjects were less likely than the other subjects to ask a nearby person for help. This inability to ask for assistance appears to stem from socially anxious people's fear that the other person might not respond favorably to the request for help.

Not only do socially anxious people fear that others will think poorly of them, they also tend to interpret whatever feedback they get about the other person's impression of them in a negative light. This was demonstrated in a study in which college students were asked to work on a series of tasks with other subjects (DePaulo, Kenny, Hoover, Webb, & Oliver, 1987). When later asked what they believed the other students thought of them, the socially anxious students felt they were less liked and had come across as less competent than did the nonanxious subjects. Subjects in another experiment carried on what they believed to be a two-way discussion via a television hook-up (Pozo, Carver, Wellens, & Scheier, 1991). In reality, all subjects watched a prerecorded videotape of a confederate posing as a subject. In this way, all subjects received identical feedback—in this case, in the form of facial expressions—from their partner while they were talking. Although the feedback was identical, socially anxious subjects were more likely than the nonanxious subjects to interpret the other person's facial expressions as indicating disapproval.

In short, people high in social anxiety expect their social interactions to go poorly and look for evidence that the other person is rejecting them. And this pessimistic approach to social encounters probably creates even more difficulties. Other people may not like the shy person's lack of confidence, thus leading to the social rejection the socially anxious person fears in the first place. In addition, because they feel the other person dislikes them, socially anxious people may cut conversations short or avoid them altogether. As a result, they may nip pleasant interactions and potential friendships in the bud before they have a chance to bloom.

Explaining Social Anxiety

Why do shy people become so anxious in certain social situations? What are they afraid of? Many researchers believe that **evaluation apprehension** is the underlying cause of social anxiety. In other words, socially anxious people are afraid of what other people think of them. In particular, they fear negative evaluation. Socially anxious people worry that the person they are talking with is going to find them foolish, boring, or immature. Situations that lend themselves to being evaluated by others are particularly anxiety-provoking. Thus, just thinking about going out on a blind date, giving a speech in front of a large audience, or meeting people for the first time can be a nightmarish experience for someone high in social anxiety.

This evaluation apprehension leads socially anxious people to take steps to reduce their fear of what others think of them. Often socially anxious people avoid the social encounter altogether. They skip parties where they might not know anyone, avoid blind dates, and opt for a term paper instead of a class presentation. When getting out of the situation is not realistic, shy people will do what they can to reduce the *amount* of social interaction. One way they do this is to avoid eye contact (Cheek & Buss, 1981; Garcia, Stinson, Ickes, Bissonnette, & Briggs, 1991; Pilkonis, 1977b). Making eye contact with someone signals a readiness or willingness to talk. By refusing to give this signal, shy people tell those around them that they would prefer to avoid social interaction. In this way socially anxious people limit the opportunities for others to evaluate them.

However, when their efforts to avoid potentially awkward social situations fail, shy people do what they can to keep the conversation short and nonthreatening. Subjects in one experiment were asked to tell four stories about themselves to an interviewer (DePaulo, Epstein, & LeMay, 1990). Some of the subjects believed the interviewer was going to use these stories to evaluate them afterward, whereas other subjects thought they would be free to leave after telling their stories. The socially anxious subjects who thought they were going to be evaluated told shorter and less revealing stories about themselves than did the other subjects. Apparently these shy subjects were worried about creating a poor impression in the mind of the interviewer.

Subjects in another experiment were asked to engage in a five-minute "get-acquainted" conversation with someone they had just met (Leary, Knight, & Johnson, 1987). When researchers examined tapes of these conversations, they found that the socially anxious subjects were more likely to engage in a whole range of verbal behavior than were nonanxious subjects. For example, subjects high in social anxiety were more likely to agree with what the other person said and to merely restate or clarify their partner's remarks when it was their turn to talk. This interactive style allows socially anxious people to create an image of politeness and interest without becoming too involved in the conversation. In this way shy people hope to minimize the amount of evaluation by their conversation partners and, in particular, to reduce the chances that this other person will find something objectionable about them.

In short, the shy person's interaction style is a type of self-protective strategy. Because they are so concerned with negative evaluations, socially anxious people do what they can to control the impressions others have of them (Schlenker & Leary, 1982; Shepperd & Arkin, 1990). Thus, shy people deliberately keep conversations short and pleasant and avoid potentially controversial or embarrassing topics. In this way they reduce the likelihood that the other person will form a negative impression of them.

Although this picture of the shy person may sound rather hopeless, one research finding suggests that socially anxious people may not be as incapable of carrying on a conversation as they seem. Researchers sometimes find that shy people do not have much difficulty interacting with others once they get started. That is, for at least some shy people, it's *initiating* a conversation that seems to be the real stumbling block (Curran, Wallander, & Fischetti, 1980; Paulhus & Martin, 1987; Pilkonis, 1977b). Shy and nonshy subjects in one study were left alone to carry on a conversation with a member of the opposite sex (Pilkonis, 1977b). Although the nonshy subjects spoke more often and were more likely to break periods of silence than the shy subjects, there was no difference in how long these two kinds of subjects spoke when they did say something.

Observations like these have led some researchers to speculate that what socially anxious people really lack is confidence in their ability to make a good impression (Hill, 1989; Leary & Atherton, 1986; Maddux, Norton, & Leary, 1988). Fear that they might say the wrong thing often keeps shy people from saying anything. Consequently, therapy programs designed to help people overcome problems with shyness often focus on developing the clients' belief that they are capable of saying the right thing and of making a good impression (Glass & Shea, 1986; Haemmerlie & Montgomery, 1986). Shy people who lack social skills can be taught how to carry on a conversation, but for many people who suffer from high levels of social anxiety the key may be developing confidence that social encounters will be more successful than most shy people now expect them to be.

Summary

1. The research presented in this chapter represents but a small fraction of the work being conducted on personality traits. Nonetheless, some important features of this research are illustrated in these examples. For example, research on need for Achievement demonstrates how programs of research can be derived from specific features of a more comprehensive trait theory. In addition, the issue of test validity, one that often complicates the lives of trait researchers, surfaces in

recent research on Type A behavior and health. Research in all three of the areas examined in this chapter demonstrates how understanding individual differences in personality traits can help us deal with important social and personal issues.

2. Perhaps because our society places such emphasis on achievement and success in business settings, need for Achievement has remained an important research topic for four decades. McClelland identified some of the characteristics of people scoring high in need for Achievement. He used this information to predict who would become the business leaders of tomorrow and which nations would show economic growth. This led McClelland to establish programs to train people in need for Achievement and thereby improve the economy of underdeveloped nations. Subsequent investigators have examined other personality variables that contribute to a resultant achievement motivation and the role of attributions for success and failure.

3. In contrast to the other variables examined here, research on Type A behavior patterns developed out of some atheoretical predictions about who suffers heart attacks. Early researchers found a strong link between Type A behavior and cardiovascular problems, but later studies did not always replicate these findings. Two explanations for this failure concern the way researchers measure Type A and identifying which Type A components are related to health problems. Numerous investigations by personality psychologists find support for the notion that differences in a need for control underlie differences between Type A and Type B people. Among other behaviors related to this personality trait, Type A people generally perform better in achievement situations than do Type B's.

4. Research on socially anxious people has identified a number of characteristic behaviors that interfere with the shy person's ability to interact effectively with others. Shy people tend to be self-conscious during social encounters, are reluctant to ask others for help, and often interpret feedback from their conversation partners as rejection. Research suggests that socially anxious people suffer from evaluation apprehension. Shy people try to avoid negative evaluation from others by limiting their social interactions or by keeping these interactions short and pleasant. The socially anxious person's lack of confidence makes initiating conversations especially difficult for them.

Key Terms

need for Achievement The motive to engage in and succeed at entrepreneurial achievement behavior.

resultant achievement motivation The tendency to achieve as determined by the tendencies to approach success and to avoid failure.

fear of success A trait dimension indicating the extent to which people anticipate that negative consequences will follow from achievement.

Type A–Type B A trait dimension indicating the extent to which a person typically acts in a driving, time-urgent manner.

Potential for Hostility The component of the Type A pattern concerned with the tendency to express anger and irritability over minor frustrations.

social anxiety A trait dimension indicating the extent to which people experience anxiety during social encounters or when anticipating social encounters.

evaluation apprehension A strong concern about receiving negative evaluation from others.

Suggested Readings

Leary, M. R. (1983). *Understanding social anxiety: Social, personality and clinical perspectives.* Beverly Hills, CA: Sage. This is a clear introduction to theory and research on social anxiety. Much of Leary's initial work on social anxiety laid the foundation for later research in this area.

McClelland, D. C. (1961). *The achieving society.* Princeton, NJ: D. Van Nostrand. Of all the many books and articles McClelland has written on need for Achievement, this one still best summarizes his thinking and pioneering work in this area.

Strube, M. J. (Ed.) (1990). Special issue: Type A behavior. *Journal of Social Behavior and Personality, 5* (1). The articles in this special issue address several current issues in Type A research. The issue includes articles on hostility, gender differences, Type A in children, and the heritability of Type A.

The Biological Approach
Theory, Application, and Assessment

9

Have you ever been told that you look or act like one of your parents? Perhaps one of your mother's friends has said, "You're your mother's son (daughter) all right." My brother's quick temper has often been described as "inherited from his father." I know one couple who were more interested in learning about the family of their daughter's fiancé than about the fiancé. They told me that meeting the new in-laws would help them see what their future grandchildren would be like. As these examples suggest, the notion that children inherit characteristics from their parents is widely held in this society. Not only do people accept that parents pass physical characteristics, such as eye color or height, through their genes, but we often expect children's personalities to resemble their parents'.

Although conventional wisdom has acknowledged the role of biology in the development of personality for years, the same cannot be said for many psychologists. Thirty to 40 years ago many academic psychologists looked at all healthy newborns as blank slates, perhaps limited by differences in intelligence or physical skills but otherwise equally likely to develop into any kind of adult personality. Different adult personalities were attributed to differences in experiences, particularly in the way parents raised their children during early years. However, this view has slowly changed over the past several decades. No reputable psychologist would argue that people are born with their adult personalities intact, but today few psychologists would deny that personality isn't at least partly the result of inherited biological differences.

This acceptance of a genetic influence on personality has coincided with a growing recognition that personality cannot be separated from other biological factors. Recent evidence tells us that not all people have identical physiological functioning. That is, we can identify differences between people in terms of brain-wave activity, hormone levels, heart-rate responsiveness and other physiological features. More important for personality psychologists, researchers find these biological differences often translate into differences in behavior. We'll review an example of this later in this chapter when we look at individual differences in brain-wave patterns. We also have seen in recent years a growing recognition that human personality, like other human features, is the product of many generations of evolutionary development. Just as biologists find it useful to ask about the evolutionary function of the physical characteristics of a species, some psychologists have found this same question useful in understanding certain features of personality.

This growing acceptance of a biological influence on personality is partly a reflection of behaviorism's declining influence over the thinking of academic psychologists. As described in Chapter 13, early behaviorists tended to ignore individual differences among newborns, and a few even claimed that with enough control over the child's experiences they could shape a child into whatever personality they wanted. Almost no behaviorist would argue such an extreme position today. The movement away from the "blank slate" position also has been stimulated by research demonstrating rather clearly that at least some of our personality is inherited from our parents. This research is reviewed in the next chapter.

In this chapter, we'll look at three ways psychologists have utilized biological concepts to explain personality. First, we'll examine Hans Eysenck's description of personality, which has been an influential model in personality research for several decades. From the beginning, Eysenck has maintained that the individual differences in personality he describes are based in physiological differences. Second, we will look at individual differences in general dispositions, called temperaments. A strong case can be made that temperaments are based in biological differences. Psychologists have been successful in identifying some of these differences in temperaments among very young babies. Finally, we'll examine a fairly new area of personality research called evolutionary personality psychology. Psychologists using this approach borrow the concept of natural selection from biology to explain a large number of relatively stable human behaviors.

What each of these three theoretical perspectives makes clear is that a complete understanding of human personality requires us to go beyond some of the traditional boundaries of the discipline. In short, it may no longer be useful to think of our personality as somehow separate from our physiological makeup.

Hans Eysenck's Theory of Personality

More than 30 years ago, when the conventional wisdom in personality psychology traced an individual's personality to his or her experiences, a respected psychologist argued that personality was, in fact, determined more by biological makeup than by any actions or mistakes made by one's parents. Although Hans Eysenck's (pronounced Eye-Zinc) theory of personality has always been accorded respect within the field, his claims about such a large biological determinant of personality initially were met by many with a mix of skepticism and tolerance. But today Eysenck's emphasis on biological aspects of individual differences is increasingly compatible with the growing recognition of biology's role in personality.

The Structure of Personality

Like Raymond Cattell and other psychologists described in Chapter 7, Eysenck has been concerned with discovering the underlying structure of personality

Hans J. Eysenck
1916–

If our heredity plays a large role in determining personality, as Eysenck has argued, then Hans Eysenck may have been born to be the center of attention in whatever field he chose to enter. Eysenck was born in Germany in 1916 into a family of celebrities. His father, Eduard Eysenck, was an accomplished actor and singer, something of a matinee idol in Europe. His mother, whose stage name was Helga Molander, was also a silent film star. They planned a glamorous career in the entertainment field for Hans, who at age 8 had a small role in a motion picture. However, like many Hollywood marriages today, Eysenck's parents divorced when he was young (only later to marry other show business people). Most of Eysenck's early years were spent with his grandmother in Berlin.

Upon graduating from public school in Berlin, the rebellious Eysenck decided

not only to pursue a career in physics and astronomy, much to his family's displeasure, but to do so abroad. After a year in France, he moved to England where he eventually completed his Ph.D. at the University of London. Like so many others at the time, Eysenck left Germany in 1934 in part to escape the rise of the Nazis. "Faced with the choice of having to join the Nazi storm troops if I wanted to go to a university," he wrote, "I knew that there was no future for me in my unhappy homeland" (Eysenck, 1982, p. 289). After military service in World War II, Eysenck returned to the University of London, where he has spent most of his career.

Although he never pursued the career in show business his parents desired, this does not mean he has avoided the public's eye. In addition to his widely respected work and high level of productivity (more than 50 books), Eysenck often appears to seek out and dive right into some of the biggest controversies in psychology. In 1952 he published a paper challenging the effectiveness of psychotherapy. He was especially critical of psychoanalysis, pointing out that empirical evidence at the time showed psychoanalysis to be no better than receiving no treatment at all. Because of his early acknowledgment that individual differences in intelligence are largely inherited, Eysenck was often unfairly associated with those who argued that blacks are inherently less intelligent than whites. In 1980 he published a book arguing that the case for

Continued

cigarettes as a cause of health problems is not strong. Critics were particularly harsh when they discovered that some of this work was sponsored by American tobacco companies.

This lifelong combative style caused one biographer to call Eysenck the "controversialist in the intellectual world" (Gibson, 1981, p. 253). Eysenck would no doubt enjoy this title. "From the days of opposition to Nazism in my early youth, through my stand against Freudianism and projective techniques, to my advocacy of behavior therapy and genetic studies, to more recent issues, I have usually been against the establishment and in favor of the rebels," he wrote. "[But] I prefer to think that on these issues the majority were wrong, and I was right" (1982, p. 298).

traits. Also like these trait researchers, Eysenck has employed factor analysis to identify the basic number of what he calls types, or supertraits. However, unlike Cattell, Eysenck's conclusion after years of research is that all traits can be subsumed within three basic personality dimensions. He calls these three dimensions extraversion-introversion, neuroticism, and psychoticism.

Eysenck's research strategy begins by dividing the elements of personality into various units that can be arranged hierarchically (see Figure 9.1). The basic structure in this scheme is the *specific response* level, which consists of specific behaviors. For example, if we watch a man spend the afternoon talking and laughing with friends, we would be observing a specific response. If this man spends many afternoons each week having a good time with friends, we have evidence for the second level in Eysenck's model, a *habitual response*. But it is likely that this man doesn't limit himself to socializing just in the afternoon and just with these friends. Suppose this man also devotes a large part of his weekends and quite a few evenings to his social life. If you watch long enough, you might find that he lives for social gatherings, discussion groups, parties, and so on. You might conclude, in Eysenck's terms, that this person exhibits the *trait* of sociability. Finally, Eysenck argues that traits such as sociability are part of a still larger dimension of personality. That is, people who are sociable also tend to be impulsive, active, lively, and excitable. All of these traits combine to form the *supertrait* Eysenck calls **extraversion.**

How many of these supertraits are there? Originally, Eysenck's factor analytic research yielded evidence for two basic dimensions that could subsume all other traits: *extraversion-introversion* and *neuroticism*. Because the dimensions are independent of one another, people who score on the extraversion end of the first dimension can score either high or low on the second dimension. Further, as shown in Figure 9.2, someone who scores high on extraversion and low on neuroticism possesses different traits than does a person who scores high on both extraversion and neuroticism.

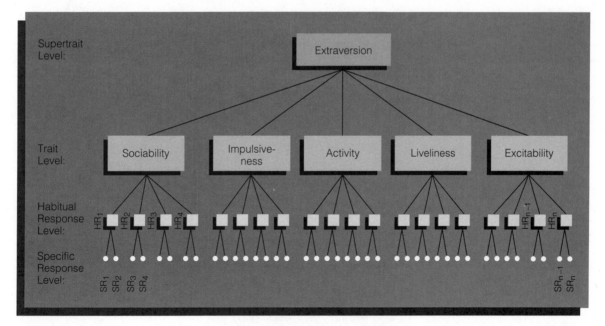

Figure 9.1

Eysenck's Hierarchical Model of Personality

Adapted from Eysenck (1982); reprinted by permission of Charles C Thomas, Publishers.

Where do you suppose you fall in this model? If you are the prototypic extravert, then Eysenck describes you as "outgoing, impulsive and uninhibited, having many social contacts and frequently taking part in group activities. The typical extravert is sociable, likes parties, has many friends, needs to have people to talk to, and does not like reading or studying by himself" (Eysenck & Eysenck, 1968, p. 6). An introvert is "a quiet, retiring sort of person, introspective, fond of books rather than people; he is reserved and distant except to intimate friends" (p. 6). Of course, most people fall somewhere between these two extremes, but each of us is perhaps a little more of one than the other.

Eysenck argues that extraverts and introverts differ not only in terms of behavior but also in their physiological makeup. Eysenck (1967) originally maintained that extraverts and introverts have different levels of cerebral cortex arousal when in a nonstimulating, resting state. Although it may sound backward at first, he proposed that extraverts generally have a *lower* level of cortical arousal than do introverts. Extraverts seek out highly arousing social behavior *because* their cortical arousal is well below their desired level when doing nothing. In a sense, highly extraverted people are simply trying to avoid unpleasant boredom.

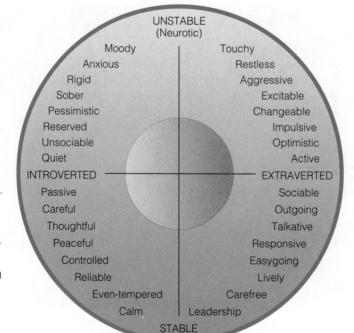

Figure 9.2

Traits Associated with Eysenck's Two Major Personality Dimensions

Adapted from Eysenck and Eysenck (1968); reprinted by permission of Educational and Industrial Testing Service.

Their problem is feeding their need for stimulation. Introverts have the opposite problem. They typically operate at an above-optimal cortical arousal level. These people select solitude and nonstimulating environments in an effort to keep their already-high arousal level from becoming too aversive. For these reasons, extraverts enjoy a noisy party that introverts can't wait to leave.

Unfortunately, a great deal of research has failed to uncover the different level of base-rate cortical arousal proposed by Eysenck. For example, introverts and extraverts show no differences in brain-wave activity when at rest or when asleep (Stelmack, 1990). But this does not mean that Eysenck's original theorizing was entirely off base. Rather, there is ample evidence that introverts are more sensitive to stimulation than extraverts are (Stelmack, 1990). That is, introverts are more quickly and strongly aroused when exposed to external stimulation. Introverts are more likely to become aroused when exposed to loud music or the stimulation found in an active social encounter. Introverts are even more responsive than extraverts when exposed to chemical stimulants, such as caffeine or nicotine.

Consequently, many researchers now describe extraverts and introverts in terms of their different sensitivity to stimulation, rather than the different base rate of cortical activity Eysenck proposed. However, the effect is essentially the same. Because of physiological differences, introverts are more quickly overwhelmed by the stimulation of a crowded social gathering, whereas extraverts are likely to find the same gathering rather pleasant. Extraverts are quickly bored by slow-moving movie plots and soft music because they are less likely to become aroused by these subtle sources of stimulation than introverts are.

The second major dimension in Eysenck's model is **neuroticism**. High scores on this dimension are "indicative of emotional lability and overreactivity. High-scoring individuals tend to be emotionally overresponsive and to have difficulties in returning to a normal state after emotional experiences" (Eysenck & Eysenck, 1968, p. 6). We sometimes refer to people who score high on this dimension as unstable or highly emotional. They often have strong emotional reactions to minor frustrations and problems and take longer to recover from these. They are more easily excited, angered, and depressed than most of us. Those falling on the other end of this dimension are less likely to fly off the handle and less prone to large swings in emotion.

Research findings later led Eysenck to add a third supertrait: **psychoticism**. People who score high on this dimension are described as "egocentric, aggressive, impersonal, cold, lacking in empathy, impulsive, lacking in concern for others, and generally unconcerned about the rights and welfare of other people" (Eysenck, 1982, p. 11). Needless to say, people scoring particularly high on this dimension are good candidates for some type of judicial correction or psychotherapy.

A Biological Basis for Personality

Eysenck (1990) points to three arguments when making the case that individual differences in personality are based in biology. First, he notes the consistency of extraversion-introversion over time. Several studies find that a person's level of this individual difference remains fairly stable over a period of many years (Scarr, 1969). Subjects in one study showed a consistent level of extraversion-introversion over a period of 45 years (Conley, 1984, 1985). Of course, this finding alone does not establish that extraversion-introversion is determined through biology. It is possible that people remain in similar environments throughout their lives or throughout the time period in which this personality trait is developed.

Therefore, Eysenck also uses the results of cross-cultural research to make his point. Researchers find the same three dimensions of personality—extraversion-introversion, neuroticism, and psychoticism—in research conducted in many different countries with different cultural backgrounds and histories (Barrett & Eysenck, 1984). Moreover, Eysenck argues that the three "superfactors" appear not only in his research but also in the work of other investigators using different data-gathering methods (Eysenck & Long, 1986). "Such cross-cultural unanimity would be unlikely if biological factors did not play a predominant part," Eysenck reasons. "The great differences in culture, education, and environment generally would be expected to produce a variety of different personality dimensions" (1990, p. 246).

Third, Eysenck points to the results of several studies indicating that genetics plays an important role in determining a person's level of each of the three personality dimensions. As presented in detail in the next chapter, this research

How do you spend your spare time? If you're an extravert, it probably never occurs to you to take a long walk by yourself. If you're an introvert, you may rely on a long walk to reduce your arousal level after an intense and active day.

suggests strongly that each of us inherited a predisposition to be introverted or extraverted.

After examining the evidence from all of these sources, and no doubt adding a bit of his own intuition, Eysenck (1982) asserted that about two thirds of the variance in personality development can be traced to biological factors. This is not to say that environmental factors do not play a role, particularly in shaping how general personality orientations are expressed. And Eysenck certainly can expect some disagreement about the two-thirds figure even from those who promote the idea that personality is influenced by one's genetic makeup. Nonetheless, as the evidence reviewed in the next chapter makes clear, biology probably sets limits on how much we can change an introverted friend into a highly sociable individual or the likelihood of shaping that impulsive, outgoing child into a calmer, easygoing adult.

Temperament

If you were to spend a few minutes watching toddlers in a nursery school, one of the first observations you might make is that even before they are a year old, children seem to be different. If you were to spend a week working in the nursery, you most likely would be able to identify the active babies, the ones who cry frequently, and (hopefully) a few who are usually quiet and happy. Although it is possible that these differences are the result of different treatment the children receive at home, a growing number of researchers are convinced these general behavioral styles may be present at birth. Further, they argue that these general styles are relatively stable and influence the development of personality traits throughout a person's life.

But does this mean that some people are born to be sociable and others born to be shy? Probably not. Instead, most researchers agree it is more likely that we are born with broad dispositions toward certain types of behaviors. They refer to these general behavioral dispositions as **temperaments**. The concept of temperaments has been around for a long time in personality theory. Allport described temperament as "the characteristic phenomena of an individual's emotional nature" (1961, p. 34). Today researchers generally think of temperaments as general patterns of behavior and mood that can be expressed in many different ways and that, depending on one's experiences, develop into different personality traits. How these general dispositions develop into stable personality traits depends on a complex interplay of one's genetic predispositions and the environment that a person grows up in.

We can understand how this interplay unfolds by examining the work of two different teams of personality researchers. First, we'll look at the three-dimension temperament model of Arnold Buss and Robert Plomin. This will be followed by a look at the research of some developmental psychologists, led by Jerome Kagan, who have identified what they call "inhibited" children.

The Buss-Plomin Temperament Model

Buss and Plomin (1975) describe temperament in terms of style (*how* a response is made) in contrast to content (*which* response is made). They argue that it is not so important to know that a person frequently gives speeches in front of large groups. Rather, we can get a better idea of the person's temperament by examining whether he or she speaks quickly or slowly, with great emphasis or in a restrained manner. Moreover, temperaments are broad personality dispositions rather than specific personality traits. How general behavioral dispositions develop into specific traits depends on how those dispositions interact with the environment the person grows up in.

How many of these general temperaments are there? Buss and Plomin (1975) originally identified four such dispositions. Later they reduced this to just three (Buss & Plomin, 1984, 1986). These three dispositions are activity, emotionality, and sociability. *Activity* refers to the person's general level of energy output.

Temperament

The following is the EAS Temperament Survey for Adults, developed by Buss and Plomin (1984). To assess your own temperament, rate each of the items using the following scale:

1 = Not at all characteristic of me
2 = Somewhat uncharacteristic of me
3 = Neither characteristic nor uncharacteristic of me
4 = Somewhat characteristic of me
5 = Very characteristic of me

_____ 1. I like to be with people. (s)
_____ 2. I usually seem to be in a hurry. (Ac)
_____ 3. I am easily frightened. (F)
_____ 4. I frequently get distressed. (D)
_____ 5. When displeased, I let people know it right away. (An)
_____ 6. I am something of a loner. (S)
_____ 7. I like to keep busy all the time. (Ac)
_____ 8. I am known as hot-blooded and quick-tempered. (An)
_____ 9. I often feel frustrated. (D)
_____ 10. My life is fast-paced. (Ac)
_____ 11. Everyday events make us troubled and fretful. (D)

Continued

Children high in this temperament move around a lot, prefer games that require a great deal of activity, and tend to fidget and squirm when forced to sit still for an extended period of time. Adults with a high level of activity temperament are always on the go, prefer active to quiet pastimes, and keep busy most of the time.

Emotionality refers to the intensity of one's emotional reactions. Children who cry frequently and easily become frightened and aroused to anger are high in this temperament. Adults who easily become upset and have a "quick temper" are high in general emotionality. Finally, *sociability* relates to a person's general tendency to affiliate and interact with others. Sociable children seek out others to play with. They enjoy and are more responsive to people. Adults with this temperament have a lot of friends and enjoy social encounters. You can get an idea of how you compare on these three temperaments by completing the scale on pages 276–277.

Temperament, continued

_____ 12. I often feel insecure. (F)
_____ 13. There are many things that annoy me. (An)
_____ 14. When I get scared, I panic. (F)
_____ 15. I prefer working with others rather than alone. (S)
_____ 16. I get emotionally upset easily. (D)
_____ 17. I often feel as if I'm bursting with energy. (Ac)
_____ 18. It takes a lot to make me mad. (An)
_____ 19. I have fewer fears than most people my age. (F)
_____ 20. I find people more stimulating than anything else. (S)

To obtain your scores, first reverse the value you gave items 6, 18, and 19 (that is, 5 = 1, 4 = 2, 3 = 3, 2 = 4, 1 = 5). Then use the letters in the parentheses following each item to identify which subscale the item belongs to. (Note that the researchers have divided the Emotionality dimension into three parts.) Sum the items for each of the scales to obtain your five scores. To get a better idea of what these scores mean, compare your scores with the averages Buss and Plomin obtained for adults, as reported below.

	Women	Men
Emotionality		
Distress	10.08	9.72
Fearfulness	10.60	8.92
Anger	10.28	10.80
Activity	13.40	12.80
Sociability	15.24	14.60

Two questions addressed in Buss and Plomin's research are: Where do these temperaments come from? and How do they develop into stable personality traits? The answer to the first question, according to these researchers, is that temperaments are largely inherited. In contrast to the approach taken by many physicians and psychologists a few decades ago, it is now widely agreed that not all babies are born alike. Parents with difficult-to-manage babies often are troubled by descriptions of the "typical" baby who sleeps whenever put into a crib, eats meals on a regular schedule, and responds to parental attention with a calm, loving reaction. Fortunately, most popular baby books today assure parents that some babies are going to be more active and more emotional than others. Research using a variety of methods (reviewed in the next chapter) has produced considerable evidence that the three temperaments identified by Buss and Plomin are to a large degree inherited (Buss & Plomin, 1984; Neale & Stevenson, 1989).

But how do these general dispositions translate into specific adult personality traits? Buss and Plomin (1975) argue that while the child's general level of emotionality points the development of personality in a certain direction, the course of the development also is influenced by the environment the child grows up in. For example, a highly emotional child has a better chance of becoming an aggressive adult than does one low in this temperament. But parents who encourage problem-solving skills over the expression of anger may turn the highly emotional child into a cooperative, nonaggressive adult.

One reason dispositions set the direction for adult personality is that a child's disposition influences the type of environment he or she lives in. How other people react to us, and even if they will be a part of our environment, is partly determined by our temperament. Thus, children high in sociability are likely to seek out environments with other people. Parents react differently to a baby who is constantly fussing and restless than to one who sleeps calmly. In short, temperament influences the environment and the environment influences how temperament develops into stable personality traits.

Thus, according to Buss and Plomin's model, adult personalities are determined by both inherited temperament and the environment. Two children born with identical temperaments can grow up to be two very different people. A child with a high activity level may become an aggressive, achieving, or athletic adult. But he or she probably will not become lazy and indifferent. A child does not represent a blank slate on which parents may draw whatever personality they desire. But neither is a child's personality set at birth, leaving the parents and society to settle for whatever they get.

Inhibited and Uninhibited Children

Many years ago, two developmental psychologists reported the results of an investigation on the stability of various personality traits (Kagan & Moss, 1962). Traits had been measured when the subjects were 2 or 3 years old and again when these same people were 20. Although most traits showed some change over time, one appeared noticeably stable: The researchers found that children who tended to be passive and cautious when faced with a new situation usually grew up to be adults who showed a similar pattern of shyness around strangers. Because environmental explanations of behavior were prevalent at the time, the researchers assumed this stable trait was the result of some type of "acquired fearfulness" shaped by the parents during childhood.

Today Jerome Kagan and his colleagues have a different interpretation. More recent research suggests this tendency to react to unfamiliar situations with an inhibited style is an inherited disposition (Kagan, 1989; Kagan, Reznick, & Snidman, 1986, 1988; Kagan & Snidman, 1991a, 1991b). This research indicates that approximately 10% of Caucasian American children can be classified as *inhibited* (Kagan & Snidman, 1991a). **Inhibited children** are controlled and gentle. When they throw a ball or knock over a tower of blocks, they do it in a manner that is "monitored, restrained, almost soft." Inhibited children are the ones who cling to their mothers or fathers when entering a new playroom or

Some children appear to inherit a tendency to respond to unfamiliar situations with increased arousal. When entering a new situation with new people, many of these children display what we typically call "shy" behavior.

when meeting new children. They are slow to explore new toys or equipment and may go for several minutes without saying anything.

The researchers compare these inhibited children with **uninhibited children**, who show the opposite pattern. Approximately 25% of the children in Kagan's samples fall into this category (Kagan & Snidman, 1991a). These youngsters express themselves in a "free, energetic, and spontaneous" style. They typically play with new toys right away and speak within a few minutes after entering a new play area.

On the surface, the difference between the two kinds of children appears to lie in how they experience and express anxiety. But inhibited children are not simply more afraid of everything. Rather, they are vulnerable to a specific form of anxiety generated by "unfamiliar people, settings, or challenges." Kagan refers to this as *anxiety to novelty*. Toddlers typically express their anxiety about the unfamiliar by turning away from strangers and burying their face in mother's or father's leg. As adults, they may express their discomfort in a new situation by withdrawing socially and waiting for others to speak first.

Anyone who has worked with young children can agree that some children fit the inhibited and others fit the uninhibited descriptions. But are these stable styles or just a passing phase? Can we predict from very early childhood behavior what kind of adult the child will become? Kagan and his colleagues argue that the answer is yes, because these differences in temperament appear to be biologically based. Inhibited and uninhibited children show a number of physical differences almost from the moment of birth. They differ in terms of body build, susceptibility to allergies, and even eye color (inhibited children are more likely to have blue eyes). Inhibited children are more likely than uninhibited children to show signs of irritability, sleep disturbances, and chronic constipation during the first few months of life. Newborns who show increases in such indicators as heart rate and pupil dilation when presented with unfamiliar stimuli as early as the first few days of life are more likely to be identified later as inhibited than uninhibited children (LaGasse, Gruber, & Lipsitt, 1989).

How stable are these different tendencies in response to the unfamiliar? Kagan and his colleagues have begun a series of longitudinal investigations to answer this question. One of these studies attempted to identify inhibited and uninhibited children from a group of four-month-old infants (Kagan, 1989; Kagan & Snidman, 1991a, 1991b). Trained judges looked at the babies' motor activity—arm and leg movements, arching of the back, tongue protrusions, crying—to place the children into categories. The infants with the highest levels of motor activity were expected to develop into inhibited children. All the children were tested for their level of fearfulness to unfamiliar events at ages 9, 14, and 21 months. Several tests were given at each age and the amount of anxiety expressed by the child recorded. For example, at 9 months the children saw a puppet speaking in an angry tone, and at 14 months the child was shown a large metal robot he or she could play with. The researchers recorded any indications of fear, such as crying or hiding.

The children identified as candidates for an inhibited style at age four months indeed showed more signs of fearfulness at the later testing sessions. Forty percent of the infants classified as likely inhibited children frequently expressed fear at 14 and 21 months, but none of the children identified as uninhibited did. The findings from this study support Kagan's contention that inhibited and uninhibited styles in children are fairly stable beginning at a very early age.

But do these temperaments show up later in life? A study by Reznick et al. (1986) suggests that they do. These investigators measured children's fear of unfamiliar situations at 21 months of age and again when the children reached 4. Then, when the children reached age 5½, they were brought back into the laboratory and examined in a number of situations. Experimenters coded how much the children played with unfamiliar children in the laboratory playroom. They also looked at how much the children spontaneously talked or moved

Table 9.1

Correlations Between Earlier Inhibition Measures and Behaviors at Age 5½ Years

Behavior at Age 5½ Years	Inhibition Score at Age 21 Months	Inhibition Score at Age 4 Years
Play with unfamiliar children	.43	.76
Laboratory activity level	.38	.27
Look at experimenter	.22	.41
Play with new toys	.19	.35
Spontaneous falling	.40	.32
Ball-toss riskiness	.35	.25
Social interaction in school	.34	.12
Mother's rating of shyness	.55	.36

Source: Taken from Reznick et al. (1986), with permission.
Note: The higher the score, the better the earlier inhibition score predicts the behavior at 5½.

around when they first entered the unfamiliar lab and how often they looked at the experimenter during the laboratory exercises. The children were observed for how likely they were to either venture out and play with new toys or cling to their mothers in a new playroom, how spontaneously they allowed themselves to fall onto a mattress when playing a falling game, and how risky they were in a ball-tossing game (either setting the target basket close by or at a more challenging distance). Finally, the researchers observed how much the children interacted with others or kept to themselves during free-play time in kindergarten, and they asked the mothers to rate their children on level of shyness.

The researchers compared the behavior of the 5½-year-olds to the earlier inhibition scores. The results are shown in Table 9.1. As seen in the table, the children who had shown an inhibited behavior pattern at each of the two earlier testing times showed the same pattern at age 5½. In other words, the toddler who clung to mother or father in a new situation showed a similar style of behavior when examined four years later.

Studies like these suggest that inhibited children are likely to exhibit a similar pattern of anxiety when responding to unfamiliar situations throughout early childhood. Does this mean inhibited children are sentenced to become shy adults? Kagan argues that this need not be the case. Like other temperament researchers, he and his colleagues emphasize that the environment still determines the degree to which this biological tendency shapes the development of adult personality. Personality is "neither fixed permanently by biology nor shaped entirely by social interaction," Kagan wrote. "An infant's temperament renders some outcomes very likely, some moderately likely, and some unlikely — although not impossible, depending on experience" (Kagan & Snidman, 1991b, p. 856). Parents of inhibited children can do their offspring a favor by becoming sensitive to the child's discomfort in unfamiliar settings and by teaching the child how to deal with new situations and people. Research with adults indicates that many business leaders, community workers, and entertainers have learned to overcome their shyness and lead very social lives (Zimbardo, 1977).

Evolutionary Personality Psychology

Think for a moment about some recent experiences you have had with anxiety. That is, what happened to you the last two or three times you felt nervous, worrisome, or anxious? Although direct threats to one's well-being — such as experiencing an earthquake or a physical assault — are certainly sources of anxiety, these fortunately are relatively rare for most of us and probably did not make your list. Instead, if you are like most people, you probably thought of something like receiving a poor grade, talking in front of a group, making a fool of yourself at a party, or having a fight with a friend. In other words, you probably thought of at least one situation that involved some sort of negative evaluation and possibly even rejection by others. Other situations on your list may have only suggested that some sort of social rejection might be coming soon, such as forgetting to turn in an assignment or discovering that you forgot to put on your deodorant one morning. What this simple exercise illustrates is that negative evaluation by other people, either directly or potentially, is one of our most common sources of anxiety.

But why might this be the case? Is this a learned behavior? Do we fear that others will punish us or refuse to give us something we want? That's certainly possible. Or could there be a psychoanalytic basis for this anxiety? At some deep level are we reminded of a traumatic separation from our parents? Perhaps. But a recent analysis suggests that the roots of anxiety go back much further than this. According to this new approach, we react to negative social evaluation the same way our ancestors did. We inherited this tendency to become nervous and upset in certain situations because experiencing this anxiety serves an important function that has allowed human beings to survive over many generations.

This new approach has become known as *evolutionary personality theory* (Buss, 1984, 1990a, 1991). Proponents of this theory use the process of natural selection, borrowed from the theory of evolution, to explain universal human characteristics, like anxiety. These psychologists argue that many characteristics of "human nature" make sense if we understand the evolutionary function they serve. We'll return to the example of anxiety later to illustrate this position. But first, we need to examine some of the assumptions underlying evolutionary personality theory.

Natural Selection and Psychological Mechanisms

Evolutionary personality psychology is based on the theory of evolution, as developed in the field of biology for more than a century. According to evolution theory, physical features evolve because they help the species to survive the challenges of the environment and to reproduce new members of the species. The key to this process is *natural selection*. That is, some members of a species possess inherited characteristics that help them meet and survive the threats from the natural environment, such as severe climate, predators, and food shortages. These survivors are more likely than those less able to deal with the environment to reproduce and pass their inherited characteristics on to their offspring. The net result, usually over many generations, is the evolution of species-specific features. Through the process of natural selection, those species developing features that help them survive prosper, and those failing to develop these features die out. In many cases, physical features evolve because they provide solutions to a serious threat to the species' survival. For example, in humans the problem of disease was resolved by the evolution of an immune system and the potential problem of bleeding to death when cut or wounded led to the evolution of blood clotting (Buss, 1991). This is not to say that these features were created because they were needed. Rather, the theory of evolution maintains that because of these changes our species was better prepared to survive.

According to evolutionary personality theory, just as the natural selection process has led to the evolution of certain physical characteristics in humans, it also is responsible for what are called *psychological mechanisms*. These psychological mechanisms are characteristically human functions that allow us to deal effectively with common human problems or needs. Through the process of natural selection, those mechanisms that increased the chances of human survival and reproduction have been retained, and those that failed to meet the challenges to survival have not.

Psychologists have identified a large number of these mechanisms. For example, most humans have an innate fear of strangers. Evolutionary personality psychologists argue that this fear evolved to meet the problem of attack by those not belonging to our group or tribe (Buss, 1991). Similarly, the human needs for achievement, power, and intimacy described in the previous chapter may have evolved as part of human nature precisely because each contributes to our ability to survive, prosper, and reproduce. Other examples of psychological mechanisms might include a need to perceive when someone is lying to us or cheating us and a need for structure and order (Buss, 1991; Hogan, 1983). But the survival function of some of these psychological mechanisms might not be so obvious at first glance. We'll turn to an example of one such mechanism next.

Anxiety and Social Exclusion

Evolutionary personality theory maintains that human characteristics like anxiety evolved because they proved beneficial to the survival of our ancestors. But how can this be? Anxiety is an unpleasant emotional state, something a normally functioning person would prefer to avoid. Moreover, anxiety is almost always problematic. It interferes with our ability to learn new tasks, remember information, perform sexually, and so on. How can something as negative as anxiety help the species?

We can answer this question by looking at what causes anxiety. Recently, some psychologists have argued that one of the primary causes of anxiety is *social exclusion* (Baumeister & Tice, 1990). These investigators propose that all humans have a strong need to belong to groups and to be in relationships. Consequently, when we experience exclusion or rejection from social groups we suffer great distress. This distress is not just limited to those relatively rare instances when we are literally rejected from a group or tossed out of a relationship. Rather, any information that suggests we might be excluded socially or that we are no longer attractive to other people is threatening to our need to belong.

As you thought about the situations that recently caused you to feel anxious, you probably recognized that most were related to a fear of social rejection. You also may have noticed that you didn't have to experience actual exclusion from a group or relationship to feel anxious. Rather, information that even hints that someday you might be rejected by others can often be enough to bring on anxiety. Events that can trigger this fear include "an unkind word from a lover or relative, criticism of one's work by a superior, any suggestion that one is unattractive or losing one's looks, and almost any sort of candidacy or application for membership" (Baumeister & Tice, 1990, p. 167).

Thinking about anxiety as fear of social rejection helps us understand why people feel anxious when they have to give a speech in front of an audience or when they discover that first gray hair. The speaker is afraid the audience members will evaluate him or her negatively, a form of social rejection. The thirtyish adult discovering a gray hair worries about his or her attractiveness to others. Although outright social rejection is not common, fear of what others will think of us may be an everyday experience.

This social exclusion explanation of anxiety also fits nicely with evolutionary personality theory. Primitive people who lived together in small groups were more likely to survive and reproduce than those living alone. An isolated person would be more susceptible to injury, illness, lack of shelter, and limited resources and would be less able to mate and raise offspring than individuals living in groups or tribes. Consequently, anything that motivates people to avoid behaviors that might lead to their exclusion from the group would help the species survive. Anxiety serves this purpose. Thus, evolutionary personality psychologists argue that anxiety evolved to meet the needs of the species.

Proponents of this view cite other pieces of evidence for the evolutionary roots of anxiety. For example, although expressed in different ways, anxiety is found in nearly all cultures (Barlow, 1988). Moreover, the kinds of behavior that lead to social exclusion are typically those that impair the survival of the species (Buss, 1990b). These include adultery, aggression, and taking valuable resources away from others. In this sense, evolutionary theory crosses paths with Sigmund Freud. Freud also argued that primitive people came to live in groups and developed laws against many sexual and aggressive behaviors so that the species might survive. Although Freud was concerned with repressing unconscious impulses, his analysis is in many ways similar to that of more recent evolutionary theorists.

In short, what we call "human nature" can be thought of as a large number of psychological mechanisms that have allowed humankind to survive as long as we have. Advocates of this approach do not argue that all human characteristics must necessarily be beneficial. It is possible that some of our psychological mechanisms could someday contribute to the extinction of the species. But in the meantime, evolutionary personality psychology appears to provide a fruitful new approach for understanding some basic features of human personality.

Application: Children's Temperaments and School

Most of us have been exposed at one time or another to a parent's or grandparent's description of the strict and very regimented way teachers used to run their classes "when I was a kid." According to these stories, all children were treated alike. Each was expected to sit quietly and read during reading period, to work at the pace set by the teacher, and above all, to pay full attention to the teacher at all times. Any deviations from the routine were met with strict and sometimes severe punishment.

Although the accuracy of these descriptions might be challenged at times, the point is that teachers do not approach their job the same way they did a few generations ago. There are no doubt many differences in teaching style today and many reasons for these changes. But one important reason for changes in the way teachers look at their task is an awareness that not all children approach school and learning in the same way. Because children are born with different temperaments, some jump right in and begin participating in lessons, whereas others are slow to warm up to new tasks. Some students have difficulty focusing their attention on any one activity for very long, whereas others become frustrated when forced to move on to a new assignment before they are ready.

In fact, the transition from the familiarities of home to the unfamiliar classroom setting is just the kind of event that is likely to bring out differences in temperament. This was illustrated in a study in which researchers used measures of inhibition taken at age 21 months to predict how children would react to their first day of kindergarten (Gersten, 1989). Observers watched the children during a relatively unstructured free-play period their first day of school. The children who had earlier been identified as inhibited responded to this new and unfamiliar situation very differently than the children identified as uninhibited. The inhibited children were more likely to spend this time by themselves watching the other children. They also were less likely to play with other children, touch other children, offer a toy to one of their classmates, or even to laugh.

Clearly inhibited and uninhibited children respond very differently to the first day of school, and researchers find that these differences often continue throughout the school year (Gersten, 1989). However, researchers have identified other temperamental differences that also may affect how a child performs in school. Thomas and Chess (1977) identified nine of these differences. They maintain that children's temperament can vary in terms of activity level, approach or withdrawal, adaptability, distractibility, intensity, mood, persistence, rhythmicity, and threshold (see Table 9.2).

Research with these nine temperament dimensions led to the identification of three basic patterns (Thomas & Chess, 1977). First, there is the *easy child*, who approaches rather than withdraws from new situations, is adaptive, and generally experiences a positive mood. Most teachers probably would prefer an entire room full of these students. However, classrooms are also likely to include some examples of the *difficult child*. These children tend to withdraw rather than approach new situations, are typically low in adaptability, and often are intense and in a negative mood. Finally, a classroom is also likely to include some children who fall in the third general pattern, the *slow-to-warm-up child*. These children are similar to the inhibited children identified by Kagan and his colleagues. They tend to withdraw from unfamiliar situations and are slow to adapt to a new kind of academic task or a new activity.

In a 6-year study of children primarily from middle-class backgrounds, Thomas and Chess (1977) found that about two thirds of the elementary school children in their study could be identified with one of these three styles. Forty percent of the students in their sample fell into the easy-child category, 10% in the difficult-child group, and 15% into the slow-to-warm-up category. This means that the typical elementary school class contains a mix of children with different temperamental patterns.

Temperament and Academic Performance

Clearly, individual differences in children's temperament have important implications for how the children interact with others and eventually for their personal adjustment (Chess & Thomas, 1986; Gersten, 1989; Keogh, 1986; Thomas & Chess, 1977). However, a large number of studies now suggest that a child's temperament may also have an impact on how well that child does in school (Cowen, Wyman, & Work, 1992; Keogh, 1986; Lerner, Lerner, & Zabski, 1985; Martin, 1985). Generally this research finds that children with a difficult-child temperament pattern and those with a slow-to-warm-up temperament pattern perform more poorly than students identified with the easy-child pattern. These differences are most likely to show up in teachers' evaluations of the students and in grades (Keogh, 1986). However, differences related to temperament also are found in standardized achievement tests. Moreover, research indicates that temperament is not related to intelligence (Keogh, 1986). Thus, different levels of performance by children of different temperament do not merely reflect the teacher's biased perceptions or differences in the child's abilities.

Why, then, does temperament appear related to how well a child does in school? There are probably several reasons. First, students' behavior evokes different responses from teachers. The student who is attentive, adaptive, seemingly eager to learn, and in a positive mood is going to draw a different reaction

Table 9.2

Thomas and Chess's Nine Temperament Dimensions

Activity Level	General level of motor activity during such periods as eating, playing, walking, or crawling.
Rhythmicity	Predictable or unpredictable patterns of behaviors, such as sleeping and hunger. Also known as regularity.
Approach or Withdrawal	Initial response to new situations or experiences, either to approach eagerly or to pull away and wait.
Adaptability	Ability to respond to a new or altered situation (after the initial reaction).
Threshold of Responsiveness	Amount of stimulation necessary to evoke a response. Includes reactions to new sensations, objects, or people.
Intensity of Reaction	Amount of energy behind response, regardless of type of response.
Quality of Mood	General mood level, either pleasant and friendly or unpleasant and unfriendly.
Distractibility	Ability to stay with ongoing behavior in the face of environmental distractors.
Attention Span and Persistence	How long child can focus his or her attention on one task; how long child persists at a task in the face of obstacles.

from the typical elementary school teacher than the student who is irritable, easily distracted, and withdrawn. Working with the former student probably will be pleasant and rewarding; working with the latter may be frustrating and demanding. Perhaps quite unintentionally, teachers may naturally work more closely and more attentively with some students than others. As a result, opportunities for learning and achievement may be shaped by the child's temperament.

In addition, some temperaments probably are more compatible with the requirements of the typical classroom than others. For example, in most classes children who are attentive, adaptable, and persistent are likely to do better than those who are low on these temperament dimensions. On the other hand, children with a short attention span and children who are easily distracted may have difficulty completing assignments or paying enough attention to learn lessons the first time. Children who take a long time to adapt to new situations often may find themselves behind the rest of the class. Moreover, children's reactions to these difficulties can lead to further problems. Children who fall behind or do poorly on assignments may become discouraged or give up, thus adding to their academic problems.

Finally, researchers have uncovered some evidence that teachers often misinterpret temperamental differences in their students (Chess & Thomas, 1986;

Keogh, 1986). Slow-to-warm-up children may be seen as unmotivated when they fail to eagerly attack a new assignment or as unintelligent when they require several tries to master a new task. A highly active student might be identified as a troublemaker. An easily distracted student might be seen as uninterested in learning. A large amount of research demonstrates that teachers' explanations for their students' behavior can affect how the teacher interacts with the student and subsequently how well the student does in school (Cooper & Good, 1983).

The impact of a teacher's misinterpretation of temperamental differences is illustrated in the case of an elementary school student who approached school-work with a high-intensity, high-persistence temperament (Chess & Thomas, 1986). This boy had a long attention span and preferred to spend an extensive amount of time absorbed in one lesson before moving on to the next. Unfortunately, the teacher's schedule rarely allowed for this. The boy became upset whenever the teacher, concerned about the other students' shorter attention spans, interrupted his lessons. The teacher interpreted the boy's reaction as an indication of some underlying behavior problem. Fortunately, the problem was resolved when the boy's parents transferred him to a school that encouraged the kind of persistent and intense style of involvement that had been a problem in the earlier class. This example leads to the next important point — that differences in temperament can help or hinder academic performance, depending on the demands of the situation.

The "Goodness of Fit" Model

We might be tempted at this point to ask, What temperament characteristics contribute to better school performance? However, this probably is not the right question. Instead, most researchers in this area prefer to ask, What kind of environment and procedures are most conducive to learning for this student, given his or her temperament? The second question reflects the thinking behind what is known as the **Goodness of Fit Model**. According to the model, how well a child does in school is partly a function of how well the expectations and demands of the learning environment match the child's "capabilities, characteristics, and style of behaving" (Thomas & Chess, 1977). In other words, not all children come to school with the same learning styles or abilities. We can't do much to change a child's temperament. But if lessons and assignments are presented in a way that matches the child's learning style, an optimal amount of learning can take place. The results of several studies find support for the Goodness of Fit Model (Keogh, 1986; Lerner, 1983; Lerner, Lerner, & Zabski, 1985). Students get higher grades and better evaluations from teachers when the student's temperament matches the teacher's expectations and demands.

The Goodness of Fit Model thus provides an obvious strategy for improved teaching. Classroom assignments that require extensive concentration create a problem for the easily distracted girl with a short attention span. However, this girl probably will have little difficulty mastering the assignment if the same material is presented in short, easily processed segments. A slow-to-warm-up boy will fall behind when his teacher works at a pace set for the average member of the class. But if allowed to progress at his own pace, the boy eventually will come around and do as well as his classmates.

Fortunately, researchers find that today most teachers are aware of differences in temperament and take steps to adapt their teaching to meet the students' individual styles (Chess & Thomas, 1986). Although time and resources may limit teachers' ability to meet the individual needs of all their students, research on temperamental differences in children clearly has direct implications for improvements in elementary school teaching.

Assessment:
Brain Electrical Activity and
Cerebral Asymmetry

The next time you're talking to some friends, you might try this quick experiment. Ask your friends some reflective questions, such as "How do you feel when you are anxious?" or "Picture and describe the most joyous scene you have recently been in." When most people engage in a little reflective thought, they tend to look off to one side. Some people consistently, although not always, glance to the right, whereas others tend to look to the left. As described later, the significance of this difference lies in what it may tell us about your friend's tendency to experience happiness or sadness. This is because which direction people look when contemplating may be a general indicator of the brain-activity patterns psychologists associate with emotion.

The notion that personality differences might be determined through physiological measures has been around a long time. Freud suggested that one day scientists might discover the neurological underpinnings of personality. Similarly, Allport argued that future technological advances would allow researchers to identify the differences in the central nervous system associated with different traits. Personality researchers have utilized various physiological measures in their experiments for many years. For example, you may recall from Chapter 6 how researchers use physiological indicators of arousal, such as heart rate and galvanic skin response, to test their ideas about anxiety and coping. In this section we'll look at another example of how psychologists use physiological measures in personality research. These researchers examine differences in brain-activity level.

Measuring Brain Activity

How can we measure brain activity without going into a person's skull? Fortunately, technology has developed relatively unintrusive procedures for measuring brain-activity level in normal humans. Most often, researchers use an instrument called an *electroencephalograph* (EEG) to measure electrical activity in different parts of the human brain (Davidson, 1988). This procedure has been

Researchers measure brain activity levels with an instrument known as an EEG. This information may tell us about the person's tendency to experience positive or negative emotions.

particularly useful to personality researchers for several reasons. First, the procedure is relatively simple and does not harm the subject in any way. Typically, small electrodes are attached to the subject's head with hair clips and elastic straps. Subjects report that the procedure is not uncomfortable, although sometimes electrode paste can leave messy spots in their hair. In addition, the EEG allows researchers to record brain activity in very quick intervals. Some instruments can measure this activity within milliseconds. This sensitivity is important when looking at emotions, which often change very rapidly.

Most electroencephalographs automatically record brain activity. EEG data are usually described in terms of cycles per second, or waves. One kind of wave identified through this process, known as an *alpha wave*, has proven particularly useful for research on personality and emotion. The lower the alpha-wave activity, the more activation in that region of the brain.

Cerebral Asymmetry

Although EEG data can be used to assess activity level in many different regions of the brain, recent research on alpha-wave levels in the anterior (front) regions of the cerebral hemisphere has proven particularly useful in understanding individual differences in emotion. This region has considerable connections with other parts of the brain that researchers now know play an important role in regulating emotions. Of particular importance is the finding that the anterior region of a person's right cerebral hemisphere often shows a different activity level than the anterior region of that same person's left cerebral hemisphere. Researchers refer to this difference in right and left hemisphere activity as **cerebral asymmetry**.

Recent research suggests that different patterns of cerebral asymmetry are associated with differences in emotional experience. More specifically, higher activation in the left hemisphere has been associated with *positive* moods, whereas higher activation in the right hemisphere is indicative of *negative* moods. This difference was demonstrated in a recent experiment in which researchers showed emotion-arousing films to subjects while taking EEG measures of right and left hemisphere brain activity (Davidson, Ekman, Saron, Senulis, & Friesen, 1990). When subjects experienced feelings of happiness and disgust, as determined by their facial expression, the researchers found increased activation in the left and right cerebral hemispheres, respectively.

Similar patterns have been found in children less than a year old. For example, in one study with 10-month-old infants, smiling was associated with higher left hemisphere activity, whereas crying was associated with higher right hemispheric activity (Fox & Davidson, 1988). In other experiments, infants showed increases in left hemisphere activity when their mother reached down to pick them up (Fox & Davidson, 1987), when they heard laughter (Davidson & Fox, 1982), and when they tasted something sweet (Fox & Davidson, 1986). In all cases, the children experiencing a positive emotion had relatively more activity in their left hemisphere than in the right. Because these results are found in children who have not yet reached their first birthday, researchers argue that this association between cerebral asymmetry and emotion is something we are born with, rather than the result of our learning experiences.

Individual Differences in Cerebral Asymmetry

More recent research has taken the association between cerebral asymmetry and emotion one step further. Investigators also find higher activation levels in one hemisphere over the other even when subjects are in a relatively nonemotional resting state. However, which hemisphere displays the higher activity level is not the same in all people. That is, some people tend to have a higher level of left hemisphere activity in the resting state, whereas others tend to have more right hemisphere activity. Moreover, like other individual differences, differences in cerebral asymmetry tend to be fairly stable over time. If you show a higher level of activity in one hemisphere over the other today, you probably will show the same pattern when taking an EEG test next week or even next year.

This observation leads to another intriguing question. Because left and right hemispheric activity is associated with positive and negative moods, can we use EEG data to predict who is more likely to experience certain kinds of moods or even mood disturbances? Some initial data on this question are promising. Subjects in one study were identified as having either higher left hemisphere or higher right hemisphere activity when in a nonemotional, restful state (Davidson & Tomarken, 1989). These subjects then watch films designed to elicit certain emotions, such as happiness or fear. As expected, subjects who tended to have a higher level of left hemisphere activity when resting were more responsive to the positive mood films, whereas the subjects with the higher right hemisphere activity levels reacted more to the films that produced negative moods.

Again, similar patterns can be found in infants. Ten-month-old infants in one study were identified as having either higher left hemisphere or higher right hemisphere activity when resting (Davidson & Fox, 1989). The babies also were divided into those who cried and those who did not cry when separated from their mothers. As expected, the criers tended to be those with higher right hemisphere activity while the noncriers were those with higher left hemisphere activity.

Some researchers explain these findings in terms of thresholds (Davidson & Tomarken, 1989). People with a higher right hemisphere activity level require a much less intense negative event before they experience fear or sadness than people who do not start out with this high level of activation. On the other hand, people who generally have a higher level of left hemisphere activity require a less intense positive experience before they experience happiness.

Finally, we can ask if this physiological difference might play a role in the development of emotional disorders. Some research findings suggest that it may. Depressed patients in one study showed more right-side activation than did nondepressed subjects (Davidson, Chapman, & Chapman, 1987). More important, researchers in another study examined EEG measures of people who currently were not depressed but who had suffered from previous bouts of depression (Henriques & Davidson, 1990). These subjects tended to have less left hemispheric activity in the anterior region of the brain when resting than a group of subjects who had never suffered from depression. This finding suggests that individual differences in cerebral asymmetry may play a role in depression. Clearly, whether we suffer from depression probably depends on many factors, including the kinds of experiences we have. But it may be that some people require fewer or less intense negative experiences before succumbing to feelings of depression.

In summary, the results from several studies suggest that inherent physiological differences in the relative activity levels of the right and left anterior regions of our cerebral hemispheres may play a role in our emotional reactions to the events we encounter in life, perhaps even positioning some people close to a threshold for emotional disorders. Let's return now to the eye drift example at the beginning of this discussion. Although not nearly as reliable as EEG data, research suggests that right-handed people who typically glance to the left when engaged in reflective thought are likely to show a higher level of right hemisphere activation when resting. Those who tend to glance to the right are more likely to be higher in left hemispheric activity (Davidson, 1991; Gur & Reivich, 1980). Of course, many other variables affect emotion, but this observation suggests that those who glance to the left may have a lower threshold for experiencing negative emotion while those who look to the right are more likely to experience positive feelings.

Strengths and Criticisms
of the Biological Approach

Strengths

One of the strengths of the biological approach is that it provides a bridge between the study of personality and the discipline of biology. For too many years, personality psychologists often ignored the biological roots of human behavior. But it has become increasingly difficult to ignore the fact that we are the product of an evolutionary history and our individual genetic makeup. Human behavior is influenced by many factors, one of which is biology. By incorporating what biologists know about such concepts as evolution and genetics, personality psychologists come closer to understanding what makes each of us the kind of person we are.

The biological approach also has succeeded in identifying some realistic parameters for psychologists interested in behavior change. The "blank slate" image of humankind can be very appealing. If the newborn personality is like clay, then with enough knowledge, resources, and effort we should be able to mold that personality in any way we want. If all babies are essentially alike, then with enough research psychologists should be able to advise parents and teachers on the "correct" way to raise all children and teach all students. But buying into this description of personality has its down side as well. Parents with difficult-to-control babies have blamed themselves for not knowing how to raise their child. Highly active children have been punished for not sitting as still as their friends or classmates. Advocates of the biological approach argue that our inherited biological differences probably place limits on the kind of children and adults we become. Some people are born with a tendency to become more introverted than others, and there is probably very little a parent, teacher, or spouse can do to turn an introvert into an extravert.

Another strength of the biological approach is that most of its advocates are academic psychologists with a strong interest in testing their ideas through research. Consequently, investigators have generated empirical support for many of the hypotheses advanced from this perspective. In addition, psychologists from the biological approach have often modified their theories as a result of research findings. For example, Eysenck outlined a comprehensive model of personality several decades ago. He and others conducted research on many of the predictions generated by this model. Much of this work has supported Eysenck's ideas, but some ideas have been altered to better account for the research findings.

Criticisms

Advocates of the biological approach often face inherent limits on their ability to test some of their ideas. Evolutionary personality psychologists in particular must often argue from the relatively weak position of analogy and reasonable deduction. Some human behaviors may resemble what we observe in lower animals, but how does a researcher demonstrate that the two behaviors serve the same function? A reasonable case can be made that anxiety helps the species survive because it prevents social isolation. But how can you test this hypothesis directly? Direct manipulation of behavior is usually out of the question for researchers in this area, thus making demonstrations of cause-effect relationships difficult if not impossible. As a result, the research support for many of the ideas postulated by evolutionary personality psychologists remains relatively weak.

Another criticism is directed at theory and research on temperament. Students and researchers may be bewildered because of the lack of an agreed-on model. Buss and Plomin identify three basic temperament dimensions (although originally they talked about four). Kagan and his colleagues look at only one dimension, yet other researchers have identified nine (see Table 9.2). Students have a right to ask which of these is correct. More important, it is difficult to make comparisons across investigations when researchers rely on different names and descriptions for these temperament dimensions. For example, is the inhibited child Kagan studies the same as the slow-to-warm-up child education researchers often examine? We can hope that clearer answers about the number and description of basic temperaments will be forthcoming as researchers continue to work in this area.

Finally, like the trait approach, the biological approach offers very few suggestions for personality change. Although there are probably plenty of ideas from this approach that are useful for psychotherapists, there are no schools of psychotherapy based on this perspective. On the contrary, the message from the biological approach is that we need to be more aware of some of the limitations on how much we can change people and that therapists might do better to recognize that not all clients will respond identically to their treatments.

Summary

1. Hans Eysenck has been a proponent of biological influences on personality for many years. Eysenck argues that personality can be divided along three primary dimensions. He calls these extraversion-introversion, neuroticism, and psychoticism. Research suggests that introverts are more sensitive to stimulation than extraverts are. Eysenck argues that these differences are based in inherited biological differences.

2. Many personality researchers have identified general inherited dispositions called temperaments. The Buss-Plomin temperament model identifies three temperament dimensions: activity, emotionality, and sociability. Buss and Plomin argue that temperament is largely inherited and that these inherited dispositions interact with experiences to form adult personality traits. Developmental psychologist Jerome Kagan has identified what he calls inhibited and uninhibited children. The former show a fear of novel or unfamiliar situations that the latter seem to lack. There is evidence that this tendency is inherited and that it remains fairly stable throughout childhood.

3. Evolutionary personality psychology uses the concept of natural selection to explain the development and survival function of human personality characteristics. These theorists point out that anxiety often results from an event suggesting potential social rejection. They argue that because social isolation decreases the chances of survival and reproducing, the evolution of anxiety has served to help the species survive.

4. Research on temperament has important implications for teaching. Research finds that children identified with a difficult temperament pattern and those identified with a slow-to-warm-up pattern perform more poorly in school than children identified with an easy temperament pattern. The Goodness of Fit Model suggests that children will learn best when the demands of the learning environment match the child's temperament.

5. Personality researchers have often used physiological measures in their research. Recently researchers have used EEG data to look at individual differences in emotions. They find differences in the activity levels of the right and left halves of the cerebral hemispheres are associated with differences in positive and negative mood. Some research indicates that people inherit different base-rate levels of brain activity in the two hemispheres and that this difference may make them more vulnerable to negative or positive emotional experiences.

6. One strength of the biological approach to personality is that it ties personality psychology to the discipline of biology. In addition, research in this area has identified realistic limitations on the "blank slate" model of personality development. Another strength of the biological approach is its strong emphasis on research. Criticisms of the approach include the difficulty researchers often have in testing some of their ideas directly. Other criticisms are that there is no agreed-upon model for temperament researchers and that the biological approach provides little information about behavior change.

Key Terms

extraversion A dimension of personality concerned with a person's general level of activity and sociability.

neuroticism A dimension of personality concerned with a person's general level of emotional stability.

psychoticism A dimension of personality concerned with a person's general level of egocentric and impersonal behavior.

temperaments General behavioral predispositions present in infancy and assumed to be inherited.

inhibited/uninhibited children Children who exhibit a strong anxiety about novel and unfamiliar situations, and those who show very little of this anxiety.

Goodness of Fit Model A model proposing that a child performs best when the demands of the environment match with his or her temperament.

cerebral asymmetry Higher levels of brain activity in one cerebral hemisphere than the other.

Suggested Readings

Buss, D. M. (1991). Evolutionary personality psychology. *Annual review of psychology, 42,* 459–491. A review of evolutionary personality theory, including an in-depth explanation of the theory and some of the competing predictions that can be made when applying the concept of natural selection to understanding human behavior. This chapter also summarizes some recent empirical work stemming from this theory.

Eysenck, H. J. (1982). *Personality, genetics, and behavior: Selected papers.* New York: Praeger. A collection of some of Hans Eysenck's writings, highlighting his work in personality, behavior therapy, genetics, and social issues. The book includes an original opening chapter in which Eysenck summarizes his theory of personality and concludes with a brief autobiography.

Kagan, J., & Snidman, N. (1991). Temperamental factors in human development. *American Psychologist, 46,* 856–862. Summary of Kagan's research on inhibited and uninhibited children. Describes the most recent findings from Kagan's longitudinal research on inhibited children.

The Biological Approach
Relevant Research

10

Today most psychologists acknowledge that biology plays an important role in human personality. However, many psychologists have come to accept this conclusion rather reluctantly. There are many reasons for this resistance. One is that the "blank slate" view of humankind has great appeal. If we accept that personality is formed largely or exclusively by one's experiences, then it is possible to shape a child into the kind of adult we want and to change personality traits that create problems. Perhaps another reason some psychologists have not eagerly embraced the biological approaches is that they remain leery of inappropriate and even offensive interpretations that come from placing too much emphasis on biological determinants of personality. For example, in the past some people have argued against social programs by maintaining that certain racial or gender differences are the result of biological rather than cultural factors.

Of course, accepting a biological component to personality does not mean that personality is fixed at birth. Those who resign themselves with "that's the way men/women are" or "it's just my nature" are foolishly ignoring the power of experience. But it would be equally foolish to ignore the wealth of research data indicating the role biology plays in personality. Perhaps the most persuasive case an advocate of the biological approach can make is to point to some of the recent research findings in this area. We'll review some of that evidence in this chapter. As with research from other approaches to personality, the studies reported here sometimes are subject to criticisms and alternate interpretations. However, taken together, the findings from these investigations make it difficult to ignore the biological determinants of personality we inherited from our parents and our ancestors.

We'll begin by looking at research on the heritability of personality characteristics. More specifically, we'll address the question of how researchers determine how much of our personalities is inherited from our parents. Investigators have used a variety of methods to produce consistent evidence for a strong genetic influence on personality. However, these research findings are not without their critics, and identifying precisely the strength of the genetic component remains elusive.

Next we'll review research generated from Hans Eysenck's theory of personality. Specifically, we'll look at some of the differences between extraverts and introverts. This research suggests that your level of extraversion-introversion affects a wide range of behavior, including how happy you are and where you sit in the library.

Finally, we'll look at an application of evolutionary personality theory. According to this theory, men and women should differ in what they look for in a potential mate. Research with a variety of cultural groups finds some support for the evolutionary theory predictions.

Heritability of Personality Traits

How much of your personality is the result of your genetic makeup, and how much is the result of the environment you grew up in? This "nature-nurture" question is one of the oldest and most enduring issues in psychology. Of course, most people readily accept that both genetic background and experiences are important in shaping personality. Parents often point to personality traits their children "got from me," but few would deny that the way they raise their children also plays a large role in what kind of adults the children will become. Thus, the question becomes not *which* of these, genetics or environment, shapes our personalities, but rather *to what extent* and *how* our personalities are shaped by each.

So we might rephrase the question this way: To what degree was the mold for your adult personality already cast by the time you were born? Researchers now agree that relatively stable abilities and aptitudes, such as intelligence, appear to be largely inherited (cf. Bouchard & McGue, 1981; Gourlay, 1979). This is not to say that a highly intelligent child cannot be born to relatively unintelligent parents or that a child's environment plays no role in intellectual development. But it does appear we are born with a potential for intelligence that combines with environmental influences to determine adult intelligence levels. Similarly, certain psychological disorders appear to have a genetic component (Kety, Rosenthal, Wender, & Schulsinger, 1976; Schulsinger, 1972). Again, this does not mean some people are born to be schizophrenic or depressed, but rather that some people are born with a higher susceptibility to these disorders than are others.

But what about personality traits? Are people born to be aggressive or extraverted? The answer appears to be a qualified yes. Genetics may very well influence these and other personality traits. However, collecting information on

Identical twins not only share physical features but also have similar personalities. Researchers attribute this similarity in part to genetic influences, although the extent of genetic influence on personality continues to be debated.

this issue is not easy, and many questions remain about how to interpret the data that are available.

Separating Environmental from Genetic Influences

Psychologists working on the environment-genetics question have a somewhat different task facing them than do those working in other areas of personality research. For technological and ethical reasons, it is not possible to manipulate people's genes and observe the kind of adults they become. Instead, these researchers must rely on less direct and more controversial means of examining the question. Like detectives trying to piece together a picture of how we got to where we are, these researchers use innovative, sometimes clever experimental procedures to track down the roots of adult personalities. Each method has its limitations and weaknesses, but data from a number of sources suggest a significant role for genetics in the development of our personalities.

The most obvious source of information on this question is the similarity of parents and children. Aggressive parents often have aggressive offspring, shy

Figure 10.1

Twin-Study Re-
search Diagram

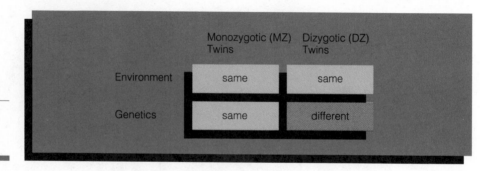

children often come from homes with shy parents. Similarly, we often see brothers who are both outgoing or sisters who both are sensitive and caring. Casual observers look at these relationships and often assume the children inherited these traits from their parents. Unfortunately, there is an obvious alternative explanation for these similarities. Members of a family not only share genes, they share living environments as well. Siblings' personalities may be similar because the parents raised them in the same basic manner. Children of introverted parents might become introverted because of the calm and quiet home they grow up in.

In most cases, therefore, shared genes and shared environments seem hope-lessly confounded. Can we peel one of these influences away from the other? Fortunately, there are ways. The most popular procedure used to examine the role of genetics and the role of environment in personality trait research is the **twin-study method**. This method takes advantage of a naturally occurring phenomenon: the two types of human twins. Some twins are **monozygotic** (MZ); that is, the two babies come from the same fertilized egg. These are the twins that look alike physically, the ones we commonly call identical twins. The important point for researchers is that MZ twins have identical genes. The other type, **dizygotic** (DZ) twins, come from different eggs. These two babies, com-monly called fraternal twins, are no more alike genetically than any two siblings.

The logic behind the twin-study method is illustrated in Figure 10.1. We assume that two same-sex DZ twins and two MZ twins (who are always the same sex) share very similar environments. That is, twin pairs, regardless of what type, are the same age and the same sex and live in the same house under the same rules. Therefore, the extent to which the environment is responsible for their personalities is going to be about the same for both types of twin pairs. However, if there is also a genetic influence on personality, we would expect the MZ twins to be more like each other than are the DZ twins. This is because the MZ twins also have identical genes, but the DZ twins do not.

Researchers using the twin-study method give personality trait measures to both members of both kinds of twins. They then look at how similar the twin brothers and sisters are on the traits. If the trait scores for the MZ twin pairs are more highly correlated than the scores for the DZ twin pairs, then we have evidence for genetic influence on personality. Because the environmental influ-

Table 10.1

Correlations from Twin Study

	MZ Twins	DZ Twins
Altruism	.53	.25
Empathy	.54	.20
Nurturance	.49	.14
Aggressiveness	.40	.04
Assertiveness	.52	.20

Source: Taken from Rushton, Fulker, Neale, Nias, & Eysenck, (1986), with permission.

ence is roughly the same for both kinds of twins, it is assumed that the MZ twins are more alike one another because they also have identical genes.

Twin-study research has generated correlation tables similar to the one found in Table 10.1. In this example, adult MZ and DZ twin pairs were compared on five personality traits (Rushton, Fulker, Neale, Nias, & Eysenck, 1986). As seen in the table, the MZ twin pairs were more similar than the DZ twin pairs in each case. When all of the studies of this type are examined together, MZ twins' scores tend to correlate on average about .50 whereas DZ twin correlations are in the .25 to .30 range (Loehlin & Nichols, 1976; Nichols, 1978). Behavior genetics researchers plug these numbers into formulas to determine that about 40% of the stability in our adult personalities can be attributed to what we inherit from our parents (Plomin, Chipuer, & Loehlin, 1990).

Other methods for teasing apart genetic and environmental influences also find evidence for genetic influence, but usually not as strong as the twin-study data. One example comes from research with another naturally occurring phenomenon: adoptions. Children raised from birth by someone other than their biological parents create situations in which genetic and environmental influences are not confounded. For example, think of a family in which parents raise one child they adopted and one they gave birth to. Which child should have a personality similar to the parents'? If genes are playing a role, we would expect the biological offspring to be more like the parents, because that child shares not only the environment but also some genes with the parents. In fact, this is what researchers have found (Scarr, Webber, Weinberg, & Wittig, 1981). However, calculations with the data from these studies suggest the genetic influence may be less than that suggested by the twin-study data. In fact, data from adoption studies suggest that the heritability of personality is about half what the twin-study data suggest (Plomin, Chipuer, & Loehlin, 1990).

Table 10.2

Correlations for Twins Raised Apart and Twins Raised Together

	Identical Twins Raised Apart	Identical Twins Raised Together
Extraversion	.61	.51
Neuroticism	.53	.50
Intelligence	.72	.86
Differential Personality Questionnaire	.65	.53

Source: Taken from Rowe (1987), with permission.

But the adoption situation provides even more opportunities to test the genetic-environmental influence question. For example, what would you expect to find if you compared the personalities of the adopted children with those of their real mothers? The children have shared no environment with the mothers but still are linked by genes. When the personality scores of adopted children are compared with those of their adoptive parents and their biological mothers, the children look more like the biological mothers, whom they have never known (Loehlin, Willerman, & Horn, 1982, 1987). Again, although the strength of the relationship is weaker than that suggested by the twin-study data, we have evidence from yet another source that genetics plays at least some role in the formation of adult personalities.

Finally, it is possible to combine the twin-study and adoption situations. Although rare, some researchers have taken advantage of situations in which MZ twins are separated from their parents at birth and in addition are raised in two different households. The twins in these pairs share genes, but not environments. These twins are then compared with MZ twins raised in the same household, who share both genes and environments. Rowe (1987) has summarized the findings of studies using this method. As shown in Table 10.2, the MZ twins tend to be quite similar to one another, regardless of being raised with or separated from their twin brother or sister. The obvious explanation for this similarity is that the twins share genes that shaped their personalities in a similar manner regardless of the environments they grew up in.

One team of researchers took this methodology one step further (Tellegen et al., 1988). They compared MZ twins reared together and reared apart with DZ twins reared together and reared apart. When the numbers from these studies are entered into formulas, researchers estimate that about 50% of differences in personality can be attributed to differences in genetic makeup.

In summary, researchers have used a variety of clever and sometimes time-consuming procedures to separate the influence of genetics on personality from the influence of the environment. Although the exact extent of the genetic influence is still uncertain, the consistency of the findings from so many different sources suggests that adult personalities are at least partly determined by heredity. However, the book is far from closed on this issue. As seen in the next section, there are reasons to challenge some of the conclusions behavior geneticists draw from their data.

Problems with Genetics Research

The strongest and most consistent evidence in favor of genetic influence on personality comes from twin-study research. However, researchers using this method make two key assumptions. The first is that twin pairs can be accurately identified as MZ or DZ twins. Many "identical" twins may in fact be DZ twins who look very much alike. Fortunately, biological advances have made this less of a problem than it once was. Today zygosity can be determined in almost all cases through blood tests.

The second assumption presents a bigger problem. Researchers assume that MZ and DZ twins have equally similar environments. However, there is evidence that MZ twins share more of their environment than DZ twins (Lytton, 1977; Scarr & Carter-Saltzman, 1979). Identical twins may be treated more alike than DZ twins. They often are thought of as one unit—dressed alike, given identical presents, and so on. DZ twins grow up in similar environments, but they usually are allowed to dress differently, join different clubs, and have different friends. It may even be the case that DZ twins experience environments that are even *less* similar than typical for siblings (Hoffman, 1985). This is because parents may look for and emphasize their differences (for example, "Don is the studious one, John is the troublemaker").

If this is the case, then we would have to modify Figure 10.1. The environmental influence on personality traits may not be *as* similar for DZ twins as it is for MZ twins, which creates a problem when interpreting the twin-study findings. We can't be certain if the higher correlations between MZ twins are caused by greater genetic similarities or greater environmental similarities. This interpretation problem may explain why data from twin-study research suggest a larger role for genetic influences than is found with other procedures (Plomin, Chipuer, & Loehlin, 1990).

But some of these other procedures also rest on questionable assumptions (Hoffman, 1985). Adoptions are not random events. Families who adopt children are different from those who do not. Further, there are likely to be many unique features with a situation in which twins are separated from their parents and raised apart. Perhaps more misleading is the assumption that parents treat an adopted child the same way they do their biological offspring. It is likely parents have different expectancies for adopted children: Because they don't know the parents, they may have few preconceived ideas about how the child's personality will unfold.

There are some additional problems with genetics research. Genetics may influence only certain personality traits and then only during certain stages of life. One study found that many differences in MZ twin and DZ twin correlations didn't show up until the twins reached adulthood (Dworkin, Burke, Maher, & Gottesman, 1976). Another study found the extent to which a trait is genetically determined may be different for males and females (Rose, 1988). Further, if genetics plays such an important role, we would expect the correlations between family members' personality scores to change as biological relationships become more distant. For example, we would expect two sisters to be more alike than two cousins. However, at least one team of researchers failed to uncover any such relationship (Price, Vandenberg, Iyer, & Williams, 1982).

So where does this leave us? Exactly how or how much our genes determine our adult personalities remains an open question. One recent review concluded that genetics probably accounts for about 20% of the variance of adult personality, but this figure is subject to change as more research data are collected (Plomin, Chipuer, & Loehlin, 1990). At any rate, it seems foolish at this point to ignore the relatively strong case that genetics has *some* influence on personality. It probably also is foolish to think that the nature-nurture debate is going to go away any time soon.

Extraversion-Introversion

Few personality variables have received as much attention from researchers and theorists for as long as extraversion and introversion. Clearly, this aspect of Hans Eysenck's personality theory has drawn more attention than any other. As described in Chapter 9, extraverts are less sensitive to stimulation than introverts are. This is why extraverts can drink more coffee than introverts without being overtaken by the effects of caffeine. It also explains why it is not uncommon to find extraverts at loud social gatherings or in the middle of a crowd, while introverts seek out solitary activities and gravitate to a quiet corner at a party.

Space allows us to examine only three of the many topics investigated by researchers in this area. First, we'll tie individual differences in extraversion-introversion to the research covered in the previous section by looking at the evidence for the heritability of this personality variable. Next, we'll look at research examining one of the basic differences between introverts and extraverts postulated by Eysenck: preference for arousal. Finally, we'll address this question: Who is happier, introverts or extraverts?

The Heritability of Extraversion

If you are an introvert, it's likely you've been given some of the following pieces of advice: "You need to get out more often," "Why can't you be more sociable?" or "Loosen up and enjoy yourself a little." Extraverts probably have heard some of these: "There's more to life than having fun all the time," "Can't you think a little before you do something?" or "Slow down and enjoy life." In short, whether you are introverted or extraverted, someone probably has asked you to try to become more of the other. Even the most extreme extravert probably can sit still for a few minutes, and the most introverted person you know occasionally cuts loose and has a good time with friends. But is it possible for an extravert to become permanently more introverted? Can you raise your child to be less introverted or less extraverted?

The answer to these questions depends on what causes a person to become an extravert or an introvert. Eysenck has championed the role of genetics in answering this question. People are said to be born with a general level of cortical activity or, according to more recent descriptions, a sensitivity to stimulation. This inherited difference in physiology remains fairly constant throughout one's life and eventually develops into the adult behavior styles of extraversion or introversion. Of course, each person who inherits a predisposition toward introversion will develop a slightly different style of dealing with his or her heightened sensitivity to stimulation. But most people eventually take on many of the characteristics described by Eysenck. Because of their inherited physiological differences, it is unlikely an introvert will come to enjoy social interactions to the same degree as someone born with a relatively low sensitivity to arousal or that an extravert will ever find a life of quiet and solitude very appealing.

Eysenck (1990) points to data from many different sources when making the case that individual differences in extraversion-introversion are based in biology (Chapter 9). Some of the strongest evidence for this position comes from research on the genetic heritability of extraversion-introversion. Although little evidence for heritability was available when Eysenck first introduced his theory of personality, today an impressive body of work appears to support Eysenck on this point.

As described earlier, researchers often used the twin-study method to determine the heritability of personality variables. Consequently, much of the evidence for the heritability of extraversion-introversion comes from research comparing correlations between pairs of monozygotic (MZ) twins with correlations between pairs of dizygotic (DZ) twins. Studies using this procedure have found consistent evidence for a genetic component of extraversion-introversion (Baker & Daniels, 1990; Eaves & Eysenck, 1975; Floderus-Myrhed, Pedersen, & Rasmuson, 1980; Neale, Rushton, & Fulker, 1986; Rose, Koskenvuo, Kaprio, Sarna, & Langinvainio, 1988; Scarr, 1969). In fact, the findings suggest such a strong genetic component for extraversion-introversion that some researchers are convinced the heritability estimates for this personality variable are somehow exaggerated (Plomin, Chipuer, & Loehlin, 1990).

Nonetheless, two of these studies deserve special attention. Floderus-Myrhed et al. (1980) gave a version of Eysenck's Personality Inventory to 12,898 adult twin pairs in Sweden. This number represents virtually all of the contactable twins born in Sweden between the years 1926 and 1958. Similarly, Rose and colleagues (1988) tested 7,144 adult twin pairs in Finland, representing nearly every living twin in that country born before 1958. Several features of these samples make them particularly important. Not only are the samples large, but they represent nearly every twin in these two countries. This means we don't have to worry about only a certain kind of person volunteering to participate in the study. In addition, for some unknown reason, the number of DZ twins born in

Table 10.3

Within-Pair Extraversion Correlations for MZ and DZ Twins

	Males		Females	
	MZ Twins	DZ Twins	MZ Twins	DZ Twins
Swedish sample	.47	.20	.54	.21
Finnish sample	.46	.15	.48	.14

Source: Taken from Floderus-Myrhed, Pederson, & Rasmuson, (1980) and Rose, Koskenvuo, Kaprio, Sarna, & Langinvainio, (1988).

these countries during the years studied was significantly higher than elsewhere in the world. Thus, DZ twin pairs are more proportionally represented in these samples than in other research.

When the within-pair correlations for DZ and MZ twins are compared, considerable evidence for a genetic component for extraversion-introversion is found. As shown in Table 10.3, the monozygotic twins were more like one another than were the dizygotic twins, arguing in favor of a genetic influence. Beyond this, the researchers in the Finnish study examined the amount of social contact between the members of the twin pairs as well as the amount of social contact they engaged in generally to see if these environmental influences might not account for the findings. Although the researchers did find that MZ twins were more likely to stay in communication with one another, this factor alone was not sufficient to explain the differences in MZ and DZ correlations on the extraversion-introversion measure.

Another study takes the twin-study method one step further (Pedersen, Plomin, McClearn, & Friberg, 1988). As in the earlier studies, the investigators compared MZ and DZ twins who grew up together. However, these researchers also located 95 pairs of MZ twins and 220 pairs of DZ twins reared apart. Again, a positive correlation between the extraversion-introversion scores of identical twins who were separated at birth and reared in different environments would provide strong evidence for a genetic component for this personality variable. As shown in Table 10.4, there was a relatively strong correlation between the scores of MZ twins reared in separate environments, albeit not as strong as MZ twins reared together.

We can conclude from this research that how introverted or extraverted you are may have been largely determined by the set of genes you inherited. This is not to say that you can't be more outgoing at times if you are highly introverted or learn to stop and introspect for a few minutes if you're an extravert. But how often you act in either of these styles probably was determined largely by the genetic

Table 10.4

Within-Pair Correlations of Extraversion Scores for Twins Reared Apart and Together

Twins Reared Apart		Twins Reared Together	
MZ Twins	DZ Twins	MZ Twins	DZ Twins
.30	.04	.54	.06

Source: Taken from Pedersen et al. (1988).

hand you were dealt many years ago. The studies also support the speculations Eysenck made many years ago about the nature and causes of individual differences.

Extraversion and Preferred Arousal Level

Imagine it's a few days before a big test in one of your classes. You've put off preparing for the exam long enough, so tonight you'll go to the library and spend a few hours behind the books. There are two study areas in this library. One contains a series of one-person desks where you can isolate yourself behind the quiet of the bookstacks. Few people walk by these desks, and the room is relatively free of whispers, photocopy machines, and other library noises. The other study area consists of long tables, sofas, and easy chairs. You can easily scan the room to see who else is there. Many people pass by on their way to other parts of the library, and short conversations with those passing through are common. Which of these study areas will you choose?

Your choice in this situation depends in part on whether you are an extravert or an introvert. One team of researchers demonstrated this phenomenon when they asked students studying in the two kinds of library rooms just described to complete the Eysenck Personality Inventory (Campbell, 1983; Campbell & Hawley, 1982). Students in the noisy, open room were more likely to be extraverts, whereas the ones in the isolated, quiet room were more likely to be introverts. Those in the noisy room said they preferred the amount of noise and the opportunities for socializing. The others said they chose the quiet room to get away from these distractions.

These findings are entirely consistent with Eysenck's and other theorists' descriptions of extraversion-introversion. Introverted students already are operating at a near optimal arousal level. They also are more sensitive to stimulation. Thus, an introvert in a noisy room is probably going to be so disturbed by all the

Is this student an introvert or an extravert? According to research, his choice of study areas provides a clue. Extraverts prefer this type of open study area where opportunities for interruptions and occasional social stimulation are possible.

activity that he or she will have a difficult time studying. On the other hand, the understimulated extravert probably finds the quiet room boring. Unless the study material is particularly exciting, the extravert probably will take a number of breaks, look around for distractors, and generally have a difficult time keeping his or her mind on the task.

This difference in preferred stimulation level also is found in more controlled laboratory experiments (cf. Geen, 1983b). For example, extraverts more quickly press a button to change slides on a visual learning task, presumably because they more quickly become bored with the pictures and designs (Brebner & Cooper, 1978). In another study, extraverts and introverts worked on a word-memory task while listening to noise through earphones (Geen, 1984). When given the opportunity, introverted subjects set their earphones at considerably lower levels than did extraverts. However, some introverts were forced to listen to loud noise, while some extraverts listened to soft noise. Consistent with Eysenck's model, the introverts did worse when exposed to higher levels of stimulation, whereas the extraverts performed worse when listening to the softer noise.

This last finding helps to explain why some students can only study with the stereo and a TV blaring, whereas other students have to find a quiet library room and then stuff their ears with those yellow foam things to block out any remaining noise. Too much stimulation makes it difficult to concentrate, and even extraverts can reach a point when they have to turn their radios down. But for introverts this point comes much earlier. Of course, the other side of the coin is that too little stimulation also interferes with performance. While it may take many hours of solitude to bring an introvert to this point, a few minutes in quiet isolation might be tough on a high extravert.

Extraversion and Happiness

Clearly, extraverts and introverts lead different lives. We are more apt to find extraverts at parties, visiting friends, going places, and doing things. Introverts are more likely to spend time alone doing quiet, low-stimulation tasks. Who do you suppose is happier? Not surprisingly, I usually find introverts guess introverts, whereas extraverts can't imagine how anyone could lead a life as boring as the introverted style.

Although introverts may have difficulty understanding this at first, researchers find that on average extraverts report higher levels of *subjective well-being* than introverts (Costa & McCrae, 1980; Headey & Wearing, 1989; Larsen & Kasimatis, 1990; Mayo, 1983). In one investigation, extraverts and introverts were asked to provide a daily mood report for 84 consecutive days (Larsen & Kasimatis, 1990). As shown in Figure 10.2, the researchers found an interesting pattern when they compared moods on days of the week. Perhaps not surprisingly, Monday was the students' least favorite day, with the week becoming progressively better as Saturday approached. But the figure also illustrates that no matter what the day of the week, extraverts reported higher levels of positive mood than introverts. As with other personality variables, this pattern seems to be fairly stable over time. One team of researchers found that extraversion test scores could significantly predict levels of positive affect measured two years later (Headey & Wearing, 1989).

If extraverts experience more happiness generally than introverts, why might this be the case? Researchers have uncovered at least two reasons. First, extraverts tend to socialize more than introverts. Extraverts tend to be more active and more vigorous in their social lives. They have more friends and they interact with those friends more often.

There are several reasons why this increase in social activity leads to positive affect. Researchers have found repeatedly that social contact is closely tied to feelings of well-being (Diener, 1984). Interacting with friends is usually a pleasant experience, as are other extraverted behaviors, such as going to dances, parties, and football games. Many basic needs, such as feeling competent and worthwhile, also are satisfied in social settings. In addition, friends often serve as a buffer against stress (Cohen & Wills, 1985). Handling problems alone may be more difficult than getting a friend's support when in need. In short, in most cases interacting with others is a positive experience.

The second explanation for extraverts' higher levels of positive affect is that extraverts may be more sensitive than introverts to information about rewards (Gray, 1981; Strelau, 1987). If this is the case, then an extravert told that he or she

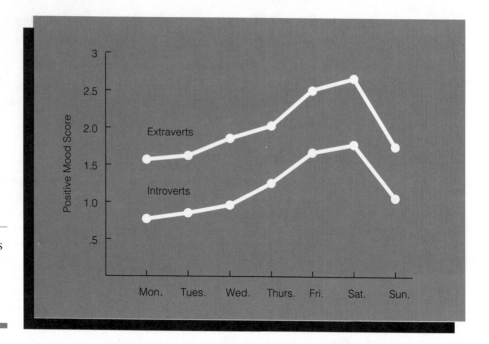

Figure 10.2

Happiness Ratings
of Extraverts and
Introverts

Adapted from Larsen and
Kasimatis (1990).

did well on a test will be happier with this news than an introvert receiving the same grade. In a laboratory test of this hypothesis, extraverts and introverts were given a test of "Syncretic Skill," supposedly a newly discovered type of intelligence (Larsen & Ketelaar, 1989). Although the test was bogus, subjects received information indicating either that they had done well on the test or that they had done poorly. Mood measures indicated that extraverts were much happier than introverts after receiving the positive feedback. Interestingly, extraverts and introverts did not differ in mood when they received negative feedback. Subjects in another study were asked simply to imagine themselves in a series of positive (winning a lottery) and negative (expelled from school) situations (Larsen & Ketelaar, 1991). Again, extraverts were put in a much better mood than introverts when they imagined the happy event, but did not differ from introverts when thinking about the unhappy event.

Does this mean extraverts are always happier than introverts? Not necessarily. We can understand why this is the case by looking more closely at what researchers mean by subjective well-being, or happiness. Many researchers today find it convenient to divide subjective well-being into *positive* and *negative* affect. That is, there is more to being happy than having no problems. We have to engage in positive experiences, do the things that give us pleasure. On the other hand, being happy also means avoiding negative experiences. It's good to like your job, but having an irritating boss can take away from the enjoyment of going to work. In short, overall happiness is obtained by increasing positive affect and decreasing negative affect.

If we apply this concept to what we know of extraversion, we can see why extraverts are not always happier than introverts. This is because extraverts are not only more sociable than introverts, they also tend to be more impulsive. Extraverts are more likely to act on the spur of the moment, to respond to what they are feeling without pausing to think. And this impulsivity can create problems. Saying the first thing that comes to mind is often not a good idea. Doing what feels good at the moment without considering the eventual consequences also is fraught with danger. Anyone who has enjoyed a trip to the beach or an evening with friends instead of writing a term paper can appreciate the problem of acting impulsively.

The result of this impulsivity is that extraverts also experience more mood swings than introverts do (Larsen & Kasimatis, 1990). While their high level of sociability might contribute to positive affect, extraverts' high level of impulsivity might bring them a pack of problems, thus contributing to greater negative affect. This conclusion was supported in a study in which students high and low in sociability and impulsivity filled out daily positive and negative well-being measures for six to eight weeks (Emmons & Diener, 1986). As expected, whereas high sociability led to more positive affect, high impulsivity led to more negative affect.

In summary, extraversion appears to be a two-edged sword. Extraverts are more likely than introverts to have friends and have fun. But they also are more likely to act before thinking and get themselves into trouble. Introverts may not always reap the benefits of social interactions, but they also avoid the price of social blunders.

Evolutionary Theory and Mate Selection

Imagine that, like thousands of people today, you decide to look for a romantic partner through the personal want ads. You call the "lonely hearts" number to place your ad and find that you are faced with two tasks. First, you must describe yourself in a way that will make you attractive to others. Second, you must identify the kind of person you are looking for. What do you say?

Researchers examining these kinds of ads have uncovered valuable information about gender roles and the nature of romantic relationships. This research finds that how people describe themselves and the kind of person they are looking for depends largely on whether they are male or female. For example, one study revealed that women were more likely than men to identify themselves as physically attractive and to say they were looking for someone who was older and could provide financial security (Harrison & Saeed, 1977). Fortunately, these requests fit rather well with what the men said about themselves. The men in the study tended to say they were looking for someone who was younger and physically attractive. The men also were more likely than the women to describe themselves as someone who could provide financial security.

Besides the practical uses for someone looking for a romantic partner, do the results of studies like this one tell us something about the nature of personality?

According to advocates of evolutionary personality theory, the answer is yes. These psychologists think of romantic relationships in terms of male and female members of a species getting together to (eventually) reproduce. Consequently, choosing a romantic partner is based in part on concerns for *parental investment* (Traivers, 1972). That is, as members of a species, we are concerned about reproducing and passing our genes along to the next generation. Because of this concern, we select mates who are likely to be a part of successful reproduction and raising of the children.

However, evolutionary personality psychologists also argue that males and females have different ideas about parental investment. Because they bear and in most cases raise the offspring, females are more selective about whom they choose to mate and reproduce with. In contrast, in many species males are free to attempt to reproduce with as many females as they can. Frequent mating with many different females increases the probability of passing along one's genes to the next generation. In evolutionary terms, the investment in selecting a mate is larger for the female than for the male. She has more to lose by making a poor choice than he does. Because they have different ideas about parental investment, evolutionary personality theory predicts that males and females look for very different characteristics in their mates.

What do men look for in a woman? What do women want in a man? Complete answers to these commonly asked questions have eluded the most insightful of us. Although they cannot explain everything, evolutionary personality psychologists argue that men and women select their mates based in part on what serves the needs of the species. As described next, research tends to support many of their speculations.

What Men Look for in Women

From an evolutionary perspective, men can best serve the needs of the species by reproducing as frequently as possible (Buss, 1991). Consequently, males should be attracted to females with "high reproductive value." In other words, a man should select a woman who is likely to give him many children. But what outward signs do we have of a woman's likely fertility? One indicator is the woman's age. A young wife has the potential to produce more offspring than does an older wife. Thus, some evolutionary personality psychologists predict that men will prefer younger women to older women (Buss, 1991). Moreover, physical features associated with young adult females, such as "smooth skin, good muscle tone, lustrous hair, and full lips," provide "cues to female reproductive capacity" (Buss, 1991, p. 2). Not coincidently, these physical attributes are the ones our society associates with beauty.

Consequently, evolutionary personality psychologists predict that men will prefer mates who are physically attractive and probably younger than they are. But can the same reasoning be applied to women? Probably not. If anything, as described later, a young male probably is less likely than an older man to provide her and the offspring with the kinds of material resources she seeks from a partner. Thus, according to the theory, men are more likely than women to use physical attractiveness to select their marriage partner. In addition, we would expect most couples to consist of an older husband and a younger wife.

Research tends to support these speculations. Married couples were asked how much importance they placed on various characteristics when choosing their spouse (Buss & Barnes, 1986). As expected, husbands were more likely than their wives to rate *physically attractive* and *good looking* as features they looked for in a marriage partner. This finding is consistent with what is now a large amount of research on the importance men and women place on physical attractiveness when selecting a dating partner. Psychologists investigating this question have examined "lonely hearts" advertisements, experimental subjects' reactions to randomly assigned attractive and unattractive lab partners, and correlations between how attractive a person is and measures of his or her popularity with members of the opposite sex. A recent review of research using these and other methodologies found strong support for the gender difference predicted from evolutionary personality theory (Feingold, 1990). That is, regardless of which experimental procedure is used, researchers find that men are more likely to consider a woman's physical attractiveness when selecting a dating partner than vice versa.

Some psychologists take this observation one step further and argue that women compete for a man's attention by emphasizing their physical attractiveness (Buss, 1988). In evolutionary personality theory this is known as *intrasexual selection* — the competition among members of the same gender for mating access to the best members of the opposite gender. If men select partners who are youthful and beautiful, then a woman can improve her chances of pairing up with the most desirable partner by emphasizing these attributes. To test this possibility, newlyweds in one study were asked to describe what they did to attract their spouse when they first began dating (Buss, 1988). As predicted, the women were more likely than the men to report that they altered their appearance (such as with makeup and jewelry), wore stylish clothes, wore sexy clothes, and kept themselves clean and groomed.

In short, there is abundant evidence that men are more likely than women to look at physical attractiveness when selecting a dating or marriage partner. However, there is one important limitation of the studies reviewed so far. That is, they tell us a lot about the preferences of *American* men and women (and primarily university students), but not about men and women in other cultures. To make a strong case for the evolutionary personality position, we need to demonstrate that this effect is not limited to certain social or cultural groups. For example, if men were found to rely on physical attractiveness more than women only in Western cultures, then a strong argument could be made that this difference reflects social learning patterns rather than an inherited human characteristic.

To solve this problem, one team of researchers conducted an elaborate cross-cultural investigation (Buss, 1989). The researchers looked at gender differences in mate selection in 37 cultural groups. These groups were located in 33 different countries, on six continents and five islands, and included people from cultural backgrounds very different from Americans, such as South African Zulus, Gujarati

Table 10.5

Mean Age Differences in Years between Preferred Age of First Marriage for Spouse and for Self in 37 Cultures

Sample	Males	Females
Africa		
Nigeria	−6.45	4.90
South Africa (Whites)	−2.30	3.50
South Africa (Zulus)	−3.33	3.76
Zambia	−7.38	4.14
Asia		
China	−2.05	3.45
India	−3.06	3.29
Indonesia	−2.72	4.69
Iran	−4.02	5.10
Israel (Jewish)	−2.88	3.95
Israel (Palestinian)	−3.75	3.71
Japan	−2.37	3.05
Taiwan	−3.13	3.78
Eastern Europe		
Bulgaria	−3.13	4.18
Estonia	−2.19	2.85
Poland	−2.85	3.38
Yugoslavia	−2.47	3.61
Western Europe		
Belgium	−2.53	2.46
Finland	−0.38	2.83
France	−1.94	4.00
		Continued

Source: Taken from Buss (1989) with permission.
Note: Negative values indicate a preference for a younger mate; positive values indicate a preference for an older mate.

Indians, and Santa Catarina Brazilians. Subjects in each of these samples were asked about what they considered the ideal age for themselves and their partner when marrying. Subjects also were asked how important each of 18 personality traits were for choosing a potential mate (for example, *intelligence, good financial prospect,* and *good looks*).

The findings provide strong support for evolutionary personality theory. As shown in Table 10.5, in each of the 37 samples males preferred mates who were younger than they were. This is consistent with the notion that a younger female partner represents a greater reproductive capacity. The researchers uncovered

Table 10.5

Mean Age Differences in Years between Preferred Age of First Marriage for Spouse and for Self in 37 Cultures, *continued*

Sample	Males	Females
Western Europe, continued		
Germany	−2.52	3.70
Great Britain	−1.92	2.26
Greece	−3.36	4.54
Ireland	−2.07	2.78
Italy	−2.76	3.24
Netherlands	−1.01	2.72
Norway	−1.91	3.12
Spain	−1.46	2.60
Sweden	−2.34	2.91
North America		
Canada (English)	−1.53	2.72
Canada (French)	−1.22	1.82
USA (Mainland)	−1.65	2.54
USA (Hawaiian)	−1.92	3.30
Oceania		
Australia	−1.77	2.86
New Zealand	−1.59	2.91
South America		
Brazil	−2.94	3.94
Colombia	−4.45	4.51
Venezuela	−2.99	3.62
Mean	−2.66	3.42

additional evidence for this preference when they looked at the *actual* age at which people first married. Information about the age of marrying couples was available in 27 of the 33 countries. These data confirmed that men in all of these cultures not only said they preferred younger partners but also, on average, actually married women younger than themselves. Although the investigators made no predictions about the females' preferences, the women in all 37 cultures said they preferred an older partner.

More evidence for the evolutionary personality position was found when the researchers looked at the importance men and women placed on physical attractiveness when selecting a mate. Males said that *good looks* were more important than did females in each of the 37 cultures. This difference was statistically significant in all but three of the samples. Thus, the tendency for men to prefer youthful and physically attractive women when looking for marriage partners appears to be fairly universal despite differences in cultures and social norms. Evolutionary personality psychologists interpret such findings as evidence for universal characteristics handed down from our ancestors.

What Women Look for in Men

According to evolutionary personality theory, men prefer a female partner who provides maximal opportunity for successful reproduction. But women have a different role to play in reproduction and child rearing. Consequently, they look for different features in their partners. According to the parental investment analysis, women prefer to mate with men who can provide for their offspring (Traivers, 1972). In nonhuman species, this may simply mean a mate who can provide food and protection. In humans, this means providing the financial resources required for raising the children. Some men are better able to do this than others. Men also differ in their ability to take care of and nurture their sons and daughters as well as their ability to transfer status or power to their children. Evolutionary personality psychologists argue that women prefer to mate with men who possess these abilities.

Again, some research supports this speculation. When investigators asked married couples to describe what they found attractive in their spouse, women were more likely than men to identify such characteristics as *dependable, good earning capacity, ambitious,* and *career-oriented* (Buss & Barnes, 1986). In another study, women going through a divorce were more likely than their former spouses to say they left the marriage because they were seeking a better financial situation (Sheets & Braver, 1991). The women in this study also indicated that they were concerned about finding a better situation in which to raise their children. Finally, undergraduate women said they found the dominant man in an interaction they observed more sexually attractive and a more desirable date than the meek man (Sadalla, Kendrick, & Vershure, 1987). According to evolutionary personality theorists, a dominant man is better able to provide needed resources for his family than is a man at the bottom of the pecking order. A dominant man is more likely to rise to the top of an organization and thereby acquire financial security and other benefits.

Other research suggests that men are aware of these preferences and, like women, compete among themselves for the most desirable partner. Newlywed husbands in one study were more likely than their spouses to say that they bragged about their financial resources as a way of catching the future wives' attention (Buss, 1988). In other words, to impress their potential mates, the men let it be known that they made a lot of money or went out of their way to show off a new car or condominium.

In sum, research finds patterns of attraction that support evolutionary theory's predictions about what women find attractive in men. But once again, we need to ask if the findings are limited to American samples. Data from the 37-sample cross-cultural study described earlier indicate that women around the world report similar preferences (Buss, 1989). As shown in Table 10-6, women in each sample were more likely than men to want their spouse to be a *good financial prospect*. Only in Spain did this difference fail to reach statistical significance. Similar patterns were found when the men and women rated the importance of such characteristics as *ambition* and *industriousness* in a partner. In short, there appears to be a nearly universal tendency for women to look for men who can provide them with good financial resources. These findings are entirely in line with what we would expect from the evolutionary personality position.

Conclusions and Limitations

Research findings on what men and women look for in members of the opposite sex tend to be consistent with the predictions from evolutionary personality psychology. Men around the world seem to prefer younger and more physically attractive women, whereas women look for a man who can provide the material resources they need to raise their children. However, as intuitive and consistent as these findings may be, there are many reasons to take them with at least a grain of salt.

First, as described in the previous chapter, researchers testing these hypotheses are necessarily limited in their ability to make strong tests of causal relationships. That is, because they cannot manipulate such variables as gender and physical attractiveness these investigators are unable to rule out many alternative explanations for their research findings. For example, differences in the ages men and women marry simply may have to do with differences in maturity level, with women becoming physically and perhaps emotionally mature more quickly than men. Moreover, investigations have not always produced findings entirely consistent with evolutionary personality theory's predictions. For example, some evolutionary theorists argue that men should place a greater value on their spouse's chastity when choosing a marriage partner than women should. Although researchers find this to be the case in many societies, this gender difference is not found in all cultures (Buss, 1989).

In addition, many characteristics that men and women look for in a potential partner may overshadow instincts inherited from our ancestors. The basic needs of animals in the wild may be quite different from the needs of men and women in modern society. For example, many women probably prefer a partner who spends time with them rather than one devoted to rising to the top of the corporate ladder. This is not to say that tendencies passed down from our ancestors do not influence our choices. The research suggests that they do. But our preferences for a physically attractive woman or a dominant man might play a relatively small role in this process. In addition, common sense tells us there are many exceptions to the rule. Many women no doubt prefer a man who is more sensitive than dominant. Many men prefer an older woman to a less mature partner.

Finally, evolutionary personality psychology is limited to heterosexual mating choices. The prediction of partner choice based on parental investment says

Table 10.6

Importance of "Good Financial Prospect" When Selecting a Mate

Sample	Males	Females
Africa		
Nigeria	1.37	2.30
South Africa (Whites)	0.94	1.73
South Africa (Zulus)	0.70	1.14
Zambia	1.46	2.33
Asia		
China	1.10	1.56
India	1.60	2.00
Indonesia	1.42	2.55
Iran	1.25	2.04
Israel (Jewish)	1.31	1.82
Israel (Palestinian)	1.28	1.67
Japan	0.92	2.29
Taiwan	1.25	2.21
Eastern Europe		
Bulgaria	1.16	1.64
Estonia	1.31	1.51
Poland	1.09	1.74
Yugoslavia	1.27	1.66
Western Europe		
Belgium	0.95	1.36
Finland	0.65	1.18

Continued

Source: Taken from Buss (1989) with permission.
Note: Subjects rated on a scale from 0 (Unimportant) to 3 (Indispensable).

little or nothing about choices for homosexuals. The analysis also may not apply to women who are past their reproductive years and older men who are interested in an intimate relationship, but not in raising a family.

Summary

1. Research examining the influence of genetics and the environment in forming adult personalities suggests that both sources play a role. Psychologists have used a variety of methods to pin down these roles, most notably the twin-study

Table 10.6

Importance of "Good Financial Prospect" When Selecting a Mate, *continued*

Sample	Males	Females
Western Europe, continued		
France	1.22	1.68
Germany	1.14	1.81
Great Britain	0.67	1.16
Greece	1.16	1.92
Ireland	0.82	1.67
Italy	0.87	1.33
Netherlands	0.69	0.94
Norway	1.10	1.42
Spain	1.25	1.39
Sweden	1.18	1.75
North America		
Canada (English)	1.02	1.91
Canada (French)	1.47	1.94
USA (Mainland)	1.08	1.96
USA (Hawaiian)	1.50	2.10
Oceania		
Australia	0.69	1.54
New Zealand	1.35	1.63
South America		
Brazil	1.24	1.91
Colombia	1.72	2.21
Venezuela	1.66	2.26

method. However, problems surface in interpreting these studies, particularly with some of the underlying assumptions of the methods. Nonetheless, the cumulation of evidence argues strongly for a significant heritability component in adult personality.

2. Extraversion-introversion is probably the most widely researched aspect of Eysenck's personality theory. Evidence indicates that this personality variable has a large heritability component. Consistent with Eysenck's theory, researchers find extraverts tend to seek out stimulating environments and perform better in these environments than introverts. Research also finds that extraverts generally are happier than introverts. However, extraverts also are more likely to experience negative affect than introverts.

3. Evolutionary personality theory predicts that men and women look for different features when selecting a potential mate. Consistent with this hypothesis, research shows that men are more likely to consider physical attractiveness when selecting a dating partner or spouse. In addition, men are more likely to prefer a younger partner. Research also indicates that women prefer a man who possesses the resources necessary for raising a family. Cross-cultural research indicates that these preferences may be universal.

Key Terms

twin-study method A procedure for examining the role of genetics on personality, in which pairs of monozygotic and dizygotic twins are compared.

monozygotic twins Twins conceived from the same fertilized egg, commonly referred to as identical twins.

dizygotic twins Twins conceived from two different fertilized eggs, commonly referred to as fraternal twins.

Suggested Readings

Buss, D. M. (Ed.) (1990). Special issue: Biological foundations of personality: Evolution, behavioral genetics, and psychophysiology. *Journal of Personality*, 58(1). The articles in this special issue address many of the topics examined here. The volume includes articles on genetics and personality, extraversion-introversion, and evolutionary personality psychology.

Plomin, R., Chipuer, H. M., & Loehlin, J. C. (1990). Behavioral genetics and personality. In L. A. Pervin (Ed.), *Handbook of personality: Theory and research* (pp. 225-243). New York: Guilford. An excellent review of research on the heritability of personality. The authors address many of the issues surrounding this research. This review assumes a basic understanding of the procedures reviewed in this chapter but is written clearly.

The Humanistic Approach
Theory, Application, and Assessment

Not long ago I was involved in a discussion about Jim Morrison, the leader of the 1960s rock group, The Doors. For a few years Morrison was a rock legend who personified counterculture thinking. But he also abused his body with drugs and alcohol and died of an apparent heart attack at age 27. One man in this discussion blamed Morrison's self-destructive behavior and death on society. He argued that Morrison's alienation from his parents, harassment by police, and pressure from record-industry executives pushed the singer to his tragic death. A woman in the group disagreed. She argued no one forced Jim Morrison to take outrageous doses of dangerous drugs or go on daily drinking binges. For that matter no one kept him in the recording business. If it was that much hassle, he easily could have gotten out.

Which of these views do you suppose is more "humanistic"? You may be surprised to find that the woman who blamed Morrison's problems on himself is probably more aligned with humanistic psychology's view than is the man who pointed to society and the hassles Morrison faced. This is not to say humanistic psychologists are insensitive to the problems society tosses our way. But failure to take personal responsibility for how we react to those problems is completely foreign to the humanistic approach to personality and mental health.

This perspective is easier to understand if we look at the circumstances that gave birth to the humanistic view. By around the middle of the 20th century, two major views of humanity had emerged from the discipline of psychology. One was the Freudian concept. According to this approach, we are all victims of unconscious sexual and aggressive instincts that constantly influence our behavior. The other view came from the behaviorists (discussed in Chapter 13), who, in the extreme, view humans as little more than large, complex rats. Just as a rat is conditioned to respond to laboratory stimuli, humans are said to respond to stimuli in our living environments over which we have no control. We act the way we do because of the situation we are in or the situations we have been in before, not because of some personal choice or direction.

However, many psychologists had difficulty accepting either of these conceptions of human nature. In particular, important aspects of human personality such as free will and human dignity were missing from the Freudians' and behaviorists' descriptions. Behavior was said to be under the control of id impulses or learning histories, rather than personal choices. In response to these concerns, a "third force" began to develop among personality theorists. The *humanistic* approach (sometimes, perhaps incorrectly, referred to as *existential* or *phenomenological* psychology) paints a much different picture of our species.

The key distinction between the humanistic approach and other theories of personality is that people are assumed to be largely responsible for their actions. Although we sometimes respond automatically to events in the environment and may at times be motivated by unconscious impulses, we have the power to determine our own destiny and to decide our actions at almost any given moment. We have free will. Jim Morrison may have found himself under tremendous pressure and difficulties. But how he responded to that situation was his own choice. Had Morrison seen a humanistic therapist, he probably would have been encouraged to accept this responsibility and make choices about his life style consistent with his individuality and personal needs.

The "third force" in American psychology caught on rapidly with a large number of psychotherapists and personality theorists. The emphasis on individuality and personal expression of the 1960s (which gave rise to the counterculture movement personified by Jim Morrison) provided fertile soil for the growth of humanistic psychology. The election of prominent humanistic psychologist Abraham Maslow to president of the American Psychological Association in 1967 symbolized the acceptance of the humanistic approach as a legitimate alternative perspective. But before exploring in depth what this alternative view is all about, let's examine where the humanistic approach came from.

The Roots of Humanistic Psychology

Although humanistic psychology evolved from many sources, its roots lie primarily in two areas: existential philosophy, which is decidedly European in flavor, and the work of some American psychologists, most notably Carl Rogers and Abraham Maslow. Existential philosophy has developed over the past few centuries. Although difficult to describe, partially because there is no one existential philosophy or agreed-upon definition, this philosophy addresses many of the questions that later became cornerstones of the humanistic approach. Some of these include the meaning of our existence, the role of free will, and the uniqueness of the human being.

A group of psychologists, primarily European, align themselves so closely with existential philosophers that they have adopted the label "existential psychologists." They rely heavily on the works of the great existential philosophers — such as Friedrich Nietzsche, Soren Kierkegaard, and Jean-Paul Sartre — in developing their theories of personality. Among the more prominent existential psychologists are Ludwig Binswanger, Medard Boss, Viktor Frankl, R. D. Laing, and Rollo May. Existential psychotherapy often centers around resolving existential anxiety — the feelings of dread and panic that follow the realization that there is no meaning to one's life. Therapy often involves development of a mature approach to life, with an emphasis on the freedom to choose and develop a life style that reduces feelings of emptiness, anxiety, and boredom.

Personality theorists obtain their insights into the nature of human functioning from a variety of sources. Existential psychologist Viktor Frankl's personal experiences with tragedy and suffering provided the unique insights into human nature and the human condition that later became the foundation for his theory of personality and approach to psychotherapy.

Frankl was imprisoned in a Nazi concentration camp in 1939. In his book *Man's Search for Meaning*, he describes his three years at Auschwitz and Dachau—the malnourishment, the disease and suffering, the cruelty of his captors, the uncertainty of his fate and that of his family and friends, and the ever-present possibility of his own death. He later calculated his odds of surviving the ordeal at less than 1 in 28. Upon his release, Frankl discovered that he had indeed been the only member of his family to survive.

Yet out of this tragedy—indeed, *because* of this tragedy—Frankl developed *logotherapy*. Like other existential therapies, the basic goal of logotherapy is to help clients find meaning in their lives. Frankl's concentration camp experiences had made him keenly aware of the question of life's meaning. "My comrades' . . . question was, 'Will we survive the camp? For if not, all this suffering has no meaning,'" he recalled. "The question which beset me was 'Has all this suffering, this dying around us, a meaning? For, if not, then ultimately there is no meaning to survival'" (1959, p. 183).

Frankl calls this feeling that life has no meaning the "existential vacuum." The focus of logotherapy is to help people understand that *they* must take responsibility for finding the meaning in their own lives. "Man should not ask what the meaning of his life is, but rather must recognize that it is *he* who is asked," Frankl wrote. "Each man is questioned by life, and he can only answer to life by *answering for* his own life" (1959, p. 172).

At the same time existential philosophy began influencing some psychologists' views, two American psychologists were writing about their personal transitions from traditional psychology approaches to a humanistic perspective. Early failures as a psychotherapist led Carl Rogers to realize that he, the therapist, was incapable of deciding for clients what their problems were or how to solve them. "It began to occur to me," Rogers reflected many years later, "that unless I had a need to demonstrate my own cleverness and learning, I would do better to rely upon the client for the direction of movement in the [therapeutic] process" (1967, p. 359).

The turning point for Abraham Maslow came while he was watching a World War II parade — "a poor, pathetic parade . . . Boy Scouts and fat people in old uniforms and a flag and someone playing a flute off-key." The parade was supposed to promote American patriotism and the war effort. Instead, it crystallized for Maslow how little psychology had contributed to the understanding of human behavior. He became determined "to prove that human beings are capable of something grander than war and prejudice and hatred." We needed a science of psychology to "consider all the problems that nonscientists have been handling — religion, poetry, values, philosophy, art" (in Hall, 1968, pp. 54–55).

Promoting this new approach to understanding human behavior became a lifetime's work for Rogers and Maslow. Their writings found a receptive audience among psychologists also bothered by the limitations and deficiencies they saw in other approaches. We will review the theories of both of these theorists after first identifying some of the key elements of the humanistic approach.

Key Elements of the Humanistic Approach

Describing humanistic psychology presents one difficulty in that there are no agreed-upon definitions of what constitutes a humanistic personality theory. This was made obvious in the 1960s and early 1970s when it seemed nearly everyone identified himself or herself as "humanistic" in an effort to capitalize on the popularity of the approach. As a result, the humanistic approach became associated with faddish therapies that promised to solve problems and provide the key to happiness for the price of a paperback book. Efforts to exploit the humanistic association have faded in recent years as the popularity of humanistic psychology has faded, but there remain a large number of psychologists who identify themselves with this perspective. Although no clear criteria exist for identifying which approaches to psychotherapy should and should not fall into the humanistic category, I think it is safe to say that the following four elements are central to the general viewpoint to which we apply the "humanistic" label. These four are: (1) an emphasis on personal responsibility; (2) an emphasis on the "here and now"; (3) a focus on the phenomenology of the individual; and (4) an emphasis on personal growth.

Personal Responsibility

Although we may try to deny it, we are ultimately responsible for what happens to us. This idea, borrowed from existential philosophers, is a cornerstone of the humanistic approach to personality and is illustrated in the way we commonly use the phrase "I have to." We say, "I have to go to class," "I have to meet some friends," "I have to take care of my children," and so forth. But the truth is, we don't *have to* do any of this. Within limits, there is practically nothing we *have to* do. Humanistic psychologists argue that our behaviors represent personal choices of what we want to do at a particular moment. People *choose to* remain in relationships, they do not have to. We *choose to* act passively, we could decide to act forcefully. We choose to go to work, call our friends, leave a party, or send a Christmas present. We do not have to do any of these things. The price we pay for making some of these choices can be steep, but they are choices nonetheless.

Unlike the Freudian or behavioral views of people at the mercy of forces they cannot control, humanistic psychologists conceive of people as active shapers of their own lives, with freedom to change limited only by physical constraints. A typical goal of humanistic psychotherapy is to get clients to accept that they have the power to do or to be whatever they desire. But, as Erich Fromm observed, for many this freedom is frightening.

The Here and Now

Think about the last time you walked to a class or some other appointment. Perhaps you spent the time thinking about what you did last weekend or ruminating over an embarrassing incident. Maybe you rehearsed something you wanted to say to someone or thought about how nice it will be to get through this week. A humanistic psychologist might say that what you really did was to lose 10 minutes. You failed to experience fully the 10 minutes that life handed you. You could have experienced the fresh air, appreciated the blue sky, or learned something from observing or talking with other people.

According to the humanistic perspective, we can't become fully functioning individuals until we learn to live our lives as they happen. Some reflection on one's past or future can be helpful, but most people spend far too much time thinking about the past or planning for the future. Time spent on these activities is time lost, for you can live life fully only if you live it in the *here and now*.

A popular poster reminds us that "Today Is the First Day of the Rest of Your Life." This phrase could well have been coined by a humanistic psychologist. The humanistic view maintains that we need not be victims of our past. Certainly our past experiences shape and influence who we are and how we behave. But these experiences should not dictate what we can become. Whereas psychoanalysts emphasize that adult personalities are formed in childhood, humanistic therapists reject this notion. People do not need to remain shy just because they "have always been that way." You do not have to remain in an unhappy relationship simply because you don't know what else to do. Your past has guided you to where you are today, but it is not an anchor. You cannot live for today as long as you are tied to the past.

The Phenomenology of the Individual

No one knows you better than yourself, according to humanistic psychologists. It therefore is absurd for therapists to listen to clients, decide what their problems are, and force them to accept the therapist's interpretation of what should be changed and how it should be changed. Instead, humanistic therapists strive to develop an appreciation for where the clients are "coming from" and to provide whatever the clients need to help themselves.

Some people find this approach to therapy a bit puzzling at first. What about disturbed people incapable of understanding their problems? And if the answers were easy and therapy the client's job anyway, why would anyone need to see a psychotherapist? The reply is that whereas some people may not be able to understand the source of their difficulties right now, the therapist also has no access to this information. During the course of therapy, clients come to understand themselves and develop an appropriate strategy for resolving their problems. You may have had a similar experience when dealing with personal problems. Friends offer advice, but allowing someone else to decide what is best for you is unsatisfying and probably ineffective. If you are like many people, it was only when you weighed the advice of others and came to a decision on your own that you were able to resolve the problem.

Personal Growth

According to humanistic psychology, there is more to life than simply having all of your immediate needs met. Suppose tomorrow you inherited several million dollars, settled down with someone who will admire and love you always, and were promised a long and healthy life. Would you be happy? For how long? Humanistic theorists maintain that people are not content when their immediate needs have been met. Rather, they are motivated to continue their development in a positive manner. If left alone, unencumbered by life's difficulties, we will eventually progress toward some ultimately satisfying state of being. Carl Rogers refers to this as becoming a "fully functioning" individual. Abraham Maslow borrowed the term *self-actualization* to describe it. We become self-actualized as we become "more what one idiosyncratically is, to become everything that one is capable of becoming" (Maslow, 1970, p. 46).

Whether one calls it a growth tendency, a drive toward self-actualization, or a forward-moving directional tendency, it is the mainspring of life.

CARL ROGERS

This growth process is assumed to be the natural manner of human development. That is, we progress toward this satisfying state unless certain problems prevent us from doing so. When these obstacles block our growth, humanistic psychotherapy can be helpful. However, the therapist does not put clients back on track. Only the client can do that. Rather, the therapist allows clients to overcome their problems and continue growing. Rogers describes this ever-unfolding of one's self as a "process of becoming."

Carl Rogers

Humanistic psychology could ask for no better example of living life fully than the career of Carl Rogers. His role as a shaper of the humanistic perspective spanned several decades. He pioneered the application of humanistic psychology to psychotherapy and was the first therapist to popularize a "person-centered" approach (Rogers, 1951). Rogers later became an important figure in the growth of encounter groups as a means of therapy (Rogers, 1970) and expanded what he learned from psychotherapy into a general theory of personality (Rogers, 1961). Later in his career, Rogers expanded the humanistic approach to social issues (Rogers, 1977). According to Rogers, the humanistic perspective of human nature

Carl R. Rogers
1902–1987

Like the inevitable unfolding of one's true self that he promoted, Carl Rogers's interest in science and his concern for people carried him from Midwest farm boy to leader of the humanistic revolution in psychology. Carl was a shy but very intelligent boy growing up in Illinois. He had a particular fondness for science, and by the time he was 13 had developed a reputation as the local expert on biology and agriculture. Ironically, the Rogers household was anything but warm and affectionate. Openly expressing emotions, later a key feature in Rogerian therapy, was not allowed. As a result, like two of his siblings, Carl developed an ulcer by age 15.

Rogers went to his mother and father's alma mater, the University of Wisconsin, to study agriculture in 1919. He planned a career in farming but soon found agriculture unchallenging. He took a correspondence course in psychology one summer but found it boring. Finally, he settled on religious studies. When he left Wisconsin with his new wife Helen in 1924, he went to Union Theological Sem-

inary in New York to prepare for a career as a minister.

Two developments in New York again changed the direction of his life. First, intensely studying theology caused him to question his own religious beliefs. "The Christian religion satisfies very different psychological needs in different men," he observed. "The important thing is not the religion but the man" (in Kirschenbaum, 1979, p. 45). The second development was a renewed introduction to psychology. While at the seminary, Rogers and several classmates took psychology courses across the street at Columbia University. These classmates included Theodore Newcomb and Ernest Hilgard, who also went on to become important figures in psychology.

A career in theology promised Rogers an opportunity to help people, but his faith continued to wane. "It would be a horrible thing to have to profess to a set of beliefs in order to remain in one's profession," he said. "I wanted to find a field in which I could be sure my freedom of thought would not be limited" (in Kirschenbaum, 1979, pp. 51–52). Much to his parents' dismay, he left the church to pursue graduate study in psychology at Columbia.

After graduation, Rogers worked at a child guidance clinic in Rochester. Later he joined the faculty at Ohio State University and the University of Chicago before returning to the University of Wisconsin in 1957. Throughout this time Rogers battled with the established

Continued

Freudian approach to psychotherapy and the dominant behavioral influence in academia. But in time he began to win many of these battles. When the American Psychological Association handed out its first annual award for distinguished scientific contribution in 1956, Carl Rogers was the recipient.

In 1963 Rogers moved to La Jolla, California, where he founded the Center for Studies of the Person. The thread that ties Rogers's career together is his genuine concern for people. "Rogers seemed ordinary," a colleague wrote. "He was not a sparkling conversationalist. [But] he would certainly listen to *you*, and with real interest" (Gendlin, 1988, p. 127). Rogers devoted the last 15 years of his life to the issues of social conflict and world peace. Even in his eighties, he led workshops and communication groups in such places as the Soviet Union and South Africa. Rogers continued to write extensively and shape the discipline of psychology until his death in February 1987.

could be used to improve education (Rogers, 1969) and ensure world peace (Rogers, 1982). For many people, Rogers's optimistic view of humanity and belief in each individual's potential for fulfillment and happiness provide a pleasant alternative to some of the approaches to personality covered thus far.

The Fully Functioning Person

"The good life," Rogers said, "is a *process*, not a state of being. It is a direction, not a destination" (1961, p. 186). Like other humanistic theorists, Rogers maintained that we naturally strive to reach an optimal sense of ourselves and a satisfaction with our lives. But this good life is not a static state. To be **fully functioning** means to be open to the constant flow of our existence.

So how does one enter this process? What are the characteristics of a fully functioning person? First, fully functioning people are open to their experiences. They strive to experience life to its fullest. They prefer to see what adventure life will throw their way each day and then appreciate the uniqueness of that experience. Second, fully functioning people open their eyes to what is going on in the here and now. They live each moment as it comes. Third, fully functioning people trust their own feelings. If something feels like the right thing to do, they do it. They aren't held back by standards they learned long ago or concern for what others might think.

Unlike Freud, Rogers believes all people are basically good. Of course, people are sometimes hostile and cruel. But Rogers maintains that if allowed to be what we are, unburdened by life's problems, all of us can fulfill our potential as loving, trustworthy people. Fully functioning people accept and occasionally express their anger. To do otherwise would be to deny a part of human emotion. But

Life, at its best, is a flowing, changing process in which nothing is fixed. It is always in a process of becoming.

CARL ROGERS

constructive, affectionate impulses have an increasingly large influence on their behavior as they grow.

Fully functioning people are less prone to conform to societal demands than are most people. Instead, they are sensitive to their own interests, values, and needs. They experience their feelings, both positive and negative, more deeply and more intensely than the rest of us. Because of this sensitivity, fully functioning people experience a greater richness in their lives. They "live more intimately with their feelings of pain, but also more vividly with their feelings of ecstasy" (Rogers, 1961, p. 195). They know anger and fear more deeply than most of us. But it's the price they pay to also feel love and joy more intensely. Opening one's self up to all of our emotions is preferable to stifling the feelings that define each of us. Fully functioning people live their lives, they don't just pass through them.

Anxiety and Defense

If we all have the potential to be fully functioning, constructive members of society, why is there so much unhappiness in the world? Why doesn't everyone get the maximum enjoyment out of life? Rogers was well aware that we often fall short of becoming happy, fully functioning adults. Our fall from happiness often begins when we experience anxiety and respond with various psychological defenses. The defenses succeed in reducing anxiety, but in the process we also lose touch with who we are and reduce our ability to experience life's richness.

According to Rogers, anxiety results when we come into contact with information that is inconsistent with the way we conceive of ourselves. Your self-concept may include the belief that you are a good tennis player, a kind person, a good student, or a pleasant conversationalist. But occasionally you receive information that contradicts your self-concept. For example, you may think of yourself as the kind of person everybody likes. But one day you overhear someone say what a jerk he thinks you are. How would you react?

First, let's describe how a fully functioning person would react. If you were fully functioning, you would be willing to accept this information. Here is someone who does not like you. You might want to think about this new information for a while and then incorporate it into your self-concept. You might recognize now that while you are a fine person, not everyone is going to find you pleasant and wonderful. Unfortunately, most of us are not capable of such a well-adjusted reaction. More commonly, the information leads to anxiety. You believe you are liked by everyone, and here is some evidence that not everyone likes you.

If the information is very threatening to a central part of your self-concept, the anxiety is difficult to manage. This is where Rogers's theory takes on a slight Freudian flavor. Rogers proposed that people receive information inconsistent with their self-concepts at a level somewhere below consciousness. Because we are not consciously aware of the inconsistency, Rogers called this process **subception**, rather than perception. If the information were not threatening, it might enter conscious awareness. However, because the information contradicts the self-concept, it creates anxiety. To deal with the anxiety, people use defense processes to keep the information from entering consciousness.

The most common defense process is distortion. In this example, you might convince yourself that the person was in a bad mood or is just a rude person. This distorted message does not contradict your self-concept and thereby reduces the anxiety. In more extreme cases, you might even resort to outright denial. No, you might convince yourself, he wasn't really talking about me, but someone else with a name that sounds like mine.

An interesting twist on this part of Rogers's theory is that anxiety can also result from positive information, if that information is inconsistent with our self-concepts. For example, people who consider themselves socially unattractive may use defenses when they hear that someone is attracted to them. They might tell themselves the admirer is just being polite or maybe is scheming to get something from them.

Distortion and denial succeed in the short-run in that they effectively reduce anxiety. But each use takes us farther and farther away from experiencing life fully. In severe cases, people replace reality with fantasy. A man may think of himself as the world's most desirable bachelor when in fact there are no objective reasons to draw this conclusion. A student with poor grades might convince herself that she is a genius whose thoughts are simply too sophisticated for her instructors to understand. When the incongruence between the self-concept and reality is so large that the defense processes cannot operate adequately, the person experiences what Rogers calls a state of *disorganization*. When this happens, protection against inconsistent information collapses. The result is extreme anxiety.

Conditions of Worth and Unconditional Positive Regard

According to Rogers, it is difficult to accept and incorporate inconsistent information into our self-concepts. But why is this so? Rogers's answer is that most of us have grown up in an atmosphere of **conditional positive regard**. As children, our parents and "significant others" provide love and support, but not unconditionally. That is, most parents love their children as long as the children do what is expected of them. When parents disapprove of children's behavior, they withhold their love. The children get the message they are loved, but only when they do what their parents want. The positive regard the children need and want is conditional upon their behavior.

As a result of this conditional positive regard, children learn to abandon their true feelings and desires and to accept only that part of themselves their parents have deemed appropriate. They deny their weaknesses and faults. Ultimately, children become less and less aware of themselves and less able to become fully functioning in the future. As adults we continue this process of incorporating into our self-concepts only those aspects that are likely to win the approval, and thus the love and support, of significant other people in our lives. Certainly there are parts of each of us that, if revealed to loved ones, would bring on disapproval and possibly rejection. So instead of accepting and expressing these thoughts and desires, we deny or distort them. We keep them out of our self-concepts. Thus, we lose touch with our feelings and become less fully functioning, which "is the basic

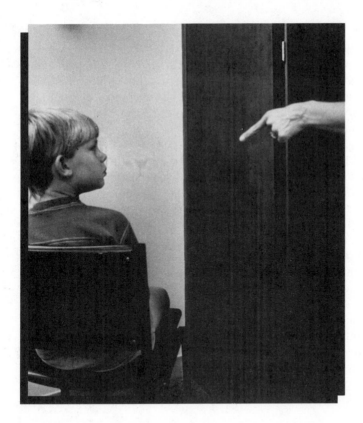

Is the child a bad boy, or has he merely done a bad thing? Rogers argues that parents should provide children with unconditional positive regard: Although the boy may have done something the mother did not like, he is still loved and prized by her.

estrangement of man," Rogers said. "He has not been true to himself for the sake of preserving the positive regard of others" (1959, p. 226).

The question then becomes: How can we come to accept our faults and weaknesses, when we know they may not be accepted by others? According to Rogers, we need **unconditional positive regard** to accept all parts of our personality. With unconditional positive regard we know we will be accepted, loved, and "prized," no matter what we do. Parents can communicate to their child that although they don't approve of a specific behavior, they will always love and accept the child. Under these conditions, children no longer feel a need to deny those parts of themselves that might otherwise have led to a withdrawal of positive regard. They are free to experience all of themselves, free to incorporate faults and weaknesses into their self-concepts, free to experience all of life.

Parents are not the only source of unconditional positive regard, and growing up in a family without this acceptance does not condemn a person to a less than full life. Therapists also can incorporate the notion of an unconditional positive environment during psychotherapy. Through the use of such an environment, and other therapy procedures developed by Rogers, adults also can get themselves back on the track toward self-fulfillment and happiness. We'll examine this approach to therapy later in this chapter.

Abraham Maslow

Maslow spent most of his career trying to fill in the gaps he found in other approaches to understanding human personality. When most psychotherapists were directing their attention to why people develop psychological disorders, Maslow wondered how psychology might facilitate the happy, healthy side of personality. "Freud supplied to us the sick half of psychology," he wrote, "and we must now fill it out with the healthy half" (1968, p. 5).

Maslow replaced Freud's pessimistic and dismal view of human nature with an optimistic and uplifting portrayal. He also criticized psychologists who focused their attention on only one aspect of the individual. Looking at one type of response to a specific stimulus or examining one personality trait at a time causes researchers to ignore the most important part of personality — the person. Many psychologists see the tree but miss the forest. Further, Maslow argued that we cannot understand a person by looking at a small slice of human functioning as if it existed independently from the whole. For example, hunger is not merely an indication that the digestive system is at work, but also affects all aspects of a person's behavior.

Maslow acknowledged the existence of unconscious motives but focused his attention on conscious aspects of personality. He conceived of people as free-willed individuals always seeking to satisfy their innate motives in a manner that fits their individual style, as well as the unique demands of their environment. It was this optimistic, psychologically healthy, and whole person that Maslow promoted during his lifetime.

I'm someone who likes plowing new ground then walking away from it. I get bored. I like discovery, not proving.
ABRAHAM MASLOW

Motivation and the Hierarchy of Needs

For a moment, contrast the concerns of the typical middle-class American today with those of the typical blue-collar worker during the Great Depression of the 1930s. Today's financially secure professionals fret over their relationships and their standing in the social community. Many seem to be concerned about where their lives are going, others find satisfaction working in community service projects and other charitable organizations. They read novels, get involved with social causes, and perhaps take classes to develop writing skills or their appreciation for the arts. Things were very different when nearly a third of the work force lost their jobs in the 1930s. Feeding oneself and one's family became the dominant need of many Americans. A job, any job, was of primary importance. Spending time contemplating the direction of one's life and experimenting with various avenues to express one's potential were luxuries reserved for those who did not have to worry about day-to-day existence.

The people in this example differ in their behavior because of differences in motivation. Maslow's theory of personality centers around understanding these differences. He identified two basic types of motives. One is a **deficiency motive**, which results from a lack of some needed object. Such needs as hunger and thirst and the need for respect from others fall into this category. Deficiency

Abraham H. Maslow
1908–1970

The changes and developments in Abraham Maslow's personal and professional life resemble in many ways the personal growth he described in his theory of personality. Although generally regarded as a warm and gregarious adult, Maslow had a cold and lonely childhood. "I was the little Jewish boy in the non-Jewish neighborhood," he recalled. "I was isolated and unhappy. I grew up in libraries and among books, without friends" (in Hall, 1968, p. 37).

His professional career also started out on a path far from his eventual position as the father of humanistic psychology. His parents, uneducated Russian immigrants, encouraged Maslow to go to law school. He went to City College of New York in this pursuit but found it uninteresting and dropped out during

the first year. Maslow went to Cornell and then to the University of Wisconsin to study psychology. Ironically, what initially attracted him to psychology was behaviorism, particularly the works of John B. Watson. "I was so excited about Watson's program," he said. "I was confident that here was a real road to travel, solving one problem after another and changing the world" (in Hall, 1968, p. 37). Although his enthusiasm for behaviorism would eventually wane, Maslow's desire to solve the world's problems through psychology never diminished.

Maslow stayed at Wisconsin to finish his Ph.D. in 1934. He remained a loyal behaviorist throughout this period, working closely with Harry Harlow in his animal lab. After graduation, Maslow went to Columbia University to work with the famous learning theorist E. L. Thorndike. But with the birth of his first daughter, Maslow went through a mystical experience similar to the peak experiences he later studied. Looking at his newborn child, Maslow realized that behaviorism was incapable of providing the understanding of human behavior that he now needed. "I looked at this tiny, mysterious thing and felt so stupid," he said. "I was stunned by the mystery and

Continued

by the sense of not really being in control. . . . Anyone who had a baby couldn't be a behaviorist" (in Hall, 1968, p. 56).

After Columbia, Maslow taught at Brooklyn College for 14 years, where he came into contact with Karen Horney, Erich Fromm, and Alfred Adler. Most important, he met Max Wertheimer, one of the founders of Gestalt psychology, and Ruth Benedict, a cultural anthropologist. It was his desire to better understand these two people, who he called "the most remarkable human beings," that led him to his exploration of self-actualized people (Maslow, 1970).

Maslow moved to Brandeis University in 1951 and remained there until shortly before his death in 1970. He hoped to leave a new movement in psychology and personality as his legacy. "I like to be the first runner in the relay race," he once said. "Then I like to pass on the baton to the next man" (in Hall, 1968, p. 56).

motives are satisfied once the needed object has been obtained. These needs are similar to those described by psychologists, including Freud, who see human motivation in terms of tension reduction, with the return to a tensionless state the ultimate aim of the motivating system.

The more interesting needs are those Maslow called **growth needs**, which include the unselfish giving of love to others and the development of potential as a human being. Unlike deficiency needs, these needs are not satisfied once the target object has been found. Rather, the satisfaction comes from the growth that provides the expression of this motive. Unlike the tension we feel when we are hungry, striving to satisfy our potential can be quite enjoyable and may even lead to an increase in, rather than a satiation of, the need.

Maslow's Need Hierarchy   Maslow is probably most famous for his **hierarchy of needs**. He argued that human motives can be placed in a hierarchy of prominence. That is, some needs demand satisfaction before others. Maslow placed these needs into five hierarchical levels, as diagrammed in Figure 11.1. Although there are exceptions, typically we satisfy the needs at the lower levels before becoming concerned with the needs at higher levels. For example, if you are hungry, your behavior will center around obtaining food. Until this need is met, you will not be very concerned about making new friends or developing a romantic relationship. Of course, once satisfied the lower need may return, causing you to divert your attention to it again. But over the course of a lifetime, most of us progress up the hierarchy, until satisfying our need for self-actualization dominates our actions. According to Maslow, only a fraction of a percent of us ultimately attain the state of self-actualization.

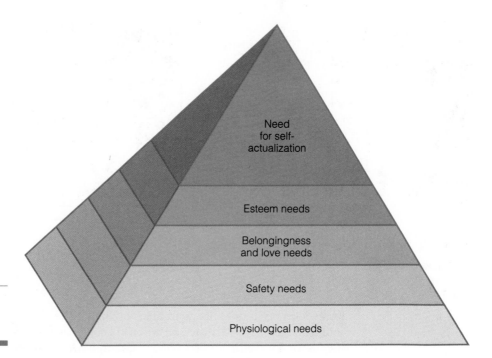

Figure 11.1

Maslow's Hier-
archy of Needs

Physiological Needs   Physiological needs, including hunger, thirst, air, and sleep, are the most demanding, in that they must be satisfied before moving on to higher-level needs. Throughout history — and, unfortunately, in many places today — many people's lives have centered around meeting these basic needs. Finding enough food and water for survival takes priority to concerns about, say, gaining the respect of peers or developing potential as an artist.

Safety Needs   When physiological needs are met, we become increasingly motivated by our safety needs. These include the need for security, stability, protection, freedom from fear or chaos, and the need for structure and order. These needs are most evident when the future is unpredictable or when stability of the political or social order is threatened. People who perceive these threats to security may build large savings accounts or seek out a job with a lot of security rather than a better but riskier position. Sometimes they seek out the predictable orderliness of organized religion or the military. Thus, people stuck at the safety need level in their personal development may put up with an unhappy marriage or a military dictatorship if these situations provide stability or a sense of security.

Belongingness and Love Needs   For most middle-class American adults, the need for food and water and the need for security and stability are fairly well satisfied. Most of us have jobs, homes, and food on the table. But satisfaction of these

Operating at Different Levels on the Hierarchy of Needs

lower-level needs does not guarantee happiness. The need for friendship and love soon emerges. "Now the person will feel keenly, as never before, the absence of friends, or a sweetheart, or a wife, or children," Maslow wrote. "He will hunger for affectionate relations with people, . . . for a place in his group or family" (1970, p. 43). Although some adults remain slaves to their safety needs and devote most of their energy to their careers, most people eventually find such work unsatisfying if it means sacrificing time spent with friends and loved ones.

Maslow identified two kinds of love. *D-love*, like hunger, is based on a deficiency. We need this love to satisfy the emptiness we experience without it. It is a selfish love, concerned with taking, not giving. But it is a necessary step in the development of the second type of love, B-love. *B-love* is a nonpossessive, unselfish love based on a growth need rather than a deficiency. We can never satisfy our need for B-love simply with the presence of a loved one. Rather, B-love is experienced and enjoyed and grows with this other person. It is a "love for the Being of another person."

Esteem Needs Although thousands of poets and songwriters might disagree, there is more to life than love. Satisfaction of our belongingness and love needs will direct attention to our esteem needs. Maslow divided these into two basic types: the need to perceive oneself as competent and achieving and the need for admiration and respect. He cautioned that this respect must be deserved. We cannot lie or cheat our way into positions of respect and authority. Even with money, spouse, and friends, failing to satisfy our need for self-respect and admiration will result in feelings of inferiority, helplessness, and discouragement.

The Need for Self-Actualization Nearly every culture has a story of someone who, by virtue of a magic lamp or contact with a supernatural being, receives everything he or she wishes. Inevitably, granting wishes of wealth, love, and power isn't enough to produce happiness in these characters. For, as Maslow explained, when all of these lower-level needs are satisfied, a new discontent and restlessness develops. People who obtain all of the obvious sources of happiness and contentment in our society turn their attention to developing themselves to their full potential. "A musician must make music, an artist must paint, a poet must write, if he is to be ultimately at peace with himself," Maslow wrote. "What a man *can* be, he *must* be. He must be true to his own nature" (1970, p. 46).

When all our lower-level needs are satisfied, we begin to ask ourselves what we want out of life, where our lives are headed, what we want to accomplish. The answers to these questions are different for each of us. Maslow believed very few adults ever reach this state of **self-actualization**, the point at which their potential is fully developed. But we all have the need to move toward that potential. Most of us will eventually direct some attention toward that goal, perhaps in ways we may not now be able to imagine.

Misconceptions about Maslow's Need Hierarchy   Maslow was quick to point out that his initial five-level need hierarchy oversimplifies the relationship between needs and behavior. Although the order of the needs makes sense for most of us, there are some notable exceptions. For example, some people need to satisfy their needs for self-esteem and respect before they can enter a love relationship. Some artists are so intent on expressing their creative desires that they sacrifice satisfaction of some lower-level needs. Painting or writing may be more important than a steady income or a constant source of food. And occasionally we hear about martyrs who sacrifice life itself for a value or an ideal.

Another common misconception about the need hierarchy is the assumption that our physiological needs must be satisfied 100% before we can turn to higher needs. More accurately, Maslow said our needs are only partially satisfied at any given moment. He estimated that for the average American, 85% of our physiological needs, 70% of our safety needs, 50% of our belongingness and love needs, 40% of our self-esteem needs, and 10% of our self-actualization needs are satisfied. Of course, how well our lower needs are satisfied determines how much those needs influence our behavior.

Although Maslow described the need hierarchy as universal, he readily admitted that the means of satisfying a particular need vary across cultures. A person can win self-esteem and respect from others in our society by becoming a doctor or political leader. But in other societies this esteem is awarded for good hunting or farming skills. Maslow argued that these differences are somewhat superficial. The basic needs themselves, not the manner in which they are satisfied, remain the same across cultures.

Finally, another oversimplification of Maslow's theory is that any given behavior is motivated by a single need. Maslow argued that behavior is the result of multiple motivations. He gave the example of sexual intercourse. Someone might say this is motivated by the need for sexual release. But Maslow argued that the same behavior also may be motivated by a need to win or express affection, a sense of conquest or mastery, or a desire to feel masculine or feminine. People have sex to satisfy any one of these needs or to satisfy all of them.

Self-Actualization

For each of the following statements, indicate the extent to which the statement applies to you, using this four-point scale:

1 = Disagree
2 = Disagree somewhat
3 = Agree somewhat
4 = Agree

_____ 1. I do not feel ashamed of any of my emotions.
_____ 2. I feel I must do what others expect of me.
_____ 3. I believe that people are essentially good and can be trusted.
_____ 4. I feel free to be angry at those I love.
_____ 5. It is always necessary that others approve of what I do.
_____ 6. I don't accept my own weaknesses.
_____ 7. I can like people without having to approve of them.
_____ 8. I fear failure.
_____ 9. I avoid attempts to analyze and simplify complex domains.
_____ 10. It is better to be yourself than to be popular.
_____ 11. I have no mission in life to which I feel especially dedicated.
_____ 12. I can express my feelings even when they may result in undesirable consequences.
_____ 13. I do not feel responsible to help anybody.
_____ 14. I am bothered by fears of being inadequate.
_____ 15. I am loved because I give love.

To calculate your score, first reverse the values for items 2, 5, 6, 8, 9, 11, 13, and 14 (1 = 4, 2 = 3, 3 = 2, 4 = 1). Then add the values for all 15 items. The test you have taken is a short measure of self-actualization developed by Jones and Crandall (1986). You can compare your score with the following norms they found for college students:

	Mean	Standard Deviation
Males	45.02	4.95
Females	46.07	4.79

The higher the score, the more self-actualized you are said to be at this point in your life.

The Study of Psychologically Healthy People

Psychologists have long identified and studied people who suffer from psychological disorders. But what do you do if you are Abraham Maslow and want to identify and study psychologically *healthy* people? Maslow began by selecting people who appeared to be psychologically healthy. In terms of the need hierarchy, these were people who had most completely satisfied their need for self-actualization. Some of them were contemporaries of Maslow who consented to being interviewed. But others were historical figures who seemed to have lived a self-actualized life style. Maslow used historical documents to gather information about such seemingly self-actualized people as Thomas Jefferson, Albert Einstein, Eleanor Roosevelt, and Albert Schweitzer. Maslow acknowledged that his procedures were far from methodologically rigorous. Rather than statistical or other quantitative analyses, Maslow provided "holistic analysis" — general impressions from his efforts to understand these people in depth. He developed a list of characteristics that seemed to recur in the personalities of these psychologically healthy people.

What are self-actualized people like? For one thing, they tend to accept themselves for what they are. They admit to their weaknesses, although not without making an effort to improve. Because of this self-acceptance, self-actualized people do not worry excessively or feel guilty about the bad things they have done. Instead, they accept the parts of themselves that need improvement. Self-actualized people are not perfect, but they respect and feel good about themselves for what they are.

Psychologically healthy people also are less restricted by cultural norms and customs than is the average person. Whereas most of us are concerned about doing the "proper" thing, self-actualized people feel free to express their desires, even when those desires run counter to what society says they are supposed to do. It is not that they are insensitive to social pressures. On the contrary, Maslow described them as very perceptive. They are simply less inhibited and more spontaneous than most of us. Society provides a long list of rules about how our lives should progress: go to school, get a job, make some money, buy a house and car, raise a family, and on and on. Further, there are rules about how to act in public, how to spend our leisure time, how to dress, how to eat, and so on. However, psychologically healthy people are less likely than the rest of us to conform to what society mandates, unless they feel their own goals and desires would be met in the process. They are "ruled by the laws of their own character rather than by the rules of society" (Maslow, 1970, p. 174).

Maslow described every psychologically healthy person he studied as creative. However, he distinguished between the traditional definition of creativity, which is based on producing something traditionally associated with talent (for example, a poem) and *self-actualizing creativity*. A well-known painter is not necessarily self-actualized. The paintings might spring more from an innate talent than from a healthy personality. Self-actualizing creativity is revealed in the way people approach routine parts of life with a spontaneity that allows them to perform daily tasks in an unconventional manner. A self-actualized teacher develops innovative ways to communicate ideas to students. A self-actualized

Self-actualizing individuals have more free will than average people.
ABRAHAM MASLOW

339

business person thinks of clever ways to improve business and devises new solutions to old problems.

In essence, self-actualizing creativity is a way of approaching life. Maslow compared it with the spontaneous way a child examines and discovers the world, ever in awe and admiration of the little things that make it such an interesting place. Maslow suggested that we all might continue to express this self-actualizing creativity if we didn't succumb to *enculturalization*, which inhibits our spontaneity. Somehow psychologically healthy people retain or rediscover the fresh and naive way of looking at life.

Maslow discovered several other characteristics common to psychologically healthy people. It may surprise you to find these people have relatively few friends. But the friendships they have are deep and rewarding. They have a "philosophical, unhostile" sense of humor. They poke fun at the human condition, including themselves, rather than at any particular person or group. Self-actualized people have a strong need for privacy. And, like Rogers's fully functioning people, they express a continued appreciation for life's experiences.

A final feature Maslow discovered in psychologically healthy people is how often they have what he called a peak experience. A **peak experience** is one in which time and place are transcended, in which people lose their anxieties and experience a unity of self with the universe and a momentary feeling of power and wonder. However, consistent with the humanistic notion of individuality, peak experiences are different for each person. Maslow likens them to "a visit to a personally defined Heaven." Peak experiences are growth experiences, for afterward people report feeling more spontaneous, more appreciative of life, and less concerned with whatever problems they may have had.

Psychologically healthy people are not the only ones who have these experiences. After all, most of us on occasion experience emotional growth and wrestle with higher-level concerns. But peak experiences for self-actualized people tend to be more intense and occur more often. However, even in the self-actualized group, Maslow found there were "peakers" and "nonpeakers." Each of these types of psychologically healthy people serves a different function in society. The nonpeaking self-actualizers are "the social world improvers, the politicians, the workers of society, the reformers, the crusaders." They have their feet planted firmly on the ground and have a clear direction in life. On the other hand, the peakers "are more likely to write the poetry, the music, the philosophies, and the religions" (1970, p. 165). The two types of self-actualizers play different roles in society, but both are on the way to fulfilling their potentials, each marching to a slightly different drummer.

A New Direction in the Humanistic Approach: The Psychology of Optimal Experience

What makes people happy? This question threads its way through much of the writings of the humanistic personality theorists. Of course, these theorists are concerned with more than the relatively superficial signs of happiness, such as a good job, a nice car, or an attractive family. And, as Maslow argued, people are not content simply because they have no pressing problems. Rather, much of humanistic personality theory focuses on the individual's quest to attain a sense of meaning and personal satisfaction in his or her life. Humanistic psychotherapy may help clients work toward a sense of contentment and self-actualization. But what about finding happiness in the everyday, routine activities in life? Can people structure the events in their daily lives in a way that promotes a sense of personal fulfillment and self-worth?

Optimal Experience

One starting point for answering these questions is simply to ask people to describe the activities that make them happy. This is one of the strategies for understanding human happiness employed by psychologist Mihaly Csikszentmihalyi (1990; Csikszentmihalyi & Csikszentmihalyi, 1988). Try it on yourself. Think of a time when you felt alive and totally engaged in an activity, when what you were doing was more than pleasurable, but truly enjoyable. What were you doing? When Csikszentmihalyi (1990) asked people to identify these experiences, he found a great variety of answers. Some people talked about mountain climbing, others about playing tennis, others about performing surgery. But when he asked these people to *describe* the experience, he found they used surprisingly similar terms.

Csikszentmihalyi's subjects talked about becoming so involved in what they were doing that nothing else seemed to matter. Climbing the mountain or performing the surgery demanded all of their attention. Although each step seemed to flow almost automatically to the next, the task was almost always challenging and demanded the subject's full concentration. Reaching the goal provided a sense of mastery, but the real pleasure came from the process rather than the achievement.

Csikszentmihalyi refers to these moments as **optimal experience**. Because people typically say these experiences feel as if they are caught in a natural, almost effortless movement from one step in the process to the next, Csikszentmihalyi has come to refer to this experience as *flow*. Optimal experiences are intensely enjoyable, but they usually are not restful, relaxing moments. On the contrary, most often flow experiences are quite demanding. "The best moments usually occur when a person's body or mind is stretched to its limits in a voluntary effort to accomplish something difficult and worthwhile," Csikszentmihalyi (1990) explains. "Optimal experience is thus something that we *make* happen" (p. 3).

Interestingly, the flow experience is described in fairly identical terms by people of all ages, in all cultures. After examining thousands of descriptions of their most satisfying and enjoyable moments, Csikszentmihalyi (1990) identified eight characteristics of the flow experience. These are listed in Table 11.1. Not every flow experience contains each of these eight. But any flow experience you might be thinking about probably includes many of these components. The flow experience that comes to mind for me happens when I become lost in my writing. I sometimes find myself writing for hours, almost totally unaware of anything

Table 11.1

Eight Components of Optimal Experience

1. **The Activity Is Challenging and Requires Skill**. The task is sufficiently challenging to demand full attention, but not so difficult that it denies a sense of accomplishment.

2. **One's Attention Is Completely Absorbed by the Activity**. People stop being aware of themselves as separate from their actions, which seem spontaneous and automatic.

3. **The Activity Has Clear Goals**. There is a direction, a logical point to work toward.

4. **There Is Clear Feedback**. We need to know if we have succeeded at reaching our goal, even if this is only self-confirmation.

5. **One Can Concentrate Only on the Task at Hand**. During flow we pay no attention to the unpleasant parts of life.

6. **One Achieves a Sense of Personal Control**. People in flow enjoy the experience of exercising control over their environments.

7. **One Loses Self-Consciousness**. With attention focused on the activity and the goals, there is little opportunity to think about one's self.

8. **One Loses a Sense of Time**. Usually hours pass by in what seems like minutes, but the opposite can also occur.

around me. I become so absorbed in what I'm doing that I've written through ringing telephones and important meetings. When I finally stop after three or four hours, it always seems as if I had been working only 10 minutes.

Optimal Experience and Happiness in Everyday Activities

If flow experiences make us happy, then understanding how to incorporate such experiences in our lives may provide an avenue for increasing happiness. Like other humanistic theorists, Csikszentmihalyi recognizes that many people suffer from the anxiety that comes from a sense that their lives have no meaning. Society provides many sources of relief from this feeling. Some people seek happiness by acquiring material possessions. Some turn to fitness centers and plastic surgery in an effort to hang on to youth. Others try out new and seemingly mystical religions. But Csikszentmihalyi (1990) argues that none of these diversions brings permanent happiness. True happiness comes when we take personal responsibility for finding meaning and enjoyment in our ongoing experiences. That is, we can enjoy life to its fullest by discovering what it is that makes us feel alive and then doing it.

Of course, in a perfect world we could all do what we wanted when we wanted. But reality does not allow us the luxury of such simple solutions. The common lament of the 1990s seems to be that we face so many demands yet have so little free time. This brings us to an important question: When are people more likely to experience flow—at work or during leisure hours? Most of us answer quickly that we are happier during time away from work. In fact, people often point to their long working hours as a cause of their lack of happiness. However, researchers find this is not the case. Flowlike experiences are far more likely to happen when people are at work than during their off hours (Csikszentmihalyi & LeFevre, 1989). Csikszentmihalyi argues that most of us simply buy into the conventional wisdom that says work is work and play is play. Consequently, we fail to recognize the frequency with which our jobs provide us with a sense of mastery, accomplishment, and enrichment.

Fortunately, this is not true of all people. A woman I know, a writer, keeps her computer near her bed so that she can turn to her work even before her first cup of coffee in the morning. Friends say she often has to be pried away from her writing at night. She doesn't understand the fuss. She loves what she does for a living. Time spent writing is time spent learning and growing. Each day her work provides more challenges and more opportunities for personal development. Movie maker and comedian Woody Allen provides another example. Friends and colleagues are constantly amazed at the energy and attention he gives to his movies. "I love to work," he once said. "I'd work seven days a week. I don't care about hours. When we solve this problem, whether it's five o'clock or ten at night, then we move on to something else. Hours or days mean nothing" (in Lax, 1991, p. 337). Woody Allen clearly experiences flow when he's working. That his movies also provide money and fame seems to be secondary.

Of course, not everyone can be a writer or a movie maker. What about the average person who puts in 40 hours a week at a less glamorous profession? Csikszentmihalyi argues that nearly any job can become a flow experience if we approach it the right way. Even mowing the lawn or making dinner can be a source of happiness if we think of these as challenges and take pride and satisfaction in a job well done. Rather than thinking of such jobs as something we have to do or something others expect us to do, we can approach these daily tasks by searching for what we can get out of them. "The most important step in emancipating oneself from social controls," Csikszentmihalyi explained, "is the ability to find rewards in the events of each moment" (1990, p. 19).

This advice also applies to students. Researchers in one study identified high school students who studied and participated in their classes not because they wanted good grades but because they found the process genuinely interesting and satisfying (Wong & Csikszentmihalyi, 1991). Interestingly, these students' grades were not particularly high. But these intrinsically motivated students did tend to take more advanced courses than the grade-driven students, probably because they wanted to learn more about the subjects they found most interesting. In short, they appeared to enjoy the learning experience itself, rather than the rewards promised for doing the work.

In sum, Csikszentmihalyi's prescription for happiness contains many of the elements traditionally embraced by humanistic personality psychology. Flow experiences require people to live in the present, to get the most out of their lives in the "here and now." Achieving the goal is not the point. Rather, it is the struggle and experience along the way that provides the enjoyment. Happiness comes from taking control of your life, rather than caving in to conventional standards or demands from others. In the flow state, people are intensely in touch with themselves and their experiences. They feel a sense of mastery and a sense of finding themselves. Like the peak experiences described by Maslow, flow experiences are occasions for personal growth.

Application: Person-Centered Therapy and Job Satisfaction

Obviously, the works of Rogers and Maslow have had a great impact on psychology and personality theory. In this section we'll examine two applications of humanistic personality theory. First we'll look at Rogers's contribution to treating psychological disorders. Then we'll explore some of the ways Maslow's theory of motivation and the hierarchy of needs have been applied to working environments and the issue of job satisfaction.

Person-Centered Therapy

Carl Rogers's personality theory presents an interesting challenge to traditional approaches to psychotherapy. According to Rogers, a therapist cannot possibly understand clients as well as clients understand themselves. Further, he maintained clients are responsible for changing themselves—the therapist isn't responsible for this. So, what is left for therapists to do with clients who come to them with problems?

Rogers's answer was that a therapist's job is not to change the client, but rather to provide an atmosphere within which clients are able to help themselves. Rogers believed each of us grows and develops in a positive, self-actualizing fashion unless our progress is in some way impeded. The therapist's job is to allow the client to get back on that positive growth track and to continue progressing in a positive direction. After successful Rogerian therapy, clients should be more open to personal experience, more able to accept all aspects of themselves, and therefore less likely to use distortion and denial when faced with information incongruent with their self-concepts. By the end of the therapy sessions, clients should be more fully functioning and happier people.

How is this accomplished? First, therapists must create the proper relationship with their clients, or as Rogers put it, "a relationship which this person may use for his own personal growth" (1961, p. 32). The most important rule here is to be open and genuine with clients. Therapists have to be themselves, rather than play the role of therapist they were taught in graduate school. This means being honest with clients, even if that includes being very frank (but not cruel) at times. Entering a genuine relationship with another person is necessary for clients to explore their feelings openly and thereby come to understand and overcome their problems. Rogers believed clients can always tell when a therapist isn't being genuine with them.

The proper therapeutic relationship also requires unconditional positive regard. Therapists must accept and "prize" their clients for what they are. Clients must feel free to express and accept all of their thoughts and feelings during therapy without fear of rejection from the therapist. Clients can overcome defenses and come to grips with experiences that have been denied or distorted only when they feel the freedom to identify and express all of their feelings, not just those that are socially acceptable.

Unconditional positive regard does not mean therapists must approve of everything clients say and do, especially acts that may hurt the client or someone else. Indeed, in the safe atmosphere provided by the therapist, clients may disclose some disturbing information about themselves. But because therapists accept clients with positive regard despite these faults and weaknesses, clients learn to acknowledge these aspects of themselves, too. They can't begin to change these things until they've acknowledged their existence.

In addition to providing an accepting relationship, therapists can help clients understand themselves better through a process of reflection. Rather than interpret what clients really mean, as a Freudian therapist might, a Rogerian therapist helps clients listen to what they are saying. Part of this comes about when clients are given the opportunity to put their feelings into words. Rogers believed the process of translating vague feelings into precise words helps clients crystallize those feelings. Clients listen to their words and examine their thoughts, perhaps for the first time. One technique a therapist can use to facilitate this process is to restate the client's statements. Some people mistakenly think this means the therapist must repeat the clients' words back to him or her verbatim. But as the following excerpt demonstrates, the goal is to help clients explore their thoughts and feelings by directing their attention to what they are saying. In this example, Rogers is working with a woman who is struggling with her sense of personal identity.

Client: I suppose I want to know just what to do, but then maybe nobody could give me that.

Therapist: You realize that you are probably looking for immediate answers that nobody could give you.

C: I just don't know. I don't know what I'm looking for. It's just that I wonder if I'm insane sometimes. I think I'm nuts.

T: It just gives you concern that you're as far from normal as you feel you are.

C: That's right. It's silly to tell me not to worry because I do worry. It's my life. . . . Well, I don't know how I can change my concept of myself—because that's the way I feel.

T: You feel very different from others and you don't see how you can fix that.

C: I realize, of course, that it all began a long time ago—because everything begins somewhere. I wasn't just—somehow or other something failed somewhere along the line. And I guess we sort of have to get at it, a sort of re-education. But I don't feel as though I can do it myself.

T: You realize that the roots must go a long way back, and that at some point you will have to start in reworking it, but you're not sure whether you can do it.

C: That's right. It's just the idea that I can see myself going through life this way, fifty, sixty, and seventy years old — still thinking these horrible thoughts. And it just doesn't seem worthwhile — I mean, it's so ridiculous. While everybody else is going their way and living life, I'm sort of at the edge, and looking on. It just isn't right.

T: The future doesn't look very bright when you look at it that way.

C: No. I know I'm lacking in courage, that's the big thing I'm lacking. That must be it, 'cause other people aren't swayed so easily. . . . It's a hard thing to explain these things. It's just as though — it's — true but I laugh at it in a way. . . . It's a very confused feeling.

T: Logically, you realize that courage is one of your deficiencies, but inside yourself you find yourself laughing at that notion and feeling that it doesn't really have anything to do with you. Is that it?

C: That's right. I always sort of make myself different. That's it. (1947, pp. 138–140)

The therapist never tells clients what they really mean to say. Instead, therapists offer restatements of what they believe they are hearing, but these are only suggestions for the client to agree with or reject. If the process is effective, clients come to see themselves as others do and eventually accept or modify what they see. Clients may come to understand that they have been distorting or denying parts of their experiences. For example, a man may realize he has been trying to live up to his father's impossibly high expectations, or a woman may come to understand she is afraid to commit herself to a serious relationship. In the freedom provided by the therapist's unconditional support, clients peel away their defenses, accept who they are, and begin to appreciate all of life's experiences.

Job Satisfaction and the Hierarchy of Needs

Think for a moment of two or three careers you would like to have some day (maybe you already work at one of these). Now ask yourself what it is about each of these jobs that makes it appealing. That is, what do you hope to gain from it that you can't get from just any job? Now, take the answers to this last question and apply them to Maslow's hierarchy of needs. Which of the five levels of needs will your chosen occupation satisfy? If you find a job attractive because it pays a lot of money or provides good job security, then the job probably will satisfy your safety needs. On the other hand, a job may appeal to you because it brings respect and admiration or allows you to express yourself artistically.

The point of this exercise is that your occupation provides an important source of need satisfaction. Besides sleeping, there is no single activity that will take up more of your adult life than your job. Maslow argued that to spend 40 hours a week at a job that pays well but doesn't allow for development of personal potential is a tragic waste. "Finding one's lifework is a little like finding one's mate," he wrote. "If you are unhappy with your work, you have lost one of the most important means of self-fulfillment" (1971, p. 185).

Is the job a chore that must be endured 8 hours a day, or does this man get more out of his work than just a paycheck? According to Maslow, occupations should provide opportunities for personal growth and the satisfaction of higher-order needs. Besides money, a job can satisfy our needs for belongingness, self-esteem, and respect for others.

Maslow was critical of job counselors who direct young people into careers simply because they pay well or fit the needs of the job market. A better approach would be to match a person's unique talents and potential to the job that allows the expression and development of that potential. A career can provide an avenue for personal growth as well as a means of paying the bills.

Of course, we probably cannot structure society so that all people work at jobs that satisfy all of their personal needs. But Maslow encouraged employers to design working environments in a manner that helps to satisfy as many needs as possible. This not only is good for the worker but also creates job satisfaction, which translates into the worker doing better work for the employer. Maslow claimed that some employers incorrectly believe they can create job satisfaction by supplying only job security and a steady income. A steady job is appreciated by someone facing unemployment. But for most professionals today, job satisfaction requires more than a good income. Just as the satisfaction of a need in one's life stimulates the next need, satisfaction of basic needs on the job leads to dissatisfaction if higher needs are ignored.

Maslow referred to the rearrangement of an organization to help employees satisfy higher-level needs as *Eupsychian management*. For example, an employer might structure jobs so that people have the opportunity to develop feelings of self-worth about what they do for a living. Workers move toward satisfying their esteem needs when they take pride in their job performance. In addition, workers might be given opportunities to suggest creative solutions to some of the problems they see. An employer might also foster a sense of belongingness and feelings of camaraderie among workers.

Maslow's work has influenced the way many organizational psychologists look at job satisfaction. Many have adopted or expanded some of Maslow's concepts in their own theories (Alderfer, 1972). In addition, the need hierarchy model has generated a great deal of research in industrial and business settings. However, to date the support for Maslow's theory has been mixed at best (Wahba & Bridwell, 1976). The difficulty researchers have had in finding empirical support for Maslow's concepts stems in part from their difficulty in developing precise operational definitions and adequate measures for such concepts as "self-actualization." Nonetheless, Maslow's influence on psychologists working in industrial-organizational settings has been significant.

Assessment: The Q-Sort Technique

Unlike many humanistic therapists, Carl Rogers was strongly in favor of conducting research on the effectiveness of person-centered psychotherapy. He was aware that therapy sessions often are declared a success after the therapist and client agree the client has shown improvement. But without evidence demonstrating therapeutic change, therapists and clients are in danger of fooling themselves. Further, Rogers believed that research into change during psychotherapy would help therapists better understand the process and thereby improve on how they work with clients.

But how does a therapist establish that a client is more fully functioning or closer to self-actualization after a few months of therapy? One technique that has proven useful in this task is an assessment procedure called the **Q-Sort**, developed by Stephenson (1953). Rogers saw that the Q-Sort was similar to some assessment methods he had tried during his early work with children, and he quickly adopted it.

Psychologists often create their own Q-Sort materials to fit their needs, but Block's (1961) California Q-Sort is a good example of a Q-Sort used by humanistic therapists. The materials for this test are not very elaborate. They consist of a deck of 100 cards. A self-descriptive phrase is printed on each card, such as "is a talkative individual," "seeks reassurance from others," or "has high aspiration level for self."

If you were a client about to begin a series of sessions with a Rogerian therapist, you might be instructed to read the cards and sort them into categories. On the first sort, you would be asked to place the cards into nine categories according to how much you believe the description on the card applies to you.

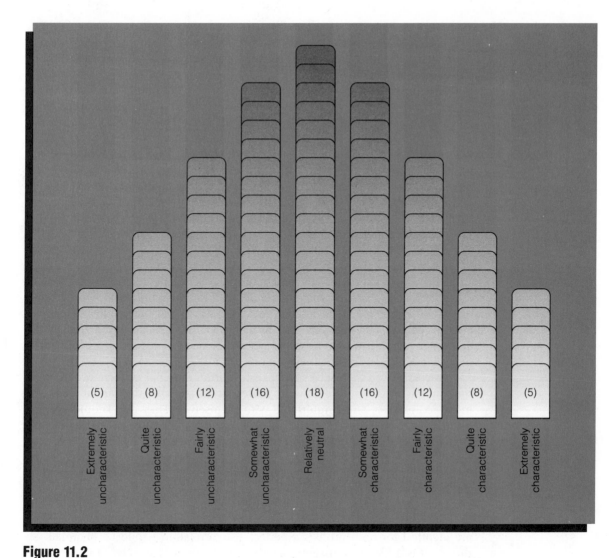

Figure 11.2

Distribution of Cards in Block's Q-Sort

The nine categories represent points on a normal distribution (see Figure 11.2), with the categories on the extreme ends representing those characteristics most descriptive of you (Category 9) and least descriptive of you (Category 1).

For example, let's suppose the description on the first card is "is a talkative individual." If this phrase describes you very well, you would place the card in Category 9 or 8. If this phrase describes you only slightly, you might put it in Category 6. If you think you are a very quiet person, you might place the card in

Category 1 or 2. There is a limit to how many cards can be placed in each category so that indecisive subjects are forced to select cards that are most descriptive of them. In this manner, you provide the therapist and yourself with a profile of your self-concept.

After recording the positions of the cards, you would be asked to shuffle the deck and take the test again. However, this time you would distribute the cards according to your "ideal" self. For example, if "is a talkative individual" does not describe you very well, but you want to become more talkative, you would move this card to a higher category when you sort your ideal self. When you have laid out descriptions of your "real" and "ideal" selves, you and the therapist can compare the two profiles. By assigning each card a number from 1 to 9 according to the category you placed it in, you can compute a correlation coefficient between your real self and your ideal self.

The Q-Sort technique fits very nicely with Rogers's theory for several reasons. Consistent with Rogers's assumption that clients know themselves best, clients are allowed to describe themselves however they please. A therapist will not always agree with a client's placement of the Q-Sort cards. For example, a client might describe herself as socially aware, polite, and sensitive to the needs of others when a perceptive therapist sees right away that her crude insensitivity may be part of her problem. But humanistic therapists maintain that in the appropriate therapeutic atmosphere clients come to see themselves in a more realistic manner and adjust their Q-Sorts accordingly.

As clients free themselves from distortion and denial of their experiences, they should obtain a more accurate understanding of who they are and become more accepting of and comfortable with themselves. They also should become more aware of the sources of their problems, which may turn out to be different from the ones they thought had driven them into therapy. In addition, clients can work to change themselves where appropriate, to become more like the person they want to be. Alternatively, they may modify their ideal selves to be more in line with the way they really are.

In a correlational analysis of Q-Sort responses, a psychologically healthy person is one whose real and ideal selves are very similar. If the category values are identical for both profiles a perfect 1.0 correlation would be obtained, although it is difficult to imagine people just like their ideal selves in every way. Clients whose real and ideal selves are completely unrelated would have a zero correlation. Clients' profiles can also be negatively correlated, if their real and ideal selves are at opposite extremes on many of the descriptions. Obviously, the farther the correlation is from 1.0, the less accepting people are of themselves and the less fully functioning.

To help illustrate how the Q-Sort can be used to track progress during psychotherapy, let's look at one of Rogers's clients (Rogers, 1961). This 40-year-old woman came to Rogers with problems that included an unhappy marriage and guilt about her daughter's psychological problems. The woman attended 40 therapy sessions over the course of 5½ months and returned a few months later for some additional sessions. She completed the real- and ideal-self Q-Sorts at the beginning and at various stages of her treatment. She also completed the Q-Sort

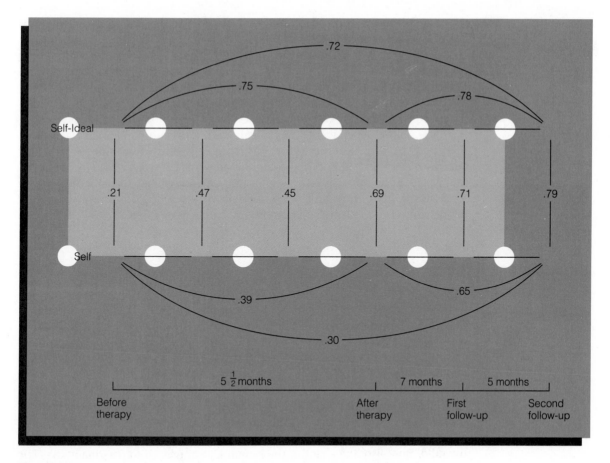

Figure 11.3

Changing Real and Ideal Self Q-Sorts for a 40-Year-Old Female Client

From Rogers (1955), with permission.

at two follow-up sessions, 7 and 12 months after her therapy. The correlations among the various Q-Sorts are presented in Figure 11.3.

Several important changes in the way the woman viewed her real self and her ideal self occurred during her treatment. First, there was a significant increase in the congruence between her real and ideal selves over the course of the therapy sessions that continued to grow after she discontinued therapy. At the beginning of her treatment, her real- and ideal-self Q-Sorts were quite discrepant, correlating at only .21. In other words, when she first entered Carl Rogers's door she did not see herself at all as the kind of person she wanted to be. However, as therapy progressed, the two descriptions became more and more similar. In particular, this client changed the way she viewed herself. We can tell this from the low correlation (.30) between the way she described herself at the beginning of the therapy and the way she described herself at the end. Thus, through the exploration of her feelings in these person-centered sessions, this woman came to see herself in very different, presumably more accurate, terms.

There were also some noticeable, but less dramatic, changes in the way she described her ideal self. She may have come to realize through therapy that the goals she set for herself were far too ideal. It is not uncommon for clients to enter therapy expecting near perfection of themselves and to consider themselves failures when they fall short of these impossible goals. It is clear from this example that Rogers's therapy was successful in bringing the client's real and ideal selves closer together. She no doubt was better able to experience life as a fully functioning person more than she had been before entering therapy.

Strengths and Criticisms of the Humanistic Approach

The humanistic movement hit psychology like a storm in the 1960s. Therapists of every perspective were converted to the person-centered approach. Humanistically oriented encounter groups and workshops sprang up everywhere. Psychologists applied many of the ideas proposed by Rogers and Maslow to such areas as education and the workplace. Then, almost as quickly as it arrived, the "third force" movement seemed to fade in the late 1970s. Many converts became disenchanted, some humanistically oriented programs were declared failures, and the number of popular paperbacks capitalizing on the movement began to dwindle. But, also like a storm, the humanistic approach to personality has left reminders of its presence. A large number of psychotherapists still identify themselves as humanistic in their orientation (Spett, 1983), while many others have adopted Rogerian techniques in their practice. Humanistic psychologists still enjoy an active division in the American Psychological Association and publish their own journal. While the movement never came close to replacing the well-entrenched psychoanalytic or behavioral approaches, it remains an appealing alternative view of human nature for many therapists. This ebb and flow of popularity suggests that the humanistic approach, like other approaches to personality, has both strengths and points for criticism.

Strengths

Because personality theorists often dwell on psychological problems, the humanists' positive approach offers a welcomed alternative. The writings of Rogers and Maslow remain popular with each new generation struggling through the higher growth needs postulated by Maslow. We should also credit these theorists for drawing the attention of many personality researchers to the healthy side of personality. Today it is not uncommon for researchers to investigate such topics as creativity, happiness, and sense of well-being.

Not surprisingly, humanistic psychology has had a huge impact on the way psychologists and counselors approach therapy. Many therapists identify themselves as "humanistic." More important, several aspects of the humanistic approach to therapy have been adopted or modified in some form by a large number of therapists from other theoretical perspectives. Many therapists adopt Rogers's emphasis on making the client the center of therapy. In addition, many therapists include in their practices such Rogerian techniques as therapist empathy, positive regard for clients, giving clients responsibility for change, and self-disclosure by client and therapist. In addition, the humanistic approach sparked the growth of encounter groups in the 1960s. Variations of encounter groups remain today in the form of group therapy and other self-improvement, personal-growth therapies.

Humanistic psychology's influence has not been limited to psychology and psychotherapy. Students in such disciplines as education, communication, and business are often introduced to Rogers and Maslow. Many employers and organizational psychologists are concerned about promoting job satisfaction by taking care of employees' higher needs. And many teachers and parents have adopted or modified some of Rogers's suggestions for education and child rearing. Because they focus on issues that many of us address in our lives — fulfilling personal potential, living in the here and now, finding happiness and meaning in life — books by Maslow, Rogers, and other humanistic psychologists continue to sell in popular bookstores.

Criticisms

Like all influential personality theories, humanistic psychology has its critics. One area of controversy centers around humanistic psychology's reliance on the concept of free will to explain human behavior. Some psychologists argue that this reliance renders the humanistic approach unfit for scientific study. Science relies on the notion that events are determined by other events. Thus, the science of behavior relies on the assumption that behavior is determined and therefore predictable. However, if we accept the idea that sometimes behavior is caused by free will, which is not subject to these laws of determination, these assumptions fall apart. How can we scientifically test whether free will exists or not? Because we can explain any behavior as caused by "free will," no investigation will ever fail to support a free will interpretation. Free will by definition is not under the control of any observable or predictable force. It is not determined, it is not predictable.

These observations do not mean free will does not exist, only that it is not a concept that can be explored through scientific inquiry. Maslow was aware of this problem but challenged the necessity of relying on the scientific method to understand human personality. "The uniqueness of the individual does not fit into what we know of science," he wrote. "Then so much the worse for that conception of science. It, too, will have to endure recreation" (Maslow, 1968, p. 13).

Another criticism of the humanistic approach is that many key concepts are poorly defined. What, exactly, is "self-actualization" or "fully functioning" or

Neither the Bible nor the prophets — neither Freud nor research — neither the revelations of God nor men — can take precedence over my own direct experience.

CARL ROGERS

"becoming"? How do we know if we're having a "peak experience" or just a particularly good time? Maslow (1968) responded that we simply don't know enough about self-actualization and personal growth to provide clear definitions. But this defense is far from satisfying for most researchers. Such vagueness prevents psychologists from adequately studying many humanistic concepts. How can we investigate self-actualization if we can't decide who's got it and who hasn't? Because most psychologists are trained as careful researchers, the inability to pin down humanistic concepts causes many to challenge the usefulness of the approach.

Rogers, Maslow, and other humanistic psychologists have provided research findings to support their views. However, the data on which many of these studies are based have been challenged by more experimentally oriented psychologists. Although Rogers is to be commended for his efforts to assess the effectiveness of person-centered therapy, he still relied too heavily on his intuitive feelings to satisfy many hard-nosed researchers. Similarly, Maslow selected people for his list of "self-actualized" individuals based on his own subjective impressions. Because of these weak data, much of what humanistic theorists say must be taken more as a matter of faith than scientific fact. Psychologists and lay readers probably embrace the humanistic approach because it is consistent with their own observations and values, not because they are persuaded by the evidence.

Other problems people have with the humanistic approach concern the effectiveness of humanistic psychotherapy techniques or the usefulness of these techniques for dealing with all kinds of people and problems. For example, some psychologists question the appropriateness of always relying on clients to make accurate appraisals of themselves. Surely there are times when clients are not able or willing to provide therapists with accurate information for these judgments. Rogers argues that under the proper circumstances clients come to understand themselves better. But many therapists question this.

Some have argued that the usefulness of humanistic psychotherapy is limited to a narrow band of problems people want to resolve in therapy. Creating the proper atmosphere for personal growth might be of value for many of Rogers's clients but may provide little help to someone with an extreme psychological disorder. Similarly, reflecting on one's values and direction in life might prove beneficial for well-educated, middle-class clients. But would it make sense to engage in the same type of therapy with someone living in a severe disturbance-inducing environment or struggling with a psychophysiological disorder? Person-centered therapy may be useful for working out certain kinds of adjustment problems, but not for dealing with the myriad of serious psychological disturbances that cause people to seek therapy.

Finally, humanistic psychologists have been criticized for making some overly naive assumptions about human nature. For example, most humanists assume that all people are basically good. Although this is more a theological than an empirical question, many 20th-century Americans find the premise difficult to accept. Another assumption many find difficult to swallow is that each of us has a desire to fulfill some hidden potential. Maslow's description of self-actualization implies that each of us is somehow predestined to become, for example, a painter, a poet, or a carpenter. The key is discovering which of these true selves lies bottled up inside waiting to develop. This predeterministic tone seems to contradict the general free will emphasis of the humanistic approach.

Summary

1. The humanistic approach to personality grew out of discontent with the psychoanalytic and behavioral descriptions of human nature that were prominent in the 1950s and 1960s. Humanistic psychology has its roots in European existential philosophy and the works of some American psychologists, most notably Carl Rogers and Abraham Maslow.

2. Although many approaches to psychotherapy have been described as humanistic, four criteria seem important for classifying a theory under this label. These criteria are an emphasis on personal responsibility, an emphasis on the here and now, focusing on the phenomenology of the individual, and emphasizing personal growth.

3. Carl Rogers introduced the notion of a fully functioning person. According to his theory, we all progress toward a state of fulfillment and happiness unless derailed by some of life's obstacles. People who encounter evidence that contradicts their self-concepts often rely on distortion and denial to avoid the anxiety this might create. People who grow up in families that give only conditional positive regard may come to deny certain aspects of themselves. Rogers advocates the use of unconditional positive regard by parents and therapists to overcome this denial.

4. Abraham Maslow introduced a hierarchy of human needs. According to this concept, people progress up the hierarchy as lower needs are satisfied. In addition, Maslow examined psychologically healthy people. He found several characteristics typical of these self-actualized people, including the tendency by some to have frequent peak experiences.

5. One recent outgrowth of the humanistic approach to personality has been outlined by Mihaly Csikszentmihalyi. He finds people describe the happiest and most rewarding moments in their lives in terms of a "flow" experience. Csikszentmihalyi argues that turning one's life into a series of challenging and absorbing tasks, what he calls optimal experiences, is the key to happiness and personal fulfillment.

6. One of Rogers's contributions to psychology is the person-centered approach to psychotherapy. Rogers said the therapist's job is to create the proper atmosphere for clients' growth. This can be done by entering a genuine relationship with clients, providing unconditional positive regard, and helping clients hear what they are saying. Maslow's hierarchy of needs concept has been applied to the problem of job satisfaction. He argued that one's career provides an opportunity for personal growth and that employers should arrange working situations to better meet employees' higher-order needs.

7. Many person-centered therapists have adopted the Q-Sort assessment procedure. This procedure allows therapists and clients to see discrepancies between clients' images of themselves and the ideal self they would like to be. Therapists can administer the Q-Sort at various points during treatment to measure therapy progress. Improvement is seen when clients close the gap between their real and ideal selves.

8. Among the strengths found in the humanistic approach to personality are the attention it gives to the positive side of personality and the influence it has had on psychotherapy procedures and such areas as communication and job satisfaction. Criticisms include the unscientific reliance on free will to explain behavior and the difficulty in dealing with many of the poorly defined constructs used by humanistic theorists. Some therapists have challenged the appropriateness of relying on clients to make therapy judgments and the usefulness of person-centered therapy for many types of clients and psychological problems. Finally, the humanistic approach has been criticized for making many naive assumptions about human nature.

Key Terms

fully functioning person A psychologically healthy individual who is able to enjoy life as completely as possible.

subception The perception of information at a less-than-conscious level.

conditional/unconditional positive regard Acceptance and respect for people either only when they act as we desire (conditional) or regardless of their behavior (unconditional).

deficiency motive A need that is reduced when the object of the need is attained.

growth need A need that leads to personal growth and that persists after the need object is attained.

hierarchy of needs In Maslow's theory, the order in which human needs demand attention.

self-actualization A state of personal growth in which people fulfill their true potential.

peak experience An intense emotional experience characterized by feelings of satisfaction and personal growth.

optimal experience A state of happiness and satisfaction characterized by absorption in a challenging and personally rewarding task.

Q-Sort An assessment procedure in which subjects distribute personal descriptions along a continuum.

Suggested Readings

Csikszentmihalyi, M. (1990). *Flow: The psychology of optimal experience*. New York: Harper Perennial. Csikszentmihalyi describes his theory of personal happiness, based on many years of research with thousands of people. In an easy-to-read style, he explains how to find happiness and personal satisfaction in physical activities, thoughtful activities, one's work, and even tragedy.

Frankl, V. E. (1959). *Man's search for meaning: An introduction to logotherapy.* New York: Pocket. I have yet to find a student who didn't appreciate this book. Viktor Frankl dramatically describes his tragic experiences in Nazi concentration camps and how he wrestled with existential issues during this ordeal. Frankl explains how his personal search for meaning and his approach to psychotherapy evolved from these experiences.

Maslow, A. H. (1970). *Motivation and personality* (2nd ed). New York: Harper & Row. This is probably the most complete and best-written statement of Maslow's theory, including his hierarchy of needs and study of psychologically healthy people. Maslow shows that he is a talented, albeit flowery, writer throughout this book.

Rogers, C. R. (1961). *On becoming a person.* Boston: Houghton Mifflin. Among Rogers's many books, this one probably best captures the flavor of his writing and thinking. In addition, the book provides a fairly comprehensive picture of Rogers's theory of personality, particularly as it applies to person-centered psychotherapy.

The Humanistic Approach
Relevant Research

The rapid growth of humanistic psychology converts a few decades ago was fanned in part by the contrast with research-oriented approaches to understanding human behavior that had become so prominent in American universities. Humanistic psychologists argued that people cannot be reduced to a set of numbers. Scores on a battery of personality tests don't capture a person's inner strength, feelings, and character. Most important, finding a person's place along a trait continuum erases that person's uniqueness and individuality. As the name implies, the third force in psychology was developed to attend to the "human" element lost in number-crunching approaches.

Ironically, this strength also proves to be one of humanistic psychology's weaknesses. Critics sometimes refer to the approach as "soft" psychology. Flowery descriptions of one's unique character are fine, but they are of little value when trying to find empirical support for the theory. Clinical observations and intuitive feelings by humanistic therapists may provide insights into personality and the therapy process, but they cannot replace reliable assessment procedures. This is not to say that humanistic psychologists do not conduct research. On the contrary, Carl Rogers continually evaluated the effectiveness of person-centered therapy. But on the whole, advocates of the humanistic perspective probably have generated less empirical research than have psychologists from the other approaches covered in this book.

Nonetheless, Rogers, Maslow, and other humanistic psychologists *have* introduced a number of intriguing concepts and hypotheses about human personality that have generated or promoted a great deal of empirical research. Although some of the original research on these topics was conducted by humanistic psychologists, in most cases the better empirical work was done by researchers outside the humanistic circle. A good example of this is research on self-disclosure, the first topic we'll explore in this chapter. Rogers and other therapists argued that the act of revealing personal information has important psychological consequences. Stimulated by this early theorizing, self-disclosure has been a widely researched topic for more than three decades now. Most of this work has been conducted by psychologists who probably would shun the "humanistic" label. Nonetheless, the findings from this research have important implications for humanistic theory and therapy.

Similarly, research on the other three topics we'll examine in this chapter—loneliness, real-ideal self congruence, and self-esteem—was inspired in part by humanistic writers but largely conducted by more empirically oriented academic psychologists. Of course, there is some irony in this situation. The cold, empirical approach to understanding personality once rejected by many humanistic types has subsequently served to promote many of the concepts central to the humanistic perspective.

Self-Disclosure

Imagine you are with someone you don't know very well but who seems to be a pleasant person. You both have some time to kill, so you begin to talk. The conversation begins casually with a discussion about the classes you're taking. However, soon this person begins to talk about some of the difficulties she has been having with her parents. You find yourself talking about similar experiences you have had. Before the conversation is over, you learn quite a lot about this person's past history—problems with her family, with dating, with her self-confidence. You reveal that you, too, sometimes have difficulty relating with members of the opposite sex. Perhaps you tell this person about an embarrassing dating situation you've been in. When the conversation ends, you feel good about this other person and maybe even about yourself.

Most of us have been in this kind of conversation. If you think back to your own experience like this one, you may recall that the conversation began with relatively impersonal topics and gradually worked toward more private information. Most likely, the conversation was anything but one-sided. You and this other person probably took turns sharing information about yourselves. And it's quite possible you left the conversation feeling good about your new acquaintance, while perceiving that person also felt good about you. This may well have been the first step toward a long-lasting friendship. Finally, the whole encounter may have put you in a pleasant mood that kept you in good spirits for the rest of the day.

According to self-disclosure theory and research, these feelings are typical after two people share personal information. People engage in **self-disclosure** when they reveal intimate information about themselves to another person. The discloser considers the information personal, and the choice of who to disclose to is fairly selective.

A better understanding of self-disclosure processes and consequences promises insights into a number of important questions for psychology. For example, how should you talk about yourself when first meeting potential friends? How should clients and therapists deal with intimate information during psychotherapy? Should therapists be open and honest with their feelings or remain professional and impersonal? Should you retain your personal secrets, or would you be better off to talk to somebody about them? We'll look at research findings that help to answer each of these questions. But first, let's explore the roots of this research, which are, not surprisingly, found in the work of some humanistic psychologists.

Jourard's Transparent Self

Carl Rogers, Abraham Maslow, and many other humanistic theorists were concerned with the role of self-disclosure in personal adjustment and the psychotherapy process. For example, Rogers (1961) suggested that disclosing openly to another person in the context of a trusting relationship is an important part of coming to understand oneself and thereby becoming more fully functioning. However, self-disclosure became a well-promoted feature of humanistic psychotherapy largely because of the work of another humanistic psychologist, Sidney Jourard.

According to Jourard (1971), frequent and open self-disclosure is the sign of a healthy personality. But Jourard also saw self-disclosure as a primary means for achieving personal adjustment. It is precisely *because* a person self-discloses, inside and outside of a therapy situation, that he or she returns to a path of personal growth. "[It] is not until I am my real self and I act my real self that my real self is in a position to grow," he wrote. "People's selves stop growing when they repress them" (1971, p. 32).

Facts are always friendly. Every bit of evidence one can acquire, in any area, leads one that much closer to what is true.
CARL ROGERS

Thus, the ultimate means of becoming a well-adjusted, fully functioning person is to make ourselves "transparent" — to allow others to see all of us, to hide nothing. Most of us spend an excessive amount of time and effort avoiding disclosure for fear of becoming embarrassed or not being respected and loved by everyone around us. If you are like most people, you go to great lengths to keep certain people from finding out about your bad habits, the parts of your character that they might not like. But transparent people have already revealed their true selves, so they have nothing to be anxious about.

More important, Jourard argued, it is *only* through self-disclosure that we can truly come to know ourselves. It is easy to hide our true feelings and beliefs behind a wall of denial and distortion as long as we are never forced to put those ideas into words. There is something about the act of saying to another person just what we feel and think that brings our feelings out in the open for everyone — including ourselves — to see. Until we are open and transparent to others, we can never be open and transparent to ourselves. And if we are not aware of all aspects of ourselves, we cannot grow and become fully self-actualized.

Naturally, Jourard and others have applied the concept of the transparent self to the therapy situation. Clients benefit most from therapy when they are allowed to engage in a genuine self-disclosing interaction with the therapist, who also must be as transparent as possible. In this type of interaction, clients feel free to explore their true feelings and move toward becoming their true, perhaps hidden, selves. Today, therapists from many different orientations acknowledge the important role self-disclosure plays in the psychotherapeutic process (Derlega, Margulis, & Winstead, 1987).

Disclosure Reciprocity

If you are like me, you have had the unfortunate experience of being stuck on a plane or a bus sitting next to a stranger who wanted to tell you all about his or her life. During a recent plane trip the woman next to me described her relationship

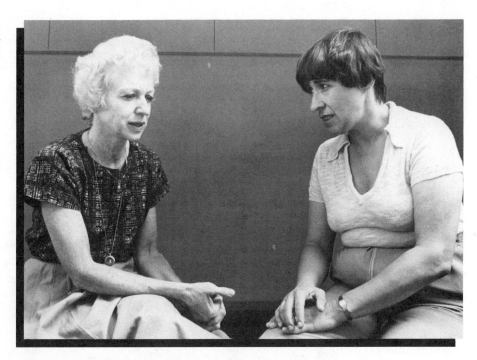

Self-disclosure plays a key role in the development of personal relationships. However, researchers find that this is rarely one-sided. Instead, relationships develop as each person reveals intimate information about himself or herself at roughly the same level of intimacy.

with her husband, problems in raising her child, her opinions on drugs, sex education, and abortion—all without a single bit of encouragement or comparable disclosure from me.

What is notable about this "stranger on the bus" phenomenon is that it violates society's rules for the way social interaction is supposed to progress. Like many social behaviors, the way we reveal information about ourselves to others is governed by a set of unstated but understood rules. Occasionally, parents teach us these rules directly ("Don't stare at people"), but more often we are not aware of the modeling and conditioning that teach us what is expected and what is not appropriate when interacting with other people.

One of these rules is reflected in what Jourard called the *dyadic effect*. He observed that when one person disclosed personal information in a conversation, the other person almost always reciprocated. Later investigators identified this as the rule of **disclosure reciprocity**. According to this social rule, people involved in a get-acquainted conversation reveal information about themselves at roughly the same level of intimacy. I reveal personal information to you as long as you continue to match that level of intimacy by revealing similarly personal informa-

Figure 12.1

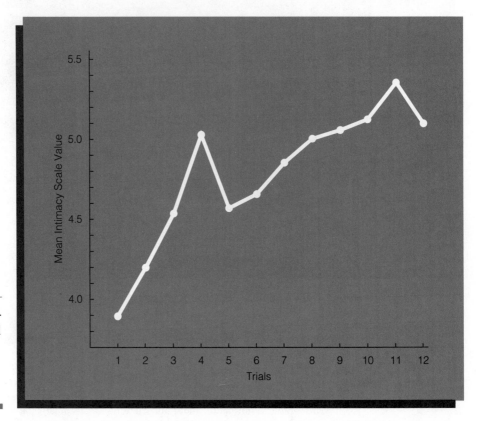

Progression of Intimacy During Dyad Conversation

Adapted from Davis (1976); reprinted by permission of the author.

tion about yourself. It is unlikely that you will reveal something very personal about yourself to someone who passively sits there listening, telling nothing about himself or herself.

The rule of disclosure reciprocity was demonstrated in an experiment in which undergraduate students were randomly paired with a member of the same sex whom they did not know (Davis, 1976). Subjects were told to get to know one another by taking turns volunteering information about themselves. They were given a list of 72 discussion topics, previously ranked for level of intimacy, ranging from fairly trivial to extremely revealing. The winner of a coin toss began by talking for one minute on any one of the topics. The partner then talked for one minute on any one of the remaining topics. This procedure continued until both partners had spoken on 12 different topics.

Several aspects of how people use self-disclosure in their daily interactions were demonstrated in this experiment. First, as shown in Figure 12.1, subjects selected increasingly intimate topics as the interaction progressed. They typically began with something safe, perhaps discussing their favorite movies or foods. But they soon moved on to more personal areas, such as problems with their parents or ways in which they felt personally inadequate. Second, subjects tended to match their partners' intimacy levels. That is, if one person spoke on either trivial or intimate topics, the partner also spoke on trivial or intimate topics. This is the rule of disclosure reciprocity. Third, one member of the dyad appeared to take responsibility for setting the intimacy level, with the partner simply matching that level of disclosure. Further examination of the conversations found that it was the more disclosing of the two who set the pace. That person typically chose a topic slightly more intimate than the one previously discussed. The partner, in turn, tended to reciprocate by also moving one step up the self-disclosure ladder.

Several subsequent studies using similar procedures have also produced evidence for disclosure reciprocity in conversations among strangers (Davis, 1977, 1978; Taylor & Belgrave, 1986). In one study, passengers waiting in an airport wrote intimate messages back to a student supposedly collecting hand-writing samples after the student had revealed something intimate first (see Box 12.1). Children as young as eight years old seem to understand and follow the disclosure reciprocity rule (Cohn & Strassberg, 1983).

Why do we reciprocate disclosure intimacy? Jourard (1971) believed that self-disclosure resulted from feelings of attraction and trust. When people disclose information about themselves to us, we are attracted to them, and a feeling of trust develops. We respond to these feelings by disclosing personal information back to that person, thus creating the reciprocity effect. Consistent with this explanation, several studies have found that we disclose to people we like and we like those who disclose to us (Jourard & Friedman, 1970; Worthy, Gary, & Kahn, 1969).

However, liking the other person appears to be only part of the story. Another reason we reciprocate self-disclosure is that people disclose at the level of intimacy they feel is appropriate for the situation. If the situation is unusual or novel, we often take our cue from the other person. We match our partner's intimacy level because that person has provided us with information about what the norm is for the particular situation. If new acquaintances reveal very little or very much about themselves, this tells us something about how we are supposed to behave. Consistent with this explanation, subjects in disclosure experiments sometimes match their partner's intimate disclosures even when they don't particularly like the person (Derlega, Harris, & Chaikin, 1973; Ehrlich & Graeven, 1971; Lynn, 1978). Even when their partners revealed something negative about themselves, the subjects in these studies apparently concluded that intimate disclosure was appropriate and responded with something personal about themselves.

Self-Disclosure Among Friends and Romantic Partners

If you've been trying to apply the disclosure reciprocity rule to a recent conversation you've had with a friend, you may have found that it doesn't seem to work. One of you may have done most of the talking while the other one listened. When a friend calls and says "I need to talk," we usually listen with no apparent need to interrupt with personal examples of our own.

Researchers also soon became aware that the rule of disclosure reciprocity did not seem to apply to good friends. They recognized that after a certain level of intimacy is reached in a relationship and the associated trust has been established, a friend may disclose with the knowledge that the other person's acceptance will

No man can come to know himself except as an outcome of disclosing himself to another person.

SIDNEY JOURARD

Box 12.1

Self-Disclosure at the Airport

You're waiting through a long layover in an airport lounge, when a stranger sits next to you and starts a conversation. How intimate do you suppose this interaction is likely to become? Although most of us have a rule against disclosing too much personal information to someone we've just met, your level of self-disclosure is likely to be determined by how disclosing the other person is first. Research suggests that the rule of disclosure reciprocity may be so strong that intimate disclosure even in this situation is likely to evoke an increased amount of disclosure in most of us.

To test this notion, student experimenters approached adults sitting alone in Boston's Logan Airport (Rubin, 1975). The experimenters explained that they were collecting handwriting samples to compare with their own handwriting as part of a school project. Subjects were shown a data collection sheet with a space for a sample of the experimenter's handwriting and a space for the subject's handwriting. The experimenter began by writing one of three messages in the appropriate space. After writing their name and year in college, the students sometimes wrote a relatively low-intimacy message: "I'm in the process of collecting handwriting samples for a school project. I think I will stay here a while longer and then call it a day." However, for other subjects they wrote a moderately revealing message: "Lately I've been thinking about my relationships with other people. I've made several good friends during the past few years, but I still feel lonely a lot of the time." Finally, some subjects read a fairly intimate message: "Lately I've been thinking about how I really feel about myself. I think that I'm pretty well adjusted, but I occasionally have some questions about my sexual adequacy."

The student then handed the sheet to the subjects, telling them to write whatever they wanted in the appropriate space. How would you react to the students' messages? When judges later coded the subjects' messages, they found the predicted reciprocity effect. The more intimate the student's message, the more intimate the subject's response. For example, one woman wrote: "I'm a grandmother but I too have been thinking of myself — where I've been — what to do — I too question my identity." Another woman gave this advice: "I'm a career woman and well adjusted to handling both adequately. All of us have questions regarding our sexual adequacy — but love and much more in living is so much more important than sex." Finally, one subject took the opportunity to disclose a personal crisis: "I'm supposed to be a respectable housewife, but guess what? I am at the Logan Airport now, going back to Laketown to my impotent husband. I just left my lover in Boston."

It's possible these subjects disclosed so freely because they knew they would never see the experimenter again. Researchers sometimes refer to this as the "passing stranger" or the "stranger on the bus" effect. Most of us have suffered through plane or bus trips sitting next to people who unload their personal problems or tell us all about their families and life plans. Nonetheless, even in these unique circumstances, the rule of disclosure reciprocity still appears to be operating.

be there (Altman & Taylor, 1973). There is no need for the other person to constantly reciprocate in an effort to reassure his or her disclosing friend about the nature of the relationship.

Research comparing self-disclosure patterns among friends and those among strangers finds support for this notion. Subjects in one study exchanged written messages either with a stranger or a very close friend (Derlega, Wilson, & Chaikin, 1976). The subjects matched their partner's level of intimacy when they thought they were exchanging messages with a stranger, but they felt no need to recipro-cate an intimate message when it came from their close friend. Another study found the highest level of disclosure reciprocity came from pairs who knew each other somewhat but who were still in the process of developing their relationship (Won-Doornink, 1985). Apparently these people had made a commitment to learn more about one another, but they didn't know each other well enough yet to assume that the trust and reciprocated intimacy would be there.

However, these findings do not mean that strangers disclose more to each other than do friends. On the contrary, friends are much more likely to talk about such intimate topics as interpersonal relationships, self-concepts, and sexual experiences (Rubin & Shenker, 1978). In one demonstration of this difference, researchers recorded (with permission) the telephone conversations of female college students (Hornstein & Truesdell, 1988). The students talked about signifi-cantly more intimate information when they interacted with their friends than when speaking on the phone with someone they identified as only an acquain-tance. Conversations among good friends also include many noticeable signs of intimacy lacking from conversations with strangers (Hornstein, 1985). These signs include the use of familiar terms, laughing at similar points, and under-standing when to speak and when the conversation is coming to an end.

Studies with couples in long-term romantic relationships find similar pat-terns. The amount of self-disclosure in a marriage is a strong predictor of marital satisfaction (Hendrick, 1981). The more couples talk to one another about what's personal and important to them, the better each of them feels about the marriage. Of course, it may also be that couples disclose *because* they feel good about each other. However, researchers note that it is not necessarily the case that people who disclose a lot have better luck in romance than those who do not. Rather, they find that couples in good relationships usually have selectively chosen one another to disclose to, rather than being high disclosers generally (Prager, 1986). Finally, as with good friends, married couples do not feel the need to reciprocate their partner's disclosure level during a conversation (Morton, 1978).

Disclosing Men and Disclosing Women

Not long ago my wife made an interesting observation about one of my male friends. "He interacts with people like a woman," she said. I immediately under-stood her point. My friend's voice is deep and masculine, and he doesn't use feminine hand gestures. But he often fills our conversations with fairly revealing information about his thoughts and feelings. This behavior would be appropriate, my wife continued, if my friend were a female. But high levels of self-disclosure seemed inappropriate for a male.

Jourard (1971) came to a similar conclusion about the different levels of intimate disclosure appropriate for men and women in this society. Naturally, Jourard was quite critical of the nonexpressive role that American men have been cast in. "The male role," he explained, "requires man to appear tough, objective, striving, achieving, unsentimental, and emotionally unexpressive" (1971, p. 35). Consistent with Jourard's observations, several investigations have found that females tend to disclose more intimately and to more people than males do (Hood & Back, 1971; Snell, Miller, & Belk, 1988; Taylor & Hinds, 1985). But why should this be so? According to Jourard, men learn as they grow up that it is not appropriate to be as expressive and disclosing as females. They fear being ridiculed or rejected if they express too many of their true feelings.

Unfortunately, some research supports these observations (Chelune, 1976a; Derlega & Chaikin, 1976). In one study, subjects read about someone who was either highly disclosing (for example, talked about his or her mother's nervous breakdown) or not very disclosing about personal problems (Derlega & Chaikin, 1976). Half the subjects thought they were reading about a male, and half thought the person was a female. The subjects who thought they were reading about a female rated that person better adjusted when she was disclosing. However, when they thought the discloser was a male, personal disclosure was seen as a sign of poor psychological adjustment.

Other studies suggest at least a few exceptions to this rule. The freedom women feel to disclose may be limited by the nature of what they are talking about. Highly disclosing women in one study were liked more than less disclosing women when talking about a parent's suicide or about their sexual attitudes. However, women who disclosed about their personal aggressiveness were liked less (Kleinke & Kahn, 1980). Similarly, self-disclosing men were seen as well adjusted as long as they disclosed on masculine topics (Cunningham, Strassberg, & Haan, 1986).

What these studies seem to suggest is that men and women are seen as most well adjusted and are liked the most when they disclose within the appropriate societal roles for their gender. For men this usually means withholding information; for women, being open and disclosing, but only on those topics society deems appropriate for women to discuss. The result is an unfortunate limitation on people's ability to be expressive and disclosing. American men have learned to avoid too much emotional expression with one another. The "manly" thing to do is to be friendly but avoid intimacy. Women feel freer to express themselves with their friends, but within limits. Perhaps as traditional male and female roles continue to erode, both men and women will feel free to interact with their friends at whatever level of intimacy they choose.

Self-Disclosure and Personal Adjustment

How much self-disclosure is optimal? Are those who are open and genuine with everyone the most well adjusted and happiest people? Rogers (1961) and Jourard (1959, 1971) argued that the personal growth process, or becoming self-actualized, requires that we openly disclose to others. As long as we hide parts of ourselves from others, they will remain hidden from us as well.

Rogers and Jourard also insisted on the therapeutic value of self-disclosure. Part of what a therapist provides is the opportunity to be genuine and open in an interpersonal relationship. You may have noticed that you felt better after disclosing something you kept bottled up inside to a friend. We often speak of the need to "get something off my chest." Thus, one key to effective therapy from the humanistic perspective is providing an atmosphere in which clients feel they can express whatever they want. This allows them to release bottled-up emotions and to better understand themselves as they move toward self-actualization.

Some research supports the idea that self-disclosure is related to personal adjustment. For example, people who suffer from anxiety tend to disclose less intimate information than those who are not anxious (Post, Wittmaier, & Radin, 1978). But does this mean the more disclosure the better? Think of how people would react if you *always* told them exactly what you were thinking. They'd soon be afraid to ask "How are you?" for fear of an unwanted, although probably genuine, description of your feelings and problems that day.

Observations like these have led some researchers to argue that sometimes disclosure is appropriate and shows good personal adjustment, but that on other occasions self-disclosure is inappropriate and indicative of interpersonal problems (Chelune, 1977, 1979; Cozby, 1972). The most well-adjusted people may be those high in *disclosure flexibility*. These people know when to talk about themselves and when to adapt their level of disclosure accordingly. For example, talking about feelings of inadequacy and embarrassing moments might be appropriate when having a long conversation with your fiancé, but not when meeting with a prospective employer on a job interview. Similarly, remaining courteous but professional will be well received at the job interview, but this nondisclosing style will stifle the development of your relationship if you always use it with your fiancé.

Several investigations provide support for this notion. People who understand the rules of when to disclose and when it is inappropriate fare better in several indicators of personal adjustment. For example, people high in disclosure flexibility are more socially perceptive (Chelune, 1977), are less likely to be neurotic (Chelune & Figueroa, 1981), and are liked more by the people they interact with (Neimeyer & Banikiotes, 1981) than are people without this social awareness. These findings suggest that self-disclosure can lead to better adjustment, but only if the person understands when to disclose and to whom.

Disclosing Traumatic Experiences: Health and Adjustment

Subjects in a recent study were asked to write anonymously about an upsetting or traumatic experience they have had, something they may have kept inside for years and told no one about (Pennebaker, 1989). One of the interesting findings from this and other studies like it is that nearly everyone can readily describe a secret trauma. Subjects write about personal failures and humiliations, illegal activities, drug and alcohol problems, and experiences with sexual abuse, such as rape and incest. They often express guilt over some regrettable action or great sadness about a personal loss or problem. About 25% of the subjects cry.

Self-Concealment

We all have secrets or information about ourselves that we typically do not disclose to others. But some people are more likely to discuss personal information with friends and relatives than others are. To see how you compare with other people on this dimension, complete the following inventory. Use a five-point scale to indicate the extent to which you agree with each statement, with 1 = strongly disagree and 5 = strongly agree.

_____ 1. I have an important secret that I haven't shared with anyone.
_____ 2. If I shared all my secrets with my friends, they'd like me less.
_____ 3. There are lots of things about me that I keep to myself.
_____ 4. Some of my secrets have really tormented me.
_____ 5. When something bad happens to me, I tend to keep it to myself.
_____ 6. I'm often afraid I'll reveal something I don't want to.
_____ 7. Telling a secret often backfires and I wish I hadn't told it.
_____ 8. I have a secret that is so private I would lie if anybody asked me about it.
_____ 9. My secrets are too embarrassing to share with others.
_____ 10. I have negative thoughts about myself that I never share with anyone.

You have just completed the Self-Concealment Scale, developed by Larson and Chastain (1990). The scale was designed to measure the extent to which people typically conceal or disclose personal information that they perceive as distressing and negative. To calculate your score, simply add your answer values together. Larson and Chastain report a mean score of 25.92 and a standard deviation of 7.30 when they administered the scale to a broad sample of adults. The higher the score, the more the tendency to self-conceal.

What advice does psychology have for people carrying around these emotional secrets? Should they bare their souls to someone or keep things under wraps? An interesting line of research suggests that carrying such secrets around with us may be hazardous to our physical health. James Pennebaker and his colleagues argue that many of us have experienced traumatic events in our lives (Pennebaker, 1989; Pennebaker & Hoover, 1986). Because it is customary to not burden others with our problems and because it might be too embarrassing to discuss them, most of us have not talked to many people—perhaps not to anyone—about our most traumatic experiences. But not talking about such an experience does not mean that we are unaffected by it. Several studies now suggest that holding emotions associated with traumatic experiences inside can be far worse for us than disclosing these feelings.

Researchers in one of these studies contacted people who had suffered the tragedy of losing a spouse either through an accidental death or because of suicide (Pennebaker & O'Heeron, 1984). Certainly such a tragedy has a tremendous impact on a person's life and must generate many thoughts and emotions. The researchers asked the subjects how much they had discussed the death with friends and about their health since the death. They found the more people had talked about the tragedy, the fewer health problems they had. Put another way, *not* talking to others about the disturbing experience was associated with *increased* health problems.

If it is the case that most of us actively conceal information about past traumatic events, then we might all be better off seeking out a close friend and talking about these secrets. To test this notion, Pennebaker and Beall (1986) asked a group of healthy undergraduates to write about themselves for 15 minutes each night for four consecutive November nights (the first part of the school year). Some of these students were instructed to write about relatively trivial topics (for example, a description of their living room). However, others were asked to write about an experience they found personally upsetting.

What impact did this writing exercise have on the students? First, measures of blood pressure and self-reported mood indicated that writing about a traumatic experience led to more stress and more negative moods immediately after the disclosure. This finding is consistent with past research (Pennebaker & Chew, 1985; Pennebaker, Hughes, & O'Heeron, 1987). It's not surprising that reliving a distressing event had more of an emotional impact than writing about a relatively trivial aspect of one's life. However, the investigators recontacted the students in May, six months after they had written about their experiences. Students were asked about how many illnesses they had had during the six months and about how many days they had been restricted because of an illness during this period. In addition, the number of visits each student had made to the campus health center was recorded.

The differences between the two groups are shown in Table 12.1. Students in the trivial-topic group had a significant increase in number of days restricted by illness and number of visits to the health center, but not the students who had written about their traumatic secrets. Similarly, only the disclosing students showed a decrease in the number of illnesses. In other words, although writing about their problems created some mild, short-term discomfort, it appears that the act of disclosing, even in the relatively mild form used in this experiment, was successful in improving the health of the already healthy college students. Similar results were obtained when researchers asked freshmen to write about the problems and emotions they encountered leaving home and adjusting to the student life style (Pennebaker, Colder, & Sharp, 1990). Subjects who wrote about these thoughts and emotions for three consecutive nights made fewer visits to the health center over the next several months than those who wrote about trivial topics.

Why does this disclosure of traumatic experiences, even when only written anonymously, result in such health benefits? Pennebaker (1989) argues that actively inhibiting thoughts and feelings about traumatic experiences requires a great deal of physiological work. Over time this results in a cumulative stress on the body, which means an increased likelihood of illness and other stress-related

Table 12.1

Long-Term Effects of Self-Disclosure on Health

	Trivial Topics Condition	Traumatic Topics Condition
Change in number of illnesses (before–after study)	+0.18	−0.60
Change in number of days restricted by illness	+4.00	+0.70
Number of visits to health center		
Before study	0.33	0.54
Following study	1.33	0.54

Source: Taken from Pennebaker and Beall (1986).

problems. Confronting the trauma releases the body from this work, resulting in a lowering of stress and an improved outlook for one's health.

But researchers find the benefits of disclosing traumatic experiences is not limited to physical health. One study revealed that people who tended to conceal negative information about themselves were more likely to suffer from depression and anxiety (Larson & Chastain, 1990). Such findings clearly have implications for psychotherapy. Pennebaker (1989) argues that talking or writing about traumatic events is an important step in working through trauma. Like Jourard, he maintains that putting our emotions into words allows us to better understand our feelings and perhaps to find meaning in our experience.

A pair of recent investigations tested this notion directly (Donnelly & Murray, 1991; Murray, Lamnin, & Carver, 1989). As in earlier studies, some subjects either wrote about traumatic experiences or wrote on trivial topics. In addition, other subjects discussed their traumatic experiences orally with a psychotherapist. Although the researchers found that both writing about the trauma and discussing it with a therapist helped subjects feel better about the experience and about themselves, the sessions with the therapist left the subjects in a better emotional state. That is, as in earlier studies, subjects who wrote about traumatic events had a short-term increase in negative emotion. However, those who expressed their feelings orally to a therapist did not show this effect. These findings suggest that although simply expressing one's emotions in words is one reason psychotherapy works for some people, there are additional benefits that come from talking with a trained therapist.

In summary, more than three decades of research on self-disclosure has discovered a great deal about how and why people reveal intimate information about themselves to others. In some cases, this research has found support for some of the ideas promoted by the humanistic personality theorists. For example, self-disclosure may help people come to understand themselves better and may be an important part of the psychotherapy process. Other humanistic positions have not fared as well. For example, people who make themselves "transparent" to others may not be as well adjusted as those who understand when to disclose and when to not disclose. Nonetheless, work on self-disclosure provides one example of how humanistic personality psychology has had an impact on the direction of personality research.

Loneliness

From time to time, we have all felt the pain of loneliness. Each of us has suffered through a time when there was no one to talk to, when everyone else seemed to be with someone while we were alone, when all of our relationships seemed superficial. Loneliness is a widespread problem in American society. One random survey of adults found 26% reported feeling "very lonely or remote from other people" during the preceding few weeks (Bradburn, 1969). Ironically, loneliness has become epidemic on college campuses. Despite the presence of people seemingly everywhere, 75% of the freshmen contacted at a large university two weeks into the school year said they had experienced loneliness since school began (Cutrona, 1982). More than 40% said their loneliness had been either moderate or severe.

Humanistic psychologists have been concerned with loneliness for a number of reasons. Humanistic psychology's rise in popularity in the 1960s may have been caused in part by an increase in feelings of alienation and loneliness that had begun to creep into the lives of many Americans (Bühler & Allen, 1972). People faced with an increasingly dehumanized, mechanistic society welcomed the humanists' emphasis on the individual with all of his or her unique potential. "I believe that individuals nowadays are probably more aware of their inner loneliness than has ever been true before in history," Carl Rogers wrote. "I see this as a surfacing of loneliness — just as we are probably more aware of interpersonal relationships than ever before" (1970, p. 106).

Some humanistic psychologists expect this concern with loneliness and interpersonal relations will continue as our society becomes more affluent. This prediction is based on Abraham Maslow's hierarchy of needs. As many members of our society become less concerned with the basic needs of shelter and job security, the need to develop meaningful and long-lasting relationships becomes more important. "When one is scrabbling for a living, uncertain as to where the next meal will come from, there is little time or inclination to discover that one is alienated from others in some deep sense," Rogers wrote. "But as affluence develops, and mobility, and the growth of increasingly transitory interpersonal systems instead of a settled life in the ancestral home town, men are more and more aware of their loneliness" (1970, pp. 106–107).

Some existential psychologists believe feelings of loneliness reflect a deeper concern about existential questions of alienation and a search for meaning in one's life (Sadler & Johnson, 1980). Humanistic therapists often help clients develop meaningful encounters to overcome loneliness (Moustakas, 1961, 1968). Perhaps the most notable development in this area was the growth of encounter groups in the late 1960s and early 1970s. Within the safe confines of the group, humanistic therapists helped members discover the richness of intimate interpersonal encounters with others and thereby learn something about themselves.

It would be incorrect to say that only humanistic psychologists have shown an interest in the phenomenon of loneliness. Psychoanalytic psychologists such as Frieda Fromm-Reichman (1959), Harry Stack Sullivan (1953), and Erich Fromm (1956/1974) also have written about the causes and effects of loneliness. Most recent research on loneliness has been conducted by investigators interested in interpersonal interaction patterns rather than humanistic psychology per se. Nonetheless, the research reviewed in this section has implications for many of the humanistic psychologists' concerns, particularly for therapists working with clients suffering from loneliness.

Defining and Measuring Loneliness

Loneliness is not the same as isolation. Some of the loneliest people are surrounded by others most of the day. Rather, loneliness concerns our perception of how much social interaction we have and the quality of that interaction. One team of investigators explained: "*Loneliness* occurs when a person's network of social relationships is *smaller* or *less satisfying* than the person desires" (Peplau, Russell, & Heim, 1979, p. 55, italics added). You can have very little contact with people, but if you are satisfied with that contact, you won't feel lonely. On the other hand, you may have many friends, yet still feel a need for more or deeper friendships and thus become lonely.

This description of loneliness helps to explain why some people who live in virtual isolation from other human beings find the solitude enjoyable, whereas other people who are surrounded by and who constantly interact with others experience loneliness. I commonly hear college students complain that while they have a lot of acquaintances and people to hang around with, they don't have many real *friends*. For these students, the unmet need to interact with that special person in an intimate and honest way can create intense feelings of being alone.

Loneliness is often caused by the circumstances people find themselves in, such as moving into a new city or attending a new school. But researchers soon discovered that loneliness can also be conceived of as a fairly stable personality trait. Although each of us feels lonely on occasion, and these feelings of loneliness come and go as circumstances change, each of us also appears to maintain a fairly stable susceptibility to these feelings. Thus, we can also think of loneliness as a personality variable. Some people are highly susceptible to feelings of loneliness and seem to chronically suffer from not having enough close friends. Other people are relatively immune from loneliness. Although they may experience loneliness in certain situations, feeling as if they have too few friends is rarely a problem.

Several personality inventories have been developed to assess the extent to which people generally feel lonely (Rubenstein & Shaver, 1980; Russell, Peplau,

& Cutrona, 1980; Russell, Peplau, & Ferguson, 1978; Schmidt & Sermat, 1983). Research with these scales (see pages 374–375) indicates that people who feel lonely today probably will feel lonely several weeks from now as well (Weeks, Michela, Peplau, & Bragg, 1980).

The Causes of Loneliness

This observation led investigators to the next question: What is it about chronically lonely people that keeps them in this state? Thus far, researchers have identified two characteristics of lonely people that seem to contribute to their loneliness. Lonely people tend to approach social interactions with overly harsh assessments of themselves and others. In addition, many lonely people lack some basic social skills, which may keep them from developing lasting friendships with others.

Negative Assessments of Self and Others No doubt you've met people you seemed to like right away and others who took a long time to understand and appreciate. We are naturally drawn to someone who comes across friendly and self-confident. Chances are good you'll want to get together with this person again and possibly develop a more personal relationship. However, you are much less likely to become friends with someone who is aloof and self-conscious and seems to show no interest in you. Yet investigators find that lonely people, who need friends the most, often come across like the latter example.

Correlations between measures of loneliness and other personality variables paint a drab and sullen picture of lonely people. High scores on loneliness scales are related to high scores on social anxiety and self-consciousness and low levels of self-esteem and assertiveness (Bruch, Kaflowitz, & Pearl, 1988; Jones, Freemon, & Goswick, 1981; Solano & Koester, 1989). Lonely people also are more likely to be introverted, anxious, and sensitive to rejection (Russell, Peplau, & Cutrona, 1980) and more likely to suffer from depression (Gerson & Perlman, 1979; Weeks, Michela, Peplau, & Bragg, 1980). Lonely people spend less time with friends, date less frequently, attend fewer parties, and have fewer close friends than do nonlonely people (Hoover, Skuja, & Cosper, 1979). They report difficulties making friends, initiating social activity, and participating in groups (Horowitz & de Sales French, 1979). Acquaintances of lonely people confirm the accuracy of these assessments. College students say their relationships with lonely people are noticeably less intimate than are those with nonlonely people (Williams & Solano, 1983).

What is it about lonely people that creates this unfriendly impression? One possibility is that they approach interpersonal encounters with excessively harsh assessments of both themselves and others (Goswick & Jones, 1981; Hanley-Dunn, Maxwell, & Santos, 1985; Jones, Freemon, & Goswick, 1981; Jones, Sansone, & Helm, 1983; Levin & Stokes, 1986). People who score high on loneliness measures tend to enter conversations with new acquaintances expecting that the other person won't like them. After all, they don't think very highly of themselves, why should this other person? Because of this, they show little interest in getting to know other people and are quick to end the conversation and move on to something else.

Loneliness

Schmidt and Sermat (1983) designed an inventory to measure loneliness in four types of situations: friendships, relationships with families, romantic-sexual relationships, and relationships with larger groups. You can take this shortened version of the Differential Loneliness Scale (student version) to assess your own level of loneliness in each of these areas.

Indicate T (true) or F (false) for each of the following statements depending on whether it accurately describes you or your situation. If an item is not applicable because you are not currently involved in the situation, score it F.

_____ 1. I feel close to members of my family.

_____ 2. I have a lover or spouse (boyfriend, girlfriend, husband, or wife) with whom I can discuss my important problems and worries.

_____ 3. I feel I really do not have much in common with the larger community in which I live.

_____ 4. I have little contact with members of my family.

_____ 5. I do not get along very well with my family.

_____ 6. I am now involved in a romantic or marital relationship where both of us are making a genuine effort at cooperation.

_____ 7. I have a good relationship with most members of my immediate family.

_____ 8. I do not feel that I can turn to my friends living around me for help when I need it.

_____ 9. No one in the community where I live seems to care much about me.

_____ 10. I allow myself to become close to friends.

Continued

These negative expectations also may lead lonely people to interpret any small sign as rejection. Subjects in one experiment spent five minutes talking with a stranger (Frankel & Prentice-Dunn, 1990). Later subjects saw a videotape of this person's evaluation of them. The videotape contained positive and negative comments. As expected, the lonely subjects paid attention to and recalled the negative feedback better than the nonlonely subjects. Because they believe their interactions have gone worse than they probably have, lonely people may be less likely than nonlonely people to pursue a friendship with someone they've met or seek out other people to do things with.

Given this negative approach to social interactions, it is not surprising that these people have such a difficult time making friends. This finding also helps to

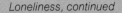
explain why loneliness is a problem for many students on crowded college campuses. With so many potential friends around, there is little reason to seek out and nurture the friendship of someone who appears to act so unfriendly.

Loneliness and Social Skills   You may be one of those lucky people for whom conversation comes easily. You may enjoy meeting and getting to know new people, effortlessly finding out about them while occasionally talking about yourself. If you are like this, then it may be difficult to understand people who have difficulty interacting with others. Even for people who are not shy and who would like to meet new friends, engaging in more than a short and trivial conversation can be a chore. What these people may lack are basic social skills,

Sometimes the loneliest people are those who are surrounded by others. But it would be wrong to assume that this man is feeling lonely. Some people need relatively little social contact to meet their needs.

the knowledge of *how* to carry on a conversation that both you and the other person will find valuable and enjoyable.

Several studies implicate just such a lack of social skills as part of what keeps lonely people in their cycle of loneliness. The best way to develop social skills is to practice conversing with others. Yet people without social skills may have such a difficult time developing relationships that they have little opportunity to develop their social skills. They never learn how to initiate an interaction or how to keep the conversation lively, and so their difficulty making friends continues.

Consider the interaction style one team of researchers found when they examined conversations with lonely and nonlonely people (Jones, Hobbs, & Hockenbury, 1982). Subjects who scored high on loneliness measures showed relatively little interest in their partners. They asked fewer questions about their partners, often failed to comment on what the partner said, and made fewer references to the partner. Instead, these lonely people were more likely to talk about themselves and introduce new topics unrelated to their partner's interests. Another study found that lonely people were more likely to give advice to strangers and less likely to acknowledge what the other person said when talking with their roommates (Sloan & Solano, 1984). In addition, lonely people tend to take on a "passive interpersonal role" (Vitkus & Horowitz, 1987). That is, they don't make much of an effort to get involved in a conversation. Little wonder, then, that we often fail to enjoy conversations with lonely people. It's not that lonely people are intentionally rude, but rather that they don't understand how their interaction style turns away potential friends.

Other researchers have examined the way lonely and nonlonely people use self-disclosure. You will recall most people understand and follow social rules about when and how much to disclose about themselves. However, people who suffer from loneliness are not very aware of these rules (Chelune, Sultan, & Williams, 1980; Solano & Koester, 1989; Wittenberg & Reis, 1986). Because of this, they may disclose too much when it is not called for or fail to reveal enough about themselves when the other person expects it. Consequently, others may see them as either weird or aloof and respond accordingly.

Similar findings emerge when researchers examine the *amount* of self-disclosure used by lonely and nonlonely people. Lonely people generally reveal less about themselves than do their partners (Berg & Peplau, 1982; Sloan & Solano, 1984). Lack of self-disclosure may be a particular problem for lonely people when interacting with members of the opposite sex. In one study, lonely people selected relatively nonintimate topics to talk about in a mixed-sex conversation (Solano, Batten, & Parish, 1982). Not surprisingly, the lonely subjects' partners reciprocated with nonintimate topics as well. Imagine how this might work on a first date. Instead of allowing their dates to get to know something intimate about themselves, lonely people might keep the conversation centered on how they are doing in certain classes or where they went on their vacation. Of course, revealing too much about themselves too soon will put people off. But failing to progress past the most nonintimate topics on a date probably means a second date is not forthcoming.

In summary, lonely people appear caught in a cycle that perpetuates their problems and helps to explain why feelings of loneliness tend to be fairly stable over time. Lonely people fail to develop close friendships because they approach conversations with negative expectancies and because they lack the necessary social skills. Interacting with these people often is not enjoyable, and so they have difficulty establishing social relations that might help them develop their social skills and thereby break out of their loneliness cycle. Initial efforts to provide lonely people with a way out of this pattern through basic social skills training have been promising (Rook & Peplau, 1982; Young, 1982). These programs provide some hope that loneliness need not be the chronic condition that now traps millions of people in a self-perpetuating cycle of despair.

Real-Ideal Self Congruence

Let's pause here for a quick exercise. Select the five descriptions from the following list that best describe you:

Creative	Insightful
Decisive	Self-confident
Disciplined	Sensitive
Friendly	Shy
Independent	Socially skilled

Now, go back over the list and select five terms you would *like* to have describe you. That is, if you could reconstruct your personality in whatever way you wanted, how would you like to measure up on these dimensions? The interesting part of this exercise is not so much what you think you are or what you would like to be, but, in Carl Rogers's terms, how similar your real and ideal selves are — your **real-ideal self congruence.** If your description of what you are is very similar to what you would like to be, then we would say there is a high congruence between these two selves. However, if what you perceive yourself to be is not at all like the person you have always hoped to be, then your real-ideal self congruence is low. A large gap between real and ideal selves is often the source of dreams, but it also is typical of clients who seek out Rogerian psychotherapy.

According to Rogers, if you understand who you are and who you want to be, and if you then bring these two together, you are on your way to becoming well adjusted and fully functioning. Therapy is said to be working as the gap closes between what people see themselves to be and what they want to be. Clients may come to see that they expect too much of themselves and thus bring their ideal self more in line with their real self. Or during the course of therapy they may become more open and accepting of who they are and hence stop aspiring to be something they are not.

Thus, one measure of well-being within a Rogerian framework is the extent to which a person's real and ideal selves are similar. Karen Horney (1950) shared Rogers's concern for falling short of one's ideal self. According to Horney, psychologically healthy people strive to reach an ideal self that is reasonably attainable. On the other hand, neurotics set unreachable standards for themselves and therefore are perpetually short of what they think they want to be.

Given this emphasis on changing real and ideal selves during psychotherapy, it should not be surprising that the original research on this topic looked at clients undergoing Rogerian therapy (Rogers & Dymond, 1954). However, more recent findings from developmental psychology have thrown a curve at the idea that a small real-ideal self discrepancy is indicative of a well-adjusted person. Just how researchers have come to account for all of these discrepant findings illustrates the complexity of human behavior and the importance of examining personality from more than one perspective.

Real-Ideal Self Congruence and Adjustment

The Rogerian position is fairly straightforward: The more congruence between a person's real and ideal selves, the better adjusted that person is. Early research on the progress of therapy clients uncovered a great deal of support for this position. For example, researchers in one study used a Q-Sort to measure real-ideal self congruence just before clients began person-centered therapy (Butler & Haigh, 1954). The correlation between the real and ideal selves ranged from .59 for one client, a fairly substantial correlation, to − .47 for another, a strongly negative correlation. The average for all clients was − .01. This finding means that before entering therapy, there was virtually no relationship between what these clients saw themselves to be and what they wanted to be.

The clients were given the Q-Sort again after several weeks of counseling. Although some clients still showed small or negative correlations between their real and ideal Q-Sorts, the average correlation after therapy was .34. In 22 of the 25 cases, clients showed an increase in similarity between their real and ideal selves. When these clients were tested once again several months after completing counseling, the average correlation between real and ideal selves was .31, indicating the long-term nature of the change. A Q-Sort given to a control group not seeking counseling showed no change in real-ideal congruence over the same period of time.

A more elaborate investigation of how real and ideal selves change during therapy used six groups of subjects (Butler, 1968). Three groups received person-centered therapy, a fourth received treatment based on Alfred Adler's approach, and two groups served as controls. One control group was made up of subjects who suffered from no apparent psychological problems. The second control group was comprised of people who had sought psychotherapy but had been placed on a 10-week waiting list. This group was tested at the beginning and the end of the 10-week waiting period.

Why was this latter group included in the study? Because these subjects were suffering from psychological distress at the time of the first testing, they were similar to subjects receiving therapy. It is crucial to demonstrate that these people do not show the same changes over time as those in therapy. Otherwise, the improvements found in the therapy clients could be attributed to time rather than therapy. However, if the subjects receiving therapy improve, but the ones on the waiting list do not, then we have evidence for the effectiveness of the treatment.

The results of the study are presented in Table 12.2. All three of the person-centered therapy groups and the group receiving Adlerian therapy showed noticeable improvement in reducing their real- and ideal-self discrepancies. However, the two control groups showed virtually no change over the course of the study. This suggests that the therapy, and not just time, was responsible for the reduction in discrepancy in the other clients.

As always, we should remember that these are average correlations. Although the majority of clients were helped, there are always clients who show no improvement or who show even greater discrepancy as therapy progresses. However, by and large, these studies provide evidence for the efficacy of person-centered therapy and the Rogerian notion of personal adjustment as defined by real-ideal self congruence.

But is real-ideal self congruence a useful indicator of adjustment only for clients undergoing psychotherapy? The answer appears to be no. Researchers in one study compared normal subjects with high and low real-ideal self congruence for how they scored on the Minnesota Multiphasic Personality Inventory and the California Psychological Inventory (Gough, Fioravanti, & Lazzari, 1983). Low real-ideal congruence was associated with self-doubt, social withdrawal, anxiety, and depression. In another investigation, Air Force officers with high and low congruence were compared (Gough, Lazzari, & Fioravanti, 1978). The officers with a high congruence between their real and ideal selves were described by others as cooperative, adaptable, outgoing, and efficient. Those with low congruence were

When I accept myself as I am, then I change.
CARL ROGERS

Table 12.2

Mean Real-Ideal Self Correlations for Six Groups of Subjects

Group	Type of Therapy	Initial Real-Ideal Self Correlation	Final Real-Ideal Self Correlation
Therapy	Person-centered	−.04	.32
Therapy	Person-centered	.05	.44
Therapy — 10 weeks	Person-centered	.04	.26
Therapy	Adlerian	.05	.35
Normal control	None	.58	.59
Client control	None	−.04	.03

Source: From Butler (1968); reprinted by permission of *Psychotherapy*.

seen as slow, awkward, confused, and unfriendly. Similar patterns are found when looking at real-ideal self congruence and ratings of life satisfaction among college students, particularly when students perceive a large difference between what they are and what they *don't* want to be (Ogilvie, 1987).

Why is real-ideal self congruence associated with good adjustment? Rogers maintained it was because people with little discrepancy between what they are and what they want to be have come to understand and accept themselves and no longer hold themselves up to impossibly high standards. More recently, E. Tory Higgins and his colleagues have described this relationship in terms of vulnerability to emotional distress (Higgins, 1989a, 1989b; Higgins, Bond, Klein, & Strauman, 1986). According to this interpretation, people with a large discrepancy between their real and ideal selves are more likely to interpret negative information in a manner that highlights this discrepancy and makes them aware of their feelings of low self-worth. In other words, people who see a large gap between what they are and what they want to be are constantly reminded of this fact. They see ads with attractive people on television and think about how much less attractive they are than they would like to be. People who have come to appreciate who they are pay less attention to this information.

Although Higgins and his colleagues base their interpretation on a cognitive model of personality (Chapter 15), many of his research findings are consistent with Rogers's description of how real- and ideal-self discrepancy relates to personal adjustment. For example, subjects with a large discrepancy between their real and ideal selves were found to have the lowest levels of self-esteem (Moretti & Higgins, 1990). Other studies find that a large inconsistency between one's real and ideal selves may indicate a vulnerability to a wide variety of psychological disorders, including eating disorders (Strauman, Vookles, Berenstein, Chaiken, & Higgins, 1991), depression and anxiety (Higgins, Klein, & Strauman, 1985; Strauman, 1989).

In sum, evidence from a variety of studies provides support for Rogers's theory. If the way you see yourself is similar to the way you would like to be, then you probably are well on your way to being a well-adjusted, fully functioning person. If not, Rogerian psychotherapy may be effective in bringing your real and ideal selves closer together and thereby returning you to the path of well-being and happiness. Unfortunately, as we will see in the next section, the relationship between real-ideal self discrepancy and personal adjustment is not this simple.

Real-Ideal Self Congruence and Cognitive Development

The first dent in the Rogerian package on real-ideal self congruence was reported by researchers who measured real-ideal self congruence in hospital patients (Achenbach & Zigler, 1963). The investigators divided patients into those high in social competence and those low in social competence, as based on measures of intelligence, occupation, employment history, and so on. Not surprisingly, people high in social competence scored differently on the real-ideal congruency measures than did those low in social competence. The surprise was that the socially competent people had *greater* discrepancies between their real and ideal selves than did the less socially competent ones.

A similar contradiction was uncovered in research on students at different age levels (Katz & Zigler, 1967). We would expect from the Rogerian position that the older and more mature the student, the more similar the person's real and ideal selves. However, when fifth-, eighth-, and eleventh-graders were compared, the older students had the *largest* discrepancies between real and ideal selves. Further, the more intelligent the student, the more the student's real and ideal selves differed. Similarly, larger real-ideal self discrepancies have been found in children who approach tasks in a thoughtful and mature manner (Katz, Zigler, & Zalk, 1975), in those who are less egocentric in their thoughts (Leahy & Huard, 1976), and in those who use more mature judgment about moral issues (Leahy, 1981).

In short, research on congruence between real and ideal selves has resulted in two basic findings which, unfortunately, show little congruence. A large number of studies indicate that a high level of real-ideal self congruence is indicative of a well-adjusted, happy person. But another considerable amount of work suggests real-ideal self congruence is indicative of immaturity, poor social competence, and low intelligence. How can this be resolved?

One solution to this puzzle is suggested if we think about the subjects in terms of their cognitive development (Katz & Zigler, 1967). There are two parts to this explanation. First, as we mature and develop intellectually, we develop the capacity for internalizing the standards and values we live by. The older we get, the more likely we are to become aware of how our behavior fails to meet those standards and the more likely we are to experience guilt. In other words, a mature person is aware of the difference between behavior (real self) and internal standards of behavior (ideal self). Parents who have pleaded with four-year-olds to do what they are supposed to do understand this gap all too well. Most four-year-olds are incapable of developing clear internal standards of behavior and then comparing what they do with those standards. Parents must act as enforcers of the rules and overseers of activities until children develop the cognitive maturity to do these things for themselves.

The second part of the explanation concerns complexity of thought patterns. At higher levels of cognitive development, people use more cognitive categories and make finer distinctions when perceiving events. Intelligent, mature people don't see the world in simple, black-and-white categories. Because they see much finer distinctions, they are more likely than less mature people to see differences between their real and ideal selves. It may be that less mature people also have large differences between their real and ideal selves, but they aren't able to perceive them as well as people who have a higher level of cognitive development. Again, ask young children to describe their performance at a game or activity and you may be surprised to find that they all think they have done very well, objective evidence to the contrary. For these children, their real selves are doing just fine when compared to their ideal selves.

So it seems higher levels of cognitive development are a mixed blessing. While cognitive maturity brings better self-perception and greater ability to deal with problems, it also brings a greater awareness of our limits and the capacity for self-derogation, guilt, and anxiety. Some people retain feelings of self-worth because they do not see their shortcomings. Others are keenly aware of how they differ from what they would like to be. Clients who report low levels of real-ideal self congruence at the beginning of therapy have sufficient cognitive maturity to recognize the difficulties in their lives and the discrepancy between how they see themselves and what they would like to be. However, if Rogers is correct, they also have the ability to resolve many of their problems and bring their real selves and ideal selves more in line with one another.

Self-Esteem

If there is a single concept that threads its way through the writings of the humanistic psychologists, it may be how the individual feels about himself or herself. A central goal of Rogerian psychotherapy is to get clients to accept and appreciate themselves for what they are. Maslow wrote about the need for self-respect and admiration and the need to feel content about who we are and what we do with our lives. He identified these as some of the higher-order needs leading to happiness and contentment. In short, humanistic personality theory is concerned about the individual's **self-esteem**. Most researchers draw a distinction between *self-esteem* and *self-concept*. Your self-concept is the cumulation of what you perceive to be your personal characteristics, that is, the kind of person you believe yourself to be. Self-esteem refers to your evaluation of your self-concept. In essence, do you like the kind of person you believe yourself to be?

Although we often speak of self-esteem in our everyday conversations, researchers face several challenges when trying to identify and measure this concept. One problem is that the way we feel about ourselves can change from one situation to the next. Most people get a little down on themselves when they act in a way they know they shouldn't, and most of us can't help but think well of ourselves when someone heaps praise on us for a job well done. Probably everyone has occasional good and bad self-esteem days. Because of this variability, some researchers examine what they call *state*, as compared with *trait*, self-esteem (Heatherton & Polivy, 1991).

However, as with other personality variables, we also can identify a relatively stable level of self-esteem in most people. That is, some people are prone to more positive self-evaluations than others. They may have bad days and disappoint themselves on occasion, but in general they like themselves and feel good about who they are and what they do. These people score high on measures of self-esteem. We also can identify people who frequently experience negative self-evaluations. Although these low self-esteem people also have good days and feel good about much of what they do, compared to others they seem to lack a basic confidence in themselves and appreciation for who they are.

Another issue facing personality researchers concerns global versus domain-specific self-esteem. Very few people feel entirely good or bad about themselves. All of us can point to deficiencies and weaknesses, and all of us can identify things we like about ourselves. Researchers often find it useful to break self-esteem into specific areas. For example, one widely used self-esteem scale, the *Tennessee Self-Concept Scale,* generates separate scores for how test takers feel about themselves in the family, physical, social, moral, and personal parts of their lives (Marsh & Richards, 1988). Although identifying specific areas of self-esteem may provide researchers and therapists with additional insight into a person's feelings about himself or herself, researchers typically assess a person's overall self-esteem, or *global self-esteem*. The research reviewed in this chapter is concerned with the subjects' global self-esteem.

Perhaps because how we feel about ourselves is a central concern of psycho-therapists, educators, parents, and others, a large amount of research has been conducted on the topic of self-esteem. We'll try to get a flavor of some of that research by looking at two recent areas of self-esteem research here. We'll examine how self-esteem affects our reactions to failure and some differences in what motivates high and low self-esteem people.

Self-Esteem and Reaction to Failure

Although many people dislike it, evaluation has become an unavoidable part of most of our lives. After only a few years of elementary school, most students have become accustomed to having their schoolwork evaluated by teachers. Evaluation by a superior is commonplace in the business world today, if not overtly in the form of an annual evaluation, then implicitly in the size of one's raise. Any type of competition, from sports to chess to gardening, brings with it the possibility of both victory and defeat as we compare our abilities and accomplishments against those of others. All of this evaluation means that each of us has experienced our share of successes and failures. But not all people react the same to these evaluations. In particular, research suggests that your self-esteem level plays an important role in how you respond to this information.

Low Self-Esteem and Failure   Several laboratory experiments have looked at how high and low self-esteem people react to being told they have done well or poorly on a test (Brockner, 1979; Shrauger & Rosenberg, 1970; Shrauger & Sorman, 1977). Subjects in these studies usually take a test supposedly measuring some intellectual ability, or work on a task that is either relatively easy or relatively difficult. Researchers then give bogus feedback to subjects indicating that they have done either very well or rather poorly. Subjects are then given a second task to work on. Investigators find that low self-esteem subjects don't try as hard, perform more poorly, and are more likely to give up on the second task when they think they have failed the first test. In contrast, high self-esteem people typically work just as hard regardless of how they think they performed on the first test.

The importance of such findings to the lives of college students was illustrated in a study examining students' reactions to their midterm exam grades (Brockner, Derr, & Laing, 1987). Students took a self-esteem test at the beginning of the semester, but the experimenters did not inform the students about the results or purpose of the test at that time. The students took their first exam for the class five weeks into the term and received their grade for the exam one week later. The researchers found that high and low self-esteem students performed almost identically on this test. The investigators then divided the students into those who had done well on the test (received an A or a B) and those who had not done as well (received a C or lower). The researchers wanted to know if the low self-esteem students would react to their low score on the test with the same decrease in motivation low self-esteem laboratory subjects showed when told they had done poorly. That is, would they more or less "give up" on the class and perform more poorly on the next test?

As shown in Figure 12.2, the answer is yes. Low self-esteem subjects who did well on the first test continued to perform as well as the high self-esteem subjects on the second test. However, low self-esteem subjects who had not done well on the first test did significantly worse than their high self-esteem counterparts on the second exam. Another investigation found low self-esteem students also experienced stronger negative emotions (for example, sadness) and reported less motivation to try on the next test than high self-esteem students when both groups did poorly on a midterm exam (Kernis, Brockner, & Frankel, 1989).

Yet another study found that low self-esteem people did not have to actually experience a failure to show these negative effects, but rather only had to imagine that they had failed (Campbell & Fairey, 1985). Subjects in this experiment were asked to imagine they had done well or poorly on a 25-item anagram test. Low self-esteem subjects who imagined failing said they expected to do poorly on the real test, and indeed performed more poorly on the test compared to low self-esteem subjects who first imagined they had done well.

Explaining the Different Reactions   A substantial amount of research demonstrates that people low in self-esteem become discouraged and unmotivated when they receive negative feedback about a performance. However, high self-esteem people seem relatively unphased when told they have not done well on a test or when they discover they can't do well on a challenging task. How can we explain this difference?

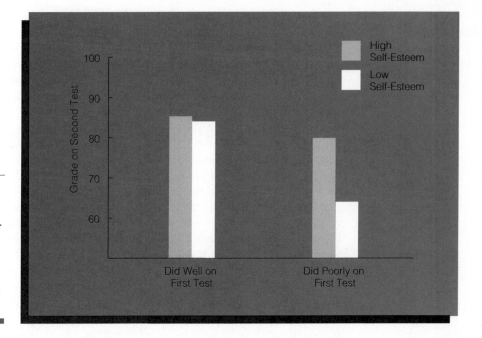

Figure 12.2

Performance on Second Test as a Function of Self-Esteem and Performance on First Test.

Adapted from Brockner et al. (1987).

One explanation for these different reactions to failure is that people are more likely to accept feedback consistent with their self-concepts (McFarlin & Blascovich, 1981). Someone with a low self-esteem probably expects to fail, or believes that he or she is the kind of person who fails more than succeeds. Consequently, it is easier for low self-esteem people to believe feedback confirming their negative self-images than information that violates their expectations.

Another way to look at this is to say that the negative feedback reminds low self-esteem people of the negative evaluations they have of themselves (Kernis et al., 1989). This feedback triggers associations with other negative thoughts, reminding the low self-esteem person of other faults and weaknesses. According to this explanation, people low in self-esteem become discouraged and unmotivated generally after receiving information about failing on a specific task. This explanation helps us understand why low self-esteem people perform more poorly on a task even when they have just imagined what it would be like to fail first.

But we can also turn this question around. What is it about *high* self-esteem people that *prevents* them from becoming discouraged after failure? Why don't they give up or look for their reinforcement elsewhere when they fail a test or do poorly at work? Some recent research indicates that high self-esteem people have developed personal strategies for blunting the effect of negative feedback. Included in this arsenal is a tendency to respond to failure by focusing attention on their good qualities rather than what they have done wrong. Thus, whereas negative feedback causes the people low in self-esteem to think about their faults and failures, this same feedback can lead high self-esteem people to think about their abilities and achievements.

The high self-esteem strategy was demonstrated in some recent experiments (Brown & Gallagher, 1992; Brown & Smart, 1991; Schlenker, Weigold, & Hallam, 1990). As in earlier studies, subjects in one experiment received feedback indicating they had performed either well or poorly on an achievement test (Brown & Smart, 1991). Subjects then were asked how well a series of adjectives described them. Some adjectives were related to achievement situations (for example, competent, intelligent), and others were relevant for social situations (for example, sincere, kind). The results for the social-attribute ratings are shown in Figure 12.3. As expected, the low self-esteem subjects tended to rate themselves poorly after discovering they had failed the test. However, the high self-esteem subjects actually rated themselves *higher* on their social attributes after failing than when they thought they had done well on the test.

These results demonstrate one tactic high self-esteem people use to maintain their feelings of high self-worth even in the face of negative feedback. When told they did not do well in one area, these subjects reminded themselves of how well they do in other areas. It is important to recognize that these high self-esteem subjects did not simply ignore the test feedback and enhance their feelings of self-worth in achievement areas. Instead, they appeared to think about what they were good at rather than where they occasionally fall down. If they mess up at work, high self-esteem people might remind themselves that they have a lot of friends. If they lose badly at handball, they might recall how well they play chess. This strategy keeps high self-esteem people feeling good about themselves even when faced with life's inevitable downturns.

Self-Enhancement and Self-Protection Motives

I recently encountered a situation that illustrates another important difference between high and low self-esteem people. As a Little League manager watching the members of my new team playing catch, I became particularly impressed with one player. This boy clearly was able to throw the ball faster, farther, and more accurately than most players his age. As a rule, nearly every Little Leaguer wants to be a pitcher. And so I was a little surprised to find that this boy quickly turned me down when I asked him if he wanted to try pitching sometime. He clearly had the talent but was adamant in his decision to not pitch. As I learned more about this player during the season and by talking to his parents, I came to understand his decision. Although the pitcher is the center of attention during the game and provides the greatest opportunity to show off what you can do, it was this very spotlight that the boy wanted to avoid. Despite his abilities, the boy suffered from low self-esteem. The possibility that he might not do well in front of everyone was far too threatening for him to take advantage of the possibility that he might perform quite well.

As this example illustrates, high self-esteem and low self-esteem people may be motivated by very different concerns. More specifically, some researchers have proposed that people high in self-esteem are motivated by a concern for *self-enhancement* (Baumeister, Tice, & Hutton, 1989). That is, high self-esteem people are interested in enhancing their prestige and public image. They want others to think well of them, to admire them, and to praise them when they do something well.

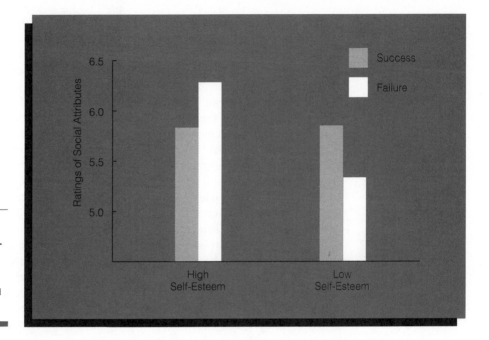

Figure 12.3

Ratings of Social Attributes Following Success and Failure.

Adapted from Brown and Smart (1991).

But certainly people low in self-esteem want this admiration as well. We all enjoy hearing others say nice things about us, and knowing that other people respect and admire us. Nonetheless, many investigations suggest that low self-esteem people are much less likely than those high in self-esteem to take advantage of opportunities to show off and let others see how good they are. Why is this? The answer is that people low in self-esteem are likely to be motivated by a concern for *self-protection*. In other words, these people are concerned about protecting themselves from public humiliation and embarrassment. Opportunities to be in the public spotlight create the possibility of drawing praise and admiration from others. But these same opportunities also carry the risk that we will fail or look foolish, thus leading to public dislike or ridicule. When push comes to shove, the low self-esteem person's need for self-protection is likely to win out over his or her need to look good.

The different motives behind high self-esteem and low self-esteem people's behavior has been illustrated in a series of experiments on a phenomenon known as *self-handicapping* (Baumeister & Tice, 1990; Harris & Snyder, 1986; Rhodewalt, Morf, Hazlett, & Fairfield, 1991; Tice, 1991). People self-handicap when they deliberately hurt their chances of performing well on a task, such as by not preparing well for a test or turning up distracting music while working on a task requiring concentration. These actions obviously reduce the person's chances for success, but they also provide a reasonable excuse in case of failure. If I don't practice at all the week before a tennis tournament, then I can say that my poor showing reflects the lack of practice rather than a lack of ability. It's not as good as winning, but it's better than losing without an excuse.

If low self-esteem people are concerned about self-protection, we might speculate they would be prone to self-handicap when they are concerned about a negative evaluation. Indeed, there is some evidence for this (Harris & Snyder, 1986). However, there is also evidence that high self-esteem people often self-handicap (Baumeister & Tice, 1990). Why might someone with a high self-esteem deliberately create obstacles for himself or herself? The answer is that self-handicapping also provides an opportunity for self-enhancement. Beating your opponent at tennis even without practicing, or doing well on the concentration test even when distracting music is blaring, is more impressive than doing well after a great deal of practice or under ideal circumstances.

We might conclude from this analysis that people with a low self-esteem sometimes create obstacles for themselves because of their concern for self-protection, whereas people with a high self-esteem do this because of their need for self-enhancement. A recent set of studies found support for this prediction (Tice, 1991). Subjects in one of these studies were given as much time as they wanted to practice on a hand-and-eye coordination task before being tested. Low self-esteem subjects self-handicapped (that is, practiced very little) when they were told the test was designed to identify people who are deficient in this ability. On the other hand, the high self-esteem subjects reduced their amount of practicing when told the test could only identify people who were good at this kind of task.

In summary, the research reviewed here illustrates some of the important difference between high and low self-esteem people. Because they are worried about negative feedback, people with a low self-esteem are likely to avoid situations in which they might look bad in front of others. If avoiding evaluation is not possible, low self-esteem people often create obstacles or excuses in an effort to reduce the impact of any negative feedback. However, when all of their efforts fail and negative feedback comes, low self-esteem people are likely to become discouraged and upset. In contrast, people with a high self-esteem are eager to perform well in front of others and do what they can to receive praise and admiration. Although high self-esteem people obviously do not like to fail, they seem to have strategies at hand that keep their self-esteems high even when objective feedback might argue otherwise.

Summary

1. Although humanistic psychologists often shun empirical research, research on topics introduced or promoted by these psychologists has provided insight into some important aspects of humanistic personality theory.

2. Sidney Jourard and other humanistic therapists argued that self-disclosure is an important aspect of mental health and therefore should be part of the psychotherapy process. Research on self-disclosure finds that people tend to follow social rules concerning when and how to reveal information about themselves.

Foremost among these is the rule of disclosure reciprocity. People in a get-acquainted situation tend to match the intimacy level of the person they are talking to. However, friends who have already shared intimate information in a reciprocal manner need not always return to this pattern. Other studies find men and women are restricted in what they disclose by what society deems appropriate. The most well-adjusted people may be those who understand when self-disclosure is appropriate and when it is not. Finally, holding traumatic secrets inside may take its toll on a person's health.

3. Loneliness is not the same as isolation. Researchers define loneliness as a discrepancy between the amount and quality of social contact we desire and the amount and quality we receive. Although loneliness is influenced by social situations, people tend to suffer from loneliness at a fairly stable level. Research on chronically lonely people indicates that they approach conversations with an overly harsh assessment of themselves and others and that they lack some basic social skills. Because of this tendency, they inadvertently stifle social interactions and discourage potential friends.

4. Carl Rogers argued that well-adjusted people show little discrepancy between their real selves and their ideal selves. Consistent with this part of his theory, progress in therapy has been tied to increased congruence between the way clients see themselves and the way they would like to be. However, other studies indicate that larger discrepancies between real and ideal selves are associated with greater maturity and intelligence. These contradictory findings can be reconciled by understanding that cognitive maturity provides the ability to see real- and ideal-self discrepancies.

5. A great deal of research has been conducted on individual differences in self-esteem. One example of this is research on how high and low self-esteem people react to failure. This research finds that low self-esteem people become discouraged and unmotivated when they receive negative feedback, whereas high self-esteem people employ tactics to blunt the effects of failure. Researchers also find that high self-esteem people often are motivated by a concern for self-enhancement and low self-esteem people often are more concerned about self-protection.

Key Terms

self-disclosure The act of revealing intimate information about oneself to another person.

disclosure reciprocity Matching a conversation partner's self-disclosing intimacy level.

loneliness Unpleasant feelings brought about by a perceived discrepancy between desired and achieved social interaction.

real-ideal self congruence The extent to which a person's perception of himself or herself resembles the way he or she would like to be.

self-esteem Evaluation of one's self-concept, usually measured in terms of a relatively stable and global assessment of how a person feels about himself or herself.

Suggested Readings

Baumeister, R. F., Tice, D. M., & Hutton, D. G. (1989). Self-presentational motivations and personality differences in self-esteem. *Journal of Personality 57*, 547–579. The authors present the case that high and low self-esteem individuals differ in terms of their self-presentation motives. Past research is reviewed in support of this position.

Derlega, V. J., & Berg, J. H. (Eds.). (1987). *Self-disclosure: Theory, research, and therapy.* New York: Plenum. This edited volume contains chapters written by some of the leading researchers in the self-disclosure area. Chapters review research on several aspects of self-disclosure and its applications, with particular relevance for the role self-disclosure plays in psychotherapy.

Jourard, S. M. (1971). *The transparent self* (2nd ed.). New York: Van Nostrand. A very readable book in which humanistic psychotherapist Sidney Jourard argues that we should all strive to make ourselves "transparent" through self-disclosure. Jourard relates self-disclosure to a wide range of topics, including mental health, gender roles, physical health, psychotherapy, and health professionals.

Pennebaker, J. W. (1989). Confession, inhibition, and disease. In L. Berkowitz (Ed.), *Advances in experimental social psychology Vol. 22* (pp. 211–244). New York: Academic Press. Pennebaker reviews the theory and research on the effects of concealing or disclosing traumatic experiences. He draws from several theoretical models to explain the effects of disclosure and discusses the implications of this research for such areas as psychotherapy and education.

The Behavioral/Social Learning Approach

Theory, Application, and Assessment

13

What do the following scenes have in common? A hospital patient suffering from depression makes his bed in the morning, dresses himself, and shows up to breakfast on time. A staff member hands the patient three tickets for completing these three acts. A third-grade student sits in front of a video display screen. Math problems are presented on the screen in a preprogrammed order. She presses buttons to indicate her answers and receives immediate feedback as to whether she has solved the problem. An animal trainer is preparing a new dog for a circus act. He wants the animal to play a song on a small piano by learning to press the right keys. He begins by giving the hungry dog a piece of food whenever it sits in front of the piano. Finally, a college student declines her friends' request to join them at a cocktail lounge after dinner. She knows people will be smoking there and is trying to break her habit.

In each of these scenes, someone is attempting to modify behavior by applying basic principles from behaviorism. The list of psychology topics that have been examined from a behaviorist's perspective includes attitude change, language acquisition, psychotherapy, student-teacher interactions, problem solving, gender roles, and job satisfaction. Naturally, such a far-reaching approach to the understanding of human behavior also provides a model for explaining why people engage in consistent behavior patterns, that is, personality.

Early behaviorists limited their descriptions of personality to consistent patterns in observable behaviors. Later theorists expanded this position to include more cognitive and social features. In particular, Albert Bandura and Julian Rotter developed their own "social learning" theories of personality. These theories include such nonobservable concepts as thoughts, values, expectancies, and individual perceptions. However, because these later theories were built on a behaviorist foundation, we will consider them together in this chapter.

Behaviorism

In 1913 a young and brash psychologist named John B. Watson published an article entitled "Psychology as the Behaviorist Views It." This article signaled the beginning of a new movement in psychology — behaviorism. By 1924, with the

John B. Watson
1878–1958

As a child growing up in Greenville, South Carolina, John Broadus Watson exhibited two characteristics that would later come to shape his career — he was a fighter and a builder. He once wrote that his favorite activity in elementary school was fighting with classmates "until one or the other drew blood." But by age 12 he also had become something of a master carpenter. Later, during his first few years as a psychology professor, he built his own 10-room house virtually by himself.

Watson's lack of enthusiasm for contemporary standards also surfaced early. In grammar school, "I was lazy, somewhat insubordinate, and, so far as I know, I never made above a passing grade." He also found that "little of my college life interested me . . . I was unsocial and had few close friends" (1936, p. 271). Watson bragged about being the only student to pass the Greek exam his senior year at Furman University. His secret was to cram the entire day before the test, powered only by a quart of Coca-Cola. "Today," he reported years

Continued

publication of his book *Behaviorism*, Watson had made significant progress in his effort to redefine the discipline. He argued that if psychology were to be a science, then psychologists must stop examining mental states. Researchers who concerned themselves with consciousness, the mind, and thoughts were not engaging in legitimate scientific study. Only the observable was reasonable subject matter for a science. Because our subjective inner feelings cannot be observed or measured in any kind of agreed-upon, accurate manner, they have no place in an objective science. The sooner psychology abandons these topics, Watson maintained, the sooner it can become a respectable member of the scientific community.

What, then, was the appropriate subject matter for psychology? Watson's answer was overt behavior — that which can be observed, predicted, and eventu-

later, " . . . I couldn't to save my life write the Greek alphabet or conjugate a verb" (1936, p. 272).

Watson began his doctoral work in philosophy at the University of Chicago, in part because Princeton required a reading knowledge of Greek. He soon switched to psychology, where, unlike his classmates, he preferred working with rats instead of human subjects. "Can't I find out by watching their behavior," he asked, "everything the other students are finding out?" (1936, p. 276).

Watson joined the faculty at Johns Hopkins University in 1908, where he began his quest to replace the psychology of the day with his new behavioral approach. His views received a surprisingly warm welcome from many scholars and academics, and in 1912 he was invited to give a series of public lectures on his theory at Columbia University. He published an influential paper, "Psychology as the Behaviorist Views It," in 1913 and his first book in 1914. Within a few years, behaviorism swept over the discipline.

Watson was elected president of the American Psychological Association in 1915. Watson the fighter had taken on contemporary psychology and won, while Watson the builder had constructed an approach to the understanding of human behavior that would change the discipline of psychology for many decades to come.

But his academic career was cut short in 1920. Watson suddenly divorced his wife of 17 years and married Rosalie Rayner, with whom he had conducted the Little Albert experiments. The scandal that surrounded these actions forced Watson out of an intolerant Johns Hopkins and into the business world, where he eventually settled into a successful career in advertising. After writing a few popular articles, and a book in 1925, Watson severed his ties with psychology while still in his early 40s. But more than 60 years later, the foundation he built for the behavioral approach to personality still stands.

ally controlled by scientists. We should recognize just how much of psychology Watson was ready to jettison in his quest. Emotions, thoughts, expectancies, values, reasoning, insight, the unconscious, and the like were of interest to behaviorists only if they could be defined in terms of observable behaviors. Thus, according to Watson, thinking was simply a variant of verbal behavior, a "subvocal speech," as evidenced by the small vocal-cord movements he claimed accompanied it.

At about this same time, other researchers had begun to examine basic processes of conditioning, or learning. Watson embraced these principles as the key to understanding human behavior. Like Watson, these researchers focused their efforts on predicting overt behaviors without introducing inner mental states to explain their findings. The famous Russian physiologist Ivan Pavlov demonstrated that animals could be made to respond to stimuli in their environment by pairing these stimuli with other events. This process soon became known as *classical conditioning*. At the same time, other psychologists were exploring what today is known as *operant conditioning*. For example, Edward Thorndike found that animals were less likely to repeat behaviors that met with negative consequences than were animals given no rewards or punishments.

This work convinced Watson that a few key conditioning principles would suffice to explain almost any human behavior. Personality, according to Watson, was "the end product of our habit systems." In other words, over the course of our lives we are conditioned to respond to certain stimuli in more or less predictable ways. You might have been conditioned by parents and teachers to respond to challenges with increased effort. Someone else might have learned to give up or try something new. Because each of us has a unique history of experiences that have shaped our characteristic responses to stimuli, each adult has developed a slightly different personality.

Watson had tremendous faith in the power of basic conditioning principles. His most outrageous claim, which he admitted went "beyond my facts," was that given enough control over the environment, psychologists could mold a child into whatever kind of adult they wanted. "Give me a dozen healthy infants, well formed, and my own specified world to bring them up in," he wrote. "I'll guarantee to take any one at random and train him to become any type of specialist I might select—doctor, lawyer, artist, merchant-chief, and, yes, even beggarman and thief" (1924/1970, p. 104). This he promised regardless of the child's inherited abilities, intelligence, or ancestry. Although somewhat frightening in its implications for controlling human behavior, this type of thinking found a receptive audience among Americans who believed in the tradition of equal opportunity for all, regardless of background or social class.

Skinner's Radical Behaviorism

If I am right about human behavior, an individual is only the way in which a species and a culture produce more of a species and a culture.

B. F. SKINNER

Watson's legacy was perhaps best personified by the career of one influential psychologist, B. F. Skinner. Skinner, who identified his particular brand of behaviorism as **radical behaviorism**, took a small step away from the more extreme position Watson advocated. He did not deny the existence or usefulness of subjective introspection, but rather challenged the extent to which we are able to observe the inner causes of our own behavior. For example, suppose you usually are uncomfortable at social events. As you prepare for a party one evening, you begin to feel nervous. It's going to be a big party and you don't think you will know very many people. At the last minute your anxiety becomes intense and you decide to stay home. Why did you skip the party? Most people would answer that they skipped the party because they felt anxious. But Skinner argued that such an interpretation is incorrect. Behavior "does not change because [you feel] anxious," he explained. "It changes because of the aversive contingencies which generate the condition felt as anxiety. The change in feeling and the change in behavior have a common cause" (1974, p. 68).

B. F. Skinner
1904–1990

When Burrhus Frederick Skinner was born in Susquehanna, Pennsylvania, in 1904, his father, a lawyer, announced the birth in the local paper as "The town has a new law firm: Wm. A. Skinner & Son." But all of his father's efforts to shape his son into the legal profession failed. After growing up in a "warm and stable" home, Skinner went to Hamilton College to study English. He planned a career as a professional writer, not a lawyer. This ambition was reinforced the summer before his senior year when an instructor introduced Skinner to the poet Robert Frost. Frost asked to see some of Skinner's work. Skinner sent three short stories, and several months later received a letter from Frost encouraging him to continue writing.

Skinner devoted the 2 years after his graduation to writing, first at home and later in Greenwich Village in New York. At the end of this time he realized he had produced nothing and was not likely to become a great novelist. "I was to remain interested in human behavior, but the literary method had failed me," he wrote. "I would turn to the scientific. The relevant science appeared to be psychology, though I had only the vaguest idea of what that meant" (Skinner, 1967, p. 395).

So Skinner went to Harvard to study psychology. He immersed himself in his studies, rising at six each morning to hit the books. After teaching at the University of Minnesota and Indiana University, Skinner returned to Harvard in 1948, where he remained the rest of his career. Literature's loss was psychology's gain. A survey of psychology historians taken at about the time of his death ranked Skinner as the most influential of all contemporary psychologists (Korn, Davis, & Davis, 1991).

Although his work in psychology earned him numerous professional awards and recognitions, Skinner never relinquished his interest in literature. In the 1940s he returned to fiction, writing a novel, *Walden Two*, about a utopian society based on the principles of reinforcement Skinner had found in his laboratory experiments. "It was pretty obviously a venture in self-therapy," Skinner wrote, sounding more psychoanalytic than behavioristic. "I was struggling to reconcile two aspects of my own behavior represented by [the characters] Burris and Frazier" (1967, p. 403).

Nonetheless, Skinner remained an adamant believer in the power of the environment and an unwavering critic of

Continued

In other words, when we introduced an inner cause for behavior, like anxiety, we may think we have identified the cause of the behavior, but we are mistaken. When you say you began eating because you were hungry, you have only put a label on your behavior — you have not explained *why* you are eating. Similarly, saying that people behave the way they do because they are friendly or aggressive or introverted does not explain where these behaviors come from. Although radically different in many ways, Skinner's view is much like Freud's in one respect. Both maintained that people simply do not know the reason for many of their behaviors, although we often think we do. Just as mathematicians and artists often cannot describe the process they go through in solving a problem or creating a piece of art, we also are not aware of the internal processes that guide much of our behavior. We often notice what we are thinking or feeling when the behavior occurs and mistakenly assume that the thought or feeling caused the behavior.

Naturally, Skinner's theory and some of the implications derived from it are highly controversial. For example, Skinner described happiness as "a by-product of operant reinforcement." The things that bring happiness are the ones that reinforce us. In his most controversial work, *Beyond Freedom and Dignity* (1971), Skinner argued that it is time we moved beyond the illusion of personal freedom and the so-called dignity we award ourselves for our actions. We don't freely choose to do something as the result of inner moral decisions, but rather as a response to environmental demands. We attribute dignity to people for admirable behavior, but because behavior is under the control of external contingencies, dignity is also an illusion. If you rush into a burning building to save people, it is not because you are heroic or foolish, but because you have a history of exposure to reinforcements and contingencies in similar situations that makes this behavior likely to occur.

Although many behaviorists do not agree with everything Skinner said, all acknowledge the importance of conditioning as a determinant of human behavior. Therefore, an understanding of basic conditioning processes is necessary for an appreciation of the behavioral approach to personality.

Basic Principles of Conditioning

Behaviorists explain behavior, for both humans and lower animals, in terms of learning experiences, or conditioning. They do not deny the influence of genetics but downplay its importance relative to the power of different conditioning experiences. It is convenient to divide conditioning into two categories: classical, or Pavlovian, conditioning and operant, or instrumental, conditioning.

Classical Conditioning

Classical conditioning begins with an existing *stimulus-response (S-R)* association. For example, some people jump (response) whenever they see a spider (stimulus). Although you may not be aware of them, your behavior repertoire contains many of these S-R associations. For example, you might feel faint when you see blood, or want to eat whenever you smell chocolate, or become nervous when you find yourself more than a few feet off the ground.

In his classic demonstration of conditioning, Pavlov used the S-R association of food and salivation. He presented hungry dogs in his laboratory with meat powder (stimulus), to which they would always salivate (response). Because this S-R association existed without any conditioning from Pavlov, we call the meat powder the *unconditioned stimulus* (UCS) and the salivation the *unconditioned response* (UCR). Then Pavlov paired the old, unconditioned stimulus with a new, *conditioned stimulus* (CS). Whenever he presented the meat powder to the dogs, he also sounded a bell. After several trials of presenting the meat powder and the bell together, Pavlov simply sounded the bell without the powder. What happened? As nearly every psychology student knows, the dogs began to salivate to the sound of the bell, even though no meat powder had been presented. The salivation had become the *conditioned response* (CR), part of a new S-R association (bell tone and salivation) in the dogs' behavioral repertoire.

The classical conditioning procedure is diagramed in Figure 13.1. Once the new S-R association is established, it can be used to condition still another S-R association. For example, if you paired a green light with Pavlov's bell tone, after a while the dogs would start to salivate when the green light came on. In this example the bell is the unconditioned stimulus paired with the salivation, the unconditioned response. After the pairing, the green light has become the conditioned stimulus and the salivation the conditioned response. This process of building on one conditioned S-R association with another is called *second-order conditioning.*

Because the stimuli and events you experience are often inadvertently paired with other aspects of the environment, you probably are not aware of the many S-R associations that influence your behavior. Research suggests that our preferences in food, clothing, and even friends can be determined through this process. A friend of mine guesses that he enjoys country and western music because his father used to play it on Saturday, his favorite day of the week. In one experiment, anxious subjects found another person unattractive after sitting in a waiting room

I fell in love with two or three women who looked as my mother must have looked when I was a child, and I think breasts are beautiful, but so far as I'm concerned, Darwin and Pavlov offer a better explanation than Sophocles and Freud.

B. F. SKINNER

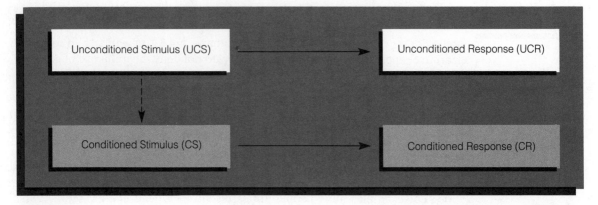

Figure 13.1

Classical Conditioning Diagram

with him or her (Riordan & Tedeschi, 1983). The researchers reasoned that the association of the anxiety with the other person created a negative response to him or her.

However, researchers also have uncovered several limitations of the power of classical conditioning. Without additional learning, conditioned S-R associations probably will not last. For a new S-R association to persist, the two stimuli must be paired occasionally or otherwise reinforced (as explained in the next section). Pavlov found the presentation of the bell tone alone resulted in fewer and fewer drops of saliva, until finally the dogs failed to salivate to the tone at all. This gradual disappearance of the conditioned S-R association is called **extinction**. Moreover, two events presented together will not always produce an association (Rescorla, 1988). Some stimuli are easily associable, whereas others might be impossible. Recent research also suggests that these associations might not be formed as automatically as earlier descriptions led some behaviorists to believe (Rescorla, 1988).

Operant Conditioning

At about the time Pavlov was demonstrating classical conditioning in Russia, American psychologists were investigating another type of learning through association. Edward Thorndike put some stray cats into "puzzle boxes." To escape from the box and thereby obtain a piece of fish, hungry cats had to engage in a particular combination of actions. Before long the cats learned what they had to do to receive their reward. These observations helped Thorndike (1911) formulate the *law of effect*—that behaviors are more likely to be repeated if they lead to

satisfying consequences and less likely to be repeated if they lead to unsatisfying

Much of what we know about the basic principles of conditioning was first demonstrated with laboratory animals. Here a researcher uses operant conditioning to teach a rat to press a bar. The rat receives positive reinforcement (a pellet of food) whenever it presses the bar.

consequences. Thorndike's cats repeated the required behaviors because they led to the satisfying consequences of escape and food.

At first glance, Thorndike's observations hardly seem insightful. Do you know any parents who don't occasionally try rewards and punishments to mold their children's behavior? Teachers, judges, and employers also regularly rely on the connection between actions and consequences to shape behavior. But vague feelings that such a connection exists are not the same as understanding how this learning works or the most efficient and productive way to utilize it. Ask a group of parents the best way to deal with a problem child and you will soon understand how little agreement there is among nonscientists on how to use rewards and punishments.

This poor understanding of basic learning principles is unfortunate, given the power of conditioning processes. It is especially tragic because several decades of research have provided psychologists with a relatively good understanding of how these processes work and how to use them most effectively. Most notably, Skinner (1953) outlined the principles through which reinforcement and punish-

Box 13.1

Schedules of Reinforcement

Why do some behaviors continue even though they are rarely reinforced? The answer has to do with the **schedule of reinforcement** used to maintain the behavior. After a behavior is learned, it need not be reinforced on every occasion to remain in an organism's repertoire. Instead, a behavior may be reinforced intermittently with one of several types of schedules, each producing slightly different results. Schedules of reinforcement may be either *ratio* or *interval*. That is, the reinforcement of the behavior may depend on the number of times it occurs (ratio) or on the length of time between reinforcements (interval). In addition, a schedule of reinforcement may be either *fixed* or *variable*. An organism may be reinforced every *n*th time the behavior is emitted (a fixed ratio schedule) or when the behavior is emitted after a fixed period of time has passed (a fixed interval schedule). Under a variable ratio schedule, the organism is reinforced on an average of once every *n*th time. Thus, a rat may receive a food pellet after 5 bar presses and then after 15, so that the reward comes on an average of every 10th response. Finally, with a variable interval schedule, the organism is reinforced after an average period of time has passed. For example, a rat may receive a food pellet for pressing the bar after 45 seconds and then for pressing after 1 minute and 15 seconds, to obtain a reward after an average of 1 minute has passed.

Understanding the different effects of the various schedules of reinforcement can help to explain why some behaviors tend to persist with little reinforcement. If we define the strength of a response in terms of how long it takes to extinguish, then we can demonstrate a seemingly paradoxical feature of operant conditioning—that the less frequently reinforced behaviors are the strongest. For example, a child passing a video arcade may ask Mom for a quarter. Suppose one mother always gives in and hands the child a quarter (fixed ratio = 1). Suppose a different mother repeatedly says no until the child's incessant whining forces her to reach into her purse and give the child the money (variable ratio = 20). One day both of these mothers decide to stop rewarding this behavior regardless of what the child does. Which child would stop asking for the quarter first? The child who was reinforced with a quarter on every trial will soon learn that no more quarters are coming, and the behavior will extinguish in a short period of time. The second child, however, is used to not getting reinforced for every request and probably will persist at the unrewarded behavior for a longer period of time before learning that the reinforcement has stopped. Research has also shown that behaviors maintained on variable schedules are particularly resistant to extinction, for again, the organism has experienced long stretches between reinforcements. This research helps explain why some problem behaviors in children persist even though parents and teachers insist that the child is rarely reinforced for the action.

ment shape and control behavior. Unlike classical conditioning, which begins with an existing S-R bond, operant conditioning begins with behaviors the organism (human or lower animal) emits spontaneously. We can observe these operant behaviors when a laboratory rat is placed in a new cage. The animal moves about, scratches, sniffs, and claws in a haphazard manner, for none of these responses has been reinforced or punished. However, if one of these behaviors is always followed by a pellet of food, then its frequency will increase.

Operant conditioning concerns the effect certain kinds of consequences have on the frequency of behavior. A consequence that increases the frequency of a behavior that precedes it is called a *reinforcement*; one that decreases it is called a *punishment*. Whether a consequence is reinforcing or punishing varies according to the person and the situation. If you are hungry, strawberry ice cream probably is a reinforcement. But if you don't like strawberry ice cream or if you are cold, the ice cream may serve as a punishment.

Psychologists have discovered two basic reinforcement strategies for increasing the frequency of a behavior. With *positive reinforcement*, the behavior increases because it is followed by a reward. Hungry rats that receive a pellet of food every time they press a bar will begin to press the bar frequently. Students who receive an A after studying for a test may begin studying that hard for all of their tests. We also can increase the frequency of a behavior by using *negative reinforcement*, the removal or lessening of an unpleasant stimulus. Rats that can turn off an electric shock by pulling a string will quickly learn to pull the string. People whose headaches go away when they take a few minutes to relax will soon learn to relax.

*Happiness is a . . .
byproduct of operant re-
inforcement. The things
which make us happy
are the things which
reinforce us.*

B. F. SKINNER

Too often people confuse negative reinforcement with punishment. In fact, they produce opposite effects. Although both deal with aversive stimuli, negative reinforcement is designed to *increase* the frequency of a behavior, and punishment is designed to *decrease* it. If a rat is shocked every time it touches a bar (punishment), it will start to touch the bar less often. We'll explore the appropriate and inappropriate ways to use punishment after first examining a few more features of reinforcement.

Shaping   Suppose you are hired to work with patients in a psychiatric hospital. Your job is to get reluctant patients more involved in some of the activities on the ward. You start with one patient who has never participated in any of the ward activities. Your goal is to get him into the daily art therapy sessions. Positive reinforcement seems the right tool. Every time the patient joins in at one of the voluntary art sessions, you will reward him with coupons for free items in the hospital store. The patient skips art therapy the first day. So, no reward. He skips art therapy the rest of the week. Still no reward. You wait two months and still the patient has not attended one of the sessions. By now one of the problems encountered when using operant conditioning is apparent to you: A behavior can be reinforced only after it is emitted.

Does this mean operant conditioning is useless in this situation? Fortunately, the answer is no. A behavior therapist working with the reluctant patient might utilize a technique known as **shaping**, in which successive approximations of the desired behavior are reinforced. For example, you might reward the withdrawn

Most parents understand that rewarding the good things their children do leads to an increase in those good behaviors. With a better understanding of the appropriate uses of reinforcement and punishment, parents can become more efficient shapers of their children's behaviors.

patient for getting out of bed and sitting among the other patients. Once this behavior is established, you might reinforce him only when he is near or in the art therapy room. From here rewards might be limited to time spent in the room during the sessions and later to time spent attending to and participating in the sessions. Shaping is particularly useful when teaching complex behaviors. Children will learn to enjoy reading if each step along the way is reinforced. If learning the alphabet, letter sounds, and short words is difficult and unpleasant, it is unlikely the child will move on to reading sentences and stories.

Generalization and Discrimination   Operant conditioning would be rather limited if every different situation required learning a new response. Fortunately, because of a process called **generalization**, this is not the case. For example, pigeons trained to peck at large red circles to receive food also will peck at small orange circles, although not as frequently. We call this tendency to make a learned response to a stimulus similar to the one used for conditioning *stimulus generalization*. This process helps explain why personality characteristics generalize across situations. A child rewarded for acting politely around relatives probably will act politely around other new acquaintances. The polite response has been generalized from the stimulus of the relative to the new stimulus, the stranger. When we observe polite behavior consistently across situations, we say this pattern is part of the child's personality.

As long as the generalized response is met with reinforcement, the behavior is likely to continue. But if the pigeon is not rewarded for pecking at orange circles, it will soon learn to discriminate between the rewarded and nonrewarded stimuli and will peck only at the red ones. Similarly, the polite child may come in contact with adults who punish friendly behavior with harshness. Soon the child will learn to discriminate between people who are friendly and people who aren't. This process is called **discrimination**. The difference between a good and a great tennis player or between a second-string baseball player and a star may be the ability to make fine discriminations between those actions that lead to a reinforcement (a winning shot or a home run) and those that do not.

Reducing Unwanted Behaviors The other side of operant conditioning is the reduction of unwanted behaviors. Teachers and parents are keenly aware of the need to reduce the frequency with which students and children do certain things. They are quick to turn to operant conditioning when children cause problems and get into trouble. Unfortunately, a poor understanding of how to use operant conditioning to reduce unwanted behaviors probably leaves most teachers and parents frustrated.

As with the task of increasing desired behaviors, operant conditioning provides two methods for decreasing undesired behaviors. The most efficient method is to cease reinforcement and thereby allow the behavior to extinguish. We often fail to see how we unintentionally reinforce problem behaviors. For example, a teacher may attempt to punish a child who acts up in class by criticizing the child in front of the other students. The teacher may not realize that the attention the child gains from other students in the form of laughter and classroom status has turned the intended punishment into a reinforcement. An observant teacher might take disruptive children out into the hall for discipline, thereby removing the reinforcer.

Alternatively, we can use **punishment** to eliminate unwanted behaviors. In theory, a behavior followed by an aversive stimulus, such as an electric shock, is less likely to be repeated in the future. The effects of punishment can be demonstrated in laboratory animals, and therapists have had some success applying this technique in special cases (such as shocking autistic children whenever they strike themselves). But research also shows the effectiveness of punishment is limited to some specific conditions.

First, punishment does not teach appropriate behaviors; it can only decrease the frequency of undesired ones. Rather than simply punish a child for hitting another student, it's better to help the child learn alternative ways to deal with frustrating situations.

Second, to be effective punishment must be delivered immediately and consistently. A parent needs to punish the problem behavior as soon as possible after it happens, not "when your father gets home." The punishment also must be fairly intense and should be administered after every instance of the undesired

Table 13.1

Operant Conditioning Procedures

Procedure	Purpose	Application
Positive reinforcement	Increase behavior	Give reward following behavior
Negative reinforcement	Increase behavior	Remove aversive stimulus following behavior
Extinction	Decrease behavior	Do not reward behavior
Punishment	Decrease behavior	Give aversive stimulus following behavior

behavior. Parents who sometimes let their children use bad language, but other times decide to punish such talk, probably will have little success in changing their children's vocabulary.

Finally, punishment can have negative side effects. Although parents or therapists intend to suppress a certain response, a child might associate other behaviors with the punishment. For example, a child who is punished for hitting a toy against a window may stop playing with toys altogether. In addition, through classical conditioning, aversive feelings that accompany the punishment may be associated with the person doing the punishing. Children who are spanked by their parents may associate the parent with the pain of the spanking. Another side effect is that undesirable behaviors may be learned through modeling. For example, children who are spanked may learn that physical aggression is okay as long as you are bigger and stronger. Finally, punishment can create negative emotions, such as fear and anxiety, strong enough to interfere with learning the appropriate response.

Taken together, these factors make punishment one of the least desirable choices for behavior therapists seeking to change problem behaviors. At most punishment can temporarily suppress an undesirable response long enough for the therapist to begin reinforcing a desired, hopefully incompatible, behavior.

In summary, the behaviorist description of personality is different from that provided by the other approaches in several ways. Behaviorists focus on observable behaviors and consider consistent behavior patterns the result of conditioning experiences. Classical and operant conditioning are the processes responsible for these behavior patterns. If this explanation seems too simple to you, you are not alone. Many adherents of behaviorism also find the radical behaviorist position too limited. We'll look at their expanded versions of this approach next.

Social Learning Theory

It is difficult to overstate the impact behaviorism had on psychology and subsequently the field of personality. Watson and his followers provided a scientific, easily testable account of human behavior that complemented the growing empirical flavor of psychology in American universities. The basic principles of learning were so universal they could be tested on lower animals. The image many people have of the lab-coated psychologist, pencil in hand, watching rats running through mazes comes from this era.

But somewhere in the 1950s or 1960s some of the enthusiasm for behaviorism began to wane. Many psychologists who still accepted the basic principles of behaviorism began to question the assertion that all human learning takes place as a result of classical or operant conditioning. "The prospects for survival would be slim indeed if one could learn only from the consequences of trial and error," Albert Bandura wrote. "One does not teach children to swim, adolescents to drive automobiles, and novice medical students to perform surgery by having them discover the requisite behavior from the consequences of their successes and failures" (1986, p. 20).

These psychologists also began to question whether behaviorism was too limited in the scope of its subject matter. For example, why couldn't "internal" events like thoughts and attitudes be conditioned the same as overt behaviors? Paranoid people who believe evil agents are out to get them might have been reinforced in the past for these beliefs. If this were the case, then behavioral models of psychotherapy could also be applied to treating these patients.

Arthur Staats (1975, 1981) helped build one of the bridges between Watson's behaviorism and more recent social learning theories. Appropriately, Staats called his theory of personality *social behaviorism*. He introduced the notion of "behavior environment-behavior interactions." That is, not only does the environment influence our behavior, but that behavior then determines the kind of environment we find ourselves in, which can then influence behavior, and so on. Staats also recognized that people often provide themselves with their own reinforcers in the absence of visible external rewards. In addition, he was among the first to describe how internal concepts such as attitudes and self-concept — foreign words to strict behaviorists — could be developed and changed through same conditioning principles used to develop and change overt behaviors.

Two prominent theories emerged from this movement to expand the strict behaviorist position. Albert Bandura and Julian Rotter each developed comprehensive models to explain human personality in more far-reaching terms than is possible with the limitations of classic behaviorism. Coincidentally, both of these theorists initially referred to their approaches as "social learning" theories. While they share a common heritage, each takes a different focus in explaining consistent behavior patterns.

Albert Bandura's Social-Cognitive Theory

Albert Bandura (1977a, 1986) rejects the radical behaviorist view of human beings as passive recipients of whatever stimuli life throws their way. Certainly

Albert Bandura

1925–

Albert Bandura was born in 1925 in Mundare, a small farming community located among the wheat fields in Alberta, Canada. He attended the only school in the area, a combined elementary and high school with a total of about 20 students and two teachers. Summer jobs included filling in holes in the highways of the Yukon. Bandura stayed in Canada for his undergraduate education, receiving his B.A. degree from the University of British Columbia in 1949.

Bandura's graduate training reflects the bridging of different areas of psychology evident in his later theorizing. He chose to get his Ph.D. from the University of Iowa because of its strong tradition of research in learning theory. Among the Iowa faculty members who influenced Bandura was the learning theorist Kenneth Spence. Bandura received his Ph.D. in 1952. The research emphasis at Iowa gave him the conviction that psychologists should "conceptualize clinical phenomena in ways that would make them amenable to experimental tests" (Evans, 1976, p. 243).

After a year of clinical internship in Wichita, Bandura accepted a position at Stanford University in 1953 and has remained there ever since. While at Stanford he has continued to build bridges between traditional learning theory and cognitive personality theories, between clinical psychology and empirically oriented approaches to understanding personality. Bandura has received numerous professional honors, including election to the presidency of the American Psychological Association in 1974.

people respond to environmental events, and certainly they often learn characteristic behaviors as the result of rewards and punishments. But people possess other capacities that are "distinctly human." By reducing the process by which people grow and change to the way a rat learns to press a bar for a pellet of food, strict behaviorists overlook some of the most important causes of human behavior and sources of human personality. Because these overlooked causes generally involve thinking and symbolic processing of information, Bandura recently has referred to his approach as a social *cognitive* view.

Reciprocal Determinism Bandura introduces a new twist to the question of whether behavior is determined by internal or by external forces. He argues that there are both internal and external determinants of behavior, but behavior is not determined exclusively by either or by a simple combination. Instead, Bandura introduces the concept of **reciprocal determinism**. That is, external determinants of behavior, such as rewards and punishments, and internal determinants, such as beliefs, thoughts, and expectations, are part of a system of interacting influences that affect not only behavior but the various parts of the system as well. Put more simply, each part of the system—behaviors, external factors, and internal factors—influences each of the other parts.

Some examples will help clarify what Bandura means. Unlike Skinner, Bandura maintains that internal factors, such as our expectancies, affect our behavior. Suppose someone you don't like much asks you to play racquetball. You can just imagine what a dismal afternoon you would have with this person. Thus, your *internal* expectation probably will cause you to reject the invitation. But what would happen if this person offered to buy you that new, expensive racket you've been eyeing if you play with him? Suddenly the *external* inducement is powerful enough to determine your behavior, and you say, "Let's play." Now, imagine further that you have one of the most enjoyable sets of racquetball ever. You're evenly matched with this person, and he even cracks a few jokes to make the afternoon fun. You actually look forward to playing with him again. The behavior in this case has changed your expectations, which will affect future behavior, and so on.

The reciprocal determinism process is diagramed in Figure 13.2. You may notice the arrows point in both directions, indicating that each of the three variables in the model is capable of influencing each of the other variables. This situation is very different from radical behaviorism, which limits explanations of human behavior to a two-factor, one-way model, in which external events cause behavior. Not only can the environment affect behavior in Bandura's model, but the opposite effect is also possible. For example, a rude person's behavior at a party can lead those around her to create an environment with punishments and few rewards. In this case the behavior has changed the environment. Bandura draws a distinction between the *potential environment*, which is the same for everyone in a situation, and the *actual environment*, the one we create with our behaviors. A friendly person at the same party might create an environment of many rewards and few punishments. Bandura would agree with those who claim we create our own opportunities. He might add that we also can create our own defeating circumstances.

But how can we predict which of the three parts in the reciprocal determinism model is going to influence which other part? This depends on the strength of each of the variables. At times environmental forces are most powerful, at other times internal forces dominate. The example used in an earlier chapter of high- and low-self-esteem people fleeing a burning building illustrates how environmental factors can override internal individual factors on occasion. Though at times we can mold our environment to meet our needs, other times we are faced with environmental factors we cannot control. We often create our own opportunities and defeats, but they also can be created for us.

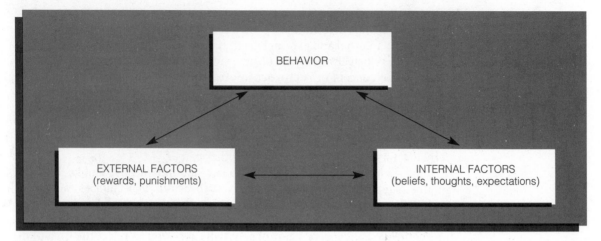

Figure 13.2

Bandura's Reciprocal Determinism Model

Cognitive Influences on Behavior   Clearly a major difference between Bandura's theory and the strict behaviorist approach is Bandura's emphasis on cognitive (internal) aspects of human personality. Bandura rejects the idea of people as large, complex rats. Instead, he identifies several features unique to human functioning that must be considered in understanding personality.

Unlike lower animals, people use symbols and forethought as guides for future action. Instead of working our way through rewards and punishments in a trial-and-error fashion every time we face a new problem, we imagine possible outcomes, calculate probabilities, set goals, and develop strategies. We do all of this in our mind without engaging in random actions and waiting to see which will be rewarded or punished. Of course, past experiences with reinforcements or punishments affect these judgments. But think about the way you prepare for a vacation. Most likely you think about several options of where and when to go, how to get there, who to go with, what to bring, what to do when you arrive, and so on. You probably don't jump in a car and head in a certain direction because once before such behavior was reinforced.

Bandura also argues that most behavior is performed *in the absence* of external reinforcements and punishments. Except for extreme situations like a prisoner-of-war camp, most of our daily actions are controlled by what Bandura calls **self-regulation**. He challenges the radical behaviorist assertion that we can be swayed into performing just about any action if the environmental contingencies are altered appropriately. You've probably seen people hold to their beliefs in spite of external pressure to change. "Anyone who attempted to change a pacifist into an aggressor or a devout religionist into an atheist," Bandura wrote, "would quickly come to appreciate the existence of personal sources of behavioral control'' (1977a, pp. 128–129).

Although people often work to obtain external rewards, Bandura argues that we also work toward self-imposed goals with internal rewards. For example, many amateur runners push themselves to reach a certain distance at a certain pace. Few expect to win races, but instead work to meet their own goals and maintain their personal standards. The reward comes from the feelings of accomplishment and self-worth just for finishing the race. Self-regulation also includes self-punishment. When we fail to maintain personal standards, we often degrade and feel bad about ourselves. For example, you may have chastised yourself for being rude to a stranger or not sticking to your diet, even when no one else seemed to notice.

Observational Learning   Perhaps social learning theory's most important contribution to the understanding of human behavior and personality is the concept of vicarious or **observational learning**. Bandura argues that learning is not limited to classical and operant conditioning. We also can learn by observing or reading or hearing about other people's behavior. Many behaviors are too complex to be learned through the slow process of reinforcement and punishment. For example, we don't teach pilots to fly by putting them in the cockpit and reinforcing correct behaviors and punishing incorrect ones. Bandura maintains that children would never learn to talk during their preschool years if they had to be reinforced for every correct utterance. Instead, the pilots and the toddlers watch others fly and talk, noting which behaviors lead to rewards.

Bandura draws an important distinction between *learning* and *performance*. Behaviors learned through observational methods need not be performed. This idea again clashes with the radical behaviorists, who maintain that we cannot learn something until we have actually engaged in that behavior. But think for a moment of some of the behaviors you could perform if you wanted to, even though you never have. For example, although you probably have never picked up a pistol and shot another human being, you've observed this behavior in movies often enough for it to be part of your behavioral repertoire. You might even know to stand with your feet apart and to hold the weapon at eye level with both hands in front of you, just like the actors portraying police do. Fortunately, most of us will never perform this behavior, but it nonetheless is one we probably have learned through observation.

Why do we perform some of the behaviors we have learned through observation but not others? The answer lies in our expectations about the consequences of the performance. That is, do you believe the action will be rewarded or punished? In the case of shooting another person, most of us expect this behavior to lead to punishment, if not in a legal sense, then through self-punishment in the form of guilt and lowered feelings of worth.

But if we have never performed the behavior, where do we get our expectations about its consequences? Again, from observing others. Your perception of what will happen to you is based on whether your model was rewarded or punished after engaging in the behavior. For example, a high school boy may watch an older friend ask someone for a date. He pays close attention to how the friend engages the potential date in conversation, what is said, and so on. If the friend's behavior is rewarded (a date is made), the boy may believe that he, too, will be rewarded if he acts just like his friend. Most likely, he'll soon get his courage up and ask a girl he's interested in for a date. But what if the boy watches his friend get turned down? It's unlikely he will imitate the punished behavior. In both cases the boy paid close enough attention to *learn* how his friend went about asking for a date. But whether he will *perform* the behavior depends on whether he thinks he'll be rewarded or punished, which he also learned from his friend's example.

In a classic experiment with important social implications, Bandura (1965) demonstrated this learning-performance distinction. Nursery school children watched a television program in which an adult model performed four novel aggressive acts on an adult-size plastic Bobo doll:

> First, the model laid the Bobo doll on its side, sat on it, and punched it in the nose while remarking, "Pow, right in the nose, boom, boom." The model then raised the doll and pommeled it on the head with a mallet. Each response was accompanied by the verbalization, "Sockeroo . . . stay down." Following the mallet aggression, the model kicked the doll about the room, and these responses were interspersed with the comment, "Fly away." Finally, the model threw rubber balls at the Bobo doll, each strike punctuated with "Bang." (pp. 590–591)

The children saw one of three endings to the film. Some saw a second adult reward the aggressive model with soft drinks, candy, and lots of praise. Others saw the model spanked with a rolled-up magazine while being warned not to act aggressively again. A third group was given no information about the consequences of the aggressive behavior. Next, each child was left alone for 10 minutes of free playing time. Among the many toys in the room were a Bobo doll and all the materials needed (for example, a mallet) to perform the aggressive acts they had seen. An experimenter watched through a one-way window to see how many of the four acts of aggression the children would perform spontaneously. Finally, each child was offered fruit juice and small toys for each of the four aggressive acts he or she could perform for the experimenter. This was done to see if the children *could* perform the behavior if they wanted to — that is, had they learned the responses from watching the model?

The results are shown in Figure 13.3. Nearly all the children in all three groups could perform the behaviors when asked. However, as Bandura predicted, whether they chose to perform the behavior when left alone depended on the consequences they expected. Although all of them had *learned* how to act aggressively, the children who had seen the model rewarded were significantly more likely to *perform* the behaviors than were those who had seen the model punished.

We learn more than aggressive behavior by watching some of the many models in our lives. Much of what we have learned about acting friendly, seductively, or professionally has come from combining various features of the many people we have seen act this way. Bandura explains that this is why siblings exposed to the same parental models often develop very different personalities.

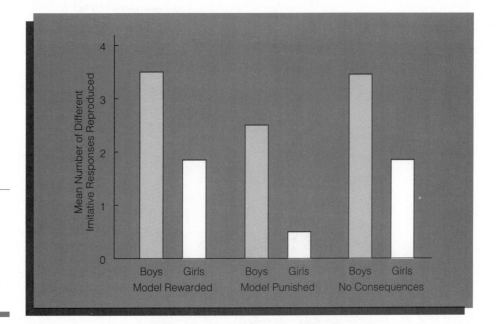

Figure 13.3

Mean Number of Aggressive Responses Performed

Adapted from Bandura (1965); reprinted by permission of the author.

The children draw from the behavior modeled by many different people—parents, siblings, friends, television characters—and each develops a unique pattern of behavioral responses and expectancies.

In summary, Bandura's social-cognitive theory expands on the classic behaviorist position in many ways. Whereas behaviorism focuses on the way the environment affects behavior, Bandura's theory examines the interactions between internal events, the environment, and behavior. Behaviorism limits its study to observable events, whereas the social-cognitive model looks at internal features such as expectancies and imagined consequences. Whereas behaviorists explain the acquisition of new behaviors through classical and operant conditioning, Bandura's theory adds observational learning. Bandura's social-cognitive theory does not represent a rejection of behaviorism as much as an elaboration of its basic concepts.

Julian Rotter's Social Learning Theory

Julian Rotter (1954, 1982; Rotter, Chance, & Phares, 1972) is another personality theorist who found the behaviorist approach to personality useful but questioned the narrowness of the radical behaviorist position. Like Bandura, Rotter concluded that the principles used to explain the behavior of lower animals are too limited to cover complex human behaviors. He argues that to predict what people will do in a certain situation we have to take into account such cognitive variables as perceptions, expectancies, and values.

Julian B. Rotter
1916–

Julian Rotter credits his introduction to psychology to the Avenue J Library in Brooklyn, where he spent a great deal of his grade school and high school years. One day, after exhausting most of the books in other sections of the library, he wandered over to the "Philosophy and Psychology" shelf. Among the first books he encountered there were Alfred Adler's *Understanding Human Nature* and Sigmund Freud's *Psychopathology of Everyday Life*. From that point on, he was hooked. However, he decided to major in chemistry at Brooklyn College, because "there was no profession of psychology that I knew of. And in 1933, in the depths of the Great Depression, one majored in a subject one could use to make a living" (1982, p. 343).

But circumstances, combined with a high reinforcement value for studying psychology, eventually made a career in psychology possible. When Rotter discovered during his junior year that Alfred Adler was teaching at the Long Island School of Medicine, he began attending the lectures. Eventually Adler invited Rotter to attend the monthly meetings of the Society of Individual Psychology held in Adler's home. Unfortunately, Adler died the next year.

Nonetheless, by then Rotter's enthusiasm for psychology dictated that he go to graduate school. He chose the University of Iowa so that he could study with the famous Gestalt psychologist Kurt Lewin. He went to the University of Indiana for his Ph.D., because it was one of the few schools at the time to offer a degree in clinical psychology. However, there were few academic positions available when Rotter graduated in 1941. After working in a hospital for a year, Rotter served as a psychologist in the Army and later the Air Force during World War II. The need for clinical psychologists was high following the war, but their numbers were few. Rotter took a position at Ohio State University, finally fulfilling his ambition to be a professional academic psychologist. He stayed there until 1963 when he moved to the University of Connecticut.

Behavior Potential   Imagine that someone has just insulted you at a party. How do you respond? You have several courses of action to choose from. You might attempt to top the remark with something clever and witty. You could calmly say the behavior was out of line and ask for an apology. You could punch the person in the face or simply leave the scene. The key to predicting what you will do in this situation lies in understanding what Rotter referred to as the *behavior potential* for each option. The **behavior potential** is the likelihood of a given behavior occurring in a particular situation. Each possible response to the insult has a different behavior potential. If you decide to hit the insulter, it means the behavior potential for that response was stronger than for any of the other possible responses.

The question then becomes: What determines the strength of the behavior potential? According to Rotter, two variables need to be considered: expectancy and reinforcement value (Figure 13.4). In short, we calculate the probability that an action will result in a given reinforcer and the value that reinforcer has for us. If the odds of being reinforced for a certain course of action are slim or if the possible reinforcement to be gained is not particularly prized, then the behavior potential is weak. On the other hand, if we expect to receive something of value for a behavior, we'll probably perform it.

Expectancy   Before you decide to stay up all night studying for an exam, you probably ask yourself what the likelihood is that the all-nighter will help you do better on the test. Similarly, when debating whether to attend a dance, you probably try to figure out the probability that you will have a good time. Rotter refers to these estimations as *expectancies*. Obviously, we base our expectancies largely on how things turned out the last time we were in this situation. If you always do well after studying all night, you probably will have a high expectancy of receiving the reward again. If you never seem to enjoy yourself at a dance, the expectancy of being rewarded for going to the dance is slim.

This is where Rotter and radical behaviorists disagree when interpreting the same event. Both recognize that people are more likely to engage in a behavior when it is reinforced. Radical behaviorists say that an operant conditioning association or habit has been strengthened by the experience. However, Rotter explains this same phenomenon in terms of changes in expectancy. The more often people are reinforced for a certain behavior (for example, studying all night and receiving an A), the stronger their expectancy that the behavior will be reinforced in the future. On the other hand, when behaviors are not reinforced (studying all night and receiving a low grade), the expectancy of reward is decreased. Of course, expectancies are not necessarily accurate. For example, you may expect that studying for your SAT will result in a higher score, even though in reality the studying may have little effect. In this case, your expectancy probably will predict your behavior better than the actual contingencies.

After you have been in the same situation many times, you probably develop a great deal of confidence in your expectancies for rewards. If you always have a great time at parties, you expect that going to a party will be rewarded again this weekend. But how can expectancies explain behavior in situations we encounter for the first time? Rotter explains that the expectancy in this case is based on

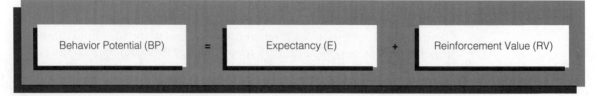

| Behavior Potential (BP) | = | Expectancy (E) | + | Reinforcement Value (RV) |

Figure 13.4

Rotter's Basic Formula for Predicting Behavior

experiences in a similar situation. The recent graduate who was rewarded for staying up all night to write papers in college probably expects that staying up all night to finish a report for the boss will lead to similar rewards. This example illustrates how expectancies lead to stable behavior patterns. We might call this person a procrastinator or perhaps say he is diligent because the same style of behavior appears repeatedly. According to Rotter, the consistency in this person's behavior is the result of well-defined and stable expectancies.

Beyond this, Rotter (1966) proposes that in new situations we rely on *generalized expectancies*. These are general beliefs either that our actions will lead to reinforcements and punishments or that they will have little effect on the rewards and punishments we receive. Subsequent research on this concept, some of which is reviewed in the next chapter, indicates that people can be placed along a continuum of what has been called generalized **locus of control**. At one end of this trait dimension we find people with an extreme internal orientation — those who generally believe that what happens to them is the result of their own actions. On the other end we find people who hold an extreme external orientation — those who generally maintain that what happens to them is the result of forces outside their control, such as chance or powerful others. Of course, most of us fall somewhere between the two extremes.

In novel or ambiguous situations, we use these generalized expectancies to calculate behavior potentials. If you are the kind of person who typically says "I think I can do it" in a new situation, Rotter would say you are relying on your generalized belief that you have the ability to make things happen. If you more often have doubts in new situations, then you probably fall on the other end of the locus of control dimension.

Reinforcement Value   Suppose a college student named Chuck is trying to decide whom to ask out this Friday. He believes there is a high probability that Alice will say yes if he asks her out and a low probability that Barbara will go out with him. Nonetheless, he still decides to ask Barbara. Why? Rotter would explain this choice by looking at the reinforcement value for each of the options. Chuck might

Table 13.2

Calculating Behavior Potential Example

Option	Possible Outcome	Expectancy	Value	Behavior Potential
Ask for apology	Apology	High	High	High
Insult back	Laughter	Low	High	Average
Leave the party	Feel foolish	Average	Low	Low
Punch in face	Bloodshed	Low	Low	Low

ask Barbara to go out with him because a date with her is much more valuable to him than is a date with Alice.

Rotter defines *reinforcement value* as the degree to which we prefer one reinforcer over another if the likelihood of obtaining each were equal. Naturally, the reinforcement value we assign a certain reward can vary from situation to situation and across time. When we are lonely, social contact holds a higher reinforcement value than when we aren't. Yet there are relatively stable individual differences in how much we value one reinforcer over another. Some people always take free baseball tickets over free ballet tickets. Hence, consistent behavior patterns also can be traced to relatively stable feelings about what certain rewards are worth. Some people almost always go to great lengths to achieve something, even if the likelihood of reaching the goal is small. We might call these people obsessive or driven because of this consistent pattern. But using Rotter's model, their personalities can be explained in terms of the consistently high value they put on achievement.

Rotter maintained that reinforcement value is independent of expectancy. That is, whether something holds a high or a low reinforcement value for you tells us nothing about your expectancy of obtaining that reinforcer. So, what do we need to know to predict how a person will respond to a given situation? Returning to the insult situation, we would need to understand what you expected to happen with each of the possible responses and how much you valued those reactions. One possibility is diagramed in Table 13.2. In this case, asking for an apology is the likely behavior because the person expects to receive an apology back and that apology is highly valued. Naturally, someone with a different history of experiences in such situations and with different feelings about the values of the rewards would likely respond in a different manner than you. This is, of course, what we call differences in personality.

Application: Behavior Modification and Self-Efficacy Therapy

One of the appeals of strict behaviorism is its presentation of a simple, rational model of human nature. Looking at the world through behaviorism glasses, everything makes sense. Employees work hard when they are reinforced properly. Children stop fighting when aggressive behavior is punished and working together is reinforced. But what about some of the seemingly irrational behaviors enacted by people suffering from psychological disorders? How can basic conditioning principles explain a fear of stairs or a belief that people are out to get you? As we will see, not only can behaviorists account for these and other abnormal behaviors, many psychotherapy techniques are based on basic conditioning principles.

Explaining Psychological Disorders

John B. Watson was the first to demonstrate how seemingly "abnormal" behaviors are created through normal conditioning procedures. Watson used classical conditioning to create a fear of white rats in an 11-month-old baby known as Little Albert (Watson & Rayner, 1920). As shown in Figure 13.5, Watson began with the stimulus-response association between a loud noise and fear present in most infants. That is, whenever Watson would make the loud noise, Albert would cry and show other signs of fear. Next, Watson showed Albert a white rat, each time accompanied by the loud noise. Soon Albert was responding to the white rat with fear responses (crying, crawling away) similar to those he had made to the loud noise, even when the noise was not sounded. Watson demonstrated that what appeared to be an abnormal fear of white rats in an infant could be explained by knowing the past conditioning of the child.

Behaviorists argue that many of our seemingly irrational fears may have been developed in a similar manner. For example, we may not recall when bridges or snakes were ever associated with an existing fear. But such associations could have taken place a long time ago or even without our awareness. However, there is a problem with this explanation. As Pavlov discovered, the new associations formed through classical conditioning extinguish once the pairing is removed. Why, then, do phobias not just become extinct on their own without the need for psychological intervention? The answer is that operant conditioning may take over to keep the phobia operating. Let's take the example of a three-year-old girl who falls off a tall slide. The pain and fear she experiences are paired with the sight of the slide, and those feelings reemerge the next time she approaches a slide. Her fear and anxiety increase as she gets closer and closer to it. Quite likely, she'll decide to turn away and try the slide some other time, thereby reducing the fear and anxiety. What has happened in this situation is that the act of avoiding the slide has been reinforced through negative reinforcement. Running away was followed by a reduction in the aversive stimulus, the feelings of fear and anxiety. If this avoidance behavior is reinforced a few more times, the girl could develop a strong fear of slides. This fear might then be generalized to a fear of all high places, and years later the woman may be forced to seek therapy for this debilitating phobia.

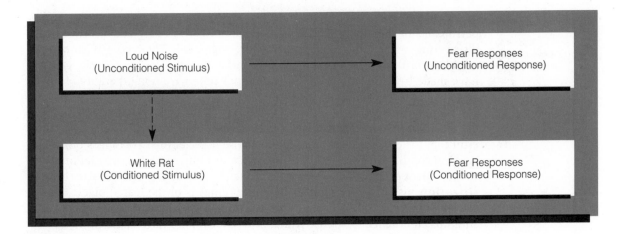

Figure 13.5

Diagram of Little Albert's Classical Conditioning

Behaviorists view other problem behaviors as the result of a learning history that somehow reinforced the wrong behavior. For example, a very introverted boy may have found the only escape from criticism and ridicule he received at home was to avoid social contact as much as possible (negative reinforcement), a behavior he then generalized to other people. An aggressive girl might have been reinforced for her aggressive behavior by earning the "respect" of other children who allowed her to have her own way most of the time. A man suffering from paranoid delusions may believe he has thwarted a plan to capture him by staying in his house all day, thereby rewarding the behavior.

Behavior theorists also explain a lack of appropriate behaviors in some psychological patients as the result of too little reinforcement. For example, if a woman's efforts to initiate conversations with others are never rewarded, she'll probably stop trying. Similarly, sometimes appropriate behaviors extinguish if they are not reinforced. Thus, a person who once enjoyed working with others but who does not enjoy it any longer can be expected to stop acting cooperatively.

Behavior Modification

If we accept that a problem behavior is the result of unusual conditioning experiences, then another principle of behaviorism should follow: Problem behaviors can be changed through the same basic conditioning principles. Consequently, several therapy procedures, generally grouped under the label **behavior modification**, have been developed from behaviorist theory and research. These procedures differ from more traditional therapies in several respects. The treatment usually lasts for several weeks, as compared to perhaps years. The focus is on changing a few well-defined behaviors, rather than changing the entire personality of the client. And behavior therapists are often unconcerned with discovering where the problem behavior originated. Their goal is simply to remove it or replace it with a more appropriate set of responses. These features have made behavior modification techniques popular among therapists from a variety of theoretical orientations.

Classical Conditioning Applications   Pairing one stimulus with another is a powerful tool for creating new stimulus-response associations. Therapists often use classical conditioning to eliminate or replace stimulus-response associations that cause a client problems. One example of such a treatment is **systematic desensitization**, used to cure phobias by pairing images of the feared object with a relaxation response. The idea is to replace the old association between the feared stimulus and the fear response with a new association between the stimulus and relaxation (Wolpe, 1958). The clients and therapists begin the treatment by creating a list of imagined scenes ranging from mildly arousing to highly anxiety-provoking. For example, people afraid of heights might begin their list with the scene of standing on a two-foot-high footstool. The next scene might be walking up a flight of stairs, followed by a scene of standing on an eight-foot ladder. Last on the hierarchy come the highly anxiety-provoking scenes, such as looking out from the top floor of a skyscraper or flying in a small airplane.

After clients complete relaxation training, they imagine the scenes while practicing relaxing. One step at a time, they slowly move through the list until they can imagine the scene without feeling anxious. In theory, the fear response is being replaced with a new, incompatible response — relaxation. If this therapy works, clients who used to be mildly anxious when thinking about standing on a two-foot-high stool can imagine (and eventually perform) looking out over the city from the top of a tall building without experiencing fear.

Aversion therapy is another example of classical conditioning used to alter problem behaviors. Here therapists try to rid their clients of undesirable behaviors by pairing aversive images with the behavior. For example, for a client trying to quit smoking, the image of a cigarette might be paired with images of becoming nauseated and vomiting.

Operant Conditioning Applications   Sometimes therapy can be as basic as reinforcing desired behaviors and punishing undesirable ones. However, this is more difficult than it may sound. Behavior modification therapists must begin this treatment by identifying the target behavior and defining it in specific operational terms. For example, what would you reinforce or punish when a child's problem is "acting too immature"? A behavior therapist probably would interview parents and teachers to determine which specific immature behaviors they wanted to reduce. Next, the therapist probably would want to determine a baseline of behavior frequency. How do you know if you're reducing the frequency of a behavior if you don't know how often it occurs now? For example, through observation or interviews, the therapist might find that a child throws an average of two and a half tantrums per week.

Once we know how often the behavior occurs under the current system of rewards and punishments, we change the contingencies. If it is a desired behavior, the environment is altered so that the client is rewarded for it. If it is an undesired behavior, punishment or a reduction of reinforcement is introduced. Ideally, appropriate responses are reinforced while the undesired behavior is being extinguished or punished. In the case of the child throwing tantrums, parents might be told to stop rewarding the action with their attention and concern. In addition, punishments might be introduced, such as not allowing the child to watch television for one day after a tantrum. At the same time, the child should be reinforced for handling frustrating situations in an appropriate way, such as seeking help instead of throwing a tantrum. The frequency of the target behavior is monitored throughout the therapy. After a few weeks, the therapist can see if the treatment is working or if adjustments need to be made. If the child is down to one tantrum a week, the treatment probably will continue for a few more weeks until the tantrums disappear entirely. If they are still occurring at two and a half times a week, a new therapy program may have to be developed.

A therapist who wants to change a large number of behaviors for a large number of people at once might use another treatment system based on operant conditioning called a *token economy*. People in a well-defined institutional unit, such as a psychiatric ward or a class, are given the opportunity to earn tokens (for example, poker chips) worth a certain number of points. They can exchange these tokens for more tangible rewards, such as snack food or extra privileges. Psychiatric ward patients might be given two tokens for making their beds in the morning, five for attending therapy sessions on time, ten for doing their assigned work on the ward, and so on. When clients show inappropriate behaviors, they might be punished by having tokens taken away.

Biofeedback represents another example of using operant conditioning to treat psychological problems. Biofeedback requires special equipment that provides information about somatic processes. This information is not readily perceivable without the equipment and therefore is difficult to control. For example, a woman suffering from anxiety might use a machine that tells her when she is tightening and relaxing certain facial and back muscles she otherwise is not aware of. After several muscle relaxation sessions with the immediate feedback of the machine, she may be able to reduce tension on her own and thereby overcome her anxiety. In operant conditioning terms, she was reinforced for producing the response that lowered her muscle tension, as indicated by the machine. As with other reinforced behaviors, she soon learned to make the relaxation response. Other bodily indicators that may be controlled through biofeedback include blood pressure, heart rate, and brain waves.

Self-Efficacy

Every year millions of Americans seek professional help to stop smoking or lose weight. Although many of these people go several weeks without cigarettes or succeed in dropping a few pounds, only a small percent permanently end their habit or keep the lost pounds off. What is it about these few successful cases that separates them from all the others? The answer may lie in what Albert Bandura calls *self-efficacy*. People stop smoking and overeating when they convince themselves they can do it. Smokers frequently explain that they have tried to quit but just can't. From a social learning analysis, one reason these smokers are unable to quit their habit is precisely because they believe they cannot.

Self-efficacy refers to the belief that one can have an impact on the environment. According to Bandura (1977b), people aren't likely to alter their behavior until they make a clear decision to change and expend some effort. Behavior modification procedures do not change people as much as they provide the method for people to change themselves once they have decided to do so.

In essence, therapy is not likely to work unless the client expects it to. Bandura (1977b) draws a distinction between outcome expectations and efficacy expectations. An *outcome expectation* is the extent to which people believe their actions will lead to a certain outcome. An *efficacy expectation* is the extent to which they believe they can bring about the particular outcome. Simply put, it is the difference between believing that something can happen and believing that you can make it happen. For example, you may hold the *outcome* expectation that if you devote several hours to studying each night and abandon social life on weekends, you will get straight A's throughout college. However, you may also hold the *efficacy* expectation that you are incapable of such devoted work and sacrifice.

Bandura argues that efficacy expectations are better predictors of behavior. Whether people make an effort to cope with problems and how long they persist in their efforts to change are determined by the extent to which they believe they are capable of such change. Students are unlikely to make the effort for straight A's if they don't think it possible. Therapy clients are unlikely to stop smoking, lose weight, or overcome a fear of flying if they don't believe they are capable of doing it.

Where do efficacy expectations come from, and how can therapists change their clients' beliefs about their abilities? Bandura (1977b) describes four sources. The most important of these is *performance accomplishments*: successful attempts to achieve the outcome in the past. Sky divers suddenly struck with fear before a jump may tell themselves that they've done this many times before without incident and therefore can do it again. On the other hand, a history of failures often leads to low efficacy expectations. People with a fear of heights who have never been able to climb a ladder without coming back down in a fit of anxiety probably will conclude they can't perform this behavior.

Although not as powerful as actual past performances, *vicarious experiences* also alter efficacy expectations. Seeing other people perform a behavior without adverse effects can lead us to believe that we can do it too. People who are afraid to speak in front of an audience may change their efficacy expectation from "I can't do that" to "maybe I can" after seeing other members of a public speaking class give their speeches without disastrous results. When you tell yourself something like "If he can do it, so can I," you are changing your efficacy expectation through vicarious experience.

A less effective way to alter efficacy expectations is through *verbal persuasion*. Telling someone who is reluctant to stand up to the boss "you can do it" might convince the person to assert his or her rights. However, this expectation will be easily eliminated if the actual performance isn't met with the expected result.

Finally, *emotional arousal* can be a source of efficacy expectations. A woman who has difficulty approaching men may find her heart begins beating rapidly and her palms start perspiring as she picks up the phone to call a man to ask for a date. If she interprets these physiological responses as signs of anxiety, she may decide she is too nervous to go through with it. However, if she notices how calm she is just before dialing, she may decide she is more courageous than she realized.

The key to a successful treatment program, then, is changing a client's efficacy expectation through one or more of these means. For example, Bandura, Adams, and Beyer (1977) helped snake-phobic subjects overcome their fear of the reptiles by taking them through the process of touching and picking up snakes (performance accomplishments) and/or watching someone else go through this procedure (vicarious experience). In nearly every case, whether the subjects believed they could approach and touch the snakes was the best predictor of whether they would actually do it. Other studies have found that self-efficacy beliefs play an important role in clients' ability to deal with a wide variety of psychological problems. These include post-traumatic stress disorder (Solomon, Weisenberg, Schwarzwald, & Mikulincer, 1988), test anxiety (Smith, 1989), drug addiction (DiClemente, 1986), and coping with the fear of sexual assault (Ozer & Bandura, 1990).

In summary, although behaviorists and social learning theorists often are associated with animal laboratories and academic research, what they have discovered about the causes of behavior has tremendous implications for helping people who have problem behaviors. Behavior modification techniques are widely used by psychologists, social workers, teachers, and others in helping professions. Since outlined by Bandura more than a decade ago, self-efficacy theory has proven useful in developing successful therapy programs (cf. Harvey, 1986). Because of their relatively high success rate in dealing with many problem behaviors, and the relative ease with which therapists and helping professionals learn and apply these techniques, therapy procedures evolving from the behavioral/social learning approach to personality probably will remain popular for a long time.

Assessment: Behavior Observation Methods

Let's begin this section by thinking about one of your bad habits. Unless you are quite different from the rest of us, you probably smoke, chew your nails, eat junk food, lose your temper, use harsh language, talk too much, or engage in some other behavior that you probably would like to change. Now, imagine that you seek out a behavior therapist for help with this problem. This therapist asks you a simple question: How often do you engage in the behavior? If you have been keeping track, you may be able to say exactly how many cigarettes you smoke per day or how often you chew your nails each week. But most likely your answer will be far from precise. Behavior therapists need to know how often a behavior occurs now so that they can determine if the treatment program is effective. Yet too often their clients explain they do this unwanted behavior "every once in a while," "not too often," or "all the time."

Unlike those who practice other approaches to psychotherapy, behavior therapists typically do not spend much time trying to discover the true cause of the client's problem. Instead, the focus is on observable behaviors. Other therapists may see the behavior as a sign of some underlying problem, but for behavior therapists, the behavior *is* the problem. Therefore, objective and reliable assessment of behavior is critical. Behavior therapists use assessment procedures for a variety of purposes. Obviously, they want to determine how often a problem behavior occurs. But they also may want to find out something about the events surrounding the behavior. Does the client smoke alone or with other people? Do the tantrums occur at a certain time of day or after a certain kind of experience, such as a scolding? These data can be very helpful in designing treatment programs. Finally, therapists probably will want to monitor the therapy's progress and make some judgment about its success. They will base this judgment on how often the target behavior occurs before and after the introduction of the treatment.

Behavior therapists have developed a variety of methods for obtaining this information. This was illustrated in a survey of members of a professional behavior therapist organization (Swan & MacDonald, 1978). Members were asked which assessment procedures they used in their work. The results are shown in Table 13.3. A few members indicated they occasionally used personality inventories and even projective tests. Quite likely, these therapists would be looked at with disfavor by the "pure" behaviorists in the group. What is clear from this list is that few behavior therapists rely on any one method for obtaining information about behavior frequency. Let's look at a few of the more popular assessment procedures in depth.

Direct Observation

The most obvious way to find out how often a behavior occurs is to observe the person directly. Although a therapist usually can't watch a client all day long, it is often possible to observe a sample of a person's behavior to obtain an idea of the frequency of the target behavior. For example, if you wanted to know how much time a girl spends interacting with children her own age, you might watch the child playing on the playground for several recesses. Sometimes psychologists create somewhat artificial settings in which to make their observations. For example, a therapist might stage a party for patients on the ward or a dance for clients suffering from acute shyness. Occasionally therapists ask clients to role-play. A therapist helping clients become more assertive might ask a man in a therapy group to imagine that another member of the group has just cut in front of him in line. The client then acts out what he would do in that situation. In this case, the way the client acts in the role-playing exercise probably is similar to the way he acts when confronted with such a situation in real life.

Table 13.3

Behavior Therapists' Assessment Methods

Method	Percentage Using
Interview with client	89.4
Client self-monitoring	51.1
Interview with others	49.2
Direct observation *in situ*	39.6
Information from consulting professionals	36.6
Role play	34.3
Self-report measures	26.9
Personality inventories	20.2
Demographic questionnaires	20.1
Projective tests	10.1

Source: Adapted from Swan and MacDonald (1978); reprinted by permission of the Association for the Advancement of Behavior Therapy.

However, good behavioral assessment requires more than simply observing a person. If the information is to be useful, the therapist should follow certain procedures. First, the behaviors to be observed must be defined as precisely as possible. This is fairly simple when talking about the number of cigarettes smoked. But what if the target behavior is "appropriate classroom responses"? In this case, the therapist might define appropriate responses as those relevant to the topic being discussed or those in which the child waits for teacher recognition before speaking. But even these definitions leave considerable room for observer interpretation. A good definition includes examples of behaviors to be counted and rules for dealing with borderline cases.

One way to improve the accuracy of behavior observation is to have two or more observers independently code the same behaviors. For example, two judges can watch the same child during the same set of recesses. If the two are largely in agreement on how often they counted the target behavior, then we can have confidence that the count is fairly accurate. However, if one coder sees few behaviors while a second coder sees many, we have little indication about how often the target behavior actually occurs. One solution to part of this problem is to videotape the behavior so that many different judges can observe the same behavior. Videotapes also allow the therapist to analyze the person's actions more precisely and more efficiently at a later, convenient time.

Psychologists working with children often use direct observation. This procedure allows them to assess how a child plays alone, how parents interact with their child, or how well a child interacts with other children. Many psychologists have also discovered the value of videotaping behavior samples for more extensive observation and coding later.

Behavior therapists also must be aware of the problem of bias. Although they strive for objective data based on observable events, behaviorists are aware that they can unintentionally (of course, not unconsciously) see what they want or what they expect to see. To guard against this problem, therapists should define behaviors in a manner that minimizes subjective judgment. If possible, a therapist might even use observers who don't know what the therapist expects to find.

Self-Monitoring

Although direct observation provides a relatively accurate assessment of the frequency of target behaviors, it often is too costly and time-consuming to be useful. An alternative is *self-monitoring*, having clients observe themselves. However, simply asking clients how often they engage in a behavior probably won't be much help. Clients often have a distorted idea about how often a behavior occurs. In addition, usually it is important to understand the circumstances surrounding the behavior. Are there places the client is particularly likely to smoke, such as in a restaurant or at a party? Is the smoking associated with a certain time of day, a certain type of activity, or a certain mood? With accurate information, a therapist

DIET COUNSELOR

I KEPT A LOG OF EVERYTHING I ATE THIS WEEK, BUT NOW I'VE GOT WRITER'S CRAMP.

© 1988 by NEA, inc   THAVES 9-15

Self-Monitoring

can develop a treatment that includes, for example, not going to cocktail lounges where everyone seems to be smoking or an alternative activity for when the client begins to feel overstressed at work.

Unfortunately, few clients can provide accurate information about these variables from memory. Therefore, therapists often ask clients to observe and record their behaviors for a period of time. Clients sometimes are surprised by what they find. For example, people trying to watch their weight may not have realized that they eat more when they're alone, when watching television, or after they've had a drink. An interesting benefit of the self-monitoring method is that watching your own behavior can be therapeutic in itself. For example, clients forced to pay attention to their eating or smoking sometimes show improvement during the first few weeks of the process, before the treatment has even begun (Mahoney & Arnkoff, 1979). Naturally, self-monitoring is also used to assess progress throughout the treatment period to determine the success of the therapy. One problem that sometimes surfaces is the client's honesty. Clients may not want to admit to their therapists that they increased their smoking or lost their temper several times in one week. Therapists who suspect a problem may want to use other assessment methods, such as the one discussed next.

Observation by Others

Some clients are unwilling or just unable to provide accurate information about themselves. For example, self-monitoring probably is inappropriate with children or those with severe psychological disorders. In these cases, it may be possible to rely on other people to make the observations. For example, parents and teachers often can record the frequency of a child's problem behaviors. It is best if these people actually observe for a period of time rather than relying on their memories. Thus, a teacher might be asked to record each time she punishes a child for inappropriate classroom behavior. Therapists in mental health settings can use

425

nurses and aides as observers to record the occurrence of patients' behaviors. Although this process can introduce bias, it provides the most accurate assessment of a client's behavior in some situations.

Many psychologists use these reports to complement data obtained through other methods. For example, children sometimes act differently in the presence of a therapist than they do at home. A client may be able to role-play the appropriate behaviors when confronting a belligerent boss but may become timid when facing the real boss at work. Getting family members involved in the process can have other advantages, such as making these members aware of the extent of the client's problem and aware of how their reactions might be affecting his or her behavior.

Self-Report Measures

Some behavior therapists include self-report inventories among their assessment tools, although these may be less accurate than actual observation. These inventories are usually different from the ones trait theorists use. Behaviorists typically are not interested in determining the strength of some underlying construct. Instead, a behaviorist's self-report inventory might ask people *how often* they engage in specific behaviors, rather than how they feel about things.

Behavior therapists use the self-report inventory found on pages 427–428 to measure the extent to which clients engage in assertive behavior. You may notice that the test items deal primarily with descriptions of behaviors. Note also that the test is not constructed to hide its intentions, as trait inventories sometimes are. When clients understand which behaviors are being measured, they can make an effort to provide as accurate a description of themselves as possible. Self-report inventories are often used in conjunction with other assessment methods and can be used throughout the treatment program to monitor the progress of the therapy.

Strengths and Criticisms
of the Behavioral/Social Learning Approach

Behaviorism roared onto the psychology scene in the 1920s and took a grip on the discipline that didn't loosen for several decades. Although humanistic psychologists tried to dethrone the behaviorists' view of human nature in the 1960s, behaviorism remains alive and well today. The social learning theories promoted by Bandura and Rotter seem more popular than ever. Obviously, the behavioral/social learning approach to personality could not have withstood this test of time without some unique strengths. Of course, no theory as influential as behaviorism can hope to escape criticism, either.

Strengths

One reason for the endurance of the behavioral/social learning approach is its solid foundation in empirical research. This contrasts with other approaches to

Assertiveness

Behavior therapists have devoted a great deal of attention to assertive behavior. Many people have difficulty asserting their rights; they have a hard time complaining to a waitress or telling their boss that they're being treated unfairly. In behavioral terms, these people need to increase the frequency of their assertive behaviors in appropriate situations. Assertiveness training often consists of modeling others' assertive behavior, role-playing assertive responses, and receiving immediate reinforcement for appropriate assertive actions. Alberti and Emmons (1974) designed the following inventory to measure assertive behavior. In a successful treatment program, the client's score should increase as therapy progresses.

ASSERTIVENESS INVENTORY
The following questions will be helpful in assessing your assertiveness. Be honest in your responses. All you have to do is draw a circle around the number that describes you best. For some questions, the assertive end of the scale is at 0; for others, at 4.
Key: 0 means *no* or *never*, 1 means *somewhat* or *sometimes*, 2 means *average*, 3 means *usually* or *a good deal*, and 4 means *practically always* or *entirely*.

1. When a person is highly unfair, do you call it to his attention? 0 1 2 3 4
2. Do you find it difficult to make decisions? 0 1 2 3 4
3. Are you openly critical of others' ideas, opinions, behavior? 0 1 2 3 4
4. Do you speak out in protest when someone takes your place in line? . . 0 1 2 3 4
5. Do you often avoid people or situations for fear of embarrassment? . . 0 1 2 3 4
6. Do you usually have confidence in your own judgment? 0 1 2 3 4
7. Do you insist that your spouse or roommate take on a fair share of household chores? 0 1 2 3 4
8. Are you prone to "fly off the handle"? 0 1 2 3 4
9. When a salesman makes an effort, do you find it hard to say "No" even though the merchandise is not really what you want? 0 1 2 3 4
10. When a latecomer is waited on before you are, do you call attention to the situation? 0 1 2 3 4
11. Are you reluctant to speak up in a discussion or debate? 0 1 2 3 4
12. If a person has borrowed money (or a book, garment, thing of value) and is overdue in returning it, do you mention it? 0 1 2 3 4
13. Do you continue to pursue an argument after the other person has had enough? 0 1 2 3 4
14. Do you generally express what you feel? 0 1 2 3 4
15. Are you disturbed if someone watches you at work? 0 1 2 3 4
16. If someone keeps kicking or bumping your chair in a movie or a lecture, do you ask the person to stop? 0 1 2 3 4
17. Do you find it difficult to keep eye contact when talking to another person? 0 1 2 3 4

continued

18. In a good restaurant, when your meal is improperly prepared or served, do you ask the waiter-waitress to correct the situation?...... 0 1 2 3 4
19. When you discover merchandise is faulty, do you return it for an adjustment?.. 0 1 2 3 4
20. Do you show your anger by name-calling or obscenities?.......... 0 1 2 3 4
21. Do you try to be a wallflower or a piece of the furniture in social situations?.. 0 1 2 3 4
22. Do you insist that your landlord (mechanic, repairman, etc.) make repairs, adjustments or replacements which are his responsibility?.. 0 1 2 3 4
23. Do you often step in and make decisions for others?............... 0 1 2 3 4
24. Are you able openly to express love and affection?................ 0 1 2 3 4
25. Are you able to ask your friends for small favors or help?........... 0 1 2 3 4
26. Do you think you always have the right answer?................... 0 1 2 3 4
27. When you differ with a person you respect, are you able to speak up for your own viewpoint?.. 0 1 2 3 4
28. Are you able to refuse unreasonable requests made by friends? 0 1 2 3 4
29. Do you have difficulty complimenting or praising others?........... 0 1 2 3 4
30. If you are disturbed by someone smoking near you, can you say so?.. 0 1 2 3 4
31. Do you shout or use bullying tactics to get others to do as you wish? .. 0 1 2 3 4
32. Do you finish other people's sentences for them?.................. 0 1 2 3 4
33. Do you get into physical fights with others, especially with strangers?.. 0 1 2 3 4
34. At family meals, do you control the conversation?.................. 0 1 2 3 4
35. When you meet a stranger, are you the first to introduce yourself and begin a conversation?....................................... 0 1 2 3 4

personality sometimes based on intuition or data gathered from biased samples. Skinner, Bandura, and Rotter based their descriptions of human personality on empirical research findings and relied on empirical data in the development and refinement of their theories. Critics often challenge the existence of Freud's Oedipus complex, but it would be difficult to deny that behaviors can be changed through operant and classical conditioning. Instead, criticism centers on the interpretation and application of these principles and on gaps in the overall approach.

Another strength of the behavioral/social learning approach lies in the development of some useful therapeutic procedures. Behavior modification procedures, although controversial at times, have several advantages over other therapy approaches. One advantage is the use of baseline data and objective criteria for determining success or failure. Other approaches often begin treatment without first determining the level of the problem; the therapy is declared a success when the therapist or the client decides there has been some improvement. In addition, behavior modification may be the most useful approach when working with certain populations, such as children, mentally disabled people, or severely emotionally disturbed patients. Members of some of these groups would have a difficult time discussing abstract psychoanalytic concepts or dealing with some of the existential questions posed by humanistic therapists. Behavior modification also is relatively quick and easy to administer. Treatment often lasts a matter of weeks, compared with months or years with other approaches. The basic methods can be taught to parents, teachers, and hospital personnel, who can then carry out the therapy without the therapist present. This means that more people can benefit from therapy procedures at a lower cost than is possible with most other types of psychotherapy.

The social learning theories of Bandura and Rotter added cognitive variables to the behavioral approach and thereby expanded the range of phenomena explained by this perspective. These theories have helped to fill in the gaps many psychologists find in the radical behavioral position. Social learning models of personality allow us to understand thoughts, expectancies, values, and the like along with basic behavior conditioning principles within one consistent framework. In addition, the introduction of these cognitive elements has helped to link behavioral personality theory with some of the more recent cognitive approaches to personality. These approaches, covered in Chapter 15, have been strongly influenced by the work of the social learning theorists.

Criticisms

A persistent criticism of the behavioral/social learning approach is that it is too narrow in its description of human personality. Many psychologists feel that while the approach touches on several crucial aspects of human experience such as thinking, emotion, and levels of consciousness, it does so in a very limited way. Critics are particularly concerned with the Skinnerian brand of behaviorism that rejects the usefulness of looking at inner feelings and intuition. Humanistically oriented psychologists have difficulty with the behaviorists' rejection of free will as a determinant of behavior. Others criticize the behavioral/social learning approach for giving inadequate attention to the role of heredity. In addition, recent research points to limits on how easily certain behaviors can be conditioned. For example, it is more difficult to create a fear of food in animals by pairing the food with electric shocks than it is to create an avoidance of the food by pairing it with nausea (Garcia & Koelling, 1966; Seligman & Hager, 1972). Thus, behaviorists may need to recognize the limits of the conditioning principles they promote so widely.

Another criticism, directed primarily at the Skinnerian position, is that human beings are much more complex than the laboratory animals used in behavioral research. These critics challenge the way behaviorists use laboratory rat data to explain human behavior. As Bandura and some of the social learning theorists recognize, people are capable of considering alternative courses of action, of weighing the probabilities and values of different reinforcers, of looking at long-term goals, and so forth. These critics do not deny that we often respond to stimuli in an automatic fashion or that some of our behaviors are conditioned. But they maintain that these are the least important and least interesting human behaviors. An example of the difficulty in generalizing from animal data to human behavior is seen in research on the effects of extrinsic reinforcers on intrinsically motivated behavior. Researchers have found consistently that paying people to engage in a behavior they already enjoy typically results in a *reduction* in the frequency of the behavior (cf. Deci & Ryan, 1987). People seem to redefine the behavior as work instead of play ("I play the piano *because* I am paid") and therefore lose interest in it unless paid.

Despite the success of behavior therapists in dealing with many problem behaviors, some critics argue that too often these therapists distort the real therapy issues when they reduce everything to observable behaviors. For example, a client who complains that he has no meaning in his life might be asked to define this abstract issue in terms of the frequency of measurable behaviors. A behavior therapist might count the number of times the person engages in pleasant activities and set up a treatment program that rewards the client for going to parties, talking with friends, reading good books, and so on. These activities might make the person feel better. But critics might argue that the therapy has not addressed the client's real problem, but instead has simply made his life a little happier or has temporarily diverted his attention from his concern for finding meaning in life.

A final criticism concerns the effects of some behavior modification procedures. Some critics charge that the positive effects of some procedures are short-lived and that clients will resume their problem behaviors once the treatment is over. This may be a particular concern with the token economy method (Greene, Sternberg, & Lepper, 1976; Levine & Fasnacht, 1974). Clients may make their beds or do their work as long as they receive token rewards. But they may stop these behaviors as soon as they leave the institutional setting and the rewards are no longer offered. Similarly, carefully controlled research indicates biofeedback may not be nearly as effective as many of the earlier adherents claimed (Roberts, 1985). In addition, critics sometimes challenge the behaviorists' explanations for why behavior modification procedures work. For example, systematic desensitization may be effective for reasons other than the pairing of incompatible responses to feared stimuli. The procedure may work simply because the clients expect that it will be effective (Kazdin & Wilcoxon, 1976). Similarly, the positive effects found in biofeedback treatments may be attributable to the relaxation induced in the procedure rather than the actual feedback of somatic processes (Lindholm & Lowry, 1978).

Summary

1. Behaviorism was introduced by John B. Watson in the 1920s and has withstood numerous challenges and the test of time to remain an influential approach to the understanding of human behavior and personality. In its most extreme form, behaviorism limits psychology to the study of observable behaviors. Classical and operant conditioning are used by behaviorists to explain the development and maintenance of behaviors. Personality is described as the end result of one's history of conditioning. B. F. Skinner later became the spokesperson for what has come to be called radical behaviorism. He rejected the use of inner states, such as anxiety, as explanations of behavior in favor of observable external events.

2. Traditional behaviorism identifies two basic forms of conditioning. Classical conditioning occurs when a new stimulus is paired with an existing stimulus-response bond. Operant conditioning results when a behavior is followed by either reinforcement or punishment.

3. Later social learning theorists expanded on the basic behaviorist position. Albert Bandura proposes that internal states, the environment, and behavior all affect one another. He maintains that people often regulate their own behavior and that we engage in purposeful, future-oriented thinking. Bandura has added to classical and operant conditioning the notion that we learn through observing others, although whether we perform the behaviors we learn depends on our expectancies for rewards or punishments.

4. Julian Rotter argues that the probability of engaging in a behavior changes after rewards and punishments because our expectancies change. He uses these expectancies and the values given to particular reinforcers to predict which of many behavior options will be enacted.

5. Behavior modification therapists apply basic conditioning principles when dealing with their clients. Some of these, such as systematic desensitization, are based on classical conditioning. Others, such as token economies, are based on operant conditioning. Bandura has identified the client's feelings of self-efficacy as a crucial variable in the psychotherapy progress. Whether clients expect to succeed is an important determinant of therapy success. These expectancies come from a variety of sources, including past performance accomplishments and vicarious learning.

6. Unlike personality approaches that interpret assessment data as a sign of some underlying construct, behavior therapists see the behavior as the focus of their treatment. Behavioral assessment includes a variety of techniques, including direct observation, self-monitoring, observations by others, and self-report measures. Each of these techniques can provide useful data for determining baseline frequencies, the conditions under which the target behavior occurs, and the success of the treatment procedure.

7. The behavioral/social learning approach has its strengths and its criticisms. Among the strengths are its empirical base and the useful therapeutic procedures it has generated. The criticisms include the inappropriate attention given to free will and heredity. People also have criticized the way behavior therapists interpret problems into observable behaviors and some of the claims of how effective these procedures are.

Key Terms

radical behaviorism An extreme form of the behaviorist view that argues against using inner states as explanations for behaviors.

classical conditioning Learning resulting from pairing a conditioned stimulus with a new, unconditioned stimulus.

extinction Weakening of a learned association through the removal of reinforcement or pairing.

operant conditioning Learning resulting from the response an organism receives following a behavior.

schedule of reinforcement The frequency and conditions under which a learned response is reinforced.

shaping The use of operant conditioning to obtain a response by reinforcing successive approximations of the desired behavior.

generalization The tendency to respond to stimuli similar to the one used in the initial conditioning.

discrimination A learned tendency to respond only to stimuli that result in reinforcement and not to similar, but unrewarded, stimuli.

punishment A process to decrease the frequency of an undesired behavior by following the occurrence of the behavior with an aversive stimulus.

reciprocal determinism The notion that external determinants of behavior, internal determinants of behavior, and behavior all influence one another.

self-regulation The ability to develop and apply rewards and punishments for internal standards of behavior.

observational learning Learning that results from watching or hearing about a person modeling the behavior.

behavior potential The likelihood that a given behavior will be performed.

locus of control A personality trait indicating the extent to which people generally perceive that they have control over events in their lives.

behavior modification Therapy procedures based on operant conditioning and classical conditioning principles.

systematic desensitization A procedure for treating phobias in which relaxation is paired with images of the feared object.

self-efficacy A person's expectancy that he or she can successfully perform a given behavior.

Suggested Readings

Harvey, J. H. (Ed.). (1986). Special issue: Self-efficacy theory in contemporary psychology. *Journal of Social and Clinical Psychology, 4*(3). This issue presents analyses of Bandura's self-efficacy theory and research applying self-efficacy to such areas as social anxiety, depression, career choice, addictive behavior, and athletic performance.

Rotter, J. B. (1982). *The development and applications of social learning theory: Selected papers.* New York: Praeger. This is a collection of Julian Rotter's most important papers, illustrating the origins and development of his social learning theory. The book includes an overview by Rotter, a brief autobiography, and a comprehensive bibliography.

Skinner, B. F. (1971). *Beyond freedom and dignity.* New York: Bantam. This book inevitably generates controversy and discussion. B. F. Skinner uses his radical behaviorist position to argue that we should abandon the notion that people freely choose their behaviors. He also argues that because our concept of human dignity is based on this illusion of freedom, it also is a myth.

Skinner, B. F. (1990). Can psychology be a science of mind? *American Psychologist, 45,* 1206–1210. Skinner outlines the philosophical underpinnings of his approach to understanding human behavior. This article was based on Skinner's last public address, a keynote speech at the 1990 American Psychological Association convention, and was completed August 17, 1990, the evening before his death.

The Behavioral/Social Learning Approach
Relevant Research

People often think of behaviorists as aloof, data-oriented scientists more concerned with how many times a rat presses a bar than with the people in their lives. While it's true that these researchers often attend to minute experimental details and precise theoretical issues that seem overly esoteric to an outside observer, this does not mean they have lost sight of the human element or their goal of improving the human condition. Even B. F. Skinner, spokesperson for the radical behaviorists, wrote extensively on how we can use the information coming out of those laboratories to overcome many of the problems facing society today. This concern for application can be seen in each of the four research topics reviewed in this chapter. Each has something to say about pressing social problems or personal lifestyle issues.

Many men and women today are concerned about how gender roles shape and restrict their behavior. In increasing numbers, women are abandoning traditional gender roles to take important positions in business and government. Some men are experimenting with nontraditional male roles, such as taking on child-rearing responsibilities. But understanding why we make some of the gender-related choices we do requires an examination of how operant and observational learning shape those choices. We'll look at these processes and how individual differences in masculinity and femininity are related to personal adjustment and the way we interact with others.

As more people become concerned about violence in our society, psychologists have focused their attention on the impact aggressive models have on aggressive behavior. Bandura's observational learning model helps to explain some of this process. We'll look at this model and the question of how mass media violence affects the behavior of those who consume it.

Applying animal research findings to human beings is a standard feature of the behavioral approach to personality. A particularly fruitful example of this application is the work on learned helplessness. From some surprising observations of dogs in a classical conditioning experiment, researchers have developed a theory with implications for depression and adjustment among the elderly.

Finally, we'll look at the aspect of Rotter's social learning theory that has inspired the most research. The concept of individual differences in generalized expectancies, known today as locus of control, has been the topic of an enormous amount of personality research. Some of these findings provide important information about how our expectancies are related to personal adjustment and our health.

Individual Differences in Sex-Role Behavior

I would like to describe two friends of mine. The first is a very caring and loving person. This friend never forgets my birthday, is sensitive to my needs and moods, and is the person I seek out first when I need someone to talk to. This friend also confides in me and is not afraid to share intimate feelings. My other friend is on the way to becoming a leader in the business world. This friend knows how to be assertive when necessary, how to express opinions directly, and how to get others to do what is needed for the company. Unlike the first person I described, this one sometimes has difficulty being intimate with others or sharing feelings. I've never seen this friend cry.

Unless you've already caught on to my point here, you probably imagined the first person I described as a woman and the second one as a man, even though I never identified the gender of either. This doesn't mean you're gullible or a sexist, but rather that you are aware of the sex-role stereotypes that affect the way men and women behave in this culture. Traditional stereotypes portray men as aggressive, independent, and unemotional, and women as passive, dependent, and affectionate. Much has been written recently about changes in these sex roles, with men being told it is all right to show emotion and women being encouraged to be assertive and businesslike. However, while some gender restrictions may have loosened in the past few decades, sex roles remain a part of our culture and, although different in each case, probably a part of every culture (Williams & Best, 1982).

Why do women tend to behave in certain ways and men in others? Although biological differences between the sexes may play some role, behaviorists and social learning theorists maintain gender differences are the result of a lifelong process of sex-role socialization. Children and adults acquire and maintain sex-appropriate behaviors largely through operant conditioning and observational learning. You can see the effects of operant conditioning whenever young children act in gender-inappropriate ways. For example, boys often tease one another for crying, playing with dolls, or showing an interest in cooking or sewing. Similarly, playmates make fun of girls when they act like tomboys. At the same time, boys are rewarded with camaraderie and parental nods for playing football and standing up to those who try to push them around. And girls win approval for showing an interest in caring for babies and for acting sweet and cute. This pattern of rewards and punishments soon shapes the amount of time children spend engaging in traditionally masculine and feminine behaviors.

You can appreciate the difficulty in changing these behavior patterns when you realize how early this operant conditioning starts. Consider what one team of researchers found when they interviewed parents of sons and daughters within 24 hours after the birth of their first child (Rubin, Provenzano, & Luria, 1974).

Sex typing . . . is the process through which a culture transforms male and female children into masculine and feminine adults.

SANDRA BEM

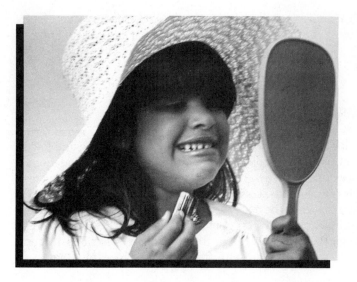

Most little girls occasionally play "dress up." Girls put on their mother's clothes, jewelry, and makeup after identifying that this is something females, but not males, do. We would not expect to find little boys imitating this behavior.

Parents rated daughters as softer, finer featured, smaller, and less attentive than sons. In addition, parents of daughters described their child as beautiful, pretty, or cute and said that the child resembled the mother more than did parents of sons. In reality, the newborns did not differ in terms of weight, length, or measures of general health. Another group of experimenters looked at the toys and clothing of boys and girls from ages 5 months to 25 months (Pomerleau, Bolduc, Malcuit, & Cossette, 1990). They found the girls were more likely to have dolls and toy furniture than the boys. However, the boys were more likely to have sports equipment, toy tools, and toy cars and trucks. Perhaps not surprisingly, the girls were more likely to have pink clothing, and the boys blue. Clearly, boys and girls are treated differently beginning at a very early age.

Within a few years, impressions of what is appropriate for boys and girls are communicated to the child. By the time children enter kindergarten, they are well aware of sex-role expectations (Vogel, Lake, Evans, & Karraker, 1991; Williams, Bennett, & Best, 1975). With parents *and* peers holding these expectancies, children are surrounded by people ready to reward gender-appropriate behaviors and punish inappropriate ones.

Sex-role behaviors also are acquired through observational learning. There certainly is no shortage of models exhibiting gender-appropriate behaviors. Children have the opportunity to learn which behaviors are expected of men and which are expected of women by watching parents, neighbors, siblings, play-mates, and television characters (see Box 14.1). When children are very young, parents probably are the most influential models, which may be why people's sex-role behavior tends to resemble that of their mother or father (Jackson, Ialongo, & Stollak, 1986). Later, children are more likely to take their cue about appropriate and inappropriate behavior from their friends.

However, this finding does not mean boys imitate only male models and girls only female models. Instead, the child must first notice that a certain behavior is

Box 14.1

Sex-Role Models in the Mass Media

We learn sex-role behaviors from a variety of models. Naturally, parents, siblings, and peers provide much of this information. But we also are exposed almost daily to role models via mass media outlets. A few decades of consciousness-raising has helped to rewrite children's books that used to portray only men as doctors and only women as child raisers. But these and similar messages remain in other popular outlets. For example, men and women typically are portrayed very differently in television commercials (O'Donnell & O'Donnell, 1978). Women are often depicted as housewives who are highly emotional, inept at handling money, and constantly gossiping or nagging. Few men on commercials are concerned with the cleanliness of their toilet bowl or if the family liked their fried chicken, but many women are.

Men and women also are portrayed differently in magazine advertisements (Venkatesan & Losco, 1975), children's toy promotions (Schwartz & Markham, 1985), and comic strips (Chavez, 1985). Boys almost never play with dolls in toy ads. Women characters rarely appear in comic strips; when they do they usually are pictured working in the kitchen, doing the shopping or engaging in some other stereotypic activity.

What effect do these stereotypic portrayals have upon our behavior? To answer this, one team of researchers compared the type of television shows college students watched with their levels of masculinity and femininity (Ross, Anderson, & Wisocki, 1982). The more students watched shows in which men and women were depicted in stereotypic ways, the more likely they were to be masculine or feminine themselves. Of course, it's possible these students chose the programs they did because of their sextype. But consider an experiment by Jennings, Geis, and Brown (1980). These researchers presented women with a series of commercials that showed women either in traditional or nontraditional roles. Women who saw the nontraditional portrayals later showed more independence in their judgments and greater self-confidence when presenting a speech than did the women who saw only traditional role behavior. This finding suggests that television models not only influence our gender-related behavior, but that changes in the way these models behave might also help to break down some of the gender stereotypes prevalent in our society today.

performed more often by one gender than the other (Bussey & Bandura, 1984; Perry & Bussey, 1979). Boys and girls may notice that men, but rarely women, work on mechanical things. When an appliance needs fixing, father is usually the one to do it. All the garage mechanics seem to be men, and if someone on television uses a screwdriver or a wrench, it almost always is a male. Children are likely to conclude that males are rewarded for mechanical behavior, but females are not. Thus, boys are more likely to get involved with mechanical things, anticipating rewards, whereas girls tend to seek out other activities. At this point operant conditioning may also come into play, such as when a father rewards his son for showing an interest in cars while laughing when his daughter asks to help with an oil change.

Masculinity-Femininity

After a lifetime of socialization through operant and observational learning, we should not be surprised that most adult men and women act in gender-appropriate ways. But even a casual observation of the people you meet in the next few hours will confirm there are large individual differences in the extent to which people act masculine and feminine. Although men generally are more aggressive and independent than women, there are many exceptions. Similarly, finding women who do not fit the stereotypic affectionate, emotional, and sensitive pattern is not difficult.

As with other individual differences, personality psychologists are interested in identifying, measuring, and describing the way people differ in terms of their masculinity and femininity. Early scales developed to measure the **masculinity-femininity** construct were based on two assumptions. First, masculinity and femininity were assumed to represent two extreme positions on a continuum of sex-role behavior. As shown in Figure 14.1, masculinity and femininity were considered opposites. The more a person was of one, the less he or she was of the other. Each of us can be placed on this continuum, with very masculine and very feminine people on the extremes and those who are both, but not much of either, toward the middle.

The second assumption was that the more people's sex-role behavior matched the stereotype for their gender, the more psychologically healthy they were. Masculine men and feminine women were considered well adjusted. But a man who acted too much the way society said a woman was supposed to act or a woman who acted too much like a stereotypic man were said to have adjustment problems. One of the original scales on the Minnesota Multiphasic Personality Inventory (MMPI) is the MF (Masculinity-Femininity) Scale. Researchers originally maintained that scoring too high or too low for one's gender on this scale was indicative of psychological disturbances.

Androgyny

Research soon uncovered several problems with the masculinity-femininity approach. After reviewing this research, Constantinople (1973) concluded the assumptions underlying the masculinity-femininity model could not be supported. She called for a new approach for understanding individual differences in sex-role behavior.

The new approach was not long in coming. Sandra Bem (1974, 1976, 1977) introduced the concept of **androgyny**. Coupled with society's rising concern for women's issues during these years, Bem's work stimulated an immense amount of interest in sex-role research and an accompanying degree of disagreement and

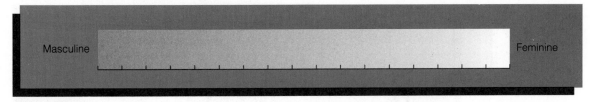

Figure 14.1

Traditional Masculinity-Femininity Model

controversy. Bem began by rejecting the notion that masculinity and femininity are opposites on a single continuum. She argued that masculinity and femininity are relatively independent traits. People can be high on both traits, on only one trait, or on neither. Further, because these traits are independent, knowing that someone is high in masculinity tells us nothing about how feminine that person is.

Bem also challenged the assumption that the most well-adjusted people are those whose gender matches their sex-type. Instead, she maintained the most well-adjusted person is one who is both masculine *and* feminine, whom she called *androgynous*. Bem argued that people who are only masculine or only feminine often lack the ability to engage in adaptive behavior. For example, masculine people do well as long as the situation calls for a masculine response. But when they are called on to act in a traditionally feminine manner, such as showing compassion or sensitivity, they falter. A well-adjusted person must have the flexibility to engage in masculine behaviors when the situation demands, as well as feminine behaviors when those are the most appropriate. "In a complex society like ours, an adult clearly has to be able to look out for himself and to get things done," Bem wrote. "But an adult also has to be able to relate to other human beings as people, to be sensitive to their needs and to be concerned about their welfare" (1976, p. 50).

Sex-Role Research

Bem's androgyny model helped to renew interest in sex-role research. The number of investigations on individual differences in masculinity and femininity ballooned during the following decade. Because the androgyny model assumes masculinity and femininity are independent traits, one of the first tasks was to develop new scales to assess each trait independently. The two most widely used scales today are the Bem Sex Role Inventory (Bem, 1974) and the Personal Attributes Questionnaire (Spence, Helmreich, & Stapp, 1974). Although some psychologists have argued that we should replace *masculinity* and *femininity* with less emotionally loaded terms, most researchers continue to use these labels (Lenney, 1991).

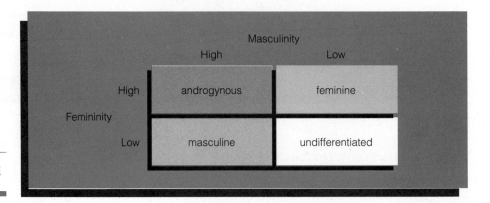

Figure 14.2

Androgyny Model

Today most sex-role inventories allow researchers to classify subjects as high or low on both a masculinity scale and a femininity scale. By using the median score as a cutoff point on each scale, researchers can place people into one of four sex-type categories, as shown in Figure 14.2. Those who score high in both masculinity and femininity are classified as *androgynous*. Those scoring high on one scale but not the other fall into either the *masculine* or the *feminine* category. Those who score low on both scales are classified as *undifferentiated*.

Which of the four categories people fall into has been tied to a large number of relevant behaviors. Two of these behaviors will be reviewed briefly here. We will begin by examining the question responsible for instigating the androgyny model in the first place, the relationship between individual differences in sex-role behavior and personal adjustment. Then we will look at research concerned with how your sex-type affects the quality of your personal relationships.

Sex-Type and Psychological Adjustment How does your sex-type affect your mental health? Despite numerous investigations into this question, no clear answer has emerged. Instead, there are at least three logical answers to how being masculine, feminine, or androgynous relates to personal adjustment.

The first, and probably least supported, description is the traditional *congruence model*. According to this model, masculine men and feminine women are the most well adjusted. Although this approach reflects old-fashioned attitudes and may even border on sexism, a case can be made. Think about all the pressure society puts on men and women to act in gender-appropriate ways. What can we conclude about people who emerge from this socialization without developing the sex-type dictated by society? Perhaps they are merely liberated from the restraints society places on most of us. But remember that the rewards and punishments for gender-appropriate behavior remain in adult life. Masculine women and feminine men probably face continual social rejection and ridicule, albeit more subtle than that imposed in the school playground. On the other hand, society is geared to give masculine men and feminine women most of the rewards in life. Thus, we might expect these people to be the happiest and most content.

Although this reasoning makes some sense, reviews of relevant research rarely find support for the congruence model (Taylor & Hall, 1982; Whitley, 1983). Masculine men and feminine women are not the most well adjusted. There may have been a time many years ago when this was the case, but we probably can safely conclude that those days are past.

The second explanation is Bem's *androgyny model*. According to this view, androgynous people are the most well adjusted because they have the ability to respond effectively in more situations than people in the other categories. People whose behavioral repertoires lack either masculine or feminine behaviors find many situations in which they are ill prepared to respond appropriately. For example, without masculine characteristics such as decisiveness and assertiveness, both men and women are likely to falter in achievement situations. On the other hand, people unable to express emotions have difficulty establishing good interpersonal relationships. Only androgynous people are capable of getting ahead on the job while relating well with friends and lovers in their leisure time.

Several investigations support the androgyny model (Bem, 1975; Bem & Lenney, 1976; Bem, Martyna, & Watson, 1976; Shaw, 1982). For example, when confronted with a baby, feminine and androgynous, but not masculine, people show appropriate nurturant behavior. On the other hand, feminine people are easily swayed by the opinions of others, whereas masculine and androgynous subjects better resist conformity pressures.

However, support for the androgyny model is mixed. Whereas many studies show the superior adaptability of androgynous people, other studies do not (Taylor & Hall, 1982; Worell, 1978). In particular, although androgynous people may be well prepared to deal with all situations, this often does not translate into a sense of well-being or high self-esteem.

A third approach, the *masculinity model*, maintains that being masculine is the key to mental health. Before rejecting this view as masculine propaganda, consider that in many ways our society is still geared toward admiring and rewarding the traits traditionally associated with men and masculinity. Stereotypically, men are independent, women are dependent. Men are achieving and powerful, women are unassertive and conforming. Men are leaders, women are followers. Given these descriptions, it makes sense that those who fit the masculine role might accomplish more and feel better about themselves than those who do not. Women do not have to abandon their femininity to get ahead in the traditionally male business world. But they may need some traditionally masculine attributes to be successful.

Several investigations find support for the masculinity model (Marsh, Antill, & Cunningham, 1987; O'Heron & Orlofsky, 1990; Orlofsky & O'Heron, 1987; Roos & Cohen, 1987). For example, because masculine people are more likely to use direct, problem-focused strategies for dealing with stress, they seem better able to deal with stressors than do people low in masculinity. Moreover, men and women high in masculinity have more confidence in their abilities and see themselves as more likely to succeed than do those low in masculinity (Dimitrovsky, Singer, & Yinon, 1989). Support for the masculinity model is particularly consistent when looking at the relationship between sex-type and self-esteem

(Whitley, 1983). Apparently, people who possess traditionally masculine attributes (such as achieving, athletic, powerful) also feel good about themselves.

So what are we to make of all this? Although the picture is far from clear, a few conclusions seem appropriate. First, very little research supports the congruence model. Second, some of the confusion may reflect the way masculinity and femininity are measured. For example, the Bem Sex Role Inventory asks people the extent to which 20 masculine and 20 feminine items describe them. Unfortunately, the masculine items tend to be more socially desirable than the feminine items (Pedhazur & Tetenbaum, 1979). It makes sense that people who describe themselves with the more flattering and positive masculine items (for example, self-reliant, ambitious) have higher self-esteem than those who describe themselves with the feminine items (for example, gullible, shy). Third, it seems quite possible that some aspects of a healthy personality, such as dealing with stress and personal achievement, are related to masculinity whereas other aspects, such as developing good interpersonal relationships, are not (Marsh & Byrne, 1991). Individual differences in sex-role behavior clearly are tied to personal adjustment and mental health in some way. However, just how these two are related remains the fuel for continued research.

Sex-Type and Interpersonal Interactions   Who would you turn to if you needed to talk to someone about a personal problem—a masculine, feminine, androgynous, or undifferentiated person? Who would you prefer for a friend? For a romantic relationship? Advertisements and TV shows often portray masculine men and feminine women as the most desirable partners for romantic encounters. Americans spend a considerable amount of money on makeup, body-building equipment, and the like to make themselves appear more feminine or masculine. But is this the road to a perfect relationship? Some research suggests it may not be.

A simple way to examine how people react to different sex-types is to ask subjects about hypothetical character sketches of masculine, feminine, androgynous, and undifferentiated people. In general, researchers using this procedure find the androgynous character is liked more than any of the others (Brooks-Gunn & Fisch, 1980; Gilbert, Deutsch, & Strahan, 1978; Jackson, 1983; Korabik, 1982; Kulick & Harackiewicz, 1979). For example, college students in one study said the androgynous person was more popular, more interesting, better adjusted, more competent, more intelligent, and more successful than people described in masculine, feminine, or undifferentiated terms (Major, Carnevale, & Deaux, 1981). Thus, in terms of first impressions, androgynous people come across quite well.

But do these impressions of hypothetical people translate into actual behaviors? To examine this question, researchers created four types of male-female pairs, based on subjects' scores on the Bem Sex Role Inventory: a masculine male and a feminine female, an androgynous female and a masculine male, a feminine female and an androgynous male, and two androgynous people (Ickes & Barnes, 1978). The couples, who did not know each other before the study, were left alone in a room for five minutes after the experimenter explained she had to get more copies of a questionnaire. The subjects were free to carry on a conversation or simply sit quietly and wait.

Table 14.1

Behaviors and Liking between Couples During 5-Minute Interactions

	Masculine Male, Feminine Female	Masculine Male, Androgynous Female	Androgynous Male, Feminine Female	Androgynous Male, Androgynous Female
Total seconds of talking	46.7	90.2	87.3	67.0
Total seconds of direct gazing	34.9	75.2	74.7	61.1
Total number of expressive gestures	1.6	7.2	4.7	4.0
Total number of expressions of positive affect (smile, laugh)	4.0	8.2	9.8	8.4
Liking rating	19.2	43.0	42.6	40.8

Source: Adapted from Ickes and Barnes (1978); reprinted by permission of William Ickes.
Note: The higher the liking rating, the more the subjects liked each other.

The subjects' behavior was recorded with a hidden video camera for later evaluation. When the experimenter returned with the questionnaire, subjects were asked to rate how much they had enjoyed the interaction. As shown in Table 14.1, the results were fairly clear. Members of the masculine male-feminine female dyads enjoyed their interactions least. These couples talked to each other less, looked at each other less, used fewer expressive gestures, and smiled and laughed less than the people in the other combinations.

These results argue against the masculine male–feminine female combination as the ideal couple. When we examine the different way masculine and feminine people approach an interpersonal encounter, some of the reasons for this become clear. The masculine style emphasizes control, self-monitoring, and self-restraint, whereas feminine people look for an active expression of feelings and warmth in their interactions. Little wonder, then, that this combination didn't work out well in this or other experiments (Ickes, Schermer, & Steeno, 1979; Lamke & Bell, 1982).

But what about long-term relationships? After the initial awkwardness, it's possible a masculine male and a feminine female will get along well once they get to know one another. However, this notion also is not supported by the evidence. One study examined combinations of sex-types among married couples and how happy the couples were with their marriages (Antill, 1983). The findings suggest that happiness comes from marrying a feminine partner. That is, when a subject's spouse was either feminine or androgynous, that person was satisfied with the relationship. Being married to a partner who lacked feminine characteristics (masculine or undifferentiated) was indicative of an unhappy marriage. Another study not only found this same pattern among married couples but discovered it also held in relationships among cohabiting heterosexuals, gay couples, and lesbian couples (Kurdek & Schmitt, 1986).

What is it that makes feminine and androgynous people preferable partners? Research suggests at least three reasons. First, look at the characteristics that make up the feminine trait. People scoring high on this scale are affectionate, compassionate, and sensitive to others' needs. Feminine people are better able to express their feelings and understand the feelings of others. It only makes sense that we turn to them when we want to talk. Second, androgynous people are more aware of and better able to express romantic feelings (Coleman & Ganong, 1985). This is because they have both the sensitivity and the understanding needed for intimacy as well as the assertiveness and willingness to take the risk needed to make things happen. Consequently, androgynous people may make the best romantic partners. This may be why one study found that the happiest married couples of all combinations were those in which both people were classified as androgynous (Zammichieli, Gilroy & Sherman, 1988). Third, because they communicate well, feminine and androgynous people are better able to resolve problems and avoid unnecessary disputes (Voelz, 1985). They are more sensitive to their partner's feelings and needs, are better able to express their own feelings, and thus are more likely to live harmoniously than people who lack these qualities.

In summary, through different experiences with operant conditioning and exposure to different models of sex-appropriate behavior, each of us becomes more or less masculine and feminine. Like other personality variables, our level of masculinity and femininity is fairly stable across situations and over time. These traits are related to personal adjustment, but research is still mixed on the exact nature of this relationship. There is somewhat more agreement that femininity and/or androgyny leads to better interpersonal relations. What *is* clear is that Bem's androgyny model has stimulated a great deal of research which has furthered our understanding of individual differences in sex-role behavior.

Observational Learning of Aggression

In July 1991, the motion picture *Boyz N the Hood* began showing at theatres around the country. Although calm was the norm at most of the theatres, many became the setting for real-life violence, including several shootings. Thirty-five people were reported wounded or injured the first night the movie was shown. A man in Chicago was killed. At least eight theatres, fearing more violence, canceled all scheduled showings. In November 1981, the motion picture *The Deer Hunter* was televised nationally. The film contains some dramatic Russian roulette scenes, in which men are shown holding pistols to their temples and pulling the trigger, hoping to miss the one chamber containing the bullet. Shortly after the movie aired, more than 25 Russian roulette deaths were reported across the

United States. In May 1981, John Hinckley tried to assassinate President Ronald Reagan. Investigators soon discovered that Hinckley had viewed the motion picture *Taxi Driver* several times before the shooting. The film portrays the life of a man who falls in love with a young prostitute, played by Jodie Foster, and who later attempts to shoot a presidential candidate. The subsequent investigation uncovered that Hinckley also had a strong attraction to Jodie Foster.

These tragic incidents are examples of one of the most widely researched aspects of Albert Bandura's social learning theory, the relationship between modeled aggression and performance of aggression. Research in this area not only demonstrates how people often learn behaviors through observing models but also raises some important questions about the portrayal of aggression in the mass media.

Bandura's Four-Step Model

Three decades of research has demonstrated conclusively that people exposed to aggressive models sometimes imitate the aggressive behavior. This finding holds true for children (Bandura, 1965) as well as adults (Baron & Kepner, 1970). But clearly, simple exposure to an aggressive model is not enough to turn us into violent people. Anyone who has watched television or attended a few movies recently undoubtedly has seen some murders, beatings, shootings, and the like. Yet rarely do we leave the theatre in search of victims.

Why, then, do people sometimes imitate aggression when most of the time they do not? Bandura (1973) explains that observational learning and performance of aggression consist of four interrelated processes. People must go through each of these steps before exposure to aggression leads them to act aggressively. They must attend to the aggressive action, remember the information, enact what they have seen, and expect that rewards will be forthcoming. Fortunately, most of the time various circumstances prevent people from moving through the entire process. Let's look at each of these steps more closely.

First, for observational learning to take place, people must *attend* to the significant features of the model's behavior. We can sit in front of violent TV programs all day long, but the aggressive models will have little or no impact unless we pay attention to them. Children who watch a lot of television probably have seen so many TV characters punched in the face or shot that only the most graphic and spectacular action will grab their attention. Children in one study imitated aggressive models only when the acts were carried out quite vigorously (Parton & Geshuri, 1971). The investigators reasoned that the less intense action failed to hold the children's attention sufficiently. A viewer's mental state also can make him or her more attentive to the aggression. Frustrated children in one experiment were more likely than nonfrustrated children to attend to an aggressive model (Parker & Rogers, 1981). The frustration seemed to make them more receptive to the information about attacking whoever got in their way (recall the connection between frustration and aggression described in Chapter 6).

But attending to an aggressive act is only the first necessary step in the observational learning process. People also must *remember* information about the model's behavior. You are not likely to recall any one aggressive behavior you saw

Research indicates that children learn aggression by imitating aggressive models. Rehearsing aggression, as when children play with toy guns, is one step in this process.

on television a few years ago unless the behavior was quite gripping. And if you can't recall what the act was, you are not likely to imitate the aggressive model. Unfortunately, while most aggressive acts we witness soon fade from our memories, not all do. Practice keeps the aggression fresh in our minds. For example, children who play with toy guns and other pieces of plastic combat equipment may embed the actions of their aggressive heroes permanently into their memories. Thinking about or mentally rehearsing the action also helps us remember.

The importance of selective recall was demonstrated in a study with first- and second-grade children (Slife & Rychlak, 1982). The researchers asked the children how much they liked each of the aggressive acts they saw on a videotape. They also determined which of the toys used by the aggressive model each child liked and disliked. Then, as in Bandura's classic study, the children were watched for 5 minutes through a one-way window while they played in a room containing all of the equipment necessary to imitate the aggressive acts they had just seen. As shown in Table 14.2, the children were most likely to imitate the aggression when it was an act they liked and when it was conducted with a toy they liked. The researchers argued that these are the acts the children remember. This also helps to explain why the boys in the study were more aggressive than the girls: They liked and recalled the aggressive behavior more than the girls did.

The third step in Bandura's model is that people must *enact* what they have seen. Remember that Bandura draws a distinction between learning and performance. One reason we don't carry out every aggressive act we notice and recall is that we may lack the ability to do so. For example, few of us can imitate the

Table 14.2

Mean Number of Aggressive Acts Imitated

	Boys	Girls
Liked toy–liked act	8.50	2.56
Liked toy–disliked act	1.00	.88
Disliked toy–liked act	2.44	.81
Disliked toy–disliked act	1.06	.63

Source: From Slife and Rychlak (1982); reprinted by permission of Brent D. Slife.

behavior of a martial arts champion, even after watching a dozen Chuck Norris movies. We also must have the opportunity to carry out the act. I may remember from repeated exposure in movies how to hold and fire a gun at an attacker. But because I don't have access to a gun and because I hope I am never in a situation where a gun would be useful, shooting someone with a handgun is one learned behavior I probably will never enact.

Finally, people must *expect* that the aggressive act will lead to a reward and not be punished. As described in the previous chapter, we not only learn what to do from an aggressive model, but we also learn something about what is likely to happen to us as a result of acting out the aggression. If our model is rewarded, such as being declared a hero and awarded public praise, we may expect that we, too, would be rewarded. If the model is punished, perhaps being arrested or getting beat up by someone even more aggressive, we probably will expect we also would be punished if we tried something like that.

Information about rewards and punishments is communicated in a number of ways. Parents who punish children for fighting may communicate that bigger and stronger people can do what they want, which may be why punishment is related to *more* aggression in children, not less (Felson & Russo, 1988). Children also are more likely to imitate aggressive acts when other children are doing so (O'Neal, Macdonald, Cloninger, & Levine, 1979). The reward in this case may come from the approval of the other children.

People also are more likely to imitate aggressive behavior that is portrayed as justified (Berkowitz & Powers, 1979; Geen, 1981). We are rewarded with a sense of justice when we see villains get what is coming to them. Children are more likely to imitate a superhero who smacks around a bad guy for the good of society than they are a supervillain who acts violently only for his own good. Inevitably, the bad guy is punished. But the aggressive behavior of the good guy is rewarded. The lesson is that the hero's behavior is warranted and therefore good. Unfortunately, people usually believe *their* side is the good and just one. Therefore, like the superhero, aggression may seem an appropriate solution to their problems. This observation leads us to the next issue—the impact of mass media violence.

Mass Media Aggression and Aggressive Behavior

If you watch even a small amount of television, you surely are aware that the average American receives a heavy dose of modeled aggression almost daily. For several decades, many people have been concerned about how this constant exposure to stabbings, shootings, beatings, and so on affects children. The average 10-year-old in this country may spend more time per week in front of a television than in a classroom (Gerbner & Gross, 1976), a pattern that has not changed in more than 20 years (Liebert & Sprafkin, 1988). Although today the action may consist of a monster being killed by a superhero's laser beam instead of a bank robber felled by a bullet from a sheriff's gun, more aggression is shown on Saturday morning "children's" entertainment than on prime-time television (National Institute of Mental Health, 1982). One estimate claimed the average American child will view about 18,000 murders on television before age 18.

As the examples at the beginning of this section suggest, there are some very convincing instances of people witnessing and then imitating an aggressive act. The problem is we can't determine conclusively that viewing the aggressive act actually caused the person to behave aggressively. For example, it is possible the people who imitated the Russian roulette scene from *The Deer Hunter* would have taken their lives in some other manner if they hadn't seen the movie, or that John Hinckley would have committed some other violent act if he hadn't watched *Taxi Driver*. After all, millions of people saw these movies without reacting this way. Although most of us find it difficult to not see a link between viewing aggression and performing aggression in these examples, they supply only weak evidence for this relationship.

Fortunately, we don't have to rely on this circumstantial evidence. Researchers have provided us with a wealth of experimental data concerning the impact of viewing aggression on performing aggression. Although a few researchers still urge caution in interpreting these studies (Freedman, 1984, 1986), the vast majority find the causal link irrefutable: Viewing aggression increases the likelihood of acting aggressively, especially over a short time span (Friedrich-Cofer & Huston, 1986; Geen, 1983a; Geen & Thomas, 1986; Huesmann & Malamuth, 1986; Wood, Wong, & Chachere, 1991). Today researchers concentrate on understanding the theoretical reasons for this relationship and on identifying variables that increase or decrease the effect.

Most of the evidence suggesting that watching aggression increases aggression comes from controlled laboratory research. Typically, subjects watch a segment from either a violent or an arousing but nonviolent program. Then they are given the opportunity to aggress against another person, usually by administering electric shocks they believe are hurting another subject. In almost all cases, researchers find the subjects who watched the violent program act more aggressively than those who saw the nonviolent program. As impressive as this body of research is, it contains some serious limitations. The effects are short-lived, and the opportunity to hurt another person provided by the experimenter is unique.

Therefore, it is reasonable to wonder how much these studies tell us about the impact of aggressive movies and television shows in real-life situations.

In response to this problem, several investigators have conducted long-term field studies to gauge the impact of exposure to violence and aggressive behavior outside the laboratory (Eron, 1987; McCarthy, Langner, Gersten, Eisenberg, & Orzeck, 1975; Singer & Singer, 1981). In each case, the researchers used the amount and kind of television that children watched at one point in their lives to predict how aggressive the children would be later in life. They uncovered significant evidence in each study indicating that watching a lot of aggressive television does lead to more aggression in children and adults.

Consider the impressive study conducted by Eron and his colleagues (Eron, 1987; Huesmann, Eron, Dubow, & Seebauer, 1987; Lefkowitz, Eron, Walder, & Huesmann, 1977). First, they measured how much television a group of eight-year-old children watched. They then examined aggressive behavior in these same subjects 22 years later, at age 30. The researchers found a significant relationship between the amount of television the subjects watched as children and the likelihood that they would have been convicted for criminal behavior by age 30. As shown in Figure 14.3, the seriousness of the criminal act was directly related to the amount of television watched. The more TV the eight-year-old had watched, the more serious was the adult crime.

One potential difficulty in interpreting this research concerns the possibility that the children watched television *because* they were aggressive, not the other way around. Research has shown that aggressive people prefer aggressive television programs (Fenigstein, 1979). However, when researchers control for the child's initial aggressiveness level statistically, the findings still suggest that watching television *causes* the later aggressive behavior (Lefkowitz et al., 1977; Singer & Singer, 1981).

In short, watching aggressive models on television appears to increase the likelihood of aggressive behavior over the short run and over many years. Some of this relationship can be explained through Bandura's social learning model. However, closer examination suggests this may be only part of the picture. In many cases the aggression displayed by subjects is not the same kind shown in the experimental film (Geen & Thomas, 1986). To account for this observation, some researchers suggest that aggressive memories are primed by the presentation of violent cues in aggressive programs (Berkowitz, 1984, 1986; Bushman & Geen, 1990; Huesmann, 1986). The violent cues found in mass media aggression activate aggressive associations in a person's memory. Because these aggressive ideas, feelings, and memories are highly activated immediately after viewing an aggressive program, the chances of engaging in some kind of aggressive act increase.

A large number of studies support this reasoning (Carlson, Marcus-Newhall, & Miller, 1990). Second- and third-grade boys were shown either violent or nonviolent films in one study (Josephson, 1987). Some of the boys were later shown a cue from the violent film (a walkie-talkie like the one used by snipers in the film) just before playing hockey. The boys who had seen the violent film *and* saw the walkie-talkie engaged in more aggression during the game (tripping opponents, hitting with their stick) than the other boys. One team of investigators

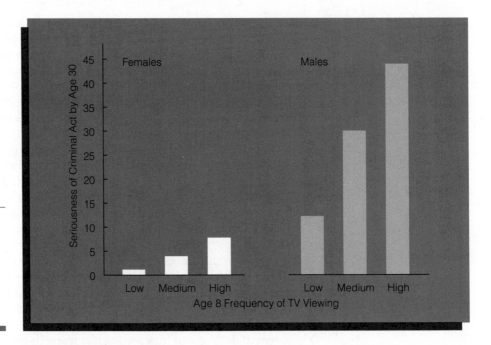

Figure 14.3

Seriousness of Criminal Act at Age 30 as a Function of Frequency of TV Viewing at Age 8

even found that playing an aggression-oriented video game increased feelings of hostility and anxiety in a group of college students (Anderson & Ford, 1986).

One interesting investigation examined the relationship between homicide rates and the highly publicized violence associated with championship boxing matches (Phillips, 1983). Anyone who has sat through 15 (or fewer) rounds of a heavyweight championship fight will agree that aggression is being modeled. In addition, the prefight publicity, with its verbal attacks and aggressive language ("I'm gonna knock his head off"), and the postfight highlights add to the climate of aggression and provide numerous aggressive cues. The researcher compared the expected homicide rate (for the time of year, day of week, and so on) and the actual homicide rate in the United States following the 18 heavyweight championship fights held from 1973 to 1978. As shown in Table 14.3, murders increased by an average of 12.46% over the expected rate 3 days after the fight. The largest increases came after the most widely publicized and most widely seen fights, with the famous Ali-Frazier fight associated with an increase of more than 26 murders.

In summary, few aggression researchers doubt that watching aggressive models increases the likelihood of some people acting aggressively in some situations. Bandura's four-step model explains when an aggressive act will be imitated and when it will not. However, this model does not explain why exposure to aggressive television leads to aggressive acts not demonstrated in the program. Many researchers today explain this relationship in terms of activated aggressive memory links that increase the probability of acting aggressively.

Table 14.3

Fluctuation of U.S. Homicide Rate 3 Days after Heavyweight Fights

Name of Fight	Observed Number of Homicides	Expected Number of Homicides	Observed Minus Expected
Foreman/Frazier	55	42.10	12.90
Foreman/Roman	46	49.43	−3.43
Foreman/Norton	55	54.33	.67
Ali/Foreman	102	82.01	19.99
Ali/Wepner	44	46.78	−2.78
Ali/Lyle	54	47.03	6.97
Ali/Bugner	106	82.93	23.07
Ali/Frazier	108	81.69	26.31
Ali/Coopman	54	45.02	8.98
Ali/Young	41	43.62	−2.62
Ali/Dunn	50	41.47	8.53
Ali/Norton	64	52.57	11.43
Ali/Evangelista	36	42.11	−6.11
Ali/Shavers	66	66.86	−.86
Spinks/Ali	89	78.96	10.04
Holmes/Norton	53	48.97	4.03
Ali/Spinks	59	52.25	6.75
Holmes/Evangelista	52	50.24	1.76

Source: Adapted from Phillips (1983); reprinted by permission of the American Sociological Association.

Learned Helplessness

Consider the following three cases. A woman is fired from her job because her employer believes the position is too demanding for her abilities. After a few frustrating weeks of job hunting, she decides to just stay home. She stops going out with friends and shuts down other parts of her life she once enjoyed — dancing, movies, jogging — almost completely. She becomes more and more depressed, develops lower and lower self-esteem, and has little faith in her ability to get another job. An elderly man is moved to an old-age home and told the staff will take care of all the chores he used to do. He no longer has to cook for himself or clean his room or even do the shopping. Shortly after the move he becomes less active. He is less talkative and less cheerful. His health begins to fail. Finally, a fourth-grade boy fails a math test. He becomes frustrated and distressed on his next few math assignments and eventually refuses to even try. He begins to do poorly in other subjects and soon loses interest in any part of school.

What these three hypothetical people have in common is that they are all examples of what researchers refer to as **learned helplessness**. Psychology's interest in learned helplessness began with the curious behavior of some dogs in a classical conditioning study and evolved into one of learning theory's most widely applied concepts.

Learning to Be Helpless

Like so many of the topics to come out of the behaviorist tradition, research on learned helplessness began with research on laboratory animals. In the original learned helplessness experiments, harnessed dogs were subjected to a series of electric shocks from which they could not escape (Overmier & Seligman, 1967; Seligman & Maier, 1967). After several trials of inescapable electric shock, the animals were placed in an avoidance learning situation. This consisted of learning to avoid shocks by jumping over a small partition to the other side of a shuttle-box whenever a signal sounded (Figure 14.4). Naturally, dogs that had not gone through the earlier shock experience scurried about frantically when the electric shock came on and quickly learned to leap over the barrier to safety whenever they heard the signal. But the researchers were totally surprised by the response of the dogs that had gone through the inescapable shock experience. These dogs also ran around for a few seconds after the shock came on. But then the dogs stopped moving. "To our surprise, it lay down and quietly whined," a researcher explained, describing one of the dogs. "After one minute of this we turned the shock off; the dog had failed to cross the barrier and had not escaped from the shock" (Seligman, 1975, p. 22).

What had happened to these dogs? According to the researchers, the dogs had learned they were helpless. During the inescapable shock trials, they had tried various moves to avoid the shock and found that none was rewarded. The dogs eventually learned there was nothing they could do to turn off the shock and became resigned to their helplessness. But this was no surprise; it's probably the most reasonable response to inescapable shock. The problem became apparent when the dogs experienced shock in the shuttle-box situation — shock from which they *could* escape. In behavioral terms, the dogs inappropriately generalized what they had learned in the first situation to the second situation. Although the dogs could have easily escaped the shock in the shuttle-box, they responded with the helplessness they had learned earlier. In fact, the researchers had to physically move the dogs into the other side of the shuttle-box to show them the shock was escapable before the animals would learn the simple response.

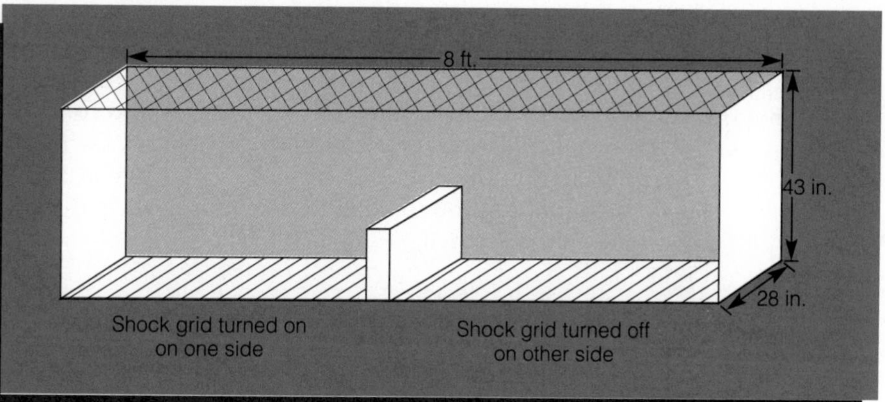

Figure 14.4

Learned Helplessness in Humans

Soon psychologists wondered if learned helplessness could be found in people as well as lower animals. Ethically, we can't put human volunteers in a harness and subject them to inescapable shock. But with a few modifications in the basic procedure, researchers figured out a way to test if humans also were susceptible to this effect (Hiroto, 1974; Hiroto & Seligman, 1975). Instead of inescapable shock, irritating (but not painful) loud noise was used. Subjects were told they could turn off the noise by solving a problem (for example, pressing some buttons in the correct sequence). Some subjects quickly worked through dozens of these problems, turning off each noise blast by figuring out the answer. However, other subjects were given problems for which there were no solutions. Like the dogs in the earlier studies, these subjects soon learned there was no way to escape the aversive stimulus.

But would these subjects generalize their feelings of helplessness to other situations? Subjects were taken out of the noise situation and given a different kind of problem to work on. The ones who had found the earlier problems solvable had little difficulty with the new problems. In fact, they did no worse than a comparison group of subjects who had received no noise. However, subjects who had felt helpless to turn off the noise performed significantly worse on the second set of problems. Like the dogs in the shuttle-box, they appeared to have inappropriately generalized their perception of helplessness in one situation to a new, controllable situation.

Numerous replications of this experiment have confirmed that humans are as susceptible as other animals to learned helplessness (cf. Garber & Seligman, 1980; Maier & Seligman, 1976). People learn they are helpless in the initial uncontrollable setting and can't break out of that association in subsequent situations. Later researchers demonstrated that the initial uncontrollable experience might not even be necessary to develop learned helplessness. People can simply be told they are helpless to overcome a serious obstacle (Maier & Seligman, 1976) or can learn through observation that they are helpless (Brown & Inouye, 1978; DeVellis, DeVellis, & McCauley, 1978). Imagine your reaction if you see several people with ability similar to yours trying and failing to pass an important test. Consistent with Bandura's social learning theory, you may also conclude you can't pass the test, even though you have not tried ("There's no use in trying, nobody ever passes that test"). These feelings of helplessness might then be generalized to a new situation, and you could suffer from learned helplessness without ever experiencing failure yourself.

Some Applications of Learned Helplessness

Since it was first demonstrated in humans about a decade and a half ago, learned helplessness has been studied in hundreds of investigations and used to explain a wide variety of human problems. Perhaps one reason for the continued popularity of learned helplessness theory is that it has provided psychologists with useful insight into two of the most important human problems we wrestle with today: adjustment among the elderly and depression.

Learned Helplessness in the Elderly   We commonly assume in Western society that elderly people deserve to rest after a lifetime of hard work. Retirement is structured to relieve the elderly of their daily concerns and responsibilities. Old-age homes often are designed to provide this relief by taking care of the cooking and cleaning and structuring residents' daily activities. But is this approach really in the best interests of the retired person? If we apply a learned helplessness analysis to this situation, we see that old-age homes may be taking away the elderly persons' control over their daily experiences. For formerly active people used to exercising a great deal of control, living under such conditions may be similar to the experience of laboratory subjects presented with uncontrollable noise or the dogs with their inescapable shock. And, like the laboratory subjects, the elderly may generalize this perception of uncontrollability to other areas of their lives. In short, the lack of motivation and activity seen in many retired people may be a form of highly generalized learned helplessness.

One team of investigators tested this possibility with residents on two floors of an old-age home (Langer & Rodin, 1976). With the administrators' cooperation, they altered the usual treatment given to one of these groups. The researchers increased the amount of responsibility and control usually exercised by these residents in several ways. Administrators gave a presentation urging the residents to take control of their lives. Here is an excerpt from that talk:

> You have the responsibility of caring for yourselves, of deciding whether or not you want to make this a home you can be proud of and happy in. You should be deciding how you want your rooms to be arranged—whether you want the staff to help you rearrange the furniture. You should be deciding how you want to spend your time, for example, whether you want to be visiting friends or whether you want to be watching television, listening to the radio, writing, reading, or planning social events. In other words, it's your life and you can make of it whatever you want. (p. 194)

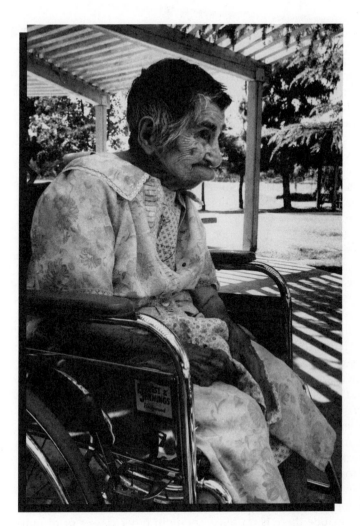

Residents of old-age homes often have many of their daily tasks, such as cooking and cleaning, taken care of by the staff. However, a learned helplessness analysis suggests that this reduction in control may lead to problems with adjustment and health for the elderly.

In addition, subjects were offered a small plant as a gift. They decided whether they wanted a plant and which plant they wanted and were told they were responsible for taking care of it.

Residents on the other floor served as the comparison group. They listened to a talk about allowing the staff to take care of things for them. They were given a plant, chosen by the staff, and were told the staff would take care of the plant for them. The differences between the two floors were soon evident. Within a few weeks, the residents in the responsibility-induced condition reported feeling happier. Staff members noted they were visiting more and sitting around less. Nurses, who did not know a study was going on, reported 93% of these residents showed improved adjustment. Only 21% of the residents in the comparison group showed improvement. But the effects of the treatment did not stop there.

The researchers returned to the old-age home 18 months later to find that many of these differences in happiness and activity level remained (Rodin & Langer, 1977). Most dramatically, only 15% of the responsibility-induced residents had died during the 18-month period, compared to 30% of the comparison group. Several subsequent investigations have discovered similar advantages when elderly people are allowed to retain control over their lives (Baltes & Baltes, 1986). This does not mean we should abandon those who genuinely need some assistance, but sometimes letting senior citizens take care of themselves as much as possible may be in everyone's best interests.

Learned Helplessness and Depression   Soon after the demonstration of learned helplessness in humans, researchers noticed the parallels between helpless laboratory subjects and depressed people (Seligman, 1976). Clinical psychologists have long observed that depressed patients often act as if they are helpless to control what happens to them (Beck, 1972). For example, severely depressed patients sometimes lack the motivation even to get out of bed in the morning. They may say there is no use trying, that nothing they do will turn out well. Like the dog that lies whimpering in the shuttle-box, they seem to have given up on their ability to do anything about their problems.

According to Seligman (1975), depression sometimes develops in a manner similar to the way laboratory subjects acquire learned helplessness. That is, people perceive a lack of control over one important part of their lives and inappropriately generalize that perception to other situations. For example, a college student might have difficulty in a particular class. No matter how hard she tries, she can't improve her test scores. At first she studies harder and gets help from others in the class, but it doesn't seem to help. If it's important to her to do well in school, she may continue her efforts to change her grade. However, at some point she may decide that no matter what she does, she can't avoid the bad grade that is bound to come at the end of the term. In other words, she has learned that she is helpless in this class. She may become mildly depressed.

Unless other information is forthcoming to counteract these feelings, this student may soon conclude there is no sense trying in other classes or in non-academic areas, such as sports or friendships. She may decide she lacks control over most of life's outcomes and eventually may lose the motivation to get up in the morning. In learned helplessness terms, she has inappropriately generalized her feelings of helplessness in one situation she can't control to others that she might be able to control.

Consistent with this interpretation of depression, subjects who go through the relatively simple inescapable noise experience in the laboratory show significant increases in depressive feelings (Burger & Arkin, 1980; Gatchel, Paulus, & Maples, 1975; Miller & Seligman, 1975). Fortunately, research also suggests a treatment. Subjects who experience success at controlling outcomes soon overcome these feelings of helplessness (Klein & Seligman, 1976). Thus, the failing student may need to do well in other classes to appreciate that she still has the ability to succeed in school and make friends.

Learned helplessness remains one of the leading models for understanding depression. However, like many topics in personality, the original theory has evolved in recent years to include many more cognitive features. As we'll discover in Chapter 16, whether people fall into learned helplessness and depression may depend not only on a perception of no control but also on how they explain that lack of control.

Locus of Control

When you get a low grade on a test, is it because the instructor asked stupid questions or because you didn't prepare adequately? If you're in good health, is it because you take care of yourself or because you're lucky? Are lonely people without friends because they don't try to meet people or because they don't have many opportunities? The way you answer these questions provides a clue about where you fall on the widely researched personality dimension of locus of control.

Research on locus of control developed out of Julian Rotter's concept of generalized expectancies. Rotter proposed that in a new situation we base our expectancies of what will happen on general beliefs about our ability to influence events. If you answered that the low grade was due to inadequate preparation, that good health comes from taking care of yourself, and that loneliness is the result of poor effort, then you probably hold what is called an *internal* locus of control orientation. Your generalized expectancy is that people can have an impact on what happens to them and that the good and bad experiences of your life are generally of your own making. On the other hand, if you feel that low grades usually are the fault of the instructor, that health is a matter of luck, and that people are lonely because of the circumstances they find themselves in, then you probably fall on the *external* end of the locus of control dimension. More than most people, you believe that what happens to you and others is outside your control.

Neither an internal nor an external orientation is necessarily accurate. Rather, where people fall along this dimension allows locus of control researchers to predict a large number of behaviors, including how they'll do in school, whether they'll vote in the next election, and how soon they'll recover from their next illness. If we consider the role of expectancies in Rotter's model, the extensive application of this individual difference makes sense. According to Rotter, the likelihood that we will engage in a particular behavior is largely determined by our perception of whether that action will have an effect. Therefore, we should not be surprised to find that people who believe they can control most situations act differently from those who believe they can't. No surprise, either, that psychologists working in education, psychotherapy, industrial settings, and other applied areas have found the locus of control concept so useful.

Measuring Locus of Control

In 1966, Rotter published a 29-item scale to measure individual differences in locus of control. Since that time, hundreds of investigators have used this scale to examine how internals and externals differ on a wide variety of behaviors (Lefcourt, 1982; Phares, 1976). Like other personality traits, locus of control

Locus of Control

The concept of locus of control has received a great deal of attention from personality researchers. An area of controversy surrounding this research, however, has been the development of a measure for locus of control. Recently, Delroy Paulhus (1983) designed a scale to measure three different "spheres" of locus of control: the sphere of perceived control over personal achievement situations, such as passing a test or building a bookcase; the sphere of perceived control over interpersonal encounters; and the sphere of perceived control over social and political matters, such as corruption in government or the development of future wars. Paulhus (1983; Paulhus & Christie, 1981) found that people may have a strong perception of control in one or two of these areas, but not in the other(s). For example, he found that the extent to which students perceived themselves as having control over personal achievement and interpersonal situations could not predict whether the person would vote in a local election; only the sociopolitical scale score could.

Below is the personal efficacy subscale from Paulhus's locus of control measure. For each item, indicate the extent to which the statement applies to you, using the following scale:

1 = Disagree strongly	5 = Agree slightly
2 = Disagree	6 = Agree
3 = Disagree slightly	7 = Agree strongly
4 = Neither agree nor disagree	

Continued

scores are fairly stable over time but not immune to change. For example, people tend to become more internal after attending college (Wolfle & Robertshaw, 1982). Women who get divorced become more external for a time but return to a locus of control level similar to married women after a few years (Doherty, 1983).

Since the publication of Rotter's original scale, researchers have created several additional locus of control inventories. This work reflects two trends in locus of control research. One of these is to examine locus of control differences along more than one dimension. Several investigators argue that examining one generalized locus of control score may be misleading (Collins, 1974; Levenson, 1981; Paulhus, 1983). For example, you might feel very internal about personal matters in your life, such as getting a job, but believe you have little ability to affect government or change "the system." Unfortunately, Rotter's scale combines all of these feelings into one global trait, thus making it difficult to interpret an internal or external score. In response to this difficulty, many newer scales derive locus of control scores for different aspects of a person's life (see box above).

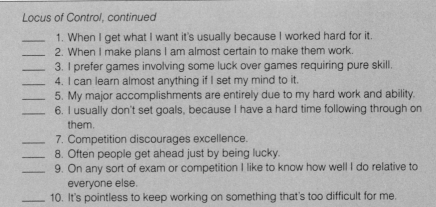

Locus of Control, continued

____ 1. When I get what I want it's usually because I worked hard for it.
____ 2. When I make plans I am almost certain to make them work.
____ 3. I prefer games involving some luck over games requiring pure skill.
____ 4. I can learn almost anything if I set my mind to it.
____ 5. My major accomplishments are entirely due to my hard work and ability.
____ 6. I usually don't set goals, because I have a hard time following through on them.
____ 7. Competition discourages excellence.
____ 8. Often people get ahead just by being lucky.
____ 9. On any sort of exam or competition I like to know how well I do relative to everyone else.
____ 10. It's pointless to keep working on something that's too difficult for me.

To determine your score, reverse the point values for items 3, 6, 7, 8, and 10 (1 = 7; 2 = 6; 3 = 5; 5 = 3; 6 = 2; 7 = 1). Then add the point values for each of the 10 items together. A recent sample of college students found a mean of 51.8 for males and 52.2 for females, with a standard deviation of about 6 for each. The higher your score, the more you tend to believe that you are generally responsible for what happens to you in achievement situations. If you scored considerably above average, you tend to give yourself credit for your successes and to accept responsibility for your failures. Low scores are associated with externality. Scoring low on this scale indicates you tend to believe that forces beyond your control, for example, more powerful people or chance, are responsible for what happens to you.

A second trend in locus of control measurement is the development of scales for narrowly defined situations. For example, Crandall, Katkovsky, and Crandall (1965) developed a scale to assess children's locus of control beliefs about academic behavior. Their scale measures specifically the extent to which children believe that what happens to them in the classroom, such as getting praise from a teacher or receiving a low grade, is the result of their own actions. Another team of researchers developed the Health Locus of Control Scales to measure the extent to which people feel their actions affect their health (Wallston & Wallston, 1981). Yet another scale was developed to measure how much control people believe they have within their marriage (Miller, Lefcourt, & Ware, 1983).

The advantage of using one of these specific locus of control measures is that researchers can better predict behavior in that particular situation than they can with a more general locus of control measure. But there is a price to pay for this added predictability. The usefulness of these scores is limited to the specific domains they are designed for. For example, knowing how much control people feel they have in their marriage tells us a lot about how people will act toward their spouse, but almost nothing about how they will act in an achievement situation. However, because Rotter's locus of control score reflects a general tendency to be internal or external, knowing how people score on this test tells us a little about how people will behave both in their marriage and on the job. The choice of how to measure locus of control therefore probably reflects the researcher's purposes.

Research on Locus of Control

Because of the tremendous amount of research on locus of control, even a brief introduction to each of the areas researched would be impossible here. Master's theses with titles that begin "Locus of Control and . . ." probably would take an entire book to cover. Instead, we'll look at two examples of how individual differences in locus of control affect behavior. First we'll examine the relationship between locus of control and personal adjustment. Then we'll look at how whether you're an internal or an external is related to your health.

Locus of Control and Personal Adjustment   Who is happier: internals, who believe they can control almost everything, or externals, who recognize all the limits outside forces place on them? Which person is more productive, better liked, and better adjusted? Of course, how you answer this question may depend on whether your locus of control score indicates you are an internal or an external. On the one hand, I often hear people argue that internals probably work harder and interact more effectively because they feel they can control events. But just because people believe they are in control of what happens to them does not mean they actually exercise control. Highly internal people might believe there is nothing they can't attain with a little effort. They may invest their efforts inefficiently chasing rainbows and even operate on a set of beliefs that aren't consistent with reality. On the other hand, externals argue that they understand their limits and work to attain only what is reasonably attainable. However, people who give up in the face of setbacks, who say there is nothing they can do to correct the situation, probably also are not exhibiting good mental health.

Obviously, there is no simple answer to whether internals or externals are better adjusted. However, an overview of research findings suggests that, with a few exceptions, generally it's better to be internal than external. This pattern is found in research on psychological disorders, achievement, and psychotherapy results. Let's look at each briefly.

Psychological Disorders   In general, people suffering from psychological disorders are more external than internal (cf. Lefcourt, 1982; Phares, 1976; Strickland, 1978). For example, locus of control scores correlate with measures of anxiety, with external subjects showing the highest anxiety levels. However, there are some notable exceptions to this pattern. For example, young females suffering from the eating disorder anorexia nervosa may be more internal than external (Hood, Moore, & Garner, 1982).

Researchers have been particularly interested in the relationship between locus of control and depression (cf. Benassi, Sweeney, & Dufour, 1988; Rehm &

O'Hara, 1979). Benassi et al. (1988) recently reviewed all of the relevant published studies on this relationship between 1966 and 1986. The combined results of 97 studies yielded an average correlation of .31, indicating that external scores are associated with higher levels of depression. As discussed in Chapter 7, this is an impressively significant correlation.

These findings are consistent with learned helplessness research, in which a perceived inability to control the experimental task leads to higher depression levels. It may be that externals often find themselves in the place of the learned helplessness subject who feels unable to control important events. Consider the findings of a study in which recently diagnosed cancer patients were tested for level of depression (Marks, Richardson, Graham, & Levine, 1986). For internal patients, discovering that the disease was more severe than originally thought did not cause them to become more depressed. However, the more severe the diagnosis for the external patients, the more depressed they became. It seems the internal patients maintained a belief that there still was something they could do to control the course of the disease, and this belief shielded them from giving up and becoming depressed about their situation.

A dramatic example of how locus of control is related to depression was demonstrated in a study of suicidal patients (Melges & Weisz, 1971). Patients who had recently attempted suicide were asked to relive the events that took place immediately before the attempt. Patients were left alone with a tape recorder and asked to describe in the present tense what had happened to them during this time. Analysis of the recordings revealed that patients describe themselves in more external terms as they relive becoming more suicidal. Other studies find suicide attempters often experience an increase in events outside their personal control prior to the attempt (Slater & Depue, 1981) and that external college students report more suicidal thoughts than internals report (Burger, 1984). Finally, as shown in Table 14.4, the rate of suicide in a country correlates .68 with the average locus of control score for that country's citizens, again with external scores indicating a higher rate of suicide (Boor, 1976).

Taken together, these studies suggest that locus of control is related to some forms of psychological disturbance, particularly depression. But we need to add two notes of caution when interpreting these findings. First, the vast majority of people scoring on the external end of locus of control scales are happy and well adjusted. Locus of control may play a role in the development of some disorders, but obviously there are many other variables. Second, because the relationship is correlational, it is difficult to make strong statements about external locus of control *causing* the disorders. It may be that externals are susceptible to depression, but it also is possible that depressed people become more external.

Achievement One sign of adjustment in Western society is achievement in school and in one's career. Although high achievers are by no means shielded from psychological problems, we often point to a deteriorating job performance as a sign of problems and improved performance in school or work as evidence that a therapy client is getting better. Studies consistently show internal students perform better on academic achievement measures, such as grades and teacher ratings, than externals perform (cf. Findley & Cooper, 1983). This finding is true

Table 14.4

Mean I-E Scores and Suicide Rates for 10 Countries

Country	Mean I-E Score	Annual Suicide Rate per 100,000
New Zealand	10.1	8.3
Israel	10.3	6.8
United States	10.3	11.7
Italy	10.5	6.0
Canada	10.9	12.2
Australia	10.9	12.5
West Germany	10.9	20.9
France	11.0	15.4
Japan	12.1	16.8
Sweden	14.6	20.3

Source: Adapted from Boor (1976); reprinted by permission of the *Journal of Social Psychology*, a publication of the Helen Dwight Reid Educational Foundation.

of elementary, high school, and college students, but the relationship is especially strong among adolescents.

Why do internals do better in school? One reason may be that they see themselves as responsible for their achievements. Internal students are more likely to believe that studying for a test will pay off, whereas externals are more likely to feel that nothing they do will affect their test scores. Another reason may be the way internals and externals respond to feedback (Gilmor & Reid, 1978, 1979). Internal students are likely to attribute a high test score to their abilities or to studying hard, whereas externals who receive an A might say they were lucky or that the test was easy. Internals also appear better able to adjust their expectancies for upcoming tests, which means they have a better idea of how to prepare for the next exam. On the other hand, externals are more likely to make excuses following a poor performance (Basgall & Snyder, 1988). An external student who fails a test beceause he didn't study might conclude the teacher is an unfair grader or doesn't like his writing style. This probably means he also will not study for the next test and probably will meet with the same result.

Psychotherapy Because external locus of control scores are associated with psychological disorders, we should not be surprised to find that clients tend to become more internal as they pass through successful psychotherapy (cf. Strickland, 1978). Consider the case of Israeli soldiers suffering from post-traumatic stress disorder following their experiences with intense combat (Solomon, Mikulincer, & Avitzur, 1988). These men suffered from a variety of distress symptoms often found after a profoundly stressful experience. When tested shortly after combat, the soldiers scored fairly external on locus of control measures. However, as they recovered from the stress over the next 3 years they became increasingly internal. Part of the soldiers' difficulties appeared to be related to their perception of losing control. But as they came to see the control they could exercise over important parts of their lives, they took a step toward recovery.

Does this mean that therapists should focus on giving clients more control over therapy, similar to what Carl Rogers suggested (Chapter 11)? Not necessarily. Several studies indicate that although internals perform better when they see themselves in control of the situation, externals may do better when they perceive outside agents are in charge (Burger, 1981; Houston, 1972; Rotter & Mulry, 1965). When applied to therapy, the most effective procedures might be those that match the client's locus of control orientation. Internals may respond well when given control over their treatment, but externals might be uncomfortable with this control and may do better when treatment is in the therapist's hands.

Consistent with this reasoning, internals in one assertiveness training group showed little improvement (Schwartz & Higgins, 1979). However, the externals in this same group showed significant improvement. What the therapists discovered was that they had structured their group in such a way that the internals felt control over their treatment had been taken away. Therapies designed to help clients stop smoking also seem to work better with a good locus of control fit (Best, 1975; Best & Steffy, 1975). Internals showed the most improvement when they could administer their own aversive stimulus, whereas externals did best when the therapist was in control.

In summary, information from a number of sources indicates that locus of control is related to personal adjustment. Although there are many exceptions, internals tend to do better on most indicators of adjustment than do externals. This finding does not mean that holding an external locus of control orientation causes psychological problems. But it does suggest perception of control is a piece in the mental health puzzle. At the least, therapists probably should be alerted to the problems associated with an overly external orientation and perhaps make changing these perceptions a goal of the treatment.

Locus of Control and Health   At first glance, people often find no obvious reason why internals and externals should be any different in their health. If anything, some argue that the high-achieving internals may put themselves under excessive stress and pay the price with their health. Yet a growing amount of research indicates the more internal you are, the healthier you are likely to be (Strickland, 1978, 1979). Even a study of business executives in high-stress positions found that those who remained healthy were more internal than were those who suffered from illnesses (Kobasa, 1979).

How can this finding be explained with what we know of locus of control differences? Researchers have uncovered two important differences in the health behaviors of internals and externals. First, internals take more steps to overcome health problems when they develop. We all occasionally suffer from illnesses and other health difficulties. But whether these turn out to be passing nuisances or major debilitations may depend on how we handle the situation. Because internals believe they control what happens to them, they believe they can do something about their health problems. On the other hand, externals believe there is little they can do to change the situation, and thus are less apt to try. One way internals react to poor health is to seek out information about their illnesses. For example, one study found internal tuberculosis patients took the trouble to learn more about their disease than did external patients (Seeman & Evans, 1962). Similarly, internal college students made aware of the dangers of hypertension sought out more information about the disease than did externals (Wallston, Maides, & Wallston, 1976).

This desire to know more about one's health problems can translate into taking more action to get better. For example, internal diabetes patients stay on their diets and keep medical records more faithfully than do externals. Most likely, this behavior results in a quicker recovery. One of the most frustrating problems health care professionals face is lack of patient cooperation. Many people simply will not take medicine or keep up with a therapy program. The medical community has even developed television spots urging those suffering from high blood pressure to continue with their medication. This noncooperative attitude sounds like an external locus of control orientation. Many people apparently believe there is little they can do to improve their health and suffer the consequences of this belief.

The second major difference between the ways that internals and externals deal with their health has to do with preventative actions. Internals are more likely to take actions that will keep them healthy (Seeman, Seeman, & Sayles, 1985). For example, internals may be more successful than externals at quitting smoking (Shipley, 1981). Smokers often justify their habit with externally oriented arguments—they might get hit by a truck tomorrow anyway, some nonsmokers get lung cancer, too, and so on. Because externals don't believe what happens to them is the result of their actions, they are less likely to accept the link between their smoking and their health.

Similar findings are obtained in weight-reduction research. Many obese people fail to lose weight, although they realize obesity is a health hazard. They often give up, arguing that nothing they try seems to help. One difference between successful and unsuccessful dieters may be their locus of control orientation. Internals tend to have more success with reduction programs, particularly those oriented toward self-control of eating (Balch & Ross, 1975; Wallston, Maides, & Wallston, 1976). In addition, because they see a relationship between what they do and how they feel, internals probably are more likely than externals to try health-maintaining exercise programs, such as aerobics or jogging (Sonstroem & Walker, 1973). Internals are even more likely to use the seat belt in their car, one simple action that reduces their chances of being hurt in an accident.

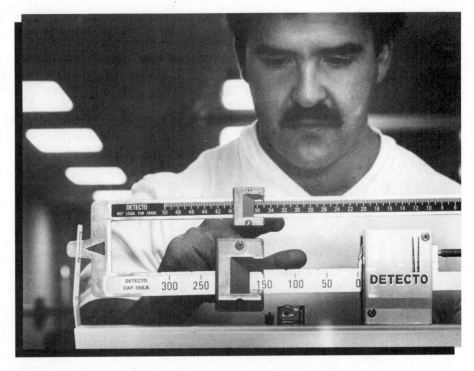

Of the millions who try to lose weight each year, only a small number of people succeed in taking it off and keeping it off. One variable that may affect a diet's success or failure is the extent to which the dieter believes he or she is capable of losing the weight.

Although exceptions are found on occasion (cf. Wallston & Wallston, 1981), the pattern of research findings is relatively clear. Internals believe people can do something about their health. They try to stay healthy when they can and work to understand their illness and overcome it when they become ill. Externals are less likely to acknowledge that what they do has much impact on their health. When they become ill, they depend on doctors and other health professionals to make them well again. Given these differences, it is easier to see how differences in locus of control translate into differences in health.

Summary

1. One of the striking similarities of the four topics covered in this chapter is the extent to which they touch on important social and lifestyle issues. This research tells us a great deal about sexual equality, aggression, depression, treatment of the elderly, and personal health. The research reminds us that psychology ultimately has a lot to say about how to improve the human condition.

2. From the day we are born, most of us face tremendous socialization pressures to take on the sex roles deemed appropriate by society. Through a combination of operant conditioning and observational learning, boys tend to act like other boys and girls like other girls. Research on individual differences in sex-role behavior was stifled originally by a model that viewed masculinity and femininity as polar opposites. Sandra Bem's androgyny model sees these as two independent traits and argues that the most well-adjusted people are those who are androgynous, that is, high in both masculinity and femininity. Research has not always supported this position, and it may be that only masculinity is related to good adjustment. However, being feminine and/or androgynous appears to be the key to good interpersonal relations.

3. Researchers agree that exposure to aggressive models increases a person's likelihood of acting aggressively. Bandura's four-step model helps to explain why people sometimes imitate aggressive acts they see and sometimes do not. Before people imitate aggression they must attend to the act, recall it, have the opportunity to engage in the behavior, and believe the aggression will lead to rewards. Research from laboratory and long-term field studies indicates that exposure to mass media violence increases aggressive behavior. Bandura's model cannot account for all of these findings, and recent researchers have pointed to the priming effect of the violent cues found in violent television programs.

4. Like much behavioral research, work on learned helplessness began with experiments on laboratory animals. Researchers observed that dogs who learned they were helpless to escape shock in one situation inappropriately generalized this perception of helplessness to a new situation. Subsequent research found that humans also are susceptible to this effect. Learned helplessness theory has applications for treatment of the elderly and for understanding and treating depression. Research suggests that elderly people may adjust better to old-age institutions when they are allowed to retain some control over their situation. Depression may develop for many people when they perceive a lack of control over an important part of their lives and then inappropriately generalize that perception to other aspects of their lives.

5. The most widely researched aspect of Rotter's social learning theory is the notion of individual differences in generalized expectancies, or locus of control. At one end of this dimension we find internals, who generally believe they control what happens to them. On the other end are externals, who generally hold that what happens to them is under the control of outside forces. Recent researchers have found it useful to measure locus of control beliefs for specific situations, although the usefulness of these scores outside of the situation is limited. Internals generally do better than externals on measures of personal adjustment and health. Because they believe they can influence events, internals are more likely than externals to take actions to overcome health problems as well as take actions to prevent illnesses.

Key Terms

masculinity-femininity A personality trait indicating the extent to which a person possesses sex-typed characteristics, with masculine characteristics at one end of the trait continuum and feminine characteristics at the other end.

androgyny A personality trait consisting of masculine as well as feminine characteristics.

learned helplessness The cognitive, motivational, and emotional deficits that follow a perceived lack of control over important aversive events.

Suggested Readings

Huesmann, R. L., & Malamuth, N. M. (Eds.) (1986). Special issue: Media violence and antisocial behavior. *Journal of Social Issues, 42*(3). This excellent collection of articles reviews the current status of longstanding questions about the effects of media violence. Chapters include discussions of the immediate effects of media violence, naturalistic studies, efforts to reduce media violence, legal issues, and methodological issues.

Lefcourt, H. M. (Ed.) (1981–1984). *Research with the locus of control concept* (Vols. 1–3). New York: Academic Press. These three volumes contain reviews of research programs examining various aspects and applications of locus of control. The volumes are divided into chapters dealing with assessment of locus of control, the application of locus of control to social problems, and recent extensions and limitations of the locus of control concept.

Shaver, P., & Hendrick, C. (Eds.) (1987). *Sex and gender*. Beverly Hills, CA: Sage. Chapters in this book examine sex roles and individual differences in sex-role behavior from several different perspectives. Topics include the role of genetics, androgyny, the influence of parents' values and roles, and a cross-cultural look at sex-role stereotypes.

The Cognitive Approach
Theory, Application, and Assessment

I went to a social gathering with a friend of mine recently. We talked with old friends, met some new people, mingled about sampling conversations, music, food, and drink. As is our custom, we immediately shared our perceptions after leaving the party. "Did you notice how casually some people were dressed?" my friend asked. Actually, I hadn't. I asked him what he thought of a man we both had met. "Wasn't he the most arrogant person?" I asked. My friend hadn't seen anything to indicate so. As we continued to exchange impressions, I began to wonder if my friend had been at the same party interacting with the same people I had. I couldn't believe he hadn't noticed how weird the music was or seen how ill at ease the hostess seemed to be. My friend didn't understand how I had failed to recognize the architecture of the house or even the furniture I sat on. "I guess we learned one lesson," I said. "Never go to a party at their house again." My friend stared at me in disbelief. "Are you kidding?" he said. "I had a great time!"

How can two people participate in the same situation yet leave with very different impressions of what happened? The answer from the cognitive approach to personality is that my friend and I have very different ways of processing information. While I was attending to and processing information about the weirdness of the music and the arrogance of the guests, my friend entered the party prepared to notice clothing styles and furniture. Because we attended to different features of the party, we had very different perceptions of it and very different experiences. These different perceptions no doubt affected how we acted that night and how we will respond to future invitations.

The cognitive approach to personality explains differences in personality as differences in the way people process information. Because I have developed relatively stable ways of processing information in social settings, I probably respond to parties and the like nearly the same way every time. Other people respond differently than I do because they consistently see something different from what I see.

Although cognitive models of personality have become popular only recently, they are not entirely new. For example, an early predecessor is found in Kurt Lewin's (1938) "field theory" of behavior. He described differences in the way people organize representations of the elements in their lives within their own cognitive "life space." A more recent, and for the purposes of this book, more important cognitive personality theory was that of George Kelly. Since the publication of his book *The Psychology of Personal Constructs* in 1955, Kelly's work has evolved into a rich source of ideas and concepts for current cognitive theorists and practitioners (Jankowicz, 1987; Landfield, 1984). Walter Mischel, one of these current theorists, has given Kelly much of the credit for launching this new perspective. "What has surprised me . . . [is] the accuracy with which he anticipated the directions into which psychology would move two decades later," Mischel said. "Virtually every point of George Kelly's theorizing in the 1950s has proved to be a prophetic preface for psychology . . . for many years to come" (1980, pp. 85–86).

It is interesting that Kelly did not conceive of himself as a cognitive psychologist. "I have been so puzzled over the early labeling of personal construct theory as cognitive," he wrote, "that several years ago I set out to write another short book to make it clear that I wanted no part of cognitive theory" (1969, p. 216). Nonetheless, Kelly's theory has become the starting point for many of the approaches to personality we now identify as "cognitive." Kelly was among the first to explain stable individual differences in behavior in terms of stable differences in the way people perceive and process information about their worlds.

Kelly identified the cognitive structures in his theory as "personal constructs." More recent theorists have introduced other cognitive structures, such as "prototypes" and "schemas." As we will see, because much of this work is relatively new, basic questions are still being asked and the overall perspective still has many gaps to fill before it is as comprehensive as some of the other personality approaches. Nonetheless, the recent surge in interest in cognitive theories indicates that it will remain a major perspective from which to understand human personality in the coming years.

George Kelly's Personal Construct Theory

I do not regard my career in psychology as a "calling." Everything around us "calls," if we choose to heed. It was I who got myself into it and I who have pursued it.

GEORGE KELLY

George Kelly's approach to personality begins with a unique conception of humankind. He rejected the need for motivational concepts to explain human behavior. Whereas Freud saw people as largely controlled by their unconscious impulses, and Skinner saw them as large organisms passively reacting to environmental stimuli, Kelly presented a *man-as-scientist* conception. We need not ask what initiates behavior, he said, for a person is "a form of motion" and "movement is the essence of human life." The human motion that interested Kelly the most is the way people, like scientists, generate and test hypotheses about their worlds and generate new ideas about what the world is like. Because no two people see the world the same, no two people behave the same or have the same personality.

According to Kelly, we are motivated to make sense of all the stimuli that impinge on us as we pass through the world. Like scientists trying to predict and control events, we want to understand the world so that we can predict and control what happens to us. For example, suppose you generate a hypothesis about what one of your instructors is like, based on past observations. You maintain that this man is stuffy and arrogant. Whenever you see this instructor you collect more information and compare it to your hypothesis. If it is verified

George Kelly
1905–1967

George Alexander Kelly was born in a farming community near Wichita, Kansas, in 1905. He attended Friends University in Wichita for three years before graduating from Park College in Missouri in 1926. His active participation in intercollegiate debate during these years helped him develop a keen ability to challenge arguments and conventional positions. However, this ability may have kept him from turning to psychology for many years. He described his first psychology course as boring and unconvincing. The instructor spent considerable time discussing learning theories, but Kelly was unimpressed. "The most I could make of it was that the S was what you had to have in order to account for the R, and the R was put there so the S would have something to account for," he wrote. "I never did find

out what that arrow stood for" (1969, pp. 46–47). He also was skeptical when he first read Freud. "I don't remember which one of Freud's books I was trying to read," he recalled, "but I do remember the mounting feeling of incredulity that anyone could write such nonsense, much less publish it" (1969, p. 47).

After graduating with a degree in physics and mathematics, Kelly went to the University of Kansas to study educational sociology. After a series of odd jobs, including teaching speech and working as an aeronautical engineer, he went to the University of Edinburgh to study education in 1929. While there he developed a growing interest in psychology, and in 1931 received his Ph.D. in psychology from the University of Iowa. Kelly spent the next 10 years at Fort Hays Kansas State College. During these years he set up a network of clinics to provide psychological services to the poor and destitute dustbowl victims of the 1930s. "I listened to people in trouble," he wrote, "and tried to help them figure out what they could do about it" (1969, p. 50). He soon came to see that what these people needed most was an explanation for what had happened to them and an ability to predict what would happen to them in the future. Personal construct theory evolved from this insight. After serving in the Navy in World War II, Kelly spent a year at the University of Maryland and then 20 years at Ohio State University. He moved to Brandeis University in 1965, where he died soon afterward.

(the instructor acts the way arrogant people act), you continue using it. If not (you find out that outside of the classroom he is a warm and charming man), you discard the hypothesis and replace it with a new one. Kelly described this process as template matching. Our ideas about what the world is like are similar to transparent templates. We place the templates over the events we encounter. If they match, we retain the templates; if not, we modify them for a better prediction next time.

Kelly called the cognitive structures we use to interpret and predict events **personal constructs**. No two people use identical personal constructs, and no two people organize their constructs in an identical manner. According to Kelly, personal constructs are bipolar. That is, we classify relevant objects in an either/or fashion with each construct. For example, I might apply personal constructs of friendly-unfriendly, tall-short, intelligent-stupid, masculine-feminine, and so on in constructing my image of a new acquaintance. This is not to say we see the world as black and white with no shades of gray. After applying the original black-and-white construct we can use other bipolar constructs to determine the extent of the blackness or whiteness. Thus, after determining that this new acquaintance is "intelligent," I might then apply an "academically intelligent-commonsense intelligent" construct to get an even clearer picture of what this person is like. Each construct also has a *range of convenience*, which restricts the items for which it is useful. For example, my "intelligent-stupid" construct is useful with people, but describing a table would be outside its range of convenience.

How can personal constructs be used to explain personality differences? Kelly maintained that differences in our behavior largely result from differences in the way people "construe the world." For example, if you and I interact with Adam, I might use friendly-unfriendly, fun-loving–stuffy, and outgoing-shy constructs in forming my template for Adam's behavior. You might interpret Adam in terms of refined-gross, sensitive-insensitive, and intelligent-stupid constructs. After we both talk to Adam for a while, I might act as if I'm interacting with a friendly, fun-loving, and outgoing person. You might respond to Adam as if dealing with a gross, insensitive, and stupid person. We're both in the same situation, but because we interpret that situation very differently, we respond in very different ways. In addition, because you and I tend to use these same constructs when meeting other people, we probably have very different characteristic ways of interacting with others. Thus, the relatively stable patterns in our behavior are the result of the relatively stable way we construe the world.

The Fundamental Postulate and Corollaries

Kelly (1955) presented his theory of personality in a highly organized and structured manner rarely seen in the social sciences. He began with one basic postulate upon which his entire theory is based, followed by 11 corollaries that elaborate on the theory (see Table 15.1). The *Fundamental Postulate*, as he called it, states that "a person's processes are psychologically channelized by the ways in which he anticipates events" (1955, p. 46). This postulate forms the cornerstone

Table 15.1

George Kelly's Fundamental Postulate and Eleven Corollaries

Fundamental Postulate: A person's processes are psychologically channelized by the ways in which he anticipates events.

Construction Corollary: A person anticipates events by construing their replications.

Individuality Corollary: Persons differ from each other in their construction of events.

Organization Corollary: Each person characteristically evolves, for his convenience in anticipating events, a construction system embracing ordinal relationships between constructs.

Dichotomy Corollary: A person's construction system is composed of a finite number of dichotomous constructs.

Choice Corollary: A person chooses for himself that alternative in a dichotomous construct through which he anticipates the greater possibility for extension and definition of his system.

Range Corollary: A construct is convenient for the anticipation of a finite range of events only.

Experience Corollary: A person's construction system varies as he successively construes the replications of events.

Modulation Corollary: The variation in a person's construction system is limited by the permeability of the constructs within whose range of convenience the variants lie.

Fragmentation Corollary: A person may successively employ a variety of construction subsystems which are inferentially incompatible with each other.

Commonality Corollary: To the extent that one person employs a construction of experience which is similar to that employed by another, his psychological processes are similar to those of the other person.

Sociality Corollary: To the extent that one person construes the construction processes of another, he may play a role in a social process involving the other person.

Source: Taken from Kelly (1955), with permission.

for Kelly's theory because it identifies the basic force behind personality and behavior in a way quite different from other major perspectives. Kelly rejected the idea that past conflicts or external stimuli are the basic shapers of our behavior. He argued that we are tied to our past experiences only in the sense that they have helped to develop our constructs and expectancies for the future.

What did he replace these concepts with? Kelly liked to call it *anticipation*. He explained in his *Construction Corollary* that we anticipate events by "construing their replications." That is, it is impossible to enter every situation as if it were unique. Without expectancies we would be overwhelmed by the flood of information. We would be confused and unable to predict anything. Therefore, we rely on our past experiences to help us organize and anticipate what will happen in the future. In this way we know what information to pay attention to and what to ignore. For example, from past experiences you may have learned that talkative-quiet is a useful construct when first meeting people. Consequently, you probably would use this construct when meeting someone new. After deciding whether this person is talkative or quiet, you would be better able to predict how he or she is likely to act in the future and decide how you are going to act accordingly.

To get a rough idea of your own construct system, ask yourself what things you are interested in learning about people when you first meet them. The first few things that come to mind are likely to be the constructs you initially use to anticipate others' behavior. For example, you might use the constructs athletic–not athletic, good sense of humor–humorless, and independent–dependent when you meet someone new. Someone else might use the constructs studious-lazy, charming-obnoxious, and neat-sloppy. It is also possible that two people use the same constructs but construe the world differently. That is, I might think someone intelligent, and you might see the same person as stupid. Further, two people's constructs might be similar on one pole but not the other. For example, I might use an outgoing-reserved construct, whereas you use an outgoing-melancholy construct. Thus, what I see as reserved behavior, you see as melancholy. All of these examples illustrate Kelly's *Individuality Corollary*, which states that we each construe the world differently.

But Kelly argued that you and I have different personalities not only because we use different constructs. We also organize our constructs differently. According to Kelly's *Organization Corollary*, some constructs are more important than others in interpreting our worlds. Kelly calls these the *superordinate* personal constructs and compares them to the less important *subordinate* constructs. These two types of constructs can be organized in one of two ways. A subordinate construct may be subsumed within one side of the superordinate construct, like this:

Friendly-Unfriendly
/
Outgoing-Quiet

In this case, people are judged as either friendly or unfriendly. If judged as friendly, they are then judged as either outgoing or quiet. If this were your construct organization, you could not see an unfriendly person as either outgoing or quiet, just unfriendly. But you also might organize these constructs this way:

Friendly-Unfriendly
/ \
Outgoing-Quiet   Outgoing-Quiet

In this case, whether you judge people as friendly or unfriendly, you can further judge them as either outgoing or quiet. Of course, it also is possible to use outgoing-quiet as the superordinate construct and friendly-unfriendly as the subordinate one. That structure would look like this:

Outgoing-Quiet

Friendly-Unfriendly　　　Friendly-Unfriendly

In this case, you might first decide if a person were outgoing or quiet and then further refine this perception with the second construct. Thus, after deciding someone is a quiet person, you might want to know if she is a quiet-friendly person or a quiet-unfriendly one. It even is possible for the same person to use different construct organizations at different times. Kelly argues that construct arrangement "characterizes the personality" even more than which constructs we use.

However, occasionally our constructs are inadequate for predicting events. We may construe situations incorrectly and find that we are unable to anticipate what will happen next. Kelly argued that this is inevitable in our ever-changing world. Therefore, construct systems should not be thought of as stagnant or perfect. In healthy people, new constructs are constantly generated to replace old, inadequate ones. Kelly argues that these constructions should be thought of as hypotheses in need of testing rather than as representations of fact.

This constant reconstruction of anticipations, which Kelly describes in the *Experience Corollary*, allows us to better predict future events. If you anticipate that a conversation with George is going to be boring but find that it is interesting, you probably will alter your anticipation of future encounters with George. Failure to do so would result in an increasing inability to predict events in George's presence. You may have experienced this when you said to someone, "I just don't understand you anymore." As we'll discuss shortly, this person's unpredictable behavior probably caused you great distress.

Kelly's theory also helps us understand why two people can get along well even though they seem so different on the surface. According to the *Sociality Corollary*, the better one person understands the way another sees the world, the better the two will interact. This is not to say that people must have similar constructs to have harmonious interpersonal relations. Rather, if you and I are to get along, I need to be able to anticipate the way you construe the world. Indeed, researchers find that people with similar construct systems often make the best friends (Duck, 1979). Kelly also suggested that this process plays an important role in psychotherapy. Therapists are of the most benefit to their clients when they understand clients' construct systems.

Finally, in a direct challenge to the behavioral perspective, Kelly asserted that two people can have similar personalities without going through similar experiences. According to the *Commonality Corollary*, all people need is to construe the world in a similar manner to have similar personalities. Kelly described "cultures" as groups of people who construe their experiences in basically the same way. The "culture shock" often experienced when encountering people from a different society is the result of general differences in the way people from different cultures construe events.

Box 15.1

Construct Similarity and Friendship

Of all the many people you encounter, only a small handful will become your friends. Certainly there are many reasons for this—similarity of interests, opportunity to interact, and so on. But people also become friends because they tend to see the world in a similar manner. One area of research to come out of Kelly's personal construct theory is concerned with understanding why friendships develop and why they sometimes dissolve (Duck, 1973, 1979). This research grew out of two of Kelly's corollaries. First, the Commonality Corollary states that people with similar construct systems construe the world in a similar manner. Second, the Sociality Corollary maintains that we may "play a role" in the "social processes" of another person if we understand how that person construes the world. In other words, we must understand where people are coming from before we can interact with them effectively.

If Kelly is correct, then people who share a perception of what the world is like are more likely to get along and eventually become friends than are those who construe the world differently. To test this notion, researchers have used Rep Test profiles and scores from other personality tests to predict who will become friends and who will not (Duck & Craig, 1978; Duck & Spencer, 1972). These investigators found that incoming college students initially choose friends based on obvious similarities in personalities and interests. For example, freshmen look for friends who also like to dance, like baseball, like rock music, and so on. However, over the course of several months they learn more about how the other students construe the world. By the end of the school year, freshmen are less likely to select friends based on superficial similarities and instead are likely to name classmates with similar Rep Test profiles as their best friends. Although you and your close friends probably share a lot of interests and activities, these similarities alone may not be enough to create a deep, long-lasting friendship. Unless the two of you agree on the way things are, it is unlikely you will "connect" in very many serious conversations.

Researchers also find support for this theory when examining friendship breakups. When students at one school were encouraged to move off campus their sophomore year, they were more likely to pair up with their freshman roommate when the two students had similar Rep Test profiles (Duck & Allison, 1978). When the two saw the world differently, the friendship tended to fade. Construct similarity also can explain why some romantic relationships last while others do not. Couples can be attracted to each other initially for a number of reasons. But over time, the relationships with a shared view of the world are the ones most likely to last. For example, one study found that the more couples shared construct structures, the happier they were with their marriages (Neimeyer, 1984). Apparently, construct similarity can hold a marriage together, even after passions fade.

Psychological Problems

Like many other personality theorists, Kelly was a practicing psychotherapist who used his theory of personality to understand psychological problems. However, unlike many theorists, Kelly rejected the idea that psychological disorders are caused by past traumatic experiences. Rather, people suffer from psychological problems because of defects in their construct systems. Past experiences with an unloving parent or a tragic incident may help explain why people construe the world as they do, but they are not the *cause* of the problems. Kelly also had little interest in developing complex diagnostic schemes for classifying various disorders; he described all disorders in terms of faulty construct systems.

Kelly did agree with Freud on one point. He maintained that anxiety is the "most common of all clinic commodities." According to Kelly, anxiety occurs when we can't predict future events. In Kelly's terms, we are aware that important events lie outside the range of convenience of our personal constructs. We all have had this experience on occasion. For example, you'll probably be more anxious going to a job interview when you have no idea of who you will meet or what kinds of questions they'll ask. Similarly, when you can't understand why others treat you the way they do or you don't know how to behave in certain situations, you become confused, disoriented, and anxious.

Why do our constructs sometimes fail us when trying to predict future events? Kelly explained that sometimes people develop impermeable constructs. An *impermeable construct* does not easily allow new elements into its existing range of convenience. For example, suppose a woman uses an accomplishable-impossible construct to evaluate the various tasks she encounters at work. If this construct suddenly were to become impermeable, new jobs that came along could not be added to her "accomplishable tasks" category. She'd probably insist on doing things the way she always has done them, even when circumstances change. Eventually her ability to do her job would decline, and she probably would become confused and anxious. If a person's entire construct system were to become impermeable, that person would be unable to learn from any new experiences. Without learning and subsequent construct modifications, the person's ability to anticipate events would continue to decrease as the world became more and more unpredictable and out of control.

Construct systems also can be incomplete, thus limiting the ability to make fine distinctions and accurate predictions. For example, some people see the world as consisting of friends and enemies. They have no subordinate constructs to delineate degrees of friendship (intimate friend–occasional chum) or types of enemies (friendly rival–dangerous opponent). These people soon find that they can anticipate very little of what other people will do. A "friend" may not invite them to a party, whereas an "enemy" might suggest a game of tennis.

Construct systems may be incomplete simply from lack of experience. Most of us have gone through the adjustment problems associated with starting a new job, attending a new school, or moving to a new city. Some of the difficulties we have during these first days may be attributed to a lack of appropriate constructs to deal with the new situations and new people we encounter. Most people eventually adjust their constructs and deal with the new situations effectively.

However, some people can't adjust and may eventually turn to psychotherapy to help make sense of their world again.

Cognitive Personality Variables

Although Kelly and other theorists introduced cognitive structures to account for individual differences in personality several decades ago, the use of cognitive explanations by personality psychologists has blossomed only in the last 15 or 20 years. During this time the field of psychology generally has witnessed a remarkable surge in interest in cognitive variables to explain a host of phenomena (Cantor, 1990). In keeping with this trend, many personality psychologists have introduced cognitive constructs to account for stable patterns of behavior. We will describe some of the more useful of these constructs here. These include Mischel's cognitive person variables, prototypes, schemas, and cognitive representations of the self.

Cognitive Person Variables

As described in Chapter 7, Walter Mischel has long been a critic of the trait approach to personality. He argues that trait measures account for only a small percentage of behavior variance and that there is little evidence for cross-situational consistency of behavior. Does this mean he denies the existence of personality? No. Mischel (1973, 1979) has offered a reconceptualization of personality that borrows heavily from cognitive psychology and social learning theory (Chapter 13). Rather than attribute consistency of behavior to traits, Mischel proposes that we examine the cognitions people use to interpret their worlds and to calculate their plans of action. He calls these relatively stable features *cognitive person variables*.

Mischel uses the five cognitive person variables listed in Table 15.2 to account for stable individual differences in our behavior. First, we each possess cognitive and behavioral *construction competencies*. These represent our potentials. Over the course of a lifetime, we develop the potential to perform a large number of organized behaviors, from riding a bicycle to carrying out an experiment. These competencies come from a number of sources, including basic conditioning processes and observational learning. However, Mischel emphasizes the cognitive component at work here. Our past experiences are not preserved exactly as they happened in our memory. Rather, we create our own conceptions of what happened, and these memories often undergo additional transformations as we think about what happened and have new experiences.

The second cognitive person variable is *encoding strategies and personal constructs*. Like Kelly, Mischel points out that people attend to, interpret, and categorize events differently. Two people learn from and respond to the same situation differently because cognitively they are having different experiences.

Although it is important to know what people are capable of doing and how they categorize events, Mischel argues that specific prediction of their behavior

Table 15.2

Mischel's Cognitive Person Variables

Construction competencies: The ability to construct (generate) particular cognitions and behaviors — refers to what the subject knows and *can* do.

Encoding strategies and personal constructs: The units used for categorizing events and for self-descriptions.

Behavior-outcome and stimulus-outcome expectancies: The expectancies people hold for particular situations.

Subjective stimulus values: Motivating and arousing stimuli, incentives, and aversions.

Self-regulatory systems and plans: The rules and self-reactions people hold for their performances and for the organization of complex behavior sequences.

Source: From Mischel (1973). Reprinted by permission.

requires an understanding of the third cognitive person variable, the *behavior-outcome and stimulus-outcome expectancies*. As Rotter described in his social learning theory (Chapter 13), through our experiences we develop expectancies that a given response will lead to a given outcome. Mischel calls these *behavior-outcome* expectancies. If raising my voice at a child rarely causes the child to stop crying, I should develop the expectancy that yelling does not stop the crying. Eventually I'll stop raising my voice and instead will turn to another plan of action I think is more likely to work. Mischel suggests that "maladaptive" behaviors are those for which the person holds a behavior-outcome expectancy inconsistent with the realities of the situation. For example, some people continually react to frustration with violence despite negative reactions to their outbursts. In cognitive terms, these people hold the inaccurate expectancy that violent behavior will take care of the frustrating situation.

Stimulus-outcome expectancies refer to our perceived likelihood that a certain event will lead to another event. Mischel uses this concept to explain many examples of classical conditioning. For example, you may have an association between dark rooms and fear. We can explain this in terms of your expectancy that bad things are likely to happen in dark places. Although this association may have been generated from a past experience in a dark place, as the behaviorists argue, Mischel maintains that this is but one of many possible sources for the expectancy.

Even with similar expectancies, people may react to events differently because of differences in their *subjective stimulus values*, Mischel's fourth cognitive person variable. For example, both you and I may expect that giving my aunt a compliment will result in a hug or a kiss. But whereas you enjoy this type of social contact, I don't. Guess who is likely to pay my aunt a compliment? Like Rotter, Mischel describes differences in stimulus value as relatively stable but points out that the value of any particular event or outcome depends largely on the conditions in which it occurs. Sometimes I welcome a hug and a kiss, other times not.

Self-regulatory systems and plans constitute the last cognitive person variable that guides our behavior. Although we obviously respond to external rewards and punishments, Mischel argues, like Bandura, that we adopt our own "contingency rules." Through self-praise and self-reinforcement, we motivate our own behavior through cognitive processes in the absence of, and sometimes in spite of, external contingencies.

Through these five cognitive variables Mischel can account for stable patterns in people's behavior without resorting to the traditional trait concept. Although he is dealing with the same phenomena that personality theorists from other approaches deal with, he explains these through differences in cognitive structures and processes. For example, changes in behavior following reinforcement are changes in expectancies, not changes in stimulus-response bonds. More recently, Mischel and his colleagues have introduced another cognitive structure to account for individual differences in behavior. We'll turn to that work next.

Prototypes

If I ask you to imagine an extravert, a genius, or an athlete, you probably will have no difficulty describing the three people that come to mind almost immediately. If I then ask you if your best friend is an extravert, a genius, or an athlete, you probably would compare your friend to the three people that came to mind earlier. Thus, the more your friend resembles the example of an extravert you imagined, the more likely you will say that he or she is an extravert.

The images of people you imagined in the preceding example represent what Mischel and some of his colleagues refer to as **prototypes** (Cantor & Mischel, 1979; Mischel, 1979, 1984). The basic framework for the prototype approach to personality comes from earlier work by cognitive psychologists, most notably Rosch (1978). These researchers proposed that people use prototypic examples when judging whether a given object belongs in a cognitive category. The more the object resembles the prototype, the more likely we are to say that it belongs in that category. For example, for the category "fruit" you may imagine an apple or an orange as your prototypic example. A nectarine and an apricot are close enough to these prototypes to be easily classified with them. But you may have been confused the first time someone told you that a tomato or an avocado was a fruit. This is because these fruits are so different from apples and oranges that they don't appear to belong in the same category, unless it is a more abstract grouping, such as "food."

Prototypes can also be used to categorize people. A prototypic person may be a combination of stereotypic features that describe no particular person, or it may be a specific individual who represents the epitome of members of that group. For example, you may use Michael Jordan as your prototype for the category "basketball players." When you say that someone doesn't look like a basketball player, you mean that person doesn't look much like Jordan. Cantor and Mischel (1979) suggest that these person categories can be arranged in a hierarchical fashion, as shown in Figure 15.1. Thus, you can have a prototype for "basketball players" and a prototype for "athletes." Becoming more specific, you can also have a prototype for "basketball centers." Which of these prototypes you use depends on your needs in a given situation.

How can we use the prototype concept to understand personality? Each of us forms unique prototypes for the categories of interest to us, and these different ways of perceiving result in different behaviors (Cantor, 1981). That is, because you and I have different prototypes and different categories for classifying information, we may identify the same people in very different ways. It follows that we also will interact with these people in very different ways. And because prototypes are relatively stable cognitive structures, these individual differences in our behavior also will be relatively stable.

An example will help illustrate the point. A high school student, Bob, has somewhat long, unkempt hair. He sits in the back of the room and rarely shows an interest in what the teacher is saying. Bob's English teacher has identified him as a troublemaker, a potentially disruptive student probably headed for a life of crime. The teacher has a prototype of "troublemaker" that he has found useful in several years of teaching, and Bob seems very much like that prototypic troublemaker. Consequently, he is quick to discipline Bob, is antagonistic whenever they interact, and grades Bob's work with an expectancy that it will be poor. On the other hand, Bob's history teacher finds that Bob matches her prototype of the "withdrawn student," who needs additional attention and encouragement. She calls on Bob whenever possible and gives positive responses to any sign that he is trying to learn. She grades Bob's work with an eye to his potential, which she believes is hidden by his withdrawn nature.

The student in this example might attribute the differences he sees in the two teachers' behaviors to some type or trait difference. The English teacher might be dismissed as "mean," whereas the history teacher probably would be seen as a "nice person." From a trait perspective, the two teachers' behaviors would fit these trait descriptions. However, from a cognitive perspective, we would say their behaviors stem from the use of different prototypes and different cognitive categories.

Even when two people use the same cognitive categories, they may classify people according to such widely different prototypes that their behaviors will be quite different. For example, my prototype of a "friendly person," a "criminal," or an "intelligent person" probably is different from yours. A man with a sharp wit and quick comebacks might fit my prototype of an "intelligent person," but he might be more like your "showoff" prototype. You might find a woman who uses big words and discusses philosophy better matches your "intelligent person" prototype, but she might be the prototypic "showoff" to me.

The use of prototypes has advantages and disadvantages. "The advantage of categorizing is that it allows thought and prevents us from being overwhelmed by a flood of stimuli," Mischel wrote. "The disadvantage is that it allows stereotyping and may lead us to view and treat people on the basis of the types or categories into which we squeeze them rather than on the basis of each individual's uniqueness" (1979, p. 747). When our use of prototypes is fairly accurate, they

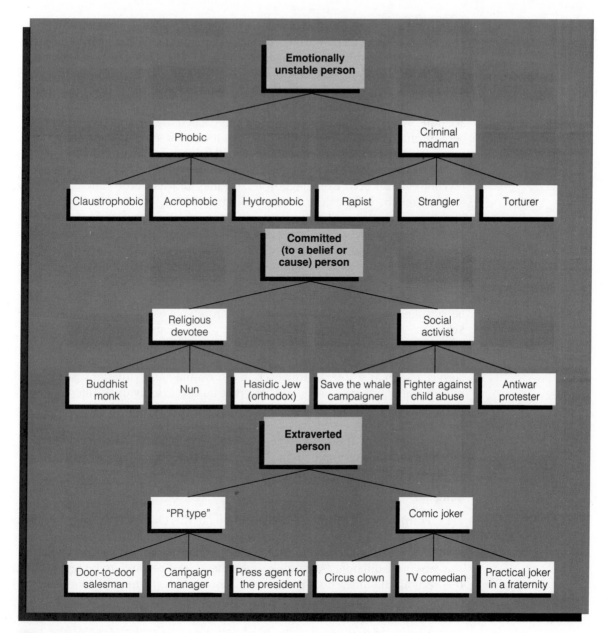

Figure 15.1

Examples of Prototype Hierarchies

Adapted from Cantor & Mischel (1979).

help us make sense of the world and interact with it effectively. How could we possibly have time to approach each person without any preconceived notions to guide our interpretation of his or her behavior? Of course, the problem is that sometimes we react to the categories we place people in rather than the way they really are. Once you decide a man is a prototypic "jerk," there is not much he can do to change your impression of him. In addition, our use of prototypes is far from accurate. Anyone who has mistakenly approached another shopper for advice because that person happened to look like their prototype of "store clerk" can appreciate the problems of inaccurate classification.

Some psychologists have extended the prototype concept to describe the way psychotherapists decide on diagnostic categories for psychiatric patients (Cantor, Smith, French, & Mezzich, 1980; Genero & Cantor, 1987). They argue that therapists essentially compare new patients with their prototypes for various diagnostic categories. After years of experience with patients, psychotherapists develop a "paranoid schizophrenic" prototype, an "obsessive-compulsive" prototype, and so on. The more a new patient resembles a particular prototype, the more likely he or she will be diagnosed into that category.

The use of prototypes is not limited to categorizing people. Situations also can be classified into categories according to prototypic cases (Cantor, Mischel, & Schwartz, 1982). If I categorize a gathering of people as a "party," my behavior will be different than if the situation resembles my prototype for an "informal business meeting." People tend to act alike in situations that are easy to classify correctly, such as a funeral. However, in more ambiguous situations, such as an office gathering that is part party and part business, individual differences are likely to surface (Schutte, Kenrick, & Sadalla, 1985). That is, if I tend to categorize such events as "parties," I will act differently from someone who tends to see these gatherings as "business." The differences in our behaviors reflect the different use of prototypes that help to shape our personalities.

Schemas

Let's return now to the scene at the beginning of this chapter — the one in which my friend and I came away from the party with completely different impressions. Although we were exposed to essentially the same people and events, what we saw was quite different. According to the theory and research to be reviewed in this section, the differences in our reactions can be explained by differences in schemas. **Schemas** are hypothetical cognitive structures that help us perceive, organize, process, and utilize information. Because there are so many stimuli to attend to in most situations, we need some way to make sense of the mass confusion around us. Imagine what the world must look like to a baby — what psychologist William James once referred to as a "buzzing, blooming confusion." The baby has not yet developed ways to know what out of this confusion to pay attention to and what to ignore. The mass of stimuli doesn't go away — think about all the sounds and sights currently bombarding your senses. But through the use of schemas, we have developed systems for identifying and attending to what is important and ignoring the rest.

Thus, one of the main functions of schemas is to help us perceive features in our environment. Naturally, when something extremely important happens or someone possesses an attention-grabbing feature, everyone notices. For example, if a seven-foot-tall man attends a party, everyone probably notices his height. But less conspicuous features of an environment probably will not be noticed unless we enter the situation with a readiness to process that information. Thus, I seldom notice how tall most people are. However, a friend of mine is very aware of other people's heights (she is short). In schema theory terms, the reason she pays attention to height is that she has a well-developed schema for processing this information. Because I use other schemas to process information about people, she and I often have different impressions of people.

Beyond helping to perceive certain features in our environment, schemas provide us with a structure within which to organize and process this information. For example, I can incorporate a new piece of information about my mother into my existing knowledge about her because I have a well-defined "mother" schema. I can give you a well-organized description of her because the information is organized into one well-formed cognitive structure, rather than scattered about as bits of information in various unrelated schemas. I also should be able to process information about my mother more readily than information about a woman I have never met. For example, when asked if my mother is sociable, I should be able to answer more readily than if asked if the queen of England is sociable. Without a strong schema for the queen, it will take me longer to process information about her. Finally, because my "mother" schema provides me with a framework within which to process and organize information about her, it is easier for me to utilize this information. I should be able to recall information about my mother more readily than information stored loosely in my memory.

As with other cognitive structures, we can use schemas to explain personality differences. That is, schemas are relatively stable and thus are responsible for relatively stable ways of perceiving and utilizing information. They also are different for each of us. Schemas cause us to process information about the world in a relatively stable manner, which results in relatively stable individual differences in our behavior.

Cognitive Representations of the Self

Although personality psychologists have demonstrated the importance of cognitive structures such as prototypes and schemas for height, criminals, English literature, and mothers, perhaps the most important cognitive structures are those that deal with the ways we think about ourselves. Beginning at a very early age, each of us develops a cognitive representation of who we are. Psychologists sometimes refer to this representation as our self-concept.

Psychologists don't always agree in their descriptions of how the self is represented in our cognitions, but few deny that cognitive representations of the self play a central role in the way we process information and thus in how we interact with the world around us. As they find with other personality constructs, researchers find that our self-concepts are relatively stable over time (Markus &

Kunda, 1986). We'll look at two examples of how the self is represented in our cognitive structures — self-schemas and possible selves.

Self-Schemas   Self-schemas are "cognitive generalizations about the self, derived from past experience, that organize and guide the processing of self-related information" (Markus, 1977, p. 64). Your self-schema consists of those aspects of your behavior that are the most important to you. Because each part of your life is not equally important, not everything you do becomes part of your self-schema (Markus, 1983). For example, if both you and I occasionally play baseball and write poetry, we can't assume that these two activities play an equally important role in our self-schemas. Baseball might be an important part of my self-schema, but not poetry, whereas the opposite might be the case for you.

If you could see your self-schema, what would it look like? An example of how a self-schema fits in with other schemas is shown in Figure 15.2. Basic pieces of information make up the core of your self-schema. This includes your name, representations of your physical appearance, and representations of your relationships with significant people, such as your spouse and parents. These are features in nearly everyone's self-schema. More important for understanding individual differences are particularistic self-schema features (Markus & Sentis, 1982; Markus & Smith, 1981). For example, athletes probably include information about sports in their self-schemas, but there are many people who don't (see, for example, Box 15.2). As shown in Figure 15.2, each of us also possesses schemas that are not relevant enough to be part of our self-schemas. For example, a person might have a schema for religion that doesn't become part of his or her self-schema until after a religious conversion.

Trait concepts, such as independence or friendliness, also can be part of your self-schema. That is, you might think of yourself as a friendly person. You frequently evaluate your behavior and the actions of others by asking if that was a friendly thing to do. On the other hand, it might never occur to me to evaluate my actions in terms of friendliness. In this example, friendliness is a feature of your self-schema, but not mine. Because the elements that comprise self-schemas vary from person to person, we all process information about ourselves differently.

Evidence for Self-Schemas   Yes or no: Are you an independent person? When faced with this question on a personality inventory, some people answer immediately and decisively; others have to pause to think about what it means to be independent and whether they possess those qualities. In taking the various personality tests in this book, you probably found some items that were easy to answer and some for which you simply couldn't make up your mind. According to a self-schema analysis, the items that were easy to answer are those for which you have a well-defined schema. People who say yes immediately when asked if they are independent have a strong schema for independence that is part of their self-schema. The schema enables them to understand the question and respond immediately. People without a strong independence schema lack the cognitive structure to respond with such quick and certain information processing.

Much of the early research on self-schemas was based on this reasoning. For example, preliminary research for one experiment found that how independent

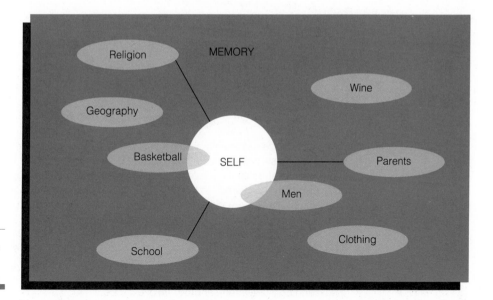

Figure 15.2

Example of a Self-Schema Diagram

or dependent people felt themselves to be was an important element in many people's self-schemas (Markus, 1977). Based on this initial phase of the study, subjects were classified as possessing either a strong "independence" schema or a strong "dependence" schema or as aschematics (those with neither schema). Three to four weeks later, these subjects participated in an experiment in which adjectives were presented on a screen one at a time. Their task was to press one of two buttons, labeled either ME or NOT ME, to indicate whether the adjective was self-descriptive. A clock connected to the buttons told the experimenter how quickly the subjects made these decisions.

Fifteen of the adjectives had been determined earlier to be related to independence and nonconformity, and 15 to dependence and conformity. The researchers wanted to see how quickly subjects in each of the three schema groups would respond to these 30 adjectives. As Figure 15.3 shows, subjects with strong independence schemas pressed the ME button quickly on the independence-related adjectives but took longer to respond on the dependence-related adjectives. Dependence-schema subjects showed the opposite pattern. Aschematics showed no difference in making these judgments for any of the types of words.

The findings demonstrate that people process information more rapidly when they have a strong cognitive structure related to that information. Subjects for whom independence is a part of their self-schemas could quickly process information about being independent. However, because these subjects lacked a strong cognitive structure to help them process information about being dependent, they were not able to answer those questions as readily. This is not to say that people without certain schemas are any less intelligent or that they have a slower cognitive tempo. They simply process information differently.

Box 15.2

Self-Schema and Exercise

The past decade has seen a growing awareness of the benefits of exercise. Surveys indicate that most Americans are convinced that exercise is good for their physical and mental health and that the majority of adults periodically take up jogging, swimming, aerobic dancing, or some other type of exercise program. However, a large number of adults rarely, if ever, exercise, and about half of those who begin an exercise program quit within the first year.

Why do some people succeed in making exercise a part of their lives, while others fail? One explanation looks at the extent to which people incorporate exercise into their self-schemas. That is, if you identify yourself as an exerciser and begin to process relevant information about yourself in terms of that self-concept, then you also are likely to begin and continue a regular program of exercise.

To test this notion, one researcher used questionnaire responses to divide subjects into those who were schematic as exercisers, those who were schematic as nonexercisers, and those who were aschematic on this dimension (Kendzierski, 1990). Subjects then were tested to determine if the schematic and aschematic subjects processed exercise-relevant information differently. Consistent with expectations, the investigator found the exercise-schematic subjects were more likely to say that exercise-relevant words described them. More important, because exercise was a part of their self-schemas, these subjects responded to the words more quickly than the other subjects.

Additional research finds that exercise-schematic people are more likely to begin exercise programs and more likely to stick with them than nonschematics or those who are nonexercise schematic (Kendzierski, 1988, 1990). These findings suggest that health professionals might want to work on getting people to incorporate exercise into their self-concepts, rather than trying to convince them to squeeze some exercise into their days. Chances are, if you think of yourself as a "basketball player" or a "gymnast," you probably are going to be healthier and more physically fit than people who do not see themselves as exercisers or athletes.

In addition to allowing for rapid processing of schema-relevant information, self-schemas provide a framework for organizing and storing relevant information. Consequently, we would expect people to retrieve information from memory more readily when they have a strong schema for the topic than when the information is stored in a less organized manner. To test this hypothesis, researchers presented college students with a series of 40 questions on a video screen (Rogers, Kuiper, & Kirker, 1977). The subjects were to answer each

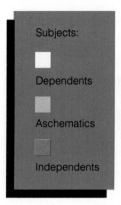

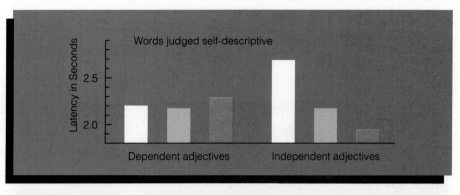

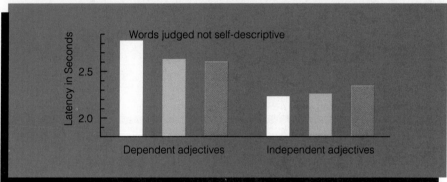

Figure 15.3

Mean Response Latencies for Adjectives

Adapted from Markus (1977); reprinted by permission.

question by pressing a YES or a NO button as quickly as possible. Subjects could answer 30 of the questions easily without using their self-schemas to process the information (see Table 15.3). For these questions, subjects simply answered whether a word was printed in big letters, whether it rhymed with another word, or whether it meant the same thing as another word. However, for 10 of the words, subjects had to decide whether the word described them. That is, they had to process the information through their self-schemas.

What the subjects were not told was that afterward they would be asked to recall as many of the 40 words as possible. The results, presented in Table 15.3, show that subjects remembered significantly more of the words from the self-reference questions than from any of the other three types of processing. The researchers argue that this is because subjects processed this information through their self-schemas, and it was therefore more readily available for recall than was the information processed in other ways.

Table 15.3

Mean Number of Words Recalled for Four Types of Adjectives

Task	Cue Question	Manipulation	Mean Number of Units Recalled
Structural	Big letters?	The adjective was either presented in the same size as the question or twice as large.	.34
Phonemic	Rhymes with XXXX?	XXXX was a word that either rhymed or did not rhyme with the adjective.	.68
Semantic	Means same as YYYY?	YYYY was either a synonym or unrelated word to the presented adjective.	1.33
Self-referent	Describes you?	Subjects simply responded *yes* or *no* to indicate the self-reference quality of the presented adjective.	2.84

Source: Adapted from Rogers, Kuiper, and Kirker (1977); reprinted by permission.

Might this finding be due to the fact that the self-referent question was harder, thus causing subjects to think about it more? Apparently not. When subjects are asked if the word describes the experimenter (Kuiper & Rogers, 1979) or Walter Cronkite (Lord, 1980), they don't recall the words as well as when they are asked about themselves. Because subjects presumably have less well-defined schemas for the experimenter or for Walter Cronkite, they recall the words less readily. Nor can the better recall of self-referent words be explained simply in terms of the words' ability to generate emotion. When researchers compared recall of self-referent words with recall of equally emotional words processed another way, the self-referent words were still recalled more readily (McCaul & Maki, 1984). In short, the accessibility and superior organization of information about ourselves seems to make information processed through the self-schema more accessible than information processed in other ways (Karylowski, 1990; Klein & Loftus, 1988; Klein, Loftus, & Burton, 1989).

Possible Selves Suppose two college students, Denise and Carlos, receive an identical poor grade in a course on deductive logic and argumentation. Neither person is pleased with the grade, but Denise quickly dismisses it as a bad semester, while Carlos frets about the grade for weeks. Denise turns her attention to the next term, but Carlos looks over his final exam several times and thinks about taking another course in this area. Although many explanations can be suggested to account for the two students' different reactions, a key piece of information may be that Carlos is thinking about going to law school and becoming a trial attorney someday, but Denise is not. A negative evaluation of his deductive logic and argumentation skills means something quite different to Carlos than it does to Denise. Further, his aspiration to become an attorney leads Carlos to a different course of action than that which Denise takes.

What this example illustrates is that our behavior is directed by cognitive representations of the self beyond the way we think of ourselves at the moment. Rather, we also think about our potential and have cognitive representations of what we might become someday. You might think about a future self with a lot of friends, with a medical degree, or with a physically fit body. However, sometimes we also think about the selves we fear we might become, such as the self that is unemployed, physically ill, or lonely and depressed.

Recently, some personality psychologists have begun to refer to these images of what we might become as our "possible selves" (Cantor, Markus, Niedenthal, & Nurius, 1986; Markus & Nurius, 1986; Ruvolo & Markus, 1992). **Possible selves** are the cognitive representations of the kinds of people we think we might become someday. These include roles and occupations we aspire to or fear we might fall into, such as police officer, alcoholic, or community leader. Possible selves also include the attributes we think we might possess in the future, such as being a warm and loving person, an overworked and underappreciated person, or a contributor to society. In a sense, possible selves represent our dreams and aspirations as well as our fears and anxieties.

Possible selves serve two important functions (Markus & Nurius, 1986). First, possible selves provide incentives for future behavior. We make decisions based on whether we anticipate that our actions will take us closer to or farther away from becoming one of our future selves. For example, a woman might enter an MBA program because this action moves her closer to becoming the powerful business executive she now sees as one of her possible selves. On the other hand, a man might stop seeing some unsavory acquaintances if he thinks the association might lead him down the path to the criminal self he fears he might become.

The second function of possible selves is to help us interpret the meaning of our behavior and the events in our lives. For example, a man with a possible self of a professional baseball player will attach a very different meaning to hitting a home run than someone who does not possess this possible self. A woman with a possible self of cancer patient will react differently to small changes in her health than someone without this cognitive representation. In other words, sometimes what happens to us also affects how we progress toward becoming one or more of our possible selves. These cases are likely to lead to greater attention and a stronger emotional reaction than when the information is not relevant for our possible selves.

An example of how possible selves relate to potential problem behaviors was demonstrated in a study examining the possible selves of juvenile delinquents (Oyserman & Markus, 1990). Adolescence is a time in which young men and women typically develop a sense of the kind of person they want to become. Significantly, more than one third of the 13- to 16-year-olds in this study had developed a possible self of "a criminal." In addition, relatively few of these subjects possessed possible selves for such conventional goals as having a job or getting along in school. If these possible selves are indicative of the goals, fears, and aspirations of these adolescents, then it is perhaps not surprising that youthful offenders often become adult criminals.

In summary, in recent years psychologists have introduced a number of cognitive variables to account for individual differences in personality. These include Mischel's cognitive person variables, prototypes, schemas, self-schemas, and possible selves. In each case the cognitive structure influences the information we attend to, how we interpret the information, and how well we recall the information. Because each of us has different cognitive structures, we respond to our worlds in unique but characteristic ways.

Application: Cognitive Psychotherapy

Just as the last few decades have witnessed an increase in the acceptance of cognitive approaches to personality, they also have seen a tremendous increase in the popularity of cognitive approaches to psychotherapy. As the name implies, the focus of cognitive psychotherapy is the client's thoughts. Although there are many different therapies that fall under this heading, each identifies inappropriate thoughts as the cause of debilitating mood disorders and self-defeating behavior. For example, the reason people become anxious and depressed is that they harbor anxiety-provoking and depressing thoughts. Consequently, the goal of most cognitive therapies is to help clients recognize these self-defeating thoughts and replace them with more appropriate ones. Sometimes this process is referred to as **cognitive restructuring**. A cognitive therapist's role usually falls somewhere between that of the intrusive Freudian therapist and the Rogerian therapist who relies on the client for clinical progress. Although clients must come to see how their cognitions affect their emotions and behaviors, the therapist plays an active role in this process.

As with cognitive personality theory, George Kelly was an early pioneer in the cognitive approach to treating psychological disorders (Kelly, 1955, 1969). According to Kelly, people seek out therapists when they are unable to construe the world with their existing set of constructs. Kelly's goal as a psychotherapist was to help clients develop new constructs, reshape construct hierarchies, and modify old constructs so that they were better able to predict events. He used a variety of methods to meet this goal. If clients' constructs seemed particularly vague (or "loose" in Kelly's terms), he asked them to define the constructs more clearly and provide examples of elements that did and did not fit the categories. In this manner, clients were forced to attend to their process of construing the world and to test its accuracy for predicting events.

Kelly also developed a procedure called **fixed-role therapy**. Here a team of therapists creates an imaginary person for clients to role-play. They design a brief biographic sketch of a person whose construct system might benefit the client. By pretending to be this other person and perceive the world the way this person might, clients "try on" the new constructs. If these constructs are helpful, clients may continue to use them after the role playing. For example, suppose you

The best scientist is one who approaches his subject [as] intimately as a clinician . . . and the best clinician is one who invites his client to join him in a controlled investigation of life.

GEORGE KELLY

conclude that your client tends to see the world in rigid "friend-enemy" terms. Everyone she meets is either for her or against her. Consequently, she has difficulty socializing with people or interacting with her coworkers on the job. As soon as a friend does something she dislikes, she assumes the person is out to get her. You might ask this client to role-play a character who sees some good in everyone and is quick to forgive and forget. If the procedure is successful, your client may see that there are other, more efficient ways to look at the world. Using these new constructs should afford her more predictability and thereby decrease anxiety.

Albert Ellis's Rational Emotive Therapy

One of the earliest advocates of cognitive therapy was Albert Ellis, who developed *rational emotive therapy* (Ellis & Harper, 1975). According to Ellis, people become depressed, anxious, upset, and the like because of faulty reasoning and the reliance on irrational beliefs. Ellis describes this as an A-B-C process. For example, suppose your boyfriend/girlfriend calls tonight and tells you the relationship is over. This is the A, which Ellis calls the **a**ctivating experience. However, when clients seek out psychotherapy they usually identify the reason as the C, the emotional **c**onsequence. In this case, you probably are depressed, guilty, angry, and so on. But how did you get logically from A to C? Why should a personal setback or loss cause such strong negative emotions? The answer is that you have used a middle step in this sequence, B — the irrational **b**elief. The only way you could logically conclude from breaking up with your partner that you should be depressed is that you are also saying to yourself something like "It is necessary for me to be loved and approved by virtually every person in my life." Of course, when isolated like this the belief is obviously irrational. But these irrational beliefs are so entrenched in our thoughts that it often takes professional help to see the flaws in our thinking.

Ellis maintains that each of us harbors a large number of these irrational beliefs. Imagine that you fail an important class (A). If you then fall back on the irrational belief "I need to do well at everything to be considered worthwhile" (B), you'll lead yourself to the conclusion that this is a catastrophe and therefore become excessively anxious (C). A rational-emotive therapist would argue that while this certainly is an unfortunate event, and something you'd prefer didn't happen, it does not warrant extreme anxiety. Expecting everything to work out well all the time will only lead to disappointment and frustration. Some of the more commonly used irrational beliefs are listed in Table 15.4. Ellis (1987) says some of these beliefs are blatantly irrational and therefore more easily identified and corrected during therapy. However, other beliefs are more subtle or tricky and therefore more resistant to change.

Ellis's goal in psychotherapy is twofold. First, he forces clients to see how they are relying on irrational beliefs and thereby see the fault in their reasoning. Second, he works to replace irrational beliefs with rational ones. For example, instead of deciding that your romantic breakup is a reason to be depressed, you might tell yourself that while you enjoy a stable romantic relationship and wish this one could have continued, you know that not all relationships work out. You

Table 15.4

Some Common Irrational Beliefs

Obvious Irrational Beliefs
"Because I strongly desire to perform important tasks competently and successfully, I *absolutely must* perform them well at all times."
"Because I strongly desire to be approved by people I find significant, I *absolutely must* always have their approval."
"Because I strongly desire people to treat me considerately and fairly, they *absolutely must* at all times and under all conditions do so."
"Because I strongly desire to have a safe, comfortable, and satisfying life, the conditions under which I live *absolutely must* at all times be easy, convenient, and gratifying."

Subtle and Tricky Irrational Beliefs
"Because I strongly desire to perform important tasks competently and successfully, and because I want to succeed at them only *some of* the time, I *absolutely must* perform these tasks well."
"Because I strongly desire to be approved by people I find significant, and because I only want *a little* approval from them, I *absolutely must* have it."
"Because I strongly desire people to treat me considerately and fairly, and because I am almost always considerate and fair to others, they *absolutely must* treat me well."
"Because I strongly desire to have a safe, comfortable, and satisfying life, and because I am a nice person who tries to help others lead this kind of life, the conditions under which I live *absolutely must* be easy, convenient, and gratifying."

Source: Taken from Ellis (1987), with permission.

also know that this doesn't mean no one else can love you or that you are never going to have a good relationship again. Thus, while the A statement is the same — "I broke up with my partner" — the B statement is different. Because the situation is identified as unpleasant but not catastrophic, there is no need to become overly depressed, the old C.

You can see how Ellis works to change these faulty thoughts in the following sample, taken from one of his therapy sessions with a young woman (Ellis, 1971):

> *Client:* Well, this is all a part of something that's bothered me for a long time. I'm always afraid of making a mistake.
>
> *Ellis:* Why? What's the horror?

C: I don't know.

E: You're saying that you're a bitch, you're a louse when you make a mistake.

C: But this is the way I've always been. Every time I make a mistake, I die a thousand deaths over it.

E: You blame yourself. But why? What's the horror? Is it going to make you better next time? Is it going to make you make fewer mistakes?

C: No.

E: Then why blame yourself? Why are you a louse for making a mistake? Who said so?

C: I guess it's one of those feelings I have.

E: One of those *beliefs*. The belief is: "I am a louse!" And then you get the feeling: "Oh, how awful! How shameful!" But the feeling follows the belief. And again, you're saying, "I should be different; I *shouldn't* make mistakes!" Instead of: "Oh, look: I made a mistake. It's undesirable to make mistakes. Now, how am I going to stop making one next time?" . . .

C: It might all go back to, as you said, the need for approval. If I don't make mistakes, then people will look up to me. If I do it all perfectly—

E: Yes, that's part of it. That is the erroneous belief: that if you never make mistakes everybody will love you and that it is necessary that they do. . . . But is it true? Suppose you never did make mistakes—*would* people love you? They'd sometimes hate your guts, wouldn't they?

Ellis challenges clients to identify their irrational beliefs and see how these beliefs lead them to their faulty conclusions. Of course, this is not easy. Most of us can readily identify what's wrong with our friends' thinking, but it's quite another matter when we're the ones with an emotional problem. "Virtually all people are born with very strong tendencies to think crookedly about their important desires and preferences," Ellis wrote. " . . . [But] I also hold that RET (Rational Emotive Therapy) has notable techniques of showing people how to increase their self-actualizing and how to minimize their self-sabotaging thoughts, feelings, and behaviors" (1987, pp. 373–374).

Self-Instructional Training

Like all therapists, cognitive psychologists help clients overcome the problems that caused them to seek professional help. But this typically is only one goal of cognitive therapy. It's important to help clients recognize they are not worthless because they failed a class. But how long until these clients run into another personal setback, another failure? Because we can never avoid potentially distressing situations, cognitive psychologists often teach clients how to prepare for and deal with potential problem situations in the future. If people learn how not to use self-defeating thoughts, they can avoid some of the emotional problems that may have plagued them throughout their lives.

Donald Meichenbaum's *self-instructional training* is a good example of such an approach. Self-instructional training is part of a larger cognitive therapy program (Meichenbaum, 1977, 1985; Meichenbaum & Cameron, 1983). Like Ellis, Meichenbaum identifies the thoughts that drive clients' disturbing emotions and

Internal monologue

helps them recognize and replace these with more adaptive thinking. But Meichenbaum also helps clients develop specific cognitive strategies for dealing with the kinds of situations that frequently cause them problems.

One reason for recurrent problems is that some people typically engage in self-defeating thinking. For example, a man who suffers from shyness probably approaches a dance telling himself something like "I don't know why I'm going to this stupid dance. No one ever wants to dance with me. When they do I usually look so awkward on the dance floor I'm sure people are staring at me. And when the dance is over I never know what to say." This man has set himself up to fail. At the first sign his prophecy is coming true, he will conclude that things are going as poorly as anticipated. All the nervousness and embarrassment he dreaded is likely to follow.

What can be done for this man? Meichenbaum recommends replacing these self-defeating thoughts with more appropriate, positive ones. This is not to say the man should unrealistically expect that everything will go well. But rather he should be prepared for some disappointments and failures and learn to interpret these in appropriate ways. Meichenbaum describes this process as "inoculation." Like a medical vaccine that prevents a patient from becoming ill, self-instructional training is designed to keep negative thoughts from creating undue psychological distress.

Meichenbaum helps clients prepare *internal monologues* for each step of the stressful experience. For example, a woman who suffers from stage fright will learn to say to herself before a performance, "Think about what you can do, not about getting nervous" or "You have a plan to deal with this." As she is about to walk out on stage, she may think, "A little tenseness is OK, it's just a reminder to use my coping skills." During the performance she may remind herself, "You can do it, you're doing fine so far." Finally, she rewards herself afterward with "You're making improvements every time" or "You still had some difficulty there, something to work on for next time."

Once clients see the effectiveness of self-instructional training for one problem, they often develop appropriate internal monologues for other problems that arise. The college actress who overcame her stage fright with this procedure may adopt a similar strategy when facing job interviews a few years later.

In summary, cognitive psychotherapy procedures have witnessed a surge in popularity in recent years. Like any approach to psychotherapy, they do not work for everyone and may be limited to psychological problems that are based in irrational and self-defeating thinking. Nonetheless, the success many therapists have had with this approach has been encouraging (Meichenbaum & Jaemko, 1983). A recent review of studies comparing cognitive therapy for depression with other types of therapy concluded that the cognitive approach was more successful than behavior therapy, drug treatments, and of course, no treatment (Dobson, 1989). Other studies indicate that cognitive therapies also are effective for treating clients suffering from anxiety and panic disorders (Beck, 1991).

Assessment: The Rep Test

Because the focus of his therapy was identifying and correcting inadequate personal constructs, George Kelly created a problem for himself: How does one go about measuring a person's personal constructs? Of course, a therapist might obtain some idea of a client's personal construct system during the course of therapy interviews. But Kelly and his colleagues needed a more efficient way to examine construct systems that could then be communicated fairly easily to the client. Kelly's response to this problem was to develop the Role Construct Repertory Test, or the **Rep Test** for short. The Rep Test is really a variety of procedures Kelly introduced to assess personal construct systems. Kelly initially was interested in measuring therapy clients' personal constructs. Subsequent researchers, however, have modified the Rep Test procedures to examine such diverse phenomena as urban planning and the study of primitive tribes' folk beliefs (cf. Neimeyer & Neimeyer, 1981).

Forms of the Rep Test

Each Rep Test form presents clients with elements from their lives. Usually this means a list of important people from various parts of their lives. Clients then identify the constructs they use to place these elements into categories. Through a series of these exercises, the therapist obtains a list of what probably are the client's most frequently used constructs.

The *Minimum Context Form* of the Rep Test is presented in abbreviated form on pages 496–497. Therapists using this form ask clients to provide a list of 24 people from various personal experiences — for example, a teacher they liked and one they disliked, a person who was hard to understand, the most successful person they know, the most interesting person they know, and so on. Although someone may fall into more than one category, a name can be used only once.

Personal Constructs

The following is an abbreviated version of Kelly's Rep Test, the Minimum Context Form. By taking a few minutes to complete the test, you can obtain a quick idea of the constructs you use to organize information about the people you know and meet. After you complete the test, you may want to compare your responses with those of other people. No doubt you will find a few overlapping constructs and many that you hadn't thought of. Of course, these differences in personal constructs represent differences in personality that should translate into relatively stable individual differences in your behavior.

To begin, write down the names of the following 12 people. Although a person may fit into more than one category, you need to compile a list of 12 *different* people.

1. A teacher you liked _____
2. A teacher you disliked _____
3. Your wife (husband) or boyfriend (girlfriend) _____
4. An employer, supervisor, or officer you found hard to get along with _____
5. An employer, supervisor, or officer you liked _____
6. Your mother _____
7. Your father _____
8. Brother (or someone like a brother) nearest your age _____
9. Sister (or someone like a sister) nearest your age _____
10. A person with whom you have worked who was easy to get along with _____

Continued

Clients are then presented with three of the names from this list and asked, "In what important way are two of these people alike but different from the third?" A client might say, for example, that two of them are warm people and that the third person is cold. In Kelly's terms, this client used a warm-cold construct to categorize the three people. The process is repeated with three different names from the list. Perhaps this time the client will divide them along "intelligent-unintelligent" or "generous-miserly" constructs. Kelly suggests that about 20 such trials or "sorts" will provide the therapist with a useful sample of the client's principal constructs.

Kelly introduced several additional Rep Test procedures. In the *Full Context Form*, the people's names are written on separate cards and subjects are asked to put the cards into groups of people that are alike. Naturally, the therapist asks clients their reasons for grouping people together, in order to identify the constructs they used. In the *Sequential Form*, the tester takes away one of the cards used in the Minimum Context Form, replaces it with a new one, and asks, "*Now, what would you say is an important way in which two of these people are alike but different from the third?*" This approach can be useful in identifying clients' difficulties in applying new constructs to new situations.

    Two other forms of the Rep Test examine more directly the way people envision themselves in regard to these constructs. In the *Self-Identification Form*, clients are presented with their name along with two names from the list. Again they are asked how two of the three are alike and one is different. In the *Personal Role Form*, the therapist asks clients to imagine themselves in a situation with the other two people: "Now suppose that the three of you were all together by yourselves for an evening. What kind of place might it be? What would happen? How would you yourself be likely to be acting? How would each of the others be likely to be acting?'' This allows the tester to examine how clients' constructs translate into actual behavior.

The purpose of all these forms of the Rep Test is to provide testers with a list of some of the client's personal constructs so that they can assess the way the client perceives and interprets events. Many therapists and researchers have modified and expanded Kelly's Rep Test procedures to fit their own needs (Bannister & Mair, 1968; Fransella & Bannister, 1977; Neimeyer & Neimeyer, 1981), but they all are interested in the same goal—to obtain a better understanding of how clients construe the world.

Assumptions Underlying the Rep Test

Kelly (1955) acknowledged that therapists must make several assumptions when using the Rep Test to measure personal constructs. One is that the constructs clients provide are not limited to the people on the list, but that they will apply to new people in new situations. In Kelly's terms, the constructs are assumed to be *permeable*. If a client used the constructs elicited by the test only for the people on the list, this would be of little value to a therapist seeking to understand how the person sees the world in general.

Another assumption built into the Rep Test is that the constructs it elicits have some degree of permanence—that is, that clients are not using these constructs for the first time in the testing session and never again. If the test is to be a measure of stable personality characteristics, the constructs listed must be those that clients use on a regular basis. A related assumption is that the people on the list are representative of the kind of people clients are likely to deal with in their daily lives. Constructs used only for unique people that clients rarely encounter are of little use in understanding how clients deal with the majority of people they interact with.

Kelly's ''most precarious assumption'' is that people are able to adequately describe the constructs they use. The Rep Test unfortunately is subject to the inherent limits of our language. Although clients may supply words that come close to what they mean, these words may be inadequate. Kelly does not assume that words necessarily exist for describing these constructs. In fact, he describes ''preverbal'' constructs, those developed prior to learning to speak. And even when clients do use appropriate words, therapists may interpret those words differently. For example, a client's definition of ''aggressive'' may be quite different from a therapist's. In this case the therapist may still end up with false impressions of how the client views the world.

Given the Rep Test's limitations, the best advice seems to be, as with most assessment procedures, to consider it as but one source of information about how clients construe the world. For example, a therapist who knows what to look for can obtain valuable information about clients' construct systems by paying attention during interviews. Or, as Kelly advised: ''If you don't know what's wrong with a client, ask him; he may tell you'' (1955, p. 201).

Clinical Analysis with the Rep Test

In addition to a list of clients' constructs, the Rep Test gives a therapist an idea about the number of constructs in clients' construct systems. Some people develop problems because they tend to view the world with a small number of frequently used constructs. For example, a woman might categorize everyone she knows with a "good-bad" construct. If she doesn't use additional constructs that allow her to make finer distinctions, she'll have great difficulty predicting what people will do. Not all people put into the "good people" category will behave alike, and without further constructs, it's difficult to predict their behavior reliably.

Therapists should also look out for what Kelly referred to as *preemptive constructs*. For example, a man might describe two people as alike because "they are both women" but be unable to verbalize this construct much further. This suggests that he sees all women as being alike and women are not like men in any way. "This carries the further implication," Kelly wrote, "that when one has said that a person is a woman he has said all that can be said about her" (1955, p. 239). A man who holds this type of preemptive construct probably will have difficulty predicting women's behavior and therefore have trouble interacting with them.

Finally, therapists can obtain valuable information from the Rep Test about how clients perceive themselves. When using Rep Test forms that include the client's name, therapists can note where clients place themselves along such dimensions as good-bad, strong-weak, outgoing-withdrawn, and so on.

Therapists may also note how accurate clients' perceptions of themselves are. Meek clients who place themselves in categories with "leaders" and "dominant people" are clearly having difficulty construing the world and are no doubt unable to predict with much accuracy how others will treat them.

In summary, the Rep Test is a collection of procedures therapists and researchers can use to assess the constructs that clients or research subjects typically use to construe the events in their lives. Testers should be aware of several assumptions built into the procedure, including clients' abilities to adequately describe the constructs they use. Nonetheless, for the alert therapist, the Rep Test can be a rich source of information about how clients perceive the world and why they have developed difficulties in predicting events.

Strengths and Criticisms of the Cognitive Approach

Because the cognitive approach is a relatively new approach to personality, many of its strengths and weaknesses may have yet to surface. As personality psychologists become more accustomed to thinking of personality in terms of differences in cognitions and as more research is conducted, stronger evaluations will be forthcoming. However, Kelly's theory has been around for almost four decades now, and enough research has been conducted on concepts like prototypes and schemas to form some initial evaluations.

Strengths

A strength of the cognitive approach is that many of the ideas evolved out of and were developed through empirical research findings. In particular, the concepts of prototype and schema were proposed to account for research findings and then subjected to additional research. Rather than initially asserting the applicability of these constructs, researchers more typically have demonstrated their ability to account for personality phenomena in empirical investigations. This contrasts with the approach taken by other personality theorists, perhaps most notably the psychoanalysts, who sometimes discuss the usefulness of their theory and constructs without the support of research findings.

Cognitive personality theorists can be credited with taking the trait approach one step further in their effort to explain why certain people demonstrate certain personality characteristics. Rather than simply identifying traits and predicting behavior, cognitive theorists have introduced cognitive structures to explain these stable individual differences in behavior. Basically, a trait can be explained in terms of a stable manner of processing information. For example, Type A and Type B subjects were compared in one study for how quickly they indicated if a trait did or did not describe them (Strube et al., 1986). Both Type A's and Type B's responded more quickly when describing traits related to their personality styles. This finding indicates that Type A's and Type B's differ in part because of differences in cognitive structures.

Another strength of the cognitive approach is that it fits well with the current mood, or *Zeitgeist*, of psychology. Researchers in other areas of psychology, such as developmental and social psychologists, are working on related lines of cognitive research that often complement and extend what is known from the personality perspective. As described earlier, cognitive approaches to psychotherapy have become particularly popular in recent years.

A refreshing feature of Kelly's personality theory is his acknowledgment of its limits. He recognized many of the assumptions built into his approach and suggested there are parts of personality that his theory may not be able to explain. Kelly went so far as to state that his theory will be useful only until a better theory is developed to replace it. After the grand assertions of some personality theorists, Kelly's attitude is a little breath of fresh air.

Criticisms

A frequent criticism of the cognitive approach is that the concepts are too vague for empirical research. What exactly *is* a "personal construct" or a "prototype"? How do we know if a schema is being used? How many schemas are there, and how are they related? More important, how can we demonstrate their influence on behavior if we have only a vague idea of what they are? Some of the answers may come with more research, but the nature of cognitions probably renders them more nebulous than many constructs used by personality theorists.

A related problem is the questionable need to introduce these vague concepts to account for individual differences in behavior. For example, behaviorists might argue that they can explain the same phenomena with fewer constructs. Introducing personal schemas or prototypes may be unnecessary at best and perhaps even a confusing obstacle to understanding personality. Applying the law of parsimony, it is incumbent upon cognitive theorists to demonstrate how their approach can explain personality better than other, less complicated approaches.

Perhaps because the cognitive approach is in an early stage of development, there is no single model to organize and guide theory and research. Basic questions about how various cognitive structures relate to each other and to other aspects of information processing, such as memory, remain unanswered. A related problem concerns the relationship between the various cognitive structures different theorists have introduced. Is a personal construct different than a schema? How do these terms differ from a prototype? A comprehensive model would help researchers understand precisely what these terms mean and how they are related.

Finally, better methods for measuring cognitive constructs are needed. Kelly's Rep Test remains more descriptive than quantitative and relies on subjective impressions rather than objective scores. Researchers and therapists need better measures for the number of cognitions and their relative strengths to better predict behavior and make comparisons between subjects or clients.

Summary

1. The cognitive approach to personality describes consistent behavior patterns in terms of individual differences in the way people process information. George Kelly was an early pioneer for this approach with his personal construct theory. Kelly maintained that we are motivated to make sense out of our worlds. He compared people to scientists, always striving for better predictions about what will happen to them. Kelly described the cognitive structures we use in this regard as personal constructs. He examined the personal constructs people use to predict behavior and the structure of their construct systems. Kelly maintained that psychological problems stem from anxiety, which results from a person's inability to predict events.

2. Walter Mischel introduced five cognitive person variables to explain stable patterns of behavior. He also borrowed the concept of prototypes to account for some of these differences. According to this approach, we often categorize people and places according to how well they fit our prototypic examples of members of that category. Personality differences are due in part to the use of different prototypes. Other psychologists have identified schemas as the cognitive structures responsible for individual differences in the way we process information. Schemas help us perceive, organize, and store information.

3. Perhaps the most important cognitive structures for personality psychologists are the cognitive representations we have of our selves. Much research in this area is concerned with self-schemas. Studies demonstrate that we perceive information more readily and recall it better when it is relevant to our self-schemas. More recently psychologists have argued that cognitive representations of future selves also guide our behavior.

4. Cognitive approaches to psychotherapy have become increasingly popular in the last decade. These therapies focus on changing the clients' thoughts. Albert Ellis, an early advocate of this approach, argues that people have emotional problems when they use irrational beliefs. He helps clients to see how they use these beliefs and to replace them with more rational ones. In self-instructional training, clients learn to replace negative internal statements with more appropriate, positive statements.

5. Kelly introduced the Rep Test to measure individual differences in personal constructs. Test takers typically develop a list of people in their lives and then divide these people into various categories. This helps the therapist see the constructs clients use to make sense of the world. Kelly acknowledged several assumptions behind this approach, including that people can adequately communicate the constructs they use. He also maintained that therapists can use Rep Test results to identify how their clients' construct systems are faulty.

6. Among the strengths of the cognitive approach to personality is its strong empirical background. The approach also fits nicely with the current trend in psychology toward cognitive explanations of behavior. The cognitive approach also appears to elaborate and extend the trait approach.

7. The cognitive approach also has been subjected to some criticisms. Some critics have complained that many of the concepts used by cognitive theorists are too vague. Others have questioned whether it is always necessary to introduce cognitions to explain behavior. The cognitive approach also suffers from the lack of a general model to organize all of the work that falls under this approach. Finally, if the cognitive approach is to prosper, psychologists need to develop better methods for assessing cognitive structures.

Key Terms

personal constructs In Kelly's theory, the bipolar cognitive structures through which people process information.

prototype A cognitive structure representing a typical case from a cognitive category.

schema A hypothetical cognitive structure used to process information.

self-schema A schema consisting of aspects of a person's life most important to him or her.

possible selves Cognitive representations of the kind of people we think we might become some day.

cognitive restructuring Psychotherapy procedures designed to alter the thoughts people use and the way they process information.

fixed-role therapy A psychotherapy procedure introduced by Kelly, in which clients act out a role suggested by therapists.

Rep Test The Role Construct Repertory Test, designed by Kelly to assess personal constructs.

Suggested Readings

Ellis, A. (1987). The impossibility of achieving consistently good mental health. *American Psychologist, 42,* 364–375. Albert Ellis addresses the question of why people continue to cling to self-defeating irrational beliefs. This article provides a nice taste of Ellis's rational emotive therapy, a recent elaboration of his theory, and his head-on approach to dealing with irrational thinking.

Jankowicz, A. D. (1987). Whatever became of George Kelly? Applications and implications. *American Psychologist, 42,* 481–487. This article examines the influence of Kelly's theory since Kelly's death 20 years earlier. The author traces the growing interest in personal construct theory among industrial-organizational psychologists and occupational counselors.

The Cognitive Approach
Relevant Research

16

If you think back to the first chapter, you may recall a discussion of the story about the blind men trying to describe an elephant. The point was that obtaining a complete understanding of human personality may require that we examine personality from several different perspectives. While each perspective offers useful information, each also provides only a limited view of this complex topic. This lesson is illustrated clearly in the research covered in this section. Each of the four topics presented here examines an area of research covered elsewhere in this book. Although the research covered earlier provides important insight into human behavior in each of these areas, we can add to our understanding by looking at each research question from a cognitive perspective.

First, we will revisit the topic of sex-type behavior and androgyny from Chapter 14. Psychologists from the behavioral/social learning approach often describe gender-related behaviors in terms of operant conditioning and observational learning. However, masculine and feminine people may also differ in terms of the way they process information along gender-related lines.

Next, questions about communication and how people cope with stress have surfaced in many places throughout this book. The cognitive perspective provides yet another way to look at these questions. In particular, some cognitive personality researchers examine stable differences in the number of constructs people typically use to make sense of the world. Among other applications, research on cognitive complexity provides insight into how people communicate and how they deal with stressful events.

Because depression is a major mental health problem today, we should not be surprised to find that psychologists from nearly every perspective have something to say about this disorder. According to the cognitive approach, people develop depression because they maintain depressing thoughts. We'll look at research on one aspect of this cognitive explanation, the use of depressive schemas.

Finally, we will return to the topic of learned helplessness. The original research, covered in the behavioral/social learning chapters, explained why laboratory animals sometimes act as if they are helpless and depressed. However, the original researchers in this area soon found they were unable to account for helplessness in human beings without also examining a person's cognitions.

Androgyny Revisited: Gender Schema Theory

Why do men and women tend to act differently? This is a question we have touched on in several places in this book. For example, you may recall from Chapter 12 that women use self-disclosure more than men do. Society's reaction to men who disclose too frequently keeps many men from sharing intimate feelings with others. In Chapter 8 we learned that whereas men and women once approached achievement situations differently, today's college women have caught up with their male counterparts in terms of achievement motivation. The most extensive analysis of gender-related behavior was an examination of individual differences in masculinity and femininity, covered in Chapter 14. Much of this research was stimulated by Sandra Bem's androgyny model. Bem argued that masculinity and femininity are independent dimensions and that the most well-adjusted people in today's society are those high on both of these. Bem called these people with both masculine and feminine personality attributes *androgynous*.

But putting a label on a style of behavior does not explain why the person acts that way (Locksley & Colten, 1979). A behavioral/social learning analysis of sex-role behavior suggests that people become masculine, feminine, androgynous, or undifferentiated through operant, classical, and observational learning. People act masculine because they have been reinforced for doing so or because they have learned through observation that masculine behavior will be reinforced. However, if we approach this question from a cognitive perspective, another explanation can be offered. It may be that masculine and feminine people act the way they do because they have different styles of processing information. Sandra Bem also has come to this conclusion and has introduced a cognitive analysis of sex-type differences called *gender schema* theory.

Gender Schema Theory

According to **gender schema** theory (Bem, 1979, 1981, 1985, 1987), people who are either highly masculine or highly feminine are *sex-typed*. Although there are many schemas with which to process information and make sense of the world, sex-typed people are more likely than most to perceive, evaluate, and organize information in terms of gender. For example, sex-typed people are more likely to notice if that new guy is masculine or if that blouse is feminine. On the other hand, androgynous and undifferentiated people do not have a strong schema for processing information along gender-related lines. They occasionally classify people or objects as masculine or feminine, but they do not consider this an important way to sort out information.

Because sex-typed people tend to see the world in masculine-feminine terms, we would expect them to behave differently than non-sex-typed people. Someone who is highly sensitive to gender-related information is going to attend to and recall that information more readily than someone who is less sensitive to this kind of information. Thus, a highly masculine male pays attention to subtle differences in how men and women act. It is important for him to act in

Researchers would probably identify this female mechanic as androgynous. According to Bem's gender schema theory, she does not process information about the world in terms of maleness and femaleness. For her, "mechanic" is not something that only men do.

gender-appropriate ways because he is more sensitive to the rewards and punishments associated with gender-related behavior. Whereas an androgynous man might see no reason why he can't enjoy ballet, a sex-typed man identifies ballet as something women, not men, enjoy.

Bem (1981) described gender schema as "a generalized readiness to process information on the basis of sex-linked associations." If sex-typed and non-sex-typed people differ in the strength of their gender schemas, then we would expect them to differ in their readiness to process information in terms of gender. This readiness to process gender information should show up in many places. For example, sex-typed people should recall gender-related information better. We also would expect them to more often describe people and behavior in terms of being masculine and feminine. They probably also are more likely to notice inconsistencies in stereotypic gender-related behavior, such as a woman physician or a male secretary. In short, there are many ways to test the predictions derived from gender schema theory. We'll look at some of those next.

Evidence for Gender Schema Theory   Bem (1981) reasoned that one way sex-typed and non-sex-typed people should differ is in the way they organize information in their minds. To test this hypothesis, she borrowed a technique developed by memory researchers called *clustering*. To get an idea of how clustering works, pause for 2 minutes to write down the names of as many kinds of birds as you can think of. If you are like most people, you probably began with a list of common birds, such as sparrows, robins, and blue jays. But soon you reached a blank. At this point, you might have expected the list to grow slowly one name at a time until time expired. But instead you probably found names of birds arriving in groups. Perhaps you remembered *chicken*. Then suddenly *duck*, *goose*, and *turkey*. You may have thought of *parrot*, then suddenly *parakeet*, *cockatiel*, and

The feminist prescription, then, is not that the individual be androgynous, but that society be gender aschematic.

SANDRA BEM

toucan. The reason these groups of birds appeared on your list together, or clustered, is that you organize and store this information together in your mind.

Returning to gender schema theory, we would expect that if sex-typed people organize and store information in terms of gender, then they should cluster this information on a free-recall task according to gender-related categories. To test this hypothesis, Bem (1981) presented subjects with a list of 61 words in random order. The words consisted of proper names (Henry, Debra), animal names (gorilla, butterfly), verbs (hurling, blushing), and articles of clothing (trousers, bikini). Some of the words within each category were masculine-oriented, and some were feminine-oriented. Subjects then were given eight minutes to write down as many words as they could remember in any order.

Bem divided the subjects into sex-typed (masculine males and feminine females), cross-sex-typed (feminine males and masculine females), androgynous, and undifferentiated categories. As shown in Figure 16.1, sex-typed subjects were considerably more likely to cluster the words on their list according to gender than were subjects in the other three groups. As explained by gender schema theory, when people with a strong gender schema recalled *gorilla*, they were likely to recall another masculine animal next, such as *eagle*, because they classified these words not just in terms of animals but also whether they are masculine or feminine animals. On the other hand, non-sex-typed subjects were just as likely to cluster *gorilla* with *butterfly* as they were with *eagle*, because whether the animal is associated with masculinity or femininity didn't figure into the way they classified and stored the information in memory.

A second way to demonstrate information-processing differences for sex-typed and non-sex-typed people is to look at the speed with which gender-related information is processed. If sex-typed people process information through a strong gender schema, then we would expect them to perceive and work with gender information more efficiently. To test this prediction, Bem (1981) administered the Bem Sex Role Inventory in a slightly different way. The 60 adjectives on the inventory were projected on a screen one at a time. Subjects responded by pressing a ME or NOT ME button, depending on how well the adjective described them. The time it took subjects to press the button was recorded for each word.

Bem reasoned that subjects with a strong gender schema would respond to the gender-related words on the inventory more quickly than other subjects. Consistent with this prediction, sex-typed subjects were quicker than others when deciding if a schema-consistent adjective described them, but slower when deciding about a schema-inconsistent adjective. That is, masculine men could decide right away if they were assertive or self-sufficient but had a more difficult time deciding if they were affectionate or compassionate. In gender schema terms, they had a readily available schema for processing the masculine words, but not the other words.

Evidence for gender schema theory comes from a number of other areas as well. For example, sex-typed women use feminine constructs more frequently than androgynous women when placing people into categories on Kelly's Rep Test (Tunnell, 1981). When sex-typed people want to know how they have done on a task, they prefer to compare their scores with those of members of their own

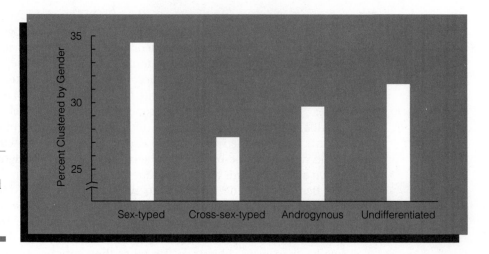

Figure 16.1

Mean Percentage of Clustered-Word Pairs

Taken from Bem (1981a).

sex, even when gender has nothing to do with the task (Miller, 1984). Sex-typed people also tend to cluster their responses to self-descriptive statements into masculine and feminine categories (Larsen & Seidman, 1986). This indicates that the masculine-feminine dimension is one of the first these people use when evaluating themselves. Sex-typed people are more likely than others to identify someone they have read about as being either a man or a woman, even when this information is not relevant to the task at hand (Frable, 1989). Finally, androgynous people are less likely to confuse members of the opposite sex with one another than are sex-typed people (Frable & Bem, 1985; Stangor, 1988). For sex-typed people, which gender category a person belongs to is the important piece of information, whereas non-sex-typed people identify and classify others along different lines.

In summary, we have evidence from a variety of sources indicating that sex-typed people differ from non-sex-typed people in the way they process information. Research reviewed in Chapter 14 already has demonstrated that these people also differ in their behavior. Unfortunately, subsequent research has begun to challenge some of the support and assumptions underlying gender schema theory. Two issues that still need resolving concern problems with replication and different interpretations of gender schema.

Continuing Issues

Although researchers sometimes replicate Bem's original work on gender schemas (Mills, 1983), several investigators have not (Ruble & Stangor, 1986). For example, two teams of researchers have been unable to replicate the clustering effect (Deaux, Kite, & Lewis, 1985; Edwards & Spence, 1987). Why the effect sometimes appears and yet other times does not is not clear. One difficulty facing researchers is that sex-typed people categorize information along dimensions besides gender. Instead of dividing animals into masculine and feminine categories, subjects may use mammal-bird or domestic-wild groupings that override or

How would you describe the way the two men in this picture are acting? A person with a strong gender schema might identify this behavior as typically "masculine." This is, sex-typed people might automatically process this action as something only men do. Such a characterization probably would not occur to a gender aschematic person.

hide their usually strong use of gender information. Whereas sex-typed people are more likely to process information along gender-related lines, there may be limited circumstances in which this tendency affects their behavior.

Another issue concerns the way researchers conceptualize gender schema. Bem describes both masculine men and feminine women as possessing a strong gender schema. However, other researchers have found it useful to think of sex-typed men as those with a masculine schema and sex-typed women as those with a feminine schema (Markus, Crane, Bernstein, & Siladi, 1982; Payne, Connor, & Colletti, 1987). In support of this interpretation, masculine subjects in one study recalled masculine words readily but not feminine words, whereas feminine subjects did the opposite (Markus et al., 1982). Yet a third interpretation is offered by psychologists who challenge the idea of grouping together all gender-related behaviors under global descriptions like "masculine" and "feminine" (Edwards & Spence, 1987; Spence, 1985). These researchers advocate looking instead at many different cognitive dimensions.

Unfortunately, at this point evidence exists for each of these interpretations. What *is* clear is that examining sex-type behavior and androgyny from a cognitive perspective has provided additional insight into these behaviors, even if researchers don't always agree on what that insight is.

Cognitive Complexity

Each of us knows someone who can communicate with anyone. The person that comes to mind for me seems to understand what I'm saying before anyone else does. Sometimes she even states my feelings for me better than I could have described them myself. I've noticed that she also expresses her ideas in a way that makes them easy to understand. Whether she's playing with children or speaking with an elderly person, the conversation goes smoothly. I've often thought she would make a good teacher. She probably could see the extent of a student's understanding right away and then adapt her presentation to that level.

What is it that makes one person so much better a communicator than others? There are no doubt many qualities that contribute to effective communication skills. However, one of the most important is suggested by Kelly's personal construct theory. Shortly after Kelly published his theory, researchers began to examine individual differences in cognitive complexity (Bieri, 1955). **Cognitive complexity** refers to how elaborate or simple a person's system of personal constructs is. One simple indicator of cognitive complexity is the number of constructs in a person's system (Crockett, 1965; O'Keefe & Sypher, 1981). Some people process nearly every person and every situation with a very limited number of constructs, whereas others have a large number of constructs at hand with which to make sense of new people they meet or new situations they encounter. Some investigators determine cognitive complexity by examining not only the number of constructs in a system but also how they are related to one another (Linville, 1987; Schroder, Driver, & Steufert, 1967). More complex systems contain highly interrelated constructs so that information gained from using one construct affects the use of other constructs.

To illustrate how cognitive complexity affects behavior, let's imagine how people high and low in cognitive complexity might evaluate new people they meet. A person with low cognitive complexity might look at each new acquaintance only as either a "fun person" or a "not-fun person." This makes sense when meeting people at a party, but not when meeting potential business associates. More cognitively complex people use a number of constructs, depending on the situation. They might process information about the person at the party in terms of how much fun he or she is but might use "professional–not professional" and "trustworthy–suspicious" constructs when meeting people on the job. In addition, after determining that the party acquaintance is a "fun" person, cognitively complex people might then use a series of additional constructs to obtain a greater understanding of this new person.

How does cognitive complexity relate to personality? As described in the previous chapter, Kelly explained personality differences in terms of the different sets of personal constructs we use to make sense of the world. You and I have different personalities because we use different constructs or use them a different

Cognitive Complexity in Politicians and World Leaders

Most of us have on occasion accused a political leader of being overly simple-minded or failing to see the complexities of an issue. In some cases, we may be correct. Psychologist Philip Tetlock and his colleagues have examined the cognitive complexity of politicians and public figures from around the world (Tetlock, 1983a). They begin by coding speeches and other public statements from these people for the degree of complex or simple thinking the statements reflect. The researchers find that cognitive complexity is related to the speaker's political ideology. For example, conservative United States senators make significantly fewer complex statements when describing the issues of the day than do moderate and liberal senators (Tetlock, 1983b). A similar pattern is found when examining members of the British House of Commons (Tetlock, 1984). Moderate socialists interpret issues in a more cognitively complex manner than do their moderate conservative colleagues. Extremists from either side tend to see things in the most simple manner.

Tetlock also demonstrated that the complexity and integration of public statements by American and Soviet leaders could predict the state of relations between the two nations throughout the four decades following World War II (Tetlock, 1985). For example, when statements by American presidents suggested a complex and well-integrated cognitive structure, the likelihood of cooperative relations with the Soviet Union increased. A similar pattern emerged when examining statements by Soviet leaders.

Although this pattern may reflect efforts to manipulate public opinion, it also indicates that the way superpower leaders view the world is related to their ability to deal with other nations. "Policy makers who think about . . . disputes in simple, black-white terms will tend to be especially suspicious of coordinative solutions to conflicts," Tetlock wrote, "and prone to resort to pressure tactics to coerce concessions from the other side" (1985, p. 1579). On the other hand, more cognitively complex leaders may be better able to see disputes from the other country's perspective and thereby seek out compromises that satisfy everyone's needs to some degree.

way. But another important difference that makes your personality different from mine is the complexity of the construct systems you and I typically use.

We can see how cognitive complexity influences behavior by observing young children. Kindergartners probably have a limited number of constructs at their disposal when making sense of their worlds. Another child is either "a friend" or "not a friend." A game is either "fun" or "not fun." Because the children do not have constructs that allow them to make finer distinctions than this, they cannot see the world in any other way. Consequently, all playmates who fall into the "friend" category are treated alike, as are all children who fall into the "not-friend" group.

However, as the child grows, so do the number of constructs in his or her system. One researcher found kindergarten children used an average of 4.4 constructs to describe a brother or a sister (Bigner, 1974). However, second-graders used 6.2 constructs, fourth-graders 8.1, and sixth-graders 9.8. Older children not only can see others as "friend–not friend," but also may use a "good friend–sometimes friend" or "friend for playing–friend for sharing" construct to further differentiate people. Naturally, because the older children see the world in a different way than do the younger children, they behave differently.

By the time we reach adulthood, we tend to construe the world with a fairly predictable number of personal constructs. As with other fairly stable individual differences, researchers have developed tests to determine the extent to which a person is cognitively complex or cognitively simple (see page 513). Two examples of how this individual difference relates to behavior will be examined here. First, a series of studies suggest that the complexity of your construct system affects the way you interact with others. Second, some research indicates that cognitive complexity may play an important role in how well you cope with stressful events.

Cognitive Complexity and Communication

Kelly's Sociality Corollary suggests that ideal communication takes place when one person understands how another person sees the world. If I know how you construe your world, then I'll have better luck explaining a new idea in a way that makes sense to you. However, if you and I are on different wavelengths, then you may not understand what I am saying, and I probably won't understand your reactions.

How does this notion apply to the concept of cognitive complexity? Understanding how another person construes the world requires that we have constructs in our system that allow us to see the world the way they do. Therefore, people with many constructs at their disposal are more likely to see the world the way I do than are people low in cognitive complexity. A person with a limited number of constructs simply doesn't have the tools to see the world the way many others do.

You can quickly obtain an idea of a person's cognitive complexity by asking that person to give directions with his or her back turned. For example, in one experiment one subject looked at a completed drawing of an unusually shaped model while another subject sat before the unassembled model pieces (Hale, 1980). The subject with the drawing had to explain to the other subject, through oral instructions only, how to put the model together. Cognitively complex subjects did a better job on this task than did those low in cognitive complexity. The cognitively complex subjects had within their construct systems the constructs needed to understand the task from the other person's perspective.

There are other reasons cognitively complex people make better communicators. Cognitively complex people are more sensitive to the perspective taken by other people (Clark & Delia, 1977; Hale & Delia, 1976). They hear about another

Cognitive Complexity

Although researchers have developed several ways to measure cognitive complexity, one of the easiest and most popular methods was introduced by Crockett (1965). To test yourself with this method, think of a person you like and a person you dislike. Next, take five minutes each to write a description of these two people. Pay particular attention to the person's "habits, beliefs, ways of treating others, mannerisms, and similar attributes." When you have finished both descriptions, count the number of different constructs you have used to describe each person. Any aspect of the person's personality or behavior counts ("She is introverted," "He talks too much"), but not physical characteristics. Add the number of constructs for the two descriptions together for your score.

Researchers typically obtain a large range of scores from college students with this procedure. For example, scores in one study ranged from 5 to 43, with an average of 16 (Hale, 1980). Although the measure is relatively quick and simple, many researchers find it the superior method for assessing cognitive complexity (O'Keefe & Sypher, 1981). Of course, number of constructs is only one part of cognitive complexity. For example, sometimes researchers look at the structure of the construct system or how well integrated or interrelated the constructs are. Nonetheless, it seems safe to conclude that people who approach the world with a small number of constructs see things differently than do those who have a large number of possible ways to interpret events at their disposal.

person's experiences and understand what that person is feeling. Further, because they have a construct system that meshes well with other construct systems, they are better able to process and recall what other people say to them. For example, cognitively complex subjects in one study remembered more of what was said in a videotaped conversation they watched than did low-complexity subjects (Neuliep & Hazleton, 1986). In a similar experiment, subjects scoring high in cognitive complexity understood a speaker's arguments better than did those scoring low (Beatty & Payne, 1984).

This ability to understand where someone else is coming from and explain things in terms this other person will understand is one of the most important qualifications of a good teacher. A cognitively complex person is better able to take the perspective of others, to see the world from their eyes. Similarly, good teachers understand the reasons students sometimes miss important points or why grasping certain concepts is difficult. Students have a better chance of understanding the point when teachers begin their explanation at the students' level. Little is learned when students and teachers are at different levels.

There are other advantages to cognitive complexity. For example, cognitively complex people are more persuasive than those low on this variable. Studies show that cognitively complex people change their arguments depending on who they are trying to persuade (Clark & Delia, 1977; Delia & Clark, 1977; O'Keefe & Delia, 1979). Cognitively complex children in one study used different arguments when talking to 6-year-old students than when trying to convince 12-year-olds (Clark & Delia, 1977). Thus, cognitively complex people are more likely to use arguments that make sense to their audiences. A cognitively complex salesperson understands that one pitch works on this customer whereas another works on that customer.

Cognitive Complexity and Coping with Stress

Parents often find it annoying yet amusing when their young children encounter a minor frustration. A 3-year-old boy upset over spilling his milk may decide that he also doesn't like anything on his plate, that his toys are all stupid, that his sister is mean, and that he never wants to go to preschool again. For children this age, life is either good or bad, things are going well or they are not. It will be a few years until the boy understands that parts of his life can still be going well even when other parts are not. Fortunately, at age three, one good event can set everything in the boy's world right again.

From a cognitive perspective, young children see the events in their lives in simple terms because they have only simple constructs with which to make sense of the world. Although adults rarely exhibit such a simple "good-bad" approach, their ability to weather the inevitable frustrations and setbacks in life may be related to the complexity of the construct system they use to make sense of these events.

Several features of cognitive complexity have implications for dealing with stress. For example, people high in cognitive complexity are better able to deal with ambiguity (Mayo & Crockett, 1964; Press, Crockett, & Delia, 1975). Because cognitively complex people are better able to make sense of events in their world, they are less likely to become anxious when confronted with unexpected or unstructured situations (Harris, 1981). Suppose an acquaintance with a simple construct system thinks of you as a "friendly" person. He expects, and finds, that you smile and act politely whenever you two interact. But, like all of us, one day you do not act friendly. Your friend is unable to make sense of your behavior. As Kelly explained, this inability to predict events results in anxiety. However, another person with a more complex construct system might be able to account for your behavior. She may have determined from earlier experiences that you are usually friendly but stress out before a big test. Your behavior is not inconsistent with her predictions, and she does not become anxious.

A recent elaboration of this research examines individual differences in *self-complexity* (Linville, 1985, 1987). As described in the previous chapter, one of the most important cognitive structures is the cognitive representation we have of ourself. Like construct systems, people have relatively stable self-concepts, which can be identified as either simple or complex. The two representations in Figures 16.2 and 16.3 illustrate this difference. Both people were asked first to list all of

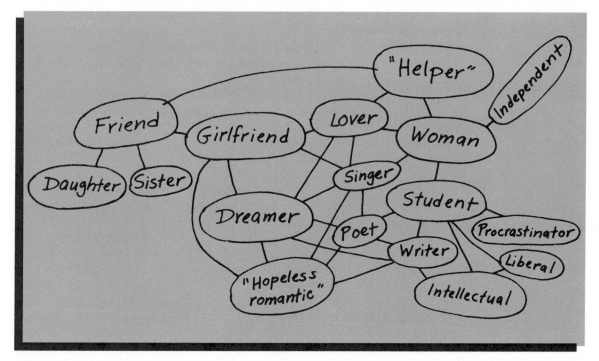

Figure 16.2

Self-Concept Drawing — Complex

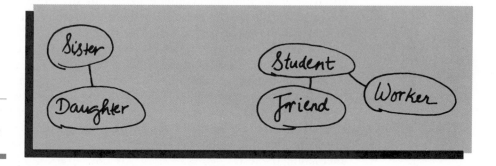

Figure 16.3

Self-Concept
Drawing — Simple

the different roles they perform in their lives. Next, they were asked to diagram how each of these roles were related. As you can see in the figure, one person has many different parts to her self-concept, and these tend to be highly related. However, the other person has relatively few parts to her self-concept, and these are not tied to many other parts.

How do these differences in self-complexity relate to coping behavior? We have all seen friends who seem to fall apart when one thing goes wrong, such as the man who is rejected by his girlfriend and decides his whole life is a mess. Like the three-year-old who reacts to one bad incident by concluding that all is wrong with the world, adults with simple self-constructs may be susceptible to large swings in their self-appraisal.

In contrast, imagine a woman who has several independent aspects to her self-concept. She sees herself as a wife, a mother, a friend, a career woman, an athlete, and a community volunteer. She also thinks of each of these parts of her life as fairly independent. What happens to this woman when she has a bad day at the office? Because her self-construct is fairly complex, she understands that trouble at the office does not mean she is a bad mother or a poor friend. She may begin to doubt her ability at work but recognizes her other good qualities and does not become depressed. Compare her to a woman with only three highly interrelated aspects to her self-concept — career woman, wife, and mother. Because each aspect makes up a large part of her overall self-concept, difficulty in any area has a greater impact on her. Further, because each aspect is tied to the others, doubts about her working ability may lead to doubts about her ability as a mother or a wife. Whereas the first woman can leave her work problems at the office, the second woman lets every problem in one part of her life affect how she feels about and functions in the other parts of her life.

Research on self-complexity supports this analysis. Low-complexity students in one study became more depressed when failing an aptitude test than did students with more complex self-concepts (Linville, 1985). In another study, subjects high in self-complexity were less likely to become depressed and experienced fewer health problems after experiencing stress than were low-complexity subjects (Linville, 1987). Because the high-complexity subjects kept their emotional reactions to one part of their lives from affecting other parts, their overall feelings about themselves were not as susceptible to changes because of one failure. Subjects in another study were placed in front of a mirror and asked to write about themselves after they had failed a simple anagram test (Dixon & Baumeister, 1991). Low-self-complexity subjects wrote fewer words and left the room more quickly than subjects high in self-complexity. The low-complexity subjects, prone to feeling bad about themselves generally after performing poorly in just one area, apparently were uncomfortable focusing attention on themselves after failing the test.

In summary, while each of us uses cognitive structures to make sense of the world, we differ in terms of the complexity of our cognitive systems. Like other personality differences, cognitive complexity is relatively stable and accounts for individual differences in behavior. Examples of these personality differences include the ability to communicate and how well one deals with stress. Research in this area demonstrates once again how knowing something about the way a person construes the world helps us predict stable patterns in that person's behavior.

Depression and Schemas

For a moment, try to think of a time when you felt depressed. One of the first things you may notice is that this is relatively easy if you already feel a little down today and relatively difficult if you feel pretty good. Depressed people not only remember sad experiences more easily but also may have difficulty keeping themselves from generating one depressing thought after another. Sad people easily recall times when they felt lonely and unloved. When I am down emotionally, I tend to think of my problems and worry about all the things that might go wrong. I remember embarrassing mishaps, things I wish I had never said, experiences I wish I could erase. Even when good things happen, depressed people look for the gray cloud to go with the silver lining. Just got accepted into a good school? Think of all that pressure and what happens if you fail. You've been invited to a party? What if you don't know anyone or you embarrass yourself there? In short, when you're depressed, your mind fills with depressing thoughts.

Depressive Schemas

These observations make it clear that depressing thoughts are tied to depressing feelings. This is why psychologists are increasingly turning to cognitive approaches to understand depression. Much of the cognitive explanation for depression has evolved from the pioneering work of Aaron Beck (1972). Although some psychologists maintain that negative thoughts are a symptom of depression, Beck argues that these thoughts *cause* people to become depressed. Specifically, he characterizes depressed people's thoughts within a **depressive cognitive triad**. Depressed people typically have negative thoughts about themselves, are pessimistic about the future, and tend to interpret ongoing experiences in a negative manner.

Beck identifies the cognitive structure that depressed people use to process information as a **depressive schema**. Not only do depressed people have thoughts that cause them to become depressed, but using this depressive schema causes them to generate even more depressing thoughts. This helps to explain why people who fall into depression often have a difficult time climbing back out.

How does a depressive schema work? Each of us faces information daily that is positive, negative, or ambiguous in terms of its emotional impact. According to a cognitive analysis, the happiest people are those who pay attention to the positive information, ignore the negative information, and interpret the ambiguous information as positively as possible. In fact, most of us have an unrealistically positive outlook on life (Taylor & Brown, 1988). Most people see themselves as better than most other people. We are unrealistically optimistic that good things will happen to us and that unfortunate events will happen to

Processing information through a depressive schema

someone else. Because most of us look at life through rose-colored glasses, we remain content and in good mental health (Alloy & Abramson, 1988).

Unfortunately, many people look at life through glasses that are tinted blue. According to depressive schema theory, depressed people process information through an active depressive schema (Kuiper & Derry, 1981; Kuiper, MacDonald, & Derry, 1983). Thus, they attend to negative information, ignore positive information, and interpret ambiguous information as depressing. Beyond this, because they use a depressive schema to process information, these people also more readily recall depressing memories and associate current experiences with past negative ones. In short, depressed people are set to process information in a way that keeps negative thoughts prominent and positive thoughts hidden or ignored. Little wonder then that these people remain depressed.

Evidence for Depressive Schemas

Researchers have developed a number of sometimes clever procedures to test various predictions from depressive schema theory. Along with clinical observations about how depressed people think and act, these experiments provide an impressive body of evidence pointing to the role of depressive schemas in the development and maintenance of depression (Ruehlman, West, & Pasahow, 1985).

Much of the evidence for depressive schemas comes from studies employing the self-schema research techniques described in the previous chapter. For example, researchers might ask depressed and nondepressed subjects to answer questions about a series of words. In one study, depressed patients responded to a list of adjectives by pressing a YES or a NO button to indicate if the word described them (Derry & Kuiper, 1981). Half of the words were related to depression (for example, *bleak*, *dismal*, *helpless*), and half were not. The researchers then surprised the subjects by giving them three minutes to recall as many of the words as they

Table 16.1

Proportion of Self-Descriptive Words Recalled with Self-Referent Processing

	Depressed Patients	Non-depressed Patients	Non-depressed Normals
Depression-associated words	.41	.18	.08
Nondepression-associated words	.16	.36	.43

Source: Taken from Derry and Kuiper (1981); reprinted by permission.
Note: The higher the number, the greater the recall.

could. The investigators reasoned that the depressed patients would recall more of the depression-associated words, because they processed this information through a depressive schema. The depressive schema should make them more likely to attend to these words, associate them with aspects of themselves, and recall them more readily later on. However, this should work only for the depression-related words. Words not associated with depression should be more difficult to recall, because they aren't processed so well with the depressive schema.

The results, shown in Table 16.1, support the predictions. The depressed patients remembered the depression-associated words better, whereas two groups of nondepressed subjects recalled the other words better. This finding has been replicated with clinically depressed patients (McDowall, 1984) and with college students after they were asked to think about some sad events in their lives (Brown & Taylor, 1986). In the latter study, the researchers apparently were able to activate the subjects' depressive schemas, thereby causing them to process information like the depressed patients.

Other research indicates that depressed people process information through a depressive schema, not just a general negative schema (Clark, Beck, & Brown, 1989; Ingram, Kendall, Smith, Donnell, & Ronan, 1987). For example, depressed subjects in one study recalled depression-related words better, but not words associated with anxiety, such as *panicked* and *nervous* (Ingram et al., 1987).

In an interesting twist to these findings, researchers find that mildly depressed people (as compared to clinically depressed people) appear to process either depressing or nondepressing information about themselves equally well (Kuiper & Derry, 1982; Kuiper & MacDonald, 1982). That is, they seem to process information through a positive schema as well as a depressive schema. Does this mean these people are balanced somewhere between depression and nondepression and all that is needed is some good news to trigger their positive schema and push them over to the nondepression side? Unfortunately, this does not appear to work (Ingram, Smith, & Brehm, 1983). It seems the ability of even mildly depressed people to interpret positive information in an ego-enhancing manner is limited by the tendency to interpret events through a depressive schema. The answer may be to change the person's thoughts directly through some of the cognitive therapy techniques described in the previous chapter.

Another set of predictions generated from depressive schema theory concerns how readily people recall experiences. Quickly think of something that happened to you in high school. Most people think of a pleasant time, perhaps hanging out with friends or a star performance in a play or an athletic event. But if you are depressed today, you may have thought of something negative, perhaps a test you failed or a time you were rejected by friends. According to the theory, people processing information through a depressive schema have greater access to the depressing memories stored there. When you are depressed, it should not take long to recall times when you were sad, lonely, ashamed, and embarrassed, because the use of a depressive schema makes these memories so accessible.

Consistent with this logic, researchers find depressed patients take less time to recall unpleasant memories than pleasant ones (Lloyd & Lishman, 1975). The opposite is found for nondepressed people. Similarly, depressed patients have difficulty remembering positive themes in stories (Breslow, Kocsis, & Belkin, 1981) but do recall negative feedback about their performances well (DeMonbreun & Craighead, 1977). Finally, depressed people have a difficult time *not* thinking about negative thoughts, even when given specific instructions to repress these cognitions (Wenzlaff, Wegner, & Roper, 1988).

This accessibility to depressing memories was demonstrated in an experiment with depressed patients (Clark & Teasdale, 1982). The patients were given a series of words (such as *train, ice, wood*) and asked to recall a real-life experience the word brought to mind. For example, a patient might describe a train ride to visit her aunt or a time she missed a train. The patients were tested twice, once when they were feeling particularly depressed and once when they were less depressed. Presumably the depressive schemas were activated more when the patients' depression levels were higher. As shown in Table 16.2, patients recalled more unhappy experiences when they were very depressed, but more happy ones when they were less depressed. As predicted from depressive schema theory, the highly activated depressive schemas appeared to make unpleasant memories more readily accessible.

Yet another prediction from the theory is that depressed people will interpret mixed or ambiguous information in the most negative light possible. This is because depressive schemas lead them to attend to and recall negative information while not processing positive information. Consequently, when depressed people are given feedback containing both positive and negative evaluations, they tend to dwell on what they did wrong while failing to give themselves enough credit for what they did right (Gotlib, 1983).

Because they focus on the negative, depressed people are less likely to benefit from positive reinforcement (Buchwald, 1977; Gotlib, 1981). Thus, if an instructor tells a depressed student he did well on five essay answers but was a little weak on one, the student will focus his attention on the one weak answer and may

Table 16.2

Type of Experience Recalled as a Function of Mood

	More Depressed Occasion	Less Depressed Occasion
Percentage happy experiences	37.7	51.1
Percentage unhappy experiences	52.3	36.7

Source: Adapted from Clark and Teasdale (1982); reprinted by permission.

conclude that his performance was poor. Focusing on the negative makes overcoming depression very difficult. We often say to depressed friends, "Look at all of your accomplishments" or "Look at all the people who like you," but this is unlikely to change their evaluations of themselves. Because depressed people are pessimistic about the future (Alloy & Ahrens, 1987; Pyszczynski, Holt, & Greenberg, 1987), they usually find the sad times they expect.

Taken together, the research findings paint a fairly consistent picture in support of the depressive schema notion. Because they process information through depressive schemas, depressed people recall depressing information and depressing memories more readily and interpret information in as negative a light as possible. All of these findings are consistent with depressive schema theory and indicate the importance of considering cognitions when battling depression.

Learned Helplessness Revisited: Attributional Model and Explanatory Style

Let's return now to the topic of learned helplessness, discussed in Chapter 14. As you recall, classical conditioning researchers first demonstrated this effect in dogs who failed to escape from electric shock after first experiencing inescapable shock. The dogs learned they were helpless in one situation and inappropriately generalized that perception to the new situation. Not long after this experiment, researchers found that people also were susceptible to the same generalizing of helpless feelings to controllable situations. Learned helplessness became a leading model for understanding depression.

However, it soon became apparent that the simple learned helplessness model used to explain animal behavior was insufficient for understanding learned helplessness in people. Human subjects reacted to some uncontrollable situations with helplessness, but not others. Feelings of helplessness generalized to some tasks, but not every task. People exposed to inescapable noise sometimes become *more* motivated than before, not less (Costello, 1978; Depue & Monroe, 1978; Roth, 1980; Wortman & Brehm, 1975).

The problems with the original model were the same ones that have led psychologists to the cognitive approach in other areas. Although basic conditioning principles can account for many behaviors and do a good job explaining the behavior of lab animals, humans are too complex to be understood in terms of simple conditioning. When you experience an uncontrollable event, most likely you begin to analyze the situation and form new expectancies for your behavior. Why can't you control this situation? Can you control similar situations? Is the situation unique, or does this lack of control say something about your abilities? In short, psychologists needed to examine cognitive variables if they were to understand learned helplessness in humans.

The Attributional Model of Learned Helplessness

In response to this need, psychologists developed the **attributional model of learned helplessness** (Abramson, Seligman, & Teasdale, 1978; Miller & Norman, 1979). According to the new model, learned helplessness in humans begins with a perception of uncontrollability. For example, a man may find he can't control the outcome of his application for a job he really wants. This is followed by asking ourselves *why* we can't control the situation. The man who failed to get the job he wanted ponders the reasons his efforts were unsuccessful. Is it because the employer did not like him? Does he lack experience or skills?

The explanations people give for their lack of control, referred to as *attributions*, then determine whether learned helplessness develops. If the man decides the employer is a jerk and that he really does possess what it takes to get a good job, he probably will continue his job quest elsewhere with no ill effects. However, if he concludes that he lacks the skills to ever advance up the job ladder, then feelings of helplessness and depression may develop.

Which attributions lead to helplessness and which do not? According to the model, we can examine these attributions along three dimensions (see Table 16.3). First, we can classify the attribution as either *internal* or *external*. You can attribute your lack of control to something personal, such as poor skills or low motivation, or to an external cause, such as an unfair test. The more internal the attribution, the more likely you will experience learned helplessness. Second, attributions can be either *stable* or *unstable*. Attributions to relatively stable causes, such as intelligence, should lead to more depression than attributions to unstable causes, such as lack of effort. Finally, attributions can be classified as either *global* or *specific*. Global attributions apply to many different situations, whereas specific attributions apply to very few. Global attributions are more likely to lead to helplessness. For example, if you attribute the loss of a job to a general lack of skills and aptitude that will keep you from getting a good job anywhere else, you may be headed for depression. However, if you fail an algebra class and conclude it's because this particular instructor used a strange and unfair grading system, it is unlikely you'll generalize feelings of helplessness to other math classes or other subjects.

Table 16.3

Examples of Attributions by a Failing Student

	Internal		External	
	Stable	**Unstable**	**Stable**	**Unstable**
Global	Lack of intelligence	Exhaustion	ETS gives unfair tests.	Today is Friday the 13th.
	Laziness	I have a cold, which makes me stupid.	People are usually unlucky on the GRE.	ETS gave experimental tests this time which were too hard for everyone.
Specific	Lack of mathematical ability	I'm fed up with math problems.	ETS gives unfair math tests.	The math test was from No. 13.
	Math always bores me.	I have a cold, which ruins my arithmetic.	People are usually unlucky on math tests.	Everyone's copy of the math test was blurred.

Source: Taken from Abramson, Seligman, and Teasdale (1978); reprinted by permission of Lyn Y. Abramson.

In short, learned helplessness begins with the perception that we can't control something important. The more we explain this lack of control in terms of internal, stable, and global attributions, the more likely we are to feel helpless and depressed.

Explanatory Style

You probably have used each of the different types of attributions listed in Table 16.3 on occasion. There are times when I can't do something and I know it's my fault. Other times I am certain my failure is due to some bad luck or maybe some temporary problem I can work out. But shortly after the publication of the attributional model of learned helplessness, researchers recognized that some people were fairly consistent in the kinds of attributions they made. For example, you may know people who always seem to blame themselves when things go wrong. Although it seems unlikely to you that they could have done anything to change the outcome, they take responsibility and apologize for letting it happen. Others seem intent on generalizing their attributions to new situations ("If I can't do this, I can't do anything"). If it rains at a picnic, one person may apologize for picking the wrong date, whereas others conclude that it always rains when they plan an outdoor activity.

What these examples illustrate is what learned helplessness researchers call *attributional style*, or more recently, **explanatory style**. That is, we can identify relatively stable tendencies to make certain kinds of attributions. Consistent with the attributional model, we can identify people who tend to make internal or external, stable or unstable, and global or specific attributions for the events in their lives (Peterson et al., 1982; Peterson & Villanova, 1988). As with other individual differences, this does not mean people with an internal attributional style always claim responsibility for what happens. But they have a tendency to do this more than most people and more than they tend to make external attributions.

As with other personality variables, explanatory style tends to be stable over time. One study found a particularly impressive amount of stability in explanatory style for negative life events (Burns & Seligman, 1989). Researchers compared the attributions elderly subjects used to explain why bad things happened to them with the attributions they made for similar events in letters and diaries from their youth. The investigators found a correlation of .54 between the kinds of attributions the elderly subjects made and the attributions they had used an average of 52 years earlier.

Because expectations affect many behaviors, explanatory style may play a role in a large number of psychological phenomena. For example, some research suggests explanatory style may be related to our health (Peterson & Seligman, 1987). In one investigation, researchers determined explanatory style by looking at personal statements written by college graduates more than 35 years earlier (Peterson, Seligman, & Vaillant, 1988). The explanatory styles of the 25-year-olds were significantly related to their health at ages 45 through 60. Those who explained unpleasant events in terms of internal, stable, and global causes were the least healthy. These people may suffer the most from unfortunate events and may make little effort to keep themselves from becoming ill or recovering once illness strikes.

Most of the research on explanatory style has been used to explain why some people are more prone to depression than others. According to the reformulated model, people who tend to make internal, stable, and global attributions are more likely to become depressed. None of us is immune from failures and other problems in life. But if we interpret such events as temporary setbacks, limited to a unique set of circumstances that we can overcome, we're not likely to develop feelings of helplessness. On the other hand, if we habitually see downturns as insurmountable, permanent, and indicative of how things are in other areas of our lives, then we may be highly vulnerable to an episode of depression.

An example of the role attributional style plays in depression is found in a study looking at students' reactions to their midterm grades (Metalsky, Halberstadt, & Abramson, 1987). The researchers measured individual differences in explanatory style at the beginning of the term for students in several introductory psychology courses. They also measured depressed mood before, immediately after, and two days after the students received their midterm exam grades. Students who had not done as well on the test as they wanted showed an increase in depressed mood immediately after receiving the grade, regardless of explanatory style. But two days later students with an unstable and specific explanatory style had recovered from their down mood. However, students with a stable and global explanatory style were still depressed. The students who shook off the bad grade recognized it as just one test in one class. The ones who remained upset saw the low grade as an indicator of how they might do on later tests and in other classes. Little wonder they remained depressed.

By now numerous studies have examined the relationship between attributions, explanatory style, and depression. Unfortunately, not all of these studies find the same results, and not all are in agreement with the attributional model (cf. Brewin, 1985; Peterson & Seligman, 1984; Peterson, Villanova, & Raps, 1985; Robins, 1988; Sweeney, Anderson, & Bailey, 1986).

Looking at reviews of all this research suggests that stable and global attributions, as well as a stable or global explanatory style, are related to increased depression. These conclusions are consistent with the attributional model. However, the evidence for a link between depression and internal attributions, or an internal explanatory style, is considerably weaker (Peterson, Villanova, & Raps, 1985; Robins, 1988).

Why don't internal-external attributions predict depression very well? Let's return to the bad grade example. You might explain a poor test performance either in terms of your low ability or because you didn't study enough. Both are internal attributions, but one is stable (low ability) and the other unstable (not studying). You might be mad at yourself for not spending enough time behind the books, but as long as you know you could have done better and should do better on the next test, making an internal-unstable attribution probably won't lead to helplessness. However, concluding that you lack ability, something with implications for the next test and maybe other classes, leads to a different reaction. Thus, just knowing someone made an internal attribution doesn't tell us much about how that person will react. Knowing whether the attribution is to a stable or an unstable cause is more important.

In addition, the internal-external concept has some theoretical problems. According to the attributional model, learned helplessness begins when people perceive they lack control. Yet if the cause of an event is internal, people often believe they have control over it. Thus, in many instances the model may be trying to explain a situation in which people perceive control over an event they perceive as uncontrollable.

Hopelessness and Depression

Recently, research on attributions and learned helplessness has spawned yet another approach to understanding depression (Abramson, Metalsky, & Alloy, 1988, 1989; Dykman & Abramson, 1990). Some psychologists have identified a specific kind of depression, called *hopelessness depression*, brought about by a specific pattern of attributions. As the name suggests, hopelessness depression is said to result from feelings that we are unable to do anything about something bad that has happened to us.

Unlike learned helplessness, which begins with a perception of no control, hopelessness depression is said to start when we experience negative life events.

That is, regardless of how much control you had over the situation, you can become depressed when you lose your job, get turned down from law school, or divorce your partner after many years of marriage. But we do not always become depressed when something bad happens to us. Rather, according to the theory, depression is most likely when the loss is something very important to us and when we attribute the reasons for the negative event to stable and global causes. The proponents of the hopelessness theory of depression also point out that some people are more prone to making stable and global attributions than others. Consistent with the research on explanatory style, these people are said to be more susceptible to depression.

In summary, simply experiencing an uncontrollable aversive event is not enough to bring about learned helplessness and depression. Instead, the reasons people give for this lack of control appear to be the key. Current evidence indicates that stable and global attributions are related to helplessness and that people who have a style of making these attributions are the most vulnerable to episodes of depression. Similar thinking has been expressed in recent theorizing about hopelessness depression. However, it is too early to tell how well research will support this theory.

Summary

1. The four examples of research presented in this chapter illustrate the increased understanding of human personality gained from examining the way people process information. Each deals with topics covered elsewhere in the book by researchers from other approaches. Examining the cognitions associated with these behaviors has added to our understanding in each of these areas. In the case of work on gender-related behavior and learned helplessness, the trek into cognitive explanations has been led by the same researchers who once explored these topics under different approaches.

2. Sandra Bem expanded her earlier research on androgyny and sex-type with gender schema theory. Sex-typed people, those high in only masculinity or femininity, are said to process information through a strong gender schema. They are more likely to perceive and process information according to gender iden-tity. In support of this theory, Bem has demonstrated that sex-typed people cluster free-recall information along gender lines. In addition, sex-typed people process masculine and feminine information more quickly. However, some re-searchers have been unsuccessful in their efforts to replicate some of these findings. In addition, different interpretations for gender schema effects have been advanced.

3. Research on cognitive complexity is concerned with how many constructs people use to make sense of the world and the relationship between constructs. People high in cognitive complexity are better communicators than are those low on this variable. They are better able to understand how other people see the world. Consequently, they also are better able to adjust their arguments to their audience and thus are probably more persuasive. Cognitively complex people also are better able to deal with stress. Because they can better accommodate ambiguity within their cognitive structures, they probably experience less anxiety than do those low in cognitive complexity. In addition, people with complex self-concepts are less likely to react in a negative manner to setbacks in one part of their lives.

4. The cognitive approach to understanding depression assumes that depressing thoughts cause depression. Depressive schema theory maintains that depressed people process information through a depressive cognitive structure. Evidence in support of this theory finds that depressed people recall depressing information and remember depressing events more readily than do nondepressed people. In addition, depressed people tend to interpret ambiguous information in a negative light. Because they attend to and recall depressing information, and because they interpret events in the most negative way possible, depressed people have difficulty breaking out of their disorder.

5. Although the original learned helplessness model explained the behavior of laboratory animals, it could not always account for findings in research with humans. An attributional model was proposed to deal with these problems. According to the model, the more people make internal, stable, and global attributions for uncontrollable aversive events, the more likely they are to suffer from depression. Researchers soon discovered stable individual differences in the way people make attributions for events. Explanatory style has been related to depression and health. Summaries of research findings suggest that whereas stable and global attributions are related to depression, the link with internal attributions is less certain. Finally, recently researchers have identified a type of depression related to feelings of hopelessness stemming from a specific pattern of attributions.

Key Terms

gender schema A cognitive structure used to process information in terms of gender-relatedness.

cognitive complexity The extent to which a person's personal construct system is elaborate or simple; usually refers to the number of personal constructs.

depressive cognitive triad In Beck's theory, the three elements that describe a depressed person's cognitions: negative views of the self, pessimism, and interpreting events in a negative manner.

depressive schema A cognitive structure that allows people to readily make negative associations.

attributional model of learned helplessness A model for understanding depression that examines the reasons people give for their perceived lack of control.

explanatory style Relatively stable tendency to make certain kinds of attributions for events, particularly those related to depression.

Suggested Readings

Abramson, L. Y., Metalsky, G. I., & Alloy, L. B. (1989). Hopelessness depression: A theory-based subtype of depression. *Psychological Review, 96,* 358–372. A detailed presentation of the latest twist in learned helplessness theory and research. The authors outline their theory of hopelessness depression and contrast the new theory with the earlier attributional model of learned helplessness.

Bem, S. L. (1985). Androgyny and gender schema theory: A conceptual and empirical integration. In T. B. Sonderegger (Ed.), *1984 Nebraska Symposium on Motivation: Psychology and gender* (pp. 179–226). Lincoln: University of Nebraska Press. Sandra Bem reviews her theory of gender schema and the research that supports it. She also compares her new gender schema model with her earlier position on androgyny, as well as commenting on some alternative viewpoints.

Kuiper, N. A., & Higgins, E. T. (Eds.) (1985). Special issue on depression. *Social Cognition, 3*(1). This collection of empirical and review papers illustrates several ways researchers are using concepts from cognitive psychology to understand depression. Topics include attributional style, self-complexity, and depressive schema research.

Conclusions and Future Directions

Not long ago, as I was searching through the stations on my car radio, I chanced upon an interview with a man who was introduced as an expert on pets. After the guest explained that pets have existed in nearly all societies throughout recorded history, the interviewer asked the obvious question: Why do people keep pets? As the expert rattled off his favorite theories and several listeners called in with their own, I found myself sliding into a type of game quite popular among personality psychologists.

Why do people keep pets? The first explanation that came to mind sounded humanistic. People have an inherent need to express and receive love and affection, I thought. Although a warm puppy can never completely satisfy this need, sometimes the affection we receive from our pets goes a long way toward making us feel loved and lovable. I suspect Abraham Maslow would have said something like that. At that point the expert on the radio said something about pets touching a hidden inner part of our psyches (his word). Of course, I thought. Perhaps pets exist in some sort of Jungian archetype tucked away in our collective unconscious. This would explain why people have kept pets in all cultures throughout history.

At that point I was hooked. The theories came fast and furiously. Maybe there is something symbolic about pets—mother's love, father's affection—that we crave. I'm sure Freud would have said so. Could attraction to pets be learned? Most of the adult pet owners I know had pets as children. Their parents and older siblings probably modeled pet-loving behaviors. And certainly few things are more rewarding than cuddling a warm and furry dog or cat. Of course, I never did come to a single satisfying answer. But the point is that I enjoyed the process.

Personality Theories as Tools

As we noted in the first chapter, each of us constantly speculates about the causes of human behavior. Coming up with explanations for why people act the way they do requires no special training, as demonstrated by the numerous theories of pet ownership I heard offered by the radio audience. Of course, the issues that concern most personality psychologists are more important than why people keep pets. But now that you have an understanding of the major approaches Western thinkers have taken to answering these kinds of questions, you probably can appreciate the value of examining this and other questions through the different lenses each of the personality theories provides. For example, each of us has explanations for why we are romantically attracted to some people but not to others. But before reading about Carl Jung's theory, it's unlikely that one of your explanations was that an image of your loved one resides in your anima or animus. However, the next time you ponder your feelings for that special person, the possibility that your collective unconscious is tugging at your heart might cross your mind.

Although at times the process can be fun and even addicting, trying to explain human behavior through the various approaches to personality is more than a game. In essence, this process is part of what psychotherapists do when working with clients. For example, suppose you are a therapist and a client comes to you for help with her stage fright. How you choose to treat this problem will depend largely on your explanation for why it developed in the first place. Is her anxiety a symptom of some underlying conflict? Perhaps the stage or the audience symbolically represents significant people or events in her past. If this is your explanation, you probably would try a psychoanalytic approach to treatment.

But you might also conclude that the client's stage fright is the result of past learning. Perhaps the fear had been classically conditioned from some negative experiences in front of an audience as a child and reinforced whenever the client declined an offer to get up on a stage. In this case, perhaps simple relaxation and desensitization therapy would be appropriate. Is the problem a lack of self-efficacy? Or perhaps the kind of internal dialogue she uses in these situations? Maybe the problem is a lack of self-esteem, resulting from an inability to define her real self as someone who occasionally fails. These explanations suggest other kinds of treatment.

The conclusion you should draw from this discussion is that psychologists rarely find one agreed-upon answer to the question of why people act the way they do. This lesson sometimes frustrates students who expect to find the "correct" theory of personality after taking an entire course on the subject. But the purpose of this book was not to provide you with *the* theory. Rather, it was designed to give you the tools with which to derive your own answers about human personality and behavior.

Of course, this does not mean you should have found each of the theories equally credible and useful. I have never met a personality psychologist who did not favor one or more of the approaches over the others. However, I also know very few psychologists who do not find at least some value in more than one approach. Remember the story of the blind men and the elephant with which we began the book. The point of the story was that while any one of the perspectives provided relevant information for describing an elephant, no one perspective gave the complete picture. Similarly, although most personality psychologists identify themselves with one of the major approaches, most also acknowledge their openness to other perspectives. In fact, I commonly find psychotherapists

Much of our lives is spent in trying to understand others and in wishing others understood us better than they do.

GORDON ALLPORT

identify themselves as "eclectic," meaning they have constructed their personal understanding of human behavior from several different schools of psychology. Thus, the question for students of personality is not "Which theory is correct?" but rather "How can each of these perspectives help me to better understand human behavior?"

Where Do We Go from Here? Future Directions in Personality Psychology

In one way the presentation of the various approaches to personality in this book reads like a historical account of the field. We began with Freud and his ground-breaking work, followed by the neo-Freudian offshoots, on through to the recent emphasis on cognitive elements. Although tempting, I won't try to predict where each field of personality will be in 10 or 20 years. Instead, I'll limit myself to identifying the directions in which each of the approaches to personality appears to be heading. Like a stockbroker who follows the ups and downs of various companies, I feel fairly confident making observations about recent trends. But as every stockbroker knows, trends change, sometimes dramatically and inexplicably. For example, during the optimism and revolutionary spirit of the 1960s numerous observers of psychology declared behaviorism dead and humanistic psychology the new king. Today those predictions seem as outdated as the love beads and hippies that also characterized those years. So, what follows is a series of educated guesses. I hope most personality psychologists would agree, but I am sure not all of them do.

The Psychoanalytic Approach

Fifty years ago, at the end of Freud's career, psychoanalysis (and the many neo-Freudian versions of it) dominated the field of psychotherapy. Since that time, and perhaps even before, the psychoanalytic approach has been the giant in the field that all newcomers feel a need to take aim at. While many of the newer approaches to personality and psychotherapy have made their inroads, declarations of the death of psychoanalysis have proved to be highly exaggerated. A large number of therapists still identify themselves as psychoanalytic, and many others accept and utilize parts of the approach. The Rorschach inkblot test and other projective measures remain immensely popular. And it is difficult to imagine a personality textbook that would not include a large section on Freud, if for no other reason than the historical foundation he laid for subsequent approaches.

If any trend in the psychoanalytic approach is apparent in the past few decades, it may be the slow decline in popularity of some of the neo-Freudian theories. At one point, studying personality meant comparing and contrasting the theories of Freud, Jung, Adler, Horney, and so on, perhaps with some attention to Allport, Murray, and a few others outside of the psychodynamic realm. Today, with the increasing acceptance of other approaches, the relative importance of the neo-Freudians appears to have declined. This is not to say that these theorists lack adherents and enthusiastic advocates. On the contrary, each of the neo-Freudian theorists covered in this book continues to have a strong following. In addition, many current personality psychologists have been influenced by these theories. But relative to other approaches, the neo-Freudians' place in the larger scheme of personality theories appears to be waning.

The Trait Approach

A quick glance through any recent personality journal will confirm that the trait approach to personality is alive and well. The number of traits identified by researchers and tests developed to measure them continues to grow at a rapid rate. However, this sign of vitality brings with it reasons for concern. As one observer noted, "Although broad traits looked promising as dimensions of personality, the number of proposed traits increased unmanageably over the years" (Fiske, 1988, p. 816). The result is a list of relatively independent collections of studies on a wide variety of personality dimensions.

This concern, and a few other recent reactions by psychologists working in the trait area, suggests the emergence of several trends in the next few years. First, in response to some of the issues raised in the trait debate (Chapter 7), I expect to see a greater emphasis on improving trait measurement. Too many scales with questionable reliability and validity have been used to predict poorly measured behaviors in the past. Second, the trait debate also may have spawned an increased interest in identifying the people for whom a trait is relevant. As discussed in Chapter 7, there is a growing awareness that traits do not apply to all people equally well. Instead of trying to predict the behavior of all people with one trait, several personality psychologists are now asking which traits are useful for predicting the behavior of which people.

A third trend already well underway is the examination of how various traits are related. The search for the "Big Five" personality factors (Chapter 7) illustrates this approach. The goal is not only to understand the underlying structure of the dimensions of personality but also to organize and perhaps synthesize the huge number of trait concepts that have proliferated in recent years. Fourth, in an effort to increase the predictability of trait measures, many psychologists appear to be narrowing the range of focus of the traits they study. Unlike the psychologists searching for broader personality dimensions at the expense of predictive power, these personality researchers seek to increase their ability to predict behaviors by focusing on more specific trait domains. For example, researchers have found they can better predict the effects of locus of control on marriage by using a test designed specifically to measure perceptions of control within a marriage relationship, rather than using a more general locus of control scale.

Each of these predicted, albeit sometimes opposing, trends represents an effort to improve the trait approach, not replace it. Despite the challenges to traits that dominated much of the dialogue about personality a decade ago, I expect that examining traits will remain a central activity among personality researchers in the future.

The Biological Approach

The ballooning interest in biological influences on personality that the field witnessed in the past decade or so shows no signs of abating. There no longer appears any debate about whether part of our personality is determined by genetics. Rather, as described in the next section, the questions now seem to be how and how much. Moreover, interest in such topics as temperament and evolutionary personality theory appear to be growing all the time.

One reason for the growing interest in biological approaches to personality is that many of the hypotheses put forth by advocates of this approach have been supported in empirical investigations. Much of this success can be tied to advances in technology that have enabled researchers to conduct necessary experiments. For example, recent technological advances allow researchers to identify specific genes linked to certain traits and disorders. It is not difficult to speculate that future technological developments will result in even more opportunities for these researchers.

It is possible that some of the lines of research spawned by the current interest in biological influences will prove to be short-lived and faddish. However, it is difficult to imagine that personality psychologists will ever return to anything approaching the "blank slate" conception of the newborn advocated by Watson and others many years ago. For the foreseeable future, I suspect personality psychology will recognize that our behavior inevitably is connected to our biological makeup.

The Humanistic Approach

Twenty to 30 years ago, proponents declared the humanistic approach psychology's "third force" that would rival and eventually replace the behavioral and psychoanalytic models of human nature. I recall browsing through the psychology section at a bookstore during this time and noticing how many authors identified their approach as "humanistic," apparently cashing in on the trend. When I checked out the psychology section at another bookstore recently, I couldn't find the word *humanistic* in even one title.

Although the humanistic approach never overthrew the more established approaches to personality, the once upstart perspective now seems to have established its own niche among psychotherapists and personality psychologists. Many psychotherapists identify their therapy style as humanistic, and many others borrow from the procedures outlined by Carl Rogers and other humanistic writers. In addition, I commonly find the works of Carl Rogers and Abraham Maslow being taught in communication, sociology, religious studies, management, philosophy, and education classes. While perhaps not as popular as it once was, the humanistic perspective seems to be firmly planted these days as one of the major approaches to understanding human behavior, and it likely will remain a refreshing and thought-provoking alternative to some of the other approaches to personality.

The Behavioral/Social Learning Approach

Since John B. Watson defiantly established his extreme behavioral view more than 70 years ago, behaviorism has been in a slow but steady state of transformation. While retaining their skepticism for less empirical approaches, behaviorists and learning theorists increasingly acknowledge the importance of concepts that might have made Watson's blood boil had he remained in the field of psychology. Around the 1950s, many prominent behaviorists began drifting to social learning and cognitive positions (Dollard & Miller, 1950). By the 1970s, the social learning theories of Arthur Staats, Albert Bandura, and Julian Rotter were widely accepted among behaviorists.

Today social learning theory seems to be blending into the cognitive approaches to personality so that the line between the two is difficult to distinguish at times. In his most recent book, Bandura identified his position as "a social cognitive theory" (Bandura, 1986). This statement seems to reflect a growing acknowledgment that traditional learning theories, social learning theories, and cognitive approaches all have something to say about personality and that limiting one's focus to any one element means limiting one's ability to understand human behavior.

The Cognitive Approach

The current popularity of the cognitive approach to understanding personality reflects a larger trend in psychology. Students come across this same theme in developmental psychology, social psychology, and abnormal psychology classes. But why the sudden "discovery" of cognition? Cognitive models for understanding behavior have been around for many decades now. Indeed, George Kelly outlined his cognitive approach to personality almost 40 years ago. This trend may simply indicate a dissatisfaction with other approaches. It may also reflect the growing sophistication many researchers have brought to investigations of cognitive processes and the provocative results this research has yielded. During the past decade or so, "cognitive psychology" has been a growing subfield within the discipline of psychology. Much of what researchers in this area have discovered about the way people process information has implications for personality. For example, research on prototypes as personality constructs stems directly from earlier work by basic cognitive psychologists.

However, I find it difficult to guess where the cognitive approach will fit in the larger scheme of personality theories 10 or 20 years from now. Because the track record is short, the current interest in cognition may be but a short-lived fascination. We also may see cognitive models of personality subsumed by social learning theories in the next few years. Then again, cognitive explanations of personality may prosper and become dominant. My guess is that any rise or fall in the popularity of the cognitive approach to personality probably will reflect the way cognition is treated in psychology generally.

Coming Together:
Signs of Growing Consensus

The theme of this chapter thus far is that no one approach to understanding personality provides a complete picture of the beast. Yet this does not mean the field is not progressing. Spurred on by research findings and persuasive advocates, several general ideas about the nature of human personality seem to be experiencing a growing acceptance among theorists of nearly all perspectives. Although again speculating about recent trends, I feel confident in identifying three areas of growing consensus. I see a growing agreement about the role of genetic influences on personality, the interaction of person and situation variables in determining personality, and the importance of thoughts outside of general awareness.

Genetic Influences

Personality theories have come a long way since John B. Watson declared he could turn any infant into whatever adult he wanted, if only given total control over the environment in which the child was raised (Chapter 13). Fifty or 60 years ago, behaviorists often promoted the idea that environmental influences could overcome whatever genetic differences people were dealt at birth. But today researchers have made a persuasive case that genetic influences cannot be easily ignored by personality theorists (Chapter 10). The nature and extent of that influence remains a source of debate, but few psychologists today deny that at least part of adult personality is influenced by genetic predispositions. Even traditional learning theorists acknowledge some of the limits genetically wired into various species of what can be classically and operantly conditioned.

But despite the growing evidence of genetic influences on personality, there remains some resistance to this view. One reason for this reluctance may be the fear some psychologists have that people will place too much emphasis on genetic influences, particularly when dealing with some important social issues. For example, if aggression is a learned behavior, as many social learning theorists maintain, then we should be able to reduce aggression through programs that alter aggression-producing environments. But support for such programs would be undercut if popular wisdom holds that some aggressive people are simply born to be aggressive.

The world we live in is largely man-made . . . but it is not well-made.

B. F. SKINNER

A similar argument can be made for differences in the behavior of men and women. If we accept the notion that gender roles are almost entirely the product of the particular culture children are raised in, then social change should eventually lead to a society in which men and women are equally assertive, nurturant, independent, and so on. But if some of these gender differences have a genetic base, then societal changes may be insufficient to bring the sexes closer together. Similarly, treatment and prevention of depression, schizophrenia, and other psychological disorders also are complicated, though far from impossible, when therapists acknowledge genetic predispositions toward susceptibility to these disorders.

Ironically, a general acceptance of a genetic influence on personality probably was delayed by the way some of the theorists advocating this position presented their arguments. As described in Chapter 9, the comments of those arguing for a large genetic influence on individual differences in intelligence were sometimes interpreted as advocating the genetic inferiority of blacks. These statements offended the sensibilities of many personality psychologists and most likely led to an increased resistance to the genetic influence notion.

Fortunately, today many of these sources of resistance are breaking down. Most personality theorists recognize that plenty of room is left for environmental variables after genetic predispositions and limits are accounted for. For example, even if women are genetically predisposed to be more nurturant than men, this does not mean men cannot become more nurturant than they currently are. Similarly, even if some people are born with a greater susceptibility to depression than others, much can be done to help these people avoid or overcome problems with depression. Today an increasing number of personality psychologists recognize that acknowledging the role of genetic influences on personality not only helps us better understand behavior but also gives us a more realistic picture on which to base our intervention programs.

Person-by-Situation Interaction

A decade or so ago, shortly after Walter Mischel launched his criticisms of personality traits, many psychologists aligned themselves with one of the extreme positions in the "person-situation" debate (Chapter 7). I commonly heard psychologists declare that trait theory is dead, that consistent behavior patterns are largely an illusion, and that what consistency there is in behavior results from placing the person in similar situations. One prominent social psychologist told me in 1977 that he "didn't believe in personality."

Although the debate continues, advocates from both sides seem increasingly willing to acknowledge the importance of both the person and the situation in determining behavior. How or how much each source does so remains a source of argument and a spur for continued research. Most trait theorists acknowledge the limits of using traits to predict behavior, and critics of the trait approach no longer seem to argue that situational variables affect all people the same. I was struck by how much psychologists have moderated their positions on this issue during a recent conversation with the social psychologist who earlier did not believe in personality. Today he identifies himself as a "social hyphen personality" psychologist.

Thoughts Outside of Awareness

Although their descriptions and explanations vary a great deal, personality theorists from nearly all of the approaches covered in this book acknowledge that thoughts outside of our awareness play an important role in determining behavior. Obviously, Freudian psychologists, who emphasize the importance of unconscious thoughts, advocate the most extreme position here. Although most psychologists do not go this far, there seems to be a growing consensus that at least some behaviors are influenced by thoughts not easily accessible to our immediate awareness.

For example, humanistic psychologists often talk about processes that keep undesirable thoughts out of awareness. Each of the neo-Freudians covered here identified underlying causes of behavior not usually apparent to the person engaging in the behavior. For example, a certain behavior might be said to reflect a need to overcome feelings of inferiority (Adler), an effort to reduce anxiety (Horney), a desire to escape the perception of personal freedom (Fromm), and so on. However, in each case the person engaging in the behavior probably would not explain it in these terms.

Similarly, cognitive psychologists describe information processing that influences our behavior but which remains at a level of consciousness somewhere below immediate awareness. For example, we are said to use self-defeating or irrational statements in a logical process that we cannot readily explain. Even behaviorists acknowledge that we often are not aware of why we do the things we do. However, radical behaviorists still maintain that efforts to examine internal thought processes as causes of behavior will only be misleading. "The crucial age-old mistake is the belief that . . . what we feel as we behave is the cause of our behaving," B. F. Skinner wrote shortly before his death. "Unfortunately, we cannot report any internal event, physical or metaphysical, accurately" (1989, p. 17).

That our behavior is sometimes influenced by thoughts outside of awareness seems to be implicitly assumed by most psychotherapists. If it were possible to easily pinpoint the thoughts that drive our unwanted behaviors or fuel our painful emotions, why would anyone need to talk to a therapist in the first place? Common experiences support this observation. For example, many of us have experienced a sudden "insight" into a personal problem that had been troubling us for some time. Where were these thoughts that suddenly came together, and where did this processing take place? We commonly speak of experiences not quite in our awareness, such as "Something about her makes me nervous" or "I can't put my finger on it, but I just don't feel right about this."

Psychoanalytic, humanistic, and cognitive therapists generally work to help clients discover (that is, bring to awareness) their troubling thoughts. Sigmund Freud described elaborate processes to bring deeply buried unconscious material into awareness. Carl Rogers talked about guiding clients through a process of discovering their true selves. Albert Ellis advocates helping clients to understand the steps in their information processing that lead them to irrational conclusions. In each case, there is the acknowledgment that thoughts now outside of awareness are responsible for the client's problem and that bringing these thoughts into awareness where they can be worked on is an important step in the therapeutic process. Even strict behavior modification therapists, who typically do not concern themselves with identifying the conditioning experiences that may have led to the current problem, acknowledge that clients often are unaware of the associations that have linked, for example, snakes with fear responses.

In short, although the nature of such thoughts and processes remains the subject matter of professional disagreements, most approaches to understanding personality acknowledge the importance of thoughts outside of immediate awareness. Because of this acknowledgment, researchers and therapists frequently look to these thoughts as the key to unlocking some of the remaining secrets about personality processes and the road to better mental health.

Conclusion

The 17 chapters in this book were devoted to describing what psychologists have discovered about personality after nearly a century of scientific inquiry. Although they differ in emphasis and style, each theory and research program remains an attempt to understand what it is that makes you different from the next person. I hope you have found some answers for why you and the people around you act the way you do. But the larger goal has been to give you the tools to prepare you to join the numerous theorists and researchers seeking a better understanding of human personality. In Chapter 1, I introduced the personality psychologists' viewpoint with the old axiom "There are few differences between people, but what differences there are really matter." I can't imagine this won't still be the case even after another century of scientific investigation. The differences between people have fascinated poets and storytellers throughout recorded history. Like the personality psychologists whose work we have explored, they (and I) continue to find personality the stuff that really matters.

Summary

1. Exploring the various approaches to personality does not identify for students *the* correct theory. Instead, exposure to each of these approaches provides students with the tools with which to examine questions about personality and human behavior. However, most psychologists find one or more of the approaches more useful for understanding behavior than others.

2. Although predictions are difficult, we can identify recent trends in personality psychology. The psychoanalytic approach continues to have a strong following, although many of the neo-Freudian theorists probably get less attention than they did a few decades ago. The trait approach remains an important part of personality psychology, but several trends within this approach can be spotted. These include improved measurement, identifying which traits apply to which people, identifying the structure and relationships among traits, and assessing narrowly focused traits to improve predictability. The popularity of the biological approach seems to be growing steadily. One reason for the recent interest in this approach can be traced to advances in technology. The humanistic approach is perhaps less popular than it once was but still retains an important place among the theories. Behaviorism has undergone a slow transformation over the past several decades. Although radical behaviorists still have an influential voice,

behaviorists are steadily moving toward the social learning theories and perhaps to cognitive approaches. The cognitive approach has surged in popularity recently, reflecting a general emphasis on cognition in psychology generally. However, predicting what will happen to this approach in the future is difficult.

3. We can identify at least three areas of growing consensus among personality psychologists. Most psychologists today acknowledge that genetics has some influence on personality. In addition, there is a growing acceptance that both the person and the situation are important in determining behavior. Finally, although descriptions and explanations differ, most personality psychologists acknowledge the importance of thoughts that lie outside of our immediate awareness.

Glossary

absorption The ability to become highly involved in sensory and imaginative experiences.

aggregate data Combining scores from more than one measure of the same concept to obtain a more reliable assessment of a variable.

anal stage The psychosexual stage of development in which the anal region is the primary erogenous zone.

androgyny A personality trait consisting of masculine as well as feminine characteristics.

anima/animus The archetype that is the feminine side of the male (anima) or the masculine side of the female (animus).

anxiety An aversive emotional state experienced as feelings of nervousness, worry, agitation, and panic.

archetypes Primordial images that predispose us to comprehend the world in a particular manner.

attributional model of learned helplessness A model for understanding depression that examines the reasons people give for their perceived lack of control.

authoritarianism A mechanism to escape the perception of freedom, characterized by striving for submission and domination.

automaton conformity A mechanism to escape the perception of freedom characterized by conforming to societal standards.

behavior modification Therapy procedures based on operant conditioning and classical conditioning principles.

behavior potential The likelihood that a given behavior will be performed.

behavior validation A method for establishing a test's validity by predicting behavior from test scores.

birth order Where people are placed among siblings according to the order of their birth.

cardinal trait A single trait that dominates a person's personality.

case study method An in-depth examination of one subject or one group.

castration anxiety The fear a boy experiences during the phallic stage of development that his father will cut off his genitals.

catharsis A release of tension or anxiety.

central traits The five or ten traits that best describe a person's personality.

classical conditioning Learning resulting from pairing a conditioned stimulus with a new, unconditioned stimulus.

cognitive complexity The extent to which a person's personal construct system is elaborate or simple; usually refers to the number of personal constructs.

cognitive restructuring Psychotherapy procedures designed to alter the thoughts people use and the way they process information.

collective unconscious The part of the unconscious mind containing material common to all members of a culture.

comparison group An experimental condition, usually a no-treatment group, that differs from other conditions in a specific way and helps to rule out alternative hypotheses.

conditional/unconditional positive regard Acceptance and respect for people either only when they act as we desire (conditional) or regardless of their behavior (unconditional).

congruent validity A method for establishing a test's validity by correlating the test scores with other measures of the same construct.

conscious In Freud's topographic model, the part of personality that contains the thoughts which we are currently aware of.

construct validity The extent to which a test measures the hypothetical construct it is designed to measure.

correlation coefficient A statistic that indicates the strength and direction of a relationship between two variables.

countertransference In psychoanalysis, the therapist's transferring of unconscious feelings about another individual to the patient.

defense mechanisms Devices the ego uses to keep threatening material out of awareness and thereby reduce or avoid anxiety.

deficiency motive A need that is reduced when the object of the need is attained.

deindividuation A state in which people are relatively unaware of themselves and their personal standards of behavior.

denial A defense mechanism in which a person denies the existence of a fact.

dependent variable The experimental variable measured by the experimenter and used to compare groups.

depressive cognitive triad In Beck's theory, the three elements that describe a depressed person's cognitions: negative views of the self, pessimism, and interpreting events in a negative manner.

depressive schema A cognitive structure that allows people to readily make negative associations.

destructiveness A mechanism to escape the perception of freedom, characterized by destructive acts.

developmental epochs The stages of personality development in Sullivan's theory.

disclosure flexibility The extent to which people typically adapt their level of self-disclosure to the situational norms.

disclosure reciprocity Matching a conversation partner's self-disclosing intimacy level.

discriminant validity A method for establishing a test's validity by demonstrating that its scores do not correlate with the scores of theoretically unrelated measures.

discrimination A learned tendency to respond only to stimuli that result in reinforcement and not to similar, but unrewarded, stimuli.

displacement A defense mechanism in which a response is directed at a nonthreatening target instead of the unconsciously preferred one.

dizygotic twins Twins conceived from two different fertilized eggs, commonly referred to as fraternal twins.

ego In Freud's structural model, the part of personality that considers external reality while mediating between the demands of the id and the superego.

emotion-focused strategies Coping strategies designed to reduce emotional distress.

experimental confound A variable that is inadvertently manipulated or allowed to vary along with the independent variable.

explanatory style Relatively stable tendency to make certain kinds of attributions for events, particularly those related to depression.

extinction Weakening of a learned association through the removal of reinforcement or pairing.

extraversion A dimension of personality concerned with a person's general level of activity and sociability.

face validity A method for establishing a test's validity, in which test items appear to measure what the test was designed to measure.

factor analysis A statistical procedure used to determine the number of dimensions in a data set.

fear of success A trait dimension indicating the extent to which people anticipate that negative consequences will follow from achievement.

field study An investigation conducted in a natural setting instead of a laboratory, with subjects who are unaware they are participating in an experiment.

fixation The tying up of psychic energy at one psychosexual stage, which results in adult behaviors characteristic of that stage.

fixed-role therapy A psychotherapy procedure introduced by Kelly, in which clients act out a role suggested by therapists.

free association A procedure used in psychoanalysis in which patients say whatever comes into their minds.

Freudian slip A seemingly innocent misstatement that reveals unconscious associations.

frustration-aggression hypothesis A theory that maintains that frustration always causes aggression and that all aggression is caused by frustration.

fully functioning person A psychologically healthy individual who is able to enjoy life as completely as possible.

functional autonomy The maintenance of a behavior pattern for reasons other than those that originally caused the behavior.

gender schema A cognitive structure used to process information in terms of gender-relatedness.

generalization The tendency to respond to stimuli similar to the one used in the initial conditioning.

genital stage The final psychosexual stage in which the ability to engage in adult sexual behavior is developed.

growth need A need that leads to personal growth and that persists after the need object is attained.

hierarchy of needs In Maslow's theory, the order in which human needs demand attention.

Human Figure Drawing test A projective test in which subjects are asked simply to draw a person.

hypothesis A formal prediction about the relationship between two or more variables that is logically derived from a theory.

hypothetical construct Imagined entities created by scientists to aid in explanation and investigation.

id In Freud's structural model, the part of personality concerned with immediate gratification of needs.

identity crisis A period in one's development characterized by a strong concern for developing a sense of self.

idiographic approach A method of studying personality through in-depth analysis of one individual and the dimensions relevant to that person's personality.

independent variable The experimental variable used to divide subjects into groups.

individuation A state in which people feel unique and differentiated from others.

inferiority complex Feelings of being vastly inferior and helpless compared to others.

intellectualization A defense mechanism in which the emotional content of threatening material is removed before bringing it into awareness.

interaction An experimental outcome in which the effect of one independent variable on the dependent variable depends on the level of another independent variable.

internal consistency The extent to which test items are interrelated and thus appear to measure the same construct.

laboratory research Highly controlled research conducted in an artificial setting created by the researcher.

latency stage The psychosexual stage of development that follows resolution of the Oedipus complex and in which sexual desires are weak.

latent content The real meaning of dreams as expressed in symbols.

learned helplessness The cognitive, motivational, and emotional deficits that follow a perceived lack of control over important aversive events.

libido The limited amount of psychic energy that powers mental activity.

locus of control A personality trait indicating the extent to which people generally perceive that they have control over events in their lives.

loneliness Unpleasant feelings brought about by a perceived discrepancy between desired and achieved social interaction.

manifest content Dream material as perceived in symbolic form.

manipulated independent variable An independent variable for which subjects have been randomly assigned to an experimental condition.

masculinity-femininity A personality trait indicating the extent to which a person possesses sex-typed characteristics, with masculine characteristics at one end of the trait continuum and feminine characteristics at the other end.

monozygotic twins Twins conceived from the same fertilized egg, commonly referred to as identical twins.

Myers-Briggs Type Indicator Popular personality test used to assess Jung's psychological types.

neodissociation theory Ernest Hilgard's theory, which maintains that consciousness is divided into aware and unaware parts during hypnosis.

neuroticism A dimension of personality concerned with a person's general level of emotional stability.

nomothetic approach A method of understanding personality that compares many people along the same personality dimensions.

nonmanipulated independent variable An independent variable for which condition assignment is determined by a characteristic of the subject.

nonrandom sample A research sample for which not all members of the target population have had an equally likely chance of being selected.

observational learning Learning that results from watching or hearing about a person modeling the behavior.

Oedipus complex A child's sexual attraction at about age 5 for their opposite-sex parent and the consequent conflicts.

operant conditioning Learning resulting from the response an organism receives following a behavior.

optimal experience A state of happiness and satisfaction characterized by absorption in a challenging and personally-rewarding task.

oral stage The psychosexual stage of development in which the mouth, lips, and tongue are the primary erogenous zone.

peak experience An intense emotional experience characterized by feelings of satisfaction and personal growth.

penis envy A girl's desire to have a penis and to be like a male.

person-by-situation approach An approach to understanding behavior that maintains behavior is a function of the person as well as the situation.

personal constructs In Kelly's theory, the bipolar cognitive structures through which people process information.

personality Consistent behavior patterns originating within the individual.

personification A mental image of oneself or of another person.

phallic stage The psychosexual stage of development in which the genital region is the primary erogenous zone and in which the Oedipus complex develops.

pleasure principle The principle on which the id operates, in which pleasure is the sole reason for behavior.

positive freedom A healthy response to the perception of freedom, characterized by spontaneity and individuality.

possible selves Cognitive representations of the kind of people we think we might become some day.

posthypnotic amnesia Hypnotic subjects' inability to recall what occurred during hypnosis after the hypnotist tells them they will not remember.

preconscious In Freud's topographic model, the part of personality that contains thoughts which can be brought into awareness with little difficulty.

press An environmental feature that interacts with psychogenic needs to determine behavior.

primordial images The images that make up the collective unconscious.

problem-focused strategies Coping strategies directed at taking care of the problem causing the anxiety.

projection A defense mechanism in which one's own unconscious thoughts and impulses are seen in other people.

projective tests Tests designed to assess unconscious material by asking subjects to respond to ambiguous stimuli.

proprium In Allport's theory, the aspect of personality containing all the features of the self.

prototype A cognitive structure representing a typical case from a cognitive category.

psychoanalysis The system of psychotherapy developed by Freud that focuses on uncovering the unconscious material responsible for the patient's disorder.

psychogenic need In Murray's theory, a relatively stable predisposition toward a type of action.

psychosexual stages of development The innate sequence of development made up of stages characterized by primary erogenous zones.

psychoticism A dimension of personality concerned with a person's general level of egocentric and impersonal behavior.

punishment A process to decrease the frequency of an undesired behavior by following the occurrence of the behavior with an aversive stimulus.

Q-Sort An assessment procedure in which subjects distribute personal descriptions along a continuum.

radical behaviorism An extreme form of the behaviorist view that argues against using inner states as explanations for behaviors.

reaction formation A defense mechanism in which people act in a manner opposite their unconscious desires.

real-ideal self congruence The extent to which a person's perception of himself or herself resembles the way he or she would like to be.

reality principle The principle on which the ego operates, in which the external consequences of an action are considered.

reciprocal determinism The notion that external determinants of behavior, internal determinants of behavior, and behavior all influence one another.

reliability The extent to which a test measures consistently.

Rep Test The Role Construct Repertory Test, designed by Kelly to assess personal constructs.

replication An investigation that finds results similar to those found in an earlier investigation.

repression A defense mechanism in which the ego pushes threatening material out of awareness and into the unconscious.

repression-sensitization A personality dimension for a person's typical response to threat, with information-avoidance behaviors at one end and information-seeking behaviors at the other.

resistance A stage in psychoanalysis in which the patient acts to prevent the therapy from progressing further.

resultant achievement motivation The tendency to achieve as determined by the tendencies to approach success and to avoid failure.

Rorschach inkblot test A projective test in which subjects are asked to describe what they see in a series of inkblots.

schedule of reinforcement The frequency and conditions under which a learned response is reinforced.

schema A hypothetical cognitive structure used to process information.

secondary traits Traits besides the central traits that also describe a person's personality.

self-actualization A state of personal growth in which people fulfill their true potential.

self-disclosure The act of revealing intimate information about oneself to another person.

self-efficacy A person's expectancy that he or she can successfully perform a given behavior.

self-esteem Evaluation of one's self-concept, usually measured in terms of a relatively stable and global assessment of how a person feels about himself or herself.

self-regulation The ability to develop and apply rewards and punishments for internal standards of behavior.

self-schema A schema consisting of aspects of a person's life most important to him or her.

shadow The archetype that contains the evil side of humanity.

shaping The use of operant conditioning to obtain a response by reinforcing successive approximations of the desired behavior.

situationism An approach to understanding behavior that maintains behavior is largely or exclusively determined by the situation rather than by personality characteristics.

social desirability The extent to which test takers tend to respond to items in a manner that presents them in a positive light.

source traits The basic dimensions of personality in Cattell's theory.

statistical significance The likelihood that a research finding represents a genuine effect rather than a chance fluctuation of measurement.

striving for superiority The primary motivational force in Adler's theory, which is the person's effort to overcome feelings of inferiority.

structural model Freud's model of personality that divides personality into the id, the ego, and the superego.

subception The perception of information at a less-than-conscious level.

sublimation A defense mechanism in which threatening unconscious impulses are channeled into socially acceptable behaviors.

subliminal psychodynamic activation A research procedure that attempts to place images into the unconscious through very rapid tachistoscopic exposure.

superego In Freud's structural model, the part of personality that represents society's values.

systematic desensitization A procedure for treating phobias in which relaxation is paired with images of the feared object.

tachistoscope An instrument capable of presenting very rapid visual images.

temperaments General behavioral predispositions present in infancy and assumed to be inherited.

test-retest reliability A measure of a test's reliability, as indicated by the correlation between scores on the same test given to the same people at different times.

Thanatos The self-destructive (death) instinct, often turned outward in the form of aggression.

Thematic Apperception Test (TAT) A projective test in which subjects are asked to tell stories about a series of ambiguous pictures.

theory A general statement about the relationship between constructs or events.

topographic model Freud's original model of personality structure, in which personality is divided into three different levels of awareness.

trait A dimension of personality used to categorize people according to the degree to which they manifest a particular characteristic.

transference A stage in psychoanalysis in which the patient transfers unconscious feelings about another individual to the therapist.

twin-study method A procedure for examining the role of genetics on personality, in which pairs of monozygotic and dizygotic twins are compared.

Type A–Type B A trait dimension indicating the extent to which a person typically acts in a driving, time-urgent manner.

unconscious In Freud's topographic model, the part of personality that contains material which cannot easily be brought into awareness.

validity The extent to which a test measures what it is designed to measure.

wish fulfillment The satisfaction of id impulses through imagining the desired object.

References

Abramson, L. Y., Metalsky, G. I., & Alloy, L. B. (1988). The hopelessness theory of depression: Does the research test the theory? In L. Y. Abramson (Ed.), *Social cognition and clinical psychology: A synthesis* (pp. 33–65). New York: Guilford.

Abramson, L. Y., Metalsky, G. I., & Alloy, L. B. (1989). Hopelessness depression: A theory-based subtype of depression. *Psychological Review, 96,* 358–372.

Abramson, L. Y., Seligman, M. E. P., & Teasdale, J. D. (1978). Learned helplessness in humans: Critique and reformulation. *Journal of Abnormal Psychology, 87,* 49–74.

Achenbach, T., & Zigler, E. (1963). Social competence and self-image disparity in psychiatric and nonpsychiatric patients. *Journal of Abnormal and Social Psychology, 67,* 197–205.

Adorno, T. W., Frenkel-Brunswick, E., Levinson, D. J., & Sanford, R. N. (1950). *The authoritarian personality.* New York: Harper & Row.

Ahadi, S., & Diener, E. (1989). Multiple determinants and effect size. *Journal of Personality and Social Psychology, 56,* 398–406.

Aiken, L. R. (1979). *Psychological testing and assessment* (3rd Ed.). Boston: Allyn and Bacon.

Alberti, R. E., & Emmons, M. L. (1974). *Your perfect right* (2nd Ed.). San Luis Obispo, CA: Impact.

Alderfer, C. P. (1972). *Existence, relatedness, and growth needs in organizational settings.* New York: Free Press.

Allen, G. J., & Condon, T. J. (1982). Whither subliminal psychodynamic activation? A reply to Silverman. *Journal of Abnormal Psychology, 91,* 131–133.

Alloy, L. B., & Abramson, L. Y. (1988). Depressive realism: Four theoretical perspectives. In L. B. Alloy (Ed.), *Cognitive processes in depression* (pp. 223–265). New York: Guilford.

Alloy, L. B., & Ahrens, A. H. (1987). Depression and pessimism for the future: Biased use of statistically relevant information in predictions for self versus others. *Journal of Personality and Social Psychology, 52,* 366–378.

Allport, G. W. (1961). *Pattern and growth in personality.* New York: Holt, Rinehart & Winston.

Allport, G. W. (1965). *Letters from Jenny.* New York: Harcourt, Brace & World.

Allport, G. W. (1967). Gordon W. Allport. In E. G. Boring & G. Lindzey (Eds.), *A history of psychology in autobiography: Vol. V* (pp. 3–25). New York: Appleton-Century-Crofts.

Allport, G. W. (1968). *The person in psychology: Selected essays.* Boston: Beacon.

Altman, I., & Taylor, D. A. (1973). *Social penetration: The development of interpersonal relationships.* New York: Holt, Rinehart & Winston.

Anderson, C. A., & Ford, C. M. (1986). Affect of the game player: Short-term effects of highly and mildly aggressive video games. *Personality and Social Psychology Bulletin, 12,* 390–402.

Anderson, C. A., & Harvey, R. J. (1988). Discriminating between problems in living: An examination of measures of depression, loneliness, shyness, and social anxiety. *Journal of Social and Clinical Psychology, 6,* 482–491.

Ansbacher, H. L., & Ansbacher, R. R. (Eds.) (1956). *The individual psychology of Alfred Adler.* New York: Basic Books.

Antill, J. K. (1983). Sex role complementarity versus similarity in married couples. *Journal of Personality and Social Psychology, 45,* 145–155.

Arkin, A. M., Antrobus, J. S., & Ellman, S. J. (1978). *The mind in sleep: Psychology and psychophysiology.* Hillsdale, NJ: Erlbaum.

Aserinsky, E., & Kleitman, N. (1953). Regularly occurring periods of eye motility and concomitant phenomena during sleep. *Science, 118,* 273–274.

Atkinson, J. W. (1957). Motivational determinants of risk-taking behavior. *Psychological Review, 64,* 359–372.

Atkinson, J. W. (1974). The mainspring of achievement oriented activity. In J. W. Atkinson & J. O. Raynor (Eds.), *Motivation and achievement* (pp. 13–14). Washington, DC: Winston.

Atkinson, J. W. (1982). Motivational determinants of thematic apperception. In A. J.

Stewart (Ed.), *Motivation and society* (pp. 3–40). San Francisco: Jossey-Bass.

Baker, L. A., & Daniels, D. (1990). Nonshared environmental influences and personality differences in adult twins. *Journal of Personality and Social Psychology, 58,* 103–110.

Balay, J., & Shevrin, H. (1988). The subliminal psychodynamic activation method: A critical review. *American Psychologist, 44,* 161–174.

Balch, P., & Ross, A. W. (1975). Predicting success in weight reduction as a function of locus of control: A unidimensional and multidimensional approach. *Journal of Consulting and Clinical Psychology, 43,* 119.

Baltes, M. M., & Baltes, P. B. (1986). *The psychology of control and aging.* Hillsdale, NJ: Erlbaum.

Bandura, A. (1965). Influences of models' reinforcement contingencies on the acquisition of imitative responses. *Journal of Personality and Social Psychology, 1,* 589–595.

Bandura, A. (1973). *Aggression: A social learning analysis.* Englewood Cliffs, NJ: Prentice-Hall.

Bandura, A. (1977a). *Social learning theory.* Englewood Cliffs, NJ: Prentice-Hall.

Bandura, A. (1977b). Self-efficacy: Toward a unifying theory of behavioral change. *Psychological Review, 84,* 191–215.

Bandura, A. (1986). *Social foundations of thought and action: A social cognitive theory.* Englewood Cliffs, NJ: Prentice-Hall.

Bandura, A., Adams, N. E., & Beyer, J. (1977). Cognitive processes mediating behavioral change. *Journal of Personality and Social Psychology, 35,* 125–139.

Bannister, D., & Mair, J. M. M. (1968). *The evaluation of personal constructs.* London: Academic Press.

Barber, T. X. (1964). Hypnotizability, suggestibility, and personality: A critical review of research findings. *Psychological Reports, 14,* 299–320.

Barber, T. X. (1970). *LSD, marihuana, yoga, and hypnosis.* Chicago: Aldine.

Barber, T. X. (1976). *Pitfalls of human research: Ten pivotal points.* New York: Pergamon Press.

Barber, T. S., & Calverly, D. S. (1964). Toward a theory of hypnotic behavior: Effects on suggestibility of defining the situation as hypnosis and defining responses to suggestion as easy. *Journal of Abnormal and Social Psychology, 68,* 585–592.

Barber, T. X., Spanos, N. P., & Chaves, J. F. (1974). *Hypnotism, imagination and human potentialities.* New York: Pergamon Press.

Barlow, D. H. (1988). *Anxiety and its disorders.* New York: Guilford.

Baron, R. A. (1978a). The influence of hostile and nonhostile humor upon physical aggression. *Personality and Social Psychology Bulletin, 4,* 77–80.

Baron, R. A. (1978b). Aggression-inhibiting influence of sexual behavior. *Journal of Personality and Social Psychology, 36,* 189–197.

Baron, R. A. (1984). Reducing organizational conflict: An incompatible response approach. *Journal of Applied Psychology, 69,* 272–279.

Baron, R. A., & Kepner, C. R. (1970). Model's behavior and attraction toward the model as determinants of adult aggressive behavior. *Journal of Personality and Social Psychology, 14,* 335–344.

Barrett, P., & Eysenck, S. B. G. (1984). The assessment of personality factors across 25 countries. *Personality and Individual Differences, 5,* 615–632.

Basgall, J. A., & Snyder, C. R. (1988). Excuses in waiting: External locus of control and reactions to success-failure feedback. *Journal of Personality and Social Psychology, 54,* 656–662.

Baumeister, R. F., & Tice, D. M. (1988). Metatraits. *Journal of Personality, 56,* 571–598.

Baumeister, R. F., & Tice, D. M. (1990). Anxiety and social exclusion. *Journal of Social and Clinical Psychology, 9,* 165–195.

Baumeister, R. F., Tice, D. M., & Hutton, D. G. (1989). Self-presentational motivations and personality differences in self-esteem. *Journal of Personality, 57,* 547–579.

Beaman, A. L., Klentz, B., Diener, E., & Svanum, S. (1979). Self-awareness and transgression in children: Two field studies. *Journal of Personality and Social Psychology, 37,* 1835–1846.

Beatty, M. J., & Payne, S. K. (1984). Listening comprehension as a function of cognitive complexity: A research note. *Communication Monographs, 51,* 85–89.

Bechtle, R. (1984). C. G. Jung and the religion of the unconscious. In J. Heaney (Ed.), *Psyche and spirit* (pp. 138–163). New York: Paulist Press.

Beck, A. T. (1972). *Depression: Causes and treatments.* Philadelphia: University of Pennsylvania Press.

Beck, A. T. (1991). Cognitive therapy: A 30-year retrospective. *American Psychologist, 46,* 368–375.

Beit-Hallahmi, B. (1980). Achievement motivation and economic growth: A replication. *Personality and Social Psychology Bulletin, 6,* 210–215.

Bem, D. J., & Allen, A. (1974). On predicting some of the people some of the time: The search for cross-situational consistencies in behavior. *Psychological Review, 81,* 506–520.

Bem, S. L. (1974). The measurement of psychological androgyny. *Journal of Consulting and Clinical Psychology, 42,* 155–162.

Bem, S. L. (1975). Sex role adaptability: One consequence of psychological androgyny. *Journal of Personality and Social Psychology, 31,* 634–643.

Bem, S. L. (1976). Probing the promise of androgyny. In A. G. Kaplan & J. P. Bean (Eds.), *Beyond sex-role stereotypes* (pp. 48–62). Boston: Little, Brown & Co.

Bem, S. L. (1977). On the utility of alternative procedures for assessing psychological androgyny. *Journal of Consulting and Clinical Psychology, 45,* 196–205.

Bem, S. L. (1979). Theory and measurement of androgyny: A reply to the Pedhazur-Tetenbaum and Locksley-Colten critiques. *Journal of Personality and Social Psychology, 37,* 1047–1054.

Bem, S. L. (1981). Gender schema theory: A cognitive account of sex-typing. *Psychological Review, 88,* 354–364.

Bem, S. L. (1985). Androgyny and gender schema theory: A conceptual and empirical integration. In T. B. Sonderegger (Ed.), *1984 Nebraska Symposium on Motivation: Psychology and Gender.* Lincoln: University of Nebraska Press.

Bem, S. L. (1987). Gender schema theory and the romantic tradition. In P. Shaver & C. Hendrick (Eds.), *Sex and gender* (pp. 251–271). Beverly Hills, CA: Sage.

Bem, S. L., & Lenney, E. (1976). Sex-typing and the avoidance of cross-sex behavior. *Journal of Personality and Social Psychology, 33,* 48–54.

Bem, S. L., Martyna, W., & Watson, C. (1976). Sex typing and androgyny: Further explorations of the expressive domain. *Journal of Personality and Social Psychology, 34,* 1016–1023.

Benassi, V. A., Sweeney, P. D., & Dufour, C. L. (1988). Is there a relationship between locus of control orientation and depression? *Journal of Abnormal Psychology, 97,* 357–367.

Berg, J. H., & Peplau, L. A. (1982). Loneliness: The relationship of self-disclosure and androgyny. *Personality and Social Psychology Bulletin, 8,* 624–630.

Berg, K. S., & Vidmar, N. (1975). Authoritarianism and recall of evidence about criminal behavior. *Journal of Research in Personality, 9,* 147–157.

Berkowitz, L. (1970). Aggressive humor as a stimulus to aggressive responses. *Journal of Personality and Social Psychology, 16,* 710–717.

Berkowitz, L. (1984). Some effects of thoughts on anti- and prosocial influences of media events: A cognitive-neoassociationist analysis. *Psychological Bulletin, 95,* 410–427.

Berkowitz, L. (1986). Situational influences on reactions to observed violence. *Journal of Social Issues, 42,* 93–106.

Berkowitz, L. (1989). Frustration-aggression hypothesis: Examination and reformulation. *Psychological Bulletin, 106,* 59–73.

Berkowitz, L., & Donnerstein, E. (1982). External validity is more than skin deep. *American Psychologist, 37,* 245–257.

Berkowitz, L., & Powers, P. C. (1979). Effects of timing and justification of witnessed aggression on the observers' punitiveness. *Journal of Research in Personality, 13,* 71–80.

Best, J. A. (1975). Tailoring smoking withdrawal procedures to personality and motivational differences. *Journal of Consulting and Clinical Psychology, 43,* 1–8.

Best, J. A., & Steffy, R. A. (1975). Smoking modification procedures for internal and external locus of control clients. *Canadian Journal of Behavioural Science, 7,* 155–165.

Bianchi, E. C. (1988). Jungian psychology and religious experience. In R. L. Moore (Ed.), *Carl Jung and Christian spirituality* (pp. 16–37). New York: Paulist Press.

Bieri, J. (1955). Cognitive complexity-simplicity and predictive behavior. *Journal of Abnormal and Social Psychology, 51,* 263–268.

Bigner, J. J. (1974). A Wernerian developmental analysis of children's descriptions of siblings. *Child Development, 45,* 317–323.

Billings, A. G., & Moos, R. H. (1981). The role of coping responses and social resources in attenuating the stress of life events. *Journal of Behavioral Medicine, 4,* 157–189.

Blass, T. (1984). Social psychology and personality: Toward a convergence. *Journal of Personality and Social Psychology, 47,* 1013–1027.

Block, J. (1961). *The Q-Sort method in personality assessment and psychiatric research.* Springfield, IL: Charles C Thomas.

Block, J. H., Gjerde, P. F., & Block, J. H. (1991). Personality antecedents of depressive tendencies in 18-year-olds: A prospective study. *Journal of Personality and Social Psychology, 60,* 726–738.

Bond, C. F., Jr., & Omar, A. S. (1990). Social anxiety, state dependence, and the next-in-line effect. *Journal of Experimental Social Psychology, 26,* 185–198.

Boor, M. (1976). Relationship of internal-external control and national suicide rates. *Journal of Social Psychology, 100,* 143–144, a publication of the Helen Dwight Reid Educational Foundation.

Botwin, M. D., & Buss, D. M. (1989). Structure of act-report data: Is the five-factor model of personality recaptured? *Journal of Personality and Social Psychology, 56,* 988–1001.

Bouchard, T. J., & McGue, M. (1981). Familial studies of intelligence: A review. *Science, 212,* 1055–1059.

Bradburn, N. (1969). *The structure of psychological well-being.* Chicago: Aldine.

Bray, R. M., & Noble, A. M. (1978). Authoritarianism and decisions of mock juries: Evidence of jury bias and group polarization. *Journal of Personality and Social Psychology, 36,* 1424–1430.

Brebner, J., & Cooper, C. (1978). Stimulus- or response-induced excitation: A comparison of behavior in introverts and extraverts. *Journal of Research in Personality, 12,* 306–311.

Breslow, R., Kocsis, J., & Belkin, B. (1981). Contribution of the depressive perspective to memory function in depression. *American Journal of Psychiatry, 138,* 227–230.

Brewin, C. R. (1985). Depression and causal attributions: What is their relation? *Psychological bulletin, 98,* 297–309.

Briggs, S. R. (1989). The optimal level of measurement of personality constructs. In D. M. Buss & N. Cantor (Eds.), *Personality psychology: Recent trends and emerging directions* (pp. 246–260). New York: Springer-Verlag.

Briggs, S. R., & Cheek, J. M. (1986). The role of factor analysis in the development and evaluation of personality scales. *Journal of Personality, 54,* 106–148.

Brockner, J. (1979). The effects of self-esteem, success-failure, and self-consciousness on task performance. *Journal of Personality and Social Psychology, 37,* 1732–1741.

Brockner, J., Derr, W. R., & Laing, W. N. (1987). Self-esteem and reactions to negative feedback: Toward greater generalizability. *Journal of Research in Personality, 21,* 318–333.

Brooks-Gunn, J., & Fisch, M. (1980). Psychological androgyny and college students' judgments of mental health. *Sex Roles, 6,* 575–580.

Brown, J., & Inouye, D. K. (1978). Learned helplessness through modeling: The role of perceived similarity in competence. *Journal of Personality and Social Psychology, 36,* 900–908.

Brown, J. D., & Gallagher, F. M. (1992). Coming to terms with failure: Private self-enhancement and public self-effacement. *Journal of Experimental Social Psychology, 28,* 3–22.

Brown, J. D., & Smart, S. A. (1991). The self and social conduct: Linking self-representations to prosocial behavior. *Journal of Personality and Social Psychology, 60,* 368–375.

Brown, J. D., & Taylor, S. E. (1986). Affect and the processing of personal information: Evidence for mood-activated self-schemata. *Journal of Experimental Social Psychology, 22,* 436–452.

Brown, R. J., & Donderi, D. C. (1986). Dream content and self-reported well-being among recurrent dreamers, past-recurrent dreamers, and nonrecurrent dreamers. *Journal of Personality and Social Psychology, 50,* 612–623.

Bruch, M. A., Kaflowitz, N. G., & Pearl, L. (1988). Mediated and nonmediated relationships of personality components to loneliness. *Journal of Social and Clinical Psychology, 6,* 346–355.

Buchwald, A. M. (1977). Depressive mood and estimates of reinforcement frequency. *Journal of Abnormal Psychology, 86,* 443–446.

Buhler, C., & Allen, M. (1972). *Introduction to humanistic psychology.* Monterey, CA: Brooks/Cole.

Burger, J. M. (1981). Locus of control, motivation, and expectancy: Predicting hypnotic susceptibility from personality variables. *Journal of Research in Personality, 15,* 523–537.

Burger, J. M. (1984). Desire for control, locus of control, and proneness to depression. *Journal of Personality, 52,* 71–89.

Burger, J. M. (1992). *Desire for control: Personality, social and clinical perspectives.* New York: Plenum.

Burger, J. M., & Arkin, R. M. (1980). Prediction, control and learned helplessness. *Journal of Personality and Social Psychology, 38,* 482–491.

Burger, J. M., & Cooper, H. M. (1979). The desirability of control. *Motivation and Emotion, 3,* 381–393.

Burns, M. O., & Seligman, M. E. P. (1989). Explanatory style across the life span: Evidence for stability over 52 years. *Journal of Personality and Social Psychology, 56,* 471–477.

Bushman, B. J., & Geen, R. G. (1990). Role of cognitive-emotional mediators and individual differences in the effects of media violence on aggression. *Journal of Personality and Social Psychology, 58,* 156–163.

Buss, A. H. (1980). *Self-consciousness and social anxiety.* San Francisco: W. H. Freeman.

Buss, A. H., & Plomin, R. (1975). *A temperament theory of personality development.* New York: Wiley.

Buss, A. H., & Plomin, R. (1984). *Temperament: Early developing personality traits.* Hillsdale, NJ: Erlbaum.

Buss, A. H., & Plomin, R. (1986). The EAS Approach to Temperament. In R. Plomin & J. Dunn (Eds.), *The study of temperament: Changes, continuities and challenges* (pp. 67–79). Hillsdale, NJ: Erlbaum.

Buss, D. M. (1984). Evolutionary biology and personality psychology. *American Psychologist, 39,* 1135–1147.

Buss, D. M. (1988). The evolution of human intrasexual competition: Tactics of mate attraction. *Journal of Personality and Social Psychology, 54,* 616–628.

Buss, D. M. (1989). Sex differences in human mate preferences: Evolutionary hypotheses tested in 37 cultures. *Behavioral and Brain Sciences, 12,* 1–49.

Buss, D. M. (1990a). Toward a biologically informed psychology of personality. *Journal of Personality, 58,* 1–16.

Buss, D. M. (1990b). The evolution of anxiety and social exclusion. *Journal of Social and Clinical Psychology, 9,* 196–201.

Buss, D. M. (1991). Evolutionary personality psychology. *Annual Review of Psychology, 42,* 459–491.

Buss, D. M., & Barnes, M. (1986). Preferences in human mate selection. *Journal of Personality and Social Psychology, 50,* 559–570.

Bussey, K., & Bandura, A. (1984). Influence of gender constancy and social power on sex-linked modeling. *Journal of Personality and Social Psychology, 47,* 1292–1302.

Butler, J. M. (1968). Self-ideal congruence in psychotherapy. *Psychotherapy: Theory, Research and Practice, 5,* 13–17.

Butler, J. M., & Haigh, G. V. (1954). Changes in the relation between self-concepts and ideal concepts consequent upon client-centered counseling. In C. R. Rogers and R. F. Dymond (Eds.), *Psychotherapy and personality change* (pp. 55–75). Chicago: University of Chicago Press.

Byrne, D. (1961). The repression-sensitization scale: Rationale, reliability, and validity. *Journal of Personality, 29,* 334–349.

Byrne, D. (1964). Repression-sensitization as a dimension of personality. In B. A. Maher (Ed.), *Progress in experimental personality research.* (Vol. 1, pp. 169–220). New York: Academic Press.

Byrne, D., Barry, J., & Nelson, D. (1963). Relation of the revised repression-sensitization scale to measures of self-description. *Psychological Reports, 13,* 323–334.

Byrne, D., Steinberg, M. A., & Schwartz, M. S. (1968). Relationship between repression-sensitization and physical illness. *Journal of Abnormal Psychology, 73,* 154–155.

Campbell, J. B. (1983). Differential relationships of extraversion, impulsivity, and sociability to study habits. *Journal of Research in Personality, 17,* 308–314.

Campbell, J. B., & Hawley, C. W. (1982). Study habits and Eysenck's theory of extraversion-introversion. *Journal of Research in Personality, 16,* 139–146.

Campbell, J. D., & Fairey, P. J. (1985). Effects of self-esteem, hypothetical explanations, and verbalization of expectancies on future performance. *Journal of Personality and Social Psychology, 48,* 1097–1111.

Cantor, N. (1981). A cognitive-social approach to personality. In N. Cantor & J. F. Kihlstrom (Eds.), *Personality, cognition, and social interaction* (pp. 23–44). Hillsdale, NJ: Erlbaum.

Cantor, N. (1990). From thought to behavior: "Having" and "doing" in the study of personality and cognition. *American Psychologist, 45,* 735–750.

Cantor, N., & Kihlstrom, J. F. (1981). *Personality, cognition, and social interaction.* Hillsdale, NJ: Erlbaum.

Cantor, N., Markus, H., Niedenthal, P., & Nurius, P. (1986). On motivation and the self-concept. In R. M. Sorrentino & E. T. Higgins (Eds.), *Handbook of motivation and cognition: Foundations of social behavior* (pp. 96–121). New York: Guilford.

Cantor, N., & Mischel, W. (1979). Prototypes in person perception. In L. Berkowitz (Ed.), *Advances in experimental social psychology* (Vol. 12, pp. 3–52). New York: Academic Press.

Cantor, N., Mischel, W., & Schwartz, J. C. (1982). A prototype analysis of psychological situations. *Cognitive Psychology, 14,* 45–77.

Cantor, N., Smith, E. E., French, R. D., & Mezzich, J. (1980). Psychiatric diagnosis as prototype categorization. *Journal of Abnormal Psychology, 89,* 181–193.

Carlson, M., Marcus-Newhall, A., & Miller, N. (1990). Effects of situational aggression cues: A quantitative review. *Journal of Personality and Social Psychology, 58,* 622–633.

Carlson, R. (1984). What's social about social psychology? Where's the person in personality research? *Journal of Personality and Social Psychology, 47,* 1304–1309.

Carlson, R., & Levy, N. (1973). Studies in Jungian typology: I. Memory, social perception and social action. *Journal of Personality, 41,* 559–576.

Carver, C. S., Coleman, E. A., & Glass, D. C. (1976). The coronary-prone behavior pattern and the suppression of fatigue on a treadmill test. *Journal of Personality and Social Psychology, 33,* 460–466.

Cattell, R. B. (1974). Raymond B. Cattell. In G. Lindzey (Ed.), *A history of psychology in autobiography: Vol. VI* (pp. 61–100). Englewood Cliffs, NJ: Prentice-Hall.

Chabot, J. A. (1973). Repression-sensitization: A critique of some neglected variables in the literature. *Psychological Bulletin, 80,* 122–129.

Chapman, A. H. (1976). *Harry Stack Sullivan: The man and his work.* New York: Putnam.

Chavez, D. (1985). Perpetuation of gender inequality: A content analysis of comic strips. *Sex Roles, 13,* 93–102.

Cheek, J. M., & Buss, A. H. (1981). Shyness and sociability. *Journal of Personality and Social Psychology, 41,* 330–339.

Chelune, G. J. (1976). Reactions to male and female disclosure at two levels. *Journal of Personality and Social Psychology, 34,* 1000–1003.

Chelune, G. J. (1977). Disclosure flexibility and social-situational perceptions. *Journal of Consulting and Clinical Psychology, 45,* 1139–1143.

Chelune, G. J. (1979). *Self-disclosure: Origins, patterns, and implications of openness in interpersonal relationships.* San Francisco: Jossey-Bass.

Chelune, G. J., & Figueroa, J. L. (1981). Self-disclosure flexibility, neuroticism, and effective interpersonal communication. *Western Journal of Speech Communication, 45,* 27–37.

Chelune, G. J., Sultan, F. E., & Williams, C. L. (1980). Loneliness, self-disclosure, and interpersonal effectiveness. *Journal of Counseling Psychology, 27,* 462–468.

Chess, S., & Thomas, A. (1986). *Temperament in clinical practice.* New York: Guilford.

Church, A. T., & Katigbak, M. S. (1989). Internal, external, and self-report structure of personality in a non-Western culture: An investigation of cross-language and cross-cultural generalizability. *Journal of Personality and Social Psychology, 57,* 857–872.

Clark, D. A., Beck, A. T., & Brown, G. (1989). Cognitive mediation in general psychiatric outpatients: A test of the content-specificity hypothesis. *Journal of Personality and Social Psychology, 56,* 958–964.

Clark, D. M., & Teasdale, J. D. (1982). Diurnal variations in clinical depression and accessibility of memories of positive and negative experiences. *Journal of Abnormal Psychology, 91,* 87–95.

Clark, R. A., & Delia, J. G. (1977). Cognitive complexity, social perspective-taking, and functional persuasive skills in second- to ninth-grade children. *Human Communication Research, 3,* 128–134.

Coe, W. C. (1978). The credibility of posthypnotic amnesia: A contextualist's view. *International Journal of Clinical and Experimental Hypnosis, 26,* 218–245.

Coe, W. C., & Sarbin, T. R. (1966). An experimental demonstration of hypnosis as role enactment. *Journal of Abnormal Psychology, 71,* 400–416.

Coe, W. C., & Sluis, A. S. E. (1989). Increasing contextual pressures to breach posthypnotic amnesia. *Journal of Personality and Social Psychology, 57,* 885–894.

Cohen, D. B. (1979). *Sleep and dreaming: Origins, nature and function.* New York: Pergamon Press.

Cohen, D. B., & Cox, C. (1975). Neuroticism in the sleep laboratory: Implications for representational and adaptive properties of dreaming. *Journal of Abnormal Psychology, 84,* 91–108.

Cohen, S., & Wills, T. A. (1985). Stress, social support, and the buffering hypothesis. *Psychological Bulletin, 98,* 310–357.

Cohn, N. B., & Strassberg, D. S. (1983). Self-disclosure reciprocity among preadolescents. *Personality and Social Psychology Bulletin, 9,* 97–102.

Coleman, M., & Ganong, L. H. (1985). Love and sex-role stereotypes: Do "macho" men and "feminine" women make better lovers? *Journal of Personality and Social Psychology, 49,* 170–176.

Collins, B. E. (1974). Four components of the Rotter Internal-External Scale: Belief in a difficult world, a just world, a predictable world, and a politically responsive world. *Journal of Personality and Social Psychology, 29,* 381–391.

Condon, T. J., & Allen, G. J. (1980). Role of psychoanalytic merging fantasies in systematic desensitization: A rigorous methodological examination. *Journal of Abnormal Psychology, 89,* 437–443.

Conley, J. J. (1984). Longitudinal consistency of adult personality: Self-reported psychological characteristics across 45 years. *Journal of Personality and Social Psychology, 47,* 1325–1333.

Conley, J. J. (1985). Longitudinal stability of personality traits: A multitrait-multimethod-multioccasion analysis. *Journal of Personality and Social Psychology, 49,* 1266–1282.

Constantinople, A. (1973). Masculinity-femininity: An exception to a famous dictum. *Psychological Bulletin, 80,* 389–407.

Contrada, R. J. (1989). Type A behavior, personality hardiness, and cardiovascular responses to stress. *Journal of Personality and Social Psychology, 57,* 895–903.

Cook, J. R. (1985). Repression-sensitization and approach-avoidance as predictors of response to a laboratory stressor. *Journal of Personality and Social Psychology, 49,* 759–773.

Cooper, H. M., & Good, T. E. (1983). *Pygmalion grows up: Studies in the expectation communication process.* New York: Longman.

Cooper, T., Detre, T., & Weiss, S. M. (1981). Coronary-prone behavior and coronary heart disease: A critical review. *Circulation, 63,* 1199–1215.

Costa, P. T., & McCrae, R. R. (1980). Influence of extraversion and neuroticism on subjective well-being: Happy and unhappy people. *Journal of Personality and Social Psychology, 38,* 668–678.

Costa, P. T., & McCrae, R. R. (1988). Personality in adulthood: A six-year longitudinal study of self-reports and spouse ratings on the NEO Personality Inventory. *Journal of Personality and Social Psychology, 54,* 853–863.

Costa, P. T., McCrae, R. R., & Arenberg, D. (1980). Enduring dispositions in adult males. *Journal of Personality and Social Psychology, 38,* 793–800.

Costello, C. G. (1978). A critical review of Seligman's laboratory experiments on learned helplessness and depression in humans. *Journal of Abnormal Psychology, 87,* 21–31.

Cowen, E. I., Wyman, P. A., & Work, W. C. (1992). The relationship between retrospective reports of early child temperament and adjustment at ages 10–12. *Journal of Abnormal Child Psychology, 20,* 39–50.

Cozby, P. C. (1972). Self-disclosure, reciprocity and liking. *Sociometry, 35,* 151–160.

Craik, K. H. (1986). Personality research methods: An historical perspective. *Journal of Personality, 54,* 18–51.

Crandall, V. C., Katkovsky, W., & Crandall, V. J. (1965). Children's beliefs in their own control of reinforcements in intellectual-academic situations. *Child Development, 36,* 91–109.

Crick, F., & Mitchison, G. (1983). The function of dream sleep. *Nature, 304,* 111–114.

Crockett, W. H. (1965). Cognitive complexity and impression formation. In B. A. Maher (Ed.), *Progress in experimental personality research* (Vol. 2). New York: Academic Press.

Cronin, D. M., Spanos, N. P., & Barber, T. X. (1971). Augmenting hypnotic suggestibility by providing favorable information about hypnosis. *American Journal of Clinical Hypnosis, 13,* 259–264.

Crowne, D. P., & Marlowe, D. (1960). A new scale of social desirability independent of psychopathology. *Journal of Consulting Psychology, 24,* 349–354.

Cunningham, J. A., Strassberg, D. S., & Haan, B. (1986). Effects of intimacy and sex-role congruency of self-disclosure. *Journal of Social and Clinical Psychology, 4,* 393–401.

Curran, J. P., Wallander, J. L., & Fischetti, M. (1980). The importance of behavioral and cognitive factors in heterosexual-social anxiety. *Journal of Personality, 48,* 285–292.

Cutrona, C. E. (1982). Transition to college: Loneliness and the process of social adjustment. In L. A. Peplau & D. Perlman (Eds.), *Loneliness.* New York: Wiley.

Csikszentmihalyi, M. (1990). *Flow: The psychology of optimal experience.* New York: Harper & Row.

Csikszentmihalyi, M., & Csikszentmihalyi, I. S. (1988). *Optimal experience: Psychological studies of flow in consciousness.* New York: Cambridge.

Csikszentmihalyi, M., & LeFevre, J. (1989). Optimal experience in work and leisure. *Journal of Personality and Social Psychology, 56,* 815–822.

Dana, R. H., & Cooper, G. W. (1964). Prediction of susceptibility to hypnosis. *Psychological Reports, 14,* 251–265.

Dattore, P. J., Shontz, F. C., & Coyne, L. (1980). Premorbid personality differentiation of cancer and noncancer groups: A test of the hypothesis of cancer proneness. *Journal of Consulting and Clinical Psychology, 48,* 388–394.

Dauber, R. B. (1984). Subliminal psychodynamic activation in depression: On the role of autonomy issues in depressed college women. *Journal of Abnormal Psychology, 93,* 9–18.

Davidson, R. J. (1988). EEG measures of cerebral asymmetry: Conceptual and methodological issues. *International Journal of Neuroscience, 39,* 71–89.

Davidson, R. J. (1991). Biological approaches to the study of personality. In V. J. Derlega, B. A. Winstead, & W. H. Jones (Eds.), *Personality: Contemporary theory and research* (pp. 87–112). Chicago: Nelson-Hall.

Davidson, R. J., Chapman, J. P., & Chapman, L. J. (1987). Task-dependent EEG asymmetry discriminates between depressed and non-depressed subjects. *Psychophysiology, 24,* 585.

Davidson, R. J., Ekman, P., Saron, C. D., Senulis, J. A., & Friesen, W. V. (1990). Approach-withdrawal and cerebral asymmetry: Emotional expression and brain physiology I. *Journal of Personality and Social Psychology, 58,* 330–341.

Davidson, R. J., & Fox, N. A. (1982). Asymmetrical brain activity discriminates between positive versus negative affective stimuli in human infants. *Science, 218,* 1235–1237.

Davidson, R. J., & Fox, N. A. (1989). Frontal brain asymmetry predicts infants' response to maternal separation. *Journal of Abnormal Psychology, 98,* 127–131.

Davidson, R. J., & Tomarken, A. J. (1989). Laterality and emotion: An electrophysiological approach. In F. Boller & J. Grafman (Eds.), *Handbook of neuropsychology, Vol. 3* (pp. 419–441). New York: Elsevier Science.

Davis, J. D. (1976). Self-disclosure in an acquaintance exercise: Responsibility for level of intimacy. *Journal of Personality and Social Psychology, 33,* 787–792.

Davis, J. D. (1977). Effects of communication about interpersonal process on the evolution of self-disclosure in dyads. *Journal of Personality and Social Psychology, 35,* 31–37.

Davis, J. D. (1978). When boy meets girl: Sex roles and the negotiation of intimacy in an acquaintance exercise. *Journal of Personality and Social Psychology, 36,* 684–692.

Deaux, K., Kite, M. E., & Lewis, L. L. (1985). Clustering and gender schemata: An uncertain link. *Personality and Social Psychology Bulletin, 11,* 387–397.

Deckers, L., & Carr, D. E. (1986). Cartoons varying in low-level pain ratings, not aggression ratings, correlate positively with funniness ratings. *Motivation and Emotion, 10,* 207–216.

Deci, E. L., & Ryan, R. M. (1987). The support of autonomy and the control of behavior. *Journal of Personality and Social Psychology, 53,* 1024–1037.

Delia, J. G., & Clark, R. A. (1977). Cognitive complexity, social perception, and the development of listener-adapted communication in six-, eight-, ten-, and twelve-year-old boys. *Communication Monographs, 44,* 326–345.

Dembroski, T. M., & Costa, P. T. (1987). Coronary-prone behavior: Components of the Type A pattern and hostility. *Journal of Personality, 55,* 211–235.

DeMonbreun, B. G., & Craighead, W. E. (1977). Distortion of perception and recall of positive and neutral feedback in depression. *Cognitive Research and Therapy, 1,* 311–329.

DePaulo, B. M., Dull, W. R., Greenberg, J. M., & Swaim, G. W. (1989). Are shy people reluctant to ask for help? *Journal of Personality and Social Psychology, 56,* 834–844.

DePaulo, B. M., Epstein, J. A., & LeMay, C. S. (1990). Responses of the socially anxious to the prospect of interpersonal evaluation. *Journal of Personality, 58,* 623–640.

DePaulo, B. M., Kenny, D. A., Hoover, C. W., Webb, W., & Oliver, P. V. (1987). Accuracy of person perception: Do people know what kinds of impressions they convey? *Journal of Personality and Social Psychology, 52*, 303–315.

Depue, R. A., & Monroe, S. M. (1978). Learned helplessness in the perspective of the depressive disorders: Conceptual and definitional issues. *Journal of Abnormal Psychology, 87*, 3–20.

Derlega, V. J., & Chaikin, A. L. (1976). Norms affecting self-disclosure in men and women. *Journal of Consulting and Clinical Psychology, 44*, 376–380.

Derlega, V. J., Harris, M. S., & Chaikin, A. L. (1973). Self-disclosure reciprocity, liking and the deviant. *Journal of Experimental Social Psychology, 9*, 277–284.

Derlega, V. J., Margulis, S. T., & Winstead, B. A. (1987). A social-psychological analysis of self-disclosure in psychotherapy. *Journal of Social and Clinical Psychology, 5*, 205–215.

Derlega, V. J., Wilson, M., & Chaikin, A. L. (1976). Friendship and disclosure reciprocity. *Journal of Personality and Social Psychology, 34*, 578–582.

Derry, P. A., & Kuiper, N. A. (1981). Schematic processing and self-reference in clinical depression. *Journal of Abnormal Psychology, 90*, 286–297.

DeVellis, R. F., Devellis, B. M., & McCauley, C. (1978). Vicarious acquisition of learned helplessness. *Journal of Personality and Social Psychology, 36*, 894–899.

DeVito, A. J. (1985). Review of Myers-Briggs Type Indicator. In J. V. Mitchell (Ed.), *The ninth mental measurements yearbook* (pp. 1029–1032). Lincoln, NE: Buros Institute of Mental Measurements.

Diamond, M. J., Gregory, J., Lenney, E., Steadman, D., & Talone, J. M. (1974). An alternative approach to personality correlates of hypnotizability: Hypnosis-specific mediational attitudes. *International Journal of Clinical and Experimental Hypnosis, 22*, 346–353.

DiClemente, C. C. (1986). Self-efficacy and the addictive behaviors. *Journal of Social and Clinical Psychology, 4*, 302–315.

Diener, E. (1976). Effects of self-awareness on antinormative behavior. *Journal of Research in Personality, 10*, 107–111.

Diener, E. (1979). Deindividuation, self-awareness, and disinhibition. *Journal of Personality and Social Psychology, 37*, 1160–1171.

Diener, E. (1980). Deindividuation: The absence of self-awareness and self-regulation in group members. In P. B. Paulus (Ed.), *Psychology of group influence* (pp. 209–242). Hillsdale, NJ: Erlbaum.

Diener, E. (1984). Subjective well-being. *Psychological Bulletin, 95*, 542–575.

Diener, E., Fraser, S. C., Beaman, A. L., & Kelem, R. T. (1976). Effects of deindividuation variables on stealing among Halloween trick-or-treaters. *Journal of Personality and Social Psychology, 33*, 178–183.

Diener, E., & Wallbom, M. (1976). Effects of self-awareness on antinormative behavior. *Journal of Research in Personality, 10*, 107–111.

Digman, J. M. (1989). Five robust trait dimensions: Development, stability, and utility. *Journal of Personality, 57*, 195–214.

Digman, J. M., & Inouye, J. (1986). Further specification of the five robust factors of personality. *Journal of Personality and Social Psychology, 50*, 116–123.

DiLalla, L. F., & Gottesman, I. I. (1991). Biological and genetic contributors to violence — Widom's untold tale. *Psychological Bulletin, 109*, 125–129.

Dimitrovsky, L., Singer, J., & Yinon, Y. (1989). Masculine and feminine traits: Their relation to suitedness for and success in training for traditionally masculine and feminine army functions. *Journal of Personality and Social Psychology, 57*, 839–847.

Dixon, T. M., & Baumeister, R. F. (1991). Escaping the self: The moderating effect of self-complexity. *Personality and Social Psychology Bulletin, 17*, 363–368.

Dobson, K. S. (1989). A meta-analysis of the efficacy of cognitive therapy for depression. *Journal of Consulting and Clinical Psychology, 57*, 414–419.

Dodge, K. A., & Crick, N. R. (1990). Social information-processing bases of aggressive behavior in children. *Personality and Social Psychology Bulletin, 16*, 8–22.

Dodge, K. A., & Somberg, D. R. (1987). Hostile attributional biases among aggressive boys are exacerbated under conditions of threats to the self. *Child Development, 58*, 213–224.

Dodge, K. A., & Tomlin, A. M. (1987). Utilization of self-schemas as a mechanism of interpretational bias in children. *Social Cognition, 5*, 280–300.

Doherty, W. J. (1983). Impact of divorce on locus of control orientation in adult women: A longitudinal study. *Journal of Personality and Social Psychology, 44*, 834–840.

Dollard, J., Doob, L., Miller, N. E., Mowrer, O. H., & Sears, R. R. (1939). *Frustration and aggression.* New Haven, CT: Yale University Press.

Dollard, J., & Miller, N. E. (1950). *Personality and psychotherapy: An analysis in terms of learning, thinking, and culture.* New York: McGraw-Hill.

Donnelly, D. A., & Murray, E. J. (1991). Cognitive and emotional changes in written essays and therapy interviews. *Journal of Social and Clinical Psychology, 10*, 334–350.

Doob, L. W., & Sears, R. R. (1939). Factors determining substitute behavior and the overt expression of aggression. *Journal of Abnormal and Social Psychology, 34*, 293–313.

Duck, S. W. (1973). *Personal relationships and personal constructs: A study of friendship formation.* London: Wiley.

Duck, S. W. (1979). The personal and interpersonal in construct theory: Social and individual aspects of relationships. In P. Stringer & D. Bannister (Eds.), *Constructs of sociality and individuality* (pp. 279–297). London: Academic Press.

Duck, S. W., & Allison, D. (1978). I liked you but I can't live with you: A study of lapsed friendships. *Social Behavior and Personality, 6,* 43–47.

Duck, S. W., & Craig, G. (1978). Personality similarity and the development of friendship: A longitudinal study. *British Journal of Social and Clinical Psychology, 17,* 237–242.

Duck, S. W., & Spencer, C. (1972). Personal constructs and friendship formation. *Journal of Personality and Social Psychology, 23,* 40–45.

Dworkin, E. S., & Efran, J. S. (1967). The angered: Their susceptibility to varieties of humor. *Journal of Personality and Social Psychology, 6,* 233–236.

Dworkin, R. H., Burke, B. W., Maher, B. A., & Gottesman, I. I. (1976). A longitudinal study of the genetics of personality. *Journal of Personality and Social Psychology, 34,* 510–518.

Dykman, B. M., & Abramson, L. Y. (1990). Contributions of basic research to the cognitive theories of depression. *Personality and Social Psychology Bulletin, 16,* 42–57.

Eaves, L., & Eysenck, H. (1975). Utilization of self-schemas as a mechanism of interpretational bias in children. *Social Cognition, 5,* 280–300.

Edwards, A. L. (1957). *The social desirability variable in personality research.* New York: Dryden.

Edwards, A. L. (1959). *Manual for the Edwards Personal Preference Schedule.* New York: The Psychological Corporation.

Edwards, V. J., & Spence, J. T. (1987). Gender-related traits, stereotypes, and schemata. *Journal of Personality and Social Psychology, 53,* 146–154.

Ehrlich, H. J., & Graeven, D. B. (1971). Reciprocal self-disclosure in a dyad. *Journal of Experimental Social Psychology, 7,* 389–400.

Ellis, A. E. (1971). *Growth through reason: Verbatim cases in rational-emotive therapy.* North Hollywood, CA: Wilshire.

Ellis, A. (1973). *Humanistic psychotherapy: The rational-emotive approach.* New York: McGraw-Hill.

Ellis, A. E. (1987). The impossibility of achieving consistently good mental health. *American Psychologist, 42,* 364–375.

Ellis, A., & Harper, R. A. (1975). *A new guide to rational living.* North Hollywood, CA: Wilshire.

Emmons, R. A., & Diener, E. (1986). Influence of impulsivity and sociability on subjective well-being. *Journal of Personality and Social Psychology, 50,* 1211–1215.

Endler, N. S., & Hunt, J. M. (1966). Sources of behavioral variance as measured by the S-R inventory of anxiousness. *Psychological Bulletin, 65,* 336–346.

Endler, N. S., & Hunt, J. M. (1968). S-R inventories of hostility and comparisons of the proportions of variance from persons, responses, and situations for hostility and anxiousness. *Journal of Personality and Social Psychology, 9,* 309–315.

Endler, N. S., & Magnusson, D. (1976). Toward an interactional psychology of personality. *Psychological Bulletin, 83,* 956–974.

Epstein, S. (1979). The stability of behavior: I. On predicting most of the people much of the time. *Journal of Personality and Social Psychology, 37,* 1097–1126.

Epstein, S. (1980). The stability of behavior: II. Implications for psychological research. *American Psychologist, 35,* 790–806.

Epstein, S. (1983). Aggregation and beyond: Some basic issues on the prediction of behavior. *Journal of Personality, 51,* 360–392.

Epstein, S. (1986). Does aggregation produce spuriously high estimates of behavior stability? *Journal of Personality and Social Psychology, 50,* 1199–1210.

Epstein, S., & Fenz, W. D. (1965). Steepness of approach and avoidance gradients in humans as a function of experience: Theory and experiment. *Journal of Experimental Psychology, 70,* 1–12.

Erikson, E. H. (1950/1963). *Childhood and society* (2nd ed.). New York: Norton.

Erikson, E. H. (1968). *Identity: Youth and crisis.* New York: Norton.

Erikson, E. H. (1975). *Life history and the historical moment.* New York: Norton.

Erickson, M. H. (1939). Experimental demonstration of the psychopathology of everyday life. *Psychoanalytic Quarterly, 8,* 338–353.

Erickson, M. H. (1967). *Advanced techniques of hypnosis and therapy: Selected papers of Milton H. Erickson.* New York: Grune & Stratton.

Eron, L. D. (1987). The development of aggressive behavior from the perspective of a developing behaviorism. *American Psychologist, 42,* 435–442.

Evans, G. W., Palsane, M. N., & Carrere, S. (1987). Type A behavior and occupational stress: A cross-cultural study of blue-collar workers. *Journal of Personality and Social Psychology, 52,* 1002–1007.

Evans, R. I. (1976). *The making of psychology.* New York: Knopf.

Eysenck, H. J. (1967). *The biological basis of personality.* Springfield, IL: Charles C. Thomas.

Eysenck, H. J. (1982). Development of a theory. In C. D. Spielberger (Ed.), *Personality, ge-*

netics and behavior (pp. 1–38). New York: Praeger.

Eysenck, H. J. (1990). Biological dimensions of personality. In L. Pervin (Ed.), *Handbook of personality theory and research* (pp. 244–276). New York: Guilford.

Eysenck, H. J., & Eysenck, S. B. G. (1968). *Manual for the Eysenck Personality Inventory.* San Diego, CA: Educational and Industrial Testing Service.

Eysenck, S. B. G., & Long, F. Y. (1986). A cross-cultural comparison of personality in adults and children: Singapore and England. *Journal of Personality and Social Psychology, 50,* 124–130.

Falbo, T. (1981). Relationships between birth category, achievement, and interpersonal orientation. *Journal of Personality and Social Psychology, 41,* 121–131.

Fazio, R. H., Cooper, M., Dayson, K., & Johnson, M. (1981). Control and the coronary-prone behavior pattern: Responses to multiple situational demands. *Personality and Social Psychology Bulletin, 7,* 97–102.

Feingold, A. (1990). Gender differences in effects of physical attractiveness on romantic attraction: A comparison across five research paradigms. *Journal of Personality and Social Psychology, 59,* 981–993.

Felson, R. B., & Russo, N. (1988). Parental punishment and sibling aggression. *Social Psychology Quarterly, 51,* 11–18.

Fenigstein, A. (1979). Does aggression cause a preference for viewing media violence? *Journal of Personality and Social Psychology, 37,* 2307–2317.

Fenigstein, A. (1987). On the nature of public and private self-consciousness. *Journal of Personality, 55,* 543–554.

Fenigstein, A., Scheier, M. F., & Buss, A. H. (1975). Public and private self-consciousness: Assessment and theory. *Journal of Consulting and Clinical Psychology, 43,* 522–527.

Fenz, W. D., & Epstein, S. (1967). Gradients of physiological arousal in parachutists as a function of an approaching jump. *Psychosomatic Medicine, 23,* 33–51.

Findley, M. J., & Cooper, H. M. (1983). Locus of control and academic achievement: A literature review. *Journal of Personality and Social Psychology, 44,* 419–427.

Fischman, J. (1987, February). Type A on trial. *Psychology Today,* pp. 42–50.

Fisher, C. B., Glenwick, D. S., & Blumenthal, R. S. (1986). Subliminal Oedipal stimuli and competitive performance: An investigation of between-groups effects and mediating subject variables. *Journal of Abnormal Psychology, 95,* 292–294.

Fiske, D. W. (1988). From inferred personalities toward personality in action. *Journal of Personality, 56,* 815–833.

Floderus-Myrhed, B., Pederson, N., & Rasmuson, I. (1980). Assessment of heritability for personality, based on a short-form of the Eysenck Personality Inventory: A study of 12,898 twin pairs. *Behavior Genetics, 10,* 153–162.

Folkman, S. (1984). Personal control and stress and coping processes: A theoretical analysis. *Journal of Personality and Social Psychology, 46,* 839–852.

Folkman, S., & Lazarus, R. S. (1980). An analysis of coping in a middle-aged community sample. *Journal of Health and Social Behavior, 21,* 219–239.

Forer, B. R. (1949). The fallacy of personal validation: A classroom demonstration of gullibility. *Journal of Abnormal and Social Psychology, 44,* 118–123.

Fox, N. A., & Davidson, R. J. (1986). Taste-elicited changes in facial signs of emotion and the asymmetry of brain electrical activity in human newborns. *Neuropsychologia, 24,* 417–422.

Fox, N. A., & Davidson, R. J. (1987). Electroencephalogram asymmetry in response to the approach of a stranger and maternal separation of 10-month-old infants. *Developmental Psychology, 23,* 233–240.

Fox, N. A., & Davidson, R. J. (1988). Patterns of electrical activity during facial signs of emotion in 10-month-old infants. *Developmental Psychology, 24,* 230–236.

Frable, D. E. S. (1989). Sex typing and gender ideology: Two facets of the individual's gender psychology that go together. *Journal of Personality and Social Psychology, 56,* 95–108.

Frable, D. E. S., & Bem, S. L. (1985). If you're gender schematic, all members of the opposite sex look alike. *Journal of Personality and Social Psychology, 49,* 459–468.

Frankel, A., & Prentice-Dunn, S. (1990). Loneliness and the processing of self-relevant information. *Journal of Social and Clinical Psychology, 9,* 303–315.

Frankl, V. E., (1959). *Man's search for meaning: An introduction to Logotherapy.* New York: Beacon.

Fransella, F., & Bannister, D. (1977). *A manual for repertory grid technique.* New York: Academic Press.

Frauman, D. C., Lynn, S. J., Hardaway, R., & Molteni, A. (1984). Effect of subliminal symbiotic activation on hypnotic rapport and susceptibility. *Journal of Abnormal Psychology, 93,* 481–483.

Freedman, J. L. (1984). Effect of television violence on aggressiveness. *Psychological Bulletin, 96,* 227–246.

Freedman, J. L. (1986). Television violence and aggression: A rejoinder. *Psychological Bulletin, 100,* 372–378.

Freedman, S. M., & Phillips, J. S. (1989). Goal utility, task satisfaction, and the self-appraisal hypothesis of Type A behavior. *Journal of Personality and Social Psychology, 56,* 465–470.

Freud, S. *The complete psychological works of Sigmund Freud* (Vols. 1–24). London: Hogarth Press.

Friedman, M., & Rosenman, R. (1974). *Type A behavior and your heart.* New York: Knopf.

Friedrich-Cofer, L., & Huston, A. C. (1986). Television violence and aggression: The debate continues. *Psychological Bulletin, 100,* 364–371.

Fromm, E. (1941/1965). *Escape from freedom.* New York: Avon.

Fromm, E. (1950). *Psychoanalysis and religion.* New Haven, CT: Yale University Press.

Fromm, E. (1956/1974). *The art of loving.* New York: Harper & Row.

Fromm, E. (1962). *Beyond the chains of illusion: My encounter with Marx and Freud.* New York: Touchstone.

Fromm, E. (1966). *You shall be as gods.* Greenwich, CT: Fawcett.

Fromm-Reichman, F. (1959). Loneliness. *Psychiatry, 22,* 1–15.

Funder, D. C., & Colvin, C. R. (1991). Explorations in behavioral consistency: Properties of persons, situations, and behaviors. *Journal of Personality and Social Psychology, 60,* 773–794.

Funder, D. C., & Ozer, D. J. (1983). Behavior as a function of the situation, *Journal of Personality and Social Psychology, 44,* 107–112.

Gale, A. (1983). Electroencephalographic studies of extraversion-introversion: A case study in the psychophysiology of individual differences. *Personality and Individual Differences, 4,* 371–380.

Garber, J., & Seligman, M. E. P. (Eds.) (1980). *Human helplessness: Theory and applications.* New York: Academic Press.

Garcia, J., & Koelling, R. A. (1966). Relation of cue to consequence in avoidance learning. *Psychometric Science, 4,* 123–124.

Garcia, S., Stinson, L., Ickes, W., Bissonnette, V., & Briggs, S. R. (1991). Shyness and physical attractiveness in mixed-sex dyads. *Journal of Personality and Social Psychology, 61,* 35–49.

Gastorf, J. W. (1980). Time urgency of the Type A behavior pattern. *Journal of Consulting and Clinical Psychology, 48,* 299.

Gatchel, R. J., Paulus, P. B., & Maples, C. W. (1975). Learned helplessness and self-reported affect. *Journal of Abnormal Psychology, 84,* 732–734.

Gayton, W. F., Bassett, J. E., Tavormina, J., & Ozmon, K. L. (1978). Repression-sensitization and health behavior. *Journal of Consulting and Clinical Psychology, 46,* 1542–1544.

Geen, R. G. (1981). Behavioral and physiological reactions to observed violence: Effects of prior exposure to aggressive stimuli. *Journal of Personality and Social Psychology, 40,* 868–875.

Geen, R. G. (1983a). Aggression and television violence. In R. G. Geen and E. I. Donnerstein (Eds.), *Aggression: Theoretical and empirical reviews* (Vol. 2, pp. 103–125). New York: Academic Press.

Geen, R. G. (1983b). The psychophysiology of extraversion-introversion. In J. T. Cacioppo & R. E. Petty (Eds.), *Social psychophysiology: A sourcebook* (pp. 391–416). New York: Guilford.

Geen, R. G. (1984). Preferred stimulation levels in introverts and extraverts: Effects on arousal and performance. *Journal of Personality and Social Psychology, 46,* 1303–1312.

Geen, R. G., & Quanty, M. B. (1977). The catharsis of aggression: An evaluation of a hypothesis. In L. Berkowitz (Ed.), *Advances in experimental social psychology* (Vol. 10, pp. 1–37). New York: Academic Press.

Geen, R. G., Stonner, D., & Shope, G. L. (1975). The facilitation of aggression by aggression: Evidence against the catharsis hypothesis. *Journal of Personality and Social Psychology, 31,* 721–726.

Geen, R. G., & Thomas, S. L. (1986). The immediate effects of media violence on behavior. *Journal of Social Issues, 42,* 7–27.

Geisler, C. (1986). The use of subliminal psychodynamic activation in the study of repression. *Journal of Personality and Social Psychology, 51,* 844–851.

Gendlin, E. T. (1988). Carl Rogers (1902–1987). *American Psychologist, 43,* 127–128.

Genero, N., & Cantor, N. (1987). Exemplar prototypes and clinical diagnosis: Toward a cognitive economy. *Journal of Social and Clinical Psychology, 5,* 59–78.

Gerbner, G., & Gross, L. (1976, April). The scary world of TV's heavy viewer. *Psychology Today,* pp. 41–44, 89.

Gergen, K. J., Gergen, M. M., & Barton, W. H. (1973, October). Deviance in the dark. *Psychology Today,* pp. 129–130.

Gerrard, M. (1982). Sex, sex guilt, and contraceptive use. *Journal of Personality and Social Psychology, 42,* 153–158.

Gerrard, M. (1987). Sex, sex guilt, and contraceptive use revisited: The 1980s. *Journal of Personality and Social Psychology, 52,* 975–980.

Gerson, A. C., & Perlman, D. (1979). Loneliness and expressive communication. *Journal of Abnormal Psychology, 88,* 258–261.

Gersten, M. (1989). Behavioral inhibition in the classroom. In J. S. Reznick (Ed.), *Perspectives on behavioral inhibition* (pp. 71–91). Chicago: University of Chicago Press.

Gfeller, J. D., Lynn, S. J., & Pribble, W. E. (1987). Enhancing hypnotic susceptibility: Interpersonal and rapport factors. *Journal of Personality and Social Psychology, 52,* 586–595.

Gibson, H. B. (1981). *Hans Eysenck: The man and his work.* London: Peter Owen.

Gilbert, L., Deutsch, C. L., & Strahan, R. F. (1978). Feminine and masculine dimensions of the typical, desirable and ideal woman and man. *Sex Roles, 4,* 767–778.

Gill, M. M., & Brenman, M. (1967). The metapsychology of regression and hypnosis. In J. E. Gordon (Ed.), *The handbook of clinical and experimental hypnosis* (pp. 281–318). New York: Macmillan.

Gilmor, T. M., & Reid, D. W. (1978). Locus of control, prediction, and performance on university examinations. *Journal of Consulting and Clinical Psychology, 46,* 565–566.

Gilmor, T. M., & Reid, D. W. (1979). Locus of control and causal attribution for positive and negative outcomes on university examinations. *Journal of Research in Personality, 13,* 154–160.

Glass, C. R., & Shea, C. A. (1986). Cognitive therapy for shyness and social anxiety. In W. H. Jones, J. M. Cheek, & S. R. Briggs (Eds.), *Shyness: Perspectives on research and treatment* (pp. 315–327). New York: Plenum.

Glass, D. C. (1977). *Behavior patterns, stress, and coronary disease.* Hillsdale, NJ: Erlbaum.

Glass, D. C., Snyder, M. L., & Hollis, J. (1974). Time urgency and the Type A coronary-prone behavior pattern. *Journal of Applied Social Psychology, 4,* 125–140.

Glisky, M. L., Tataryn, D. J., Tobias, B. A., Kihlstrom, J. F., & McConkey, K. M. (1991). *Journal of Personality and Social Psychology, 60,* 263–272.

Goldberg, L. R. (1990). An alternative "description of personality": The big-five factor structure. *Journal of Personality and Social Psychology, 59,* 1216–1229.

Gorassini, D., Sowerby, D., Creighton, A., & Fry, G. (1991). Hypnotic susceptibility enhancement through brief cognitive skill training. *Journal of Personality and Social Psychology, 61,* 289–297.

Gorassini, D. R., & Spanos, N. P. (1986). A social-cognitive skills approach to the successful modification of hypnotic susceptibility. *Journal of Personality and Social Psychology, 50,* 1004–1012.

Goswick, R. A., & Jones, W. H. (1981). Loneliness, self-concept, and adjustment. *Journal of Psychology, 88,* 258–261.

Gotay, C. C. (1981). Cooperation and competition as a function of Type A behavior. *Personality and Social Psychology Bulletin, 7,* 386–392.

Gotlib, I. H. (1981). Self-reinforcement and recall: Differential deficits in depressed and nondepressed psychiatric patients. *Journal of Abnormal Psychology, 90,* 521–530.

Gotlib, I. H. (1983). Perception and recall of interpersonal feedback: Negative bias in depression. *Cognitive Therapy and Research, 7,* 399–412.

Gough, H. G. (1956). *Manual for the California Psychological Inventory.* Palo Alto, CA: Consulting Psychologists Press.

Gough, H. G. (1987). *Manual for the California Psychological Inventory—Revised Edition.* Palo Alto, CA: Consulting Psychologists Press.

Gough, H. G., Fioravanti, M., & Lazzari, R. (1983). Some implications of self versus ideal-self congruence on the Revised Adjective Check List. *Journal of Personality and Social Psychology, 44,* 1214–1220.

Gough, H. G., Lazzari, R., & Fioravanti, M. (1978). Self versus ideal self: A comparison of five adjective check list indices. *Journal of Consulting and Clinical Psychology, 46,* 1085–1091.

Gourlay, N. (1979). Heredity versus environment: An integrative analysis. *Psychological Bulletin, 86,* 596–615.

Granberg, D. (1972). Authoritarianism and the assumption of similarity to self. *Journal of Experimental Research in Personality, 6,* 1–4.

Gray, J. A. (1981). A critique of Eysenck's theory of personality. In H. J. Eysenck (Ed.), A model for personality (pp. 246–276). New York: Springer.

Greenberg, R., Pillard, R., & Pearlman, C. (1978). The effect of dream (stage REM) deprivation on adaptation to stress. In S. Fisher & R. P. Greenberg (Eds.), *The scientific evaluation of Freud's theories and therapy* (pp. 40–48). New York: Basic Books.

Greene, D., Sternberg, B., & Lepper, M. R. (1976). Overjustification in token economy. *Journal of Personality and Social Psychology, 34,* 1219–1234.

Grove, J. R., Hanrahan, S. J., & McInman, A. (1991). Success/failure bias in attributions across involvement categories in sport. *Personality and Social Psychology Bulletin, 17,* 93–97.

Gur, R. C., & Reivich, M. (1980). Cognitive task effects on hemispheric blood flow in humans: Evidence for individual differences in hemispheric activation. *Brain and Language, 9,* 78–92.

Haber, R. A. (1980). Different strokes for different folks: Jung's typology and structured experience. *Group and Organizational Studies, 5,* 113–119.

Haemmerlie, F. M., & Montgomery, R. L. (1986). Self-perception theory and the treatment of shyness. In W. H. Jones, J. M. Cheek, & S. R. Briggs (Eds.), *Shyness: Perspectives on research and treatment* (pp. 329–342). New York: Plenum.

Hale, C. L. (1980). Cognitive complexity-simplicity as a determinant of communication effectiveness. *Communication Monographs, 47,* 304–311.

Hale, C. L., & Delia, J. G. (1976). Cognitive complexity and social perspective-taking. *Communication Monographs, 43,* 195–203.

Hall, C. S., (1953). A cognitive theory of dream symbols. *Journal of General Psychology, 48,* 169–186.

Hall, C. S. (1984). "A ubiquitous sex difference in dreams" revisited. *Journal of Personality and Social Psychology, 46,* 1109–1117.

Hall, C. S., & Domhoff, B. (1963). A ubiquitous sex difference in dreams. *Journal of Abnormal and Social Psychology, 66,* 278–280.

Hall, M. H. (1968, August). A conversation with the president of the American Psychological Association: The psychology of universality. *Psychology Today,* pp. 35–37, 54–57.

Hanley-Dunn, P., Maxwell, S. E., & Santos, J. F. (1985). Interpretation of interpersonal interaction: The influence of loneliness. *Personality and Social Psychology Bulletin, 11,* 445–456.

Hargadon, F. (1981). Tests and college admissions. *American Psychologist, 36,* 1112–1119.

Harris, D. B. (1963). *Children's drawings as measures of intellectual maturity.* New York: Harcourt, Brace & World.

Harris, M. B. (1974). Mediators between frustration and aggression in a field experiment. *Journal of Experimental Social Psychology, 10,* 561–571.

Harris, R. M. (1981). Conceptual complexity and preferred coping strategies in anticipation of temporally predictable and unpredictable threat. *Journal of Personality and Social Psychology, 41,* 380–390.

Harris, R. N., & Snyder, C. R. (1986). The role of uncertain self-esteem in self-handicapping. *Journal of Personality and Social Psychology, 51,* 451–458.

Harrison, A. A., & Saeed, L. (1977). Let's make a deal: An analysis of revelations and stipulations in lonely hearts advertisements. *Journal of Personality and Social Psychology, 35,* 257–264.

Hartshorne, H., & May, M. A. (1928). *Studies in the nature of character: Studies in deceit.* New York: Macmillan.

Harvey, J. H. (Ed.) (1986). Special issue: Self-efficacy theory in contemporary psychology. *Journal of Social and Clinical Psychology, 4*(3).

Haspel, K. C., & Harris, R. S. (1982). Effect of tachistoscopic stimulation of subconscious Oedipal wishes on competitive performance: A failure to replicate. *Journal of Abnormal Psychology, 91,* 437–443.

Hayes, S. C. (1981). Single case experimental design and empirical clinical practice. *Journal of Consulting and Clinical Psychology, 49,* 193–211.

Headey, B., & Wearing, A. (1989). Personality, life events, and subjective well-being: Toward a dynamic equilibrium model. *Journal of Personality and Social Psychology, 57,* 731–739.

Heatherton, T. F., & Polivy, J. (1991). Development and validation of a scale for measuring state self-esteem. *Journal of Personality and Social Psychology, 60,* 895–910.

Heilbrun, K. S. (1980). Silverman's subliminal psychodynamic activation: A failure to replicate. *Journal of Abnormal Psychology, 89,* 560–566.

Heilbrun, K. S. (1982). Reply to Silverman. *Journal of Abnormal Psychology, 91,* 134–135.

Helmreich, R. L., Spence, J. T., & Pend, R. S. (1988). Making it without losing it: Type A, achievement motivation, and scientific attainment revisited. *Personality and Social Psychology Bulletin, 14,* 495–504.

Hendrick, S. S. (1981). Self-disclosure and marital satisfaction. *Journal of Personality and Social Psychology, 40,* 1150–1159.

Henriques, J. B., & Davidson, R. J. (1990). Regional brain electrical asymmetries discriminate between previously depressed and healthy control subjects. *Journal of Abnormal Psychology, 99,* 22–31.

Higgins, E. T. (1989a). Self-discrepancy theory: What patterns of self-beliefs cause people to suffer? In L. Berkowitz (Ed.), *Advances in experimental social psychology, Vol. 22* (pp. 93–136). New York; Academic Press.

Higgins, E. T. (1989b). Continuities and discontinuities in self-regulatory and self-evaluative processes: A developmental theory relating self and affect. *Journal of Personality, 57,* 407–444.

Higgins, E. T., Bond, R. N., Klein, R., & Strauman, T. (1986). Self-discrepancies and emotional vulnerability: How magnitude, accessibility, and type of discrepancy influence affect. *Journal of Personality and Social Psychology, 51,* 5–15.

Higgins, E. T., Klein, R., & Strauman, T. (1985). Self-concept discrepancy theory: A psychological model for distinguishing among different aspects of depression and anxiety. *Social Cognition, 3,* 51–76.

Hilgard, E. R. (1973). A neodissociation interpretation of pain reduction in hypnosis. *Psychological Review, 80,* 396–411.

Hilgard, E. R. (1977). *Divided consciousness: Multiple controls in human thought and action.* New York: Wiley.

Hilgard, J. R. (1970). *Personality and hypnosis.* Chicago: University of Chicago Press.

Hill, G. J. (1989). An unwillingness to act: Behavioral appropriateness, situational constraint, and self-efficacy in shyness. *Journal of Personality, 57,* 871–890.

Hiroto, D. S. (1974). Locus of control and learned helplessness. *Journal of Experimental Psychology, 102,* 187–193.

Hiroto, D. S., & Seligman, M. E. P. (1975). Generality of learned helplessness in man. *Journal of Personality and Social Psychology, 31,* 311–327.

Hoffman, L. W. (1974). Fear of success in males and females: 1965 and 1971. *Journal of Consulting and Clinical Psychology, 42,* 353–358.

Hoffman, L. W. (1985). The changing genetics/socialization balance. *Journal of Social Issues, 41,* 127–148.

Hogan, R. (1983). A socioanalytic theory of personality. In M. M. Page (Ed.), *1982 Nebraska Symposium on Motivation* (pp. 55–89). Lincoln: University of Nebraska Press.

Hokanson, J. E., & Burgess, M. (1962). Critique and notes: The effects of three types of aggression on vascular processes. *Journal of Abnormal and Social Psychology, 64,* 446–449.

Hokanson, J. E., & Edelman, R. (1966). Effects of three social responses on vascular processes. *Journal of Personality and Social Psychology, 3,* 442–447.

Hokanson, J. E., & Shetler, S. (1961). The effect of overt aggression on physiological arousal. *Journal of Abnormal and Social Psychology, 63,* 446–448.

Holahan, C. J., & Moos, R. H. (1987). Personal and contextual determinants of coping strategies. *Journal of Personality and Social Psychology, 52,* 946–955.

Holmes, D. S., McGilley, B. M., & Houston, B. K. (1984). Task-related arousal of Type A and Type B persons: Level of challenge and response specificity. *Journal of Personality and Social Psychology, 46,* 1322–1327.

Hood, J., Moore, T. E., & Garner, D. M. (1982). Locus of control as a measure of ineffectiveness in anorexia nervosa. *Journal of Consulting and Clinical Psychology, 50,* 3–13.

Hood, T. C., & Back, K. W. (1971). Self-disclosure and the volunteer: A source of bias in laboratory experiments. *Journal of Personality and Social Psychology, 17,* 130–136.

Hoover, S., Skuja, A., & Cosper, J. (1979). Correlates of college students' loneliness. *Psychological Reports, 44,* 1116.

Horner, M. S. (1972). Toward an understanding of achievement-related conflicts in women. *Journal of Social Issues, 28,* 157–175.

Horney, K. (1937). *The neurotic personality of our time.* New York: Norton.

Horney, K. (1945/1966). *Our inner conflicts: A constructive theory of neurosis.* New York: Norton.

Horney, K. (1950). *Neurosis and human growth.* New York: Norton.

Horney, K. (1967). *Feminine psychology.* New York: Norton.

Hornstein, G. A. (1985). Intimacy in conversational style as a function of the degree of closeness between members of a dyad. *Journal of Personality and Social Psychology, 49,* 671–681.

Hornstein, G. A., & Truesdell, S. E. (1988). Development of intimate conversation in close relationships. *Journal of Social and Clinical Psychology, 7,* 49–64.

Horowitz, L. M., & de Sales French, R. (1979). Interpersonal problems of people who describe themselves as lonely. *Journal of Consulting and Clinical Psychology, 47,* 762–764.

Houston, B. K. (1972). Control over stress, locus of control and response to stress. *Journal of Personality and Social Psychology, 21,* 249–255.

Howard, J. H., Cunningham, D. A., & Rechnitzer, P. A. (1977). Work patterns associated with Type A behavior: A managerial population. *Human Relations, 30,* 825–836.

Howard, M. L., & Coe, W. C. (1980). The effects of context and subjects' perceived control in breaching posthypnotic amnesia. *Journal of Personality, 48,* 342–359.

Hoyt, M. F., & Singer, J. L. (1978). Psychological effects of REM ("dream") deprivation upon waking mentation. In A. M. Arkin, J. S. Antrobus, & S. J. Ellman (Eds.), *The mind in sleep: Psychology and psychophysiology* (pp. 487–510). Hillsdale, NJ: Erlbaum.

Huesmann, L. R. (1986). Psychological processes promoting the relation between exposure to media violence and aggressive behavior by the viewer. *Journal of Social Issues, 42,* 125–139.

Huesmann, L. R., Eron, L. D., Dubow, E. F., & Seebauer, E. (1987). Television viewing habits in childhood and adult aggression. *Child Development, 58,* 357–367.

Huesmann, L. R., Eron, L. D., & Yarmel, P. W. (1987). Intellectual functioning and aggression. *Journal of Personality and Social Psychology, 52,* 232–240.

Huesmann, L. R., & Malamuth, N. M. (Eds.) (1986). Media violence and antisocial behavior. *Journal of Social Issues, 42*(3).

Ickes, W., & Barnes, R. D. (1978). Boys and girls together — and alienated: On enacting stereotyped sex roles in mixed-sex dyads. *Journal of Personality and Social Psychology, 36,* 669–683.

Ickes, W., Robertson, E., Toke, W., & Teng, G. (1986). Naturalistic social cognition: Methodology, assessment, and validation. *Journal of Personality and Social Psychology, 51,* 66–82.

Ickes, W., Schermer, B., & Steeno, J. (1979). Sex and sex-role influence in same-sex dyads. *Social Psychology Quarterly, 42,* 373–385.

Iennarella, R. S., & Kaplan, M. F. (1988). Acceptance of personality descriptions by subjects: Individual and base-rate truthfulness. *Journal of Social and Clinical Psychology, 6,* 388–397.

Ingram, R. E., Kendall, P. C., Smith, T. W., Donnell, C., & Ronan, K. (1987). Cognitive specificity in emotional distress. *Journal of Personality and Social Psychology, 53,* 734–742.

Ingram, R. E., Smith, T. W., & Brehm, S. S. (1983). Depression and information processing: Self-schemata and the encoding of self-referent information. *Journal of Personality and Social Psychology, 45,* 412–420.

Jackson, L. A. (1983). The perception of androgyny and physical attractiveness: Two is better than one. *Personality and Social Psychology Bulletin, 9,* 405–413.

Jackson, L. A., Ialongo, N., & Stollak, G. E. (1986). Parental correlates of gender role: The relations between parents' masculinity, femininity, and child-rearing behaviors and their children's gender roles. *Journal of Social and Clinical Psychology, 4,* 204–224.

Jahoda, M. (1977). *Freud and the dilemmas of psychology.* New York: Basic Books.

Janda, L. H., & O'Grady, E. E. (1980). Development of a sex anxiety inventory. *Journal of Consulting and Clinical Psychology, 48,* 169–175.

Jankowicz, A. D. (1987). Whatever became of George Kelly? Applications and implications. *American Psychologist, 42,* 481–487.

Jenkins, C. D. (1971). Psychologic and social precursors of coronary disease. *New England Journal of Medicine, 284,* 244–255, 307–317.

Jenkins, C. D. (1976). Recent evidence supporting psychologic and social risk factors for coronary disease. *New England Journal of Medicine, 294,* 987–994, 1033–1038.

Jenkins, C. D., Zyzanski, S. J., & Rosenman, R. H. (1976). Risk of new myocardial infarction in middle-age men with manifest coronary heart disease. *Circulation, 53,* 342–347.

Jenkins, S. R. (1987). Need for achievement and women's careers over 14 years: Evidence for occupational structure effects. *Journal of Personality and Social Psychology, 53,* 922–932.

Jennings, J., Geis, F. L., & Brown, V. (1980). Influence of television commercials on women's self-confidence and independent judgment. *Journal of Personality and Social Psychology, 38,* 203–210.

Jensen, A. R. (1969). How much can we boost IQ and scholastic achievement? *Harvard Educational Review, 39,* 1–123.

John, O. P. (1990). The "big five" factor taxonomy: Dimensions of personality in the natural language and in questionnaires. In L. A. Pervin (Ed.), *Handbook of personality: Theory and research* (pp. 66–100). New York: Guilford.

Johnson, J. T., Cain, L. M., Falke, T. L., Hayman, J., & Perillo, E. (1985). The "Barnum effect" revisited: Cognitive and motivational factors in the acceptance of personality descriptions. *Journal of Personality and Social Psychology, 49,* 1378–1391.

Johnson, R. D., & Downing, L. L. (1979). Deindividuation and valence of cues: Effects on prosocial and antisocial behavior. *Journal of Personality and Social Psychology, 37,* 1532–1538.

Jones, A., & Crandall, R. (1986). Validation of a short index of self-actualization. *Personality and Social Psychology Bulletin, 12,* 63–73.

Jones, E. (1953–1957). *The life and work of Sigmund Freud (Vols. 1–3).* New York: Basic Books.

Jones, W. H. (1982). Loneliness and social behavior. In L. A. Peplau & D. Perlman (Eds.), *Loneliness.* New York: Wiley.

Jones, W. H., Freemon, J. E., & Goswick, R. A. (1982). The persistence of loneliness: Self and other determinants. *Journal of Personality, 49,* 27–48.

Jones, W. H., Hobbs, S. A., & Hockenbury, D. (1982). Loneliness and social skill deficits. *Journal of Personality and Social Psychology, 42,* 682–689.

Jones, W. H., Sansone, C., & Helm, B. (1983). Loneliness and interpersonal judgments. *Personality and Social Psychology Bulletin, 9,* 437–441.

Josephson, W. L. (1987). Television violence and children's aggression: Testing the priming social script, and disinhibition predictions. *Journal of Personality and Social Psychology, 53,* 882–890.

Jourard, S. M. (1971). *The transparent self* (2nd ed.). New York: Van Nostrand.

Jourard, S. M., & Friedman, R. (1970). Experimenter-subject "distance" and self-disclosure. *Journal of Personality and Social Psychology, 15,* 278–282.

Jung, C. G. *The collected works of Carl Jung* (Vols. 1–17). Princeton, NJ: Princeton University Press.

Jung, C. G. (1933). *Modern man in search of a soul.* New York: Harcourt Brace Jovanovich.

Jung, C. G. (1961). *Memories, dreams, reflections.* New York: Pantheon Books.

Jung, C. G. (1964). Approaching the unconscious. In C. G. Jung (Ed.), *Man and his symbols* (pp. 3–94). New York: Dell.

Kagan, J. (1989). Temperamental contributions to social behavior. *American Psychologist, 44,* 668–674.

Kagan, J., & Moss, H. A. (1962). *Birth to maturity.* New York: Wiley.

Kagan, J., Reznick, J. S., & Snidman, N. (1986). Temperamental inhibition in early childhood. In R. Plomin & J. Dunn (Eds.), *The study of temperament: Changes, continuities and challenges* (pp. 53–65). Hillsdale, NJ: Erlbaum.

Kagan, J., Reznick, J. S., & Snidman, N. (1988). Biological bases of childhood shyness. *Science, 240,* 167–171.

Kagan, J., & Snidman, N. (1991a). Infant predictors of inhibited and uninhibited profiles. *Psychological Science, 2,* 40–44.

Kagan, J., & Snidman, N. (1991b). Temperamental factors in human development. *American Psychologist, 46,* 856–862.

Karylowski, J. J. (1990). Social reference points and accessibility of trait-related information in self-other similarity judgments. *Journal of Personality and Social Psychology, 58,* 975–983.

Katz, P., & Zigler, E. (1967). Self-image disparity: A development approach. *Journal of Personality and Social Psychology, 5,* 186–195.

Katz, P. A., Zigler, E., & Zalk, S. R. (1975). Children's self-image disparity: The effects of age, maladjustment, and action-thought orientation. *Development Psychology, 11,* 546–550.

Kazdin, A. E., & Wilcoxon, L. A. (1976). Systematic desensitization and nonspecific treatment effects: A methodological evaluation. *Psychological Bulletin, 83,* 729–758.

Kelly, G. A. (1955). *The psychology of personal constructs.* New York: Norton.

Kelly, G. A. (1969). *Clinical psychology and personality: The selected papers of George Kelly.* New York: Wiley.

Kendzierski, D. (1988). Self-schemata and exercise. *Basic and Applied Social Psychology, 9,* 45–61.

Kendzierski, D. (1990). Exercise self-schemata: Cognitive and behavioral correlates. *Health Psychology, 9,* 69–82.

Kenrick, D. T., & Funder, D. C. (1988). Profiting from controversy: Lessons from the person-situation debate. *American Psychologist, 43,* 23–34.

Keogh, B. K. (1986). Temperament and schooling: Meaning of "Goodness of fit"? In J. V. Lerner & R. M. Lerner (Eds.), *Temperament and social interaction during infancy and childhood* (pp. 89–108). San Francisco: Jossey-Bass.

Kernis, M. H., Brockner, J., & Frankel, B. S. (1989). Self-esteem and reactions to failure: The mediating role of overgeneralization. *Journal of Personality and Social Psychology, 57,* 707–714.

Kety, S. S., Rosenthal, D., Wender, P. H., & Schulsinger, F. (1976). Studies based on a total sample of adopted individuals and their relatives. *Schizophrenia Bulletin, 2,* 413–428.

Kihlstrom, J. F. (1985). Hypnosis. *Annual Review of Psychology, 36,* 385–418.

Kilmann, R. H., & Taylor, V. (1974). A contingency approach to laboratory learning: Psychological types versus experimental norms. *Human Relations, 27,* 891–909.

Kirschenbaum, H. (1979). *On becoming Carl Rogers.* New York: Delacorte Press.

Klein, D. C., & Seligman, M. E. P. (1976). Reversal of performance deficits and perceptual deficits in learned helplessness and depression. *Journal of Abnormal Psychology, 85,* 11–26.

Klein, E. B. (1963). Stylistic components of response as related to attitude change. *Journal of Personality, 31,* 38–51.

Klein, S. B., & Loftus, J. (1988). The nature of self-referent encoding: The contributions of elaborative and organizational processes. *Journal of Personality and Social Psychology, 55,* 5–11.

Klein, S. B., Loftus, J., & Burton, H. A. (1989). Two self-reference effects: The importance of distinguishing between self-descriptiveness judgments and autobiographical retrieval in self-referent encoding. *Journal of Personality and Social Psychology, 56,* 853–865.

Kleinke, C. L., & Kahn, M. L. (1980). Perceptions of self-disclosers: Effects of sex and physical attractiveness. *Journal of Personality, 48,* 190–205.

Klinger, B. I. (1970). Effect of peer model responsiveness and length of induction procedure on hypnotic responsiveness. *Journal of Abnormal Psychology, 75,* 15–18.

Kobasa, S. C. (1979). Stressful life events, personality, and health: An inquiry into hardiness. *Journal of Personality and Social Psychology, 37,* 1–11.

Konecni, V. J., & Doob, A. N. (1972). Catharsis through displacement of aggression. *Journal of Personality and Social Psychology, 23,* 379–387.

Koppett, L. (1978, February 11). Carrying statistics to extremes. *The Sporting News,* p. 9.

Koppett, L. (1981, September 19). Statistics are best used with a grain of salt. *The Sporting News,* p. 9.

Koppett, L. (1984, November 11). A stock market theory on the ropes. *Peninsula Times Tribune,* p. A-2.

Koppett, L. (1985, January 4). The perfect stock theory collapses. *Peninsula Times Tribune,* p. A-2.

Koppitz, E. M. (1968). *Psychological evaluation of children's human figure drawings.* New York: Grune & Stratton.

Korabik, K. (1982). Sex-role orientation and impressions: A comparison of differing genders and sex roles. *Personality and Social Psychology Bulletin, 8,* 25–30.

Koriat, A., Melkman, R., Averill, J. R., & Lazarus, R. S. (1972). The self-control of emotional reactions to a stressful film. *Journal of Personality, 40,* 601–619.

Korn, J. H., Davis, R., & Davis, S. F. (1991). Historians' and chairpersons' judgments of eminence among psychologists. *American Psychologist, 46,* 789–792.

Kuhlman, T. L. (1985). A study of salience and motivational theories of humor. *Journal of Personality and Social Psychology, 49,* 281–286.

Kuiper, N. A., & Derry, P. A. (1981). The self as a cognitive prototype: An application to person perception and depression. In N. Cantor & J. F. Kihlstrom (Eds.), *Personality, cognition, and social interaction* (pp. 215–231). Hillsdale, NJ: Erlbaum.

Kuiper, N. A., & Derry, P. A. (1982). Depressed and nondepressed self-reference in mild depressives. *Journal of Personality, 50,* 67–80.

Kuiper, N. A., & Higgins, E. T. (Eds.) (1985). Special issue on depression. *Social Cognition, 3*(1).

Kuiper, N. A., & MacDonald, M. R. (1982). Self and other perception in mild depressives. *Social Cognition, 1,* 223–239.

Kuiper, N. A., MacDonald, M. R., & Derry, P. A. (1983). Parameters of a depressive self-schema. In J. Suls & A. G. Greenwald (Eds.), *Psychological perspectives on the self* (Vol. 2, pp. 191–217). Hillsdale, NJ: Erlbaum.

Kuiper, N. A., & Rogers, T. B. (1979). Encoding of personal information: Self-other differences. *Journal of Personality and Social Psychology, 37,* 499–514.

Kulick, J. A., & Harackiewicz, J. (1979). Opposite-sex interpersonal attraction as a function of the sex roles of the perceiver and the perceived. *Sex Roles, 5,* 443–452.

Kurdek, L. A., & Schmitt, J. P. (1986). Interaction of sex role self-concept with relationship quality and relationship beliefs in married, heterosexual cohabiting, gay and lesbian couples. *Journal of Personality and Social Psychology, 51,* 365–370.

LaGasse, L., Gruber, C., & Lipsitt, L. P. (1989). The infantile expression of activity in relation to later assessments. In J. S. Reznick (Ed.), *Perspectives on behavioral inhibition* (pp. 159–176). Chicago: University of Chicago Press.

Lamke, L. K., & Bell, N. J. (1982). Sex-role orientation and relationship development in same-sex dyads. *Journal of Research in Personality, 16,* 343–354.

Landfield, A. W. (1984). Personal construct psychology: A developmental perspective. *Journal of Social and Clinical Psychology, 2,* 97–107.

Langer, E. J., & Rodin, J. (1976). The effects of choice and enhanced personal responsibility for the aged: A field experiment in an institutional setting. *Journal of Personality and Social Psychology, 34,* 191–198.

Larsen, R. J., & Kasimatis, M. (1990). Individual differences in entrainment of mood to the weekly calendar. *Journal of Personality and Social Psychology, 58,* 164–171.

Larsen, R. J., & Ketelaar, T. (1989). Extraversion, neuroticism and susceptibility to positive and negative mood induction procedures. *Personality and Individual Differences, 10,* 1221–1228.

Larsen, R. J., & Ketelaar, T. (1991). Personality and susceptibility to positive and negative emotional states. *Journal of Personality and Social Psychology, 61,* 132–140.

Larsen, R. J., & Seidman, E. (1986). Gender schema theory and sex role inventories: Some conceptual and psychometric considerations. *Journal of Personality and Social Psychology, 50,* 205–211.

Larson, D. G., & Chastain, R. L. (1990). Self-concealment: Conceptualization, measurement, and health implications. *Journal of Social and Clinical Psychology, 9,* 439–455.

Lax, E. (1991). *Woody Allen: A biography.* New York: Knopf.

Lazarus, R. (1968). Emotions and adaptation. In W. J. Arnold (Ed.), *Nebraska Symposium on Motivation.* Lincoln: University of Nebraska Press.

Lazarus, R. S. (1974). Cognitive and coping processes in emotion. In B. Weiner (Ed.), *Cognitive views of human motivation* (pp. 21–32). New York: Academic Press.

Lazarus, R. S., & Folkman, S. (1984). *Stress, appraisal and coping.* New York: Springer.

Leahy, R. L. (1981). Parental practices and the development of moral judgment and self-image disparity during adolescence. *Developmental Psychology, 17,* 580–594.

Leahy, R. L., & Huard, C. (1976). Role taking and self-image disparity in children. *Developmental Psychology, 12,* 504–508.

Leak, G. K. (1974). Effects of hostility arousal and aggressive humor on catharsis and humor preference. *Journal of Personality and Social Psychology, 30,* 736–740.

Leary, M. R. (1983a). Social anxiousness: The construct and its measurement. *Journal of Personality Assessment, 47,* 66–75.

Leary, M. R. (1983b). *Understanding social anxiety: Social, personality, and clinical perspectives.* Beverly Hills, CA: Sage.

Leary, M. R. (1986). The impact of interactional impediments on social anxiety and self-presentation. *Journal of Experimental Social Psychology, 22,* 122–135.

Leary, M. R., & Atherton, S. C. (1986). Self-efficacy, social anxiety, and inhibition in interpersonal encounters. *Journal of Social and Clinical Psychology, 4,* 256–267.

Leary, M. R., Knight, P. D., & Johnson, K. A. (1987). Social anxiety and dyadic conversation: A verbal response analysis. *Journal of Social and Clinical Psychology, 34,* 50.

Leary, M. R., & Meadows, S. (1991). Predictors, elicitors, and concomitants of social blushing. *Journal of Personality and Social Psychology, 60,* 254–262.

Lee, H. (1960). *To kill a mockingbird.* Philadelphia: J. B. Lippincott.

Lefcourt, H. M. (1981–1984). *Research with the locus of control construct* (Vol. 1–3). New York: Academic Press.

Lefcourt, H. M. (1982). *Locus of control: Current trends in theory and research* (2nd ed.). Hillsdale, NJ: Erlbaum.

Lefkowitz, M. M., Eron, L. D., Walder, L. O., & Huesmann, L. R. (1977). *Growing up to be violent: A longitudinal study of the development of aggression.* New York: Pergamon Press.

Lenney, E. (1991). Sex roles: The measurement of masculinity, femininity, and androgyny. In J. P. Robinson, P. R. Shaver, & L. S. Wrightsman (Eds.), *Measures of personality and social psychological attitudes* (pp. 573–660). San Diego, CA: Academic Press.

Leon, G. R., Gillum, B., Gillum, R., & Gouze, M. (1979). Personality stability and change over a 30-year period—middle age to old age. *Journal of Consulting and Clinical Psychology, 47,* 517–524.

Lerner, J. V. (1983). The role of temperament in psychosocial adaptation in early adolescents: A test of a "goodness of fit" model. *Journal of Genetic Psychology, 143,* 149–157.

Lerner, J. V., Lerner, R. M., & Zabski, S. (1985). Temperament and elementary school children's actual and rated academic performance: A test of a "goodness of fit" model. *Journal of Child Psychology and Psychiatry, 26,* 125–136.

Levenson, H. (1981). Differentiating among internality, powerful others, and chance. In H. M. Lefcourt (Ed.), *Research with the locus of control construct* (Vol. 1, pp. 15–63). New York: Academic Press.

Levin, I., & Stokes, J. P. (1986). An examination of the relation of individual difference variables to loneliness. *Journal of Personality, 54,* 717–733.

Levine, F. M., & Fasnacht, G. (1974). Token rewards may lead to token learning. *American Psychologist, 29,* 816–820.

Lewin, K. (1938). *The conceptual representation and measurement of psychological forces.* Durham, NC: Duke University Press.

Liebert, R. M., & Sprafkin, J. (1988). *The early window: Effects of television on children and youth* (3rd ed.). New York: Pergamon Press.

Lindholm, E., & Lowry, S. (1978). Alpha productivity in humans under conditions of false feedback. *Bulletin of the Psychonomic Society, 11,* 106–108.

Lindskold, S., & Propst, L. R. (1981). Deindividuation, self-awareness, and impression management. In J. T. Tedeschi (Ed.), *Impression management theory and social psychological research* (pp. 201–221). New York: Academic Press.

Linn, R. L. (1982). Admissions testing on trial. *American Psychologist, 37,* 279–291.

Linville, P. W. (1985). Self-complexity and affective extremity: Don't put all of your eggs in one cognitive basket. *Social Cognition, 3,* 94–120.

Linville, P. W. (1987). Self-complexity as a cognitive buffer against stress-related illness and depression. *Journal of Personality and Social Psychology, 52,* 663–676.

Littig, L. W., & Yeracaris, C. A. (1965). Achievement motivation and intergenerational occupational mobility. *Journal of Personality and Social Psychology, 1,* 386–389.

Lloyd, G. G., & Lishman, W. R. (1975). Effect of depression on the speed of recall of pleasant and unpleasant experiences. *Psychological Medicine, 5,* 173–180.

Lochman, J. E. (1987). Self- and peer perceptions and attributional biases of aggressive and nonaggressive boys in dyadic interactions. *Journal of Consulting and Clinical Psychology, 55,* 404–410.

Locksley, A., & Colten. M. E. (1979). Psychological androgyny: A case of mistaken identity? *Journal of Personality and Social Psychology, 37,* 1017–1031.

Loehlin, J. C., & Nichols, R. C. (1976). *Heredity, environment, and personality.* Austin: University of Texas Press.

Loehlin, J. C., Willerman, L., & Horn, J. M. (1982). Personality resemblances between unwed mothers and their adopted-away offspring. *Journal of Personality and Social Psychology, 42,* 1089–1099.

Loehlin, J., Willerman, L., & Horn, J. M. (1987). Personality resemblance in adoptive families: A 10-year follow-up. *Journal of Personality and Social Psychology, 53,* 961–969.

Lord, C. G. (1980). Schemas and images as memory aids: Two modes of processing social information. *Journal of Personality and Social Psychology, 38,* 257–269.

Lubin, B., Larsen, R. M., & Matarazzo, J. D. (1984). Patterns of psychological test usage in the United States: 1935–1982. *American Psychologist, 39,* 451–454.

Lubin, B., Larsen, R. M., Matarazzo, J. D., & Seever, M. (1985). Psychological test usage patterns in five professional settings. *American Psychologist, 40,* 857–861.

Lynn, S. J. (1978). Three theories of self-disclosure exchange. *Journal of Experimental Social Psychology, 14,* 466–479.

Lynn, S. J., Weekes, J. R., Neufeld, V., Zivney, O., Brentar, J., & Weiss, F. (1991). Interpersonal climate and hypnotizability level: Effects on hypnotic performance, rapport, and archaic involvement. *Journal of Personality and Social Psychology, 60,* 739–743.

Lytton, H. (1977). Do parents create, or respond to, differences in twins? *Developmental Psychology, 13,* 456–459.

McCarthy, E. D., Langner, T. S., Gersten, J. C., Eisenberg, J. G., & Orzeck, L. (1975). Violence and behavior disorders. *Journal of Communication, 25,* 71–85.

McCaul, K. D., & Maki, R. H. (1984). Self-reference versus desirability ratings and memory for traits. *Journal of Personality and Social Psychology, 47,* 953–955.

McCauley, C., Woods, K., Coolidge, C., & Kulick, W. (1983). More aggressive cartoons are funnier. *Journal of Personality and Social Psychology, 44,* 817–823.

McClelland, D. C. (1961). *The achieving society.* Princeton, NJ: Van Nostrand.

McClelland, D. C. (1965). N Achievement and entrepreneurship: A longitudinal study.

Journal of Personality and Social Psychology, 1, 389–392.

McClelland, D. C. (1978). Managing motivation to expand human freedom. *American Psychologist, 33,* 201–210.

McClelland, D. C. (1980). Motive dispositions: The merits of operant and respondent measures. In L. Wheeler (Ed.), *Review of personality and social psychology* (Vol. 1, pp. 10–41). Beverly Hills, CA: Sage.

McClelland, D. C. (1985). How motives, skill, and values determine what people do. *American Psychologist, 40,* 812–825.

McClelland, D. C., Atkinson, J. W., Clark, R. A., & Lowell, E. L. (1953). *The achievement motive.* New York: Appleton-Century-Crofts.

McClelland, D. C., & Boyatzis, R. E. (1982). Leadership motive pattern and long-term success in management. *Journal of Applied Psychology, 67,* 737–743.

McClelland, D. C., & Pilon, D. A. (1983). Sources of adult motives in patterns of parent behavior in early childhood. *Journal of Personality and Social Psychology, 44,* 564–574.

McClelland, D. C., & Winter, D. G. (1969). *Motivating economic achievement.* New York: Free Press.

McCrae, R. R., & Costa, P. T., Jr. (1983). Social desirability scales: More substance than style. *Journal of Consulting and Clinical Psychology, 51,* 882–888.

McCrae, R. R., & Costa, P. T. (1986a). Personality, coping, and coping effectiveness in an adult sample. *Journal of Personality, 54,* 385–405.

McCrae, R. R., & Costa, P. T. (1986b). Clinical assessment can benefit from recent advances in personality psychology. *American Psychologist, 41,* 1001–1003.

McCrae, R. R., & Costa, P. T. (1987). Validation of the five-factor model of personality across instruments and observers. *Journal of Personality and Social Psychology, 52,* 81–90.

McCrae, R. R., Costa, P. T., & Busch, C. M. (1986). Evaluating comprehensiveness in personality systems: The California Q-Set and the five-factor model. *Journal of Personality, 54,* 430–446.

McDowall, J. (1984). Recall of pleasant and unpleasant words in depressed subjects. *Journal of Abnormal Psychology, 93,* 401–407.

McElroy, E. (1950). Methods of testing the Oedipus complex hypothesis. *Quarterly Bulletin of the British Psychological Society, 1,* 364–365.

McFarlin, D. B., & Blascovich, J. (1981). Effects of self-esteem and performance feedback on future affective preferences and cognitive expectations. *Journal of Personality and Social Psychology, 40,* 521–531.

McGhee, P. E. (1979). *Humor: Its origin and development.* San Francisco: W. H. Freeman.

McGrath, M. J., & Cohen, D. B. (1978). REM sleep facilitation of adaptive waking behavior: A review of the literature. *Psychological Bulletin, 85,* 24–57.

Maddux, J. E., Norton, L. W., & Leary, M. R. (1987). Cognitive components of social anxiety: An investigation of the integration of self-presentation theory and self-efficacy theory. *Journal of Social and Clinical Psychology, 6,* 180–190.

Magnusson, D. (1990). Personality development from an interactional perspective. In L. A. Pervin (Ed.), *Handbook of personality: Theory and research* (pp. 193–222). New York: Guilford.

Mahoney, M. J., & Arnkoff, D. B. (1979). Self-management. In O. F. Pomerleau & J. P. Brady (Eds.), *Behavioral medicine: Theory and practice.* Baltimore: Williams & Wilkins.

Maier, S. F., & Seligman, M. E. P. (1976). Learned helplessness: Theory and evidence. *Journal of Experimental Psychology: General, 105,* 3–46.

Major, B., Carnevale, P. J. D., & Deaux, K. (1981). A different perspective on androgyny: Evaluations of masculine and feminine personality characteristics. *Journal of Personality and Social Psychology, 41,* 988–1001.

Mann, L. (1981). The baiting crowd in episodes of threatened suicide. *Journal of Personality and Social Psychology, 41,* 703–709.

Mann, L., Newton, J. W., & Innes, J. M. (1982). A test between deindividuation and emergent norm theories of crowd aggression. *Journal of Personality and Social Psychology, 42,* 260–272.

Marks, G., Richardson, J. L., Graham, J. W., & Levine, A. (1986). Role of health locus of control beliefs and expectations of treatment efficacy in adjustment to cancer. *Journal of Personality and Social Psychology, 51,* 443–450.

Markus, H. (1977). Self-schemata and processing information about the self. *Journal of Personality and Social Psychology, 35,* 63–78.

Markus, H. (1983). Self-knowledge: An expanded view. *Journal of Personality, 51,* 543–565.

Markus, H., Crane, M., Bernstein, S., & Siladi, M. (1982). Self-schemas and gender. *Journal of Personality and Social Psychology, 42,* 38–50.

Markus, H., & Kunda, Z. (1986). Stability and malleability of the self-concept. *Journal of Personality and Social Psychology, 51,* 858–866.

Markus, H., & Nurius, P. (1986). Possible selves. *American Psychologist, 41,* 954–969.

Markus, H., & Sentis, K. (1982). The self and social information processing. In J. Suls (Ed.), *Psychological perspectives on the self* (Vol. 1, pp. 41–70). Hillsdale, NJ: Erlbaum.

Markus, H., & Smith, J. (1981). The influence of self-schemata on the perception of others. In N. Cantor & J. F. Kihlstrom (Eds.), *Personality,* *cognition, and social interaction* (pp. 233–262). Hillsdale, NJ: Erlbaum.

Marsh, H. W., Antill, J. K., & Cunningham, J. D. (1987). Masculinity, femininity, and androgyny: Relations to self-esteem and social desirability. *Journal of Personality, 55,* 661–683.

Marsh, H. W., & Byrne, B. M. (1991). Differentiated additive androgyny model: Relations between masculinity, femininity, and multiple dimensions of self-concept. *Journal of Personality and Social Psychology, 61,* 811–828.

Marsh, H. W., & Richards, G. E. (1988). Tennessee Self Concept Scale: Reliability, internal structure, and construct validity. *Journal of Personality and Social Psychology, 55,* 612–624.

Martin, R. P. (1985). Temperament: A review of research with implications for the school psychologist. *School Psychology Review, 12,* 266–275.

Maslach, C. (1974). Social and personal bases of individuation. *Journal of Personality and Social Psychology, 29,* 411–425.

Maslach, C., Santee, R. T., & Wade, C. (1987). Individuation, gender role, and dissent: Personality mediators of situational forces. *Journal of Personality and Social Psychology, 53,* 1088–1093.

Maslach, C., Stapp, J., & Santee, R. T. (1985). Individuation: Conceptual analysis and assessment. *Journal of Personality and Social Psychology, 49,* 729–738.

Maslow, A. H. (1968). *Toward a psychology of being* (2nd ed.). New York: Van Nostrand.

Maslow, A. H. (1970). *Motivation and personality* (2nd ed.). New York: Harper & Row.

Maslow, A. H. (1971). *The farther reaches of human nature.* New York: Viking Press.

Matthews, K. A. (1982). Psychological perspectives on the Type A behavior pattern. *Psychological Bulletin, 91,* 293–323.

Matthews, K. A., & Carra, J. (1982). Suppression of menstrual distress symptoms: A study of Type A behavior. *Personality and Social Psychology Bulletin, 8,* 146–151.

Matthews, K. A., & Haynes, S. G. (1986). Type A behavior pattern and coronary risk: Update and critical evaluation. *American Journal of Epidemiology, 123,* 923–960.

Matthews, K. A., Helmreich, R. L., Beane, W. E., & Lucker, G. W. (1980). Pattern A, achievement striving, and scientific merit: Does Pattern A help or hinder? *Journal of Personality and Social Psychology, 39,* 962–967.

Matthews, K. A., & Saal, F. E. (1978). The relationship of the Type A coronary-prone behavior pattern to achievement, power, and affiliation motives. *Psychosomatic Medicine, 40,* 631–636.

Mayo, C. W., & Crockett, W. H. (1964). Cognitive complexity and primacy-recency effects in impression formation. *Journal of Abnormal and Social Psychology, 68,* 335–338.

Mayo, P. R. (1983). Personality traits and the retrieval of positive and negative memories. *Personality and Individual Differences, 4,* 465–471.

Meeker, W. B., & Barber, T. X. (1971). Toward an explanation of stage hypnosis. *Journal of Abnormal Psychology, 77,* 61–70.

Meichenbaum, D. H., (1977). *Cognitive behavior modification: An integrative approach.* New York: Plenum.

Meichenbaum, D. (1985). *Stress inoculation training.* New York: Pergamon.

Meichenbaum, D., & Cameron, R. (1983). Stress inoculation training: Toward a general paradigm for training coping skills. In D. Meichenbaum & M. E. Jaemko (Eds.), *Stress reduction and prevention* (pp. 115–157). New York: Plenum.

Meichenbaum, D. H., & Jaemko, M. (1983). *Stress reduction and prevention.* New York: Plenum.

Meissner, W. W. (1984). *Psychoanalysis and religious experience.* New Haven, CT: Yale University Press.

Melges, F. T., & Weisz, A. E. (1971). The personal future and suicidal ideation. *Journal of Nervous and Mental Disease, 153,* 244–250.

Mershon, B., & Gorsuch, R. L. (1988). Number of factors in the personality sphere: Does increase in factors increase predictability of real-life criteria? *Journal of Personality and Social Psychology, 55,* 675–680.

Metalsky, G. I., Halberstadt, L. J., & Abramson, L. Y. (1987). Vulnerability to depressive mood reactions: Toward a more powerful test of the diathesis-stress and causal mediation components of the reformulated theory of depression. *Journal of Personality and Social Psychology, 52,* 386–393.

Mettlin, C. (1976). Occupational careers and the prevention of coronary-prone behavior. *Social Science and Medicine, 10,* 367–372.

Miller, C. T. (1984). Self-schemas, gender, and social comparison: A clarification of the related attributes hypothesis. *Journal of Personality and Social Psychology, 46,* 1222–1229.

Miller, I. W., & Norman, W. H. (1979). Learned helplessness in humans: A review and attribution theory model. *Psychological Bulletin, 86,* 93–118.

Miller, N. E. (1941). The frustration-aggression hypothesis. *Psychological Review, 48,* 337–346.

Miller, P. C., Lefcourt, H. M., & Ware, E. E. (1983). The construction and development of the Miller Marital Locus of Control Scale. *Canadian Journal of Behavioural Science, 15,* 266–279.

Miller, W. R., & Seligman, M. E. P. (1975). Depression and learned helplessness in man. *Journal of Abnormal Psychology, 84,* 228–238.

Mills, C. J. (1983). Sex-typing and self-schemata effects on memory and response latency. *Journal of Personality and Social Psychology, 45,* 163–172.

Mischel, W. (1968). *Personality and assessment.* New York: Wiley.

Mischel, W. (1973). Toward a cognitive social learning reconceptualization of personality. *Psychological Review, 80,* 252–283.

Mischel, W. (1979). On the interface of cognition and personality: Beyond the person-situation debate. *American Psychologist, 34,* 740–754.

Mischel, W. (1980). George Kelly's anticipation of psychology: A personal tribute. In M. J. Mahoney (Ed.), *Psychotherapy process.* New York: Plenum.

Mischel, W. (1983). Alternatives in the pursuit of the predictability and consistency of persons: Stable data that yield unstable interpretations. *Journal of Personality, 51,* 578–604.

Mischel, W. (1984). Convergences and challenges in the search for consistency. *American Psychologist, 39,* 351–364.

Mischel, W. (1990). Personality dispositions revisited and revised: A view after three decades. In L. A. Pervin (Ed.), *Handbook of personality: Theory and research* (pp. 111–134). New York: Guilford.

Mischel, W., & Peake, P. K. (1982). Beyond déjà vu in the search for cross-situational consistency. *Psychological Review, 89,* 730–755.

Mischel, W., & Peake, P. K. (1983). Some facets of consistency: Replies to Epstein, Funder, and Bem. *Psychological Review, 90,* 394–402.

Miserandino, M., & Hoffman, J. P. (1990). *Basketball shooting improvement through attribution retraining.* Paper presented at the annual meeting of the American Psychological Association, Boston.

Mitchell, R. E., Cronkite, R. C., & Moos, R. H. (1983). Stress, coping, and depression among married couples. *Journal of Abnormal Psychology, 92,* 433–448.

Monat, A., & Lazarus, R. S. (1985). Stress and coping: Some current issues and controversies. In A. Monat & R. S. Lazarus (Eds.), *Stress and coping: An anthology* (2nd ed., pp. 1–12). New York: Columbia University Press.

Moretti, M. M., & Higgins, E. T. (1990). Relating self-discrepancy to self-esteem: The contribution of discrepancy beyond actual-self ratings. *Journal of Experimental Social Psychology, 26,* 108–123.

Morton, T. L. (1978). Intimacy and reciprocity of exchange: A comparison of spouses and strangers. *Journal of Personality and Social Psychology, 36,* 72–81.

Mosher, D. L. (1966). The development and multitrait-multimethod matrix analysis of three aspects of guilt. *Journal of Consulting Psychology, 30,* 25–29.

Mosher, D. L. (1968). Measurement of guilt in females by self-report inventories. *Journal of Consulting and Clinical Psychology, 32,* 690–695.

Mosher, D. L. (1979). The meaning and measurement of sex guilt. In C. E. Izard (Ed.), *Emotions in personality and psychopathology* (pp. 105–129). New York: Plenum.

Motley, M. T., & Camden, C. T. (1985). Non-linguistic influences on lexical selection: Evidence from double entendres. *Communication Monographs, 52,* 124–135.

Motley, M. T., Camden, C. T., & Baars, B. J. (1979). Personality and situational influences upon verbal slips: A laboratory test of Freudian and prearticulatory editing hypotheses. *Human Communication Research, 5,* 195–202.

Moustakas, C. E. (1961). *Loneliness.* Englewood Cliffs, NJ: Prentice-Hall.

Moustakas, C. E. (1968). *Individuality and encounter.* Cambridge, MA: Doyle.

Mullen, B. (1986). Atrocity as a function of lynch mob composition. *Personality and Social Psychology Bulletin, 12,* 187–197.

Murray, E. J., Lamnin, A. D., & Carver, C. S. (1989). Emotional expression in written essays and psychotherapy. *Journal of Social and Clinical Psychology, 8,* 414–429.

Murray, H. A. (1938). *Explorations in personality: A clinical and experimental study of fifty men of college age.* New York: Oxford University Press.

Murray, H. A. (1967). Henry A. Murray. In E. G. Boring & G. Lindzey (Eds.), *A history of psychology in autobiography: Vol. V* (pp. 285–310). New York: Appleton-Century-Crofts.

Musante, L., MacDougall, J. M., Dembroski, T. M., & Costa, P. T. (1989). Potential for hostility and dimensions of anger. *Health Psychology, 8,* 343–354.

Myers, M. B., & McCaulley, M. H. (1985). *Manual: A guide to the development and use of the Myers-Briggs Type Indicator.* Palo Alto, CA: Consulting Psychologists Press.

Nadon, R., Hoyt, I. P., Register, P. A., & Kihlstrom, J. F. (1991). Absorption and hypnotizability: Context effects reexamined. *Journal of Personality and Social Psychology, 60,* 144–153.

Nairn, A. (1980). *The reign of ETS: The corporation that makes up minds.* Washington, DC: Nader.

Nash, M. (1987). What, if anything, is regressed about hypnotic age regression? A review of the empirical literature. *Psychological Bulletin, 102,* 42–52.

National Institute of Mental Health (1982). *Television and behavior: Ten years of scientific progress and implications for the eighties* (Vol. 1). Washington, DC: U.S. Department of Health and Human Services.

Neale, M. C., Rushton, P., & Fulker, D. W. (1986). Heritability of item responses on the

Eysenck Personality Questionnaire. *Personality and Individual Differences, 7,* 771–779.

Neale, M. C., & Stevenson, J. (1989). Rater bias in the EASI Temperament Scales: A twin study. *Journal of Personality and Social Psychology, 56,* 446–455.

Neimeyer, G. J. (1984). Cognitive complexity and marital satisfaction. *Journal of Social and Clinical Psychology, 2,* 258–263.

Neimeyer, G. J., & Banikiotes, P. G. (1981). Self-disclosure flexibility, empathy, and perceptions of adjustment and attraction. *Journal of Counseling Psychology, 28,* 272–275.

Neimeyer, G. J., & Neimeyer, R. A. (1981). Personal construct perspectives on cognitive assessment. In T. V. Merluzzi, C. R. Glass, & M. Genest (Eds.), *Cognitive assessment* (pp. 188–232). New York: Guilford.

Neuliep, J. W., & Hazleton, V. (1986). Enhanced conversational recall and reduced conversational interference as a function of cognitive complexity. *Human Communication Research, 13,* 211–224.

Nevo, O., & Nevo, B. (1983). What do you do when asked to answer humorously? *Journal of Personality and Social Psychology, 44,* 188–194.

Nichols, R. C. (1978). Heredity and environment: Major findings from twin studies of ability, personality, and interests. *Homo, 29,* 158–173.

Nisbett, R. E., & Ross, L. D. (1980). *Human inference: Strategies and shortcomings of social judgment.* Englewood Cliffs, NJ: Prentice-Hall.

Noller, P., Law, H., & Comrey, A. L. (1987). Cattell, Comrey, and Eysenck personality factors compared: More evidence for the five robust factors? *Journal of Personality and Social Psychology, 53,* 775–782.

Nunnally, J. C. (1978). *Psychometric theory* (2nd ed.). New York: McGraw-Hill.

Ochse, R., & Plug, C. (1986). Cross-cultural investigation of the validity of Erikson's theory of personality development. *Journal of Personality and Social Psychology, 50,* 1240–1252.

O'Donnell, W. J., & O'Donnell, K. J. (1978). Update: Sex role messages in TV commercials. *Journal of Communication, 28,* 156–158.

Ogilvie, D. M. (1987). The undesired self: A neglected variable in personality research. *Journal of Personality and Social Psychology, 52,* 379–385.

O'Heron, C. A., & Orlofsky, J. L. (1990). Stereotypic and nonstereotypic sex role trait and behavior orientations, gender identity, and psychological adjustment. *Journal of Personality and Social Psychology, 58,* 134–143.

O'Keefe, B. J., & Delia, J. G. (1979). Construct comprehensiveness and cognitive complexity as predictors of the number and strategic adaptation of arguments and appeals

in a persuasive message. *Communication Monographs, 46,* 231–240.

O'Keefe, B. J., & Sypher, H. E. (1981). Cognitive complexity measures and the relationship of cognitive complexity to communication. *Human Communication Research, 8,* 72–92.

Oliver, J. M., & Burkham, R. (1982). Subliminal psychodynamic activation in depression: A failure to replicate. *Journal of Abnormal Psychology, 91,* 337–342.

O'Neal, E. C., Macdonald, P. J., Cloninger, C., & Levine, D. (1979). Coactor's behavior and imitative aggression. *Motivation and Emotion, 3,* 373–379.

Orgler, H. (1963). *Alfred Adler: The man and his work.* New York: Liveright.

Orlofsky, J. L., & O'Heron, C. A. (1987). Stereotypic and nonstereotypic sex role trait and behavior orientations: Implications for personal adjustment. *Journal of Personality and Social Psychology, 52,* 1034–1042.

Orne, M. T. (1962). On the social psychology of the psychological experiment: With particular reference to demand characteristics and their implications. *American Psychologist, 17,* 776–783.

Ortega, D. F., & Pipal, J. E. (1984). Challenge seeking and the Type A coronary-prone behavior pattern. *Journal of Personality and Social Psychology, 46,* 1328–1334.

Ovcharchyn, C. A., Johnson, H. H., & Petzel, T. P. (1981). Type A behavior, academic aspirations, and academic success. *Journal of Personality, 49,* 248–256.

Overmier, J. B., & Seligman, M. E. P. (1967). Effects of inescapable shock upon subsequent escape and avoidance learning. *Journal of Comparative and Physiological Psychology, 63,* 28–33.

Oyserman, D., & Markus, H. R. (1990). Possible selves and delinquency. *Journal of Personality and Social Psychology, 59,* 112–125.

Ozer, E. M., & Bandura, A. (1990). Mechanisms governing empowerment effects: A self-efficacy analysis. *Journal of Personality and Social Psychology, 58,* 472–486.

Pagano, D. F. (1973). Effects of task familiarity on stress responses of repressors and sensitizers. *Journal of Consulting and Clinical Psychology, 40,* 22–26.

Page, M. M. (Ed.) (1983). *1982 Nebraska Symposium on Motivation: Personality — Current theory and research.* Lincoln: University of Nebraska Press.

Parker, D. R., & Rogers, R. W. (1981). Observation and performance of aggression: Effects of multiple models and frustration. *Personality and Social Psychology Bulletin, 7,* 302–308.

Parton, D. A., & Geshuri, Y. (1971). Learning of aggression as a function of presence of a human model, response intensity, and target of the response. *Journal of Experimental Child Psychology, 20,* 304–318.

Paulhus, D. (1983). Sphere-specific measures of perceived control. *Journal of Personality and Social Psychology, 44,* 1253–1265.

Paulhus, D. L., & Christie, R. (1981). Spheres of control: An interactionist approach to assessment of perceived control. In H. Lefcourt (Ed.), *Research with the locus of control construct* (Vol. 1, pp. 161–188). New York: Academic Press.

Paulhus, D. L., & Martin, C. L. (1987). The structure of personality capabilities. *Journal of Personality and Social Psychology, 52,* 354–365.

Paunonen, S. V., Jackson, D. N., Trzebinski, J., & Forsterling, F. (1992). Personality structure across cultures: A multimethod evaluation. *Journal of Personality and Social Psychology, 62,* 447–456.

Payne, T. J., Connor, J. M., & Colletti, G. (1987). Gender-based schematic processing: An empirical investigation and reevaluation. *Journal of Personality and Social Psychology, 52,* 937–945.

Peabody, D., & Goldberg, L. R. (1989). Some determinants of factor structures from personality-trait descriptors. *Journal of Personality and Social Psychology, 57,* 552–567.

Pedersen, N. L., Plomin, R., McClearn, G. E., & Friberg, L. (1988). Neuroticism, extraversion, and related traits in adult twins reared apart and reared together. *Journal of Personality and Social Psychology, 55,* 950–957.

Pedhazur, E. J., & Tetenbaum, T. J. (1979). Bem Sex Role Inventory: A theoretical and methodological critique. *Journal of Personality and Social Psychology, 37,* 996–1016.

Pennebaker, J. W. (1989). Confession, inhibition, and disease. In L. Berkowitz (Ed.), *Advances in experimental social psychology,* (Vol. 22, pp. 211–244). New York: Academic Press.

Pennebaker, J. W., & Beall, S. K. (1986). Confronting a traumatic event: Toward an understanding of inhibition and disease. *Journal of Abnormal Psychology, 95,* 274–281.

Pennebaker, J. W., & Chew, C. H. (1985). Deception, electrodermal activity, and inhibition of behavior. *Journal of Personality and Social Psychology, 49,* 1427–1433.

Pennebaker, J. W., Colder, M., & Sharp, L. K. (1990). Accelerating the coping process. *Journal of Personality and Social Psychology, 58,* 528–537.

Pennebaker, J. W., & Hoover, C. W. (1986). Inhibition and cognition: Toward an understanding of trauma and disease. In R. J. Davidson, G. E. Schwartz, & D. Shapiro (Eds.), *Consciousness and self-regulation* (Vol. 4, pp. 107–136). New York: Plenum.

Pennebaker, J. W., Hughes, C. F., & O'Heeron, R. C. (1987). The psychophysiology of confession: Linking inhibitory and psychosomatic processes. *Journal of Personality and Social Psychology, 52,* 781–793.

Pennebaker, J. W., & O'Heeron, R. C. (1984). Confiding in others and illness rates among spouses of suicide and accidental-death victims. *Journal of Abnormal Psychology, 93,* 473–476.

Peplau, L. A., Russell, D., & Heim, M. (1979). The experience of loneliness. In I. Frieze, D. Bar-Tel, & J. Carroll (Eds.), *New approaches to social problems* (pp. 53–78). San Francisco: Jossey-Bass.

Perry, D. G., & Bussey, K. (1979). The social learning theory of sex differences: Imitation is alive and well. *Journal of Personality and Social Psychology, 37,* 1699–1712.

Perry, H. S. (1984). *Psychiatrist of America: The life of Harry Stack Sullivan.* Cambridge, MA: Belknap Press.

Peterson, C., & Seligman, M. E. P. (1984). Causal explanations as a risk factor for depression: Theory and evidence. *Psychological Review, 91,* 347–374.

Peterson, C., & Seligman, M. E. P. (1987). Explanatory style and illness. *Journal of Personality, 55,* 237–265.

Peterson, C., Seligman, M. E. P., & Vaillant, G. E. (1988). Pessimistic explanatory style is a risk factor for physical illness: A thirty-five-year longitudinal study. *Journal of Personality and Social Psychology, 55,* 23–27.

Peterson, C., Semmel, A., von Baeyer, C., Abramson, L. Y., Metalsky, G. I., & Seligman, M. E. P. (1982). The Attributional Style Questionnaire. *Cognitive Therapy and Research, 6,* 287–300.

Peterson, C., & Villanova, P. (1988). An expanded Attributional Style Questionnaire. *Journal of Abnormal Psychology, 97,* 87–89.

Peterson, C., Villanova, P., & Raps, C. S. (1985). Depression and attributions: Factors responsible for inconsistent results in the published literature. *Journal of Abnormal Psychology, 94,* 165–168.

Peterson, R. A. (1978). Review of the Rorschach. In O. K. Buros (Ed.), *Eighth mental measurements yearbook* (pp. 1042–1045). Highland Park, NJ: Gryphon.

Petty, R. E., & Brock, T. C. (1979). Effects of Barnum personality assessments on cognitive behavior. *Journal of Consulting and Clinical Psychology, 47,* 201–203.

Phares, E. J. (1976). *Locus of control in personality.* Morristown, NJ: General Learning Press.

Phillips, D. P. (1983). The impact of mass media violence on U.S. homicides. *American Sociological Review, 48,* 560–568.

Phillips, S. D., & Bruch, M. A. (1988). Shyness and dysfunction in career development. *Journal of Counseling Psychology, 35,* 159–165.

Piccione, C., Hilgard, E. R., & Zimbardo, P. G. (1989). On the degree of stability of measured hypnotizability over a 25-year period. *Journal of Personality and Social Psychology, 56,* 289–295.

Pilkonis, P. A. (1977a). Shyness, public and private, and its relationship to other measures of social behavior. *Journal of Personality, 45,* 585–595.

Pilkonis, P. A. (1977b). The behavioral consequences of shyness. *Journal of Personality, 45,* 596–611.

Pinderhughes, E. E., & Zigler, E. (1985). Cognitive and motivational determinants of children's humor responses. *Journal of Research in Personality, 19,* 185–196.

Pittner, M. S., & Houston, B. K. (1980). Response to stress, cognitive coping strategies, and the Type A behavior pattern. *Journal of Personality and Social Psychology, 39,* 147–157.

Pittner, M. S., Houston, B. K., & Spiridigliozzi, G. (1983). Control over stress, Type A behavior pattern, and response to stress. *Journal of Personality and Social Psychology, 44,* 627–637.

Playboy readers' sex survey (1983, January). *Playboy,* pp. 108, 241–250.

Plomin, R., Chipuer, H. M., & Loehlin, J. C. (1990). Behavioral genetics and personality. In L. Pervin (Ed.), Handbook of personality theory and research (pp. 225–243). New York: Guilford.

Pomerleau, A., Bolduc, D., Malcuit, G., & Cossette, L. (1990). Pink or blue: Environmental gender stereotypes in the first two years of life. *Sex Roles, 22,* 359–367.

Post, A. L., Wittmaier, B. C., & Radin, M. E. (1978). Self-disclosure as a function of state and trait anxiety. *Journal of Consulting and Clinical Psychology, 46,* 12–19.

Pozo, C., Carver, C. S., Wellens, A. R., & Scheier, M. F. (1991). Social anxiety and social perception: Construing others' reactions to the self. *Personality and Social Psychology Bulletin, 17,* 355–362.

Prager, K. J. (1986). Intimacy status: Its relationship to locus of control, self-disclosure, and anxiety in adults. *Personality and Social Psychology Bulletin, 12,* 91–109.

Prentice-Dunn, S., & Rogers, R. W. (1980). Effects of deindividuating situational cues and aggressive models on subjective deindividuation and aggression. *Journal of Personality and Social Psychology, 39,* 104–113.

Prentice-Dunn, S., & Rogers, R. W. (1983). Deindividuation and aggression. In R. G. Geen & E. I. Donnerstein (Eds.), *Aggression: Theoretical and empirical reviews* (Vol. 2, pp. 155–171). New York: Academic Press.

Press, A. N., Crockett, W. H., & Delia, J. G. (1975). Effects of cognitive complexity and of perceiver's set upon the organization of impressions. *Journal of Personality and Social Psychology, 32,* 865–872.

Price, R. A., Vandenberg, S. G., Iyer, H., & Williams, J. S. (1982). Components of variation in normal personality. *Journal of Personality and Social Psychology, 43,* 328–340.

Pyszczynski, T., Holt, K., & Greenberg, J. (1987). Depression, self-focused attention, and expectancies for positive and negative future life events for self and others. *Journal of Personality and Social Psychology, 52,* 994–1001.

Rehm, L. P., & O'Hara, M. W. (1979). Understanding depression. In I. H. Frieze, D. Bar-Tal, & J. S. Carroll (Eds.), *New approaches to social problems* (pp. 209–236). San Francisco: Jossey-Bass.

Rescorla, R. A. (1988). Pavlovian conditioning: It's not what you think it is. *American Psychologist, 43,* 151–160.

Reuman, D. A., Alwin, D. F., & Veroff, J. (1984). Assessing the validity of the achievement motive in the presence of random measurement error. *Journal of Personality and Social Psychology, 47,* 1347–1362.

Reznick, J. S., Kagan, J., Snidman, N., Gersten, M., Baak, K., & Rosenberg, A. (1986). Inhibited and uninhibited children: A follow-up study. *Child Development, 57,* 660–680.

Rhodewalt, F., & Comer, R. (1982). Coronary-prone behavior and reactance: The attractiveness of an eliminated choice. *Personality and Social Psychology Bulletin, 8,* 152–158.

Rhodewalt, F., & Davison, J. (1983). Reactance and the coronary-prone behavior pattern: The role of self-attribution in responses to reduced behavioral freedom. *Journal of Personality and Social Psychology, 44,* 220–228.

Rhodewalt, F., Morf, C., Hazlett, S., & Fairfield, M. (1991). Self-handicapping: The role of discounting and augmentation in the preservation of self-esteem. *Journal of Personality and Social Psychology, 61,* 122–131.

Riordan, C. A., & Tedeschi, J. T. (1983). Attraction in aversive environments: Some evidence for classical conditioning and negative reinforcement. *Journal of Personality and Social Psychology, 44,* 683–692.

Robbins, P. R., Tanck, R. H., & Houshi, F. (1985). Anxiety and dream symbolism. *Journal of Personality, 53,* 17–22.

Roberts, A. H. (1985). Biofeedback: Research, training, and clinical roles. *American Psychologist, 40,* 938–941.

Robins, C. J. (1988). Attributions and depression: Why is the literature so inconsistent? *Journal of Personality and Social Psychology, 54,* 880–889.

Robyak, J. E., & Patton, M. J. (1977). The effectiveness of a study skills course of students of different personality types. *Journal of Counseling Psychology, 24,* 200–207.

Roche, S. M., & McConkey, K. M. (1990). Absorption: Nature, assessment, and correlates. *Journal of Personality and Social Psychology, 59,* 91–101.

Rodin, J., & Langer, E. J. (1977). Long-term effects of a control-relevant intervention with the institutionalized aged. *Journal of Personality and Social Psychology, 35*, 897–902.

Rogers, C. R. (1947). The case of Mary Jane Tildon. In W. U. Snyder (Ed.), *Casebook of nondirective counseling* (pp. 128–203). Cambridge, MA: Houghton Mifflin.

Rogers, C. R. (1951). *Client-centered therapy: Its current practice, implications, and theory.* Boston: Houghton Mifflin.

Rogers, C. R. (1959). A theory of therapy, personality, and interpersonal relationships, as developed in the client-centered framework. In S. Koch (Ed.), *Psychology: A study of a science* (Vol. 3, pp. 184–256). New York: McGraw-Hill.

Rogers, C. R. (1961). *On becoming a person: A therapist's view of psychotherapy.* Boston: Houghton Mifflin.

Rogers, C. R. (1967). Carl R. Rogers. In E. G. Boring & G. Lindzey (Eds.), *A history of psychology in autobiography* (Vol. 5, pp. 341–384). New York: Appleton-Century-Crofts.

Rogers, C. R. (1969). *Freedom to learn: A view of what education might become.* Columbus, OH: Merrill.

Rogers, C. R. (1970). *Carl Rogers on encounter groups.* New York: Harper & Row.

Rogers, C. R. (1977). *Carl Rogers on personal power.* New York: Delacorte Press.

Rogers, C. R. (1980). *A way of being.* Boston: Houghton Mifflin.

Rogers, C. R. (1982, August). Nuclear war: A personal response. *American Psychological Association Monitor*, pp. 6–7.

Rogers, C. R., & Dymond, R. F. (1954). *Psychotherapy and personality change.* Chicago: University of Chicago Press.

Rogers, R. W., & Prentice-Dunn, S. (1981). Deindividuation and anger-mediated interracial aggression: Unmasking regressive racism. *Journal of Personality and Social Psychology, 41*, 63–73.

Rogers, T. B., Kuiper, N. A., & Kirker, W. S. (1977). Self-reference and the encoding of personal information. *Journal of Personality and Social Psychology, 35*, 677–688.

Rook, K. S., & Peplau, L. A. (1982). Perspectives on helping the lonely. In L. A. Peplau & D. Perlman (Eds.), *Loneliness.* New York: Wiley.

Roos, P. E., & Cohen, L. H. (1987). Sex roles and social support as moderators of life stress adjustment. *Journal of Personality and Social Psychology, 52*, 576–585.

Rosch, E. (1978). Principles of categorization. In E. Rosch & B. B. Lloyd (Eds.), *Cognition and categorization.* Hillsdale, NJ: Erlbaum.

Rose, R. J. (1988). Genetic and environmental variance in content dimensions of the MMPI. *Journal of Personality and Social Psychology, 55*, 302–311.

Rose, R. J., Koskenvuo, M., Kaprio, J., Sarna, S., & Langinvainio, H. (1988). Shared genes, shared experiences, and similarity of personality: Data from 14,288 adult Finnish co-twins. *Journal of Personality and Social Psychology, 54*, 161–171.

Rosenman, R. H. (1986). Current and past history of Type A behavior pattern. In T. H. Schmidt, T. M. Dembroski, & G. Blumchen (Eds.), *Biological and psychological factors in cardiovascular disease* (pp. 15–40). New York: Springer-Verlag.

Rosenman, R. H., Brand, R. J., Jenkins, C. D., Friedman, M., Straus, R., & Wurm, M. (1975). Coronary heart disease in the western collaborative group study: Final follow-up experience of 8½ years. *Journal of the American Medical Association, 233*, 872–877.

Rosenthal, R. (1979). The "file drawer problem" and tolerance for null results. *Psychological Bulletin, 86*, 638–641.

Rosenthal, R. (1990). How are we doing in soft psychology? *American Psychologist, 45*, 775–777.

Ross, L., Anderson, D. R., & Wisocki, P. A. (1982). Television viewing and adult sex-role attitudes. *Sex Roles, 8*, 589–592.

Roth, S. (1980). A revised model of learned helplessness in humans. *Journal of Personality, 48*, 103–133.

Rotter, J. B. (1954). *Social learning and clinical psychology.* Englewood Cliffs, NJ: Prentice-Hall.

Rotter, J. B. (1966). Generalized expectancies for internal versus external control of reinforcement. *Psychological Monographs, 80*, (1, Whole No. 609).

Rotter, J. B. (1982). *The development and applications of social learning theory: Selected papers.* New York: Praeger.

Rotter, J. B., Chance, J. E., & Phares, E. J. (Eds.) (1972). *Applications of a social learning theory of personality.* New York: Holt, Rinehart & Winston.

Rotter, J. B., & Mulry, R. C. (1965). Internal versus external control of reinforcement and decision time. *Journal of Personality and Social Psychology, 2*, 598–604.

Rowe, D. C. (1987). Resolving the person-situation debate: Invitation to an interdisciplinary dialogue. *American Psychologist, 42*, 218–227.

Rubenstein, C. M., & Shaver, P. (1980). Loneliness in two northern cities. In J. Hartog, J. R. Andy, & Y. A. Cohen (Eds.), *The anatomy of loneliness* (pp. 319–337). New York: International Universities Press.

Rubin, J. A., Provenzano, F. J., & Luria, Z. (1974). The eye of the beholder: Parents' views of sex of newborns. *American Journal of Orthopsychiatry, 44*, 512–519.

Rubin, Z. (1975). Disclosing oneself to a stranger: Reciprocity and its limits. *Journal of Experimental Social Psychology, 11*, 233–260.

Rubin, Z., & Shenker, S. (1978). Friendship, proximity, and self-disclosure. *Journal of Personality, 46,* 1–22.

Rubins, J. L. (1978). *Karen Horney: Gentle rebel of psychoanalysis.* New York: Dial Press.

Ruble, D. N., & Stangor, C. (1986). Stalking the elusive schema: Insights from developmental and social-psychological analyses of gender schemas. *Social Cognition, 4,* 227–261.

Ruehlman, L. S., West, S. G., & Pasahow, R. J. (1985). Depression and evaluative schemata. *Journal of Personality, 53,* 46–92.

Rushton, J. P., Fulker, D. W., Neale, M. C., Nias, D. K. B., & Eysenck, H. J. (1986). Altruism and aggression: The heritability of individual differences. *Journal of Personality and Social Psychology, 50,* 1192–1198.

Russell, D., Peplau, L. A., & Cutrona, C. E. (1980). The revised UCLA Loneliness Scale: Concurrent and discriminant validity. *Journal of Personality and Social Psychology, 39,* 472–480.

Russell, D., Peplau, L. A., & Ferguson, M. L. (1978). Developing a measure of loneliness. *Journal of Personality Assessment, 42,* 290–294.

Russell, G. W., & Drewry, B. R. (1976). Crowd size and competitive aspects of aggression in ice hockey: An archival study. *Human Relations, 29,* 723–735.

Ruvolo, A. P., & Markus, H. R. (1992). Possible selves and performance: The power of self-relevant imagery. *Social Cognition, 10,* 95–124.

Ryckman, R. M., Burns, M. J., & Robbins, M. A. (1986). Authoritarianism and sentencing strategies for low and high severity crimes. *Personality and Social Psychology Bulletin, 12,* 227–235.

Sadalla, E. K., Kendrick, D. T., & Vershure, B. (1987). Dominance and heterosexual attraction. *Journal of Personality and Social Psychology, 52,* 730–738.

Sadler, W. A., & Johnson, T. B. (1980). From loneliness to anomie. In J. Hartog, J. R. Audy, & Y. A. Cohen (Eds.), *The anatomy of loneliness* (pp. 34–64). New York: International Universities Press.

Santee, R. T., & Maslach, C. (1982). To agree or not to agree: Personal dissent amid social pressure to conform. *Journal of Personality and Social Psychology, 42,* 690–700.

Sarbin, T. R. (1988). Self-deception in the claims of hypnosis subjects. In J. S. Lockard & D. L. Paulhus (Eds.), *Self-deception: An adaptive mechanism?* (pp. 99–112). Englewood Cliffs, NJ: Prentice-Hall.

Sarbin, T. R., & Coe, W. C. (1972). *Hypnosis: A social psychological analysis of influence communication.* New York: Holt, Rinehart & Winston.

Sarbin, T. R., & Coe, W. C. (1979). Hypnosis and psychopathology: Replacing old myths with fresh metaphors. *Journal of Abnormal Psychology, 88,* 506–526.

Scarpetti, W. L. (1973). The repression-sensitization dimension in relation to impending painful stimulation. *Journal of Consulting and Clinical Psychology, 40,* 377–382.

Scarr, S. (1969). Social introversion-extraversion as a heritable response. *Child Development, 40,* 823–832.

Scarr, S., & Carter-Saltzman, L. (1979). Twin method: Defense of a critical assumption. *Behavior Genetics, 9,* 527–542.

Scarr, S., Webber, P. L., Weinberg, R. A., & Wittig, M. A. (1981). Personality resemblances among adolescents and their parents in biologically related and adoptive families. *Journal of Personality and Social Psychology, 40,* 885–898.

Scarr, S., & Weinberg, R. A. (1976). IQ test performance of black children adopted by white families. *American Psychologist, 31,* 726–739.

Scarr-Salapatek, S. (1971). Race, social class, and IQ. *Science, 174,* 1286–1295.

Scheier, M. F., & Carver, C. S. (1981). Private and public aspects of self. In L. Wheeler (Ed.), *Review of personality and social psychology* (Vol. 2, pp. 189–216). Beverly Hills, CA: Sage.

Schill, T. R. (1972). Aggression and blood pressure responses of high- and low-guilt subjects following frustration. *Journal of Consulting and Clinical Psychology, 38,* 461.

Schlenker, B. R., & Leary, M. R. (1982). Social anxiety and self-presentation: A conceptualization and model. *Psychological Bulletin, 92,* 641–669.

Schlenker, B. R., Weigold, M. F., & Hallam, J. R. (1990). Self-serving attributions in social context: Effects of self-esteem and social pressure. *Journal of Personality and Social Psychology, 58,* 855–863.

Schmidt, N., & Sermat, V. (1983). Measuring loneliness in different relationships. *Journal of Personality and Social Psychology, 44,* 1038–1047.

Schroder, H. M., Driver, M., & Streufert, S. (1967). *Human information processing.* New York: Holt, Rinehart & Winston.

Schulsinger, F. (1972). Psychopathology: Heredity and environment. *International Journal of Mental Health, 1,* 190–206.

Schutte, N. S., Kenrick, D. T., & Sadalla, E. K. (1985). The search for predictable settings: Situational prototypes, constraint, and behavioral variation. *Journal of Personality and Social Psychology, 49,* 121–128.

Schuyler, B. A., & Coe, W. C. (1981). A physiological investigation of volitional and nonvolitional experience during posthypnotic amnesia. *Journal of Personality and Social Psychology, 40,* 1160–1169.

Schwartz, D. P., Burish, T. G., O'Rourke, D. F., & Holmes, D. S. (1986). Influence of personal and universal failure on the subsequent performance of persons with Type A and

Type B behavior patterns. *Journal of Personality and Social Psychology, 51,* 459–462.

Schwartz, L. A., & Markham, W. T. (1985). Sex stereotyping in children's toy advertisements. *Sex Roles, 12,* 157–170.

Schwartz, R. D., & Higgins, R. L. (1979). Differential outcome from automated assertion training as a function of locus of control. *Journal of Consulting and Clinical Psychology, 47,* 686–694.

Sears, D. O. (1986). College sophomores in the laboratory: Influences of a narrow data base on social psychology's view of human nature. *Journal of Personality and Social Psychology, 51,* 515–530.

Sears, R. R. (1941). Non-aggressive reactions to frustration. *Psychological Review, 48,* 343–346.

Seeman, M., & Evans, J. W. (1962). Alienation and learning in a hospital setting. *American Sociological Review, 27,* 772–782.

Seeman, M., Seeman, T., & Sayles, M. (1985). Social networks and health status: A longitudinal analysis. *Social Psychology Quarterly, 48,* 237–248.

Seligman, M. E. P. (1975). *Helplessness: On depression, development and death.* San Francisco: W. H. Freeman.

Seligman, M. E. P. (1976). *Learned helplessness and depression in animals and men.* Morristown, NJ: General Learning Press.

Seligman, M. E. P., & Hager, J. L. (Eds.) (1972). *Biological boundaries of learning.* Englewood Cliffs, NJ: Prentice-Hall.

Seligman, M. E. P., & Maier, S. F. (1967). Failure to escape traumatic shock. *Journal of Experimental Psychology, 74,* 1–9.

Shaw, J. S. (1982). Psychological androgyny and stressful life events. *Journal of Personality and Social Psychology, 43,* 145–153.

Sheets, V. L., & Braver, S. L. (1991). *Men and women divorce for different reasons: A socio-evolutionary interpretation.* Paper presented at the annual meeting of the Western Psychological Association, San Francisco.

Sheldon, W. H. (1942). *The varieties of temperament: A psychology of constitutional differences.* New York: Harper & Row.

Shepperd, J. A., & Arkin, R. M. (1990). Shyness and self-presentation. In W. R. Crozier (Ed.), *Shyness and embarrassment: Perspectives from social psychology* (pp. 286–314). Cambridge: Cambridge University Press.

Shiffman, S. (1985). Coping with temptations to smoke. In S. Shiffman & T. A. Wills (Eds.), *Coping and substance use* (pp. 223–242). New York: Academic Press.

Shipley, R. H. (1981). Maintenance of smoking cessation: Effect of follow-up letters, smoking motivation, muscle tension, and locus of control. *Journal of Consulting and Clinical Psychology, 49,* 982–984.

Shrauger, J. S., & Rosenberg, S. E. (1970). Self-esteem and the effects of success and failure feedback on performance. *Journal of Personality, 38,* 404–417.

Shrauger, J. S., & Sorman, P. B. (1977). Self-evaluations, initial success and failure, and improvement as determinants of persistence. *Journal of Consulting and Clinical Psychology, 45,* 784–795.

Shurcliff, A. (1968). Judged humor, arousal, and the relief theory. *Journal of Personality and Social Psychology, 4,* 360–363.

Silverman, L. H. (1976). Psychoanalytic theory: "The reports of my death are greatly exaggerated." *American Psychologist, 31,* 621–637.

Silverman, L. H. (1982a). A comment on two subliminal psychodynamic activation studies. *Journal of Abnormal Psychology, 92,* 126–130.

Silverman, L. H. (1982b). Rejoinder to Allen and Condren's and Heilbrun's replies. *Journal of Abnormal Psychology, 91,* 136–138.

Silverman, L. H., & Fishel, A. K. (1981). The Oedipus Complex: Studies in adult male behavior. In L. Wheeler (Ed.), *Review of personality and social psychology* (Vol. 2, pp. 43–67). Beverly Hills, CA: Sage.

Silverman, L. H., Klinger, H., Lustbader, L., Farrell, J., & Martin, A. D. (1972). The effects of subliminal drive stimulation on the speech of stutterers. *Journal of Nervous and Mental Disease, 155,* 14–21.

Silverman, L. H., Ross, D. L., Adler, J. M., & Lustig, D. A. (1978). Simple research paradigm for demonstrating subliminal psychodynamic activation: Effects of Oedipal stimuli on dart-throwing accuracy in college males. *Journal of Abnormal Psychology, 87,* 341–357.

Silverman, L. H., & Weinberger, J. (1985). Mommy and I are one: Implications for psychotherapy. *American Psychologist, 40,* 1296–1308.

Singer, D. (1968). Aggression arousal, hostile humor, catharsis. *Journal of Personality and Social Psychology Monograph Supplement, 8,* 1–14.

Singer, J. L., & Singer, D. G. (1981). *Television, imagination, and aggression: A study of preschoolers.* Hillside, NJ: Erlbaum.

Skinner, B. F. (1953). *Science and human behavior.* New York: Macmillan.

Skinner, B. F. (1967). B. F. Skinner. In E. G. Boring & G. Lindzey (Eds.), *A history of psychology in autobiography* (Vol. V, pp. 387–413). New York: Appleton-Century-Crofts.

Skinner, B. F. (1971). *Beyond freedom and dignity.* New York: Bantam.

Skinner, B. F. (1974). *About behaviorism.* New York: Vintage Books.

Skinner, B. F. (1983). *A matter of consequences.* New York: Knopf.

Skinner, B. F. (1989). The origins of cognitive thought. *American Psychologist, 44,* 13–18.

Skinner, B. F. (1990). Can psychology be a science of mind? *American Psychologist, 45,* 1206–1210.

Slater, J., & Depue, R. A. (1981). The contribution of environmental events and social support to serious suicide attempts in primary depressive disorder. *Journal of Abnormal Psychology, 90,* 275–285.

Slife, B., & Rychlak, J. F. (1982). Role of affective assessment in modeling aggressive behavior. *Journal of Personality and Social Psychology, 43,* 861–868.

Sloan, W. W., & Solano, C. H. (1984). The conversational styles of lonely males with strangers and roommates. *Personality and Social Psychology Bulletin, 10,* 293–301.

Smith, D. (1982). Trends in counseling and psychotherapy. *American Psychologist, 37,* 802–809.

Smith, R. E. (1989). Effects of coping skills training on generalized self-efficacy and locus of control. *Journal of Personality and Social Psychology, 56,* 228–233.

Snell, W. E., Miller, R. S., & Belk, S. S. (1988). Development of the Emotional Self-Disclosure Scale. *Sex Roles, 18,* 59–73.

Snyder, C. R. (1988). From defenses to self-protection: An evolutionary perspective. *Journal of Social and Clinical Psychology, 6,* 155–158.

Snyder, M. (1974). The self-monitoring of expressive behavior. *Journal of Personality and Social Psychology, 30,* 526–537.

Snyder, M. (1987). *Public appearances/private realities: The psychology of self-monitoring.* New York: W. H. Freeman.

Snyder, M., & Gangestad, S. (1986). On the nature of self-monitoring: Matters of assessment, matters of validity. *Journal of Personality and Social Psychology, 51,* 125–139.

Solano, C. H., Batten, P. G., & Parish, E. A. (1982). Loneliness and patterns of self-disclosure. *Journal of Personality and Social Psychology, 43,* 524–531.

Solano, C. H., & Koester, N. H. (1989). Loneliness and communication problems: Subjective anxiety or objective skills? *Personality and Social Psychology Bulletin, 15,* 126–133.

Solomon, Z., Avitzur, E., & Mikulincer, M. (1988). Coping resources and social functioning following combat stress reaction: A longitudinal study. *Journal of Social and Clinical Psychology, 8,* 87–96.

Solomon, Z., Mikulincer, M., & Avitzur, E. (1988). Coping, locus of control, social support, and combat-related posttraumatic stress disorder: A prospective study. *Journal of Personality and Social Psychology, 55,* 279–285.

Solomon, Z., Weisenberg, M., Schwarzwald, J., & Mikulincer, M. (1988). Combat stress reaction and posttraumatic stress disorder as determinants of perceived self-efficacy in bat-tle. *Journal of Social and Clinical Psychology, 6,* 356–370.

Sonstroem, R. J., & Walker, M. I. (1973). Relationship of attitudes and locus of control to exercise and physical fitness. *Perceptual and Motor Skills, 36,* 1031–1034.

Spangler, W. D., & House, R. J. (1991). Presidential effectiveness and the leadership motive profile. *Journal of Personality and Social Psychology, 60,* 439–455.

Spanos, N. P. (1986). Hypnosis, nonvolitional responding, and multiple personality: A social psychological perspective. In B. A. Maher & W. B. Maher (Eds.), *Progress in experimental personality research* (Vol. 14, pp. 1–62). New York: Academic Press.

Spanos, N. P., & Hewitt, E. C. (1980). The hidden observer in hypnotic analgesia: Discovery or experimental creation? *Journal of Personality and Social Psychology, 39,* 1201–1214.

Spanos, N. P., & Katsanis, J. (1989). Effects of instructional set on attributions of nonvolition during hypnotic and nonhypnotic analgesia. *Journal of Personality and Social Psychology, 56,* 182–188.

Spanos, N. P., Radtke, H. L., & Dubreuil, D. L. (1982). Episodic and semantic memory in posthypnotic amnesia: A reevaluation. *Journal of Personality and Social Psychology, 43,* 565–573.

Spanos, N. P., Robertson, L. A., Menary, E. P., Brett, P. J., & Smith, J. (1987). Effects of repeated baseline testing on cognitive-skill-training-induced increments in hypnotic susceptibility. *Journal of Personality and Social Psychology, 52,* 1230–1235.

Spence, J. T. (1985). Achievement American style: The rewards and costs of individualism. *American Psychologist, 40,* 1285–1295.

Spence, J. T., & Helmreich, R. L. (1983). Achievement-related motives and behaviors. In J. T. Spence (Ed.), *Achievement and achievement motives: Psychological and sociological approaches* (pp. 7–74). San Francisco: W. H. Freeman.

Spence, J. T., Helmreich, R. L., & Stapp, J. (1974). The Personal Attributes Questionnaire: A measure of sex-role stereotypes and masculinity-femininity. *JSAS Catalog of Selected Documents in Psychology, 4,* 127 (Ms. No. 617).

Spett, M. C. (1983). All psychologists are not members of Divisions 12 and 17. *American Psychologist, 38,* 498.

Spivey, C. B., & Prentice-Dunn, S. (1990). Assessing the directionality of deindividuated behavior: Effects of deindividuation, modeling, and private self-consciousness on aggressive and prosocial responses. *Basic and Applied Social Psychology, 11,* 387–403.

Staats, A. W. (1975). *Social behaviorism.* Homewood, IL: Dorsey Press.

Staats, A. W. (1981). Paradigmatic behaviorism, unified theory, unified theory construction methods, and the Zeitgeist of separatism. *American Psychologist, 36,* 239–256.

Stangor, C. (1988). Stereotype accessibility and information processing. *Personality and Social Psychology Bulletin, 14,* 694–708.

Stava, L. J., & Jaffa, M. (1988). Some operationalizations of the neodissociation concept and their relationship to hypnotic susceptibility. *Journal of Personality and Social Psychology, 54,* 989–996.

Steinkamp, M. W. (1990). The social concomitants of competitive and impatient/aggressive components of Type A behavior pattern in preschool children: Peer responses and teacher utterances in a naturalistic setting. *Journal of Personality and Social Psychology, 59,* 1287–1295.

Stelmack, R. M. (1990). Biological bases of extraversion: Psychophysiological evidence. *Journal of Personality, 58,* 293–311.

Stephenson, W. (1953). *The study of behavior: Q-technique and its methodology.* Chicago: University of Chicago Press.

Stewart, A. J. (1982). *Motivation and society.* San Francisco: Jossey-Bass.

Strauman, T. J. (1989). Self-discrepancies in clinical depression and social phobia: Cognitive structures that underlie emotional disorders? *Journal of Abnormal Psychology, 98,* 14–22.

Strauman, T. J., Vookles, J., Berenstein, V., Chaiken, S., & Higgins, E. T. (1991). Self-discrepancies and vulnerability to body dissatisfaction and disordered eating. *Journal of Personality and Social Psychology, 61,* 946–956.

Strelau, J. (1987). Emotion as a key concept in temperament research. *Journal of Research in Personality, 21,* 510–528.

Strentz, T., & Auerbach, S. M. (1988). Adjustment to the stress of simulated captivity: Effects of emotion-focused versus problem-focused preparation on hostages differing in locus of control. *Journal of Personality and Social Psychology, 55,* 652–660.

Strickland, B. R. (1978). Internal-external expectancies and health-related behaviors. *Journal of Consulting and Clinical Psychology, 46,* 1192–1211.

Strickland, B. R. (1979). Internal-external expectancies and cardiovascular functioning. In L. C. Perlmuter & R. A. Monty (Eds.), *Choice and perceived control* (pp. 221–231). Hillsdale, NJ: Erlbaum.

Strube, M. J. (1982). Time urgency and Type A behavior: A methodological note. *Personality and Social Psychology Bulletin, 8,* 563–565.

Strube, M. J. (1987). A self-appraisal model of the Type A behavior pattern. In R. Hogan & W. Jones (Eds.), *Perspectives in personality theory* (Vol. 2, pp. 201–250). Greenwich, CT: JAI Press.

Strube, M. J., Berry, J. M., Lott, C. L., Fogelman, R., Steinhart, G., Moergen, S., & Davison, L. (1986). Self-schematic representation of the Type A and B behavior patterns. *Journal of Personality and Social Psychology, 51,* 170–180.

Strube, M. J., Berry, J. M., & Moergen, S. (1985). Relinquishment of control and the Type A behavior pattern: The role of performance evaluation. *Journal of Personality and Social Psychology, 49,* 831–842.

Strube, M. J., Boland, S. M., Manfredo, P. A., & Al-Falaij, A. (1987). Type A behavior pattern, and the self-evaluation of abilities: Empirical tests of the self-appraisal model. *Journal of Personality and Social Psychology, 52,* 956–974.

Sullivan, H. S. (1953). *The interpersonal theory of psychiatry.* New York: Norton.

Suls, J., & Fletcher, B. (1985). The relative efficacy of avoidant and nonavoidant coping strategies: A meta-analysis. *Health Psychology, 4,* 249–288.

Suls, J., & Wan, C. K. (1989). The relation between Type A behavior and chronic emotional distress: A meta-analysis. *Journal of Personality and Social Psychology, 57,* 503–512.

Swan, G. E., & MacDonald, M. L. (1978). Behavior therapy in practice: A national survey of behavior therapists. *Behavior Therapy, 9,* 799–807.

Sweeney, P. D., Anderson, K., & Bailey, S. (1986). Attributional style in depression: A meta-analytic review. *Journal of Personality and Social Psychology, 50,* 974–991.

Taylor, D. A., & Belgrave, F. Z. (1986). The effects of perceived intimacy and valence on self-disclosure reciprocity. *Personality and Social Psychology Bulletin, 12,* 247–255.

Taylor, D. A., & Hinds, M. (1985). Disclosure reciprocity and liking as a function of gender and personalism. *Sex Roles, 12,* 1137–1147.

Taylor, M. C., & Hall, J. A. (1982). Psychological androgyny: Theories, methods and conclusions. *Psychological Bulletin, 92,* 347–366.

Taylor, S. E., & Brown, J. D. (1988). Illusion and well-being: A social psychological perspective on mental health. *Psychological Bulletin, 103,* 193–210.

Tellegen, A., & Atkinson, G. (1974). Openness to absorbing and self-altering experiences ("absorption"), a trait related to hypnotic susceptibility. *Journal of Abnormal Psychology, 83,* 268–277.

Tellegen, A., Lykken, D. T., Bouchard, T. J., Wilcox, K. J., Segal, N. L., & Rich, S. (1988). Personality similarity in twins raised apart and together. *Journal of Personality and Social Psychology, 54,* 1031–1039.

Tempone, V. J., & Lamb, W. (1967). Repression-sensitization and its relation to measures of adjustment and conflict. *Journal of Consulting and Clinical Psychology, 31,* 131–136.

Tetlock, P. E. (1983a). Psychological research on foreign policy: A methodological overview. In L. Wheeler & P. Shaver (Eds.), *Review* *of personality and social psychology* (Vol. 4, pp. 45–78). Beverly Hills, CA: Sage.

Tetlock, P. E. (1983b). Cognitive style and political ideology. *Journal of Personality and Social Psychology, 45,* 118–126.

Tetlock, P. E. (1984). Cognitive style and political belief systems in the British House of Commons. *Journal of Personality and Social Psychology, 46,* 365–375.

Tetlock, P. E. (1985). Integrative complexity of American and Soviet foreign policy rhetoric: A time-series analysis. *Journal of Personality and Social Psychology, 49,* 1565–1585.

Thelen, M. H. (1969). Repression-sensitization: Its relation to adjustment and seeking psychotherapy among college students. *Journal of Consulting and Clinical Psychology, 33,* 161–165.

Thomas, A., & Chess, S. (1977). *Temperament and development.* New York: Brunner/Mazel.

Thorndike, E. L. (1911). *Animal intelligence: Experimental studies.* New York: Macmillan.

Tice, D. M. (1991). Esteem protection or enhancement? Self-handicapping motives and attributions differ by trait self-esteem. *Journal of Personality and Social Psychology, 60,* 711–725.

Tice, D. M., & Baumeister, R. F. (1990). Self-esteem, self-handicapping, and self-presentation: The strategy of inadequate practice. *Journal of Personality, 58,* 443–464.

Tresemer, D. (1976). The cumulative record of research on "fear of success." *Sex Roles, 2,* 217–236.

Trivers, R. L. (1972). Parental investment and sexual selection. In B. Campbell (Ed.), *Sexual selection and the descent of man: 1871–1971* (pp. 136–179). Chicago: Aldine.

Tunnell, G. (1981). Sex role and cognitive schemata: Person perception in feminine and androgynous women. *Journal of Personality and Social Psychology, 40,* 1126–1136.

Ulrich, R. E., Stachnik, T. J., & Stainton, N. R. (1963). Student acceptance of generalized personality interpretations. *Psychological Reports, 13,* 831–834.

Urbina, S. P., & Grey, A. (1975). Cultural and sex differences in the sex distribution of dream characters. *Journal of Cross-Cultural Psychology, 6,* 358–364.

Van Egeren, L. F. (1979). Cardiovascular changes during social competition in a mixed-motive game. *Journal of Personality and Social Psychology, 37,* 858–864.

Venkatesan, M., & Losco, J. (1975). Women in magazine ads: 1959–1971. *Journal of Advertising Research, 15,* 49–54.

Veroff, J., Depner, C., Kulka, R., & Douvan, E. (1980). Comparison of American motives: 1957 versus 1976. *Journal of Personality and Social Psychology, 39,* 1249–1262.

Vitaliano, P. P., DeWolfe, D. J., Maiuro, R. D., Russo, J., & Katon, W. (1990). Appraised changeability of a stressor as a modifier of the relationship between coping and depression: A test of the hypothesis of fit. *Journal of Personality and Social Psychology, 59,* 582–592.

Vitkus, J., & Horowitz, L. M. (1987). Poor social performance of lonely people: Lacking a skill or adopting a role? *Journal of Personality and Social Psychology, 52,* 1266–1273.

Voelz, C. J. (1985). Effects of gender role disparity on couples' decision-making processes. *Journal of Personality and Social Psychology, 49,* 1532–1540.

Vogel, D. A., Lake, M. A., Evans, S., & Karraker, K. H. (1991). Children's and adults' sex-stereotyped perceptions of infants. *Sex Roles, 24,* 605–616.

Vogel, G. W. (1975). Review of REM sleep deprivation. *Archives of General Psychiatry, 32,* 749–761.

Wahba, M. A., & Bridwell, L. G. (1976). Maslow reconsidered: A review of research on the need hierarchy theory. *Organizational Behavior and Human Performance, 15,* 212–240.

Wallach, M. A. (1960). Two correlates of symbolic sexual arousal: Level of anxiety and liking for esthetic material. *Journal of Abnormal and Social Psychology, 61,* 396–401.

Waller, N. G., & Ben-Porath, Y. S. (1987). Is it time for clinical psychology to embrace the five-factor model of personality? *American Psychologist, 42,* 887–889.

Wallston, K. A., Maides, S., & Wallston, B. S. (1976). Health-related information seeking as a function of health-related locus of control and health value. *Journal of Research in Personality, 10,* 215–222.

Wallston, K. A., & Wallston, B. S. (1981). Health locus of control scales. In H. M. Lefcourt (Ed.), *Research with the locus of control construct* (Vol. 1, pp. 189–243). New York: Academic Press.

Ward, C. H., & Eisler, R. M. (1987). Type A behavior, achievement striving, and a dysfunctional self-evaluation system. *Journal of Personality and Social Psychology, 53,* 318–326.

Ward, S. E., Leventhal, H., & Love, R. (1988). Repression revisited: Tactics used in coping with a severe health threat. *Personality and Social Psychology Bulletin, 14,* 735–746.

Watson, J. B. (1924/1970). *Behaviorism.* New York: Norton.

Watson, J. B. (1936). John Broadus Watson. In C. Murchison (Ed.), *A history of psychology in autobiography* (Vol. 3, pp. 271–281). Worcester, MA: Clark University Press.

Watson, J. B., & Rayner, R. (1920). Conditioned emotional reactions. *Journal of Experimental Psychology, 3,* 1–14.

Watson, R. I. (1973). Investigation into de-individuation using a cross-cultural survey technique. *Journal of Personality and Social Psychology, 25,* 342–345.

576

Weeks, D. G., Michela, J. L., Peplau, L. A., & Bragg, M. E. (1980). Relation between loneliness and depression: A structural equation analysis. *Journal of Personality and Social Psychology, 39,* 1238–1244.

Weidner, G., & Matthews, K. A. (1978). Reported physical symptoms elicited by unpredictable events and the Type A coronary-prone behavior pattern. *Journal of Personality and Social Psychology, 36,* 1213–1220.

Weinberger, D., Schwartz, G. E., & Davidson, R. J. (1979). Low-anxious, high-anxious, and repressive coping styles: Psychometric patterns and behavioral and physiological responses to stress. *Journal of Abnormal Psychology, 88,* 369–380.

Weinberger, J. L., & Silverman, L. H. (1987). Subliminal psychodynamic activation: A method for studying psychoanalytic dynamic propositions. In R. Hogan & W. H. Jones (Eds.), *Perspectives on Personality* (Vol. 2, pp. 251–287). Greenwich, CT: JAI Press.

Weiner, B. (1979). A theory of motivation for some classroom experiences. *Journal of Educational Psychology, 71,* 3–25.

Weiner, B. (1985). An attributional theory of achievement motivation and emotion. *Psychological Bulletin, 92,* 548–573.

Weiner, B. (1990). Attribution in personality psychology. In L. A. Pervin (Ed.), *Handbook of personality: Theory and research* (pp. 465–485). New York: Guilford.

Wender, P. H., Kety, S. S., Rosenthal, D., Schulsinger, F., Ortmann, J., & Lunde, I. (1986). Psychiatric disorders in the biological and adoptive families of adopted individuals with affective disorders. *Archives of General Psychiatry,* 923–929.

Wenzlaff, R. M., Wegner, D. M., & Roper, D. W. (1988). Depression and mental control: Resurgence of unwanted negative thoughts. *Journal of Personality and Social Psychology, 55,* 882–892.

Whitely, B. E. (1983). Sex-role orientation and self-esteem: A critical meta-analytic review. *Journal of Personality and Social Psychology, 44,* 765–778.

Whyte, L. L. (1978). *The unconscious before Freud.* New York: St. Martin's.

Wicker, F. W., Barron, W. L., & Willis, A. C. (1980). Disparagement humor: Dispositions and resolutions. *Journal of Personality and Social Psychology, 39,* 701–709.

Wickless, C., & Kirsch, I. (1989). Effects of verbal and experiential expectancy manipulations on hypnotic susceptibility. *Journal of Personality and Social Psychology, 57,* 762–768.

Williams, J. E., Bennett, S. M., & Best, D. L. (1975). Awareness and expression of sex stereotypes in young children. *Developmental Psychology, 11,* 635–642.

Williams, J. E., & Best, D. L. (1982). *Measuring sex stereotypes: A thirty-nation study.* Beverly Hills, CA: Sage.

Williams, J. G., & Solano, C. H. (1983). The social reality of feeling lonely: Friendship and reciprocation. *Personality and Social Psychology Bulletin, 9,* 237–242.

Wilson, T. D., & Linville, P. W. (1982). Improving the academic performance of college freshmen: Attribution therapy revisited. *Journal of Personality and Social Psychology, 42,* 367–376.

Wilson, T. D., & Linville, P. W. (1985). Improving the performance of college freshmen with attributional techniques. *Journal of Personality and Social Psychology, 49,* 287–293.

Winter, D. G. (1987). Leader appeal, leader performance, and the motive profiles of leaders and followers: A study of American presidents and elections. *Journal of Personality and Social Psychology, 52,* 196–202.

Wittenberg, M. T., & Reis, H. T. (1986). Loneliness, social skills, and social perception. *Personality and Social Psychology Bulletin, 12,* 121–130.

Wolfe, R. N., & Kasmer, J. A. (1988). Type versus trait: Extraversion, impulsivity, sociability, and preferences for cooperative and competitive activities. *Journal of Personality and Social Psychology, 54,* 864–871.

Wolfle, L. M., & Robertshaw, D. (1982). Effects of college attendance on locus of control. *Journal of Personality and Social Psychology, 43,* 802–810.

Wolpe, J. (1958). *Psychotherapy by reciprocal inhibition.* Stanford, CA: Stanford University Press.

Won-Doornink, M. J. (1985). Self-disclosure and reciprocity in conversation: A cross-national study. *Social Psychology Quarterly, 48,* 97–107.

Wong, M. M., & Csikszentmihalyi, M. (1991). Motivation and academic achievement: The effects of personality traits and the quality of experience. *Journal of Personality, 59,* 539–574.

Wood, W., Wong, F. Y., & Chachere, J. G. (1991). Effects of media violence on viewers' aggression in unconstrained social interaction. *Psychological Bulletin, 109,* 371–383.

Worell, J. (1978). Sex roles and psychological well-being: Perspectives on methodology. *Journal of Consulting and Clinical Psychology, 46,* 777–791.

Worthy, M., Gary, A. L., & Kahn, G. M. (1969). Self-disclosure as an exchange process. *Journal of Personality and Social Psychology, 13,* 59–63.

Wortman, C. B., & Brehm, J. W. (1975). Responses to uncontrollable outcomes: An integration of reactance theory and the learned helplessness model. In L. Berkowitz (Ed.), *Ad-*

vances in experimental social psychology, (Vol. 8, pp. 277–336). New York: Academic Press.

Wright, L. (1988). The Type A behavior pattern and coronary artery disease. *American Psychologist, 43,* 2–14.

Yarnold, P. R., Mueser, K. T., & Grimm, L. G. (1985). Interpersonal dominance of Type As in group discussions. *Journal of Abnormal Psychology, 94,* 233–236.

Young, J. E. (1982). Loneliness, depression and cognitive therapy: Theory and application. In L. A. Peplau & D. Perlman (Eds.), *Loneliness.* New York: Wiley.

Zajonc, R. B., Markus, H., & Markus, G. B. (1979). The birth order puzzle. *Journal of Personality and Social Psychology, 37,* 1325–1341.

Zammichieli, M. E., Gilroy, F. D., & Sherman, M. F. (1988). Relations between sex-role orientation and marital satisfaction. *Personality and Social Psychology Bulletin, 14,* 747–754.

Zillmann, D. (1979). *Hostility and aggression.* Hillsdale, NJ: Erlbaum.

Zillmann, D., Bryant, J., & Cantor, J. R. (1974). Brutality of assault in political cartoons affecting humor appreciation. *Journal of Research in Personality, 7,* 334–345.

Zimbardo, P. G. (1970). The human choice: Individuation, reason, and order versus deindividuation, impulse, and chaos. In W. J. Arnold & D. Levine (Eds.), *Nebraska Symposium on Motivation, 1969.* Lincoln: University of Nebraska Press.

Zimbardo, P. G. (1977). *Shyness.* Reading, MA: Addison-Wesley.

Zimbardo, P. G. (1986). The Stanford Shyness Project. In W. H. Jones, J. M. Cheek, & S. R. Briggs (Eds.), *Shyness: Perspectives on research and treatment* (pp. 17–25). New York: Plenum.

tion seeking. *Journal of Consulting and Clinical Psychology, 36,* 45–52.

Zuckerman, M. (1979). *Sensation seeking: Beyond the optimal level of arousal.* Hillsdale, NJ: Erlbaum.

Zuckerman, M., Kolin, E. A., Price, L., & Zoob, I. (1964). Development of a Sensation-Seeking Scale. *Journal of Consulting Psychology, 28,* 477–482.

Name Index

Subject Index